METHODOLOGICAL ISSUES IN ACCOUNTING RESEARCH
Theories, methods and issues

Edited by

ZAHIRUL HOQUE, PhD, CPA, FCMA
Associate Dean (research) and Professor of Accounting
Faculty of Law and Management
La Trobe University, Australia

ſSpiramus

Published in July 2006
and reprinted August 2010 by

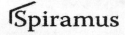
Spiramus

Spiramus Press Ltd
102 Blandford Street
London W1U 8AG
Telephone +44 20 7224 0080
www.spiramus.com

ISBN
978 1904905 12 7 Hardback
978 1904905 13 4 Paperback

Printed and bound in Great Britain by Good News Digital Books, England
Cover design: David Shaw and associates

CONTENTS

CONTENTS

PART IV   CRITICAL PERSPECTIVES

PART V   RESEARCH STRATEGIES AND DATA ANALYSIS

CONTENTS

PREFACE

What is my theory? How do I choose a theory? Why and how should I employ a particular method for collecting the empirical data? These basic questions concern everyone involved in research. Current books on research methodology lack detailed answers to these questions. In this collection, I have tried to fill this apparent gap in the literature by providing a practical guideline as to why and how to choose a particular theory or method to study organisational phenomena such as accounting practice. The chapters have been written by well-known scholars in their respective fields. Each chapter documents the latest developments and research in accounting and control systems and provides valuable insights into methodological perspectives in accounting research.

The book is primarily intended for research students and academic researchers. It can also be used for undergraduate Honours course as well as postgraduate accounting and business methodology courses. Research organisations and consulting firms in accounting and business fields may also find this book useful.

REVIEW PROCESS

This is a peer-reviewed collection of chapters. Each submitted chapter has been subject to the following review process: (a) it has been reviewed by the General Editor for its suitability for further referencing, and (b) its final acceptance for publication has been subject to double and triple blind peer review.

ACKNOWLEDGEMENTS

The contributors and I have been equal partners in the compilation of this volume. I am grateful to the contributors whose chapters are presented here. I would also like to thank Carl Upsall and his team at Spiramus for their support. I am grateful to Ms Zlatica Kovac for her editorial assistance during the project. Last, but not least, my wife, Shirin, has provided invaluable support.

Professor Zahirul Hoque, PhD (Manchester), CPA, FCMA
Deakin University
School of Accounting, Economics and Finance
Geelong, Victoria
Australia

June 2006

About the Editor

Zahirul Hoque is Professor of Accounting at the School of Accounting, Economics and Finance at Deakin University, Geelong in Australia. Before joining Deakin University, he was Professor and Head of School of Business at Charles Darwin University in the Northern Territory of Australia. He has also held positions at Griffith University Gold Campus in Australia, Victoria University of Wellington in New Zealand, and the University of Dhaka, Bangladesh. His research interests include governance and performance management, public sector reforms, accounting change, accounting for not-for-profit organisations, management accounting in less developed countries, qualitative case study research and critical discourse analysis. He is the author of the textbook *Strategic Management Accounting: Concepts, Processes and Issues* (Spiro Press, 2nd edition, 2003), the editor of the book *Handbook of Cost and Management Accounting* (Spiramus, 2005) and the co-editor (with Trevor Hopper) of the supplement *Accounting and Accountability in Emerging and Transition Economies* (Elsevier Sciences, 2004). He is the founding editor of the *Journal of Accounting & Organizational Change*. He is also on the editorial board of *Accounting, Accountability and Performance*, *Investment Management and Financial Innovations* and *AIUB Journal of Business and Economics*. He has published several articles and book chapters in many leading international journals. The editor can be contacted at zahirul.hoque@deakin.edu.au.

Notes on the Contributors

Carol Adams is a Professor of Accounting at La Trobe University, Australia. Prior to joining La Trobe University, she was professor and Head of the School of Accounting, Economics and Finance at Deakin University, Melbourne, Australia. Her current recent projects include: examining the use of the Internet as a medium for ethical, social and environmental reporting; the integration of sustainability reporting into decision making, performance management and risk management; accountability for gender issues in employment; internal sustainability reporting processes; and, sustainability reporting verification processes.

Manzurul Alam is an Associate Professor in the Department of Accounting and Finance at Monash University. He holds a MBA (Leuven) and a PhD (LSE). His current research interests focus on performance measurement, inter-firm comparison, small business development, and accounting issues in public sector organisations. He is also an Associate Editor of the *Journal of Accounting & Organizational Change*.

C. Richard Baker is Professor of Accounting at Adelphi University, Garden City, New York. Prior to joining Adelphi University, he was Professor and Chair of the Accounting Department at the University of Massachusetts Dartmouth. He has held previous academic positions at Columbia University and Fordham University in New York City. His research interests focus on the regulatory, legal and ethical aspects of accounting and auditing. He is the author of over 90 academic articles and other publications. He holds a PhD from the Graduate School of Management at UCLA and he is a Certified Public Accountant in New York State.

John Burns is Professor of Accounting at the University of Dundee, UK since July 2004, having held previous academic positions at the University of Manchester (UK) and the University of Colorado (USA), as well as Ernst and Whinney. Since 1993, his research and professional interests have primarily been in management accounting, organisational change and institutional theory. He has published numerous refereed articles and books in these areas, as well as several articles and research monographs for international professional accounting bodies. John is co-founder of the international research network, European Network for Research of Organisational and Accounting Change (ENROAC). He is also an associate editor for Management Accounting Research, and a member of the editorial boards for the Journal of Accounting and Organizational Change, and the Asia-Pacific Journal of Management Accounting.

Cristiano Busco is an Associate Professor of Management Accounting and Business Administration at the University of Siena, Italy. Formerly, he was a lecturer at the School of Accounting and Finance of the University of Manchester, UK, and visiting professor at the Leventhal School of Accounting, University of Southern California, Los Angeles. He has published some books and monograph in the field of

Management Accounting and Performance Measurements as well as articles in journals such as *Management Accounting Research, Business Horizons, Financial Management & Strategic Finance*. He is in the editorial board of *Journal of Accounting and Organizational Change*.

David Campbell is Lecturer in accounting at the University of Newcastle upon Tyne, England. His research interests include content analysis method, accounting report interrogation, social/environmental reporting and the development of corporate responsibility 'strategy' in organisations.

Christopher S. Chapman is Head of the Accounting group at Saïd Business School, University of Oxford. He is an associate editor of *Accounting, Organizations and Society*, and sits on the editorial boards of *Contemporary Accounting Research* and *Journal of Management Accounting Research*. Chris is also a member of the scientific committee of the European Institute for Advanced Studies in Management.

Robert Chenhall is Professor of Accounting at Monash University, Australia. He has wide experience in teaching management accounting in Australia, UK, Europe and the US and has consulted to a range of organization in both private and public sectors. He is on the editorial boards of *Accounting, Organisations and Society, Journal of Accounting and Public Policy, Behavioral Research in Accounting, Journal of Management Accounting Research, Management Accounting Research, European Accounting Review, Accounting and Business Research, Accounting Research Journal, Accounting and Finance* and the *Journal of Accounting & Organizational Change*.

Craig Deegan, B.Com (University of New South Wales), M.Com (Hons) (University of New South Wales), PhD (University of Queensland), FCA, is Professor of Accounting and Director of Research in the School of Accounting & Law, RMIT University, Melbourne, Australia. Craig has been within the university sector for two decades prior to which he was a chartered accountant in practice. Craig's research has tended to focus on various social and environmental accountability and financial accounting issues and he has published in a number of leading international accounting journals, including *Accounting Organizations and Society; Accounting and Business Research; Accounting, Auditing and Accountability Journal; Accounting and Finance; British Accounting Review;* and the *International Journal of Accounting*. He is also on the editorial board of a number of journals, including *Accounting, Auditing and Accountability Journal, Accounting Forum,* and *Journal of Accounting & Organizational Change*. Craig is the author of the leading financial accounting texts, *Australian Financial Accounting* and *Financial Accounting Theory*, both published by McGraw-Hill Book Company. Craig is also the author of many government and industry based reports.

Jesse Dillard, PhD., holds the Retzlaff Chair in Accounting at Portland State University and is Director of the Center for Professional Integrity and Accountability. Professor Dillard's research and teaching interests relate to the organizational management and control with specific emphasis on pubic responsibilities, ethical structures, and advanced information technology systems. His is currently the editor of *Accounting and the Public Interest* and is Associate Editor of *Accounting, Auditing, and Accountability Journal*. He has published extensively in the accounting and business literature.

Timothy J. Fogarty is Professor of Accounting and Associate Dean at The Weatherhead School of Management of Case Western Reserve University, Cleveland, Ohio, USA. He is now completing 17 years at that institution, six of which he served as department chairman. He has a variety of degrees including law and economics. His most passionate research interests are the sociology of professional accounting and the organization of accounting education. However, he is willing to work with anybody that has good ideas. He is active in most things that constitute an academic life, including service on twenty editorial boards.

Irene M. Herremans is an Associate Professor at the Haskayne School of Business and as an adjunct professor in Environmental Design at the University of Calgary. She also teaches in a Master's Degree in Sustainable Energy in Quito, Ecuador. She holds several degrees including a MBA, Masters of Science in Accounting, and a PhD that included studies in accounting, marketing, and international business. She holds a professional designation as a Certified Public Accountant. Her research interests focus on many contemporary issues including management and environmental control systems, environmental performance, intellectual capital, and performance valuation.

Trevor Hopper is currently a part-time Professor of Management Accounting at Manchester University, adjunct professor at Victoria University of Wellington, New Zealand; and Stockholm School of Economics, Sweden. He was Head of School and Director of Research and Postgraduate Studies in the School of Accounting and Finance at Manchester. Previously he worked at Wolverhampton and Sheffield Universities and as a cost accountant in industry. He has held visiting positions at the University of Michigan, Ann Arbor, USA; Queen's University, Canada; Griffith University, Gold Coast, Australia; and the Universities of Kyushu and Fukuoka, Japan. Professor Hopper is on the editorial boards of *Accounting, Accountability and Performance; Accounting, Auditing and Accountability Journal; Accounting and the Public Interest; Alternative Perspectives on Finance and Accounting; British Accounting Review; Critical Perspectives on Accounting; Journal of Accounting & Organizational Change; Management Accounting Research*; and *Qualitative Research in Accounting & Management*. He was formerly a co-editor of *British Accounting Review* and has served on the executive of the British Accounting Association. His major interests lie in the social, organisational and political aspects of management accounting. He has co-edited four books and has published extensively in professional journals, books, and international research journals including *Accounting and Business Research; Accounting, Organizations and Society; the Auditing, Accounting and Accountability*

Journal; British Accounting Review; Critical Perspectives on Accounting; Journal of Management Studies; and *Management Accounting Research.*

Julian Jones is Lecturer in Accounting at the Manchester Business School, The University of Manchester, UK. His research interests include performance measurement, outsourcing and the configuration of virtual enterprises.

Theresa J.B. Kline is a Professor in the Department of Psychology at the University of Calgary. She has an active research program in the area of team performance and her other research interests include psychometrics, organizational effectiveness, and work attitudes. Theresa has published two books on teams, *Teams that Lead* (2003) and *Remaking Teams* (1999), and one on psychometrics, *Psychological Testing* (2005), and has over 45 peer-reviewed articles. Theresa teaches statistics/methods and organizational psychology at both the undergraduate and graduate levels. She has an active organisational consulting practice with projects ranging from individual and organisational assessment to strategic alignment.

Anne Lillis is an Associate Professor of Accounting and Deputy Head of the Department of Accounting and Business Information Systems. Anne researches and teaches in Management Accounting. Her research interests focus on field studies of the design and behavioural influence of performance management and control systems. She has published both management accounting and field study method papers in leading international journals. Anne is chair of the ICAA Management Accounting Module Advisory Committee, and a member of the ICAA Academic Board. She is also actively engaged in academic and governance activities of the American Accounting Association Management Accounting Section. Prior to joining the University of Melbourne, Anne spent several years in the Australian Taxation Office, La Trobe and Deakin Universities.

Joanne Lye is a Lecturer in the Department of Accounting and Management at La Trobe University, Australia. Joanne completed her Masters degree at Massey University of New Zealand and is currently undertaking a doctorate degree through the University of Adelaide. Joanne has published in *Accounting, Auditing and Accountability Journal* and the *Australian Accounting Review* (forthcoming). She has also been an ad-hoc reviewer for *Accounting, Auditing and Accountability Journal.* Joanne teaches Accounting for Managers on the Masters of Professional Accounting. Her research interests are performance measurement and research methodology.

Maria Major, PhD (Manchester), is an Assistant Professor of Management Accounting at ISCTE – Business School, Lisbon. She holds a PhD. in Accounting from The University of Manchester. Her PhD thesis was on ABC and regulation in the telecommunications sector. She has been teaching Management Accounting to undergraduates and Accounting Theory and Research Methodology both to master and doctoral students. Her research interests lie in management accounting change both in private and public organisations. Currently she is conducting a research project funded by the Portuguese Government on management control in the healthcare sector.

Patty McNicholas is a Senior Lecturer at Monash University - Clayton campus where she teaches financial accounting. Her main research interests are the critical and social analysis of accounting with a particular focus on gender, ethnicity and cultural issues, methodological issues, ethical and environmental issues.

Jodie Moll, PhD, is a Lecturer in Accounting at the Manchester Business School, UK. Her main research interests are in the areas of issues in management control and public sector accounting. Her research is mainly qualitative and she teaches a Research and Dissertation Design course at the Business School. Jodie studied at Griffith University, Australia where she gained her PhD degree for research about Higher Education Reform and the budgetary effects on Universities. Her latest research project, funded by the ACCA, is investigating Whole of Government Accounting in the UK. She is an associate editor for the *Journal of Contemporary Accounting and Organisational Change* and is additionally active in refereeing articles for a number of leading journals.

Jamal A. Nazari is a PhD student in Accounting at Haskayne School of Business. He holds a BA in Accounting from the Ferdowsi University of Mashhad, Iran, and his Master in Accounting from the University of Tehran, Iran. Jamal's professional experience has included working as a finance executive and manager for an Investing and a Trading Company in Iran, as well as a Senior Finance Expert in automobile industry in Iran. His research interests focus on managerial accounting. He is pursuing research on contemporary issues such as intellectual capital measurement and sustainability.

Bill Nixon is Mathew Chair Professor of Management Information Systems in the Department of Accountancy and Business Finance, University of Dundee, Scotland. He has a longstanding research interest in management control systems for Research and Development, Design and Product Innovation. He is currently working in two multi-disciplinary teams on three funded research projects in New Product Design and Development.

Hector B. Perera is a Professor of Accounting at Massey University, where he has been on the faculty since 1986. He has an undergraduate degree from the University of Sri Lanka, Peradeniya, and received his PhD. from the University of Sydney, Australia. He has published in various journals, including *Journal of International of Accounting Research; Journal of Accounting Literature; International Journal of Accounting; Advances of International Accounting; Journal of Internal Financial Management and Accounting; Abacus; Accounting and Business Research; Accounting, Auditing and Accountability Journal; Accounting Education; Australian Accounting Review; and Pacific Accounting Review*. In an article appearing in a 1999 issue of the International Journal of Accounting, he was ranked fourth equal in authorship of international accounting research in US journals over the period 1980-1996. He is currently an associate editor for the *Journal of International Accounting Research*, and on the editorial boards of *Accounting, Auditing, Accountability and Performance Evaluation; Review of Accounting and Finance; and Qualitative Research in Accounting and Management*. His main areas of research and teaching interests are international and methodological issues in accounting.

Asheq R. Rahman is an Associate Professor of Accounting at Nanyang Technological University, Singapore. He has a PhD. from the University of Sydney. He has published in several academic and professional journals, which include *Abacus, Accounting, Auditing and Accountability Journal, Accounting and Business Research, Accounting Education, International Journal of Accounting, Journal of Accounting and Public Policy, Journal of International Accounting Research, Journal of International Financial Management and Accounting, Critical Perspectives in Accounting, Advances in International Accounting, the Australian Accounting Review, the Australian Accountant, the Singapore Accountant and the Accountants Journal*. He has authored and/or co-authored books and monographs, which include *Australian Accounting Standards Review Board - The Establishment of its Participatory Standard-Setting Approach; Accounting in the Asia Pacific Region; Accounting and Closer Economic Relations Agreement between New Zealand and Australia; US-GAAP and IAS harmonisation - a Singapore perspective*; and *Electronic Business Reporting*. He is also on the Editorial Committee of the *Journal of International Accounting Research* and the Editorial Board of *Abacus*. He also regularly reviews papers for the *European Accounting Review*. His areas of interest in research and teaching are Financial Accounting, Disclosure and Accounting Institutions.

Robin Roslender is Professor of Accountancy at Heriot-Watt University, Edinburgh. He previously held appointments in accountancy at the University of Stirling and behavioural science at Napier University, Edinburgh. A specialist in interdisciplinary accounting research, his 1992 monograph *Sociological Perspectives on Modern Accountancy* remains one of the founding contributions in the field. His principal research interests currently lie in the intellectual area, particularly on how it might be possible to account for workforce wellness as an organisational asset. Professor Roslender continues to make contributions to the strategic management accounting literature and to the critical accounting project, and is member of a diverse range of editorial boards including: *Accounting and the Public Interest; Accounting Education; Journal of Human Resource Costing and Accounting*; and *Journal of Marketing Management*.

Kala Saravanamuthu, PhD, is a senior lecturer in the University of New England, Australia. Her primary post-doctoral research: theorising and formulating an alternative perspective that equips researchers and practitioners alike with the tools to engage with the meaning and implications of sustainable development. This theoretical framework is based on Gandhi's interpretation of the *Advaitic Vedic* philosophy, and lessons learned from his political activities in resisting British imperialism. She hopes to inform this framework further through case-study research of communities that are experimenting with the sustainability ethos. She is a member of the Editorial Board of the Journal of Sustainable Development.

Nava Subramaniam, PhD, is a Senior Lecturer in the Department of Accounting, Finance and Economics of Griffith University. Nava's research interests include, corporate governance, management control system, auditing and accounting education. She has published in numerous journals including *Accounting and Finance, Management Accounting Research, Accounting Accountability and Performance, Australian Journal of Management* and *Australian accounting Review*. Presently, she is the Co-editor of *Accounting, Accountability and Performance* and the Associate Editor of the *Journal of Applied Management Accounting Research*, CIMA.

Susanne Trimbath, PhD, is a Senior Research Economist at the STP Advisory Services, Santa Monica, CA, USA.

Danture Wickramasinghe is a Lecturer at Manchester Business School. A PhD from the University of Manchester, he has been teaching accounting in a number of universities in the last 25 years. He has publications in *Accounting, Auditing and Accountability Journal, Critical Perspectives on Accounting, Financial Management, and Advances in Public Interest Accounting*. With an inclination to use structural and post-structural theories, his research interest lies in management control and governance in LDCs, NGO accountability, and the diffusion of 'new' management accounting. Currently, he is a guest editor of a special issue on management accounting in LDCs for *Journal of Accounting & Organizational Change*.

Reviewers of the book

The editor would like to thank the following for their assistance in the refereeing process.

Carol Adams	*La Trobe University, Melbourne, Australia*
Manzurul Alam	*Monash University, Melbourne, Australia*
Shahid Ansari	*Babson College, USA*
Jane Broadbent	*Roehampton University, London, UK*
Albie Brooks	*Victoria University, Melbourne, Australia*
Timothy J Fogarty	*Case Western Reserve University, USA*
David Campbell	*University of Newcastle upon Tyne, UK*
Robert Chenhall	*Monash University, Melbourne, Australia*
Craig Deegan	*RMIT University, Melbourne, Australia*
Jesse Dillard	*Portland State University*
William Dimovski	*Deakin University, Australia*
Andrew Goddard	*University of Southampton, UK*
Trevor Hopper	*University of Manchester, UK*
Stuart Lawrence	*University of Waikato, New Zealand*
Anne M. Lillis	*University of Melbourne, Australia*
Maria Major	*ISCTE – Business School, Lisbon, Portugal*
Lokman Mia	*Griffith University, Brisbane, Australia*
Sven Modell	*Stockholm University, Sweden*
Jodie Moll	*University of Manchester, UK*
Jan Moritsen	*Copenhagen Business School, Denmark*
Neale O'Connor	*City University of Hong Kong, PRC*
Keith Robson	*University of Cardiff, UK*
Robin Roslender	*Heriot-Watt University, UK*
John Sands	*Griffith University, Gold Coast, Australia*
Kala Saravanamuthu	*University of New England, Australia*
Prem N Sikka	*University of Essex, UK*
Randy Silver	*Deakin University, Australia*
Gary Spraakman	*York University, Canada*
Nava Subramaniam	*Griffith University, Gold Coast, Australia*
Stuart Turley	*University of Manchester, UK*
Gillian Vesty	*Victoria University, Melbourne, Australia*
Ed Vosselman	*Radboud University Nijmegen, The Netherlands*
Martin Walker	*University of Manchester, UK*
Danture Wickramansinghe	*University of Manchester, UK*
Rachid Zeffane	*University of Sharjah, UAE*

1

INTRODUCTION

Zahirul Hoque

Deakin University, Australia

1.   Introduction

A major problem confronting a researcher new to this area is which theoretical perspective is most apt. A research study can be a voyage of discovery or a choice of theoretical perspective, as well as gathering empirics or facts on a problem or situation. The aim of this edited collection of chapters is to make a contribution to advancing research methodology in accounting by critically assessing the existing theories and methods that are applied to study accounting practices.

Accounting researchers use both traditional and emergent theories to study accounting in organisations. Traditional and emergent theories offer differing insights into organisational phenomena and suffer from different shortcomings. Nevertheless, these two approaches to accounting research lead to the increase in knowledge and understanding about a phenomenon or phenomena. This book has brought these two strands of literature together in one volume. In addition to this, the book also includes chapters on research strategies, data analysis, ethical issues, and publishing work in academic journals. The book is divided into seven parts, namely: positivistic perspectives; naturalistic research approach; institutional and contextual perspectives; critical perspectives; research strategies and data analysis; ethical issues; and publishing research.

2.   Positivistic Perspectives

Research using positivistic (or traditional) perspectives or theories see 'reality' as a concrete structure and 'people' as adapters, responders, and information processors to achieve efficiency and the goal of an organisation (Morgan and Smircich, 1980). Accounting research from such perspectives, views accounting control systems, such as budgeting as a means to achieving low cost, efficient operations. Using this approach the researchers normally rely on an arms-length research method – statistically categorises key variables and then attempts to retrieve meaning by *ex post facto* interpretations of tests of significance (Tomkins and Groves, 1983, p. 362).

The second part of this book presents six chapters. Chapter 2 introduces the principles of rational choice theory and shows how the incentives of a given decision imply a certain behavioural response, one that is dictated by a desire to achieve maximum utility. The chapter also discusses the concept of bounded rationality and models of bureaucracy to show the complexity of decision processes across time and, in turn, point to the limitations of rational choice theory and the need to complement the theory with other sociological theories to embed the decision process within its cultural and institutional context. Chapter 3 discusses the human relations theory which has contributed to a broader understanding of how a variety of human aspects can affect the operation of accounting and control systems in organisations. These include: the effects of participation/consultation in decision-making processes; motivation, satisfaction and reward systems; leadership effects; organisational slack practices; and the effect of interpersonal relations among organisational members.

Within the second part, Chapter 4 focuses on a central theoretical concept in contingency theory, the nature of fit. Reviewing, in turn, Selection, Interaction and Systems forms of fit, they discuss the main assumptions and implications that each entails, followed by a discussion of the various ways in which these theoretical approaches have been tested in practice in a variety of studies of contingency theory looking at management control systems. Chapter 5 provides a summary of the commonalities and differences across the three major paradigms adopted by accounting researchers when using an agency framework: Principal-Agent, Transaction Cost Economics and Positivist (Rochester) model. Chapter 6 reviews management control literatures alongside conventional transaction cost economics (TCE) in order to address the absence of ex-post control mechanisms in TCE's rather restrictive account of governance. A review of the evolution of strategic thinking and the management control systems (MCS) literature in Chapter 7 provides a conceptual map for integrating disparate perspectives to meet the immediate challenges for MCS development.

3. Naturalistic Research Approach

It has been suggested that by the use of scientific or positivistic approaches, the researchers know little about accounting in actual practice, how it interacts with other organizational effectiveness and adaptability (Tomkins and Grove, 1983; Hopper and Powell, 1985). Tomkins and Groves (1983) suggest that the use of "scientific" methodology is appropriate only where the meanings of variables are found, or perceived, to be "stable" and "situation-independent". They further view that this approach is inappropriate for certain types of social research problems where the researcher lacks the confidence to adopt the view of the world and related set of ontological assumptions to enable the scientific approach to be used with validity. Within the naturalistic domain, Chapter 8 proposes the use of a method of research called the Grounded Theory method. In this Chapter, the authors suggest that the rationale behind the Grounded Theory method is that theory should be grounded in empirical evidence, i.e. evolve from data, rather than be developed a priori and then be tested. Glaser and Strauss (1967) suggest that most social research is primarily concerned with deductive rather than inductive reasoning, or the testing of hypotheses rather than their generation. They urged researchers to develop "grounded theory", discovering theory from data, having first shed all theoretical preconceptions about the substantive area under examination. The aim is to move from raw data, to the identification of conceptual categories and their conceptual properties, to their interrelationships, and hence to the construction of a theory or set of related hypotheses, using s systematic procedure of data coding and analysis which they labelled the constant comparative method (Glaser & Strauss, 1967). In this book, Chapter 8 expands on this issue.

4.   Institutional and Contextual Perspectives

Accounting research also investigates accounting practice from social, cultural and political standpoints within which it operates (Burchell *et al.*, 1980; Berry *et al.*, 1985; Hoque and Hopper, 1994; Covaleski and Dirsmith, 1988a, 1988b; Carpenter and Feroz, 2001; Modell, 2002, 2003, 2005). Part IV presents four chapters on institutional and contextual perspectives. Within this part, Chapter 9 explores the notion of 'organisational legitimacy' and emphasises that organisational legitimacy can be considered as a resource upon which many organisations are dependent for their survival. Chapter 10 describes institutional theory and provides a review of extant accounting research concentrating on those studies that have adopted both 'old' and 'new' institutional approaches. Chapter 11 discusses the relevance of stakeholder theory in accounting research as an alternative approach to the shareholder theory. It highlights that the success of modern business depends on sustainability which can be achieved by considering the needs of its stakeholders. Chapter 12 offers a snapshot of some of the recent attempts to conceptualise management accounting systems within its organisational context. In so doing, the chapter discusses the intensity of processes of change by looking at the evolutionary versus revolutionary patterns.

5.   Critical Perspectives

Part V focuses on critical perspectives. In this part, Chapter 13 highlights the merits of Critical Theory as a theoretical perspective or 'way of seeing' informing research in accounting. Chapter 14 discusses the labour process theory, grounded in Braverman's formulation, with an introduction to the literature that has emerged as well as a discussion of the major criticisms that have been raised as to its validity, comprehensiveness, and contemporary applicability. Chapter 15 draws on Gandhi's interpretation of the *Vedic* philosophy of living in harmony with Nature in proposing an alternative to the dominant paradigm of economic growth, which is based on the logic of control. This chapter discusses the implications of Gandhi's principles of *satyagraha* (that is, assertive search for truth through dialogue) and *swaraj* (freedom) that are applied in formulating a discursive accountability framework which engages dialectically with the individual and structure through the psychology of fear-reflectivity. Chapter 16 attempts to review and discuss the theoretical and methodological underpinnings of accounting research on power.

6.   Research Strategies and Data Analysis

Part VI presents seven chapters on research methods and data analysis. Chapter 17 is about the use of case study methods in accounting research. It discusses both case study and action research approaches through their assumptions, concepts and perspectives. Chapter 18 provides a general overview of the current qualitative landscape and some practical guidance to any student or researcher embarking on research for the first time. Chapter 19 is intended to introduce the protocol analysis method, to review its epistemic and methodological underpinnings and then to briefly consider how it has been employed by accounting researchers. Chapter 20 offers practical advice for using income and balance sheet data, along with an example using STATA commands for analysis. Chapter 21 discusses the psychometric issues regarding the design, implementation and analysis of mail surveys. Chapter 22 addresses issues of valid and reliable measurement and inference in field research. Chapter 23 introduces issues of triangulation strategy to accounting research. In Chapter 23, the authors illustrate the various forms of triangulations that can be applied in accounting research. The message of their chapter is that whilst conventional 'paradigms' can usefully explain qualitative, case study research, they need to be located in analyses embracing subjective and institutional factors for an adequate understanding of their import. As well as being a plea for greater theoretical plurality, the chapter also suggests a variety of research methods which can be developed jointly within a single study.

7.   Ethical Issues

Within Part VII, Chapter 24 outlines the basic ethical issues in human subjects research, with reference to qualitative research in accounting. It demonstrates how to deal with the application process for ethics approval. Chapter 25 examines some of the more significant methodological issues pertaining to research on accounting ethics.

8.   Publishing Research Work

In the final part, Chapter 26 offers practical advice in all aspects of the research and publication process. This ranges from generic aspects of approaching research to more focused treatments of the norms and conventions surrounding the endeavour.

I hope that the reader will find the following chapters of interest. It is not claimed that this book provides a complete review of methodological issues in accounting research. Any suggestions from the reader would be appreciated for its improvement in a future edition.

References

Berry, A. J., Capps, T., Cooper, D., Ferguson, P., Hopper, T. and Lowe, E.A. (1985), "Management control in an area of the NCB: rationales for accounting practices in a public enterprise", *Accounting, Organizations and Society*, Vol. 10, No. 1, pp. 3-28.

Burchell, S., Clubb, C., Hopwood, A.G., Hughes, T. & Nahapiet, J.E. (1980), "The Roles of Accounting in Organizations and Society", *Accounting, Organizations and Society*, Vol.5, No.1, pp. 5-28.

Carpenter, V. L. and Feroz, E. H. (2001), "Institutional theory and accounting rule choice: an analysis of four US state governments' decisions to adopt generally accepted accounting principles", *Accounting, Organisations and Society*, Vol. 26, pp. 565-596.

Chua, W. F. (1986), "Radical developments in accounting thought", *The Accounting Review*, Vol. LXI, No. 4, October, pp. 601-632.

Colville, J. (1981), "Reconstructing 'behaviourial accounting'", *Accounting, Organizations and Society*, Vol. 6, No. 2, pp. 119-132.

Covaleski, M. A. and Dirsmith, M. W. (1988a), "An institutional perspective on the rise, social transformation, and fall of a university budget category", *Administrative Science Quarterly*, Vol. 33, pp. 562-587.

Covaleski, M. A. and Dirsmith, M. W. (1988b), "The use of budgetary symbols in the political arena: an historically informed field study", *Accounting, Organisations and Society*, Vol. 13, pp. 1-24.

Glaser, B.G., and Strauss, A.L. (1967), *The Discovery of Grounded Theory: Strategies for Qualitative Research*, New York: Aldine Publishing Co.

Hopper, T. M. and Powell, A. (1985), "Making sense of research into the organizational and social aspects of management accounting: a review of its underlying assumptions", *Journal of Management Studies*, Vol. 22, No. 5, pp. 429-465.

Modell, S. (2002), "Institutional perspectives on cost allocations: integration and extension", *European Accounting Review*, Vol. 11, pp. 653-679.

Modell, S. (2003), "Goals versus institutions: the development of performance measurement in the Swedish university sector", *Management Accounting Research*, Vol. 14, pp. 333-359.

Modell, S. (2005), "Students as consumers? An institutional field-level analysis of the construction of performance measurement practices", *Accounting, Auditing and Accountability Journal*, Vol. 18, No. 4, pp. 537-563.

Morgan G. and Smircich, L. (1980), "The case for qualitative research", *The Academy of Management Review*, Vol. 5, No. 4.

Tinker, A.M., (1980), "A political economy of accounting", *Accounting, Organizations and Society*, Vol.5, No.1, pp.147-160.

Tomkins, C. and Grove, R. (1983), "The everyday accountant and researching his reality", *Accounting, Organizations and Society*, Vol. 8, No. 4, pp. 361-374.

Willmott, H.C. (1983), "Paradigms for accounting research: critical reflections on Tomkins & Groves' "Everyday accountant and researching his reality, *Accounting, Organizations and Society*, Vol.8, No.4, pp. 389-405.

2

RATIONAL CHOICE THEORY
Jodie Moll
University of Manchester, UK
Zahirul Hoque
Deakin University, Australia

Abstract: Organisational life features a range of decisions including new technologies, new products, mergers and acquisitions, discontinuation of products, and pricing, product mix. These decisions involve purposeful human action. The rational choice theory provides some insight into how and why such choices are made based on the principle of optimisation. This chapter explores the rational choice theory through its assumptions, concepts and perspectives.

Keywords: Decision-making, organisation, bounded rationality, principal agent theory, bureaucracy.

1.   Introduction

Decision making is a critical function of management. Managers are required to make decisions such as who should their suppliers be, what price should they set for their products, or should they invest in new accounting software. This chapter introduces the rational choice theory (RCT) as a basis for understanding how and why such choices are made in organisations. The chapter proceeds as follows: the key features of the theory are presented in section two; section three presents the concept of 'bounded rationality', which was developed in direct response to the narrow view of decision making offered by the economic versions of RCT; organisational links to RCT follow in section 4 including descriptions of both Weber's bureaucracy and Principal-agent theory; the paper then introduces RCT's link to accounting providing a future research agenda in section 5; and concluding remarks are offered in section 6.

2.   The Rational Decision Making Process

The term rational choice theory (RCT) is often used interchangeably with 'public choice theory', 'neoclassicism', 'expected utility theory' (Zey, 1998), 'rational actor theory' (Renwick Monroe, 2001; Zey, 1998) and 'utilitarianism' (Zafirovski, 1999). Derived from economics, RCT is a normative theory which provides an explanation of purposeful human action. The key to understanding the rational choice theory lies in 'optimisation'. Optimisation occurs when actors make decisions and take actions after assessing all of the costs and benefits of each alternative with the objective of maximising utility (or minimising disutility) (Coleman, 1990; Ryan, 1999). When the choice of action corresponds with the optimal choice it is deemed to be rational. Figure 1 outlines the typical rational decision process.

Figure 1:
A typical rational model of the decision making process with feedback control element.

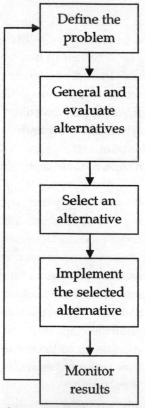

Source: Hatch, M. J. (1997), Organization Theory: Modern Symbolic and Postmodern Perspectives. Oxford University Press, Oxford, p. 273.

This decision making process is underpinned by a number of simple assumptions designed to increase its explanatory power and ability to predict decision outcomes. First, the decision process occurs as a result of a conscious effort by an individual to solve a problem (Renwick Monroe, 2001). This implies that larger social outcomes can be traced to individual actors. Second, the individual possesses complete information and foresight (e.g. demand, supply, prices) which always enable a rational choice to be made (Katona, 1964; Renwick Monroe, 2001).

Third, the individual is in pursuit of a set of pre-specified goals. Fourth, a set of alternative courses of action to any decision exists and each of these is mutually exclusive, separate and easily identified. Fifth, these preferences orderings are transitive, in the sense that an actor will have a preference of one over the other determined by which alternative is likely to maximise benefits and minimise the costs, or maximise utility. Sixth, the actor does not have any institutional or psychological factors which restrict them, or make it expensive or slow for them to implement the decision (Katona, 1964). Finally, each actor is able to make a decision without influence from others actions (Katona, 1964).

RCT has emerged as a dominant theoretical paradigm in economic, psychological (Hogarth and Reder, 1986) and political sciences (Dowding, 1994; Dowding and King, 1995). The key difference in the various strands lies in the fact that the psychology and political science strands concentrate on explaining the *process* by which choices are made, whereas the economist versions tend to focus on how the choice of a particular outcome has produced the intended consequence.

In the 1950s Simon published two seminal papers in which he outlined concerns for the simplifying assumptions upon which the economic RCT was erected. He (Simon, 1957, p. 198) argued:

> The capacity of the human mind for formulating and solving complex
> problems is very small compared with the size of the problems whose
> solution is required for objectively rational behaviour in the real world – or
> even for a reasonable approximation to such objective rationality.

He also suggested that individual decision efforts are not always aimed at providing 'optimal' decisions, but those that are satisfactory. To address these criticisms, Simon developed the concept of 'bounded rationality', which relaxed the assumptions of the economic rational model, combining the economic perspective with psychology literature.

3.   Bounded Rationality
In reality decision processes are far more complex than described by RCT. Dowding (1994) for instance, points out that all human decisions cannot be predicted by identifying the alternative which maximises utility. Using the Cuban missile crisis as an example, Dowding shows how particular individuals and their preferences can shape the decision making process. He (Dowding, 1994, p. 113) suggests that applying the RCT assumption of utility maximisation is too 'crude' and that a fuller explanation of the complexities is required to understand the process. Also related to this, RCT ignores the human capacity to make decisions in a rational manner; in particular it ignores the fact that emotional states can affect the degree of rationality of decision making. Holsti (1979; as cited in Zey, 1998) for instance suggests that the individual's capacity to make rational decisions is reduced during periods of high stress. Hechter and Kanazawa also report this concern, arguing that decisions on spouses, jobs or children are often emotionally charged and can take an emotional toll on individuals reducing their ability to choose the most rational alternative.

They (Hechter and Kanazawa, 1997) also suggest that people often act impulsively and do not calculate or appreciate all of the alternatives available (see also Smelser, 1992 for some discussion on this point). In similar vein, Miller (2000) maintains that individual actors can have short term horizons making what would seem to be the rational alternative in the short term irrational in the long term. Others have also criticised the theory for not acknowledging possible biased views or opinions (Friedrich and Opp, 2002). RCT is also said to be limited because it neglects to account for habitual decision making, much of which occurs in everyday life (Friedrich and Opp, 2002). It does not consider for instance, that each decision is not made after completing a full cost benefit of the alternatives. Where the decision mirrors a prior situation, especially where it is a low cost decision, it is not uncommon the response to imitate previous response.[1] This means that decisions can be made in a more timely fashion (for a discussion see Zey, 1998). But, it also means that decisions are made without full consideration of any of their behavioural consequences (Friedrich and Opp, 2002).

Apart from these behavioural assumptions the RCT has been criticised because it ignores the wider social, economic and political context in which organisations operate (Ansari and Euske, 1987; Burchell, et al., 1980; Chua, 1986; Covaleski and Dirsmith, 1983; Hopper, et al., 1987; Hopwood, 1983; Ogden and Bougen, 1985; Otley, 1984). Finally, Mouritsen (1994) contends that RCT's explanatory power is limited, since compliance with RCT model does not guarantee that the outcome will be rational. Mouritsen, for instance, suggests that by instilling rationality organisational learning is reduced, and existing models remain unchallenged.

To cope with this environment, Simon suggests that individuals construct a simplified model of the situation to enable them to make rational choices. Prediction of his/her behaviour thus requires knowledge of his/her psychological attributes.

4. Extending the Theory to Modern Organisations

Limitations in our computational ability, comprehension and foresight make organisations an important vehicle for the achievement of our goals. Because a group of individuals is unlikely to hold a static set of goals and are poor at communicating those goals achieving organisational goals becomes much more problematic. When presented with an organisational decision, disagreements become commonplace about which goals to pursue or which problems need solving and which knowledge is relevant to determine how the organisational goals should be achieved. The complexity of such cases renders the RCT, on its own, uninformative. Simon suggests that organisations cope with this environment, by adopting procedures and techniques that encourage improved decision making

---

[1] Eva Lindbladh and Carl Hampus Lyttkens (2002) present an interesting case study concluding that the rational choice model may be less applicable for decision making where there are limited resources.

similar to those underpinning Weber's bureaucracy. In addition, the decision making process has become increasingly complex in the modern business environment, not least because of the principal-agent relationships that pervade it. This form of relationship presents a range of problems for agents, who need to ensure that their objectives remain paramount in the decision process. To provide more robust explanations of RCT, scholars appeal to principal agency theory. The next two sections provide reviews of Weber's theory of bureacractic rationality and principal agent theory, respectively.

4.1 Weber's Theory of Bureaucratic Rationality

Weber's (1952) bureaucracy is a type of administrative structure characterised by rational-legal authority. To Weber rationality, reaching an optimal or rational decision involves satisfying both the 'zweckrationlitat' values of managers and owners and the 'wertrationalitat' concerns of other stakeholders. Traits of bureaucracy include a hierarchy of authority, an organisation bound by rules, fixed jurisdictional areas, administrative acts recorded in writing, the employee is subject to discipline, employees are selected based on their expertise, and the separation of administrative staff from ownership of the means of production. Weber rationality assumes goals are embedded within the technical-legal knowledge and thus are not the subject of debate. The implication of this for decision making is that the goals of actors employed in the organisation are consistent with the organisations. For Weber, bureaucracy represents the most rational form of organisation since it offers the possibility of logical outcomes (Ryan, 1999). In his words (1968, p. 987):

> Bureaucracy is the means of transforming social action into rationally organised action. Therefore, bureaucracy is an instrument of power for one who controls the bureaucratic apparatus.

Through this device, organisational decisions are able to be made and resources mobilised. Advocates of this theory argue that this type of structure is necessary to carry out the administration of the increasingly complex business environment and that if these bureaucratic forms did not exist, society would be chaotic and organisations would function in an inefficient and wasteful manner. While bureaucratic forms of administration may increase the effectiveness of an organisation, this type of administrative structure is also acknowledged to limit freedom, and provide structures of domination.

Weber distinguished between two types of rationality in his analysis of organisations: formal and substantive. Formal rationality is concerned with the techniques of calculation. Substantive rationality, in comparison, refers to a decision which is subject to values and ethical norms. It is the substantive rationality that gives meaning to the outcome of the formal rationality.

To date much of the criticism surrounding Weber's bureaucracy stems from its dehumanising nature, in particular its attention to conflict and evasion of rules and the chain of command (see, for instance, Gouldner, 1954; Parsons, 1956; Selznick, 1957, 1966). In reality, decision making is far more problematic because of a separation of principal and agent fostering debate over what the organisational goals are and how they can best be achieved. The principal agent model (also known as agency theory) provides some insight into this process.

4.2 Principal Agent Models

The complexity of modern day organisations where it is common for an agent to work on behalf of a principal in an organisation presents a challenge to RCT which was designed to provide insight into individual decision making.

A common criticism of RCT is that individuals will strive to maximise the profits of organisations, with little regard to the multiplicity of non-pecuniary motives which may influence that individual in making a choice. For example, in an outsourcing decision a CEO may choose to purchase from a former colleague, rather than from the lowest bidder. Or a choice may be made by a CEO based on its ability to legitimise or reinforce power relations in the organisation.

Principals face two problems in hiring agents to undertake a task (1) the agent and the principles goals are incompatible, and (2) they are faced with an asymmetric information problem, whereby they do not have full knowledge of the agents abilities, skills and expertise, or integrity (Zey, 1998). To complicate the situation further, these goals change over time. To address these such asymmetries, the principle must determine what governance structures (information systems, monitoring, incentives) are needed to ensure that the agent fulfils the principal's wishes and act in their best interest. An indepth review of this theory is provided in Chapter 5 of this text.

5. Management Accounting and RCT

Accounting practices provide calculative techniques for optimal decision making. In addition, accounting provides a basis for decision alternatives to be compared (Carruthers and Espeland, 1991). It also provides a record of the organisational choices which can help to rationalise or justify actions that have already been carried out (Burchell, *et al.*, 1980). In this sense, it could be argued that RCT pervades much of what is written about accounting; texts are written to describe accounting techniques that are an integral part of organisational decision making. In true Weberian form, Dillard and Ruchala (2005) also suggest that accounting systems foster 'administrative evil' in organisations, since they divorce action from moral context.

So if accounting systems are considered rational, why do they change? The simple answer to this is because conceptions of what is rational changes over time; RCT assumes that it is always possible to improve accounting information through the introduction of new technical developments. This suggests that personal conceptions of what is rational may be challenged when new information or techniques are presented or when the existing systems fail to provide the requisite information.

Management accounting research explicitly informed by RCT is relatively rare, with the exception of a few accounting studies which explain the form in which the management control system or elements of the management control system exist

(Burchell, *et al.*, 1980). In this section we review, briefly, several of these studies to indicate how it has been used in the discipline.

Ansari and Euske (1987) are perhaps most commonly cited for their use of RCT. In this study the authors utilised three theories, socio-political, institutional and the technical rational perspective to understand how military repair facilities introduced the depot cost and production reporting system and how this system conformed to the objectives of the system.

Carruthers and Espeland (1991) used the RCT to explain why double entry bookkeeping emerged as a dominant form of accounting. They suggest that there has been a widespread adoption of double entry bookkeeping because of its technical superiority for providing accurate and relevant information for decision-making.

Ansari and Bell (1991) employed the RCT to provide partial explanation of the role accounting played in control in International Foods, a holding corporation for a group of companies located in Pakistan. Another study that used RCT in tandem with other sociological and organisational theories is Covaleski, Dirsmith, and Michelman (1993). These researchers combined institutional and RCT theories to explain the use of case-mix accounting systems in health care organisations. From an RCT perspective they argue that the use of case mix accounting systems can lead to optimal efficiency and effectiveness by allowing for product lines to be monitored.

Jones and Dugdale (1994) drew on the RCT to explain investment decision making practices. Their study investigated the investment appraisal decision processes within the wider investment decision processes and context to understand the different reasons for the choice of a particular method to make investment decisions. In the case of Hoque and Hopper (1994) the RCT provided a partial explanation for how and why the control system was fashioned in a large nationalised jute mill in Bangladesh. More recently, Vámosi (2000) used a combination of institutional theory and RCT to explain how the concepts of market and market economy are adapted to the management accounting system in a Hungarian company.

Rahaman and Lawrence (2001) combined RCT with the socio-historical perspective and the socio-economic perspective to analyse the nature and effectiveness of accounting and financial management systems operating in the Volta River Authority in Ghana to determine the extent to which the accounting and financial systems were 'deficient'.

6.   Utilising RCT in Accounting Research

The limited use of RCT to inform our understanding of management accounting research suggests that there is still much that can be learned about the role(s) that accounting plays in constructing and making sense of everyday organisational life. How, for example, do organisations explain poor performance when accounting tools have been used to inform their decisions? Under what circumstances does accounting information dominate the decision process? What are the unintentional outcomes that can arise with using the information provided by a particular accounting technique? And, why do organisations prefer certain techniques over others, when their technical superiority is well noted in the texts? Such studies are also likely to contribute to the broader RCT literature, which has tended to focus on the economic 'outcome' approach rather than the psychology processual approach.

The simple nature of RCT acts as both its strength and weakness. It means that it is broadly relevant to a range of decision situations from including new technologies, new products, mergers and acquisitions, discontinuation of products, pricing, and product mix. In addition, it is robust in terms of its applicability to both individual and organisational decision making (Hannan, 1992; Zey, 1998). Traditionally scholars focused on the individual (i.e. the manager or the employee) as a basis for understanding organisational choice with the assumption that the analysis of individual actions would provide insight into larger social outcomes. In this regard, individual action is believed to be supportive of those outcomes that are beneficial to the organisation.

Recently, however, scholars have directed their attention to the organisation as the unit of analysis. This change in focus follows from a view that organisations are not passive recipients of the choices of its members or of institutional rules, and that they can play a fundamental role in setting the direction or timing of change in the social system (e.g. Coleman 1990; Hannan, 1992). Advocates of this view challenge whether social systems can be explained by the aggregate individual action. If, for example, individuals are rational decision makers, does this also imply that the collective organisational outcome will also be rational? According to these scholars, irrational organisational choice represents deviations in the behaviour of employees, in particular, those who have little or no incentive to comply with the chosen course of action (Hechter and Kanazawa, 1997).

But, the simplified nature of RCT comes at a cost. It means that its ability to provide indepth analysis of decision situations is limited, especially when the decision situation features multiple individuals, each able to mobilise different resources and each having different goals, priorities and assumptions about how the organisational goals should be attained. RCT is incapable of explaining such social relationships since it overlooks any data that does not fit within its assumptions (Zey, 1998). Furthermore, despite its normative focus, RCT makes no attempt to explain what the organisational aims ought to be. To make sense of the decision process and why it considers a particular action to be rational also requires knowledge of individual preferences, how they are formed and why particular meanings get attached to a situation. If such questions are the focus of study, they point to the need for RCT to be complemented with other sociological theories such as institutional theory or symbolic interactionism.

7.   Concluding Remarks

This chapter has described RCT as a theory of decision making. RCT is purposively simple, ignoring social norms and values, historical forces and painting the decision maker to be one whose actions are unaffected by emotion or habit. Typically, it was explained that the perspective is used to understand how the incentives of a given decision imply a certain behavioural response, one that is dictated by a desire to achieve maximum utility. Discussions of the concept of bounded rationality and models of bureaucracy and principal-agent followed. These discussions were designed to show the complexity of decision processes across time and in turn point to the limitations of RCT and the need to complement the theory with other sociological theories to embed the decision process within its cultural and institutional context. Fledgling RCT advocates wishing to further their knowledge of RCT should refer to the early chapters in Coleman's (1990) *Foundations of Social Theory*, Zey's (1998) *Rational Choice Theory and Organizational Theory: A Critique*, and Abell's (1991) *Rational Choice Theory*.

References

Abell, P., (1991), *Rational Choice Theory*, Elgar, Aldershot.

Ansari, S. and Bell, J. (1991), "Symbolism, collectivism and rationality in organisational control", *Accounting, Auditing & Accountability Journal*, Vol. 4, No. 2, pp. 4-27.

Ansari, S. and Euske, K. J., (1987), "Rational, rationalizing, and reifying uses of accounting data in organizations", *Accounting, Organizations and Society*, Vol. 12, No. 6, pp. 549-570.

Burchell, S., Clubb, C., Hopwood, A., Hughes, J. and Nahapiet, J. (1980), "The roles of accounting in organizations and society", *Accounting, Organizations and Society*, Vol. 5, No. 1, pp. 5-27.

Carruthers, B. G. and Espeland, W. (1991), "Accounting for rationality: double-entry bookkeeping and the rhetoric of economic rationality", *The American Journal of Sociology*, Vol. 1, July, pp. 31-69.

Chua, W. F. (1986), "Theoretical constructions of and by the real", *Accounting, Organizations and Society*, Vol. 11, No. 6, pp. 583-598.

Coleman, J. S. (1990), *Foundations of Social Theory*, Belknap, Cambridge.

Covaleski, M. A. and Dirsmith, M. W. (1983), "Budgeting as a means for control and loose coupling", *Accounting, Organizations and Society*, Vol. 8, No. 4, pp. 323-340.

Covaleski, M. A., Dirsmith, M. W. and Michelman, J. E. (1993), "An institutional theory perspective on the drg framework, case-mix accounting systems and health-care organizations", *Accounting, Organizations and Society*, Vol. 18, No. 1, pp. 65-80.

Dillard, J. and Ruchala, L. V. (2005), "The rules are no game: from instrumental rationality to administrative evil", *Accounting, Auditing & Accountability Journal*, Vol. 18, No. 5, pp. 608-630.

Dowding, K. (1994), "The compatibility of behaviouralism, rational choice and 'new Institutionalism'", *Journal of Theoretical Politics*, Vol. 6, No. 1, pp. 105-117.

Dowding, K. and King, D. (1995), *Preferences, Institutions and Rational Choice*, Oxford University Press, Oxford.

Friedrich, J. and Opp, K.-D. (2002), "Rational behaviour in everyday situations", *European Sociological Review*, Vol. 18, No. 4, pp. 401-415.

Gouldner, A. W. (1954), *Patterns of Industrial Bureaucracy*, The Free Press, New York.

Hannan, M. T. (1992), "Rationality and robustness in multilevel systems", Series, *Rationality and Robustness in Multilevel Systems*, Sage Publications, Inc., Newbury Park, CA.

Hechter, M. and Kanazawa, S. (1997), "Sociological rational choice theory", *Annual Review of Sociology*, Vol. 23, pp. 191-214.

Hogarth, R. M. and Reder, M. W., (1986), *Rational Choice*, University of Chicago Press, Chicago.

Hopper, T., Storey, J. and Willmott, H. (1987), "Accounting for accounting: towards the development of a dialectical view", *Accounting, Organizations and Society*, Vol. 12, No. 5, pp. 437-456.

Hopwood, A. G. (1983), "On trying to study accounting in the contexts in which it operates", *Accounting, Organizations and Society*, Vol. 8, No. 2-3, pp. 287-305.

Hoque, Z. and Hopper, T. (1994), "Rationality, accounting and politics: a case study of management control in a Bangladeshi Jute Mill", *Management Accounting Research*, Vol. 5, No. 1, pp. 5-30.

Jones, T. C. and Dugdale, D. (1994), "Academic and practitioner rationality: the case of investment appraisal", *British Accounting Review*, Vol. 26, pp. 3-25.

Katona, G. (1964), "Rational behavior and economic behavior", in Gore, W. and Dyson, J. W. (Ed.), *The Making of Decisions: A Reader in Administrative Behavior*, The Free Press, New York, pp. 51-63.

Miller, G. (2000), "Rational choice and dysfunctional behaviour", *Governance: An International Journal of Policy and Administration*, Vol. 13, No. 4, pp. 535-547.

Mouritsen, J. (1994), "Rationality, institutions and decision making: reflections on March and Olsen's Rediscovering Institutions", *Accounting, Organizations and Society*, Vol. 19, No. 2, pp. 193-211.

Ogden, S. and Bougen, P. (1985), "A radical perspective on the disclosure of accounting information to trade unions", *Accounting, Organizations and Society*, Vol. 10, No. 2, pp. 211-224.

Otley, D. T. (1984), "Management accounting and organization theory: a review of their inter-relationship", in Scapens, B., Otley, D. T. and Lister, R. (Ed.), *Management Accounting, Organizational Theory and Capital Budgeting: Three Surveys*, Macmillan, London, pp. 96-164.

Parsons, T. (1956), "Suggestions for a sociological approach to the theory of organizations", *Administrative Science Quarterly*, Vol. 1, No. 63-85, pp. 39-43.

Rahaman, A. S. and Lawrence, S. (2001), "Public sector accounting and financial management in developing country organisational context; a three dimensional view", *Accounting Forum*, Vol. 25, No. 2, pp. 189-210.

Renwick Monroe, K. (2001), "Paradigm shift: from rational choice to perspective", *International Political Science Review*, Vol. 22, No. 2, pp. 151-172.

Ryan, N. (1999), "Rationality and implementation analysis", *Journal of Management History*, Vol. 5, No. 1, pp. 36-52.

Selznick, P. (1957), *Leadership in Administration: A Sociological Interpretation*, Harper and Row, Publishers, Incorporated, Berkeley, CA.

Selznick, P. (1966), *TVA and Grass Roots: A Study in the Sociology of Formal Organization*, Harper and Row Publishers, Incorporated, New York.

Simon, H. A. (1957), *Administrative Behaviour*, Macmillan, New York.

Smelser, N. (1992), "The rational choice perspective", *Rationality and Society*, Vol. 4, No. 4, pp. 381-410.

Vamosi, T. S. (2000), "Continuity and change: management accounting during processes of transition", *Management Accounting Research*, Vol. 11, No. 1, pp. 27-63.

Weber, M. (1952), "The essentials of bureaucratic organization", in Merton, R. K. (Ed.), *Reader in Bureaucracy*, Free Press, New York, pp. 19-27.

Weber, M. (1968), *Basic Sociological Terms*, University of California, Berkeley.

Zafirovski, M. (1999), "What is really rational choice? Beyond the utilitarian concept of rationality", *Current Sociology*, Vol. 47, No. 1, pp. 47-113.

Zey, M. (1998), *Rational Choice Theory and Organizational Theory: A Critique*, Sage Publications, Thousand Oaks, CA.

3

THE HUMAN RELATIONS THEORY

Zahirul Hoque
Deakin University, Australia

Abstract: Human relations factors play a vital role in the working of an organisational process. This chapter illustrates the implications of human relations theory for management accounting practice. The chapter suggests that human relations is multidimensional as this approach places emphasis on the individual and the organisation, motivation, supervisory and management leadership, group dynamics, and organisational development. As accounting is influenced by human elements in both accounting policy making and its implementation, a human relations perspective is useful to understand accounting in action.

Keywords: Human relations; participation; motivation; budgets; resistance to change; behavioural accounting research.

1.   Introduction

A significant development of modern management during the 1930s and 1940s was the increase in attention to the human factors in organisations, which has later become known as the 'human relations school of management'. The human relations approach emphasises the work group and the role of the first-line supervisor in achieving organisational goals (Porter and Bigley, 1995). This chapter illustrates the implications of human relations theory for management accounting practice in organisations. The first section of this chapter discusses the meaning of human relations. Following this, it outlines the key features of human relations, and provides details of the various ways that the theory had been applied to researching management accounting practice. Finally the chapter concludes.

2.   The Meaning of Human Relations

Anytime somebody confronts a problem at work dealing with people, either individually or groups, he or she is potentially making use of human relations (DuBrin, 1984). To Carvell (1980, p. 2), 'Human relations is motivating people in groups to develop teamwork which effectively fulfils their needs and achieves organizational objectives'. From the view point of a manager or supervisor who has responsibility for leading a work group, Davis (1967) holds that 'human relations is the integration of people into a work situation that motivates them to work together productively, cooperatively, and with economic, psychological, and social satisfaction'. Thus the subject of human relations focuses on using systematic knowledge about human behaviour. Lewis (1983, p. 9) sees human relations as the study of how people treat one another in a social or a work situation.

Human relations theory places emphasis on the individual and the organisation, motivation, supervisory and management leadership, group dynamics, and organisational development. These factors have dominated the development of human relations movement in the field of management science.

3. Human Relations Movement

A few early writers such as Mayo (1933, 1941), Roethlisberger and Dickson (1939, 1945), Dalton (1950, 1959) and Kerr and Fisher (1957) provided the foundation for the human relations movement. Among these authors, the prominent human relations study was conducted by Elton Mayo between 1927 and 1932 at the Western Electric's Hawthorne plant near Chicago. The basic theme underlying this study is that employee satisfaction is a major determinant of productivity or performance. The next section outlines the two classical approaches to management that contributed to the emergence of human relations approach to management thought, what we call 'scientific management' and 'classical management theory'.

3.1. Scientific Management

In the early 1900s, Frederick W. Taylor (1911) developed the idea of efficiency and productivity of individual workers which became known as 'scientific management' in the study of management. It mainly focused on improved worker output as a result of job specialisation and mass production. To Taylor, money was the only important motivational factor in the workplace, and he introduced the idea of piece-rate pay in which each worker was paid for the amount of work he completed during the workday rather than for the time spent on the job (for details, see Moorehead and Griffin, 1995).

Taylor's Scientific Management Theory can be summarised, as follows:
- Use increasing specialisation and division of labour to make a process more efficient.
- Systematically analyse the relationship between the worker and task and redesign processes to ensure maximum efficiency, e.g. use a bigger shovel so more grain can be lifted with each action.
- Have written procedures for each task and ensure they are followed by supervision and quality control.
- Get maximum prosperity for employer and employee alike by linking pay and other rewards directly to work output.
- Select workers with the right skills and abilities for the specific task and train them thoroughly to follow the procedures (Source: http://www.mftrou.com/frederick-taylor.html).

Taylor's scientific management, however, was not well accepted by labourers because of its explicit focus on getting more output from workers (for a critical review of Taylor's scientific management, see Wrege and Perroni, 1974; Wrege and Stoka, 1978). Another contribution to management during the 1900s was known as 'classical management theory' which focused on how organisations can be structured most effectively.

3.2.   Classical Management Theory

Henry Fayol, Lyndall Urwick, and Max Weber were the major contributors to the classical management theory. Among these three scholars, Max Weber became well known for his theory of 'bureaucracy' that suggests that a bureaucracy is a logical, rational, and efficient model of organisations (Moorehead and Griffin, 1995).

Weber's 'bureaucratic' form of organisation focuses on the following aspects, as summarised by Moorhead and Griffin (1995):

- **Rules and procedures**: A consistent set of abstract rules and procedures should exist to ensure uniform performance.
- **Distinct division of labour**: Each position should be filled by an expert.
- **Hierarchy of authority**: Hierarchy in the authority structure.
- **Technical competence**: Employment and advancement should be based on merit.
- **Segregation of ownership**: Professional managers, rather than owners, should run the organisation.
- **Rights and properties of the position**: These should be associated with the organisation, not the person who holds the office.
- **Documentation**: A record of actions should be kept regarding administrative decisions, rules, and procedures.

Both scientific management and classical management theory have been criticised by many scholars because of their over-emphasis on rationality, efficiency, and standardisation. It has been suggested (Moorehead and Griffin, 1995) that these two approaches ignore the roles of individuals in organisations. Human relations theory emerged to overcome such criticisms of both scientific management and classical management theory.

3.3.   Human Relations Factors

Elton Mayo (1933) and his colleagues (Roethlisberger and Dickson, 1939) at Harvard University gave academic stature to human relations. Elton Mayo's Hawthorne experiments at the Western Electric Company (USA) suggest that an organisation is a social system and the worker is the most important element in it. Mayo and his colleagues' experiments further showed that employees are motivated not only by economic needs but also by social needs. Mayo suggests that employees achieve their basic sense of identity largely through interaction with others in the organisation, and they are as responsive to social forces as they are to economic pressures. Roethlisberger and Dickson added that 'a human problem to be brought to a human solution requires human data and human tools' (quoted in Davis, 1967,

p. 9). There is also the view that employees performed most efficiently under systems of management, which met their social as well as economic needs. Thus, human relations focus on people and their associated behaviour in an organisation.

To elaborate further, the work of Elton Mayo has emphasised the morale aspect of human relations, as Mayo maintained: 'morale is more important than the physical conditions of work' (cited in Hughes, 1970, p. 11). In this context, Hughes (1970, p. 11) remarks: 'this (morale) aspect of Mayo's work really only reinforces what any supervisor knows from his own study of people – we can get good output in poor working conditions if the human relationships are good, but we can get poor output in very good working conditions if the human relations are bad'. Porter and Bigley (1995) classify the human relations movement into five areas: the individual and the organisation; motivation; leadership; group dynamics; and organisational development. These are discussed in turn.

3.3.1. The individual and the organisation. Douglas McGregor (1960) became well known for human relations' maturity in management fields. His popular 'Theory X' and 'Theory Y' suggest that human relations cannot work at organisations with management's autocratic approach (Theory X) without supporting ideas for leading people (Theory Y).

Theory X assumes that:
- The average human being has an inherent dislike of work and will avoid it if he can.
- Because of this human characteristic of dislike of work, most people must be coerced, controlled, directed, and threatened with punishment to get them to put forth adequate effort toward the achievement of organisational objectives.
- The average human being prefers to be directed, wishes to avoid responsibility, and has relatively little ambition, wants security above all.

On the other hand, **Theory Y** assumes that:
- The average human being does not naturally dislike work; depending upon controllable conditions, work may be a natural part of their lives.
- External control and the threat of punishment are not the only means for bringing about effort toward organisational objectives. People will exercise self-direction and self-control in the service of objectives to which they are committed.
- Commitment to objectives is a function of the rewards associated with their achievement.
- The average human being learns, under proper conditions, not only to accept but to seek responsibility.
- The capacity to exercise a relatively high degree of imagination, ingenuity, and creativity in the solution of organisational problems is widely, not narrowly, distributed in the population.

- Under the conditions of modern industrial life, the intellectual potentialities of the average human being are only partially utilised.

To McGregor, industrial man and woman have a hunger for self-expression and personal creativity, and these are, according to Hopwood (1974, p. 33), what today's large organisations should be providing if they want to retain a motivated and involved groups of managers and employees. To some people, human relations is nothing but glad-handling, backslapping, and the big smile, as Davis (1967) makes it clear that this is the 'keep 'em happy' or 'nice-guy' philosophy. Further, Davis (1967, p. 11) suggests:

> Human relations is not a matter of liking people, but of doing something constructive about working relationships within the organization. Human relations does not try to make the organization into a life adjustment society, nor is it psychological paternalism. Rather, it helps get the job done.

3.3.2. Motivation and employee productivity. Employee motivation plays an important part in employee performance vis-à-vis organisational performance. This idea or theme has been central to Maslow's (1943) contribution to human relations movement entitled 'A Theory of Human Motivation'. Maslow identified human needs into the following five-levels of hierarchy:

1. Psychological needs: such as the requirements for food, water, shelter, and sleep;
2. Safety needs: actual physical safety such as a safe working environment;
3. Love needs: social or belonging needs, that is, interactions amongst human beings;
4. Esteem needs: ego needs, that is, individuals want to be seen as competent and capable by others, and
5. Self-actualising needs: the needs for self-fulfilment and personal development.

Maslow's motivation theory suggests that human beings move from one level of need to the next higher level when the lower level is satisfied, or reverted to a lower level when an upper one is blocked (Porter and Bigley, 1995).

Herzberg and his colleagues at the end of 1950s also contributed significantly to human relations movement by introducing the 'motivation-hygiene' theory, which focuses on job 'satisfiers' or 'motivators'. Herzberg *et al.* (1959) suggest that job elements such as achievement, recognition, challenging work, responsibility, and the opportunity for achievement gives individuals satisfaction, which, in turn, motivates them. In contrast, some (hygiene) factors, according to Herzberg *et al.*, dissatisfy individuals. Examples of such hygiene factors include hot, cramped office with no windows. According to Herzberg *et al.*, dissatisfiers relate to the context (the job setting or external elements such as company policy and administration, supervision, physical working conditions, relationships with others on the job, status, job security, salary, and personal life.

Table 1 exhibits a comparison between the Maslow and Herzberg theories. Table 1 shows that satisfiers and motivators relate to the higher-level needs and dissatisfiers and hygiene factors relate to lower level needs. DuBrin (1984) comments, 'one major difference between the Maslow and Herzberg theories is that, according to the former, an appeal to any level of need can be a motivator ... only appeals to higher level needs can be motivational'. Herzberg's motivation-hygiene theory was influential in the development of job design approaches such as job enlargement and job enrichment (Porter and Bigley, 1995).

Table 1
Comparison Between the Maslow and Herzberg Theories

Maslow	Herzberg
	Motivational factors
Self-actualisation	Work itself
	Achievement
	Responsibility
Self-esteem	Recognition
	Advancement
	Status
	Hygiene factors
Love (belonging and affiliation)	Interpersonal relations
	Supervision-technical
Safety and security	Company policy and administration
Physiological needs	Job security
	Working conditions
	Salary
	Personal life

Source: Derived from DuBrin (1984, p. 41).

3.3.3. Expectancy theory. Another development in the human relations approach is the expectancy theory, which assumes that people are rational human beings who choose among alternatives by selecting the one that appears the most advantageous (Vroom, 1964). The expectancy theory has the following three components:

Effort-performance outcome: Exhibits how an individual's behaviour is associated with his/her mind with a certain expectancy or subjective hunch of the probability of success. This suggests that effort-performance expectancies influence whether or not one will even strive to earn a reward. For example, self-confident people have higher effort-performance expectancies than do less self-confident people.

Performance-outcome expectancy: An individual's intention of achieving a desired outcome. This suggests that the stronger the individual's subjective probability (hunch) that performance is likely to lead to a desired outcome, the stronger the probability that the individual is likely to expend effort.

Valence: Each outcome has a value to an individual, thereby one can observe significant differences in the valence a given reward has for different people (DuBrin, 1984). Thus, valence is about a person's affective orientations towards particular outcomes. Vroom (1964, p. 15) uses this example to explain the concept of valence: 'For any pair of outcomes, x and y, a person prefers x to y, prefers y to x, or is indifferent to whether receives x or y. Preferences, then, refers to a relationship between the strength of a person's desire for, or attraction toward, two outcomes'.

The above discussion suggests that a person's motivation is a function of *expectancy, performance* and *outcome*, which can be expressed by the following formula:

Motivation = (Expectancy⇒Performance)x(Performance⇒Outcome) x valence.

Several other early research studies provide evidence to support the expectancy theory of motivation (e.g. Porter and Lawler, 1967; Galbraith and Cummings, 1967; Graen, 1969; Lawler, 1968). These researchers found that the force on an individual to engage in a specific behaviour is a function of (1) his expectations that the behaviour will result in a specific outcome; and (2) the sum of the valences, that is, personal utilities or satisfactions, that he derives from the outcomes (see the above formula) (for more details, see House, 1971).

Recent human relations literature has classified human motivation broadly into cognitive and noncognitive models. Cognitive models suggest that individuals make conscious decisions about their behaviour. In other words, individuals are driven by internal forces that guide their behaviour. Goal theory, the need for hierarchy, Herzberg's two-factors hygiene theory, and expectancy theory fall under this cognitive category of human motivation.

In contrast, noncognitive models of motivation focus on the environment rather than on the inner person for an explanation of why individuals behave as they do. Seen in such a context, rewards and punishments play an important part in the environment. Noncognitive models suggest that people engage in motivated behaviour when their behaviour leads to a reward (for further details, see DuBrin, 1984).

Katz (1964) emphasises three basic types of employee behaviour that are essential for a functioning organisation: (1) employees must be attracted to and retain within the organisation; (2) employees must perform their duties that meet some minimum level of quantity and quality of performance; and (3) there must be innovative and spontaneous behaviour amongst employees in achieving organisational objectives. Instrumental systems rewards (fringe benefits, recreational facilities, job security, pleasant working conditions, etc.), instrumental individual rewards (monetary and non-monetary rewards to individuals), and intrinsic job satisfaction are some of the motivational bases an organisation can use to improve individual employee productivity as well as organisational-wide productivity (Katz, 1964).

3.3.4. Leadership style and human relations. Leadership style plays an important part in managing human relations in an organisation. Rensis Likert's work (1961) on supervision and leadership raised the issue of the conditions under which employees could be mobilised with all the motivational force into a powerful group towards achieving organisational goals. Likert introduced the idea of 'participative group' approach in decision making and organisational design. The Likert thesis is that it is the leader's crucial role as the 'linking pin' between higher- and lower-level groups in the organisation (Porter and Bigley, 1995). According to Likert (1961, p. 103):

> *The leadership and other processes of the organization must be such as to ensure a maximum probability that in all interactions and all relationships with the organisation each member will, in the light of his background, values, and expectations, view the experience as supportive and one which builds and maintains his sense of personal worth and importance* (emphasis added originally).

Katz (1964) remarks that Likert's theory takes account of the hierarchical authority structure of organisations, but also ties in every individual in the organisation through his attachment to his own group, and presumably integrates the needs of all subgroups. There is the widely held view that participation produces high morale, which in turn, increases employee productivity. In this context, Likert suggests that a participative and group oriented approach to managing the social environment should be the preferred style of management (for further details, see Hopwood, 1974).

3.3.5. Resistance to change and human relations. Human relations theory also focuses on the dynamics of social forces and how they react to organisational change (Lewin, 1947). From an organisational point of view, we encounter two very important issues in a changed environment: why do people resist change? and what can be done to overcome such resistance?

Coch and French (1948) suggest that change can be accomplished by the use of group meetings in which management effectively communicate the need for change and stimulates group participation in planning the changes.

4. Human Relations and Organisational Behaviour

An organisation has a primary goal and operates as a unit to achieve that goal (Lewis, 1983). Organisational employees must communicate with each other and contribute action to achieve the common organisational goal. Studies using the human relations theory found that personal relations among organisational members are critical to employee productivity, which leads to achieve organisational goals.

People at work interact with each other. How do people get along with other people? Employee productivity vis-à-vis organisational performance fully depends upon employees' positive attitudes towards their jobs, supervisors or managers. Lewis (1983) suggests that human relations is vital to successful development in any work activity requiring interpersonal contacts, therefore, it is important to know how people affect each other through their behaviour. However, it should be noted that people differ because their perceptions differ (Lewis, 1983). Therefore, it is essential to learn about the nature of the organisation's workforce, their expectations, their behaviour, their personal goals, and so forth.

The organisational behavioural literature suggests that the study of people at work should not be isolated from the study of organisation (e.g. Lewis, 1983). This implies the development of the discipline, 'Organisational Behaviour'. Moorhead and Griffin (1995) define organisational behaviour as the study of human behaviour in organisational settings, the human behaviour-organisation interface, and the organisation itself. For a successful business, managers at all levels must regard the role of human relations in organisational settings because, according to Lewis (1983), if the working environment allows people to meet their basic needs and realise self-esteem, they are likely to be more satisfied and motivated and this has a spin-off effect – one relationship affects others; work affects social life, and vice versa. Such an argument tallies with Davis's (1967) view that individuals, groups, and the institution combined have influence on organisational activities which results in integration into a working social system. Davis (1967, p. 86) notes:

The result of an effective mix of human relations factors is productive motivation. This kind of motivation should get above-average performance out of average people. It develops problem solvers out of problem makers. It causes two-way human relations, meaning that managers and employees are jointly influencing each other and jointly benefiting. This is power with people rather than power over them. There is no one-way manipulation or bulldozing of one party by the other. People are treated like people, nothing more and nothing less.

Managing human relations in any organisation depends on a particular theory or philosophy of management. Carvell (1980) suggests that the relationship of management philosophy and its impact on the psychological climate of the workplace is a key factor in the study of human relations. Similarly, Davis (1967) suggests that underlying theory is a conscious guide to organisational managers' behaviour. Seen in such a context, I now discuss how theories of organisational behaviour vis-à-vis management philosophy affect the basic human relations factors in an organisation.

The organisational behavioural literature identifies the following three dominant theories of organisational behaviour: the Autocratic Theory; the Custodial Theory; and the Supportive Theory. The autocratic theory focuses on power that managers or supervisors exercise to get things done by their subordinates. To do so, an organisation sets formal policies that every employee must follow. Tight control through a formal budget is an example of such a formal authority. Douglas McGregor in his published book *The Human Side of Enterprise* in 1960 classified such an organisational behaviour or management style as *Theory X*.

On the other hand, the custodial theory places emphasis on material (economic) rewards, security, organisational dependency, and maintenance factors. Maslow's

(1943) human need-priority model emphasises a definite sequence of five basic needs of human relations, as outlined earlier in this chapter.

Table 2 summarises some important contributions of these disciplines to the human relations theory. According to Davis (1967), human relations should be looked at from the combined approach of many disciplines as exhibited in Table 2.

Table 2
Contributions of Various Disciplines in the Development of Human Relations

Disciplines	Contribution to Human Relations
Scientific Management	• Formal Organisation (Organisations without People)
Psychology	• Human Needs • Motivation • Counselling • Individual differences
Sociology	• Role Theory • Informal Organisation • Status • Group Dynamics
Organisation and Management Theory	• Objectives • Line and Staff • Authority and Responsibility • Division of Labour
Semantics	Understanding of: • communication processes, • meaning, and • listening
Social Anthropology	• Culture • Status Symbols
Philosophy	• Value Systems • Human Dignity
Economics	• Labour Theory • Productivity Concepts
Social Science (Behavioural)	Why and how people behave as they do (People without Organisations)

Source: Derived from Davis (1967, pp. 18-19)

The preceding discussion suggests that human relations is an integration of many disciplines such as scientific management, psychology, sociology, and organisation theory. Several early writers contributed significantly to the behavioural or human relations aspects of the organisation.

Some contributions of human relations to the development of behavioural research in accounting include human needs, motivation, individual differences in perceptions and attitudes, employee emotions, leadership styles, participative management and control, value systems and human dignity, and productivity and performance concepts. Argyris (1952, 1953, 1955, 1960), Simon, *et al.* (1954), Hofstede (1968), Swieringa and Moncur (1974), Hopwood (1973, 1974), Brownell (1982a, 1982b) are, among others, major contributors in behavioural accounting research. The next section discusses some of them.

5.   Accounting and Human Behaviour

Several strands of human relations theory have emerged from accounting studies based on the human relations approach. Anthony Hopwood's (1974) seminal work contributed significantly to the development of behavioural aspects of accounting research. In his 1974 book 'Accounting and Human Behaviour' Hopwood comments:

> ... the effectiveness of any accounting procedure depends ultimately upon how it influences the behaviour of people in the enterprise ... there is nothing new about such a view point: accounting have never operated in a behavioural vacuum. Just try to imagine designing and operating an accounting system on technical expertise alone. What type of information would you design information for control purposes without considering how it would fit in with the other means of influencing behaviour in organisational settings? How would you provide information to motivate superior performance without having some understanding of human needs and aspirations? And how would you manage the processes of standard setting, budgeting, and planning, all of which are essentially social in nature (pp. 1-2).

To Hopwood, accounting is about human behaviour, and its social and behavioural aspects are just as much an indispensable part of the whole as the more traditional technical aspects (Hopwood, 1974, p.14). Hopwood's viewpoints are grounded in several early behavioural research in management accounting practice such as budgeting.

6.   Human Relations Factors and Psychology-Based Budgeting Research

Budgets are generally viewed as a means for motivating individual managers and employees (Hopwood, 1974). Covaleski, Evans, Luft and Shields (2003) offer a comprehensive review of the psychology-based budgeting research. They use the following three dimensions to summarise the relationship between human relations factors and budgeting:

* Primary research questions (e.g. what are the effects of budgeting initiatives on human beings, their mental states, behaviour and performance?)
* Level of analysis (e.g. how the effects of budgeting vary across individuals rather than organisations)
* Underlying assumption about rationality (e.g. bounded rational and satisfying).

Considerable research has claimed that participation in the budget process may have either a positive or negative effect on individuals behaviour, motivation, and satisfaction (see Argyris, 1952, 1953, 1955, 1960; Simon, *et al.*, 1954; Dalton, 1959; Dearden, 1961; Hofstede, 1968; Schiff and Lewin, 1970; Dew and Gee, 1973; Swieringa and Moncur, 1974; Ashton, 1976; Otley, 1976, 1978). Using the human relations theory, researchers show how a budget can induce an active and possibly pressured organisational environment which may result in higher levels of performance. It has been suggested that both productivity and satisfaction are greater when managers and employees set objectives through active participation in the budget making process (for more details, see Hopwood, 1974).

Researchers further discovered: how superior managers use accounting information to express their own styles of leadership (Decoster and Fertakis, 1968); how subordinates react to budget-related pressure and the association of budgets with pressure, aggression, conflict, inefficiency and staff-line clashes (Hofstede, 1968); and how managers use budgets in response to prevailing environmental circumstances (Otley, 1976, 1977, 1978). Other factors studied include: personality and attitudinal variables (Swieringa and Moncur, 1974); the influence of personality factors in participative budgeting (Vroom, 1964; Brownell, 1981, 1982a, 1982b); and dysfunctional aspects of participative budgeting (Schiff and Lewin, 1970).

Schiff and Lewin (1970) suggest that managers tend to create slack in budgets through a process of understating revenues and overstating costs. Others (e.g. Lowe and Shaw, 1968; Dalton, 1961; Shillinglaw, 1964) reported similar observations (for a detailed review, see Belkaoui, 1989). Stedry (1960) suggests that many management accounting techniques such as budgeting and standard costing may not motivate employees effectively because they fail to consider the broad spectrum of needs and drives of the participants (for details, see Caplan, 1966).

Some recent studies have extended earlier research based on human relations approaches (see for instance, Brownell, 1982a, 1982b; Hirst, 1983, 1987; Dunk, 1989; Brier and Hirst, 1990; Brownell and Dunk, 1991). Brownell's (1982a) study shows that when budget participation is high (low), a high (low) budget emphasis is associated with enhanced managerial performance. Another study, Hirst (1983), suggests that when budget emphasis is high (low) and task uncertainty is low (high), job-related tension is minimised.

Thus, human relations based accounting research revealed how top-down controlling tools such as budgeting demotivate employees despite its potential benefits (Covaleski, Evans, Luft and Shields, 2003). To overcome such a problem, studies investigated how an organisation can create a favourable environment through a participative style of budgeting (for a comprehensive review on participative budgeting, see Shields and Shields, 1998). Hopwood (1974), however, criticise the heavy influence on the participative approach to the budgeting process, as he concludes:

> It is simply naïve to think that participative approaches are always more effective than more authoritarian styles of management or vice versa. The participation of managers and employees in the budgetary process, for instance, can do much to increase their

acceptance of the budget, their subsequent involvement and commitment, and the quality of the budget as an aid to decision making, but it can also have the opposite effects. The critics as well as the advocates of participative management would therefore be wise to direct their energies towards identifying the situations in which a variety of decision making styles are effective, rather than towards universalistic claims for the applicability or otherwise of any single approach (pp. 89-90).

Nevertheless, many of the above budgeting research produced mixed findings – some found positive effects of budgeting on individual's mental states, behaviour and performance, some found negative, and no significant effects (Hopwood, 1976; Kenis, 1979; Shields and Shields, 1998; cited in Covaleski *et al.*, 2003).

Covaleski et al. (2003) argue for the psychology-based accounting research and identify two assumptions in this context. The first assumption is that human behaviour is boundedly rational and satisficing. The second assumption is that human beings "seek or desire a state of internal (single-person) equilibrium that is called mental consistency, but they are often in a state of disequilibrium due in part to their bounded rationality and satisficing" (Covaleski et al., 2003, p. 22). For further details on bounded rationality see Chapter 2 of this book plus Conlisk (1996), Rabin (1998), and Shafir and LeBoeuf (2002). Using the notion of cognitive consistency of human beings research has shown how people strive for a balanced or equilibrium cognitive structure, with unbalanced or disequilibrium (e.g. Brownell. 1982a; cited in Covaleski et al., 2003).

7. Conclusion

This chapter outlined the human-relations approach and explained how the theory is utilised to understand the operation of accounting and control systems according to individuals' attitudes, behaviour and job satisfaction. The discussion suggested that an individual's behaviour influences the way they process information in control systems and increased satisfaction can sometimes result in increased productivity (Macintosh, 1985). Human relations studies from organisational social psychology have contributed to a broader understanding of how a variety of human aspects can affect the operation of accounting and control systems in organisations. These include: the effects of participation/consultation in decision-making processes; motivation, satisfaction and reward systems; leadership effects; organisational slack practices; and the effect of interpersonal relations among organisational members.

The chapter also outlined the theoretical weaknesses of the human relation approach, namely that human relations studies on accounting and control systems provide inconsistent results, the human relations works can neglect the import of individuals' understanding, values, meanings and culture, and that the approach fails to explain how accounting and control systems may be products of the socio-economic and political contexts in which the organisation operates. Using psychoanalysis within sociology, future research can explore how does accounting in action affect individuals' mental states, behaviour and performance, which in turn, affect organisational performance.

References

Argyris, C. (1952), *The Impact of Budgets on People*, Controllership Foundation, New York.

Argyris, C. (1953), "Human problems with budgets", *Harvard Business Review*, Vol. 31, January-February, pp. 97-110.

Argyris, C. (1955), "Organizational leadership and participative management", *Journal of Business*, Vol. 28, January, pp. 1-7.

Argyris, C. (1960), *Understanding Organizational Behavior*, Tavistock Publications, London.

Argyris, C. (1973), "Personality and organisation theory revisited", *Administrative Science Quarterly*, Vol. 18, pp. 141-167.

Ashton, R. H. (1976), "Deviation-amplifying feedback and unintended consequences of management accounting systems", *Accounting, Organizations and Society*, Vol. 1, No. 2, pp. 289-300.

Belkaoui, A. (1989), *Behavioural Accounting: The Research and Practical Issues*, Quorum Books, New York.

Brier, M. and Hirst, M. (1990), "The role of budgetary information in performance evaluation", *Accounting, Organizations and Society*, Vol. 15, No. 4, pp. 373-398.

Brownell, P. (1981), "Participation in budgeting, locus of control and organizational effectiveness", *The Accounting Review*, October, pp. 844-860.

Brownell, P. (1982a), "The role of accounting data in performance evaluation, budgetary participation and organizational effectiveness", *Journal of Accounting Research*, Spring, pp. 12-27.

Brownell, P. (1982b), "Participation in the budget process: when it works and when it eoesn't", *Journal of Accounting Literature*, Vol. 1, No. 2, pp. 124-153.

Brownell, P. and Dunk, A. S. (1991), "Task uncertainty and its interaction with budgetary participation and budget emphasis: some methodological issues and empirical investigation", *Accounting, Organizations and Society*, Vol. 16, No. 8, pp. 693-703.

Carvell, Fred J. (1980), *Human Relations in Business*, 2nd edition, Macmillan, New York.

Coch, L. and French, Jr. J. R. P. (1948), "Overcoming resistance to change", *Human Relations*, Vol. 1, pp. 512-532.

Conlisk, J. (1996). Why bounded rationality? *Journal of Economic Literature*, Vol. 34, June Issue, pp. 669-700.

Covaleski, M. A., Evans III, J. H., Luft, J. L. and Shields, M. D. (2003), "Budgeting research: three theoretical perspectives and criteria for selective integration", *Journal of Management Accounting Research*, Vol. 15, pp. 3-49.

Dalton, M. (1959), *Men Who Manage*, Wiley, New York.

Davis, K. (1972), *Human Behavior at Work: Human Relations and Organizational Behavior*, 4th edition, McGraw-Hill Book Company, New York.

Dearden, J. (1961), "Problems in decentralized management controls", *Harvard Business Review*, Vol. 39, No. 3, pp. 72-80.

DeCoster, D. T. and Fertakis, J. P. (1968), "Budget-induced pressure and its relationship to supervisory behavior", *Journal of Accounting Research*, Autumn, pp. 237-246.

Dew, R. B. and Gee, K. P. (1973), *Management Control and Information*, Macmillan, London.

DuBrin, A. J. (1984), *Human Relations: A Job Oriented Approach*, 3rd edition, Reston Publishing Co. Inc., Reston, Virginia.

Dunk, A. S. (1989), "Budget emphasis, budgetary participation and aanagerial performance: a note", *Accounting, Organizations and Society*, Vol. 14, No. 4, pp. 321-324.

Gailbraith, J. and Cummings, L. L. (1967), "An empirical investigation of the motivational determinants of past performance: interactive effects between instrumentality, valence, motivation and ability", *Organizational Behavior and Human Performance*, Vol. 2, pp.237-257.

Graen, G. (1969), "Instrumental theory of work , motivation: some empirical results and suggested modifications", *Journal of Applied Psychology*, Vol. 53, pp. 1-25.

Herzberg, F., Mausner, B. and Snyderman, B. B. (1959), "A hypothesis related and expanded and motivation versus hygiene", in *The Motivation to Work*, John Wiley, New York, pp. 107-119.

Hirst, M. K. (1983), "Reliance on accounting performance measures, task uncertainty, and dysfunctional behavior: some extensions", *Journal of Accounting Research*, Autumn, pp. 596-605.

Hirst, M. K. (1987), "The effects of setting budget goals and task uncertainty on performance: a theoretical analysis", *The Accounting Review*, October, pp. 774-784.

Hofstede, G. H. (1968), *The Game of Budget Control*, Tavistock, London.

Hopwood, A. G., (1973), *An Accounting System and Managerial Behaviour*, Saxon House, London.

Hopwood, A. G. (1974), *Accounting and Human Behaviour*, Accounting Age, London.

House, R. J. (1971), "A path goal theory of leader effectiveness", *Administrative Science Quarterly*, Vol. 16, pp. 321-338.

Hughes, E. W. (1970), *Human Relations in Management*, Pergamon Press, Oxford.

Katz, D. (1964), "The motivational basis of organizational behaviour", *Behavioral Science*, Vol. 9, pp. 321-333.

Kenis, I. (1979), "Effects of budgetary goal characteristics on managerial attitudes and performance", *The Accounting Review*, pp. 707-721.

Lawler, E. E. III. (1968), "A correlation-causal analysis of the relationship between expectancy attitudes and job performance", *Journal of Applied Psychology*, Vol. 52, pp. 462-468.

Lewin, K. (1947), Frontiers in group dynamics: concept, method and reality in social science; social equilibria and social change", *Human Relations*, Vol. 1, pp. 5-41.

Lewis, P. V. (1983), *Managing Human Relations*, Kent Publishing Company, Boston.

Likert, R. (1961), "An integrating principle and an overview", in *New Patterns of Management*, McGraw-Hill, New York, pp. 97-118.

Macintosh, N. B. (1985), *The Social Software of Accounting and Information Systems*, John Wiley and Sons, New York.

Maslow, A. H. (1943), "A theory of human motivation", *Psychological Review*, Vol. 50, pp. 370-396.

Mayo, E. (1933), *The Human Problems of an Industrial Civilization*, Harvard University Press, Cambridge, Mass.

Mayo, E. (1941), "Research in human relations", *Personnel*, Vol. 17, pp. 264-269.

McGregor, D. (1960), *The Human Side of Enterprise*, McGraw-Hill Book Company, New York.

Moorhead, G. and Griffin, R. W. (1995), *Organizational Behavior*, Hoghton Miffin Company, Boston.

Otley, D. T. (1977), "Behavioural aspects of budgeting", *Accounts Digest* ICAEW, London, No. 49, Summer.

Otley, D. T. (1978), "Budget use and managerial performance", *Journal of Accounting Research*, Vol. 16, Spring, pp. 122-149.

Porter, L. W. and Bigley, G. A. (Eds.) (1995). *Human Relations: Theory and Developments*, Aldershot, England: Dartmouth.

Rabin, M. (1998). "Psychology and economics". *Journal of Economic Literature*, Vol. 36, March Issue, pp. 11-46.

Roethlisbereger, F. J. and Dickson, W. J. (1939), *Management and the Worker*, Harvard University Press, Cambridge, Mass.

Roethlisberger, F. J. and Dickson, W. J. (1945), "The foreman: master and victim of double talk", *Harvard Business Review*, Vol. 23, pp. 283-298.

Schiff, M. and Lewin, A. Y. (1970), "The impact of people on budgets", *The Accounting Review*, pp. 259-268.

Schein, E. H. (1971), "The individual, the organization, and the career: a conceptual scheme", *Journal of Applied Behavioral Science*, Vol. 7, pp. 401-426.

Shafir, E. and LeBoeuf, R. (2002). "Rationality". *Annual Review of Psychology*, Vol. 53, pp. 491-517.

Simon, H., Guetzkow, H., Kozmetsky, G. and Tyndall, G. (1954), *Centralization Versus Decentralization in Organizing the Controller's Department*, Controllership, New York, NY.

Taylor, F. W. (1911), *The Principles of Scientific Management*, Harper and Brothers, New York.

Vroom, V. H. (1964), "Motivation – a point of view", in *Work and Motivation*, John Wiley, New York, pp. 8-28.

Wrege, C. D. and Perroni, A. M. (1974), "Taylor's pig-tale: a historical analysis of Frederick W. Taylor's pig-iron experiment", *Academy of Management Journal*, March, pp. 6-27.

Wrege, C. D. and Stoka, A. M. (1978), "Cooke creates a classic: the story behind Taylor's principles of scientific management", *Academic of Management Review*, October, pp. 736-749.

4

THEORISING AND TESTING FIT IN CONTINGENCY RESEARCH ON MANAGEMENT CONTROL SYSTEMS

Robert H. Chenhall
Monash University, Australia
Christopher S. Chapman
University of Oxford, UK

Abstract: In this chapter we focus on a central theoretical concept in contingency theory, the nature of fit. Reviewing in turn Selection, Interaction and Systems forms of fit we discuss the main assumptions and implications that each entails, followed by a discussion of the various ways in which these theoretical approaches have been tested in practice in a variety of studies of contingency theory looking at management control systems.

Keywords: Contingency theory, fit, method.

1. Introduction

Contingency-based studies in the area of management control systems (MCS) now comprise a substantial and diverse body of research. Whilst this literature includes studies that have adopted a wide array of empirical and statistical approaches the central issue required to inform an understanding of their contribution is the concept of 'fit'. This concept has been described as 'the heart of contingency theory' (Donaldson, 2001, p.181). In MCS research a contingency framework has been utilised to identify how MCS are best designed and implemented to 'fit' the context, or contingencies, within which MCS are employed. Fit is thus a question of alignment between three primary pieces of an organisational puzzle: (1) The characteristics of MCS, (2) Organisational Performance, and (3) Contingency factors that might affect the relationship between the first two. Figure 1 shows an overview of the basic question of contingency research together with an indication of some of the main contingency variables that have been examined in the MCS literature to date.

Figure 1
An Overview of Contingency Analysis of MCS

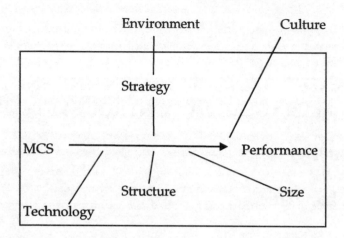

Building on the contingencies that formed the interest of classic contingency studies from the organisational literature, MCS based researchers have studied the effects of environment, technology and size on organisational structure. More recently much attention has been given to the importance of strategy as a contingency. This raises interesting questions for the contingency framework, blurring as it does the distinction between endogenous and exogenous variables. In relation to the environment, for example, notions such as enactment and selection of the environment through strategic choices raise questions as to the validity of assumptions that the environment is something external that imposes on organisations. For a comprehensive review of MCS studies that have worked with these various factors, the primary ways in which they have been conceptualised as variables amenable to study, and an overview of the resulting propositions concerning their impact, see Chenhall (2003; forthcoming).

Over time, contingency-based MCS research has been subject to a number of critiques. Otley (1980), for example, was concerned about the relative lack of attention to measuring performance, an issue that has subsequently received much more attention including the use of stock market performance information as a measure in studies such as Ittner *et al.* (2003). Chapman (1997) argued that whilst much attention had been devoted to the development of research instruments that addressed an increasingly wide variety of contingency factors, relatively less effort seemed to have been devoted addressing more processual aspects of MCS. The increasing appearance of studies building on the notion of *Interactive Control Systems* show that progress continues to be made on this front (Bisbe *et al.*, 2005). Whilst much remains to be done in these areas, such progress is cheering.

Hartmann and Moers (1999) engaged in a comprehensive review of the literature addressing questions of theoretical and statistical rigour with which contingency-based hypotheses have been put forward and subsequently tested. One of their concerns was that very often past studies had failed to elaborate their expectations regarding the nature of fit with sufficient clarity. Recent publications show that whilst a central concept, fit remains subject to ongoing and often spirited debate (e.g. Gerdin and Greve, 2004; Gerdin and Hartmann, 2005) many years after seminal discussions of the topic such as (Drazin and Van de Ven, 1985).

A particular challenge in understanding fit in terms of its theoretical and methodological implications is the fact that there is considerable and confusing variation in the use of vocabulary used to describe various forms of fit between the main writers on the subject.[2] Table 1 shows a comparison of the terms employed by two leading sources on the subject. We can see that whilst noting that the adoption of a common set of terms is helpful, Donaldson (2001) nonetheless proposes a comprehensive departure from the terms suggested by Drazin and Van de Ven (1985). His arguments in support of his suggested re-naming of Selection and Systems fit provide an excellent summary of key arguments regarding the nature of relationships being theorised and will be discussed below. In particular, his proposed renaming of Interaction fit deserves more attention here since it stresses an important argument that highlights the separation between theoretical concepts of fit and their statistical operationalisation. Partly he wishes to avoid confusion caused by the use of multiplicative interaction terms commonly used in statistical analysis of Interaction fit. His main concern is to elaborate Matching fit (very little used in MCS research) from more general approaches that use multiplicative interaction terms (the bulk of the MCS literature). Donaldson proposes Matching fit as the exemplar of contingency research, and as we will see below it offers a far more precise theorisation of the relationship between MCS, contingencies and performance.

Table 1
Abbreviated Summary of Fit Relationships

Drazin & Van de Ven	Donaldson
1. Selection fit	1. Managerial choice
2. Interaction fit	2. Congruence fit
	Matching & Interaction
3. Systems fit	3. Multifit

In this chapter we will examine the various notions of contingency fit (Selection, Matching and Interaction, Systems) that have been used to model the relationships between MCS and outcomes in the literature. Having clarified the specific assumptions underlying these different forms of fit we will briefly address some of the wider theoretical debates related to different notions of fit, and discuss briefly how they have been operationalised drawing on illustrative examples from the MCS literature.

---

[2] Confusion is also caused since writers also use of the same words in relation to different forms of fit. So, for example, Donaldson adopts the term congruence in relation to what Drazin and Van de Ven (1985) refer to as Interaction fit.

2. Selection Fit

Selection studies examine the way contextual factors are related to aspects of MCS with no explicit attempt to assess whether this association is linked to performance.[3] For example, it may be that managers find that a reliance on accounting performance measures is most useful in situations that are relatively stable and certain. Implicit in these approaches is the assumption that firms operate in situations of equilibrium. As such, researchers will observe only organisations that have taken optimal choices to ensure that MCS suit the context of the organisation. Therefore all firms are at optimal performance, given their situation, and it is not possible to identify firms that have not aligned their MCS with the requirements of their context as they will not have survived. In discussing critiques from reviewers in accounting journals that equilibrium assumptions mean that performance effects of MCS are not to be expected, Ittner and Larcker (2001) suggest this is a somewhat extreme stance, proposing instead,

> A more defensible position ... is that people learn to make good decisions and that organizations adapt by experimentation and imitation so there is at least 'fossil evidence' available for testing theories (Milgrom and Roberts (1992) quoted in Ittner and Larcker (2001, p. 399)).

Drazin and Van de Ven (1985) in discussing this recognise that the equilibrium assumptions underlying Selection fit models may apply more to some aspects of organisation than others. Arguing that in many studies there is some 'more-macro' level that imposes on the 'more-micro' level. Frequently these impositions are conditional (and hence of particular interest to contingency theorists) involving switching rules to distinguish appropriate actions and situations (such as the differential organisation of production and research and development, for example). In doing so, they bring in the issue of managerial decision. Donaldson (2001) prefers the term 'managerial decision' for this form of fit, arguing that appeals to concepts such as natural selection and survival of the fittest downplay significant aspects of managerial choice.

2.1. Testing Selection Fit

The statistical techniques used to examine research questions concerning the extent to which MCS are related to an element of context involve tests of association such as correlation analysis, or if there are multiple elements of context, multivariate techniques such as regression analysis. A distinctive feature of selection studies in MCS research is that have identified a novel aspect of MCS and shown how they relate to various contingencies. We select just two examples, Simons (1987) and

---

[3] In Gerdin and Greve's (2004) Figure 1 in which they provide a helpful classificatory framework of forms of fit, Selection fit is indicated with the bracket noting forms of fit in which MCS is the Dependent variable.

Davila (2000) to show how selection studies identify novel aspects of MCS and examine associations with context.

Simons (1987) expressed the primary concern of his study using the Null form H₀ 'Control system attributes do not differ between Prospector firms and Defender firms'. In the study he aimed to elaborate on the meaning of MCS and identified 10 specific MCS characteristics. The research focused on how these were associated with the strategic archetypes of Prospectors and Defenders. Correlations were used to identify the strength of the association between each characteristic and the strategic archetype. In addition, multiple regression (LOGIT) was used to see how well the MCS characteristics could predict firms as prospectors or defenders. The study also analysed performance effects in a separate set of analyses, but the primary interest of the study is its Selection fit hypothesis.

Davila (2000) presents a study of the role of MCS in new product development. Following a series of preliminary field studies and a careful analysis of the literature on the nature of uncertainty and its consequent information processing requirements his study puts forward two sets of Selection fit hypotheses. The study also includes a third set of hypotheses that explore Interaction fit relationships. As discussed in detail by Gerdin and Greve (2004) and Gerdin and Hartmann (2005) in particular, care must be used in mixing forms of fit since in some cases the underlying theoretical assumptions may be mutually exclusive. At a statistical level there is also the concern that if a contingency and MCS variable have been tested using correlation analysis in support of a Selection fit hypothesis then it is problematic to then test their Interaction fit with performance, since regression analysis assumes the independent variables are not significantly correlated. Davila (2000) presents an instructive example of the careful integration of Selection fit and Interaction fit. So, for example, one of his Selection fit hypotheses (supported in the study) concerns the relationship between market uncertainty and use of customer information in MCS. Customer information in MCS is then tested in Interaction with a customer focused strategy to show positive performance effects.

3.   Interaction Fit

Whilst the findings of selection fit studies have been instructive and they have generated streams of subsequent studies, the question of performance is seen as important by many accounting researchers. There is widespread interest as to whether different combinations of MCS and context have different performance outcomes. Unlike Selection approaches, Interaction approaches imply that whilst organisations are likely moving towards optimal combinations, there will be some that have not achieved this combination. Others may have changed their context, say their strategy or structure, and have yet to adjust MCS to suit the new situations. This dynamic process of moving in and out of equilibrium means that researchers can expect to identify poor performing organisations (with MCS that are not suitable for their context) at any given point in time. In considering how MCS, contingencies and performance come together Donaldson (2001) argues that his concept of

Matching fit is the most appropriate. We consider this first, and then, in a subsequent section, discuss Multiplicative Interaction fit, the approach used most often in MCS research.

3.1. Matching Fit

Matching fit assumes optimal combinations between aspects of a contextual variable and particular dimensions of an MCS. For each level of a contextual variable, there is assumed to be a unique level of an MCS variable. If these two levels 'match' then the firm is in fit, and performance is maximised. Any mismatch (in either direction) between the specific level of the contextual variable and the appropriate MCS results in a decline in performance. A Matching fit line can be conceptualised as one that joins all the points of fit derived from matching the appropriate MCS with the level of the contextual variable.

Figure 2
Matching Fit: Isoperformance

Donaldson Matching fit (Iso-performance)

Locus of control							
	C o n t r o l	Internal	5	-4	-3	-2	-1	*0*
			4	-3	-2	-1	*0*	-1
	o f		3	-2	-1	*0*	-1	-2
			2	-1	*0*	-1	-2	-3
		External	1	*0*	-1	-2	-3	-4
				1	2	3	4	5
				Low				High

Participation

For example, Figure 2 shows that in considering the locus of control of an employee there might be a unique level of budgetary participation at which performance might be maximised. In the figure the assumption is made that scales of measurement have been found at which this unique level is determined as having an equal score. Under Matching fit assumptions performance is a question of how far from fit a situation is, not where on the fit line that the match is positioned. Given this, performance is the same at any point on the line of fit, hence the use of the term Isoperformance by Donaldson (2001).

A second significant implication of this form of fit is that by contrast with more common forms of Multiplicative Interaction fit as found in MCS literature, performance is not simply a question of more (less) of an MCS variable in interaction with more (less) of a context variable. In Figure 2, faced with a locus of control score of 4 (indicating in this hypothetical case a more Internal focus), then the appropriate level of participation is also 4 (indicating a relatively high level of participation). Performance would be reduced by either less or more participation than this. As will be shown in a subsequent section, Multiplicative Interaction fit clearly differs from the idea of Matching fit, where the latter specifies a unique fit for participation at a given level of locus of control. A further issue is that matching fit can entail an expectation of curvilinear relationships, and not simply linear ones. For example, it is often suggested that more organic forms of management controls are better suited to conditions of environmental uncertainty than more formal, mechanistic controls. However, while mechanistic controls suit relative certainty and as the environment becomes more uncertain more organic systems provide for more flexible responses, it is possible that at extremely high levels of uncertainty the organisation's survival is threatened and the most suitable response is to employ more mechanistic controls to ensure that resources are conserved. Matching fit can model and test this situation by recognising the three stages on uncertainty and the curvilinear relationship with the mechanistic-organic typology.

Examples of Matching fit in the MCS literature are relatively rare. Two studies that use a deviation score rather than a multiplicative interaction term (see below) are Brownell (1982) and Frucot and Shearon (1991). In their footnote 12, Frucot and Shearon (1991) describe their approach as similar to Brownell's, being based on 'matching' their two variables of interest. Both studies examine Locus of control and budgetary participation (with the latter study adding in effects of specific aspects of Hofstede's dimensions of national culture). Both use a deviation score approach, testing the relationship between the absolute difference between the two main variables and performance. Whilst their approach does produce a different profile of performance expectations than simple multiplicative interaction (see Figure 4 below) as they argue is appropriate, it is worth noting that Figure 3 shows that they are not using Donaldson's form of Matching fit (as shown in Figure 2). The use of the term 'matching' has caused confusion in subsequent analysis of the field, with Hartmann and Moers (1999) noting on page 299 that if Matching fit was being applied, then appropriately worded hypotheses would have made reference to a single unique level of participation given locus of control.

Figure 3
Brownell, and Frucot and Shearon Deviation Score Analysis

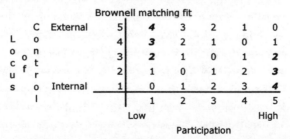

In both Brownell (1982) and Frucot and Shearon (1991) an external locus of control was scored highly, and so a high locus of control score is best served by a low participation, and vice versa. As such their theory predicts a relationship between performance and maximum deviation between variables, as opposed to minimum deviation seen in Figure 2. The salient differences with Matching fit are that there is no assessment of a theoretically optimum value, thus there is no isoperformance line of fit. Neither does their deviation score relationship allow for too much (or little) participation. In their model more (less) is strictly better. At medium levels of locus of control their operationalisation also raises the issue of equifinality, whereby there are two equally good solutions in the same situation. Given a locus of control score of 3, then the deviation score is maximised by both very low and very high participation. Donaldson (2001) argues strongly that equifinality is not a part of contingency theory, and that where it has been argued it represents a failure to consider other relevant contingencies that vary between apparently similar situations.

3.2. Testing Matching Fit

Matching fit requires measuring the deviation of the actual MCS score from the appropriate unique score of the MCS that ensures a fit at each level of the contextual variable. A common method to calculate deviation from fit is Euclidean distance. This technique first identifies the appropriate MCS score for a level of context and then subtracts the actual MCS score at that level of context. High scores indicate misfit, while a score of zero would be on the isoperformance line as indicated in Figure 2. When using Euclidean distance the fit scores for MCS and context may be determined from theory or empirical analysis.

Euclidean distance is a way of measuring the distance between the actual MCS score and the 'ideal' score that the organisation should have if it fits with the contextual variable (Drazin and Van de Ven, 1985, pp. 350-351). The formula is:

$$\text{Dist }_{IJ} = \sqrt{\sum_{S=1}^{N} (X_{IS} - X_{JS})^2}$$

- Dist_{IJ} = Euclidean Distance for the jth focal organisation to its ideal type (I) (theoretically or empirically determined)
- X_{IS} = Score of ideal (I) type organisation on the Sth contingency dimension
- X_{JS} = Score of Jth focal organisation on the Sth contingency dimension.

This may be positive (above the isoperformance line) or negative (below the isoperformance line). The technique was developed to measure multiple dimensions of fit.[4] To capture absolute distance ignoring sign effects the squared deviation scores are added and then the square root is taken. The deviation score is then associated with performance with the predication of a negative association. To determine fit it is necessary to identify the 'ideal' score. This can be done theoretically or empirically. An alternative approach that we will examine is the residual method of determining deviation from fit.

3.3. Euclidean Distance: Theoretical Approach

This approach requires the researcher to identify from theory that certain combinations of MCS and context are fits and other combinations are not. It is then necessary to identify those organisations in fit or misfit and see if this identification predicts performance. The approach can be illustrated by reference to the

---

[4] Drazin and Van de Ven (1985) note that Matching Fit, or deviation score analysis as they term it represents a bi-variate equivalent of the multivariate Systems fit approach.

isoperformance graph in Figure 2. In this approach fit is determined from theory and is represented by points along the isoperformance line. That is, each point along the isoperformance line is assumed to be optimal, as given *a priori* from theory, with fit scoring 0. Each movement or deviation away from 0 is a move into misfit (more or less MCS for a level of context) and scores -1. From Figure 2, a maximum negative score would be -4, moving in either direction away from the isoperformance line.

There are few studies in MCS research that have used deviation from the theoretical fit approach. Govindarajan (1988) provides an example where administrative procedures, defined in terms of three attributes (a budgetary style of evaluation, decentralisation and managers' locus of control) are argued to result in high performance only in firms using strategies of product differentiation. If applied in firms following strategies of cost leadership they result in a decline in performance. To test this Matching fit model the Administrative Procedures scores were standardised with end points at -1 and +1, with -1 predicted to fit with low cost (scored -1) and +1 to fit with product differentiation (scored +1). Fit was measured as the Euclidean distance between the organisational unit's scores and scores of its ideal type, identified for the unit's particular strategy. Thus, for example, a unit that has a low cost strategy (scored -1) will be in fit if it scores -1 on each of the administrative mechanisms. If one or more of the administrative scores is greater than -1, the Euclidean distance score increases and the unit moves into misfit. The Euclidean distance score is then regressed against performance. A negative association with performance supports the proposition of good fit. Govindarajan (1988) found support for fit when using the total sample. However, when examining Systems fit for the separate strategy groups, only fit for product differentiation had significant fit. In addition, the study found support for the Systems fit model when defining ideal scores within the range -1.00 and 0.50 for low-cost and +1.00 to +0.50 for product differentiation.

3.4. *Euclidean Distance: Empirical Approach*

In this approach, rather than using *a priori* theory to determine fit, an estimate of fit is determined empirically. It is assumed that organisations are in the process of moving towards fit and that the nature of fit can be determined by an examination of the relationship between MCS and the relevant contingency variable for the highest performing entities in a sample of organisations. That is, the appropriate fit score for the MCS can be determined by using the MCS scores for each level of context for the highest performers in the sample as a benchmark. Alternatively, applying regression analysis to relate MCS to context will produce a regression line that represents fit combinations of MCS for each level of context. To ensure that this relationship is truly fit, a sample of the highest performers can be used for the regression analysis of MCS on context, given sufficient numbers in the sample. In each case, the fit scores can be compared with the actual score for the MCS at the level of context, to provide a deviation score. This deviation score can be used to predict performance with high deviation scores being associated with low performance.

Selto, Renner and Young (1995) illustrate the use of the empirical approach to Euclidean distance. This is included in a test of Systems fit in their study of JIT and context (e.g. size, cultures, environment, technology), organisational structure (formality, flexibility, delegated authority, incentives), and controls (communications, information flows, management controls). Systems fit was examined by considering the effect of fit on 42 workgroups. The highest performing workgroup (a composite of efficiency, yield, defects, schedule) was taken as the benchmark for determining the ideal score on each dimension of the study, and this was subtracted from actual scores in the remaining workgroups to determine the Euclidean distance. The Euclidean distance was regressed against the outcome measures. Significant results were not found. The study examined the extent to which each difference score for context, structure and control variable were associated with outcomes. In their analysis of deviation using the mean scoring of the individual respondents making up each work group there were modest results.

3.5. Deviation From Empirically Determined Fit using Residual Analysis

An alternative approach is to use residuals from regressing MCS on context as a measure of misfit (Duncan and Moore, 1989). As in the prior approach, it is assumed that organisations are moving towards equilibrium. Those that are in fit will lie on the regression line that relates MCS to context, and the residuals will measure the extent of misfit, or the extent to which organisations are off the fit regression line. The next step is to regress the residuals on performance with the predication that there will be a negative relationship between the residuals (degree of misfit) and performance.

An example of this approach is found in Ittner, Lanen and Larcker (2002). They found that extensive use of ABC adoption in plants and improved financial performance depended on the fit of ABC with the plants' operational characteristics. Operational characteristics found to be relevant in this relationship were mixed rather than discrete (job shop) settings, high product mix facility, volume, more recent new product introductions, advanced manufacturing practices, but volume did not have an affect. Ittner and Larcker (2002) used a logit regression to show that extensive use of ABC (ABC use = +1, non-use = 0) was associated with the plant's operational characteristics. They assumed that 'all firms may be moving towards optimal practices, but at any point in time some firms will be off equilibrium'. This allows performance differences to be examined by assessing the extent to which performance is associated with deviations from 'optimal practices'. It is then shown that the residuals from the logit equation of ABC use on operational characteristics represent sub-optimal over or under investment in ABC.[5] Over- and under-

---

[5] The residuals represent the degree to which plants over and under invested in ABC. A plant making extensive use that is appropriate for the operating situation will have a low

investing are captured by positive and negative residuals, to capture potential different effects of over or under investment. These represent positions above and below the fit regression, respectively. A plant's over-investment score is the residual scored positively (the plant uses ABC extensively but it is predicted not to use ABC because the context is inappropriate) and zero if not. An under-investment is the residual scored negatively and zero if not (the plant does not use ABC extensively and it is predicted that it should use ABC). These residuals are regressed against performance with the expectation that the regression coefficients signs are negative for the positive residuals and positive for the negative residuals, and if significant indicate poor performance from mis-fit. Support for contingency effects were found when measuring performance on Return on Assets.

3.6. Multiplicative Interaction Fit

Matching and Multiplicative Interaction fit models differ, the latter being less theoretically precise. For any given level of context the Matching fit approach has only one level of the MCS variable that ensures optimal performance, all other levels of the MCS variable result in deviations from the optimal, with a consequent decline in performance. For general Multiplicative Interaction approaches (by far the majority of MCS contingency studies), relationships are expressed in more general terms, with higher (lower) values of context require higher (lower) values of MCS to achieve higher (lower) performance. Thus, for example, given a high level of uncertainty, more flexibility in budget use will produce better performance than less budget flexibility. This kind of relationship can be simply tested using a multiplicative interaction term.

Simply multiplying MCS by context produces the interaction terms for each combination of MCS and context as presented in Figure 4. If it is assumed that increasing values on these interaction terms are significantly associated with high performance then inspection of Figure 4 reveals the nature of the implied relationship between MCS, context and performance. To return to the variables used to describe Matching fit, first we note that performance is enhanced by the use of more participative budgeting at each level of locus of control, although the relative improvement is higher at higher scores of locus of control (e.g. at locus of control score 2, increasing budget participation to 5 produces a maximum of 10; whilst at locus of control score of 5 increasing budget participation to 5 produces a maximum of 25). This suggests that more participation is appropriate at all levels of locus of control, although this is accelerated at higher levels. Figure 4 then expresses a monotonic interaction between context and MCS on performance.

---

residual, while another plans also making extensive use but in inappropriate operating conditions will have a large residual (i.e. a positive residual indicating over investment). Similarly, under investment for non-users that operate in situations where they should use ABC will have larger residuals (i.e. negative residual indicating under investment) than those non-users operating in situations which do not suit ABC.

Figure 4
Interaction Fit: Monotonic Interaction

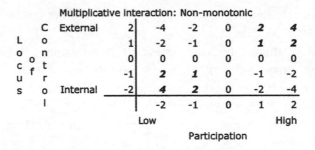

Multiplicative interaction: Monontonic

C External	5	5	10	15	20	25
o	4	4	8	12	16	20
n	3	3	6	9	12	15
t	2	2	4	6	8	10
r Internal	1	1	2	3	4	5
o		1	2	3	4	5

(Locus of control — vertical axis; Low ... High Participation — horizontal axis)

Theory might dictate that a non-monotonic relationship between the two, however. That is to say one where the effect of an interaction on performance is positive for one level of an independent variable, and negative at another. This can be seen by centring variables before producing a multiplicative interaction term. Figure 5 shows that, as locus of control increases above the mid point, the interaction term is positive for high levels of participation, but negative for low levels. Regressing these interaction terms on performance produces a coefficient, which if significant, the sign can be used to support the propositions that the slope of regression in one condition of the contingency variable group is greater than in the other.

Figure 5
Interaction Fit: Non-Monotonic Interaction

Multiplicative interaction: Non-monotonic

C External	2	-4	-2	0	2	4
o	1	-2	-1	0	1	2
n	0	0	0	0	0	0
t	-1	2	1	0	-1	-2
r Internal	-2	4	2	0	-2	-4
o		-2	-1	0	1	2

(Locus of control — vertical axis; Low ... High Participation — horizontal axis)

These two figures are intended to elaborate the intuition behind monotonic and non-monotonic interactions but, see, Luft and Shields (2003) appendix J for graphical presentations of the complete range of possible permutations and combinations of sign effects. See also Hartmann and Moers (1999) Appendix A1 for a helpful summary of forms of interaction with examples of verbal hypotheses and associated statistical tests.

3.7. Testing Multiplicative Interaction Fit

There are many examples of Multiplicative Interaction studies in the area of MCS research. Hartmann and Moers (1999) provide an extensive review of the use of interaction models and the role of moderated regression in budgetary research. We select examples of studies that have shown the strength of the interaction, the form of the interaction both monotonic and nonmonotonic. Studies that examine the strength of interaction fit relationships often also include an examination of form. It should be noted that strength examines the difference in associations between MCS and performance in different contexts (e.g. a correlation of 0.30 compared to 0.70), whilst form provides information on differences in how changes in context affect the prediction of performance by MCS (e.g. different slopes in the regressions used to predict performance from MCS, depending on context).

In their study, Abernethy and Lillis (1995) examine if manufacturing flexibility influenced the relationship between performance measures, integrative liaison devices and performance. In a test of a strength interaction their sample was split into flexible and non-flexible firms and correlations between the performance measures and performance were estimated. For efficiency-based measures there was a significance difference between the levels of correlation observed in the two groups (positive for non-flexible, and, negative for flexible subgroups). The test of strength interaction for integrative liaison devices was not found to be significant.

To test the form of the contingency model, it is usual to employ multiple regression to examine if the slope of the regression between an outcome variable (say, performance) and MCS differs in different conditions of the contextual variable. The approach is to regress the outcome variable against the MCS variable, the contingency variable and a multiplicative interaction term, constructed by multiplying the MCS by the contingency variable. As indicated earlier, form is indicated by the slope of the regression line between outcome and MCS in each condition of the contingency variable (e.g. high or low uncertainty). Both monotonic and non-monotonic relationships are possible.

Govindarajan and Gupta (1985) show a non-monotonic interaction. In their study, it is proposed that a greater reliance on long-run performance measures (e.g. sales growth, market share, new product development, R&D, personnel development, political/public affairs) to determine incentive bonuses for strategic business unit managers will have a stronger positive impact on effectiveness for units following build strategies compared to those following harvest strategies. A significant interaction term between strategy and reliance on long-term criteria within a regression equation that included main effects and the interaction indicated that the positive impact on effectiveness was stronger for build compared to harvest strategies. To test for monotonicity the partial derivative of the regression equation was calculated. That is, the change in effectiveness as a result of a change in reliance on long-term measures is equated with levels of the strategy variable. This revealed that for build strategies, a reliance on long-term criteria has a positive affect on effectiveness, while for harvest strategies a greater reliance on long-term criteria has a negative affect on effectiveness.

An example of a monotonic interaction is Chenhall (1997). In this paper it is hypothesised that the interaction between a reliance on manufacturing performance measures (MPM) will be significantly associated with organisational performance, such that profitability of entities employing more extensive TQM will be enhanced where the approach to measurement entails reliance on MPM. After establishing the significance of the interaction, the sample is split into four groups based on high and low TQM and reliance or no reliance on MPM. Using an ANOVA the effectiveness means for sub-groups could be inspected. It was shown that performance for both high and low TQM groups was positive, but the performance for firms with a reliance on MPM was greater than those that did not rely on manufacturing MPM. For the low TQM groups, performance was positive but not significantly different between groups with high or low reliance on MPM.

4.   Systems Fit

While most Selection, and Interaction fit approaches consider how performance measures are related to only one or two contextual variables, there is a view that this approach is overly molecular and that MCS design should be considered in terms of the many contextual variables that describe the operating situation (Drazin and Van de Ven, 1985). Examining how performance measures should best be designed becomes more than considering the sum of the effect of each contextual variable or their interactions. The holistic combination of performance measures and multiple contextual variables provide a Systems form of fit. The exact consequences of multiple contingencies may be difficult to predict. A contextual variable may act synergistically or antagonistically with other variables, intensifying or reducing the effects of context on a requisite aspect of MCS. A frequent consequence of such complexity is the attribution to Systems fit of an expectation that change ceases to be a gradual process of realignment[6] becoming instead a process of quantum leaps between successful archetypes.

There are two main ways that MCS researchers have testing systems fit: Euclidean Distance and Cluster analysis. We discussed Euclidean Distance under the section on Matching fit as a way of determining deviation between ideal fit and actual. The technique attempts to study how MCS and contextual variables act simultaneously to affect performance outcomes. The analysis identifies patterns of underlying dimensions of context and MCS. Ideal patterns of scores on the variables of interest are identified either from theory, or empirically from high performing firms. The Euclidean Distance formula is used to generate a single 'distance score' for each organisation that represents the sum of all the deviations across the multiple variables in the systems fit model.

Earlier we explained the use of Euclidean Distance to test Matching models of fit. In this case only one aspect of a MCS and one contextual variable are examined. In a sense the Euclidean Distance technique as an operationalisation of the systems approach can be considered as examining multiple 'matchings' between MCS variables and contextual variables. However, it is important to note that to many theorists the systems approach aims to capture the holistic pattern of

---

[6] Donaldson (2001) discusses this under the heading SARFIT Structural Adaptation to Regain Fit.

interdependencies between multiple variables and it represents more than the sum of each variable considered separately.[7] The Euclidean Distance approach to testing Systems fit is restricted to being an additive model. It adds the separate 'matching fits' of each contextual variable and as such the final distance measure is the sum if the component parts. As described above, Selto et al. (1995) and Govindarajan (1988) use Euclidean distance to measure systems fit.

In considering attempts to analyse systems fit adopting a more holistic approach, Cluster analysis has been used to identify sets or clusters of organisations that share a common profile along conceptually distinct variables that captures the complexity of organisational context. The clusters of organisations are formed such that the distance between variables within a cluster is minimised, while the distance between clusters is maximised. While this technique provides a powerful way of identifying how organisations can be grouped on the basis of similarity in contextual and MCS variables it requires the researcher to make several important decisions. The resulting clusters are thus very much the result of the choices made. With regards to the distance between clusters for example, options include the shortest distance, the maximum distance and the average distance between variables. In addition, the distance between centroids of clusters may be used; and one method sums the squares between two clusters summed over all variables (Aldenderfer and Blashfield, 1984). Clusters might be formed either by adding elements (agglomerative) or deleting them (divisive). Clusters may be formed hierarchically or non-hierachically, with the later requiring pre-specification of the number of clusters. When using cluster analysis to examine systems models, the researcher must decide on the number of clusters to represent the Systems fit concept for use in the final interpretation. This may be done on the basis of theory, say clustering organisations into the three elements of Miles and Snow's (1978) taxonomy of viable strategy: analyser, prospector and defenders. Alternatively, the technique can rely on execution rules to determine empirically the relationships between variables within groups of organisations and how they differ between groups.

An example of a theory driven cluster analysis that involves an exploratory approach to identifying configurations of firms is Chenhall and Langfield-Smith (1998). In this study it is argued that a selection of traditional and contemporary MCS fit with combinations of manufacturing practices that suit either low cost or product differentiation strategies. Cluster analysis was employed to identify configurations of strategies (product differentiation by way of customer service and flexibility, or low price), manufacturing techniques (human resource management, integrating systems, manufacturing systems innovations, quality systems, improving existing processes, team-based structures), and management accounting practices (traditional practices, benchmarking, activity-based techniques, balanced

---

[7] By contrast, Donaldson (2001) in discussing this emphasises the additive nature of contingencies, thus preferring the term multi-fit to systems fit.

scorecards, employee-based measures, strategic planning techniques). Six clusters were identified, three that emphasised product differentiation and three that were relatively more concerned with low price, although all clusters had some concern with both differentiation and low price. The performance of organisations within these clusters was determined. The results showed that that different configurations were associated with enhanced performance, thereby supporting a Systems fit interpretation.

A second example of cluster analysis that examines a more limited number of contextual variables is Gerdin (2005). This research is concerned with the way in which organisational structure and interdependence interact and how differences in MCS best fit the combinations of these variables. The study argues that organisational structure can be categorised as comprising functional (centralised, bureaucratic, rigid formalised communication), lateral (decentralised, product group focus), and simple units (centralised, small, less formalised). Interdependence is defined as sequential (one-way flows between segments) and reciprocal (two-way flows between segments). Six combinations of structure and interdependence are predicted and the type of MCS to suit is argued. The MCS are classified in terms of budgeting, standard costing, manufacturing operational information. A rudimentary MCS had low use of all practices, broad scope MCS emphasizes non-financial information and traditional MCS focuses on standard costing but not operations information. The research argues that it is possible that more than one form of MCS may suit the configurations of interdependence and structure.

Cluster analysis was used to develop categories of structure and MCS. The segments were separated into sequential and reciprocal interdependence. This provided six cells (three clusters for each category of interdependence) that were used to examine the extent to which the three dimensions of MCS were emphasised (over or under represented) in the cells. The results provided varying support for the hypothesised role of MCS in the structural-interdependence configurations. The study stressed the likelihood of some organisations not being able to bring multiple aspects of context into fit at any given time.

5. Concluding Comments

In this chapter we have briefly considered the major forms of fit[8] adopted in the MCS contingency literature. This literature addresses the relationship between MCS, performance and contingency variables that affect this relationship. The different forms of fit through which these relationships are theorised entail detailed and specific sets of expectations and assumptions. At stake are significant issues such as

---

[8] We haven't discussed Intervening variable forms of Interaction fit, however. The spread of techniques such as Partial Least Squares and Structural Equation Modelling are opening up avenues of enquiry that seek to understand how aspects of context relates to MCS by way of other intervening elements of context. Useful starting references for those seeking to pursue such issues are Chenhall (2005) and Shields, Deng and Kato (2000).

the nature of organisational equilibrium, the gradual or quantum nature of organisational change, the linearity or non-linearity of relationships. Given the far-reaching significance of the assumptions involved in concepts of fit in it is perhaps surprising that it has only recently come to the fore-front of MCS contingency debates.

Hartmann and Moers (1999), in particular, criticised the failure of many studies explicitly to state the nature of interactions that they were both expecting and testing. Many significant studies in the extant literature use the Null hypothesis form, whereby expectations are written out as not expecting to see an interaction between the variables of interest. Even if such an approach is adopted, the contribution of future studies would be greatly enhanced if they were to go on to state in their Null hypotheses what kind of interaction they were not expecting to find. The central concern in Hartmann and Moers (1999) paper is that appropriate statistical techniques are applied and their results interpreted appropriately. Gerdin and Greve (2004) widen the significance of clarity concerning studies' theorisation of fit. They point out that, given the specificity of assumptions underlying different forms of fit, the synthesis of results (both within and between studies) that are based on different forms of fit requires considerable caution in order to avoid the drawing of erroneous conclusions.

Luft and Shields (2003) in their analysis of the Management Accounting literature lament the fact that only a tiny handful of the theory consistent relationships that they found in the review comprised non-linear relationships. Much of the extant literature has adopted simple forms of Interaction fit, typically Multiplicative Interaction, with consequently linear analyses of relationships. Donaldson (2001) proposes Matching fit as the exemplar of structural contingency. Matching fit offers the challenge of thinking through in a more precise way the conceptualisation of the nature of contingency relationships. This includes enabling researchers to explore non-linear situations, where, for example, aspects of management control systems may switch between being important, less important, and then more important as the organisation moves between various aspects of a contextual variable. We hope that our detailed discussion of Matching fit here makes a compelling case for its wider adoption in future.

Our aim for the brief discussion provided in this chapter is to offer both theoretical clarification of the concept of fit, together with some practical guidance to its application in particular studies. We feel that the richness of analysis opened up is helpful in understanding why the contingency approach continues to enjoy such popularity despite suffering from ongoing critique. In particular, we see that the concept of fit is central to rebutting casual assertions that contingency research is not a strongly theoretical activity.

References

Abernethy, M. and Lillis, A. (1995). "The impact of manufacturing flexibility on management control system design", *Accounting Organizations and Society*. Vol.20, No. 4, pp. 241-258.

Aldenderfer, M. S. and Blashfield, R. K. (1984), *Cluster Analysis*, Sage Publications, Newbury Park, Ca.

Bisbe, J., Batista-Foguet, J. and Chenhall, R. H. (2005), "What do we really mean by interactive control systems? The danger of theoretical misspecification", paper presented at the *Global Management Accounting Research Symposium*, Sydney, Australia, 16-18 June.

Brownell, P. (1982). A field study examination of budgetary participation and locus of control. *The Accounting Review 57*, 766-777.

Chapman, C. S. (1997), "Reflections on a contingent view of accounting", *Accounting, Organizations and Society*, Vol. 22, No. 2, pp. 189-205.

Chenhall, R. H. (1997), "Reliance on manufacturing performance measures, total quality management and organizational performance", *Management Accounting Research*, Vol. 8, pp. 187-206.

Chenhall R.H. and Langfield-Smith, K. (1998). "The relationship between strategic priorities, management techniques and management accounting: an empirical investigation using a systems approach", *Accounting, Organizations and Society*. Vol. 23, No. 3, pp. 243-264.

Chenhall, R. H. (2003), "Management control systems design within its organizational context: Findings from contingency-based research and directions for the future", *Accounting, Organizations and Society*, Vol. 28, No. 2/3, pp. 127-168.

Chenhall, R. H. (2005), "Integrative strategic performance measurement systems: strategy, strategic alignment of manufacturing, learning and organizational performance", *Accounting, Organizations and Society*, Vol. 30, No. 5, pp. 395-422.

Chenhall, R. H. (forthcoming). "Management control systems design within its organizational context: Findings from contingency-based research and directions for the future", in Chapman, C. S., Hopwood, A. G. and Shields, M. D., *Handbook of Management Accounting Research*, Elsevier, Oxford.

Chenhall R. H. and Langfield-Smith, K. (1998a), "The relationship between strategic priorities, management techniques and management accounting: an empirical investigation using a systems approach", *Accounting, Organizations and Society*, Vol. 23, No. 3, pp. 243-264.

Davila, T. (2000), "An empirical study on the drivers of management control systems' design in new product development", *Accounting, Organizations and Society*, Vol. 25, No. 4/5, pp. 383-409.

Donaldson, L. (2001), *The contingency theory of organizations*, Sage Publications, London.

Drazin, R. and Van de Ven, A. H. (1985), "Alternative forms of fit in contingency theory", *Administrative Science Quarterly*, Vol. 30, pp. 514-539.

Duncan, K. and Moore, K. (1989), "Residual analysis: a better methodology for contingency studies in management accounting", *Journal of Management Accounting Research*, Vol. 1, pp. 89-104.

Frucot, V. and Shearon, W. T. (1991), "Budgetary participation, locus on control, and Mexican managerial performance and job satisfaction", *The Accounting Review*, Vol. 66, pp. 80-99.

Gerdin, J. (2005), "Managing accounting system design in manufacturing departments: an empirical investigation suing a multiple contingency approach", *Accounting, Organizations and Society*, Vol. 30, No. 2, pp. 99-126.

Gerdin, J. and Greve, J. (2004), "Forms of contingency fit in managerial accounting research – a critical review", *Accounting, Organizations and Society*, Vol. 29, No. 3/4, pp. 303-326.

Gerdin, J. and Hartmann, F. (2005), "The contingency paradox in management accounting research: reconciling selection and interaction models of fit", paper presented at *European Accounting Association Congress*, Gothenburg, Sweden.

Govindarajan, V. and Gupta, A. K. (1985), "Linking control systems to business unit strategy: impact on performance", *Accounting, Organizations and Society*, Vol. 10, No. 1, pp. 51-66.

Govindarajan, V. (1988), "A contingency approach to strategy implementation at the business-unit level: integrating administrative mechanisms with strategy", *Academy of Management Journal*, Vol. 31, pp. 828-853.

Hartmann, F. and Moers, F. (1999), "Testing contingency hypotheses in budgetary research: an evaluation of the moderated regression analysis", *Accounting, Organizations and Society*, Vol. 24, No. 4, pp. 291-315.

Ittner, C. and Larcker, D. (2001), "Assessing empirical research in managerial accounting: a value-based management perspective", *Journal of Accounting and Economics*, Vol. 32, No. 1-3, pp. 349-410.

Ittner, C., Lanen, W. and Larcker, D. (2002), "The association between activity-based costing and manufacturing performance", *Journal of Accounting Research*, Vol. 40, No. 3, pp. 711-726.

Ittner, C., Larcker, D. and Randall, T. (2003), "Performance implications of strategic performance measurement in financial services firms", *Accounting, Organizations and Society*, Vol. 28, No. 7/8, pp. 715-741.

Luft, J. L. and Shields, M. D. (2003), "Mapping management accounting: graphics and guidelines for theory-consistent empirical research", *Accounting, Organizations and Society*, Vol. 28, No. 2/3, pp. 169-249.

Miles, R. W. and Snow C. C. (1978), *Organizational Strategy Structure and Process*, McGraw Hill, New York.

Milgrom, P. and Roberts, J. (1992), *Economics, Organization & Management*, Prentice Hall, Englewood Cliffs, NJ.

Otley, D. (1980), "The contingency theory of management accounting: achievement and prognosis", *Accounting, Organizations and Society*, Vol. 4, No. 4, pp. 413-428.

Selto, F. H., Renner, C. J. and Young, S. M. (1995), "Assessing the organizational fit of a just-in-time manufacturing system: testing selection, interaction and systems models of contingency theory", *Accounting, Organizations and Society*, Vol. 20, No. 7/8, pp. 665-684.

Shields, M. D., Deng, F. J. and Kato, Y. (2000), "The design and effects of control systems: tests of direct- and indirect-effects models", *Accounting, Organizations and Society*, Vol. 25, No. 2, p. 185.

Simons, R. (1987), "Accounting control systems and business strategy: an empirical analysis", *Accounting, Organizations and Society*, Vol. 12, No. 4, pp. 357-374.

5

AGENCY THEORY AND ACCOUNTING RESEARCH: AN OVERVIEW OF SOME CONCEPTUAL AND EMPIRICAL ISSUES

Nava Subramaniam

Griffith University, Gold Coast, Australia

Abstract: This chapter aims to give the reader an overview of agency theory (AT) and its application in accounting research. It delineates the basic assumptions and concepts of AT and identifies the various measures that can be undertaken to minimise agency costs. The chapter also provides a summary of the commonalities and differences across the three major paradigms adopted by accounting researchers when using an agency framework: Principal-Agent, Transaction Cost Economics and Positivist (Rochester) model. Further, a review of some recent theoretical and empirical studies on the design of optimal contracts, namely those relating to implicit contracts, multi-agent and multi-period issues is undertaken. Several suggestions are made for future studies adopting an AT-based approach.

Keywords: Agency theory, agency costs, optimal contracts, performance evaluation, employee compensation.

1. Introduction

Agency Theory (AT) provides a rich theoretical premise for understanding organisational processes and design from a principal-agent perspective. In general, an agency relationship arises when one party (the principal) hires another (the agent) to perform a task. In most cases, this would involve the agent making decisions on behalf of the principal. Jensen and Meckling (1976) define the principal-agent relationship as 'a contract under which one or more persons (the principal(s)) engage another person (the agent) to perform some service on their behalf which involves delegating some decision making authority to the agent' (p.308). For example, a commonly conceptualised agency relationship is between the owners of an organisation (as the principal) and the managers (as agents). Two key underlying assumptions of AT are that the efficiency of the principal and agent relationship is impacted by individualistic and opportunistic interests held by each party, and that the situation may be exacerbated by incomplete information, and uncertainty. Consequently, the principal may elect to monitor the agent's behaviour and/or offer incentives through employment contracts that help align the agent's interest with that of the principal's. The trade-off between risk and return in turn plays a significant role in identifying optimal contracts in varying situations of uncertainty and risk preferences. Thus for researchers, the insights offered by AT help to incorporate more explicitly conflicts of interest, incentive problems, and mechanisms for controlling incentive problems in their investigations (Eisenhardt, 1989; Lambert, 2001).

Accounting researchers over the years have predominantly focused on performance evaluation and various organisational control issues including managerial incentives and behaviour. As such, the AT framework has been an attractive and useful tool to model and predict managerial and organisational outcomes in response to accounting information and practices. The objectives of this chapter are four-fold:

1. to provide an introduction to the fundamental concepts of AT including the basic (or *standard*) agency model, its underlying assumptions, and the types of agency problems faced in two common organisational relationship sets, namely, the shareholder-manager and the debtholder-shareholder relationships;

2. to delineate two common strategies available to reduce opportunistic behaviour by agents i.e. monitoring activities and incentive schemes;

3. to provide a critical evaluation of the use of AT in accounting research. In particular, various issues as raised by Baiman (1982, 1990) are discussed through a comparison of the inherent advantages and disadvantages of the three main research approaches adopted by accounting researchers, i.e. the *Principal-Agent*, the *Transaction Cost Economics* and the *Positivist*. This is followed by a review of more recent empirical studies in accounting, specifically the design of managerial employment contracts[9], and

4. to provide several suggestions for future AT research which include the need to broaden extant theoretical conceptualisations through recognition of the evolving, new forms of organisational structures and forms (Child and Rodrigues, 2003); personality differences in individual managers which may affect their motivation to work despite their incentive structure, as well as the issue of factors such as trust and organisational culture that may influence managerial behaviour and their attitudes towards incentive structures.

---

[9] Given that empirical accounting research using an AT framework is rather voluminous, the discussion in this chapter will be restricted to empirical development and findings relating to managerial performance and incentive structures. In specific, the chapter will review recent theoretical and empirical studies on the design of optimal contracts, namely implicit contracts, multi-agent and multi-period issues.

The next section provides an overview of AT's background, its fundamental assumptions and concepts, and circumstances that potentially exacerbate agency problems.

2.   Agency Theory Overview

2.1.   Background

While AT was increasingly adopted in accounting research in the 1970s and 1980s, the roots of AT are viewed to be in the information economics literature. Eisenhardt (1989) contends that AT has broadened the early (i.e. 1960s and 1970s) risk-sharing literature (Arrow, 1971; Wilson, 1968) which investigated information and risk sharing behaviour among individuals and groups. Much of this literature focused on the risk sharing problem which arises as a result of different attitudes towards risk by cooperating parties i.e. those expected to work together. By bringing in the ubiquitous agency relationship in which one party delegates decision-making responsibility to another, AT is seen to provide an additional perspective on how two or more parties with different goals and divisions of labour may behave. Managers are no longer considered to be passive reactors to information systems, but that they will behave with self-interest. Not surprisingly, given the role accounting information plays in organisational decision making, the use of an AT framework to explain and predict managerial and organisational behaviour gained the interest of the accounting researchers.

Jensen and Meckling (1976) further enriched the theoretical premise of the relationship between a principal and an agent by using the metaphor of a contract for modelling optimal relationship outcomes. Their arguments were based on earlier work by Coase (1937) and Alchian and Demsetz (1972) whereby firms are viewed as 'legal fictions which serve as a nexus for a set of contracting relationships among individuals (Jensen and Meckling, 1976, p. 310), and that the employment contracts, while serving the individual interests of the agents, also help maximise the firm's value (i.e. the principal's interests). Contracting theories thus brought into focus the importance of effective and efficient employment contracts for aligning the agent's behaviour with the principal's interests. The assumptions of effective and efficient contracts design in turn were related to a variety of factors, such as the people (e.g. self-interest, risk preferences), the organisation (e.g. goal conflict among members), and information acquisition (e.g. the availability and cost of acquiring information) (Eisenhardt, 1989). For accounting researchers, a common research issue, for example, is to identify the efficiency of a behaviour-oriented contract (e.g. salaries and organisational position) as opposed to an outcome-based contract (e.g. commission and stock options) under selected sets of assumptions.

A more detailed discussion on the origins and development of AT can be found in Eisenhardt (1989), Fama and Jensen (1983a), Lambert (2001) and Zingales (2000).

2.2. Fundamental Assumptions of AT

2.2.1. A basic principal-agent model. In its simplest form, an agency model can be viewed to comprise two parties: the principal and the agent. The principal is expected to supply the capital, bear risks and to construct incentives, while the agent is required to complete the tasks, make decisions on the principal's behalf and to bear risks (of a secondary type) (Lambert, 2001). Using Lambert's (2001, p. 6) outline of key events in a basic agency relationship, the normal sequence of events over a single time period may be viewed as follows:

I	I	I	I
Contract s(x,y) agreed upon	Agent selects actions (a)	Performance measures (x,y, etc.) observed	Agent is Paid s (x,y) Principal keeps x – s(x,y)

The sequence begins with a compensation contract between the principal and agent specifying the performance measures upon which the agent's compensation will be assessed. Let this compensation function be denoted as 's', and 'x' as the 'outcome' of the firm, and 'y' as the vector of performance measures to be used in the contract. The agent is then seen to, based on the terms of the contract, choose a vector of actions, a, which could include operating decisions, financing decisions, or investment decisions. The agent's actions, along with other exogenous factors (generally modelled as random variables) influence the realisations of the performance measures, and the outcome of the firm as well. After the performance measures are jointly observed, the agent is paid according to the terms of the contract.[10] Overall, this sequence of events is seen to proceed smoothly based on several key assumptions.

First, the outcome of the firm, i.e. x is observable and can be contracted on. Further, it is assumed that x can be measured in monetary terms and relates to a single-period. This means the firm's outcome can be easily and clearly defined by objective (monetary-based) measures such as the end-of-period cash flow or the liquidating dividend of the firm gross of the compensation paid to the agent. Another assumption is that the agent chooses the actions and the principal is not able to fully observe this choice, and there is a stochastic term attached to the agent's output. In other words, events beyond the agent's control may occur to affect the output. Thus, both the principal and the agent assume a certain amount of risk, and in general the greater the risk assumed by the agent, the higher the agent's compensation.[11]

---

[10] Note that, as highlighted by Lambert (2001, p. 7), 'this formulation implicitly assumes that the property rights to the outcome belong with the principal. A few papers consider the opposite situation in which the agent has the property rights to the outcome by allowing him to keep any "unreported income"'.

[11] The basic agency model has been extended and analysed in several ways, leading to more realistic and complex models such as dropping the assumption that outcomes might be

2.2.2. The agency problem. The basic principal-agent relationship, however, is confronted with a fundamental issue. Drawing from the traditional economics literature are the following two underlying assumptions of AT: (i) the principal and the agent are utility maximisers whereby both parties seek to maximise their returns, and (ii) it is not always that the interests of the principal and agent are aligned (Berle and Means, 1932; Jensen and Meckling, 1976). Consequently, inherent in any principal-agent situation is the 'agency problem' that the agent may not act in the best interests of the principal. For instance, the principal and agent may differ in their risk preferences resulting in the agent's actions being different to that expected by the principal. This issue is also referred to as the 'problem of risk sharing'. Unless the risk differentials are known and made clear between the parties at the outset, i.e. prior to the contract formation and factored into the compensation, the agency problem is likely to increase.

2.2.3. Information Asymmetry. Further, the agency problem is seen to exacerbate under conditions of information asymmetry, i.e. where one party has an information advantage over another party – which is characteristic of most business settings (Scott, 1997). It is usually the agent who is seen to possess the information advantage over a principal as he or she tends to be more directly involved in the day-to-day operations of a business.[12] Such private or asymmetric information generally encompasses knowledge about some exogenous variable, i.e. information relating to factors outside the agency relationship. Information asymmetry in turn may lead to two specific types of agency problems:

- Moral hazard (sometimes referred to as *hidden costs*) – which relates to a lack of effort by the agent i.e. *shirking* as a result of the principal having restricted ability to observe the performance of the manager directly, and the principal can only assess a manager's performance based on the outcome. In such situations, a manager may be tempted to shirk his or her duties e.g. consume perquisites in excess of what was agreed to or *'taking it easy on the job'* as the principal may not be able to observe the manager's actions.

- Adverse selection – which arises even when the principal is able to observe a manager's behaviour but is unable to determine if the effort extended by the agent is the most appropriate behaviour. For example, an agent may choose accounting policies that maximise reported net income in order to gain higher bonuses. At the capital market level, investors may not receive full and proper disclosure of a firm's prospects as managers may stand to gain from non-

---

observable, incorporating multi-agent and multi-period features, and whether the principal elects to conduct variance investigations at the end of a period. Examples of reviews of such studies are found in Baiman (1990), Lambert (2001) and Indjejikian (1999).

[12] A related agency problem, though not directly linked to information asymmetry, is the existence of mutual ignorance, where some key variable is unknown at the time of contracting but becomes known to one party during the contracting period.

disclosure. Other adverse selection situations include when the agent's tasks or the job itself is so highly complex (e.g. risky investment projects) and if an agent misrepresents his or her ability, the principal is not able to verify the agent's abilities either at the time of hiring or even while the agent is working on the project.

2.2.4. Agency problems in specific relationship sets. The two most common sets of agency relationship that has attracted the attention of accounting researchers are the *Shareholder-Manager* and the *Debtholder-Shareholder (Manager)* relationships.[13] Presented below is a brief description of the nature of the relationship and some examples of agency problems that may occur in each situation:

(1) *Shareholder-Manager Relationship*: This relationship centres on the issue of the separation of ownership and control, resulting in limitations to the shareholders' (i.e. owners') ability to observe management actions, which in turn gives rise to the risk that management may not always act in the best interest of the firm. For instance, opportunistic behaviour may easily occur when the manager is on a nominal fixed wage salary and the owners are not able to fully observe the manager's actions as well as naively have little restrain or influence on the manager's actions. Henderson *et al.* (2004) provide several examples of opportunistic behaviour that managers may undertake to the detriment of shareholders.

First, termed as 'excessive perquisites', the manager may indulge in unnecessary or excessive expenditures on luxury items, e.g. business trips, luxury office fittings, etc. Further, the manager may indulge in 'empire building' by attempting to expand the firm's operations, beyond the point at which the owner's expected wealth is maximised and exposing the firm to unreasonable risks. Often a manager's motivation in such cases would be to enhance his or her own reputation in the market, leading to better employment opportunities. Shirking is another opportunistic behaviour where the manager reduces his or her workload by not attending to the necessary duties and tasks. The fourth and final example relates to incorrect investment decisions because managers are generally assumed to be more risk averse than the principal (normally assumed as being risk neutral) as the manager is more dependent on the firm for his/her livelihood. Consequently, the owners who are more diversified would want to undertake more risky projects with high returns, while the manager is likely to choose projects with lower risks which would yield lower returns.

(2) *Debtholder-Shareholder(Manager) Relationship:* In this relationship, the debtholder is viewed as the principal and the agent is the manager who acts on behalf of the shareholders of the firm (i.e. managers' interests are assumed to be

---

[13] Additional discussion and reference material in this area may be found in Godfrey, *et al.* (2003), Deegan (2001) and Henderson *et al.* (2004).

aligned with the shareholders or owners). The debtholder is viewed as the principal because the assets or resources lent to the firm by the debtholder will be controlled by the manager (i.e. as the agent). Also, several assumptions are generally made. First, the manager is assumed to be either the sole owner of the firm, i.e. has interests that are totally congruent with the owners' interests. Second, the firm is a limited liability company managed by the manager as an owner. It is argued that both parties are free to reach an agreeable contract and that the relationship between them is unregulated (Henderson *et al.*, 2004). Third, it is assumed that since the value of the firm entails value of debt as well as value of equity, the agent may engage in opportunistic behaviour by attempting to transfer wealth from the debt providers to the firm (Godfrey *et al.*, 2003).

Some examples of opportunistic behaviour that could occur in debtholder-shareholder(manager) relationships are as follows. The first refers to 'excessive dividend payout'– which occurs when debt is lent to the firm on the assumption of a certain level of dividend payout, and the manager uses the borrowed funds to pay himself or herself a higher dividend. Another problem relates to 'under-investment' which occurs when the manager feels that the benefits of investing in projects with a positive NPV accrue to debtholders rather than to the owners. Another common behaviour is 'claim dilution' where the manager may borrow from other sources and promise the new debtholders a ranking equal to or higher than that held by the original debtholders. While the outcome of such transactions depend on how the newly borrowed funds are used, the potential remains for the debt of the original debtholders to become riskier and thus less valuable.

3.   Strategies to Mitigate Agency Problems

Agency problems may be mitigated through several strategies or courses of action that involve either monitoring their behaviour or providing incentives that engender behaviour congruent with the principal's interests. The costs associated with the strategies that help mitigate agency problems are called agency costs which can be classified under the following three headings:

(1)   Monitoring costs – which are the costs incurred in monitoring the agent's behaviour e.g. mandatory audit costs, investment in governance structures, formal procedures, information systems, and other oversight processes that help curb opportunistic behaviour.

(2)   Bonding costs – which relate to those initiatives that help align the agent's interest with that of the principal's including private contracting, e.g. through bonus incentive schemes or reward structures that minimise loss through underperformance or opportunistic behaviour by the agent.

(3)   Residual costs – which are all other costs incurred as a result of incongruence between the principal and agent's interests despite monitoring and bonding processes.

The two most common types of strategies for minimising agency problems directly relate to the monitoring and bonding agency costs, and are respectively classified as monitoring-related and incentive-focused strategies for further discussion in the next two sub-sections. In general, there is a trade-off between monitoring and bonding costs whereby the greater the monitoring activities, the higher the likelihood for the principal to observe and arrest any opportunistic behaviour. Consequently, this also leads to lower probability of opportunistic behaviour by agents, and the need for bonding measures (e.g. bonuses) as incentives is diminished. In other words, with increasing monitoring activities, it is not necessary for the principal to impose further risk on an agent's contract which would result in providing the agent higher incentives (and increase bonding costs).

3.1. *Monitoring strategies*

Monitoring strategies may be external or internal to the firm. Some of the common strategies include (1) undertaking external and internal audits, (2) having more independent (versus non-independent) directors on the board, and (3) designing effective budgetary and other performance evaluation systems.

3.1.1. External / Internal Audits. The provision of audited financial statements is usually regarded as a cost-effective contractual response to agency costs (DeAngelo, 1981; Watts and Zimmerman, 1986). Similarly, internal auditing may also serve as a monitoring response to agency costs (Anderson *et al.* 1993; DeFond, 1992). The annual statutory audit that is mandatory for public-listed firms is an example of how management actions may be scrutinised and validated by an independent auditor. Further, AT also suggests that the agents themselves may demand or utilise the external audit as a way to signal the quality of the company, to current and future investors as it would be in the best interests of the agents. It is argued that an agent's position is such that he or she has greater investment in the firm (as his or her job is at stake), while the company has broader range of options for investment. Interestingly, recent empirical findings by Seow (1999) and Carey *et al.* (2000) indicate that even in smaller and family business firms, there is substantial demand for voluntary audits, both external and internal.

3.1.2. Board of Directors' Composition. Fama and Jensen (1983b) examined the role of the board of directors as a monitoring device. It was argued that independent auditors will be more likely to demand higher audit quality in order to protect their reputation (Abbott and Parker, 2000; Carcello and Neal, 2000). Based on reputational capital enhancement theory, it is contended that since independent directors generally hold a high-reputation in the business community and they view the directorship as a means of further developing their reputations as expert in decision making, such directors will be prone to be more diligent in their duties (Fama and Jensen, 1983b).

3.1.3. Performance Evaluation Systems. Proponents of AT assume that performance evaluation systems are largely designed to mitigate incentive problems (Indjejikian, 1999; Kaplan and Atkinson, 1989). Budgeting, for instance, is viewed as an important, multi-faceted activity within organisations that not only enables the setting of performance targets for agents, but also facilitates monitoring and restricting agent behaviour. For example, through variance analysis a principal is able to assess agent performance and further investigate the reasons for any deviations from the budgetary target. Various studies adopting an AT framework in this area have focused on building analytical budgeting models that assess how uncertainty and information asymmetry affect the use of information-based practices such as budgeting in incentive contracts between owners and employees.[14] According to Covaleski, Evans III and Luft (2003), AT has provided 'an important conceptual advance for the study of budgeting by offering a well-defined structure in which the value of such practices (including their decision-influencing value) could be established in a rigorous, internally consistent manner' (p.13).

3.1.4. Incentive-focused Strategies. The second type of strategy to reduce opportunistic behaviour is to provide positive incentive structures to the agent. Traditionally, the types of positive incentives offered to a manager or agent would be performance related rewards such as bonuses, promotion, stock options, and other organisational perks. The use of managerial shareholding or ownership as an incentive mechanism, however, needs careful consideration with recent studies suggesting that at a certain range of managerial ownership, managers could become entrenched. The early work by Berle and Means (1932) propose that managerial shareholdings are likely to reduce agency conflicts between management and shareholders due to the implicit bonding and signalling roles of managerial shareholdings. Likewise, Jensen and Meckling (1976) suggest a *'convergence-of-interests'* hypothesis whereby it is argued that as the level of managerial shareholdings increase, the costs borne by managers for not making value-maximising decisions also increase. Hence, the convergence-of-interests perspective predicts that higher managerial shareholdings should be associated with greater congruence with owner's interests and lower agency costs.

On the other hand, the *'management entrenchment'* hypothesis as proposed by Morck, Shleifer, and Vishny (1988) suggests that the relationship between managers' ownership and the expected positive impact on their behaviour may be neither simple nor linear. It is argued that as ownership by managers increases, there will be a point when the managers become entrenched and would make decisions that maximise their wealth as opposed to the wealth of the other owners or shareholders. The ability of these owners to monitor and discipline the manager is seen to decline because managers through greater ownership levels are able to exert greater control over decision making. Faced with a less transparent management team, the other owners are likely to place contractual constraints such as debt covenants and compensation contracts, but these in turn may only further motivate management to

---

[14] In monitoring literature, the issue of whether principal is able to monitor the agent's private information, e.g. Baiman and Demski (1980) and Gale and Hellwig (1985) and the quality of the monitoring system (e.g. Kim and Suh (1992) are relevant for contract optimality.

manipulate earnings, leading to reduced earnings quality and the informativeness of earnings (Pergola, 2005). In fact, Jensen and Meckling (1976) had warned that when management equity stakes are large (or ownership is widely dispersed), managers can gain effective control and become entrenched themselves making them immune from other governance mechanisms. Further, Morck *et al.* (1988) also provide empirical evidence in support of the hypothesis whereby firm value was seen to increase with board ownership in the 0% to 5% fall, as ownership rose to 25% and then slowly rise again, as ownership level exceeded 25%. Clearly, further research is needed for a better understanding of managerial shareholding as an incentive mechanism.

4. Comparison of Research Branches

There is no doubt that the AT-based accounting research literature is vast. Not surprisingly, numerous reviews of the adoption of AT in accounting have been undertaken. For example, Baiman's (1982, 1990) literature reviews of the application of AT in management accounting provide in-depth and insightful analyses of the broad theoretical foundations and technical issues that arise when modelling management accounting problems from an AT perspective. Watts and Zimmerman (1986) surveyed AT-based financial accounting studies. In more recent years, Lambert's (2001) analyses of contracting theory and accounting, and Covaleski *et al.*'s (2003) evaluation of the use of economic theory, particularly AT in budgeting research provide comprehensive and rigorous analyses of the respective areas.

In this section of the chapter, I aim to address a number of limitations of AT-based research in accounting, namely those raised by Baiman (1990) in his review of the area. First, as shown in Figure 1, a summary of the basic assumptions, focus and criticisms of each of the three main AT branches: principal-agent, transaction cost economics and positivist (Rochester) model, is provided.[15] This is followed by a brief discussion that compares and contrasts the research issues addressed by accounting studies in each branch. Please review Baiman's (1990) paper for the full discussion.

---

[15] Eisenhardt (1989) notes that the majority of AT-based financial accounting studies tend to revolve around positivist research.

Figure 1
Comparison of the basic assumptions, focus and criticisms of the three AT branches

Principal-Agent	Transaction Cost Economics (TCE)	Positivist / Rochester Model
Basic Assumptions (1) All three branches assume that individuals are rational and act on their own self interest.		
(2) Individual actions are endogenously derived, based on well-specified preferences and beliefs. (3) Individuals have unlimited computational ability. (4) Individuals can anticipate and assess the probability of all possible future contingencies. (5) Contracts can be less costly and can be accurately enforced by the courts. (6) Contracts are comprehensive and unambiguous, i.e. for each verifiable situation actions are clearly specified.	(2) Unlike Principal-agent branch studies, individuals are assumed *not* to have unlimited computational ability. (3) Individuals are seen to face bounded rationality with limitations to their ability to acquire and process information. (4) Consequently contracts become incomplete and opportunistic behaviour becomes possible to the extent that markets conditions allow.	(2) Studies in this branch share many of the assumptions of TCE branch. The external labour and capital markets are assumed to be efficient and accurately anticipate the incentives of management. (3) The Rochester model and the principal agent branch share the need to understand how agency problems arise and the use of contractual means and organisational design to reduce opportunistic behaviour.
Focus: Formal analysis of an explicit, internally consistent model or design of an optimal employment contract.	Analysis of the effectiveness and efficiency of governance procedures put in place to limit opportunistic behaviour – given the assumption of incomplete contracts.	Understanding factors affecting observed contracts e.g. how changes in employment and financing contracts affect managerial behaviour (e.g. their investment and financing decisions).

Criticisms:		
(1) Some of the assumptions appear unrealistic, e.g. the assumptions that courts can enforce all contracts and even when all the parties may subsequently wish to recontract. (2) Most models developed to analyse the principal-agent relationship is too simple. Also, the form of contracts as a result of research findings may be too complicated and not closely related to real-world contracts.	Transaction cost variables, e.g. size and source and the concepts of equilibrium and efficiency not well defined. Further, the notion of bounded rationality is not well-defined. Theoretical analysis less rigorous than in the principal-agent research.	Similar to TCE, Transaction cost variables, e.g. size and source and the concepts of equilibrium and efficiency not well defined. Observed contracts are generally assumed to be efficient, with little emphasis on clearly identifying the motivations for the choice of the observed contractual features.

The principal-agent stream predominantly focuses on developing a general agency model. According to Eisenhardt, the 'positivist theory identifies various contract alternatives, and principal-agent theory indicates which contract is the most efficient under varying levels of outcome uncertainty, risk aversion, information and other variables' (1989, p. 60). Studies in the principle-agent stream tend to be based on theoretical deduction and mathematical proof. One of the benefits that the principal-agent stream has is that it can specify the most efficient contract alternative to adopt in a given situation. Some of the more common agency variables used in the accounting studies include outcome versus behaviour-based incentives, subjective versus objective information (e.g. accounting-based performance measures), information systems (including budgetary) and task programmability.

The transaction cost economics and the positivist (Rochester) research have both tended to identify situations where divergence in the interests of the principal and agent are evident or probable, and to evaluate the cost effectiveness of setting up governance mechanisms based on transaction costs. The transaction cost economic models, however, tend to differ slightly from the positivist research, in that capital markets which are seen to be efficient and able to accurately anticipate the incentives of management, play a more central role in the positivist branch. Many of the studies in this area are regarded as undertaking a positive accounting theory approach.[16] Jensen and Meckling (1976), for instance, examined how

---

[16] Watts and Zimmerman (1986) have made significant contributions to positive accounting theory, and they had also heavily relied on the Jensen and Meckling (1976) paper. See R. L. Watts and J. L. Zimmermann, *Positive Accounting Theory*, Prentice Hall, Englewood

corporate ownership structures (e.g. the level of equity versus debt) affects the nature of agency costs.

In sum, while the basic assumptions and focus of the AT branches differ in nature and extent, the empirical issues investigated by prior studies across the different branches share several common objectives. For instance, the identification of factors that lead to optimal contracts (i.e. the development of incentive schemes or employment contracts that create value) has been a focal research issue of prior studies. The design of monitoring mechanisms which enhance information quality and ultimately firm value has been another common research aim. Further, a fundamental insight derived from the AT framework is the existence of a trade-off between risk and incentives wherein compensation packages are seen to comprise a contingent (risky) component that induces agents (who are assumedly risk and effort averse) to work, but at the same time minimises any potential transfer of risk onto them. This notion of risk-incentive tradeoff also provided the basis for Holmstrom's (1979) *informativeness* principle that suggests that accounting and related performance measures have information value in terms of reflecting the actions and decisions taken by the employee. Consequently, a critical research issue is to understand the signal or meaning portrayed by the performance indicators (both accounting and non-accounting) about the effort and decisions of an agent, which subsequently is expected to lead to the development of optimal contracts.

Given the critical role played by performance evaluation and compensation design in agency relationships, the next section will review some recent empirical developments, particularly those that aim to address the limitations of prior studies.

4.1. Research Studies – Performance Evaluation and Compensation Issues

As noted by Baiman (1990), a major criticism of the principal-agent agency studies is that the standard or basic principal-agent conceptualisation is far too simple given that most employer-employee relationships and a firm's compensation practices are quite complex. For example, the basic agency model as presented in an earlier section of this chapter comprises a highly simple situation where the principal-agent relationship involves a single principal and a single agent in a single time period, and the incentives provided to the agent are explicit and measured in monetary terms. In reality, however, situations are normally more complicated whereby the agency relationship involves multiple agents, over multiple time periods, and the incentives to agents not always explicitly specified in their contract. Researchers have attempted to address the employment contract complexity issue by not only relaxing the assumptions of the basic agency model, but also by adopting multi-

---

Cliffs, 1986 and R. L. Watts and J. L. Zimmermann, 'Positive Accounting Theory: A Ten Year Perspective', *The Accounting Review*, January, 1990, pp. 131-156. Positive accounting theory refers to empirically tested theory that describes, explains or predicts accounting practice (Godfrey *et al.*, 2003). Much of positive accounting theory is based on neo-classical economic theory principles including utility function maximisation and achieving cost-benefit equilibrium.

method and multi-theoretical approaches. In the next three sub-sections, a brief review is provided on some recent studies in the following three areas: informal (also referred as implicit) contracts, multi-period contracts, and multi-agent contracts. A more extensive review of the earlier studies pertaining to these three research strands is provided in Baiman (1990).

4.2. Informal / Implicit Employee Contracts

In modelling the principal–agent contracts, much of the focus of prior studies to date has been on explicit contracts. However, as highlighted by Indjejikian (1999), many employer-employee relationships involve informal arrangements and understandings about an individual's duties and responsibilities, the organisation's reward systems and other aspects of an employment contract (i.e. also referred as implicit incentives or contracts). In general, implicit incentives include all elements that affect an agent's behaviour other than those relating to external incentives and monitoring factors. An agent, for instance, may view career image or reputation (implicit incentives) as being more important than explicit incentives in choosing one's actions. As such, both implicit terms and explicit factors are relevant when examining optimal contracts, i.e. in evaluating the effectiveness of incentive packages. Thus, some of the key research questions addressed in this area include: 'do firms rely on implicit or relational employment contracts to motivate and reward employees, and if so, what type of measures do they rely upon?'

Baker *et al.* (1994) examined the combined use of subjective and objective performance measures in implicit and explicit incentive contracts, respectively. It is argued that incentive contracts often include important subjective components that mitigate incentive distortions caused by imperfect objective measures. The study demonstrated that the presence of sufficiently effective explicit contracts can render all implicit contracts infeasible, even those that would otherwise yield the first-best. It is also shown that in some circumstances, objective and subjective measures are complements: neither an explicit nor an implicit contract alone yields positive profit, but an appropriate combination of the two contract types does. This suggests that an implicit arrangement can be beneficial by addressing undesirable outcomes associated with explicit contracts. Further, an implication of these results is that 'certain combinations of human resource practices (such as group piece-rates (explicit contracts) and subjective bonus plans (implicit contracts)) are much more effective when implemented together rather than singly' (Baker et al., 1994, p. 1128).

Hayes and Schaefer (2000) tested the issue of whether implicit contracts ought to be based on performance measures that are observable only to the contracting parties. They hypothesise in the first instance that 'if corporate boards optimally use both observable and unobservable (to outsiders) measures of executive performance and the unobservable measures are correlated with future firm performance, then unexplained variation in current compensation should predict future variation in firm performance' (p. 273). Using data from the Forbes Executive Compensation Surveys from 1974 through 1995, Hayes and Schaefer (2000) found that the unexplained variation in executive compensation was significantly and positively related to firm performance (as measured by return on equity). Further, a second hypothesis predicting that the informativeness of compensation for future return on equity is inversely related to the quality of observable performance measures as contracting instruments was tested. The results of regressing the interaction terms between the compensation variable and proxies for the quality of observable measures on firm performance, provide some support for the second hypothesis with unexplained variation in compensation more positively related to future return on equity when the variances of market and accounting returns are higher. Overall, the results support the notion that boards of directors use information that is not available to those outside the relationship as part of an implicit incentive compensation contract.

4.3. *Multi-period Contracts*

The efficiency of multi-period contracts has attracted significant interest with early studies such as by Lambert (1983) and Rogerson (1985) indicating that long term contracts in repeated agency contexts entail memory, and hence have attributes different to single period contracts. For instance, multi-period contracts may appear attractive as over time employees are able to learn and improve their productivity, and redesign performance evaluation and compensation programmes. Another attractiveness of multi-period contracts is that principals may use employment or future compensation as an incentive mechanism. However, when the agent has access to perfect credit markets, long-term contracts will only be effective if they encourage the acquisition and use of information that is mutually beneficial under the contract. Fudenberg *et al.* (1990), for instance, argue that long term contracts will be no better than a sequence of one-period contracts if (i) principal and agent preferences over future contracts are common knowledge, and (ii) the employee is able to borrow and save at the same rate as the principal.

Interestingly, it can be argued that in a single-period contract situation, the employee is more likely to work hard because if he or she shirks, the firm will not re-hire which also means that the firm is able to avoid separation costs. Furthermore, a critical problem in long-term contracts is the *ratchet effect* whereby when an employer tends to consider an employee's past superior performance as a guide to evaluating his current performance, an employee is tempted to under-perform in earlier years so as to avoid being held to higher (i.e. ratcheted) standard in the future (Milgrom and Roberts, 1992). Clearly, the ratchet effect is inefficient. While the employer is seen to be better off if both parties can agree to a multi-period contract without subsequent revision, this is not realistic as there are efficiency gains to be made after the fact to using the information.

On the other hand, the ratchet effect can be mitigated by linking agent compensation to some comparative performance measure, e.g. a firm- or an industry-wide measure, and if the agent shirks, he or she will be seen to be either shirking or performing below a nominal measure, i.e. below par. Alternately, the agent can be given the option to resign if nominal standards are not met in a given period, resulting in the agent being induced to meet the nominal performance target based on career incentives.

Indjejikian and Nanda (1999) have addressed the multi-period issue by testing a two-period agency model to demonstrate that the use of more aggregate performance measures and greater consolidation of responsibility helps mitigate the ratchet effect. In analysing the ratchet effect on the choice of performance measures, they consider a firm's problem of motivating a single manager to perform a single task based on either a pair of performance measures or the aggregate of the two. In illustrating the ratchet effect on responsibility assignment, managerial motivation is examined in relation to two types of activities or tasks (e.g. sales and production, two business units and divisions) over two time periods. The analyses suggest that more aggregated performance measures are subject to less ratcheting and may be preferred to single responsibility accounting systems that tend to produce detailed information. Alternately, aggregation can be facilitated by assigning multiple tasks for an employee through the creation of consolidated responsibility centres. While several prior studies have focused on how incentive pay affects agent's risk allocation and work motivation in multi-task agency settings (Holmstrom and Milgrom, 1991; Krueger, 1991; Slade, 1996), Indjejikian and Nanda's (1999) findings elucidate the mitigating effect of multi-tasks on the agent's potential to ratchet his or her performance.[17]

Dutta and Reichelstein (2003) developed a multi-period agency model to study the role of leading indicator variables in managerial performance measures. Leading indicator variables such as share price or non-financial variables usually provide a noisy forecast of the investment returns to be received in future periods. However, a standard finding in AT literature is that any informative signal is valuable for contracting purposes (Holstrom, 1979) which implies that despite their noisiness leading indicator variables are useful for contract design. This argument, on the other hand, needs further examination in a multi-period setting because in the early stages leading indicators may provide added information, but this information may be supplanted by the actual results borne in the subsequent period(s). Dutta and Reichelstein (2003) thus pose the following question: 'Does an optimal performance measure need to include a noisy forecast of future cash flows if receipt of actual cash flows in the future can be adequately rewarded at that time?'

---

[17] When agents operate in a multi-task setting, the situation becomes more complex as the trade-off between risk sharing and incentives will need to consider how agents come to distribute their efforts over several tasks and the optimality of different types of incentives. For instance, Holmstrom and Milgrom (1991) predict that the desirability of providing incentives for one activity decreases with the difficulty of measuring performance in any other activities that make competing demands on the agent's time and attention. For further discussion and empirical findings on multi-task agency issues, see Krueger (1991); Slade (1996) and Dixit (1997).

In addressing the above research question, they developed a two-period model in which both investments and managerial effort are unobservable information variables. It is argued that in addition to the familiar moral hazard problem, the principal faces the task of motivating a manager to undertake 'soft' investments. Such investments, however, are not directly contractible, but the principal can instead rely on leading indicator variables that provide a noisy forecast of the investment returns to be received in future periods. Their analysis relates the role of leading indicator variables to the duration of the manager's incentive contract. The findings suggest that 'with short-term contracts, leading indicator variables are essential in mitigating a hold-up problem resulting from the fact that investments are sunk at the end of the first period. With long-term contracts, leading indicator variables will be valuable if the manager's compensation schemes are not stationary over time' (Dutta and Reichelstein, 2003, p. 837). The leading indicator variables may then be used to match the future investment return with the current investment expenditure.

Additionally, basing compensation on a leading indicator and not the actual result tend to appear less risky, and thus will be preferred by risk averse agents, and thereby be less expensive to implement. This notion relates to the time consistency concept propounded by Kydland and Prescott (1977) whereby a time-consistent policy is 'a sequence of rules, one for each time period, which specifies policy decisions contingent on the state of the world in that period. Each decision rule has the property that it is optimal given the subsequent elements of the sequence' (Wohltmann and Kromer, 1989, pp. 1283-1284). Thus, the optimal rule decided at time point $t + k$ (where $k>0$) is simply the continuation of the rule at time point t (Wohltmann and Kromer, 1989). In a principal-agent setting, this rule would suggest that, if an agent takes an action in period t, and its effects are not realised until period $t+2$, then in period $t+1$, the employer should pay the agent a flat wage. This is because both parties will be better off if the risk on the agent's compensation were removed (or at least minimised) given that the agent has already chosen the action at time point t. One purpose then of signing a contract at time point t is to commit the principal to pay according to this scheme, for if the agent knew that he or she could renegotiate and be paid the reservation wage for certain rather than the variable compensation, then the agent would not have incentives (other than career concerns) to perform well. In other words, for the agent to choose the alternate compensation, i.e. selecting variable compensation rather than fixed wages, the agent must believe that his or her compensation will depend on the outcome, and that the outcome is stochastically related by some sort of dominance relation to his or her effort, or affected by the use of private information held by the agent.

4.4 Multi-agent Incentive Issues Such As Teamwork and Co-operative Behaviour

The use of single principal-single agent settings for analysing optimal contract design is generally criticised as being highly simplified and unrealistic. However, when the model is expanded to a multi-agent setting, the situation becomes more complex and issues arise with respect to teamwork, how agents share information and risk, and cooperate with each other (Meyer, 1995). The principal faces the basic problem of how to motivate agents to work together to reach an outcome desired by the principal and not collude to work against the principal's interests. One way is to keep the agents independent of each other and reward them individually, i.e. 'independent organisation of tasks'. Another way is for the principal to keep the agents independent but to use relative performance evaluation so that each agent is rewarded based in part on how well he or she performs relative to the other agent, i.e. a non-cooperative game or 'competitive organisation of tasks' (Ramakrishnan and Thakor, 1991). The third alternative is for the principal to induce cooperation, where the agents can decide on both effort levels and sharing of payoffs. The agents can also undertake side contracting whereby they can negotiate and agree to pool their payoffs and share them (i.e. coinsurance reasons), or exert joint effort in completing the tasks (Itoh, 1992).

Holmstrom (1982) highlights two problems in a multi-agent situation: free riding and competition. The free rider problem pertains to team situations such as where only group incentives exist, and the agent has the incentive to shirk duties, i.e. to 'free ride' while the other team member(s) work. The use of group incentives tends to be common in teamwork situations (i.e. where the joint efforts of two or more agents usually result in a single output) because it is prohibitively expensive, if not impossible, for the principal to determine the individual contribution of each agent. Competition in a team-setting encourages optimal disclosure of information among agents. Information on relative performance evaluation becomes important in situations where the incentive structure of one agent is dependent on the other agent's performance. Rather than encourage co-operation, the principal has options in designing contracts that induce agents to report on the other or to prohibit agents pooling either their efforts or their payoffs, i.e. selective intervention by the principal.

Itoh (1991) addressed the moral hazard problems in multi-agent situations where co-operation is an issue. The main objective of the analysis was to examine what factors affect the principal's decision to induce team production through interdependent incentive schemes rather than to treat the agents separately through individual based schemes. The findings suggest that two critical factors affect the principal's decision based on an incentives perspective: (i) strategic interaction between agents, and (ii) their attitudes toward performing multiple tasks. Several assumptions are made in the analysis. Each agent is able to allocate his or her own effort to various tasks; each task is independent of the other, i.e. the outcome of one task does not affect the other; and the revenues from each task only depend on the outcome on that task and no other. The agent also chooses the amount of 'help' to extend to other agents which improves the outcomes of their tasks. The principal, who cannot observe the agent's effort level, is assumed to design wage schedules contingent on outcomes.

Using a one-principal and two-agent model, Itoh (1991) then examined how a marginal change of the optimal contract in the direction of teamwork (i.e. by making wage payments to an agent contingent on the outcome of the other agent's task) affected firstly, one agent to help the other agent, and secondly, the principal's welfare. The analysis suggests that if an agent's marginal disutility of performing an additional task is zero, then team work is optimal if each agent increases his or her own effort in response to an increase in help from the other agent. On the other hand, if the assumption that agents are willing to co-operate is disregarded, then the situation is seen to become more complicated. For one, costs of inducing an agent to perform multiple tasks need to be addressed as they will be larger than the incentive costs for a specialised agent. This will result in 'the nonconvexity of the optimal task structure: the principal wants either a specialized structure or substantial teamwork' (Itoh, 1991, p.631). However, Itoh (1991) also acknowledges that the implications of these results for real management policies are limited (e.g. even if the principal would prefer a specialised task, the nature of production processes may not allow it). He further suggests that factors related to more real-world settings such as learning, reputation, information asymmetries and firm-specific human capital accumulation ought to be incorporated in future studies.

In Arya, Fellingham and Glover (1997), a one owner-two manager model is used to provide an explanation for why muted incentive contracts may be effective in motivating team members (the two managers) in a two-period contract. They demonstrate that by having the team repeat a task in the second time period, explicit (contractual) incentives can be substituted by implicit incentives team members provide to each other. In their analysis, it is assumed that only a team (group) performance measure is available, and that the use of a group performance ties a manager's incentive to the performance of the other agents, thus providing the incentive to monitor the other agents and impeding free riders. It is argued that, under the optimal two-period contract, in the first period the use of team performance measure results in explicit incentives being muted (i.e. bonuses being smaller than if individual incentives had been provided), but that the free rider problem still exists since only group performance measures are available. Thus, in the second period, the team is requested to repeat the task, but individual incentives are provided instead. According to Arya et al. (1997), individual incentives here mean 'each manager prefers to work given the other manager is working. This contract induces the managers to use implicit (self-enforcing) side contracts to overcome the free rider problem in the first period. The managers monitor each other's first period action and threaten to punish deviant behavior' (p. 9). It is also noted that in this setting it is not so much the same task is repeated but that the same team perform a task in the subsequent period.

Arya et al. (1997) also analyse a situational example in which, despite uncorrelated individual performance measures being available, it is optimal to condition each manager's pay on both managers' performance. It is assumed that this leads to the development of a group performance measure, and that using a group performance measure provides each manager with incentives to monitor and a means of punishing other managers. Thus, these results encourage mutual monitoring through the introduction of interdependencies in agents' compensation (i.e. group performance measures), even when individual performance indicators are available.

Mookherjee and Reichelsen (1997) developed a model of budgeting in hierarchical organisations. Each agent in the hierarchy receives a budget for a task. Based on his own information, the agent assigns tasks and budgets to his subordinates, who, in turn, do the same for their subordinates, and so forth. Each department's performance is measured by the difference between budgeted and actual cost. In this multi-agent setting, it is shown that a particular budget mechanism is optimal in terms of the incentives it creates and the co-ordination it achieves.

More recently, Baldenius and Melumad's analysis (2002) considered the optimal assignment of monitoring tasks in a multi-agent setting. The study examined how to assign 'monitors', i.e. non-strategic supervisors to oversee a group of agents in order to generate signals about the agents' performance that are most useful from a contracting perspective. The monitoring assignment is characterised as being either 'focused' –meaning observations by the monitor involve a few products regardless of geographic region in which they are sold, or 'dispersed' whereby observations are over many products in a limited geographic region. The results suggest that if signals generated by the same monitor are negatively correlated, then the optimal monitoring assignment will be focused because dispersed monitoring allows the firm to better utilise relative performance evaluation. By contrast, if each monitor communicates only an aggregated signal to the principal, then focused monitoring is always optimal since aggregation undermines relative performance evaluation. The study also tested team-based compensation and randomised monitoring assignments. Baldenius and Melumad (2002) demonstrate that the principal prefers team-based compensation over contracting with each agent individually unless the correlation between signals is positive and sufficiently high. In the case of randomisation, it was shown that the firm can gain from randomising the monitoring assignment, compared with the optimal linear deterministic contract. Furthermore, under randomisation, the conditional expected utility for the agent is higher when the agent is not monitored compared with the case where the agent is monitored.

In conclusion, recent AT-based accounting studies, particularly those adopting a principal-agent approach, have evolved to expand previous single period, single agent, external contract-focused models to address more complex situations involving multi-period, multi-agent relationships and informal contractual terms (i.e. implicit employer-employee work arrangements). While the literature in the area – both the theoretical and empirical research, has burgeoned considerably, much more can still be done to advance research in the area. In the following section, several suggestions are made for future AT-based accounting studies in the performance evaluation and compensation areas.

5. Directions for Future Research

First, there needs to be better understanding of how accounting-based information (that is subject to the accrual process) can be transformed into useful and reliable information for performance evaluation (Indjejikian, 1999; Lambert, 2001). For instance, how well is the market able to translate financial report information for firm valuation purposes and in turn how efficient are stock or share-based compensation schemes? Further, as noted by Lambert (2001), 'it would be interesting to compare the market's ability to 'undo' manipulations versus the compensation's ability to do so' (p.81). Improved availability of accounting-based performance measures is also seen to help in the construction of multi-period models whereby the production of interim performance information and performance measures can lead to more accurate predictions of managerial outcomes in dynamic situations. In particular, assuming that the agent has a shorter time horizon than the principal, 'forward looking' performance measures are seen to be preferred. As argued by Lambert (2001), 'if an investment project generates negative cash flows in the early years and positive cash flows in later years, he will be unwilling to invest the optimal amount if he is evaluated based on the cash flows that are realized during his tenure', (p.81). One consequence is that this would mean supplementing financial information with non-financial measures of managerial performance, but that would mean the use of more subjective measures. Other related issues with the use of accounting information and developing multi-period models include the need to consider managers' private information, and the ability to dynamically adjust budgets and targets based on arrival of accounting information between decisions.

Another area for future AT studies is to increase the analysis and development of principal-agent relationship models in relation to new and evolving forms of organisational structures (Child and Rodrigues, 2003). Organisational structure is a key factor through which the problem of 'control' has been traditionally addressed and debated. Typically, the hierarchical form of governance that has been assumed in understanding principal-agent relationships is that shareholders through the board of directors they elect have the capacity to affect managerial decisions. However, firms are increasingly entering into partnerships with other entities for reasons of entering into new or foreign markets as well as accessing technology and other resources (Child and Rodrigues, 2003). Firms can also adopt highly complex structures such as having multiple partners pooling their assets in equity-based joint ventures and sometimes joint management with some of the partners (Borys and Jemison, 1989). Consequently, a multiplicity of agency relationships is likely to arise which in turn tends to compound agency costs.

Understanding the agency roles and the impact of the different incentive and monitoring strategies also become more complex and challenging in such situations. Future research thus needs to pay more attention to the mix of incentive and monitoring strategies in the increasingly new and evolving organisational forms.

Further work can also proceed in terms of recognising the inherent limitations of understanding organisational relationships purely from an economics point of view (Bowe and Freeman, 1992; Baiman, 1990). The core assumption of the AT pertains to the individualistic and opportunistic interests of human nature. The decision maker is portrayed as a utility-maximiser, who behaves in self-serving ways to increase his utility. However, this assumption fails to address managerial behaviour in a real-world organisational context where there are other significant environmental and social imperatives. For instance, future studies may address how individual performance is affected by self-interest factors such as wages and bonuses as opposed to organisational imperatives (e.g. environmental and organisational factors such as trust and culture) that may influence individual managerial behaviour. McCauley and Kuhnert (1992) and Chan (1997), for example, argue that trust is a vital factor in task performance, and that organisational culture is also a key variable in affecting trust as well as employee attitudes to job performance. Subramaniam and Mia (2003) likewise found that managerial work-related values impact their budgetary decision-making as well as their organisational commitment. Further, Barkema and Gomez-Mejia (1998), in their review of managerial compensation and firm performance research argue that disciplines such as social comparison theory, social exchange theory, and institutional theory can help to enhance understanding of pay-setting process within firms.

Last but not least, further studies need to recognise that personality differences in individual managers may also moderate their work motivation despite incentive and monitoring structures. The assumption based on economic utilitarianism whereby self-serving and opportunistic ways predominate principal-agent choices does not adequately nor fully explain managerial behaviour and outcomes. While most individuals may impose self-restraints on self-serving behaviours, not everyone will do so, as a result of individual personality differences. For example, Tourigny et al. (2003) contend that executive or senior managers' decision making may be related to personality characteristics such as narcissism (Post, 1993) whereby the individual can become dogmatic in their world-view and ignore stakeholders' views. Narcissism can also predispose a manager to use manipulative techniques (including unethical behaviour) to achieve his or her personal ends at the expense of others. Other individual dimensions that may affect how individuals react to uncertainty (which consequently has implications for their decision-making) are their risk preferences (i.e. how risk averse a manager is) and tolerance for ambiguity. While significant work has been undertaken in examining the impact of risk preferences on managerial decision choices within the AT literature (e.g. March and Shapira, 1987; MacCrimmon and Wehrung, 1986), the impact of tolerance for ambiguity remains largely indeterminate.

Tolerance for ambiguity refers to the extent of desirability of *ambiguity* to an individual, with the greater the tolerance for *ambiguity*, the greater the preference and acceptance of ambiguous situations (Kahn and Sarin, 1988). Ghosh and Ray (1997), based on an experimental study, demonstrate that decision makers who are less risk averse and those having more tolerance for ambiguity, display greater confidence in their decision choice. Risk aversion is viewed as an attitudinal factor, while tolerance for ambiguity is a personality dimension. It is argued that risk assessments are not always based on rational calculations alone, but attitudes towards uncertainty or ambiguous situations may also affect an individual's risk assessment and decision confidence. Given that incentive structures may vary in their level of ambiguity (e.g. implicit terms may be viewed to be more ambiguous than explicit contracts), AT-based studies may further investigate how personality factors of an agent, e.g. tolerance for ambiguity affects their responses to such incentive structures.

6. Conclusions

The AT framework provides a coherent and integrated framework for understanding and analysing organisational relationships where one party delegates decision making to another party. Accounting researchers have adopted this framework extensively in understanding the impact of accounting information on individual level relationships as well as at the market level. This chapter has delineated some of the basic assumptions of AT and strategies for minimising AT associated costs. A review of the major research branches of AT and related research was also undertaken. The continuing progress in both the empirical and theoretical agency research has provided numerous insights into improving the use of accounting information and addressing related issues such as employment contract design, organisational structure, financial reporting and monitoring. No doubt, there are numerous opportunities for future studies to advance accounting research, both empirically and theoretically.

References

Abbott, L. J. and Parker, S. (2000), "Audit committee characteristics and auditor selection", *Auditing: A Journal of Practice and Theory*, Vol. 19, No. 2, pp. 47-66.

Alchian, A. and Demsetz, H. (1972), "Production, information costs and economic organization", *American Economic Review*, Vol. 62, pp. 777-795.

Anderson, D., Francis, J. and Stokes, D. (1993), "Auditing, directorships and the demand for monitoring", *Journal of Accounting and Public Policy*, Vol. 12, pp. 353-375.

Arrow, K. (1971), *Essays in the Theory of Risk Bearing*, Markham, Chicago.

Arya, A., Fellingham, J. and Glover, J. (1997), "Teams, repeated tasks, and implicit incentives", *Journal of Accounting and Economics*, Vol. 23, pp. 7-30.

Baker, G., Gibbons, R. and Murphy, K. J. (1994), "Subjective performance measures in optimal incentive contracts", *Quarterly Journal of Economics*, Vol. 109, pp. 1125-1156.

Baiman, S. (1982), "Agency research in managerial accounting: a survey", *Journal of Accounting Literature*, Vol. 18, pp. 154-213.

Baiman, S. (1990), "Agency research in managerial accounting: a second look", *Accounting Organizations in Society*, Vol. 15, No. 4, pp. 341-371.

Baiman, S. and Demski, J. (1980), "Economically optimal performance evaluation and control systems", *Journal of Accounting Research*, pp. 184-220.

Baldenius, T. and Melumad, N. (2002), "Monitoring in multiagent organizations", *Contemporary Accounting Research*, Vol. 19, No. 4, pp. 483-511.

Barkema, H. G. and Gomez-Mejia, L. R. (1998), "Managerial compensation and firm performance: a general research framework", *Academy of Management Journal*, Vol. 41, No. 2, pp. 135-145.

Berle, A. and Means, G. (1932), *The Modern Corporation and Private Property*, MacMillan Publishers, New York.

Borys, B. and Jemison, D. B. (1989), "Hybrid arrangements as strategic alliances: theoretical issues in organisational combinations", *Academy of Management. The Academy of Management Review*, Vol. 14, No. 2, pp. 234-249.

Bowie, N.E. and Freeman, R.E. (1992), *Ethics and Agency Theory: An Introduction*, Oxford University Press, New York.

Carey, P., Simnett, R. and Tanewski, G. (2000), "Voluntary demand for internal and external auditing by family business", *Auditing*, Vol. 19, pp. 37-51.

Carcello, J. and Neal, T. (2000), "Audit committee characteristics and auditor reporting", *The Accounting Review*, Vol. 75, No. 4, pp. 453-467.

Chan, M. (1997), "Some theoretical propositions pertaining to the context of trust", *The International Journal of Organizational Analysis*, Vol. 5, No. 3, pp. 227-248.

Child, J. and Rodrigues, S. (2003), 'Corporate governance and new organizational forms: issues of ouble and multiple agency", *Journal of Management and Governance*, Vol. 7, pp. 337-360.

Coase, R. (1937), "The Nature of the Firm', *Econometrica*, Vol. 4, pp. 386-405.

Covaleksi, M. A., Evans III, J. H. and Luft, J. L. (2003), "Budgeting research; three theoretical perspectives and criteria for selective integration", *Journal of Management Accounting Research*, Vol. 15, pp. 3-49.

DeAngelo, L. E. (1981), "Auditor size and auditor quality", *Journal of Accounting and Economics*, Vol. 3, No. 3, pp. 183-199.

Deegan, C. (2001), *Financial Accounting Theory*, McGraw-Hill, Australia.

DeFond, M. L. (1992), "The association between changes in client firm agency costs and auditor switching", *Auditing: A Journal of Practice and Theory*, Vol. 2, No. 1, pp. 16-31.

Dixit, A. K. (1997), "Power of incentives in private versus public organizations", *American Economic Review*, Vol. 87, pp. 378-382.

Dutta, S. and Reichelstein, S. (2003), "Leading indicator variables, performance measurement, and long-term versus short-term contracts", *Journal of Accounting Research*, Vol. 41, No. 5, pp. 837-866.

Eisenhardt, K. M. (1989), "Agency theory: an assessment and review", *Academy of Management Review*, Vol. 14, pp. 57-74.

Fama, E. and Jensen, M. (1983a), "Agency problems and Residual Claims", *Journal of Law and Economics*, Vol. 26, No.2, pp. 327-349.

Fama, E. and Jensen, M. (1983), "Separation of ownership and control", *Journal of Law and Economics*, Vol. 26, pp. 301-325.

Fudenberg, D., Holstrom, B. and Milgrom, P. (1990), "Short-term contracts in long-term agency relations", *Journal of Economic Theory*, Vol. 51, pp. 1-31.

Gale, D. and Hellwig, M. (1985), "Incentive compatible debt contracts: the one period problem", *Review of Economic Studies*, Vol. 52, No. 4, pp. 647-664.

Ghosh, D. and Ray, M. R. (1997), "Risk, ambiguity, and decision choice: some additional evidence', *Decision Sciences*, Vol. 28, No. 1, pp. 81-104.

Godfrey, J., Hodgson, A. and Holmes, S. (2003), *Accounting Theory*, 5th edition, John Wiley and Sons Ltd, Australia.

Hayes, R. M. and Schaefer, S. (2000), "Implicit contracts and explanatory power of top executive compensation for future performance", *The Rand Journal of Economics*, Vol. 31, No. 2, pp. 273-293.

Henderson, S., Peirson, G. and Harris, K. (2004), *Financial Accounting Theory*, Pearson Education, Australia.

Holmstrom, B. (1979), "Moral hazard and observability", *The Bell Journal of Economics*, Vol. 10, pp. 74-91.

Holmstrom, B. (1982), "Moral hazard in teams", *The Bell Journal of Economics*, Vol. 13, pp. 324-340.

Holmstrom, B. and Milgrom, P. (1991), "Multitask principal-agent analyses: incentive contracts, asset ownership, and job design", *Journal of Law, Economics and Organization*, Vol. 7, pp. 24-52.

Indjejikian, R. and Nanda, D. (1999), "Dynamic incentives and responsibility accounting", *Journal of Accounting and Economics*, Vol. 27, pp. 177-201.

Indjejikian, R. (1999), "Performance evaluation and compensation research: an agency perspective", *Accounting Horizons*, Vol. 13, No. 2, pp. 147-157.

Itoh, H. (1991), "Incentives to help in multi-agent situations", *Econometrica*, Vol. 59, pp. 611-636.

Itoh, H. (1992), "Cooperation in hierarchical organizations: an incentive perspective", *Journal of Law, Economics and Organisations*, Vol. 8, pp. 321-345.

Jensen, M. and Meckling, W. H. (1976), "Theory of the firm: managerial behaviour, agency costs and ownership structure", *Journal of Financial Economics*, Vol. 3, No. 4, pp. 305-360.

Kahn, B. E. and Sarin, R. K. (1988), "Modelling ambiguity in decisions under uncertainty", *Journal of Consumer Research*, Vol. 15, pp. 265-272.

Kaplan, R. and Atkinson, A. (1989), *Advanced Management Accounting*, 2nd edition, Prentice-Hall, New Jersey.

Kim S.K. and Suh, Y.S. (1992), "Conditional Monitoring Policy under moral hazard", *Management Science*, Vol. 38, No.2, pp.1106-1119.

Kydland, F. E. and Prescott, E. C. (1977), 'Rules rather than discretion: the inconsistency of optimal plans', *Journal of Political Economy*, Vol. 85, pp. 473-491.

Krueger, A. B. (1991), 'Ownership, agency and wages: an examination of franchising in the fast food industry", *Quarterly Journal of Economics*, Vol. 106, pp. 75-101.

Lambert, R. (1983), "Long-term contracting and moral hazard", *Bell Journal of Economics*, Vol. 4, No. 2, pp. 441-452.

Lambert, R. A. (2001), "Contracting theory and accounting", *Journal of Accounting and Economics*, Vol. 32, Issue 1-3, pp. 3-87.

MacCrimmon, K. and Wehrung, D. (1986), *Taking Risks: The Management of Uncertainty*, Free Press, New York.

McCauley, D. P. and Kuhnert, K. W. (1992), "A theoretical review and empirical investigation of employee trust in management", *Public Administration Quarterly*, Vol. 16, pp. 265-284.

March, J. and Shapira, Z. (1987), "Managerial perspectives on risk sharing", *Management Science*, Vol. 33, pp. 1404-1418.

Meyer, M. (1995), "Cooperation and competition in organisations: a dynamic perspective", *European Economic Review*, Vol. 39, pp. 709-722.

Milgrom, P. and Roberts, J. (1992), *Economics, Organization, and Management*, Prentice Hall, New Jersey.

Mookherjee, D. and Reichelstein, S. (1997), 'Budgeting and hierarchical control", *Journal of Accounting Research*, Vol. 35, No. 2, pp. 129-156.

Morck, R., Shleifer, A. and Vishny, R. W. (1988), "Management ownership and market valuation: an empirical analysis", *Journal of Financial Economics*, Vol. 20, No. 1 and 2, pp. 293-315.

Pergola, T. M. (2005), "Management entrenchment: can it negate the effectiveness of recently legislated governance reform?", *Journal of American Academy of Business*, Vol. 6, No. 2, pp. 177-183.

Post, J. M. (1993), "Current concepts of the narcissistic personality: implications for political psychology", *Political Psychology*, Vol. 14, pp. 99-121.

Ramakrishnan, R. and Thakor, A. (1991), "Cooperation versus competition in agency", *Journal of Law, Economics and Organisations*, Vol. 7, pp. 248-283.

Rogerson, W. (1985), "Repeated moral hazard", *Econometrica*, Vol. 53, Issue 1, pp. 69-76.

Scott, W. R. (1997), *Financial Accounting Theory*, Prentice-Hall Inc., New Jersey.

Seow, J-L. (1999), "The demand for the UK small company audit – an agency perspective", *International of Small Business Journal*, Vol. 19, No. 2, pp. 61-79.

Slade, M. E. (1996), "Multitask agency and contract choice: an empirical exploration", *International Economic Review*, Vol. 37, No.2, pp. 465-486.

Subramaniam, N. and Mia, L. (2003), "A note on work-related values, budget emphasis and commitment in functionally differentiated organisations", *Management Accounting Research*, Vol. 14, No. 4, pp. 389-408.

Kim, S. K. and Suh, Y. S. (1992), "Conditional monitoring policy under moral hazard", *Management Science*, Vol. 38, No. 8, pp. 1106-1120.

Tourigny, L., Dougan, W. L., Washbush, J. and Clements, C. (2003), "Explaining executive integrity: governance, charisma, personality and agency", *Management Decision*, Vol. 41, No. 10, pp. 1035-1049.

Watts, R. L. and Zimmerman, J. L. (1986), *Positive Accounting Theory*, Prentice Hall, New Jersey.

Watts, R. L. and Zimmerman, J. L. (1990), "Positive accounting theory: a ten year perspective", *The Accounting Review*, pp. 131-156.

Wilson, R. (1968), "On the Theory of Syndicates", *Econometrica*, Vol. 36, pp. 119-132.

Wohltmann, H. and Kromer, W. (1989), "On the notion of time-consistency", *European Economic Review*, Vol. 33, pp. 1283-1288.

Zingales, L. (2000), "In search of new foundations", *The Journal of Finance*, Vol. 55, No. 4, pp. 1623-1653.

6

TRANSACTION COST ECONOMICS GOVERNANCE AND CONTROL DECISIONS

Julian Jones
University of Manchester, UK

Abstract: Transaction Cost Economics (TCE) (Coase, 1937; Williamson 1979) makes predictions on firm size based on the relative magnitudes of transaction costs occurring in the switch from bureaucracy to market-based provision. The chapter reviews management control literatures alongside conventional TCE in order to address the absence of ex-post control mechanisms in TCE's rather restrictive account of governance. The resulting TCE-informed management accounting and control framework provides a more cohesive account of contemporary governance decisions. The chapter concludes with recent research in the field further integrating TCE with other related perspectives, and with a set of recommendations for future research to enhance our understanding of the many facets of governance and control.

Keywords: Transaction cost economics; governance; control; trust.

1. Introduction
Transaction Cost Economics: The Principles
Building on the seminal insights of Coase (1937), Williamson (1975, 1986) developed Transaction Cost Economics (TCE) to explain the boundaries of the firm in terms of the optimal choice between market and hierarchical provision. In turn, this is based on the trade-off between 'production' and so called 'information' (transaction) costs.

In many ways, Coase (1937) was the originator of transaction cost theory. By relaxing (problematic) neo-classical assumptions of perfect certainty, he allowed for the possibility of incomplete contracting and enforcement, he was thus able to go to the very heart of the firm and ask 'why firms exist'? The original proposition put forwards is that they exist because of the need to mediate the additional information costs associated with the purchase and subsequent monitoring of inputs provided from the market.

The transaction cost approach regards the transaction as the basic unit of analysis. It holds that an understanding of transaction cost economising is central to the study of organisations through assessing how their governance structures serve to economise on transaction costs.

Transaction costs occur 'when a good or service is transferred across a technologically separable interface' (Williamson, 1981). Nooteboom (1993, p.285) later elaborated considerably on the sources of transaction costs by associating them to a three-stage exchange process: contact, contract and control. At each stage, buyers and suppliers face different magnitudes of transaction costs. At the *(ex ante)* contact and contract stage, a buyer incurs search costs and the seller, marketing costs. At the contract stage, costs are incurred in preparing an agreement to counteract anticipated outcomes during execution.

In its very raw form, TCE is therefore an *ex ante* review of information costs occurring during the first two stages of contacting and contracting with external, market-based vendors. This later emerges as a major limitation and barrier to greater adoption in management accounting research.

In almost the complete reverse of agency assumptions, under TCE, transactions are executed by innately 'imperfect' human beings (Spekle, 2001) in imperfect factor markets. Decision makers are bound by limited decision-making capacity *(bounded rationality)* and seek to maximise their own utility first and foremost which can result in *opportunistic* tendencies.

1.1. Bounded rationality

Williamson and Ouchi (1981, p.350) argued that if hyper-rationality assumptions underpinning neo-classical economics were true, organisational structure would be of little economic importance. Markets would then imply no more transaction costs than firms.

Bounded rationality – a key transaction cost assumption is a behavioural construct explaining how most transactions occur with limited information (Williamson, 1986). Since there are practical limits to the amount of information the human mind can process, decision-making capacity is constrained by information on current and prospective performance. Decision quality is then a function of the attention directed to a problem and elicitation of relevant information. As the number of decisions rise, computational abilities diminish (Sarkar and Ghosh, 1997).

Nooteboom (1993) later explained how bounded rationality imposes limits during the contact, contract and control stages of governance decisions. At the contact stage, it limits opportunities for competitive positioning and search for appropriate contractors. Although decision-makers are assumed to be rational utility-maximising individuals, since they are informationally bound, they cannot foresee nor incorporate all contingencies into ex-ante contractual arrangements. Even if they could, Baiman (1990) noted that costly contracting and enforcement may provide a deterrent to their incorporation. At the control stage, bounded rationality limits abilities to monitor post-contractual performance against service level agreements. As transactions become more complex, monitoring, compliance and, where appropriate, insurance costs (due to the uncertain nature of the contractual process), also increase.

1.2.   Opportunism

Williamson (1986) defined opportunism as the incomplete or distorted disclosure of information, especially to calculated efforts to mislead, distort, disguise, obfuscate, or otherwise confuse (p. 47). In exercising opportunistic behaviour, a contracting party may not necessarily breach terms of an agreement, but would take advantage of bounded rationality. This then creates efficiency implications about whether transactions are undertaken in the market or within a firm.

Given behavioural constructs of bounded rationality and opportunism, Williamson (1986) sought to outline two further sources relating to the characteristics of transactions:

(1)   The frequency with which the transaction is performed, and
(2)   The degree of asset specificity accompanying the transaction.

1.3.   Frequency

Frequency refers to how often an asset is used or how often an activity is performed. Recurrent transactions will be organised in the market, while assets that are rarely used will be organised inside the firm.

1.4.   Asset specificity

Asset specificity relates to the extent to which assets deployed are customised to a particular environment. Williamson (1986) outlined six sources of specificity:

(i)   *Site/Location Specificity:* manufacturers are often co-located to economise on transportation and inventory costs.

(ii)   *Physical Asset Specificity:* describes the adoption of equipment for particular processes.

(iii)   *Human Asset Specificity:* refers to employee specialisation required in support of a transaction. This is created through specialised training and learning by doing. Labour then becomes a non-homogeneous input and employees no longer become substitutable.

(iv)   *Specific Investments:* include investments in research and development that would otherwise have little utility in another organisation.

(v)   *Brand name capital,* and

(vi)   *Temporal specificity:* akin to technological nonseparability, similar in nature to site specificity in which a timely on-site response is vital.

Where an agent specifically deploys assets in respect of the principal's transaction, the principal's power increases in line with the associated size of the investment, and decreases with the agent's ability to deploy those assets alternate uses. Assets that are specific to any one environment then have greater utility *inside* rather than outside the exchange relationship owing to 'quasi-rents' created by continuing the asset-specific relation (Baiman, 1990).

2.   Transaction Cost Predictions

The organisational imperative that emerges in such circumstances is this: organise transactions so as to economise on bounded rationality while simultaneously safeguard them against the hazards of opportunism (Williamson, 1985 p. 32).

The characteristics of the transaction, the contracting parties and the environment interact to distinguish between three governance mechanisms: markets, hierarchies and hybrids.

2.1.   Market

The homogeneity characteristic of non-specific, recurrent transactions with easily measurable performance attributes ensures a low score on the specificity scale. The absence of idiosyncrasy also ensures competitive supply market conditions and allows the 'invisible hand' of the market to constrain behaviour, even in conditions of exceptional uncertainty. In repeated transactions, both the client and market-based vendor have an incentive to continue market-based relations: the outsourcing client obtains uninterrupted service and the supplier, uninterrupted revenue. Under performance or opportunism threatens continuation and sacrifices opportunity revenue.

2.2.   Hierarchy

On the other end of the specificity and frequency spectrum are idiosyncratic transactions, requiring large but sporadic managerial input and specific (physical) assets and skills. These characteristics impede the smooth functioning of the market which cannot devise performance measures for transactions with largely qualitative outcomes, nor reward individuals against unspecified organisational criteria. Authoritative control mechanisms of hierarchies are then relevant in containing transactions.

2.3.   Hybrid

Hybrids lie between markets and hierarchies. They incorporate control devices of the former with contractual safeguards based on neo-classical contract law of the latter. Hybrids involve bringing together resources and governance structures of distinct organisations into shared collaborative ventures (Boyrs and Jemison, 1989). Often, they are evident in public sector reform agendas, specifically, the UK's use of Public Finance Initiatives (PFI) to reform large elements of the public sector. These involve significant capital expenditures in long-term highly specific assets (schools, hospitals, and penal institutes), significant uncertainty, the promise of long-run cash flows in return for (theoretically) cost control in procurement, the redistribution of risk and the sharing of expertise.

'Efficient' solutions are found where the buyer is dependent on long-term service provision and the provider on long-run cash inflows to recover the investments in specific assets. Reputational effects have important externality effects in constraining information costs (Williamson, 1996, p. 378). In these arrangements, the client is exceptionally dependent on the vendor for uninterrupted service, but since the vendor's assets have little salvage value outside the direct exchange relationship and the provider is dependent on the client to command credibility in obtaining further third party work, the so-called 'exchange of hostages' (Klein, 1980) counterbalances supplier power, reduces dependence, comforts buyers and advance compliance to the provisions of the arrangement (Williamson, 1983).

Yet there are a number of disadvantages to balance the merits of transaction cost investments. Their provision increases buyer dependence, fuelling search and monitoring costs for alternative supply (Nooteboom, 1993). Further, to be effective, this process requires some previously agreed to, contractually anchored, notion as to what constitutes adequate performance (Spekle, 2001). Empirically, Semlinger (1991) reports that component suppliers in the automotive sector supply products with highly transaction specific assets (moulds, dies), without obtaining, and in some cases, without wanting the safeguards prescribed by TCE.

2.4.   TCE and its critics

Williamson's depiction of self-serving, utility maximising individuals is not without its critics. Robins (1987) is Williamson's fiercest critics. According to Robins (1987), in anything other than perfect competition, optimal exchange efficiency need not always prevail. The argument he makes is that the degree to which organisations are pushed to find their most efficient structures depends on the realisation of competitive pressures and on the availability of strategic alternatives (see also Harrigan, 1984). Under non-equilibrium conditions, the competitive pressures on firms are far from certain, and the ideal organisational structure to minimise transaction costs, indeterminate.

Winter (1988) notes that sub-optimal and even dysfunctional inter-organisational arrangements can persist indefinitely. March and Simon (1958) also reported that decision makers often operate under cognitive constraints, and Demsetz (1988) uses this as a basis to attack the assumption of 'perfect knowledge'. Osborn and Hagedoorn (1997) too argue that inter-organisational relations serve a number of purposes, of which economising on transactions may only be a part. The outcome then is that strict optimising theories then become untenable and focusing on transaction costs may hide more than it reveals (p. 247).

There is increasing evidence that transaction cost reduction is not *the* ultimate objective. A cursory glance at the mainstream strategy literatures demonstrates this. Business process models such as Porter's (1985) concentrate on profitability drivers and proprietary knowledge and time competition in creating hard to imitate advantages. But proprietary business models involve non-standard interfaces that exclude or complicate access to world-class suppliers. This then creates information costs, but these do not feature in strict optimising theories such as TCE. The resource-based view invites us to pinpoint resources that are rare, valued and imitable (Prahalad and Hamel, 1990) and with this, the remit of 'coreness' becomes evident, as does the boundary between transactions that should be supported in-house or by the market. Again, these decisions occur irrespective of any information costs involved. Increasingly networks are offered as the engine providing access to proprietary resources for growth and eliminating competitiveness in resources (Thorelli, 1986, p. 46). In an influential article entitled 'Collaborate with your competitors and win', Hamel, Doz and Prahalad (1989) outlined the merits of collaborating versus competing within a network, based on whether organisations are embedded in a network (collaborate) or acting discretely (compete). The relevance then for governance and control theory is that firm size is driven not only by failure, but by *success* criteria; focus and collaborate for advantage, irrespective of transaction costs.

In the 1990s, the UK National Health Service contracted out its cleaning to private contractors with efficiency motives in mind. However, by December 2004, the Labour government admitted that, while the process had indeed delivered against the efficiency objective, the need to bid low had reduced standards, leaving hospitals dirtier than they were before. The requirement to maximise efficiency has now been supplemented with a need to include outcome performance attributes in governance decisions (Financial Times, 2 June 2005, p. 30).

Rather than setting out to displace TCE, the underlying implication is that it should not be applied indiscriminately. Robins (1987) explained how TCE provides a common framework for analysing the impact of external market constraints on different forms of organisation under specific conditions 'When transaction costs are dislodged from their position as the motive force of organisational change, the conditions that mandate more or less costly forms of governance become an integral part of the analysis' (Robins, 1987, p. 82).

Like many others (Smith, Carroll and Ashford, 1995; Chiles and McMackin, 1996; Dekker, 2004), Robins is less confident that a single theoretical perspective focusing on two stages of a three staged process of contact, contract and control (Nooteboom, 1997) is sufficiently robust to make such hard-line governance decisions.

A further significant limitation is its central focus on the characteristics of transactions to the detriment of social embeddedness. Even though the notion of trust in contractual arrangements was not an alien concept to Williamson (1975), noting that 'trust is important and businessmen rely on it much more extensively than is commonly realized' (1975, p. 108), trust is very much a salient feature of TCE.

Goodwill trust, defined as perceptions of intentions to perform in accordance with expectations (Ring and van de Ven, 1992) is increasingly reported to reduce opportunism (Sako, 1992; Das and Teng, 2001). Similarly, an in-house function that outperforms expectations may well create internal trust, raising the threshold at which market transactions appear acceptable.

Social exchanges between clients and suppliers are crucial elements in outsourcing relations (Dwyer *et al.*, 1987; Kern and Willcocks, 2000; Zaheer and Vankatraman, 1995; Nooteboom *et al.*, 1997 and van der Meer-Kooistra and Vosselman, 2000), but the traditional TCE paradigm does not incorporate any such social context into its analysis (Chiles and McMackin, 1996; Covaleski *et al.*, 2003). The result is that TCE lacks conceptual force when confronted with delicately posed, yet informal governance structures it lumps together as 'hybrid' forms.

Clearly, Coases (1937) original preoccupation with ex-ante information costs appear 'out of sync' with contemporary governance choices that encompass notions of service quality, strategic fit, economic cost efficiency and social relations.

3. Transaction Cost Principles in Management Accounting Research

Unsurprisingly, TCE has not as yet featured prominently in management accounting research (Baiman, 1990, p. 346). The focus of the remainder of this review is therefore on the limited few contributors who have made much progress in addressing these obstacles which limit its adoption in management accounting research.

The earliest paper examined is Baiman's (1990) paper concerned with agency costs. While not specifically contributing to the development of TCE, this was the earliest (successful) attempt to integrate incentive-based perspectives (from agency theory) with information cost perspectives (from TCE). By relaxing the perfect market assumption that had directed the focus of management accounting researchers towards methods of re-aligning ex-ante interests, Baiman allowed for more accurate accounts of contemporary governance decisions that today, incorporate socially induced ex-ante bargaining and associated control mechanisms.

Citing evidence of research in the automobile sector, Flynn (1987) argued that a strong relationship exists between bounded rationality and trust. Trust and commitment could direct upstream outsourcing relations between manufacturers and their component suppliers. Trust could reduce problems associated with bounded rationality, and the behavioural uncertainty associated with decision-making. Trust based relations are also prominent in sustaining successful industrial buyer-seller relationships (Milliman and Fugate, 1988, Howes *et al.*, 1989). Excluding the social element in inter-firm relations is thus cited as the greatest constraint of conventional transaction cost theory (Ghoshal and Moran, 1996; Hill, 1990). In no small way, by integrating the work on inter-firm relations (principal-agent paradigm) with intra-firm relations (from TCE), Baiman set the scene for a TCE-informed management accounting and control research.

van der Meer-Kooistra and Vosselman (2000) explicitly considered the role of social interactions in governance decisions. Leaning on control theory where trust is given explicit consideration and integrating these perspectives with TCE, the paper is able to more accurately represent contemporary organisational forms that rely on trust for their formation and control.

Spekle's (2001) paper, 'Explaining management control structure variety: a transaction cost economics perspective', is based on the premise that since management control is all about enhancing organisational effectiveness, management control theory should specify in more detail the *modus operandi* of management control structures. The paper successfully achieves this and depicts the controls, concepts and operative mechanisms of a transaction cost theory of management control.

In no small way, Baiman (1990), van der Meer-Kooistra and Vosselman (2000) and Spekle (2001) have contributed to the advancement of transaction cost theory and more specifically, set the research agenda in providing a more holistic account of governance. In so doing, enhancing its attractiveness to management accounting researchers. What then follows is an applied piece by Langfield-Smith and Smith (2003) who are among the few to test Baiman, van der Meer-Kooistra & Vosselman and Spekle's more socially adept TCE framework formally in the field.

Baiman has focused on redefining the relevance and contribution of agency theory to management accounting research, and in his 1990 paper, set out to enhance our understanding of the selection and design of management accounting systems. Baiman recognised that much could be gained by providing an integrating principal agent and transaction cost principles since the former focused on inter-firm contractual relations and the latter on intra-firm relations.

The principal-agent model was initially proposed in the economics literature (Alchian and Demsetz, 1972; Jensen, 1983; Jensen and Meckling, 1976). Here, inter-organisational relations are described as a series of control mechanisms under which one or more person(s) (principal) engages another (agent) to perform a service on their behalf (Alchian and Demsetz, 1972; Jensen, 1983; Jensen and Meckling, 1976). Central to this is the risk that without appropriate inducements and safeguards, agents shirk from responsibilities in a manner that results in disutility for principals.

Baiman believes that the principal-agent theory has, over the years, provided a coherent and useful framework to conceptualise management accounting problems. Research in this domain has centred on the role of conventional cost accounting procedures and control mechanisms in containing agency costs. Suh (1987), for example, suggested that the allocation of agency costs from one to another could be used to prevent collusive behaviour in cost allocation problems. Rajan (1992) provided a similar rationale for allocations of indirect costs. Additional research also looks at how the information that budgetary (Guilding, 2003), monitoring and transfer pricing systems produce can mitigate agency problems when incorporated into employment contracts. Others, however, argue that its historical origins in economics limit its appeal in other spheres of management accounting (Hemmer, 1996), while some go as far as to suggest that the theory is both blatant and conservative (Perrow, 1986, p. 22).

Given these qualifications, Baiman set out to compare and contrast the theoretical underpinnings of principal-agent and transaction cost theory, the most significant of which concerns the market efficiency hypothesis. Principal-agent theory assumes costless and perfect court enforcement. On the other hand, TCE's entire rationale for the existence of the firm is based on the imperfect factor markets.

This (major) departure point holds significant implications for the drafting and organisation of management accounting systems. Under transaction cost rationale, uncontracted-for contingencies that are a by-product of imperfect factor markets give rise to opportunism, and the ability to curb opportunism is largely down to investments in relation-specific assets. However, under agency theory, as contracts are assumed to be complete and self-enforcing, there is no place for ex-ante bargaining, and so the design of transactions is largely irrelevant.

Relaxing the perfect market assumption, Baiman outlined a number of scenarios under which contact, contract and control-stage contract costs associated with exchanges need not be so onerous.

Taking in the characteristics of contemporary transactions, this seems entirely plausible. Clauses increasingly allow for renegotiation of contractual terms once the contract is in place. For example, Accenture, one of the worlds's leading providers of outsourcing services today would expect to see a 10-year contract renegotiated at least twice.[18] And from this discussion of ex-post re-negotiation alone, significant implications emerge for the shape of managerial accounting research 'Admitting for the possibility of incomplete contracts and allowing for renegotiation as a way of dealing with contract incompleteness introduces a new strategic element in the choice of managerial accounting procedures that has been ignored in principal-agent models to-date' (Baiman, p. 355).

Prior to this, ex-ante contractual safeguards were the only means of realigning interests. Self-enforcing socially driven inducements had virtually no ex-ante economic value, sitting alongside the principal-agent paradigm rather uncomfortably. Although Baiman fell short of a full exposition of the potential role of socially-induced control mechanisms in replacing formal contractual safeguards, in no small way, he encouraged successive generations of managerial accounting researchers to investigate these issues further and in so doing, present a more accurate principal-agent paradigm 'Allowing for jointly observable but unverifiable information and incorporating incomplete contracts in a multiperiod setting allows concerns for trust and fairness and more generally reputation to endogenously arise' (Baiman, p. 356).

Agency and transaction cost theory both lack a conceptual understanding of the disciplining role of less formal social control mechanisms as substitutes for, or complements to, formal governance. Incorporating incentive-perspectives alongside information-cost perspectives and assigning social inducements co-equal status with information costs promises to enhance our understanding of governance and get us closer to a more realistic model of managerial accounting (Baiman, p. 367). This opened up a whole new arena for research concerned with the shape and form of management accounting systems.

---

[18] William Green, chief executive, FT, 2 June 2005.

Standard neo-classical economics and its belief in perfect court enforcement largely led research to focus on formal inter-firm control mechanisms. Today, however, management control incorporates discussions of inter *and* intra-firm accounting control mechanisms, reflecting Otley's earlier call (1994) for research to investigate relations beyond equal internal parties (p. 52) that increasingly occur within networks of suppliers and buyers.

Dropping the assumption of perfect markets and allowing for the possibility of social control mechanisms allowed quite different scenarios than those derived from complete contracting to emerge (Baiman, p. 357). This also facilitated a fundamental change in the boundaries of conventional concern for management accounting.

van der Meer-Kooistra and Vosselman (2000) were to make significant headway in this arena, reconciling transaction cost economics with practice which sees activities being transferred in less than competitive supply markets with much uncertainty alongside trust and strong dependencies. The treatment of social embeddedness is the key in this respect.

Granovetter (1985) had long described the positive association between the extent to which transactions are socially embedded and opportunism. Williamson (1993), however, is documented as claiming that social embeddedness is part of the wider institutional environment in which transactions occur, much like legal rules and the influence of trade unionism. By classifying social embeddedness as an environmental variable, Williamson essentially dismissed the notion that trust, once established, could be actively deployed to curtail opportunism (van der Meer-Kooistra and Vosselman, p. 56).

In stark contrast, rather than some exogenous variable, trust takes centre stage in van der Meer-Kooistra and Vosselman's depiction. It can be capable of being nurtured and/or deployed over time.

In much of what follows, the authors set out to showcase how trust contains information costs in market exchanges, specifically in 'hybrid' organisational arrangements characterised by a high degree of specificity, low output measurability and task programmability that would otherwise be precluded under conventional transaction cost theory.

van der Meer-Kooistra and Vosselman were not concerned with 'markets' or 'bureaucracies' *per se*, but the conditions under which transactions that encompass trust-based patterns of control emerge (Table 1). In the *contact* phase, suppliers are selected on the basis of friendships, from previous contractual relations or on the basis of a legacy (reputation) of trustworthiness. As these relations are largely socially embedded, *contracts* are far from detailed and payments not directly correlated with activity outputs. Since both share risks and rewards, *control* is achieved via the facilitation of competence trust (certification, education, reputation or through investments by contracting parties) and goodwill trust (open commitment, reciprocity and exceeding expectations) (Sako, 1992).

Table 1
Transaction Characteristics / Control

Contingency factors	Market based pattern	Bureaucracy based pattern	Trust based pattern
Transaction characteristics	Low asset specificity; high repetition; measurability of activities and output; short to medium term contract	Medium to high asset specificity which can be protected by contractual rules; low to medium repetition; measurability of activities or output based on contractual rules; medium to long term contract	High asset specificity; low repetition; activities or output cannot be measured well; long term contract
Transaction environment characteristics	Many potential transaction parties; market price contains all the market information; social embeddedness and institutional factors are not relevant	Future contingencies are more or less known; medium to high market risks; institutional factors influence the contractual rules	Future contingencies are unknown; high market risks; social embeddedness; institutional factors influence the relation
Party characteristics	Not important, because there are many parties with the same characteristics due to which switching costs are low	Competence reputation; medium risk sharing attitude; asymmetry in bargaining power	Competence reputation; experience in networks; experience with contracting parties; risk sharing attitude; no asymmetry in bargaining power

(*Source*: *van der Meer-Kooistra and Vosselman, 2000, p. 62*)

The first case – NAM (Nederlandse Aardolie Maatschappij) describes the outsourcing activities of the largest gas producer in the Netherlands with approximately 2,500 employees. The characteristics of the transaction – meticulous selection criteria, comprehensive contracts, repetitive activities and medium levels of specificity make it difficult for van der Meer-Kooistra and Vosselman to agree formally on whether the relationship encompasses strict bureaucratic or market-characteristics. This, though, is partly a reflection of the environment in which the gas producer operates. European rules do not allow selections based on trust/past social relations, but require objective and transparent search criteria.

The characteristics of the second case of outsourcing at Shell's research and technology centre in Amsterdam encompass partly repetitive and non-repetitive outputs, medium levels of specificity, a risk sharing attitude and an open commitment to exchange; transactions which clearly lend themselves to trust-based rather than market of bureaucratic control devices. What this paper has been effective at demonstrating is that elements of social embeddedness including trust and commitment are indeed control variables that have an economic purpose during the contact stage in bringing down information costs in otherwise preclusive or high risk markets and after contracts have been negotiated and drawn.

Given that transaction cost and management control theorists share a common interest in understanding purposive control, and both are committed to an explanation of control structure choice, Spekle (2001) set out to build on Baiman's (1990) and van der Meer-Kooistra and Vosselman's (2000) work in the control arena to specify the modus operandi of management control structures ...'Trying to transfer the insights accumulated (in TCE) to the domain of Management Control might well be worth the effort' (p. 420).

In doing this, Spekle related the type of control mechanism to the frequency characteristics of a transaction. Transaction-oriented, programmable activities allow ex-ante articulation of expectations via authoritative rules-based instructions and/or targets – primarily service level agreements in outsourcing relations. Less programmable transactions on the other hand are far less ill-defined. These emphasise 'general commitments' or the sketching of 'broad confines' within which performance ought to fit, rather than precise specifications, and the key issue is which control device is appropriate in these circumstances.

Leaning on the control devices from the management control literatures and transaction characteristics from TCE, Spekle was to sketch a number of alternative governance arrangements, each with their own transaction characteristics and control devices. Figure 1 is drawn here to help summarise Spekle's predictions. Point (a) in the matrix indicates the range of transactions capable of being governed in the market. These are highly programmable, non-specific transactions that take place in highly competitive markets where the 'invisible hand' is sufficient to constrain opportunism.

On the other end of the control axis lie idiosyncratic transactions with highly specific and (largely) non-programmable characteristics. Here, a decreasing pool of competent contributors in the market raises the threat of dependency and opportunism. This rules out market based control devices in favour of hierarchical governance structures and their machine-like control devices (Mintzberg, 1983), as indicated at point (b).

Between 'markets' and 'hierarchies' is the domain of 'boundary forms of control' (Simons, 1995). These encompass market discipline with bureaucratic control. In terms of ownership structure, they can encompass joint ventures and equity ownership. In terms of management control, should it not be possible to rely on the invisible hand of the market for control owing to the thinness in the market, the provision of investments that are specific to a particular transaction can keep participants sufficiently engaged. These relations, indicated at point (c) are particularly relevant where transactions are so idiosyncratic, they require specialist inputs (staff, systems, assets, etc) not hitherto (or competitively) available in the market. The costs of guarding against opportunism and the threat of appropriation of key resources are such that control devices have to focus on the prevention of undesired outcomes. Transactions performed in this range can then only be effectively governed via hierarchical control.

In many ways, these relations are the easiest to structure. However, it is more difficult to reconcile the discrepancy between practice and theory in respect of activities that fall outside of this range. These transactions, described earlier by van der Meer-Kooistra and Vosselman, encompass attributes of trust and reputation, less quantifiable outputs, and much uncertainty.

Spekle was to make significant headway in resolving this discrepancy. He described how, with experience and data on actual states of the world, uncertainty diminishes over time. With this in mind, transactions accompanied by high specificity and significant uncertainty (point (e) in the matrix) can potentially be organised on an exploratory basis. These can be highly disorganised, lack explicit guidance, characterised by an unwillingness to define responsibilities, mutual interdependency and information sharing with top management acting in a supportive, rather than a hierarchical mode. Decision-making is complex along a steep learning curve and control devices emerge and adapt with the availability of new information (p. 432). Long-term, as soon as richer insights emerge, elements of machine control are introduced to the arrangement, ultimately supplanting the exploratory form.

It is then worthwhile asking where socially-embedded principles of trust and reputation as defined specifically by Baiman (1990) and van der Meer-Kooistra and Vosselman (2000) sit within Spekles depiction of control archetypes. Evidently, they have limited economic value in hierarchical governance arrangements with machine-based control (point b), nor do they play a significant role in market-based arrangements with authoritative control devices (point a). While Spekle does not specifically advocate trusting relations in his depiction, it is inconceivable that trust based relations would not come to the fore in conditions of high specificity and idiosyncrasy.

Figure 1
Characteristics / control matrix

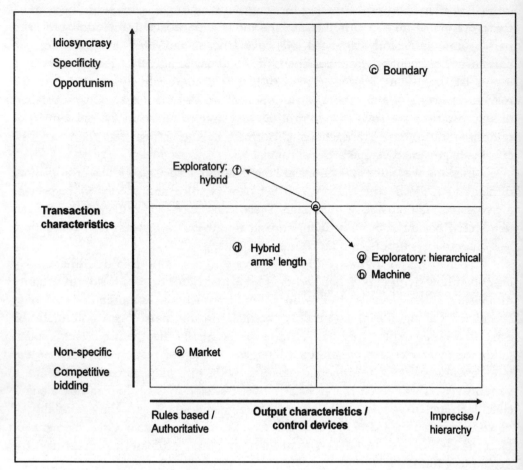

Exploratory control devices can be appropriate to govern hybrid organisational forms (point f), involving outsourcing relations with a limited number of suppliers. According to Spekle, these emerge for activities with moderate levels of specificity. Where high levels of idiosyncrasy were involved, suppliers may be being unwilling to invest in specific assets as buyers will be unable to offer long-term contracts, except in hybrid organisational arrangements where the presence of trust and reputation can provide safeguards missing in very uncompetitive supply markets. The alternative is to adopt exploratory control devices in hierarchical governance structures (point g). These transactions have with less precise output characteristics, high idiosyncrasy but manageable levels of uncertainty owing to the internal control devices.

Clearly, it is in this experimental quadrant that many contemporary transactions now take place. The review that follows by Langfield-Smith and Smith

(2003) utilise transaction cost principles in an attempt to more fully describe the conditions under which the hybrid organisational form emerge.

Langfield-Smith and Smith's (2003) paper is an explicit attempt to apply transaction cost led theory of management control to illuminate the influence of trust as a control device. It does this via case based research examining the case of IT outsourcing at an Australian electricity company.

The case (Central Energy) is particularly interesting as the company is the result of a merger of two electricity companies. Following the merger, the company was also re-organised around a holding company and four separate businesses, each with profit maximising objectives. Post-privatisation, consumers could 'shop around' for their power needs, resulting in more competition, a greater focus on customer service and reduced costs.

Within two months of the merger, a decision was made to outsource the Information Technology and Telecommunications function that was a result of the legacy of the merger. The motive was clear – an accurate assessment of costs could not be made, pricing structures between the divisions were far from transparent. There was also limited overall accountability and a belief that the company lacked effective IT capabilities to deliver to the core network and energy services business, even after bringing the two disparate IT functions together. Three proposals to undertake the activity were received from external participants – two external and one internal. Global Systems (the vendor) was successful, whereas the in-house proposal came last.

The incumbent vendor, Global Systems, faced challenges on a number of fronts: determining appropriate service levels to control the deal; getting a handle on costs and delivering cost reduction; implementing a risk-reward mechanism; managing expectations at the same time as developing trust with the client, Central.

The table below summarises the various facets of the relationship and the accompanying transaction cost explanation.

Table 2
Characteristics of Trust based Contracting

Element	Transaction Cost Explanation
Vendor provides management services while client retains ownership of IT hardware	Contains fears of loosing control, and recourse in the event of opportunism
Contract specified broad expectations, not precise contingent claims contract	Contain information costs at contact and control stage of outsourcing development
The environment	Much uncertainty; greater reliance on social embeddedness through competence trust in IT provision, regular meeting; personal relations; open-book transactions
Characteristics of the transaction	Mixed transactions: idiosyncratic and standard
Transaction frequency	Mix of programmable/non-programmable, increasing in programmability over time, no explicit performance measures indicating trust-based, exploratory/emergent control
Asset specificity: Physical assets owned by Central Vendor located on-site High human specificity	Guard against dependency/opportunism High switching costs
Cost allocation: difficulty in selecting overhead recovery rate	Rates emergent over-time; exploratory control

This paper is to be commended as a rare applied piece. Having relaxed preclusive perfect market assumptions, it is able to depict the role of exploratory control devices in facilitating market-based transactions in otherwise preclusive transaction cost environments.

4. Conclusion

This chapter set out to investigate the influence of TCE in management accounting research. Reviewing the very assumptions on which TCE bases its prescriptions, we have seen that the predictive power of TCE *per se*, is limited. The exclusion of the disciplining role of ex-post control on governance is a significant limitation. A pre-occupation with transaction cost minimisation to the exclusion of others is another.

Baiman's (1990) move formally to extend the seminal insights of Coase and Williamson into the management control domain by integrating it with principal-agent theory was a significant step forwards. Principal-Agent theory had a respected legacy in management accounting research. Integrating TCE and control theory and closing the gap between governance and control, Baiman largely prevented the death of TCE.

Further, later works of van der Meer and Spekle too have been most influential in providing a voice to social control mechanisms in governance, thereby allowing more accurate accounts of contemporary governance choices to emerge.

Today, informal social constructs are as integral in TCE as are the characteristics of transactions and transaction parties in defining transaction costs. Trust is capable of constraining uncertainty resulting from a small number of participants, and from the deployment of assets which have little utility outside direct exchange relationships. This provides management accounting researchers with a far more dynamic framework with which to examine inter-organisational relations.

Still much work needs to be done in building on earlier successes of Baiman, van der Meer-Kooistra and Vosselman and Spekle to further enhance our theoretical understanding of the many facets of governance and control. The continued preoccupation with homogeneity of outcomes is limiting. Theory continues to imply that products and services have more or less the same quality, and factors such as delivery times and reliability play hardly any role (van der Meer-Kooistra, 2000, p.54-55). Market failure is still *the* defining force in shaping boundaries, irrespective of success or failure criteria. The psychology literature represents a whole range of alternative corporate objectives, including unplanned actions, habits, routines and behavioural rules. All these undermine rational efficiency considerations (see, for example, Duhaime and Schwenk, 1985; Osborn and Hagdoorn, 1997).

For these reasons, this chapter joins the call from other researchers (Chiles and McMackin, 1996; Smith, Carroll and Ashford, 1995; Dekker, 2004) to further integrate TCE with other theoretical perspectives.

Taking the lead in this respect is Van den Bogard and Spekle (2003) who utilise TCE to help explain structure/control issues in a case of corporate restructuring at Shell. A number of problems in the restructuring process were strongly related to uncertainty and specificity dimensions. The resulting hybrid structure which was formed surprisingly incorporated many hierarchical controls associated with the old structure. The conclusion is that such hierarchical controls can be a rational response to high levels of uncertainty and specificity.

Dekker (2004) too, in a case study of a strategic alliance in the rail industry set out to test the proposition that co-ordination requirements and the social context of the alliance influence formal control structures. The paper reports that high levels of goodwill trust weakened transaction hazards and formal control mechanisms, but nonetheless, were extensively relied on to facilitate co-ordination. Interestingly, the paper concludes that the value of contracting may not necessarily lie in providing ex-post control, rather, in laying down a set of goals and methods to enable mutual planning.

Clearly, there is much scope for further research to enhance our understanding of governance and control. Further applied research such as Langfield-Smith and Smith (2003), Van den Bogard and Spekle (2003) and Dekker (2004) is one route. Another is to incorporate TCE with other perspectives along the lines of Baiman (1990), van der Meer-Kooistra & Vosselman (2000) and Spekle (2001).

References

Alchian, A., and Demsetz, H (1972) "Production, Information Costs, and Economic Organization", *America's Economic Review*, 62(July): 777-798.

Baiman, S (1990) "Agency Research In Management Accounting: a second look", *Accounting, Organizations and Society*, Vol.15, No.4, pp.341-371.

Boyrs, B and Jemison, D.B (1989) "Hybrid Arrangements as Strategic Alliances: Theoretical Issues in Organizational Combinations", *Academy of Management Review*, Vol.14, No.2, pp.234-249.

Chiles, T.H., & McMackin, J.F (1996) "Integrating variable risk preferences, trust, and transaction cost economics", *Academy of Management Review*, Vol.21, pp.73-99.

Coase, R (1937) "The Nature of The Firm", *Economica*, Vol.4, pp.386-405.

Covaleski, M A., Dirsmith, M W., and Samuel. S (2003) "Changes in the institutional environment and the institutions of governance: extending the contributions of transaction cost economics within the management control literature", *Accounting, Organizations and Society*, Vol.28, No.4, pp.417-441.

Dekker, H C (2004) "Control of inter-organisational relationships: evidence on appropriation concerns and coordination requirements", *Accounting, Organizations and Society*, Vol.29, pp.27-49.

Demsetz, H (1988) "The Theory of the Firm Revisited", *Journal of Law, Economics & Organization*, Vol.4, pp.141-161.Das, T., and Teng, B (2001) "A risk perception model of alliance structuring", *Journal of International Management*, 7, 1-29. Duhaime, I M., and Schwenk, C R (1985) "Conjectures on cognitive simplification in acquisition and divestment decision making", *Academy of Management Review*, Vol.10, pp.287-295.

Dwyer, F R., and Scurr, P H (1987) "Developing buyer-seller relationships", *Journal of Marketing*, Vol.51, pp.11-27.

Flynn, M S (1987) "The Global Automobile: Outsourcing Rediscovered", Special Report, IEEE Spectrum, pp.47-49.

Ghoshal, S., and Moran, P (1996) "Bad for Practice: A Critique of Transaction Cost Theory", *Academy of Management Review*, Vol.21, Iss.1, p.13.

Granovetter, M (1985) "Economic Action and Social Structure: A Theory of Embeddedness", *American Journal of Sociology*, Vol. 91, pp.481-510.

Guilding, C (2003) "Hotel ownership/operator structures: implications for capital budgeting process", *Management Accounting Research*, Vol.14, Iss:3, pp.179-199.

Hamel, G., Doz, Y., and Prahalad, C K (1989) "Collaborate with your competitor - and win", *Harvard Business Review*, Vol.67, No.1, pp.133-139.

Harrigan, K R (1984) "Formulating Vertical Integration Strategies", *Academy of Management Review*, Vol.9, Iss.4, pp.638-652.

Hemmer, T (1996) "Allocations of Sunk Capacity Costs and Joint Costs in a Linear Principal-Agent Model", *The Accounting Review*, Vol.71, No.3, July, pp.419-432.

Hill, C (1990) "Cooperation, Opportunism, and The Invisible Hand: Implications for Transaction Cost Theory", *Academy of Management Review*, Vol.15, pp.500-513.

Howes, J M., Mast, K F., and Swan, J E (1989) "Trust Earning Perceptions of Sellers and Buyers", *Journal of Personal Selling and Sales Management*, Vol.9, Spring, pp.1-8.

Jensen, M C (1983) "Organization Theory and Methodology", *Accounting Review*, 56 (July): pp.319:339.

Jensen, M C and Meckling W H (1976) "Theory of the Firm: Managerial Behaviour, Agency Costs and Ownership Structure", *Journal of Financial Economics*, Vol.3, pp.305-360.

Kern, T., and Willcocks, L (2000) "Exploring information technology outsourcing relationships: theory and practice", *Journal of Information Systems*, Vol.9, pp.321-350.

Klein, B (1980) "Transaction Cost Determinants of 'Unfair' Contractual Arrangements", *American Economic Review*, Vol.70, pp.356-362.

Langfield-Smith, K., and Smith, D (2003) "Management control systems and trust in outsourcing relationships", *Management Accounting Research*, Vol.14, pp.281-307.

March, J., and Simon, H (1958) "Organisations", New York: Wiley.

Milliman, R E., and Fugate, D L (1988) "Using Trust-Transference as a Persuasion Technique: An Empirical Investigation", *Journal of Personal Selling and Sales Management*, Vol.8, August, pp.1-7.

Mintzberg, H (1983) "Structures in Fives: Designing effective organizations", Englewood Cliffs: Prentice Hall.

Nooteboom, B., Berger, H., and Noorderhaven, N G (1997) "Effects of trust and governance on relational risk", *Academy of Management Journal*, Vol.40, pp.308-338.

Otley, D (1994) "Management Control in contemporary organizations: towards a wider framework", *Management Accounting Research*, Vol.5, 289-299.

Osborn, R.N., and Hagedoorn, J (1997) "The institutionalization and evolutionary dynamics of interorganizational alliances and networks", *Academy of Management Journal*, Vol.40, pp.261-278.

Perrow, C (1986) "Complex Organisations", New York: McGraw-Hill "Goals in Complex Organizations" *American Sociological Review*, Vol.26 (November): 854-865.

Porter, M (1985) "Competitive Advantage", Free Press: New York.

Prahalad, C K., and Hamel, G (1990) "The Core Competence of the Corporation", *Harvard Business Review*, May–June, pp.79 – 91.

Rajan, M (1992) "Cost allocation in multiagent settings", The *Accounting Review*, Vol.67, pp.527:545.

Ring, P., and Van de Ven, A (1992) "Structuring cooperative relationships between organizations", *Strategic Management Journal*, 13, 483-498.

Robins, J (1987) "Organisational Economics: Notes on the use of Transaction Cost Theory in the Study of Organisations", *Administrative Science Quarterly*, Vol.32, pp.68-86.

Sako, M (1992) "Prices, quality and trust: Interfirm relationships in Britain and Japan", Cambridge University Press.

Sarkar, S., and Ghosh, D (1997) "Contractor Accreditation: A Probabilistic Model", *Decision Sciences Journal*, Vol.28, Iss.2, pp.235-259.

Semlinger, K (1991), "New Developments in Subcontracting – Mixing Market and Hierarchy", in Amin. A., and Dietrich, M. (eds), "Towards a New Europe: Structural Change in the European Economy", Aldershot: Edward Elgar.

Simons, R (1995) "Levers of control: How managers use innovative control systems to drive strategic renewal", Boston: Harvard Business School Press.

Smith, K.G., Carroll, S.J., and Ashford, S.J (1995) "Intra-and interorganizational cooperation: towards a research agenda", *Academy of Management Journal*, Vol.38, pp.7-23.

Spekle, R F (2001) "Explaining management control structure variety: a transaction cost economics perspective", *Accounting, Organizations and Society*, Vol.26, pp.419-441.

Suh, Y (1987) "Collusion and noncontrollable cost allocation", *Journal of Accounting Research*, Vol.25 (Supplement), pp.22-46.

Swann, J E., Trawick, I., and Silva, D (1985) "How Industrial Salespeople Gain Customer Trust", *Industrial Marketing Management*, Vol.14, August, pp.203-211.

Swann, J E., Trawick, I F., Rink, D R., and Roberts, J J (1988) "Measuring Dimensions of Purchaser Trust of Industrial Salespeople", *Journal of Personal Selling and Sales Management*, Vol.8, May, pp.1-9.

Thorelli, H B (1986) "Networks: Between Markets and Hierarchies', *Strategic Management Journal*, Vol.7, pp.37-51.

Van den Bogard, M A., and Spekle, R F (2003) "Reinventing the hierarchy: strategy and control in the Shell Chemicals care-out", *Management Accounting Research*, Vol.14, pp.79-93.

Van der Meer-Kooistra, J., and Vosselman, E G J (2000) "Management control of interfirm transactional relationships: the case of industrial renovation and maintenance", *Accounting, Organizations and Society*, Vol.25, pp.51-77

Williamson, O (1975) "Markets and hierarchies: Analysis and antitrust implications", New York: Free Press.

Williamson, O (1979) "Transaction Cost Economics: The Governance of Contractual Relations", *American Economic Review*, Vol.61, pp.233-262.

Williamson, O (1981) "The Economics of Organization: The Transaction Cost Approach." *American Journal of Sociology*, Vol.87, pp.548-577.

Williamson, O (1985) *The Economic Institutions of Capitalism*, New York: Free Press.

Williamson, O (1986) *The Economics of the Firm and Market Organisation*, Wheatsheaf Ltd, London.

Williamson, O (1993) "Opportunism and its critics", *Managerial and decision Economics*, Vol.14, 97, 107.Williamson, O (1996) *The Mechanisms of Governance*, New York: Oxford University Press.

Williamson, O., and Ouchi, W.G (1981) "The markets and hierarchies program of research: origins, implications, prospects". In A. H Van de Ven, & W.F Joyce *Perspectives on organization design and behaviour* (pp.347-370). New York: John Wiley & Sons.

Winter, S G (1988) "On Coase, Competence and the Corporation", Journal *of Law Economics and Organisation*, Vol.4, pp.163-180.

Zaheer, A., and Venkatraman, N (1995) "Relational governance as an interorganizational strategy: an empirical test of the role of trust in economic exchange" *Strategic Management Journal*, Vol.16, pp.373-392.

7

STRATEGIC CHOICE AND MANAGEMENT CONTROL SYSTEMS: A REVIEW OF THEORIES AND CHALLENGES FOR DEVELOPMENT

Bill Nixon

University of Dundee, UK

Abstract: Implementing strategy entails aligning many reinforcing intra- and inter-firm activities. Conceptually and empirically this alignment involves many disciplines and functions. A review of the evolution of strategic thinking and the management control systems (MCS) literature provides a conceptual map for integrating disparate perspectives to meet the immediate challenges for MCS development.

Keywords: management control systems; perspectives of strategy; performance management and measurement; complementarity theory; collaboration.

1.   Introduction

There are, as the title of this chapter implies, a number of theories of both strategic choice and management control systems (MCS). An awareness of the respective theories is important since each theoretical perspective is based on a whole set of different ontological assumptions that may be diametrically opposed, such as, for example, who strategy is for and how it is formulated (Whittington, 2001). Indeed, part of the problem of aligning strategy and control relates not only to the dynamic nature and different contexts of strategy but also to the proliferation of disparate views of strategy among both academics and practitioners (Bowman *et al.*, 2002; Coad, 2005). Notwithstanding the strategy traditions that still co-exist, and the tensions between those who see strategy as a situational art and those who believe there are universal laws of strategy (Hambrick, 2003), there is at least a trend towards a broad consensus among both strategy and MCS scholars that these related activities are context and culture specific (Rumelt, 1982; Jones, 2002; Chenhall, 2003; Otley, 2003; Sigglekow, 2003; Berry *et al.*, 2005). Even when the general and more immediate environments of organisations are similar, the business strategies, organisational configurations and processes that work for each may be quite different (Miles and Snow, 2003). Consequently, the recognition of appropriate, particular, conceptual perspectives can only come from an understanding of their attributes and sensitivity to the context and key assumptions of each viewpoint. In practice, it is also the case that managers need to understand different ways of thinking about strategy and the strategic approaches of their competitors and partners.

This chapter aims to provide an overview of different perspectives of strategy and of the strategy-control interface, and some of the challenges that these perspectives present for MCS development. Hopefully, the chapter will provide a basis for further research and encourage a new eclecticism. The approach adopted is premised on the belief that MCS can play a pivotal role in linking all of the activities that alignment of strategy, structure and processes entail.

2. Perspectives of Strategy

2.1. Ten Schools of Strategy

The field of strategy is distinguished by a history of theoretical pluralism that borrows concepts from several disciplines. For example, Mintzberg and Lampel (1999) identified ten 'schools of strategy', which were more or less dominant in the last thirty or forty years and still influence most teaching and practice today. The base disciplines for the various schools of strategy include systems theory and cybernetics, economics, cognitive psychology, political science, anthropology, biology and history. However, the academic groups that have at different periods since the mid-1960s played a dominant role in developing strategic thinking have been institutionalists, economists and behaviouralists (Bowman et al., 2002). While most of the schools, notably the Cognitive, Learning, Power, Cultural and Environmental, are mainly descriptive, the Design, Planning and Positioning schools adopt a more prescriptive stance, and the Entrepreneurial and Configuration schools are both descriptive and prescriptive.

A longitudinal perspective of strategy formulation in organisations suggests that the context and process can tilt toward the features of one school or another:

> toward the entrepreneurial school during start-up or when there is the need for a dramatic turnaround, toward the learning school under dynamic conditions when prediction is well-nigh impossible, and so on (Mintzberg and Lampel, 1999, p. 27).

The absence of a single unifying paradigm of strategy, or of the 'strategic management' that it evolved into in the 1980s, reflects, in part at least, the changing nature and intensification of competition and a context that is increasingly turbulent and complex (Stacey et al., 2002; Christensen and Raynor, 2003; Prahalad and Ramaswamy, 2004). Nevertheless, there is an acknowledged need to go beyond the narrowness of each school; there is also some recent evidence of a broadening of perspective and a more eclectic approach to strategy (Mintzberg and Lampel, 1999; Bowman et al., 2002; Coad, 2005). In part, this theoretical convergence is attributable to the fundamental need to understand the whole strategy formulation process and outcomes and not just some dimensions of it; 'we have to get beyond the narrowness of each school: we need to know how strategy formation, which combines these schools and more really works' (Mintzberg and Lampel, 1999, p. 29).

2.2. Four Perspectives of Strategy

Whittington, 2001, for example, organises the various theories of strategy into four generic perspectives along two continua, relating to the strategy formulation process (Deliberate-Emergent) and outcomes (Profit Maximising-Pluralistic). The matrix (Figure 1 below) is best regarded as a useful heuristic that simplifies a complex set of issues at the expense of obscuring the overlap that exists among perspectives and the fact that the views of key protagonists associated with each of the generic approaches have become more integrated (Bowman et al., 2002; Jeremy, 2002).

Figure 1
Based on Whittington's Four Generic Perspectives on Strategy
OUTCOMES
Shareholders

Classical (1960s)	Evolutionary (1980s)
Chandler	Hannan and Freeman
Ansoff	Williamson
Sloan	Peters and Waterman
Porter	

PROCESS

Deliberate	**Emergent**
Systemic (1990s)	Processual (1970s)
Granovetter	Cyert and March
Whitley	Mintzberg
	Hamel & Prahalad
	Grant
	Pettigrew
	Weick

Stakeholders

Whittington's framework is useful because it facilitates identification of different views of strategy and research streams and reduces the possibility of both strategy and control researchers disagreeing violently whilst still perceiving themselves to be studying the same thing (Machin, 1983). The link between the ten schools of strategy and Whittington's four perspectives is a loose one partly because some schools cut across different perspectives. Nevertheless, the link exists because both the schools and perspectives are based on a common axis, namely whether the strategy formulation process is deliberate or emergent; the link is obscured because Whittington's second continuum relates to the shareholder-stakeholder tension whereas Mintzberg and Lampel use the degree of change in the external environment for their analysis. Linking the ten schools and the four perspectives is helped by the fact that Mintzberg and Lampel explicitly link the schools to theories that Whittington analyses by reference to how they address the process (deliberate-emergent) and outcomes (shareholder-stakeholder) issues. Broadly, the Planning, Position and Design schools fit mostly the Classical perspective, the Power and Entrepreneurial schools the Evolutionary perspective, the Cognitive and Learning schools the Processual perspective, and the Cultural, Configuration and Environmental schools the Systemic perspective.

The means (process) and ends (outcomes) dimensions of the matrix also help management control researchers to address an acute need, identified by Langfield-Smith's critical review of strategy and MCS, namely, 'to develop consistent classifications for controls and other contingent variables, and use established classifications of strategy' (1997, p. 228). The four generic perspectives of Figure 1 reflect, in an approximate way, the historical conceptual development of business strategy, which only emerged in the 1960s as a coherent discipline (Bowman *et al.*, 2002).

2.3. The Classical Perspective

Chandler (1962), Sloan (1963), and Ansoff (1965) established the key features of the Classical approach: attachment to a rational process of deliberate calculation and analysis, and to strategy formulation and control as the prime task of top management with strategy implementation as the responsibility of middle management, and commitment to profit maximisation as the primary aim of the business. Though the Classicists varied in their approaches, they all focused on a rich, 'institutionalist' description of the strategy process from a top manager's perspective (Whittington, 2002).

2.4. The Processualist Perspective

The Processualists followed the detailed descriptive approach of the Classicists but were more sceptical about rational strategy making. In particular, they emphasised the cognitive limits of rational action, the concept of 'bounded rationality' (Cyert and March, 1963) and the micro-politics of organisations (Pettigrew, 1973, 1983). The Classicists' perception of strategy formulation as a distinct and very deliberate activity that precedes strategy implementation contrasts sharply with the Processualists' perspective of strategies, 'emerging' gradually through the organisation's routines, actions and experiences (March, 1976; Nelson and Winter, 1982; Mintzberg, 1989, p. 31). The scepticism of the Classical rational analysis (deliberate strategy in Figure 1), that both the Processualists and Evolutionists share, is, however, attributable to different reasons. The Processualists do not subscribe to the efficiency and power of the external markets but instead emphasise the importance of internal processes as the source of sustainable superior performance. This view is exemplified by the 'resource-based' theorists, who point to the importance of exploiting distinctive internal resources, such as patterns of collaboration, tacit knowledge relationships and intangible assets that take a long time to create and cannot easily be replicated by competitors (Grant, 1991). The research approach and perspective of the Processualists, however, needs to be distinguished from the Business Process Re-Engineering (BPR) Movement that began in 1993 with the publication of *Re-Engineering the Corporation* (Hammer and Champney, 1993) and continues today with process-oriented techniques, such as Six Sigma (Harry and Schroeder, 2000) and Lean Production (Womack and Jones, 1996). The BPR movement stressed the importance of delivering value to customers and advocated an inclusive, participative process but, in practice, this translated to ruthless cost cutting and downsizing that was much more consistent with a Classical, Scientific Management approach.

Although, it is conceptually convenient to dichotomise deliberate and emergent strategies and to link them through strategy as Plans and strategy as Pattern with diagnostic and interactive controls respectively (Simons, 2000), in reality they 'form the end points of a continuum along which the strategies that are crafted in the real world may be found' (Mintzberg, 1989, p. 32). A major difference between deliberate and emergent strategy is that the latter is based primarily on incremental learning, on what Lindblom referred to as 'continual nibbling' (1959, p. 25), whereas deliberate strategy, especially the 'Grand Strategy' type, depends less on new learning (Mintzberg and Waters, 1985). The greater the learning component in the range of strategies on the deliberate-emergent spectrum, the greater the difficulty of aligning strategy and control; learning often comes from the periphery of the organisation that is a long way removed from the centre where the traditional deliberate strategy is formulated. For example, when Intel withdrew from memory chip production, it was the result of incremental, autonomous decisions taken over an extended period by the finance and production planning people. Reflecting on Intel's strategic decision to terminate memory chip production, Andy Grove, former CEO of Intel, stated that:

These people didn't have the authority to get us out of memories but they had the authority to fine-tune the production allocation process by lots of little steps. Over the course of many months their actions made it easier (for top management) to eventually pull the plug on our memory participation (Grove, 1999, p. 111).

This example of 'emergent', as opposed to 'deliberate', strategy (Mintzberg, 1989) illustrates how lower, organisational-level decisions and incremental actions can shape strategy rather than the more usual perception of strategy as the prerogative of top management and cascading down the organisation to drive operations (Jeremy, 2002). It is also consistent with the Complexity Theory view that new ideas and innovation cannot be planned in a top-down fashion, and that the role of top management, operating with only partial information and in uncertain environments, is to share in the discovery of the emerging situation and develop their assessments and responses, along with other participants (Johnson and Scholes, 2002; Stacey *et al.*, 2002). A management control system designed to support top-down planning and control is likely to be unsuitable for a more incremental, bottom-up approach (Chenhall, 2003).

2.5. The Evolutionist Perspective

The Evolutionists, like the Processualists, do not subscribe to the rational, linear approach of the Classicists. In many ways the Evolutionist perspective reflects the more turbulent, relatively unpredictable environment of the 1980s, which renders irrelevant much of the formal strategy formulation process and outcomes (Brown and Eisenhardt, 1998). However, the Evolutionists, unlike the Processualists, are committed to maximisation of shareholder wealth as the primary aim of the business (Post *et al.*, 2002; Smith, 2003) and subscribe much more to the power of market competition (Kay, 2003). Indeed, this leads some Evolutionists to the paradoxical view that the notion of strategic choice is misleading because so-called strategic decisions are largely imposed on managers by markets and a complex and uncertain environment (Jones, 2002). In a volatile and dynamic environment, all managers can do, according to Evolutionists, is to ensure that their organisations have the capability to adapt as quickly and effectively as possible to the major environmental demands of the day (Whittington, 2002).

2.6. The Systemic Perspective

The Systemic perspective shares the deliberate stance of the Classicists and the stakeholder orientation of the Processualists (Figure 1). However, Systemic theorists emphasise the influence of culture and the social context; the objectives and practices of strategy are embedded in the social systems in which they take place (Granovetter, 1985). From this perspective a whole array of personal, professional and cultural factors may cause strategists deliberately to prioritise goals other than maximisation of shareholder wealth (Swedberg *et al.*, 1987; Whittington, 1992).

2.7. Value of Generic Perspectives of Strategy

The two questions that are the basis of Whittington's four generic perspectives of strategy (who is strategy for and how is it formulated?) undoubtedly oversimplify both the conceptual views of theorists and the empirical realities that practitioners perceive. For example, the business environment of many organisations in the twenty-first century, sometimes referred to as the digital, information, connected or knowledge economy, compels managers to simultaneously pursue several strategies (Abell, 1999; Markides and Charitou, 2004), which are not exclusively in a single paradigm. Nevertheless, the matrix provides a useful overview of 'different ways of thinking about strategy in a wide range of situations' (Whittington, 2001, p. ix) and of different approaches to strategy research that conceptually cannot be separated from a discussion of management control research but, in practice, are often neglected. This happens partly because for thirty years MCS development was constrained by a conceptual framework that may have been appropriate in the 1960s, when Robert Anthony advanced his model in 1965, but this framework lagged behind conceptual and empirical developments in subsequent decades

(Hopwood, 1974a, 1974b; Hofstede, 1978; Ouchi, 1979; Merchant, 1982; Parker, 1986; Otley *et al.*, 1995; Simons, 1995; Langfield-Smith, 1997).

Anthony's seminal work in MCS reflected, in particular, the top-down, rational, linear approach of the Classical management theorists and the preoccupation of managers and consultants in the 1960s with financial planning (Bowman *et al.*, 2002). The long-standing view of Anthony and a series of co-authors, that management control is an activity that 'fits between strategy formulation and task control' (Anthony and Govindarajan, 2004, p. 6) has meant that MCS research has focused mostly on business-level strategy and on the controls needed to implement competitive strategies (Simons, 1995; Langfield-Smith, 1997), and has neglected the relevance controls required to align corporate strategy with broad environmental developments (Schreyogg and Steinmann, 1987; Coad, 2005). The wider strategic management perspective of the Classical, Processual, Evolutionary and Systemic theorists provides a helpful, conceptual way of integrating strategic formulation, management control and task control through the relevance and implementation controls for corporate (Kald *et al.*, 2000; Chakravarthy and White, 2002; Marginson, 2002; Mendoza and Saulpic, 2002) and competitive strategies (Govindarajan and Gupta, 1985; Bruggeman and Van der Stede, 1993). This integration is especially challenging when the complexity and dynamic of business obscures the boundaries between strategic planning, implementation and control. The competitive strategy focus of MCS also means that it has avoided the stakeholder-shareholder tension, which is central to corporate strategy (Smith, 2003). Yet the answer to the question, 'Who is strategy for?', is a pre-requisite to linking the reward system with performance measurement and control (Chenhall and Langfield-Smith, 2003).

The question, 'How is strategy formulated?', provides a conceptual basis for linking deliberate and emergent strategies with diagnostic and interactive controls (Simons, 1995). The different 'corporate intelligence' required for deliberate and emergent strategies has implications for MCS design and knowledge management (Hartmann and Vaassen, 2003; Bhimani and Roberts, 2004; Mouritsen and Larsen, 2005). It is also the case that the MCS, which is suitable for a single strategy, is unlikely to be suitable for parallel deliberate and emergent strategies (Markides, 1999; Chenhall, 2003; Hoque, 2004; Markides and Charitou, 2004; Berry *et al.* 2005).

3. The Strategy-Control Interface

The development of strategic thinking in the last 40 years and the emergence of four broad perspectives, or groups, reflects major changes in the salient features of the business environment in each decade since the 1960s. Management control thinking, likewise, mostly lagged behind developments in management theory (Parker, 1986). Otley *et al.*, 1995, used four perspectives to summarise developments in the MCS literature in approximately the same 40 year period (see Figure 2 below). The four perspectives, based on the transition observed by Scott (1981), from closed to open systems models, reflect both the move from a deliberate to an emergent perspective of strategy and the tension between the narrow focus of the Classicists and Evolutionists on maximisation of shareholder wealth as the primary corporate objective and the more pluralistic perspective of the Processual and Systemic theorists.

Figure 2
Perspectives of MCS derived from Otley et al., 1995
Closed Systems

Classical Management Theory	Behavioural Approaches
Woodward (1958, 1965, 1970)	Argyris (1952)
Burns and Stalker (1961)	Hopwood (1972, 1974a, 1974b)
Drucker (1964)	Vickers (1965, 1967)
Simon *et al.* (1954)	Otley and Berry (1980)
Rational Models	**Natural Models**
Systems and Contingency Approaches	Radical Perspectives
Ouchi (1979)	Chua *et al.* (1989)
Beer (1972)	**Ansari and Bell (1991)**
Lowe and Machin (1983)	Dent (1991)
Lowe and McInnes (1971)	Laughlin and Broadbent (1993)
Otley (1980)	

Open Systems

A key issue that separates the Evolutionist and Processualist, rational and natural MCS perspectives of strategic settings is the extent of the influence of the external environment on strategy and control. The Evolutionists and open system, rational MCS perspectives attribute greater influence to the external environment than do the Processualists and open system, natural MCS researchers (Otley *et al.*, 1995; Whittington, 2001; Bowman *et al.*, 2002). The development of strategic taxonomies, or the 'configurational view' of strategy (Hambrick, 2003, p. ix) is premised on the belief that although the external environments of organisations and business units differ and are constantly changing, there are a limited number of viable strategic and organisational configurations that provide a basis for sustainable competitive advantage. Whereas at least a dozen strategic and organisational typologies have appeared the literature, the two most enduring frameworks in the management and MCS literatures are the Prospector, Analyser, Defender and Reactor taxonomy of Miles and Snow (1978), and the Differentiation, Low Cost and Focus, 'generic' strategies of Porter (1980) (Langfield-Smith, 1997; Ketchen, Jr., 2003). Porter's approach is very much in the Classical tradition (Porter, 1980) and Miles and Snow fit much more into the Systems and Contingency approach (Ketchen, 2003; Miles and Snow, 2003).

Intensification of competition meant that by the early 1990s the relevance of Porter's theory was already being questioned because it was evident, for example, that 'the Japanese have made ... differentiation at low cost an entirely feasible strategy' (Lorenz, 1993, p. 10), and that 'yesterday's bases of competition have become today's price of admission and new ways of competing have developed' (McNair and Leibfried, 1992, p. 262). The relevance of Porter's dichotomy in the 'Knowledge Economy' has also been called into question by evidence that sustainable high growth and profits requires equal emphasis on innovation and value to stakeholders (Kim and Mauborgne, 2004).

In the last decade, in particular, competitive advantage accrues less to the individual firm and more to what is sometimes referred to as the 'extended enterprise' (Post *et al.*, 2002, p. 5), that is, to clusters, networks, partnerships and alliances. The MCS context and issues are very different from those in a single organisation because, notwithstanding the fact that collaborating firms share objectives, risks, rewards and arrangements for communication and co-ordination of common business, none of the partners has full control, as in a merger or a go-it-alone firm (Bamford and Ernst, 2002; Van der Meer-Kooistra and Vosselman, 2000). Competitive advantage in the 21st century is also more dependent on designing and developing knowledge-intensive, new products and services than a couple of decades ago when Porter developed his theory of competitive advantage.

Although the Prospector-Defender taxonomy of Miles and Snow (1978), is often regarded as another strategy typology similar to the Differentiation-Low Cost typology of Porter (Langfield-Smith, 1997), its perceived conceptual and empirical relevance has been more enduring (Ghoshal, 2003). This is probably because:

> *Porter's typology focuses primarily on the market activities essential to build and sustain a given strategy while our [M&S] typology focuses on the structures and managerial processes essential to follow a particular strategic approach* (Miles, 2003, pp. 100-101).

The enduring component of the Miles and Snow conceptual framework is, perhaps, not the competitive typology but rather the 'adaptive cycle', that is the dynamic process of alignment between each strategic orientation (Prospector, Analyser, Defender and Reactor) and the structure and processes appropriate to the related Entrepreneurial, Technological and Administrative requirements of implementing strategy.

Conceptually, the Miles and Snow framework links the literatures of strategy and structure with those of marketing, innovation and technology management, and systems management. Empirically, the competitive typology and adaptive cycle, together, provide a basis for understanding 'the process by which organisations continually adjust to their environments' (Miles and Snow, 2003, p. xv) and for bridging 'the gap between knowledge (of management accounting and control) and doing' (Norreklit *et al.*, in press). The strength of the Miles and Snow framework is the detailed template it provides for classifying activities and managing the dynamic relationships among strategy, structure and processes, including control, marketing and logistics, new product development and production, and the administrative systems, to maintain coherence in the adaptive process.

> *What is remarkable about this (Miles and Snow) categorization scheme is the comprehensiveness of organizational attributes – across strategic orientation, organizational features and management processes – that it captures* (Ghoshal, 2003, p. 113).

This comprehensiveness and systematic, clear integration of strategy, structure and process, especially the adaptation process, provides an excellent context for performance measurement and control. Although the scope of the Miles and Snow adaptive cycle is broader than management control, its focus on change and on-going organisational transition is especially useful to MCS because 'the difficulty of designing control systems for organisations is fundamentally that they are not static systems, but dynamic, self-controlling systems' (Otley, 2003, p. 323).

Yet despite a strong consensus that MCS concepts need to be renewed to keep pace with new industry and organisational structures, ways of competing, processes, technology and intellectual property standards (Otley, 1994; Simons, 1995; Langfield-Smith, 1997; Eisenhardt and Santos, 2002; Manzoni, 2002; Mouritsen, 2005; Nixon and Burns, 2005), the Miles and Snow framework, especially the adaptive cycle, is mostly ignored in the MCS literature. For example, Simons' 'Four Levers' model (2000) replaced the Prospector, Analyser, Defender and Reactor strategic orientations he used in previous research (Simons, 1987) with four definitions of strategy (Perspective, Position, Plan and Pattern), identified by Mintzberg (1987), but does not refer to the adaptive cycle. However, Simons' framework, and, indeed, those of Ouchi (1979), Merchant (1982), Otley (1999), and Hartmann and Vaassen (2003), complement rather than compete with the Miles and Snow framework. The need for an eclectic approach, one that draws on a portfolio of models, and the scope for integration of these frameworks is underlined by Chenhall's conclusion that scholars of control need to reflect:

> *on the work of the original organizational theorists and more recent thinking in areas such as strategy, organizational and cultural change, manufacturing, information technology and human resource management* (Chenhall, 2003, p. 161).

4. Some Challenges for MCS Development

The broad, eclectic research approach suggested by Chenhall (2003), is consistent both with the evolution of MCS from closed to open systems (Figure 2) and with major challenges that MCS development must now address, like support for activity management, for integration of 'reinforcing activities' (Porter, 1996, p. 71), performance measurements and MCS, support for simultaneous management of multiple strategies, new organisational forms, a knowledge-based view of strategy, and corporate governance issues. These six challenges are not exhaustive or in any order of urgency or relative importance. The challenges reflect, in part at least, an increasingly knowledge-intensive, dynamic external environment, a lag between the salient features of this environment in each decade since the 1960s and strategic thinking which is mostly leading developments in MCS.

4.1. MCS Support for Activity Management

Chenhall's conclusion is also consistent with the research findings of Milgrom and Roberts (1990, 1995), on the economics of systems of complementary activities and functions in the context of 'modern manufacturing' (1990, p. 511). They found that modern manufacturing companies tended to react to external changes with coherent sets of internal responses that, in turn, required central co-ordination to align activities. Porter (1996), extended the concept of coherence, alignment or 'fit' beyond manufacturing and emphasised the importance of mutually reinforcing activities in creating and sustaining competitive advantage; he pioneered activity-system maps to assess the consistency, complementarity and optimisation of the internal and external activities of the organisation. A major challenge for MCS today is to support this activity management. A problem, however, with activity maps is that:

> no two of them include the same activities (not even the same categories of activities) and because they have been constructed strictly after the fact, they cannot be used for prediction, generalization or theory building (Hambrick, 2003, p. xi).

The Strategic and MCS perspectives of Figures 1 and 2 can help this assessment of internal and external alignment and the degree of fit among strategy, structure and processes, including MCS, in particular contexts. Although the three axes of Figures 1 and 2 are very simplistic – shareholder/stakeholder orientation, deliberate (rational)/ emergent (natural) strategy formulation and open/closed system assumptions - their application can nevertheless reduce the possibility of fundamental misalignment, like trying to apply a rational, highly structured, linear MCS in a non-linear, volatile environment. Conceptually, the Figures help to determine the perspectives most appropriate to a particular configuration.

4.2. Reinforcing Activities, Performance Measurement and MCS

Kaplan and Norton, whose 'Balanced Scorecard', 1992, was one attempt to broaden the narrow financial control framework of Anthony (1965), 'formulated a generic strategy map to serve as a starting point for any organization in any industry' (Kaplan and Norton, 2004, p. xiii). In Strategy Maps, Kaplan and Norton aim to facilitate a comprehensive description of strategy so that objectives and performance measures can be established (The Balanced Scorecard, 1996, focused on this dimension) and managed (The Strategy-Focused Organization, 2001). Although Strategy Maps is more detailed and integrated than The Balanced Scorecard, it is clear that there is scope to go beyond a single generic strategy in order to specify the general character of activities for various strategic stances, such as Prospector, Defender, Analyser and Reactor. The generic strategy of Strategy Maps is also more deliberate than emergent and, together with its emphasis on sustained shareholder value as the overarching financial objective of strategy, the Kaplan and Norton framework is more in the Classical perspective than in any of the other three (Figure 1). From, say, a Processualist perspective, it is difficult to see how the Strategy Maps framework copes with a dynamic concept of alignment, or fit, and the continuous co-evolution of a bundle of mutually reinforcing activities, or 'complementarities' (Milgrom and Roberts, 1995, p. 179), like new organisational forms, processes, cultures and contexts, that, together, contribute to performance.

Nevertheless, *The Balanced Scorecard* framework, and its derivatives, have played a key role in both the performance measurement literature and practice in the last decade. Performance measurement, which was once mostly a component of MCS, has become something of a growth industry and has developed rapidly in a relatively fragmented way in different disciplines (Neely *et al.*, 2004). A clear need, and opportunity, now exists to bring together in a coherent, cogent way MCS and the disparate strands of performance measurement – in Research and Development, Design, Manufacturing, Marketing, Human Resource Management and Accounting and Finance. One possible way of achieving this integration, both in principle and in practice, could be through an inclusive performance management framework (Otley, 1999). Such a framework would avoid the negative connotations of the word 'control' but, more substantively, performance management is ultimately what strategy, structure and process are about.

4.3.   Multiple Strategies and MCS

A third challenge for MCS development is aligning MCS to changes that can quickly render detailed strategic plans and budgets obsolete. In reality, very few organisations operate in environments that are always relatively stable or constantly volatile. Instead they may face periods of relative quiescence punctuated with episodes of dramatic change, or periods of turbulence interspersed with stable intervals; it may also be the case that one area, say production, is predictable whereas another area, perhaps related technology trajectories, is very uncertain. Consequently, organisations may need to simultaneously manage 'dual strategies' (Abell, 1999, p. 73), 'populations of strategies' (Beinhocker, 1999, p. 95), or 'a portfolio of strategic options' (Williamson, 1999, p. 126). Simons' interactive and diagnostic controls represent an attempt to deal with both deliberate and emergent-type strategies in much the same way as the Analyser strategic orientation of Miles and Snow addressed the co-existence of Prospector and Defender strategies. Strategy-Control alignment is relatively simple for a single strategy, like Defender, Prospector or the generic strategy of *Strategy Maps*. 'Pity the poor managers in an Analyser though. They are walking a tight-rope, trying to be innovative at the same time they are trying to be efficient and reliable' (Hambrick, 2003, p. xi). When Miles and Snow first published *Organizational Strategy, Structure and Process* in 1978 it was possible to achieve and maintain alignment among dual strategies, a single matrix structure and processes, including the MCS. Today, however, Miles and Snow acknowledge the need for an expanded framework 'to include a new organizational form, a new "entrepreneurial" strategy and a new organizational approach both energized by a new "meta-capability" that facilitates knowledge creation and sharing' (Miles and Snow, 2003, p. xxi).

Evidence of new organisational approaches is emerging and a growing number of management researchers challenge systems thinking and the perception of the organisation as an objective pre-given realiy that can be modified, designed and controlled (Pascale, 1999; Stacey *et al.*, 2002). These complexity theorists emphasise the unpredictable aspects of systems that involve many dynamic internal and external relationships. The implications for MCS development of these dynamic relationships that are shaping new strategies and structures are still opaque (Venkatraman and Subramaniam, 2003; Henri, in press; Mouritsen and Thrane, in press; van Veen-Dirks, in press).

4.4. New Organisational Forms and Relationships

Since Chandler (1962), established the need to match strategy and structure, 'the study of corporate structure has seemed rather old-fashioned' (Whittington, 2002, p. 113). In the MCS literature 'organizational structure also appears to be overlooked as a control in its own right' (Otley, 2003, p. 320). However, in the last decade structure has once again become important as strategic thinking has evolved from the concept of strategy as a portfolio of businesses in the 1970s to a portfolio of capabilities in the 1980s and to a portfolio of relationships in the 1990s (Venkatraman and Subramaniam, 2003). Evidence supporting complementarity theory (Milgrom and Roberts, 1990, 1995) and the need to reinforce chosen strategies with an array of activities also helped to revive the importance of structure to strategy implementation and performance management. In the 1980s, organisations began to focus on core activities and to outsource non-core operations to either upstream or downstream firms that had a competitive advantage in these activities (Porter, 1980). Moves toward more horizontal and virtual organisational forms were driven in large part by the intensification of price-based competition and a perceived need to develop a fast response capability to new rivals, technologies and other environmental changes. By the end of the 1980s the number of technologies that most organisations needed to impound in their products and/or services had exceeded their capability to generate internally. In an endeavour to acquire requisite technologies and to keep abreast of pacing and emerging technologies, knowledge-intensive organisations, like pharmaceutical and bio-technology companies, formed alliances, partnerships, joint ventures, clusters and networks. Unlike outsourcing relationships that relate to non-core activities and are based on transaction-cost criteria, these relationship portfolios usually relate to the acquisition of capabilities that are core or may become so. The number of relationships and their disparate nature in terms of formality, resource commitment, arrangements for collaboration and knowledge-sharing present a formidable challenge for MCS and performance measurement (Van der Meer-Kooistra and Vosselman, 2000; Dekker, 2004).

4.5. A Knowledge-Based View (KBV) of Strategy and MCS

The portfolio of relationships view of strategy emphasises the arrangements to acquire knowledge resources. A KBV of strategy (Eisenhardt and Santos, 2002) goes beyond sourcing of capabilities and focuses on integration of external knowledge and organisational learning, including the organisational structure, culture and reward system that can facilitate internal and external knowledge transfer (Gupta and Govindarajan, 2000). Control in knowledge-intensive organisations is different from that in traditional industrial organisations; people cannot be coerced into yielding ideas and knowledge. The KBV of strategy requires 'a fundamental refocus on the control questions brought about by the central roles of knowledge, information, and communication in contemporary organizations' (Hartmann and Vaassen, 2003).

4.6. MCS, Corporate Governance and the External Control of Organisations

MCS and performance measurement mostly has an internal focus that is designed and managed relatively independently of external controls. Yet, the importance of the external environment for understanding organisations was a logical extension of open systems theory (Figure 2 above). The 'resource dependencies' view of organisations as being embedded in networks of interdependencies and social relationships (Pfeffer and Salancik, 1978; Granovetter, 1985) is especially relevant to MCS and performance measurement today because of more stringent statutory and professional governance requirements and more proactive stakeholder activities. The Sarbanes-Oxley Act 2002, (ss. 404 and 409 in particular) is one example of an external control that will almost certainly affect the internal MCS of publicly-owned companies in the USA.

Corporate governance research has also increased and spans many disciplines from accounting and finance, to management and strategy, to law, sociology and political science. Not surprisingly, perhaps, the definitions of corporate governance vary widely (Davis and Useem, 2002). A narrow financial definition may be consistent with the Classical and Evolutionist perspectives of the primary aim of strategy as maximisation of shareholder wealth. A broader definition of governance, like that of Blair, 1995, is more appropriate to the Systemic and Processualist stakeholder perspectives. Corporate governance, in Blair's view, is:

> the whole set of legal, cultural, and institutional arrangements that determine what publicly traded corporations can do, who controls them, how that control is exercised, and how the risks and returns from the activities they undertake are allocated (Blair, 1995, p. 3, as cited in Davis and Useem, 2002, p. 235).

This broad definition of governance seems to match better the complementarity theory view of MCS and performance measurement than a narrow, less inclusive, definition.

5. Conclusion

The challenges confronting MCS development suggest a need for a broad, flexible framework with sufficient breadth to accommodate the different perspectives of strategy, which are appropriate to the multiple strategies that organisations pursue, often simultaneously, in competitive, knowledge-intensive environments that require more intra- and inter-firm collaboration. The dual strategy, Analyser-type, firm is not a new concept but the structure(s) and processes, including MCS, required to support such a strategic mix have become much more complex and dynamic. The framework needs to be flexible enough to manage the on-going adaptive process and the interface among strategic directions, competitive strategies and the many activities required to reinforce implementation of these strategies. An inclusive framework of MCS is consistent with the concept of MCS as an integrating package within organisations (Malmi and Brown, 2005), the portfolio of relationships and knowledge-based views of strategy and the pervasive principle of complementarity theory that emphasises the importance of alignment and the need for an array of mutually reinforcing activities to support strategy.

In much the same way as organisations, competing in highly uncertain, dynamic environments, are pursuing simultaneously a 'population' of strategies, so, too, MCS researchers may need to adopt an approach that draws concurrently upon extant, related frameworks and 'reinforcing' perspectives in a coherent, cohesive way. A number of frameworks are referred to in this chapter that might be customised to provide component modules for an enlarged framework: frameworks, such as Whittington's Generic Perspectives of Strategy, 2001, Miles and Snow's strategic orientation typology and Adaptive Cycle, 1978, Otley's Performance Management Framework for MCS, 1999, Simons' Levers of Control, 2000, and Hartmann and Vaassen's Knowledge-based Framework for Control, 2003. This approach is likely to require 'a meta-capability of collaboration' (Miles and Snow, 2003, p. xxii) among researchers of disparate theoretical perspectives and disciplines.

References

Abell, D. F. (1999), "Competing today while preparing for tomorrow", *MIT Sloan Management Review*, Vol. 40, No. 3, Spring, pp. 73-81.

Ansari, S. L. and Bell, J. (1991), "Symbolism, collectivism and rationality in organizational control", *Accounting, Auditing and Accountability Journal*, Vol. 4, No. 2, February, pp. 4-27.

Ansoff, H. I. (1965), *Corporate Strategy: An Analytic Approach to Business Policy for Growth and Expansion*, McGraw-Hill, New York, NY.

Anthony, R. N. and Graduate School of Business Administration, Harvard University (Ed.) (1965), *Planning and Control Systems: A Framework for Analysis*, Graduate School of Business Administration, Harvard University, Boston, MA.

Anthony, R. N. and Govindarajan, V. (2004), *Management Control Systems*, 11th international edition, McGraw-Hill/Irwin, a business unit of the McGraw-Hill Companies, Inc., New York, NY.

Argyris, C. (1952), *The Impact of Budgets on People*, The Controllership Foundation, Ithaca, NY.

Bamford, J. and Ernst, D. (2002), "Managing an alliance portfolio", *The McKinsey Quarterly*, Vol. 3, pp. 28-39.

Beer, S. (1972), *Brain of the Firm*, Allen Lane, Harmondsworth, Middlesex.

Beinhocker, E. D. (1999), "Robust adaptive strategies", *MIT Sloan Management Review*, Vol. 40, No. 3, Spring, pp. 95-106.

Berry, A. J., Broadbent, J. and Otley, D. (2005), "Approaches to control," in Berry, A. J ., Broadbent, J. and Otley, D. (Eds.) (2005), *Management Control: Theories, Issues and Performance*, 2nd edition, Palgrave Macmillan, Basingstoke, Hampshire, UK, Ch. 2, pp. 17-28,

Bhimani, A. and Roberts, H. (2004), "Editorial, management accounting and knowledge management: in search of intelligibility", *Management Accounting Research*, Vol. 15, No. 1, pp. 1-4.

Blair, M. M. (1995), *Ownership and Control: Re-Thinking Corporate Governance for the Twenty-First Century*, Brookings Institution, Washington, DC, as cited by Davis, G. F. and Useem, M. (2002), "Top management, company directors and corporate control", Ch. 11, pp. 232-258, in Pettigrew, A., Thomas, H. and Whittington, R. (Eds.) (2002), *Handbook of Strategy and Management*, Sage Publications Ltd, London, UK.

Bowman, E. H., Singh, H. and Thomas, H. (2002), "The domain of strategic management: history and evolution", in Pettigrew, A., Thomas, H. and Whittington, R. (Eds.) (2002), *Handbook of Strategy and Management*, Sage Publications Ltd, London, UK, Ch. 2, pp. 31-51.

Brown, S. L. and Eisenhardt, K. M. (1998), *Competing on the Edge: Strategy as Structured Chaos*, Harvard Business School Press, Boston, MA.

Bruggeman, W. and Van der Stede, W. (1993), "Research note, fitting management control systems to competitive advantage", *British Journal of Management*, Vol. 4, No. 3, pp. 205-218.

Burns, T. and Stalker, G. M. (1961), *The Management of Innovation*, Tavistock, London, UK.

Chakravarthy, B. S. and White, R. E. (2002), "Forming, implementing and changing strategies", in Pettigrew, A., Thomas, H. and Whittington, R. (Eds.), (2002), *Handbook of Strategy and Management*, Sage Publications Ltd, London, UK, Ch. 9, pp. 182-205.

Chandler, A. D. (1962), *Strategy and Structure: Chapters in the History of American Enterprise*, MIT Press, Cambridge, MA.

Chenhall, R. H. (2003), "Management control systems design within its organizational context: Findings from contingency-based research and directions for the future", *Accounting, Organizations and Society*, Vol. 28, No. 2-3, pp. 127-168.

Chenhall, R. H. and Langfield-Smith, K. (2003), "Performance measurement and reward systems, trust and strategic change", *Journal of Management Accounting Research*, Vol. 15, January, pp. 117-143.

Christensen, C. M. and Raynor, M. E. (2003), *The Innovator's Solution: Creating and Sustaining Successful Growth*, Harvard Business School Press, Boston, MA.

Chua, W. F., Lowe, T. and Puxty, T. (1989), *Critical Perspectives in Management Control*, Macmillan, London, UK.

Coad, A. F. (2005), "Strategy and control", in Berry, A. J., Broadbent, J. and Otley, D. (Eds.) (2005), *Handbook of Strategy and Management*, 2nd edition, Palgrave Macmillan, Basingstoke, Hampshire, UK, Ch. 10, pp. 167-191.

Cyert, R. M. and March, J. G. (1963), *A Behavioural Theory of the Firm*, Prentice Hall, Englewood Cliffs, NJ.

Davis, G. F. and Useem, M. (2002), "Top management, company directors and corporate control", in Pettigrew, A., Thomas, H. and Whittington, R. (Eds.) (2002), *Handbook of Strategy and Management*, Sage Publications Ltd, London, UK, Ch. 11, pp. 232-258.

Dekker, H. C. (2004), "Control of inter-organizational relationships: evidence on appropriation concerns and coordination requirements", *Accounting, Organizations and Society*, Vol. 29, No. 1, pp. 27-49.

Dent, J. F. (1991), "Accounting and organizational cultures: a field study of the emergence of a new organizational reality", *Accounting, Organizations and Society*, Vol. 16, No. 8, pp. 705-732.

Drucker, P. (1964), "Control, controls and management", in Bonini, C. P., Jaedieke, P. K. and Wagner, H. M. (Eds.) (1964), *Management Controls: New Directions in Basic Research*, McGraw-Hill, Maidenhead, UK.

Eisenhardt, K. M. and Santos, F. M. (2002), "Knowledge-based view: a new theory of strategy?", in Pettigrew, A., Thomas, H. and Whittington, R. (Eds.) (2002), *Handbook of Strategy and Management*, Sage Publications Ltd, London, UK, Ch. 7, pp. 139-164.

Ghoshal, S. (2003), "Academic Commentary, Miles and Snow: Enduring insights for managers", *Academy of Management Executive*, Vol. 17, No. 4, November, pp. 109-114.

Govindarajan, V. and Gupta, A. K. (1985), "Linking control systems to business unit strategy: impact on performance", *Accounting, Organizations and Society*, Vol. 10, No. 1, pp. 51-66.

Granovetter, M. (1985), "Economic action and social structure: the problem of embeddedness", *American Journal of Sociology*, Vol. 91, No. 3, pp. 481-510.

Grant, R. M. (1991), "The resource-based theory of competitive advantage: implications for strategy formulation", *California Management Review*, Vol. 33, No. 3, pp. 114-122.

Grove, A. S. (1999), *Only the Paranoid Survive: How to Exploit the Crisis Points That Challenge Every Company*, Currency Doubleday, a division of Random House, Inc., New York, NY.

Gupta, A. K. and Govindarajan, V. (2000), "Knowledge flow within multinational corporations", *Strategic Management Journal*, Vol. 21, No. 4, pp. 473-496.

Hambrick, D. C. (2003), "Foreword to the classic edition, vii-xiii", in Miles, R. E. and Snow, C. C. (Eds.) (2003), *Organizational Strategy, Structure, and Process*, classic edition, Stanford Business Classics, Stanford Business Books, an imprint of Stanford University Press, Stanford.

Hamel, G. and Prahalad, C. K. (1985), "Do you really have a global strategy?", *Harvard Business Review*, July-August, pp. 139-149.

Hammer, M. and Champney, J. (1993), *Reengineering the Corporation: A Manifesto for Business Revolution*, Harper Business, a division of Harper Collins Publishers, Inc., New York, NY, reprinted (2001), Harper Collins Publishers, Inc., New York, NY.

Hannan, M.T. and Freeman, J. (1988), *Organizational Ecology*, Harvard University Press, Cambridge, MA.

Harry, M. and Schroeder, R. (2000), *Six Sigma: The Breakthrough Management Strategy Revolutionizing the World's Top Corporations*, a Currency Book, Doubleday, a division of Random House, Inc., New York, NY.

Hartmann, F. G. H. and Vaassen, E. H. J. (2003), "The changing role of management accounting and control systems: accounting for knowledge across control domains", in Bhimani, A. (Ed.) (2003), *Management Accounting in the Digital Economy*, Oxford University Press, Oxford, UK, Ch. 6, pp. 112-132.

Henri, J.-F. (Article in Press), "Organizational control systems and strategy: a resource-based perspective", *Accounting, Organizations and Society*, doi:10.1016/j.aos.2005.07.001.

Hofstede, G. H. (1978), "The poverty of management control philosophy", *Academy of Management Review*, Vol. 3, No. 3, July, pp. 450-461.

Hopwood, A. G. (1972), "An empirical study of the role of accounting data in performance evaluation", *Empirical Research in Accounting*, Supplement to *Journal of Accounting Research*, Vol. 10, pp. 156-182.

Hopwood, A. G. (1974a), "Leadership climate and the use of accounting data in performance appraisal", *Accounting Review*, pp. 485-495.

Hopwood, A. G. (1974b), *Accounting and Human Behavior*, Prentice-Hall, Englewood Cliffs, NJ.

Hoque, Z. (2004), "A contingency model of the association between strategy, environmental uncertainty and performance measurement: impact on organizational performance", *International Business Review*, Vol. 13, No. 4, pp. 485-502.

Jeremy, D. J. (2002), "Business history and strategy", in Pettigrew, A., Thomas, H. and Whittington, R. (Eds.) (2002), *Handbook of Strategy and Management*, Sage Publications Ltd, London, UK, Ch. 19, pp. 436-460.

Johnson, G. and Scholes, K. (2002), *Exploring Corporate Strategy*, 6th edition, Financial Times Prentice Hall, an imprint of Pearson Education Limited, Harlow, Essex, UK.

Jones, G. (2002), "Perspectives on strategy", in Segal-Horn, S. (Ed.) (2002), *The Strategy Reader*, Blackwell Publishers Ltd, a Blackwell Publishing Company, in association with The Open University, Oxford, UK, Ch. 20, pp. 409-429.

Kald, M., Nilsson, F. and Rapp, B. (2000), "On the strategy and management control: the importance of classifying the strategy of the business", *British Journal of Management*, Vol. 11, No. 3, pp. 197-212.

Kaplan, R. S. and Norton, D. P. (1992), "The Balanced Scorecard – measures that drive performance", *Harvard Business Review*, Vol. 70, No. 1, pp. 71-79.

Kaplan, R. S. and Norton, D. P. (1996), *Translating Strategy Into Action – The Balanced Scorecard*, Harvard Business School Press, Boston, MA.

Kaplan, R. S. and Norton, D. P. (2001), *The Strategy-Focused Organization: How Balanced Scorecard Companies Thrive in the New Business Environment*, Harvard Business School Press, Boston, MA.

Kaplan, R. S. and Norton, D. P. (2004), *Strategy Maps: Converting Intangible Assets into Tangible Outcomes*, Harvard Business School Press, Boston, MA.

Kay, J. (2003), *The Truth About Markets: Their Genius, Their Limits, Their Follies*, Allen Lane, an imprint of Penguin Books, London, UK.

Ketchen, Jr., D. J. (2003), "An interview with Raymond E. Miles and Charles C. Snow", *Academy of Management Executive*, Vol. 17, No. 4, pp. 97-104.

Ketchen, Jr., D. J. (2003), "Introduction: Raymond E. Miles and Charles C. Snow's Organizational Strategy, Structure, and Process", *Academy of Management Executive*, Vol. 17, No. 4, pp. 95-96.

Kim, W. Chan and Mauborgne, Renee, (2004), *Blue Ocean Strategy; How to Create Uncontested Market Space and Make the Competition Irrelevant*, Harvard Business School Press, Boston, Ma.

Langfield-Smith, K. (1997), "Management control systems and strategy: a critical review", *Accounting, Organizations and Society*, Vol. 22, No. 2, pp. 207-232.

Laughlin, R. C. and Broadbent, J. (1993), "Accounting and law: partners in the juridification of the public sector in the UK?", *Critical Perspectives on Accounting*, Vol. 4, No. 4, pp. 337-368.

Lindblom, C. E. (1959), "The science of muddling through", *Public Administration Review*, Vol. 19, No. 2, pp. 79-88.

Lorenz, C. (1993), "Mercedes sees the writing on the wall", *Financial Times*, 5 February, p. 10.

Lowe, E. A. and Machin, J. L. J. (Eds.), (1983), *New Perspectives in Management Control*, Macmillan, London, UK.

Lowe, E. A. and McInnes, J. M. (1971), "Control in socio-economic organizations: a rationale for the design of management control systems (Section I)", *Journal of Management Studies*, pp. 213-227.

Machin, J. L. J. (1983), "Management control systems: whence and whither?", in Lowe, E. A. and Machin, J. L. J. (Eds.), *New Perspectives in Management Control*, Macmillan, London, UK, pp. 22-42.

Malmi, T. and Brown, D. (2005), "Call for papers: Special Issue of Management Accounting Research, Accounting controls as a part of organizational control package", *Management Accounting Research*, Vol. 16, No. 3, pp. 395-396.

Manzoni, J.-F. (2002), "Management control: toward a new paradigm?", in Epstein, M. J. and Manzoni, J.-F. (Eds.), *Performance Measurement and Management Control: A Compendium of Research*, Studies in Managerial and Financial Accounting, Vol. 12, JAI, an imprint of Elsevier Science Ltd, Oxford, UK, pp. 15-46.

March, J. G. (1976), "The technology of foolishness". in March, J. and Olsen J. (Eds.), *Ambiguity and Choice in Organizations*, Universitetsforlaget, Bergen, Norway.

Marginson, D. E. W. (2002), "Management control systems and their effects on strategy formation at middle-management levels: evidence from a UK organization", *Strategic Management Journal*, Vol. 23, No. 11, pp. 1019-1031.

Markides, C. C. (1999), "A dynamic view of strategy", *MIT Sloan Management Review*, Vol. 40, No. 3, pp. 55-63.

Markides, C. and Charitou, C. D. (2004), "Competing with dual business models: a contingency approach", *Academy of Management Executive*, Vol. 18, No. 3, pp. 22-35.

McNair, C. J. and Leibfried, K. H. J. (1992), *Benchmarking: A Tool for Continuous Improvement*, Harper Business, New York, NY.

Mendoza, C. and Saulpic, O. (2002), "Strategic management and management control: designing a new theoretical framework", in Epstein, M. J. and Manzoni, J.-F. (Eds.), *Performance Measurement and Management Control: A Compendium of Research*, Studies in Managerial and Financial Accounting, Vol. 12, JAI, an imprint of Elsevier Science Ltd, Oxford, UK, pp. 131-158.

Merchant, K. A. (1982), "The control function of management", *MIT Sloan Management Review*, Vol. 23, No. 4, Summer, pp. 43-55.

Miles, R. E. (2003), "An interview with Raymond E. Miles and Charles C. Snow", in Ketchen, Jr., D. J. (Ed.) (2003), *Academy of Management Executive*, Vol. 17, No. 4, pp. 97-104.

Miles, R. E. and Snow, C. C. (1978), *Organizational Strategy, Structure, and Process*, McGraw-Hill, New York, NY.

Miles, R. E. and Snow, C. C. (2003), *Organizational Strategy, Structure, and Process*, Stanford Business Classics, Stanford Business Books, an imprint of Stanford University Press, Stanford, CA.

Milgrom, P. and Roberts, J. (1990), "The economics of modern manufacturing: technology, strategy and organization", *American Economic Review*, Vol. 80, pp. 511-528.

Milgrom, P. and Roberts, P. (1995), "Complementarities and fit: strategy, structure, and organizational change in manufacturing", *Journal of Accounting & Economics*, Vol. 19, pp. 179-208.

Mintzberg, H. (1979), *The Structuring of Organizations*, Prentice-Hall, Englewood Cliffs, NJ.

Mintzberg, H. (1987), "The strategy concept 1: five Ps for strategy", *California Management Review*, Vol. 30, No. 1, June, pp. 11-24.

Mintzberg, H. (1989), *Mintzberg on Management: Inside Our Strange World of Organizations*, Free Press, New York, NY.

Mintzberg, H. and Lampel, J. (1999), "Reflecting on the strategy process", *MIT Sloan Management Review*, Vol. 40, No. 3, Spring, pp. 21-30.

Mintzberg, H. and Waters, J. A. (1985), "On strategies, deliberate and emergent", *Strategic Management Journal*, Vol. 6. No. 1, pp. 25-37.

Mouritsen, J. (2005), "Intellectual capital and knowledge resources", in Berry, A. J., Broadbent, J. and Otley, D. (Eds.) (2005), *Handbook of Strategy and Management*, 2nd edition, Palgrave Macmillan, Basingstoke, Hampshire, UK, Ch. 12, pp. 205-229.

Mouritsen, J. and Larsen, H. T. (2005), "The 2nd wave of knowledge management: the management control of knowledge resources through intellectual capital information", *Management Accounting Research, Towards New Forms of Control*, Vol. 16, No. 3, pp. 371-394.

Mouritsen, J. and Thrane, S. (Article in Press), "Accounting, network complementarities and the development of inter-organisational relations", *Accounting, Organizations and Society*, doi:10.1016/j.aos.2005.04.002

Neely, A., Kennerly, M. and Walters, A., Cranfield School of Mangement (Eds.) (2004), *Performance Measurement and Management: Public and Private*, papers from the Fourth International Conference on Performance Measurement and Management – PMA 2004, Edinburgh international Conference Centre (EICC), UK, 28-30 July 2004, Centre for Business Performance, Cranfield School of Management, Bedfordshire, UK.

Nelson, R. R. and Winter, S. G. (1982), *An Evolutionary Theory of Economic Change*, Harvard University Press, Cambridge, MA.

Nixon, W. A. J. and Burns, J. (2005), "Introduction: management control in the 21st century", *Management Accounting Research, Towards New Forms of Control*, Vol. 16, No. 3, pp. 260-268.

Norreklit, L., Norreklit, H. and Israelsen, P. (Article in Press), "The validity of management control topoi: towards constructivist pragmatism", *Management Accounting Research*, doi:10.1016/j.mar.2005.04.002.

Otley, D. T. (1980), "The contingency theory of management accounting: achievement and prognosis," *Accounting, Organizations and Society*, Vol. 5, No. 4, pp. 413-428.

Otley, D. (1994), "Management control in contemporary organizations: towards a wider framework", *Management Accounting Research*, Vol. 5, No. 3, pp. 289-299.

Otley, D. (1999), "Performance management: a framework for management control systems research", *Management Accounting Research*, Vol. 10, No. 4, pp. 363-382.

Otley, D. (2003), "Management control and performance management: whence and whither?", *British Accounting Review*, Vol. 35, No. 4, pp. 309-326.

Otley, D. T. and Berry, A. J. (1980), "Control, organization and accounting", *Accounting, Organizations and Society*, Vol. 5, No. 2, pp. 231-246.

Otley, D., Broadbent, J. and Berry, A. (1995), "Research in management control: an overview of its development", *British Journal of Management*, Vol. 6, Special Issue, December, S31-S44.

Ouchi, W. G. (1979), "A conceptual framework for the design of organizational control mechanisms", *Management Science*, Vol. 25, No. 9, September, pp. 833-849.

Parker, L. D. (1986), *Developing Control Concepts in the 20th Century*, Garland, New York, NY.

Pascale, R. T. (1999), "Surfing the edge of chaos", *MIT Sloan Management Review*, Vol. 40, No. 3, Spring, pp. 83-94.

Peters, T. J. and Waterman, R. H. (1982), *In Search of Excellence*, Harper and Rowe, New York, NY.

Pettigrew, A. M. (1973), *The Politics of Organizational Decision-Making*, Tavistock, London, UK.

Pettigrew, A. M. (1983), *The Awakening Giant: Continuity and Change in ICI*, Blackwell, Oxford, UK.

Pfeffer, J. and Salancik, G. R. (1978), *The External Control of Organizations: A Resource Dependence Perspective*, Harper & Row, New York, NY, reprinted (2003), Stanford Business Classics, Stanford Business Books, an imprint of Stanford University Press, Stanford, CA.

Porter, M. E. (1980), *Competitive Strategy: Techniques for Analyzing Industries and Competitors*, The Free Press, New York, NY.

Porter, M. E. (1996), What is strategy?, *Harvard Business Review*, Vol. 74, No. 6, pp. 61-78.

Post, J. E., Preston, L. E. and Sachs, S. (2002), "Managing the extended enterprise: the new stakeholder view", *California Management Review*, Vol. 45, No. 1, Fall, pp. 5-28.

Prahalad, C. K. and Ramaswamy, V. (2004), *The Future of Competition: Co-Creating Unique Value with Customers*, Harvard Business School Press, Boston, MA.

Rumelt, R. P. (1982), "Diversification strategy and profitability", *Strategic Management Journal*, Vol. 3, pp. 359-369.

Sarbanes-Oxley Act 2002 (officially titled "The Public Company Accounting Reform and Investor Protection Act of 2002"), Pub. L. No. 107-204, 116 Stat. 745 (2002), in particular, ss. 404 and 409.

Schreyogg, G. and Steinmann, H. (1987), "Strategic control: a new perspective", *Academy of Management Review*, Vol. 12, No. 1, pp. 91-103.

Scott, W. R. (1981), "Developments in organization theory: 1960-1980", *American Behanioral Scientist*, pp. 407-422.

Siggelkow, N. (2003), "Change in the presence of fit: the rise, the fall, and the renaissance of Liz Claiborne", in Chakravarthy, B., Mueller-Stewens, G., Lorange, P. and Lechner, C. (Eds.) (2003), *Strategy Process: Shaping the Contours of the Field*, Blackwell Publishing Ltd, Malden, MA and Oxford, UK.

Simon, H.A., Guetzkow, H., Kozmetsky, G. and Tyndall, G. (1954), *Centralization vs. Decentralization in the Controller's Department*, Controllership Foundation, New York, NY, reprinted (1978) by Scholar's Book Co., Houston, TX.

Simons, R. (1987), "Accounting control systems and business strategy: an empirical analysis", *Accounting, Organizations and Society*, Vol. 12, No. 4, pp. 357-374.

Simons, R. (1995), *Levers of Control: How Managers Use Innovative Control Systems to Drive Strategic Renewal*, Harvard Business School Press, Boston, MA.

Simons, R. (2000), *Performance Measurement & Control Systems for Implementing Strategy: Text & Cases*, Prentice Hall, Inc., Upper Saddle River, NJ.

Sloan, A. P. (1963), *My Years With General Motors*, Sedgewick & Jackson, London, UK.

Smith, H. J. (2003), "The shareholders vs. stakeholders debate", *MIT Sloan Management Review*, Vol. 44, No. 4, Summer, pp. 85-90.

Stacey, R. D., Griffin, D. and Shaw, P. (2002), *Complexity and Management: Fad or Radical Challenge to Systems Thinking?*, Routledge, an imprint of the Taylor & Francis Group, London, UK and New York, NY.

Swedberg, R., Himmelstrand, W. and Brulin, G. (1987), "The paradigm of economic sociology", *Theory and Society*, Vol. 16, No. 2, pp. 169-213.

Van der Meer-Kooistra, J. and Vosselman, E. G. J. (2000), "Management control of interfirm transactional relationships: the case of industrial renovation and maintenance", *Accounting, Organizations and Society*, Vol. 25, No. 1, pp. 51-77.

van Veen-Dirks, P. (Article in Press), "Complementary choices and management control: field research in a flexible production environment", *Management Accounting Research*, doi: 10.1016/j.mar.2005.05.001.

Venkatraman, N. and Subramaniam, M. (2003), "Theorizing the future of strategy: questions for shaping strategy research in the knowledge economy", in Pettigrew, A., Thomas, H. and Whittington, R. (Eds.) (2002), *Handbook of Strategy and Management*, Sage Publications Ltd, London, UK, Ch. 20, pp. 461-474.

Vickers, G. (1965), *The Art of Judgement: A Study of Policy-Making*, Methuen, London, UK.

Vickers, G. (1967), *Towards a Sociology of Management*, Chapman and Hall, London, UK.

Weick, K. E. (1979), *The Social Psychology of Organizing*, 2nd edition, Random House, New York, NY.

Whitley, R. D. (1999), *Divergent Capitalisms*, Oxford University Press, Oxford, UK.

Whittington, R. (1992), "Putting Giddens into action: social systems and managerial agency", *Journal of Management Studies*, Vol. 29, No. 6, pp. 693-712.

Whittington, R. (2001), *What is Strategy – and does it matter?*, 2nd edition, Thomson Learning, London, UK.

Whittington, R. (2002), "Corporate structure: from policy to practice", in Pettigrew, A., Thomas, H. and Whittington, R. (Eds.), (2002), *Handbook of Strategy and Management*, Sage Publications Ltd, London, UK, Ch. 6, pp. 113-138.

Williamson, O. E. (1985), *The Economic Institutions of Capitalism*, The Free Press, New York, NY.

Williamson, P. J. (1999), "Strategy as options on the future", *MIT Sloan Management Review*, Vol. 40, No. 3, Spring, pp. 117-126.

Womack, J. P. and Jones, D. T. (1996), *Lean Thinking: Banish Waste and Create Wealth in Your Corporation*, Simon & Schuster, New York, NY.

Woodward, J. (1958), *Management and Technology*, HMSO, London, UK.

Woodward, J. (1965), *Industrial Organization: Theory and Practice*, Oxford University Press, Oxford, UK.

Woodward, J. and Rackham, J. (1970), *Industrial Organization: Behaviour and Control*, Oxford University Press, London, UK.

8

GROUNDED THEORY: A THEORY DISCOVERY METHOD FOR ACCOUNTING RESEARCH

Joanne Lye
La Trobe University, Australia

Hector Perera
Massey University, New Zealand

Asheq Rahman
Nanyang Technological University, Singapore

Abstract: Social scientists have been recognising the shortcomings of the scientific methodology for quite some time. The main shortcoming, according to them, has been the oversimplified deductive approach to theory development that has been adopted in the scientific methods.[19] The oversimplification occurs because some of the essential variables of reality are assumed to be constants. In a similar vein, researchers in social science have often been making calls for the adoption of the naturalistic approach to study complex human phenomena. We believe the construction of accounting phenomena belongs to this category, and suggest the use of the naturalistic approach to examine them as they may not be examinable by the structured theory driven scientific approach. Within the naturalistic domain, we propose the use of a method of research called the Grounded Theory method. The rationale behind the Grounded Theory method is that theory should be grounded in empirical evidence, i.e. evolve from data, rather than be developed *a priori* and then be tested. Since its introduction in the 1960s, the

---

[19] We use the terms 'approach' and 'methodology' interchangeably to mean the conceptual basis of research procedures, such as the inductive basis for the naturalistic approach and the deductive basis of the scientific approach. In the case of scientific approach, we believe that theories are developed through the deductive process and then tested through the inductive process of empirical methods used. So, primarily, in the scientific approach theories are developed through deductive logic and not through inductivism as some theorists claim. We use the term method or research method to identify the actual research procedures applied like case research, field studies, empirical analysis of secondary data sources, mail surveys, etc.

grounded theory method has found favour in many other disciplines, such as nursing, sociology and organisation studies. This chapter suggests Grounded Theory method could be a viable alternative available to accounting researchers to examine complex phenomena.

Keywords: naturalistic research approach; grounded theory method; divergence of grounded theory method.

1. Introduction

Scientific methodology of research has come under serious scrutiny in recent years from the proponents of both scientific and naturalistic research. Scientific researchers in the field of economics and psychology have questioned the efficacy of each other's research methods.[20] Researchers using economic paradigms have for long challenged the views of those who feel that decision-makers vary in their level of rationality while making economic decisions. They hold the utilitarian view that all decision-makers are rational utility maximisers. For example, in accounting and finance, they feel that all decision makers act efficiently to maintain rational self-interest and through their actions certain equilibria in markets are arrived at instantaneously which do not allow anyone to achieve abnormal gains at the expense of others. In other words they hold the factor of rational self-interest as a constant to examine human behaviour. However, those who examine human behaviour from a psychological viewpoint have long held the view that the factor of rationality is a variable and not a constant. Nevertheless, in using the scientific methods of research, psychologists have also controlled certain variables. For example, in accounting, human information processing researchers using experimental research hold information constant to study the variabilities in the level of rationality of individuals. More recently, researchers in both camps are moving towards a compromise that allows greater acceptance of the variability of all the factors involved in decision making. This has led to a plethora of methods under the names of case research, field studies, verbal protocol analysis, etc. Most of these methods are common to the naturalistic approach to research.

Those who favour naturalistic research methods have also suggested that decision making needs to be observed in its natural setting to be able to better appreciate the way it is done. Suggestions for the use of naturalistic methods in accounting research have intensified in recent times (e.g. Chua, 1986; Hopper, Storey and Willmott, 1987; Covaleski and Dirsmith, 1990; Hopwood, 1990; Hopwood, 1994). This view recognises that there is a need for research that studies accounting phenomena within 'everyday life', the broader social, economic and political environment, and the context of change to enrich our understanding of the social

---

[20] See *Journal of Business*, 1986, Vol. 59 No. 4, Pt. 2, for papers dealing with the perspectives of economists and psychologists on human choice behaviour. Scapens (1990) also discusses the problems arising from the utilitarian beliefs of neoclassical economics.

construction of accounting (Hopwood, 1990; Hines, 1989). Accounting, according to Perera (1994), is a socio-technical activity that involves dealing with both technical and societal factors, as well as interaction between them. Prima facie, both the scientific and naturalistic researchers have started recognising the multidirectional causality between variables in favour of the previously held unidirectional view between a dependent and an independent variable.

Given the growing acceptance of the complexity of the human choice environment, methods that are common to naturalistic studies are quite often used by or recommended for use for the scientific approach. For example, case research or field studies are often used or recommended to test deductive theories (e.g. Scapens, 1990; Keating, 1995). However, this causes confusion about what naturalistic approach is and which method of research is best suited for the naturalistic approach. Naturalistic approach is essentially an inductive approach and is best suited to gaining understanding of complex phenomena. Therefore, it is felt that the confusion caused by the use of naturalistic research methods for meeting the traditional scientific end, needs to be clarified and a method of research more akin to the naturalist approach needs to be identified. The purpose of this chapter is to clarify the position of naturalistic approach and suggest the use of a research method that is primarily naturalistic in orientation.

The rest of the chapter is organised into nine sections. The next section explicates the premise of the naturalistic approach, and its main features. The third section identifies Grounded Theory as a method that efficiently reflects the main features of the naturalistic approach. The fourth section introduces the procedures and techniques of the grounded theory craft. The fifth section explains the features of the resulting theory. The sixth section outlines possible criteria for evaluation. The seventh section provides an overview of the divergence of techniques between the originators of grounded theory. The eighth section discusses the potential of grounded theory method for application in research, in general, and accounting research, in particular. This is followed by a summary and some concluding comments in the final section.

2.   Towards a Naturalistic Approach to Research

Tomkins and Groves (1983) drew attention to the use of naturalistic research approach to discover and understand relevant social behaviour 'in its natural setting' (p. 364). Like many others, Broadbent and Guthrie (1992) reiterated the use of this approach. They reviewed the new directions on public sector research and suggested that explanations of accounting's role and how it influences and is influenced within wider organisational and social settings are required. Similarly the narrow rational utility maximisation assumption of the utilitarian models has also come under close scrutiny. Such models have failed to give comprehensive explanations for human choice behaviour and are also being seen as an impediment to understanding complex human phenomena such as decision making under ambiguity (Einhorn and Hogarth, 1986). For example, in accounting, utilitarians conducting studies about the relevance of accounting numbers to markets have found that the markets are neither efficient nor single decision-makers. Psychologists have provided an alternative to this problem arising from a single assumption about the premise of human behaviour by suggesting the need to recognise varying degrees of rationality. However, many studies based on psychology theories are experimental as they control for important variables such as the availability of information to decision-makers. This has made psychology to fail in providing comprehensive solutions. Therefore, calls have been made in both the utility-based disciplines such as economics and psychology to use methods such as case research and field studies (Hogarth and Reder, 1986). Case studies and field research have also found favour with accountants (Scapens, 1990). However, the use of these research methods is focused on testing of deductively derived theories and not generating new theories. This defeats the purpose of the examination of complex structures of human behaviour because such deductive theories are narrowly focused on specific variables through the prior biases of the theoretician.

Accounting researchers, who have adopted the naturalistic approach without explaining the methods, have also been criticised. For example, Ferreira and Merchant (1992), in their review of field research in the management accounting control area, criticised scholars for not satisfactorily explaining the research methods employed, and for not showing how the research evolved during the research process. Others, such as Scapens (1990) and Keating (1995) have blurred the distinction between what is needed in naturalistic approach and scientific approach by suggesting that methods commonly used by naturalistic researchers can also be used for testing pre-established theories. Consequently, there seems to be confusion about what naturalistic approach stands for and the methods best applicable for it.

Knowledge by definition is limited and there is no single best approach to understanding the empirical world[21] (see Chua, 1986; Laughlin, 1995; Tomkins and Groves, 1983). All research approaches are inextricably subjective (Hopper, Annissette, Dastoor, Uddin and Wickramasinghe, 1995, p. 517) because the researcher must make choices about what is to be researched, what data are to be collected and how they are to be analysed. These aspects are all affected by the researchers' value judgements. As Laughlin (1995) states, a researcher's 'insights are inevitably subjective because no knowledge is generated distinct from the observer whose reasoning and experiential powers are not uniform or determined' (p. 71).

Typically, epistemological and ontological assumptions of the researcher are often unexamined. Both Burrell and Morgan (1979) and Morgan and Smircich (1980) designed abstract classification schema for understanding key assumptions which distinguish different empirical approaches in the social sciences. The contribution of the Burrell and Morgan classification schema is discussed and acknowledged by

---

[21] In this chapter, the word empirical is used to denote facts and experiences.

Laughlin (1995). Morgan and Smircich developed six alternative views of looking at the world along an objective/subjective continuum[22] They illustrated the inter-connectedness of assumptions about ontology, human nature, epistemology and research methods. They also highlighted that in between the objectivist and subjectivist ends is a range of assumptions representing various combinations of subjectivity and objectivity.

When there is a well-founded theory that accurately describes an area of inquiry the researcher can concentrate on the collection of data applicable to the existing theory. However, many inquiries particularly in social sciences do not fit this pattern. In many cases, no relevant theories exist at all, and even when they do exist, they may be too remote or abstract to be useful in gaining much detailed guidance and assistance. The need for the scope of accounting research to be expanded from its traditional style (Abdel-Khalik and Ajinkya, 1979) to include social and political phenomena has been recognised for some time (e.g. Cooper, 1980; Tinker, 1980; Burchell et al., 1980). Consequently, increasing attention has been drawn to the use of a variety of alternative approaches to the traditional scientific approach (Macintosh and Scapens, 1990, p. 455). The terms 'qualitative methods' (Covaleski and Dirsmith, 1990, p. 544), 'naturalistic methods' (Tomkins and Groves, 1983, p. 81) and 'interpretive sociology' (Chua, 1988, p. 62) have been used to describe these alternative approaches. Generally, all of these approaches are naturalistic in orientation. However, accounting literature commonly uses the term interpretive approach to represent them.[23]

A growing appreciation for interpretive/naturalistic research methods in accounting is reflected in many recent studies, for example, Tomkins and Groves (1983), Kaplan (1983, 1984, 1986), Chua (1986, 1986b, 1988), Dirsmith et al. (1985), Covaleski and Dirsmith (1990), Arrington and Francis (1989), Macintosh and Scapens (1990) and Boland (1993). Covaleski and Dirsmith (1990) explained the contrast between traditional scientific approach and emerging interpretive perspectives as follows:

> In contrast with the traditional perspective in which reality is seen as objective, empirical and rational, and where attention is directed at better knowing and representing it, the emergent perspective sees reality as subjective, ill-structured, complex, anomaly-filled, fluid, socially constructed (p. 549).

---

[22] Strictly speaking, Morgan and Smircich's schema can be criticised on the ground that it is inappropriate to depict the relation between subjective and objective world views in terms of a continuum because no world view can be purely subjective or purely objective although the two ends of the continuum suggest that it is possible.

[23] Hereinafter, the term 'interpretive approach' is also used to represent these alternative research approaches. It is recognised, however, that the European concept of interpretive approach in its pure form has a specific meaning which may not be applicable to some of the alternative approaches.

NATURALISTIC RESEARCH APPROACH

The historical roots of the interpretive alternatives are found in Germanic philosophical interests who emphasise the role of language, interpretation, and understanding in social science (Chua, 1986, p.613). As Boland (1993, p.125) explains, the key premise of the interpretive approach is that the meaning of individuals' actions and those around them is something the researcher develops. In other words, it is an interpretation and not something given to the researcher. (The main features of the traditional scientific and interpretive research approaches are briefly outlined in Table 1).

Table 1
TRADITIONAL AND ALTERNATIVE APPROACHES TO ACCOUNTING RESEARCH

	TRADITIONAL (Scientific)	ALTERNATIVE (Interpretive-Naturalistic)
Reality	Objective, structured	Subjective, unstructured, and socially constructed
Focus	Better knowing and representing reality. (Causal determination, prediction, generalisation)	Understanding the meaning of individual's actions and those around them. (Illustration, extrapolation)
Research approach	Reductionist – theory driven	Interpretive - holistic
Research process	Linear	Non-linear
Research purpose	Theory testing	Theory discovery
Analysis	Based on the face value of data	Based on the understanding gained by interpreting data

Tomkins and Groves (1983) drew attention to the work of Morgan and Smircich in an attempt to highlight a range of different approaches to research that could be used in accounting. There has been an increasing recognition of the view that in order to provide rich explanations, the research methods must incorporate the complexities of the context that surrounds the phenomena under investigation, rather than ignore or simplify them. For example, Covaleski and Dirsmith (1990) identified the interdependencies 'among the research questions being addressed, the research approaches employed, the organisations and actions studied, and the researchers' (p. 543). The interpretive approach proposes to enhance our understanding of the phenomena under investigation by moving beneath the surface and explaining how complex and multi-faceted reality is. In this approach the social world is seen as an emergent process created by the individuals concerned. Covaleski and Dirsmith (1990) and Parker (1994) identified different methods within the interpretive research mode.

3. Grounded Theory Method

A method within the interpretive domain is Grounded Theory method. Grounded Theory has found favour in many disciplines, e.g. nursing studies (Walton, 1989), sociology (Parker, 1994) and organisational studies (Martin and Turner, 1986) due to its effectiveness in explaining the decision making processes and human behaviour within their natural settings. Its prospects lie in being able to identify significant variables and relationships between variables that are not detectable by the scientific approach and in generating theories that are grounded in reality (Parker, 1994). It is primarily inductive in form and therefore a true naturalistic procedure. Practice being the basis or source of data for the Grounded Theory method also allows the perceived gap between theories and practice to be reduced.

Grounded theory method is a way of thinking about and conceptualising data. Symbolic interactionism provides the genesis for grounded theory (Chenitz and Swanson, 1986; Baker, Wuest and Stern, 1992). Symbolic interactionism is a perspective within the interpretive approach that has its disciplinary roots in social psychology and is associated with George Herbert Mead (1934) and Herbert Blumer (1969). Blumer (1969, p. 2) articulated three premises that are fundamental to symbolic interactionism:

1. Human beings act toward things on the basis of the meanings that the things have for them.
2. The meaning of such things is derived from, or arises out of the social interaction that one has with one's fellows.
3. These meanings are handled in, and modified through, an interpretive process used by the person in dealing with the things [s]he encounters.

Central to Blumer's (1969) premises is the idea that human beings construct their reality through a process of assigning meaning to action, interaction and self-reflection. It is through these processes that those meanings become reality to actors.

To conduct research within this approach, it is necessary to understand the reality of the actors, to see the world as the actor sees it, and to illuminate unforeseen relationships.

Two sociologists, Barney Glaser and Anslem Strauss coined the term 'grounded theory', as a result of their research into American health institutions. The grounded theory method was first used by Glaser and Strauss (1965a, 1965b) in their study of patterns of organisational behaviour exhibited in hospitals with respect to dying patients. The conceptual foundation of this approach was introduced in their seminal book *The Discovery of Grounded Theory: Strategies for Qualitative Research* (1967). Subsequently, Glaser and Strauss have written individually elaborating on their original work (e.g. Glaser, 1978 and 1992, Strauss, 1987). Additionally, Strauss and Corbin (1990) in their book *Basics of Qualitative Research: Grounded Theory Procedures and Techniques*, also provide a comprehensive framework of procedures and techniques for learning qualitative analysis (see also Strauss and Corbin, 1994).[24]

Strauss and Corbin (1990) explain grounded theory as:

one that is inductively derived from the study of the phenomenon it represents. That is, it is discovered, developed, and provisionally verified through systematic data collection and analysis of data pertaining to that phenomenon. Therefore, data collection, analysis, and theory stand in reciprocal relationship with each other. One does not begin with a theory, then prove it. Rather, one begins with an area of study and what is relevant to that area is allowed to emerge (p. 23).

The distinguishing characteristic of this research approach is that the resulting theory evolves during actual research, and it does this through continuous interplay between analysis and data collection. Because of this continuous interplay differing stages of the research can be worked upon simultaneously. Through such overlap the researcher comes to understand the problem better, but more importantly, enables the researcher to manage the complexity of the grounded theory method.

The grounded theory method proposes to discover processes that occur as individuals interact with others within a particular social context. Its credibility as a research method is established through the adoption of certain procedures and techniques to ensure rigour in the research process. The discussion that follows is intended as an aid to explain the grounded theory craft.

4.   Procedures and Techniques of the Grounded Theory Method

The procedures and techniques of grounded theory, as well as the logic behind them have been explained in Glaser and Strauss (1967), Glaser (1978), Corbin and Strauss (1990), Strauss (1987), Strauss and Corbin (1990) and Charmaz (1983, 1990). There are two tenets to the grounded theory method, i.e. discovery and theoretical sensitivity. The process of *discovery* is important because the researcher must 'discover what is going on' (Glaser, 1978). To aid discovery, a vital element of grounded theory method is creativity (Strauss and Corbin, 1990). Creativity involves the ability of the researcher to code concepts and derive apt categories that represent the underlying reality of the particular study. It also allows the mind to make new insights with the data not previously seen that will lead to discovery and thus avoid 'conceptually thin and poorly validated research' (Strauss and Corbin, 1990, p. 94).

Additionally, researchers are permitted to triangulate data sources to facilitate discovery. Denzin (1970) has described triangulation of data within a method as 'the use of multiple methods in the study of the same object' (p. 301). The contribution of this is that the analyst can tap into a variety of data sources (e.g.

---

[24] Other relevant works include Corbin and Strauss (1988, 1990), Glaser (1972, 1978a), Glaser and Strauss (1964a, 1968, 1970), Strauss (1978, 1991), Strauss, Bucher, Ehelich, Sabshin and Schatzman (1963, 1964).

interviews, archival documents and newspapers) to understand the phenomenon being investigated.

Within a grounded theory based study, the researcher commences with an area of research and allows relevant theoretical concepts or theory to emerge from the data. As stated by Glaser (1978), *'conceptual specification* is the focus of grounded theory, not *conceptual definition'* (p. 64, original emphasis). This is an important point because the operational meaning of a concept emerges from the analysis by identifying dimensions and properties from the data of a particular study. Thus, specification of a concept is subject to change throughout the duration of the study. Grounded theory is a flexible approach to research in which there is little in the research process that is irreversible, for example, if at any stage, the concept labels are thought to be too specific or too general, this can be remedied. Martin and Turner (1986) emphasise that this process is a movement across levels of abstraction, not a numerical tabulation of incidents associated with a discovered concept. They go on to point out that all concepts are only more or less useful, not more or less true or valid, and that as the theory emerges, more useful concepts will remain and less useful ones will fall into disuse.

The second tenet of grounded theory is *theoretical sensitivity*. There are several procedures and techniques the researcher can utilise to enhance theoretical sensitivity. They include the constant comparative method, questioning, coding, memo-writing, theoretical sampling, the conditional matrix, review of the literature and sorting. These enable the researcher to relate systematically concepts and categories that represent and work with the data to make the necessary connections in studies employing grounded theory method (Glaser, 1978).

Coding provides the link between the data and the theoretical concepts or theory. Open coding, also called substantive coding (Strauss, 1987), is the first analytical step upon which the research process is based. Thereafter, each level of coding represents a more 'condensed abstract view' (Glaser, 1978).

The *constant comparative method* is utilised throughout the research process to identify similarities and differences, to uncover specific dimensions and to facilitate systematic development of theory. In contrasting the constant comparison method with analytic induction, Glaser and Strauss (1967) states:

> the constant comparative method is concerned with generating and plausibly suggesting (but not provisionally testing) many categories, properties, and hypotheses about general problems ... . Some of these properties may be causes, as in analytic induction but unlike analytic induction, others are conditions, consequences, dimensions, types, processes, etc. (p. 104).

Initially this method is used to compare incidents with incidents to give them the same substantive code. Substantive codes are then clustered according to their similarities and differences. Eventually, through a process of accumulated knowledge (Glaser and Strauss, 1967), categories begin to become integrated, and a core category or process that explains the data is discovered. The strategic process of moving from data to abstract categories or concepts is referred to as concept discovery (Glaser and Strauss, 1967, Glaser, 1978).

Questioning is another technique employed to open the data and to enhance theoretical sensitivity, although its nature changes at differing stages of the research process (Glaser and Strauss, 1967; Strauss and Corbin, 1990).

Memo-writing, i.e. informal memoranda written by the researcher, to the researcher, are a crucial element throughout the research process. At the early stages, the goal is to move up a notch in level of abstraction, capturing in written format thoughts and ideas that derive from the research process at each stage. They allow the researcher freedom to record observed relationships from the data without concerns about expression, punctuation and grammar. During the research process, the memos vary in content reflecting the improved theoretical sensitivity of the researcher. Glaser and Strauss (1967) suggest a rule to be followed to capture ideas: 'stop coding and record a memo on your ideas' (p. 107). According to Glaser (1978, p. 83):

> *Memos are the theorising write-up of ideas about codes and their relationships as they strike the analyst while coding. Memos lead, naturally, to abstraction or ideation. Memoing is a constant process that begins when first coding data, and continues through reading memos or literature, sorting and writing papers or monograph to the very end. Memo-writing continually captures the 'frontier of the analyst's thinking' as he goes through either his date, codes, sorts and writes … . The four basic goals in memoing are to theoretically develop **ideas** (codes), with complete **freedom** into a memo **fund**, that is highly **sortable**.*

Theoretical sampling is critical to the application process of grounded theory. Strauss and Corbin (1990, p. 176) define theoretical sampling as 'sampling on the basis of concepts that have proven theoretical relevance to the evolving theory'. Thus, it is not the people *per se*, but incidents that are important in theoretical sampling to the development of relevant concepts. Therefore, predetermined sample sizes are not appropriate because after initial selection, sampling is related to the findings of the study and where those findings take the researcher (Sandelowski, 1986).

Sampling ceases through a judgemental decision by the researcher, for example, when saturation of themes is evident (Glaser and Strauss, 1967). This occurs when the information received from participants is repetitive, and no new themes are emerging. In addition to saturation of themes, other criteria include density of the theory, integration of the theory, depth of focus, variation of process and theoretical sensitivity of the analyst (Glaser and Strauss, 1967, pp. 45-77; and Strauss and Corbin, 1990, pp. 178-179).

Another useful analytical tool for the researcher is the *Conditional Matrix* developed by Strauss and Corbin (1990) and reproduced in this chapter as Figure 1. The conditional matrix provides an explanatory framework linking a broad range of factors at various levels for identifying conditions and consequences related to the phenomenon under investigation.

Figure 1
Conditional Matrix

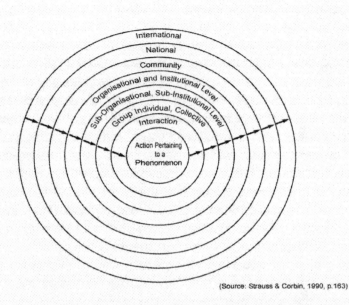

(Source: Strauss & Corbin, 1990, p.163)

Strauss and Corbin (1990, pp. 162-164) describe the general features that should be considered within each matrix level. Considerations at the broadest levels (international, national and community) include conditions such as: politics, culture, values, philosophies, economics, history, issues and problems in the environment. Each respective level should be analysed to discover the relevant factors at each level that influenced the phenomenon under investigation. Moving inward, the history, structure and problems of applicable organisations and institutions are to be identified. Next the unique features of a department or division within an organisation or institution need to be incorporated. At the collective, group and individual levels biographies of key individuals and groups would be included. This is followed by the interactional level where actors interpret meanings regarding the phenomenon through interaction with other people, also with themselves. Strauss and Corbin (1990, p. 164) state, 'interaction is carried out through processes of interaction such as debate, discussion, negotiation, and self reflection'. The innermost circle completes the matrix and includes both strategic and routine action.

Throughout data collection and analysis, the relevant *literature*, both technical and non-technical, is *reviewed* continuously. The purpose of this is to treat all literature as data that can supplement real (primary) data in a variety of ways. For example, two ways the literature (technical and non-technical) can be used are:

to direct theoretical sampling and to identify pertinent material that can be used to support emergent categories (refer Strauss and Corbin, 1990, pp. 48-56).

Sorting enables patterns to emerge from the data. In the early stages this includes sorting of codes (substantive and theoretical). In the later stages it is the sorting of memos to derive conceptual categories and the core category. No matter at what stage the sorting is undertaken, ideas which emerge during this process should be captured in memos, to avoid any ideas being lost. It is at this stage that the researcher becomes aware of how multidimensional reality is. As explained by Glaser (1978) 'it is during the sorting that the analyst appreciates to the fullest the multivariate nature of grounded theory. [S]he can just see it occurring during [her] sorts and as the multi-connections between categories occurs' (p. 118).

A diagrammatic overview of the grounded theory procedures and techniques is illustrated in Figure 2. A grounded theory study starts with the collection of data and the procedures and techniques discussed above permeate the process of abstracting from the data, through various levels of coding, until the core category is identified.[25] It is important to note that the process of abstraction under grounded theory is non-linear and iterative (Glaser and Strauss, 1967), in other words, the research does not proceed in a linear fashion from raw data to concept codes to preliminary writing on theory to the final theory (Glaser, 1978).

For a piece of research to be called a grounded theory study, it needs to employ all of the techniques and procedures. For example, in explaining the importance of theoretical memoranda, Glaser (1978) says:

> The core stage is the process of generating theory, the bedrock of theory generation, its true product is the writing of theoretical memos. If the analyst skips this stage by going directly from coding to sorting or to writing, he is not doing grounded theory (p. 83).

Strauss and Corbin (1994, p. 277) also raise similar issues.

Having to handle large amounts of non-standard data is a major difficulty in grounded theory method. This has been facilitated to some extent by the availability of software packages which are capable of assisting in data coding and sorting (Tesch, 1990), for example, NUD*IST (Richards, Richards, McGalliard and Sharrock, 1992) and ATLAS/ti (Muhr, 1992). While this is an exciting development, some caution needs to be exercised in seeking the assistance of computer software packages for grounded theory research in order to ensure that the interpretive nature of the work is not compromised.

---

[25] The conditional matrix origin is Strauss and Corbin (1990).

Figure 2
Diagramatic Overview of Grounded Theory Procedures and Techniques

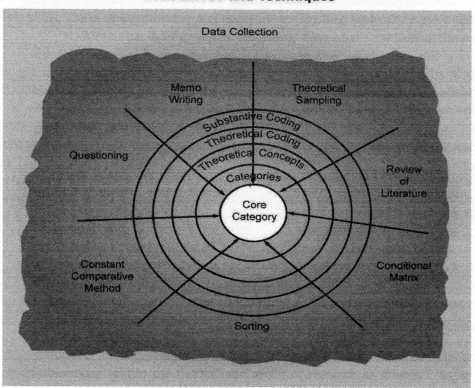

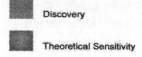 Discovery

Theoretical Sensitivity

5.   The Resulting Theory

The researcher, accepting the idea that there are multiple realities, cannot profess to discover the only reality. The grounded theory approach will enable the researcher to provide an interpretation of events derived from the participants' perspective that will be abstracted via coding at various levels to derive some core theoretical categories integrated into a theoretical framework. Thus, as stated by Strauss (1987), 'the researcher's will not be the only possible interpretation of the data ... but it will be plausible, useful, and allow its own further elaboration and verification' (p. 11). This is a distinctive position taken in interpretive research where the researcher accepts responsibility for his/her interpretive role. The researcher does not believe it sufficient merely to report or give voice to the viewpoints of the people, groups or organisations studied. Instead, the researcher assumes the further responsibility of interpreting what is observed, heard or read (Strauss and Corbin, 1994, p. 274).

Theory discovery studies have the capacity to produce novel, even unexpected, findings of theoretical importance (Ferreira and Merchant, 1992). Grounded theory studies are also useful in identifying knowledge gaps and unresolved theoretical puzzles, and specifying research programmes to develop theoretical issues.

The resulting theory is characterised by several features. First, the theory justifies itself, by providing a detailed and carefully crafted account of the area under investigation. In other words, the theory is always traceable to the data that gave rise to it. Second, the theory allows the researcher to study phenomena without having to fit them into a predetermined research design. Third, the theory aids the researcher's understanding of the phenomena under investigation, and provides a means of communicating the researcher's understanding to those in the area studied, either as a basis for discussion or as a vehicle for implementing change. Fourth, the resulting theory is an interpretation made from given perspectives as adopted by the researcher, not the formulation of some discovered aspect of a pre-existing reality 'out there'. Fifth, the theory is likely to be of great conceptual density in terms of richness of concept development and relationships, which rest on great familiarity with associated data and are checked out systematically with these data (Strauss and Corbin, 1994, p. 274). Finally, the theory is likely to lead to an enrichment of available general theories as they can be evaluated in the light of questions drawn from a new, firmly based and logically grounded theory.

6.   Evaluative Criteria

Caution needs to be exercised in the use of evaluative criteria of other research approaches, especially those that are theory based, to assess grounded theory research. As McKinnon (1988) states 'Criteria designed to guide and evaluate research using one method are not necessarily appropriate and transferable to research using alternative methods' (p. 34).

Grounded theorists (and advocates of other types of qualitative research) have redefined the evaluative criteria for studies focused on human behaviour. For example, Glaser and Strauss (1967) state:

In this book we have raised doubts about the applicability of these (the usual) canons of rigor as proper criteria for judging the credibility of theory based on the use of this methodology. We have suggested that criteria of judgment be based instead on the detailed elements of the actual strategies used for collecting, coding, analyzing, and presenting data when generating theory, and on the way in which people read the theory (p. 224).

Strauss and Corbin (1990) provide evaluative criteria for judging a grounded theory study, which relate to the research process employed and the empirical grounding of the study. The discipline expected of grounded theorists through the processes of description and specification of relationships directs them toward a high degree of rigour in handling and interpretation of data.

In discussing the quality of the theoretical accounts resulting from grounded theory, Turner (1983) suggests two criteria for judging a good theory, i.e. first, whether the theoretical accounts fit closely and adequately the social scene with which it is concerned, and second, whether they are accurate, understandable and enlightening to individuals who have some familiarity with the social phenomenon under investigation, either as participants or as 'lay' observers (p. 347).

Guba and Lincoln (1981) suggest credibility, fittingness, auditability and confirmability as strategies for achieving and evaluating rigour in qualitative research. These have also been used successfully in research that adopted grounded theory method, e.g. Walton's study in nursing (Walton, 1989). A study is credible when the descriptions and interpretations presented are recognisable by the participants or other people who might read the study. Fittingness is attained when the findings are well grounded in the participants' experiences and 'fit' the data from which they were derived representing both typical and atypical elements. Another aspect of fittingness is when a study's findings are viewed as meaningful and applicable in contexts outside the study situation. Auditability is attained when the researcher leaves a clear 'decision trail' that can be followed by another researcher. For instance, if the researcher needed to adopt any other procedures or techniques this would need to be fully elaborated in the final report. Additionally, another researcher, given the data, perspective and situation, could arrive at similar and not contradictory interpretations. Confirmability represents the criterion of neutrality and is achieved when credibility, fittingness and auditability criteria have been met in the findings of the study.

Field research is one of the common methods of data collection for grounded theory. McKinnon (1988) focused on certain criteria for evaluating validity and reliability issues of field research. She found the threats to validity and reliability arise mainly due to (1) the observer's presence in the environment, (2) observer bias in interpreting or recording events, (3) data access limitations and (4) the subject's mode of informing the researcher about the event, especially in interviews. McKinnon, however, feels that some of these difficulties can be dealt with through sufficient presence of the researcher in the field such that the researcher is seen as part of the field setting by the subjects, use of multiple data collection methods, sensitively handling the subjects and using the data collection procedures with care.

7. Pitfalls of the Approach

The use of grounded theory procedures is very time intensive, for example, note writing is a demanding task, often taking as long as or even longer than the observation itself. Further, as Patton (1990) explains, the researcher is both the greatest strength and weakness in this type of analysis. Turner (1983) states '... the quality of the final product arising from this kind of work is more directly dependent upon the quality of the research worker's understanding of the phenomena under observation than is the case with many other approaches to research' (p. 335). Researcher bias is another potential problem area. Everybody is biased by some view and it is the researcher's responsibility to control his or her bias. These concerns, however, apply in varying degrees to all research methods.

More specifically, when collecting data under grounded theory method, interviewees may be uninterested in the researcher's study, may not be aware of the macro influences, may give 'false' information, or may have difficulty in recollecting events. To apply grounded theory procedures and techniques adequately, such that the data acquired are valid and reliable, requires immense effort and time on the part of the researcher.

8. Divergence of Grounded Theory Method

In recent years, there has been a divergence of opinion between the originators of grounded theory, which became public in 1992 with Glaser publishing his book titled: *Basics of Grounded Theory Analysis: Emergence vs Forcing*. The book is a critique of Strauss and Corbin's 1990 book. This divergence can be traced to differing philosophical positions related to the originators' backgrounds. Glaser, who studied at Columbia University during the 1950s where there was a tradition of quantitative methods, was influenced by quantitative methodology as developed by Paul Lazarsfeld and Paul Merton (Goulding, 2002). The Columbian approach also 'emphasized empirical research in conjunction with the development of theory' (Strauss and Corbin, 1990, p. 25). Glaser advocates a conceptual approach to grounded theory studies based on emergence and relevance. He accepts the subjectivity within the naturalistic mode of research as inherent, as with human nature. He suggests the researcher should have trust and patience that, through emergence, a conceptual framework will materialise that will explain how participants processed a problem. The patterns are just there waiting to be discovered.

By contrast, Strauss, who studied at the University of Chicago where there was 'a long history and strong tradition in qualitative research' (Strauss and Corbin, 1990, p. 24) advocates a more objective and application oriented approach. This is manifested in Strauss and Corbin's 1990 book with its step by step approach.

An in-depth analysis highlighting differences in the two approaches is contained in Appendix 1. Two key differences relate to Strauss and Corbin's development of the paradigm model and the conditional matrix. The paradigm model first emerges under Chapter 7 on Axial Coding and is pivotal because all categories discovered must be linked to the constituent elements of the model, i.e. causal conditions, phenomenon, context, intervening conditions, action/interaction strategies and consequences. The conditional matrix is an analytical framework that subsumes the paradigm model and is a tool to integrate the findings of a grounded theory study. By identifying constituent elements the paradigm model introduced structure to the development of grounded theory. The model focuses the researcher's attention thereby impinging on the creativeness and consequently downplaying the role of other techniques such as sorting. A similar criticism applies to the application of the conditional matrix.

After the first level of open (substantive) coding the paradigm model permeates a grounded theory study. For instance Strauss and Corbin refer to three levels of coding: open, axial and selective. For each level of coding there is a relevant approach to theoretical sampling that has a specific purpose. In addition to the requirement that sampling continues until no new or relevant data emerges from participants regarding a category they also require that all of the elements in the paradigm model have been accounted for. Likewise, with each level of coding, the authors point to the differing purpose of memos and diagrams. All codes derived should be related back to both models.

For the beginning researcher the model presents difficulty because it seems contrary to the coding process. It raises such questions as 'how does the model fit in with the codes that I have derived' and 'When do I sort the codes according to the model?' It is suggested here that the researcher use the techniques of sorting and the constant comparative method to abstract from the data. Before the core category and supporting categories have all been identified the researcher is required to use the paradigm model. Thus the categories derived from a study are determined by means of the paradigm model. So, in effect, what happens is that the grounded theory discovered using this approach has a structure that is determined *a priori* even though the categories developed may not include the terms from the paradigm model. Strauss and Corbin have provided researchers with a step by step approach to conducting a grounded theory study. Their approach is prescriptive because all codes must be related to the paradigm model otherwise the grounded theory derived 'will lack density and precision' (Strauss and Corbin, 1990, p. 99).

Differences in emphasis occur with the use of questioning, constant comparative method, how to get started with a grounded theory study and theoretical sampling. Even so, the fundamental purpose of these techniques is the same. The techniques of questioning and constant comparative method are used to aid the researcher to 'open up' the data. To break through biases and ways of thinking to focus more clearly on what is significant in the data, to move to a more abstract level.

Glaser believes that a researcher should approach the research area with no predefined problem. The problem will emerge from the area to be investigated. Through analysis of the data a grounded theory will emerge, and the researcher must be patient and trust that to occur. Only codes that are relevant should emerge and theoretical sampling is a continuing guide to data collection. Once the core variable has been identified then writing commences. A grounded theory study should be evaluated on whether it fits, works and is relevant to the area being studied.

By contrast Strauss and Corbin advocate that a research question should be formulated, even if very broad, at the beginning of the study. They suggest coding to be undertaken at three levels although they acknowledge that axial and open coding may be done simultaneously. Theoretical sampling, memos and diagrams are tailored to each of the levels of coding. An essential feature of any grounded theory analysis is to capture process.

In summary, Strauss and Corbin have developed a more prescriptive approach than Glaser's more flexible approach. Yet, Strauss and Corbin's approach is easier for beginning researchers to follow and get started. However, once researchers have completed open (substantive) coding, Glaser's notions of grounded theory appear more suitable such that the essence of interpretive research, flexibility in data collection and interpretation, is not lost. This is because the paradigm model and the conditional matrix focus the attention of the researcher on specific issues. By contrast, Glaser relies on the process of sorting codes and advocates that researchers have faith in the techniques and the emergence of a theory through working with the data.

9. Application of Grounded Theory

Although grounded theory method was developed by sociologists, it has been used by researchers in many other disciplines, e.g. psychology, anthropology, education, social work and nursing. Strauss and Corbin (1994, p.275, pp.283-284) provide a list of grounded theory studies carried out by its originators and their students. Martin and Turner (1986, p. 144) explain how grounded theory has been applied to study a variety of issues and topics in organisational research, ranging from examinations of industrial organisations and cultures to hospital planning procedures to academic activities to corporate growth.[26]

It is likely to be intelligible to those in the situations observed, and gives those in the area studied a superior understanding of the nature of their own situation. If change is regarded as desirable and possible, the use of grounded theory to analyse the data directing the change will likely result in greater acceptance, compared with other approaches such as monitoring of the opinions of a few senior managers (Turner, 1983; Pasmore and Friedlander, 1982; Dunn and Swierczok, 1977). Dunn and Swierczok (1977) point out that:

> The application of grounded theories promises to contribute to improvements in the degree to which findings (i) reflect conditions actually present in particular change efforts (**internal validity**); (ii) typify conditions actually present in other change

---

[26] Refer Turner (1971), Reeves and Turner (1972), Riley and Sermsri (1974), Conrad (1978), Johnson (1981), Dunn and Swierczek (1977), Blum (1982), Rothschild-Whitt (1979), Martin (1984), Hawker (1982).

*efforts (**external validity**); (iii) contribute to the generation of new concepts by constantly comparing information obtained by different methods (**reflexivity**); and (iv) promote understanding among groups with conflicting frames of reference, including change agents, change sponsors, and change targets (**translatability**)* (p. 137).

Dunn and Swierczok (1977) also make the point that grounded theory means continuous efforts to relate existing concepts, methods, and practices such that 'experience' in its widest sense becomes available for public discussion. Grounded theories can also be relevant and possibly influential either to the 'understanding' of policy makers or to their direct action (Strauss and Corbin, 1994, p. 280).

In anticipating what the future might hold for grounded theory, Strauss and Corbin (1994) identify the following social and intellectual trends that are likely to be influencing factors:

1. the continued fragmentation of traditional social and behavioural science disciplines into subdisciplines, each with its currently distinctive issues, types of data, and often specific research procedures;
2. an increasing interest in and the presumed necessity for social research within various professions and their subunits, and directed toward an increasing or at least changing set of issues;
3. a continued reliance on qualitative methods alone or in conjunction with quantitative ones, by increasing numbers of professional and disciplinary researchers;
4. an increasing interest in theoretical interpretations of data, along with divergent definitions of theory believed to fit the nature of one's materials;
5. a continuation of the current trend of antagonism toward anything that goes by the name of science and especially toward its canons;
6. the spread of postmodernism, but a variegated spread, given that there are many and sometimes divergent direction within this general intellectual movement;
7. a continued trend toward the use of computer programs to order and interpret data, perhaps with visual and oral accomplishments;
8. in the world at large, probably a continued and even greater emphasis on individual and collective identity (nationalism, for instance), requiring improved methods for understanding the meanings and symbolization of actors (pp. 282-283).

It is interesting that the above trends are observable within accounting in varying degrees of intensity.

A knowledge of how accounting is socially constructed will increase our understanding of accounting in particular contexts (Hines, 1989). Grounded theory represents a suitable approach for handling large amounts of non-standard data generated by qualitative research in accounting, e.g. from participant observation, from observation of face-to-face interaction, from semi-structured or unstructured interviews, from case study material or from certain kinds of documentary sources. As Turner (1983) points out:

> *Qualitative social research can create severe problems of data handling and data analysis. It not only generates large amounts of data, but it generates data in a non-standard format which, in the nature of the research, can rarely be predicted in advance. It is not uncommon for researchers to find themselves overwhelmed by such large volume of data ... Grounded theory tackles some of these problems. It offers a way of attending in detail to qualitative material in order to develop systematically theories about the phenomena which have been observed.* (p. 333).

Given the comprehensive nature of its techniques and procedures, grounded theory is a valuable research approach available to accounting researchers in understanding the social construction of accounting, in particular, where the studies involve:

a. phenomena which are multi-faceted and about which little is known, e.g. the introduction of a requirement for each government department to prepare a set of financial statements using generally accepted accounting principles;

b. questions which involve dealing with social processes behind a phenomenon including the process of change, e.g. issues associated with a change in public sector accounting from a cash-based system to an accruals-based system;

c. questions which encompass a set of circumstances which cannot be explained in terms of existing theories, e.g. circumstances where the behaviour patterns of members of an organisation in relation to budget setting process appear to be different to what is assumed under existing theories;

d. questions which deal with the impact of new ideologies, e.g. the impact of the change of emphasis within the accounting profession from occupational control to product differentiation as a strategy to safeguard professional interest, upon professional activity;

e. questions which require investigating and working with organisational cultures, e.g. issues related to the effectiveness of management accounting systems within an organisation in motivating performance;

f. issues related to the values of the accounting sub-culture;

g. gender issues within the accounting profession, and

h. power issues associated with accounting standard setting, for example, the nature of power play in lobbying for/against proposed accounting standards (How is it manifested, by whom, when, where, how, with what effect?).

In the accounting literature, over the past three decades there has been a small but growing stream of studies that have employed the grounded theory approach to analyse qualitative data. Some of the papers quoting the originators of this research strategy are of a theoretical nature (see Tomkins and Groves, 1983, and Parker and Roffey, 1997). They highlight the potential of such an approach to contribute to the interpretive accounting literature and the intellectual pluralism of accounting research. Others have collected empirical evidence using the grounded theory research strategy to guide analysis of the data. For example, grounded theory methodology and methods have been used to investigate a variety of issues contributing to differing streams of the accounting literature. In the capital markets literature grounded theory studies have been undertaken to investigate corporate financial disclosure (Gibbons, Richardson and Waterhouse, 1990; Holland, 2005) and the market for information in relation to stock information flows (Barker, 1998). In the management accounting literature scholars have different motivations for adopting the grounded theory approach. Some examples of issues investigated are the dynamics of management control systems for strategic investment decisions (Slagmulder, 1997), examination of the use of information derived from the implementation of activity-based techniques (Norris, 2002), accountability and budgetary practices of local government entities (Goddard, 2004) and the process of change from cash accounting to accrual accounting in the public sector (Lye, Perera and Rahman, 2005). In addition to these studies, within the management accounting literature there is a subset of studies that has investigated accounting practices in religious organisations (Lightbody, 2000; Parker, 2001, 2002). In the auditing literature, Beattie, Fearnley and Brandt (2004) examine the process of negotiation between auditors and directors because they felt that the existing literature was under-theorised in terms of capturing the complexity of the auditor client relationship. Finally, in the accounting education literature, Stevenson-Smith (2004) used grounded theory procedures and techniques to develop a theory of assessment consequences in US accounting programmes.

Three primary motivations for adopting grounded theory can be identified. First, is to understand 'what is going on' from participants to capture their experience of a phenomenon under investigation (for example, see Gibbons et al., 1990; Barker, 1998; Holland, 2005; Lye et al., 2005). Second, the grounded theory approach is useful where existing theories fail to explain a set of circumstances (for example, see Slagmulder, 1997; Beattie et al., 2004; Goddard, 2004). Third, the research questions which involve dealing with social processes behind a phenomenon in an in-depth manner (for example, see Lightbody, 2000; Parker, 2001, 2002).

The role of theory in a grounded theory study has already been explained in the fourth section. From the analysis of studies using the grounded theory approach, it is observable that there are a number of differing ways in which the literature has been incorporated into a study. Most studies conduct a literature review broadly to define the research issue by highlighting shortcomings in the existing literature to be investigated, justify why research should be grounded in practice and the selection of the grounded theory approach. Most studies have related the findings of the substantive grounded theory back to existing literature. For example, Lye et al. (2005) and Holland (2005) in addition to using the literature to define the problem and justify the use of grounded theory, segment the grounded theory framework developed from participants and relate the findings to the relevant literature, and then link the overall grounded theory derived from the findings to the extant literature noting the contribution and differences of the derived grounded theory to existing theories. In another study, Goddard (2004) developed his grounded theory findings further by using Bourdieu's concept of 'habitus', 'a system of durable, transposable dispositions which functions as the generative basis of structured, objectively unified practices' and which 'produces individual and collective practices' (Bourdieu, 1990, p. 13, quoted in Goddard, 2004, p. 563). Finally, in contrast to most studies, Covaleski, Dirsmith, Heian and Samuel (1998) use Foucaldian methodology to probe the exercise of professional control in Big Six public accounting firms, which permeates every stage of the research process. In this study, grounded theory was an adjunct technique to the research investigation.

Finally, it can be observed from the accounting literature that the style of grounded theory methodology adopted by scholars varies. By way of illustration, some authors such as Gibbons et al. (1990) and Barker (1998) rely on the work of Glaser and Strauss (1967) and Glaser (1978). By contrast, other scholars such as Lightbody (2000) and Goddard (2004) rely on the works of Strauss and Corbin (1990, 1998). Yet another group of scholars, such as Parker (2001, 2002) and Lye et al. (2005) use a hybrid approach to their grounded theory studies. These observations reflect the intentions of the originators of grounded theory in that grounded theory is a 'general methodology for generating theory' (Glaser, 1978) that employs the same basic procedures for developing substantive theories. To a certain extent, the adoption of Glaser and Strauss (1967) and Glaser (1978) or Strauss and Corbin (1990, 1998) also depended on when the studies were commissioned. Earlier studies relied on Glaser and Strauss (1967) and Glaser (1978), whereas, the later ones relied on Strauss and Corbin (1990, 1998). However, level of complexity or desire to have more specificity in the methods may also dictate the approach chosen. For example, Lye et al. (2005) required a hybrid approach due to the broad public sector setting of accounting and an accounting change that was a construct linked to many aspects of this broad setting. They also attempted to capture the dynamism of their research setting. Eventually, what is important is that the researchers adopt a procedure that validates their assessments within the context of their research setting.

Goddard (2004) refers to the design of a 'formal' theory using Grounded Theory method. We believe that there is not enough accumulated knowledge from any of the grounded theory studies captured in our analysis to suggest they develop formal theories. They are all 'substantive' theories. They explain what happened in a particular context and in that sense each substantive theory 'fits', 'works' and is 'relevant' to its context. Glaser (1978) calls such studies 'little islands of knowledge' (p. 148). He argues for 'formal theory', but it is unclear about which is the best way to go about creating such theories. Glaser (1978, Chapter 9) discusses formal theory and states in a note to the chapter that the future of the development of grounded formal theory requires a book devoted to its methodology, 'after much more experience is gained' (p. 142, original emphasis). He also refers to strategies and problems associated with formal theory.

10. Summary and Conclusion

The grounded theory method is an interpretive/naturalistic research strategy, characterised by concurrent collection, coding and analysis of data. Several procedures and techniques critical to the method permeate this process such as: coding, theoretical sampling, constant comparative method, memo writing and sorting. The process that results in the emerging theory continues until saturation of theoretical conceptualisations is achieved, that is, control is exercised when the information received from participants is repetitive and no new themes emerge. Through sorting, an integrated theoretical framework will emerge that fits the data.

The distinguishing feature of grounded theory lies not in the mode of investigation associated with it, but in the manner in which the information collected is analysed. As Turner (1983) explains, 'For this analysis to proceed, the researcher must develop a facility for discerning abstractions in the material collected and for processing these abstractions at several levels of generality. It is also important to foster an ability to use what we might call a "creative theoretical imagination"' (p. 335).

The Grounded Theory method, as described in this paper, lays out some basic tenets of how this interpretive/naturalistic approach can be adopted to provide plausible interpretations to complex circumstances which comprise accounting phenomena. One point to note is that there are no procedures drawn yet that guide the development of formal theories from a set of grounded theories. Perhaps it is the inherent nature of this methodology to appreciate various insights of the phenomenon being researched. It should also be noted that the grounded theory method is an extremely demanding research method, yet if the procedures and techniques of the method are followed this will lead to rich insights and excellent qualitative studies emerging in the accounting literature in the future.

Appendix 1
Analysis of Grounded Theory by Strauss & Corbin (1990) and Glaser (1992)

	Chapter	Issue	Strauss & Corbin (1990)	Glaser (1992)
2/4	Getting Started	How does a researcher get started in a grounded theory study?	A research question should be formulated, even if very broad, at the beginning of the study.	The researcher should move into the area to be investigated with 'no problem' (22) and the problem will emerge from the area to be investigated.
3/5	Theoretical Sensitivity	What personal attributes of the researcher are required?	A researcher brings two sources of theoretical sensitivity to the study. First background experience that the researcher brings to the situation (professional, experiential and knowledge of the literature). Second, analytical skills and insights developed whilst conducting a grounded theory study.	Personal attributes required of the researcher include conceptual acumen, understanding and be able to give meaning to the data.
4/6	The Uses of the Literature	When do you integrate the literature with the findings?	The researcher should have some knowledge of the literature before entering the field. However, it is only after a category has emerged that the technical literature should be referred to in depth.	The literature should be reviewed and integrated *only* after the emergent theory is sufficiently developed.
5/7	Open Coding	How does the researcher develop codes to succinctly capture the meaning of the words in the data?	Researcher required to reduce data to conceptual labels by analysis on some basis (e.g. a line by line basis; sentence by sentence basis; or paragraph by paragraph) by using the techniques of comparative analysis and asking questions of	Through use of the constant comparative method derive a set of relevant categories linked by theoretical codes to develop an integrated theory. Two primary sources of codes are sociological constructs and in vivo codes.

Chapter		Issue	Strauss & Corbin (1990)	Glaser (1992)
			the data.	
6/8	Techniques for Enhancing Theoretical Sensitivity	What techniques are used to aid discovery?	The authors suggest the use of questioning and other techniques to stimulate theoretical sensitivity to aid in understanding the data.	Only the constant comparative method (used within the data) and four neutral questions are needed to develop theory from the data.
7/9	Axial Coding	How does the researcher derive theory from data collected?	Each category developed must be related to the paradigm model. Under this model causal conditions, context, intervening conditions, action/interaction, and consequences are related to the central phenomenon under investigation.	Grounded theory should emerge from the data and the analyst must be patient and trust that to occur.
8/10	Selective Coding	How is the core category discovered?	The authors outline five integrating procedures to be used in developing a conceptually integrated grounded theory.	Theory will emerge from the data, and the core category will emerge – 'it is automatic' (77).
9/11	Process	Is process a fundamental element or only relevant if it emerges?	The researcher should be aware and capture process in a grounded theory analysis.	Process is a theoretical code that will emerge if relevant.
10/12	The Conditional Matrix	Is the conditional matrix an analytical tool or only relevant if it emerges?	An analytical tool for linking factors at various levels directly to a phenomenon, particularly conditions and consequences.	Codes should be discovered from the data and what is relevant should emerge.
11/13	Theoretical Sampling	How does the researcher use theoretical sampling?	For each level of coding (open, axial and selective) there is a relevant approach to sampling that has a specific purpose.	Theoretical sampling is a continuing guide to data collection.

Chapter	Issue	Strauss & Corbin (1990)	Glaser (1992)
		Theoretical sampling continues until saturation of categories has occurred.	
12/14 Memos and Diagrams	Memos capture ideas that occur to the researcher. Does the content of memos change during the research process?	For each level of coding the authors point to the differing purpose of memos and diagrams.	As the emergent theory unfolds, the memos will change, reflecting the enhanced theoretical sensitivity of the researcher.
13/15 Writing	When does the researcher commence writing?	This chapter gives useful suggestions regarding writing in response to a series of questions anticipated by the authors.	Writing commences when the sorting is completed and an integrated theory with a core variable has been identified.
14/16 Criteria for Judging a Grounded Theory Study	What criteria are used to judge a grounded theory study?	The authors list seven criteria in question format that might need to be modified, depending upon the research project.	Assessment of grounded theory studies is achieved when the grounded theory has fit, work, relevance, modifiability, parsimony, and the scope in explanatory power.

Acknowledgements

The authors are grateful to participants at the following conferences – 20th European Accounting Association conference, Graz, 1997 and University of Waikato Forum, Beyond Accounting, Finance and Management, 1995 and staff seminar participants of the Departments of Accountancy and Sociology of Massey University. We also wish to thank Pekka Pihlanto, Kari Lukka and Markus Granlund from the Turku School of Economics and Business Administration, for their useful comments on earlier drafts of this chapter and appreciation to anonymous reviewers.

References

Abdel-Khalik, A. R. and Ajinkya, B. B. (1979), "Empirical research in accounting: a methodological viewpoint", *Accounting Education Series*, 4, American Accounting Association.

Arrington, C. E. and Francis, J. R. (1989), "Letting the chat out of the bag: deconstruction, privilege and accounting research", *Accounting, Organizations and Society*, pp. 1-28.

Baker, C., Wuest, J. and Stern, P.N. (1992), "Method slurring: the grounded theory/phenomenology example", *Journal of Advanced Nursing*, Vol. 17, pp. 1355-1360.

Barker, R. G. (1998), "The market for information – evidence from finance directors, analysts and fund managers", Vol. 29, No. 1, pp. 3-20.

Beattie, V, Fearnley, S. and Brandt, R. (2004), "A grounded theory model of auditor-client negotiations", *International Journal of Auditing*, Vol. 8, pp. 1-19.

Blum, D. B. (1982), *Life Span Changes in an Alternative Social Movement Organization: The Case of Anti-Nuclear Alliance*. Unpublished doctoral dissertation, Florida State University, Tallahassee.

Blumer, H. (1969), *Symbolic Interactionism: Perspective and Method*, Prentice Hall, Inc., Englewood Cliffs, New Jersey.

Boland, R. J. Jr. (1993), "Accounting and the Interpretive Act", *Accounting, Organizations and Society*, pp. 125-146.

Broadbent, J. and Guthrie, J. (1992), "Changes in the public sector: a review of recent 'alternative' accounting research", *Accounting, Auditing & Accountability Journal*, Vol. 5, No. 2, pp. 3-31.

Burchell, S., Clubb, C., Hopwood, A. G., Hughes, J. and Nahapiet, J. (1980), "The roles of accounting in organizations and society", *Accounting, Organizations and Society*, pp. 5-27.

Burrell, G. and Morgan, G. (1979), *Sociological Paradigms and Organisational Analysis*, Heinemann, London, pp. 21-37.

Charmaz, K. (1983), "The grounded theory method: an explication and interpretation", in Emerson, R. (Ed.), *Contemporary Field Research*, Little, Brown, Boston pp. 109-126.

Charmaz, K. (1990), "'Discovering' chronic illness: using grounded theory", *Sociology of Health and Illness*, Vol. 30, pp. 1161-1172.

Chenitz, W. C. and Swanson, J. M. (1986), *From Practice to Grounded Theory*, Addison-Wesley Publishing Company, Inc., Menlo Park, California.

Chua, W. F. (1986), "Radical developments in accounting thought", *The Accounting Review*, Vol. LXI, No. 4, p. 601, pp. 601-627.

Chua, W. F. (1986b), "Theoretical constructions of and by the real", *Accounting, Organizations and Society*, pp. 583-598.

Chua, W. F. (1988), "Interpretive sociology and management accounting research – a critical review", *Accounting, Auditing & Accountability Journal*, pp. 59-79.

Conrad, C. F. (1978), "A grounded theory of academic change", *Sociology of Education*, Vol. 51, pp. 101-112.

Cooper, D. J. (1980), "Discussion of 'Towards a political economy of accounting'", *Accounting, Organisations and Society*, pp. 269-286.

Corbin, J. and Strauss, A. (1988), *Unending Work and Care: Managing Chronic Illness at Home*, Josses-Bass, San Francisco.

Corbin, J. and Strauss, A. (1990), "Grounded theory method: procedures, canons, and evaluative criteria", *Qualitative Sociology*, Vol. 13, pp. 3-21.

Covaleski, M. A. and Dirsmith, M. W. (1990), "Dialectic tension, double reflexivity and the everyday accounting researcher: on using qualitative methods", *Accounting, Organizations and Society*, Vol. 15, No. 6, pp. 543-573.

Covaleski, M. A., Dirsmith, M. W., Heian, J. B., and Samuel, S. (1998), "The calculated and the avowed: techniques of discipline and struggles over identity in big six public accounting firms", *Administrative Science Quarterly*, Vol. 43, pp. 293-327.

Denzin, N. K. (1970), *The Research Act: A Theoretical Introduction to Sociological Methods*, Aldine, Chicago.

Dirsmith, M. W., Covaleski, M. A. and McAllister, J. (1985), "Of paradigms and metaphors in auditing thought", *Contemporary Accounting Research*, pp. 46-68.

Dunn, W. N. and Swierczok, F. W. (1977), "Planned organizational change: toward grounded theory", *Journal of Applied Behavioural Science*, Vol. 13, pp. 135-157.

Einhorn, H. J. and Hogarth R. M. (1986), "Decision making under ambiguity", *Journal of Business*, Vol. 59, Vol. 4, Pt. 2, pp. 225-250.

Extern, H. (1975), "Case study and theory in political science", in Green Stein, F.I. and Palsy, N.W. (Ed.), *Handbook of Political Science, 7, Strategies of Inquiry*, Addison-Wesley, pp. 79-137.

Ferreira, L. D. and Merchant, K. A. (1992), "Field research in management accounting and control: A review and evaluation", *Accounting, Auditing & Accountability Journal*, Vol. 5, No. 4, pp. 3-34.

Gibbons, M., Richardson, A. and Waterhouse, J. (1990), *Journal of Accounting Research*, Vol. 28, No. 1, pp. 121-143.

Glaser, B. G. and Strauss, A. L. (1965a), *Awareness of Dying*, Aldine, Chicago.

Glaser, B. G. and Strauss, A. L. (1965b), "Temporal aspects of dying as a non-scheduled status package", *American Journal of Sociology*, Vol. 71, pp. 48-59.

Glaser, B. G. and Strauss, A. L. (1967), *and The Discovery of Grounded Theory: Strategies for Qualitative Research*, Aldine Publishing Company, Aldine, New York.

Glaser, B. G. and Strauss, A. L. (1968), *Time for Dying*, Aldine, Chicago.

Glaser, B. G. and Strauss, A. L. (1970), *Status Passages*, Aldine, Chicago.

Glaser, B. G. (1972), *Experts Versus Laymen: A Study of the Patsy and the Subcontractor*, Transaction, New Brunswick, New Jersey.

Glaser, B. G. (1978), *Advances in the Methodology of Grounded Theory: Theoretical Sensitivity*, The Sociology Press, Mill Valley, California.

Glaser, B. G. (1992), *Basics of Grounded Theory Analysis*, The Sociology Press, Mill Valley, California.

Goddard, A. (2004), "Budgetary practices and accountability habitus – a grounded theory", *Accounting, Auditing & Accountability Journal*, Vol. 17, No. 4, pp. 543-577.

Goulding, C. (2002), *Grounded Theory: A Practical Guide for Management, Business and Market Researchers*, SAGE Publications Ltd, London.

Guba, E. G. and Lincoln, Y. S. (1981), *Effective Evaluation*, Jossey-Bass Limited, San Francisco.

Hawker, R. (1982), *The Interaction Between Nurses and Patients' Relatives*, Unpublished doctoral dissertation, University of Exeter, Exeter.

Hines, R. D. (1989), "The sociopolitical paradigm in financial accounting research", *Accounting, Auditing & Accountability Journal*, Vol. 2, No. 1, pp. 52-76.

Hogarth R. M. and Reder, M. W. (1986), "Editors' comments: perspectives from economics and psychology", *Journal of Business*, Vol. 59, No. 4, Pt. 2, pp.185-207.

Holland, J. (2005), "A grounded theory of corporate disclosure", *Accounting and Business Research*, Vol. 35, No. 3, pp. 249-267.

Hopper, T., Annisette, M. A., Dastoor, N., Uddin, S. N. N. and Wickramasinghe, D. P. (1995), "Some challenges and alternatives to positive accounting research (Introduction to Chapter Five)", in Jones, S., Romano, C. and Ratnatunga, J. (Eds.), *Accounting Theory: A Contemporary Review*, Harcourt Brace, Sydney, pp. 517-550.

Hopper, T., Storey, T. and Willmott, H. (1987), "Accounting for accounting: towards the development of a dialectical view" *Accounting, Organizations and Society*, Vol. 12, No. 5, pp. 437-456.

Hopwood, A. G. (1990), "Accounting and organisation change", *Accounting, Auditing & Accountability Journal*, Vol. 3, No. 1, pp. 7-17.

Hopwood, A. G. (1994), "Accounting and everyday life: an introduction", *Accounting, Organizations and Society*, Vol. 19, No. 3, pp. 299-301.

Johnson, G. (1981), *The Application of Grounded Theory to a Study of Corporate Growth*, Working Paper - 212, University of Aston Management Centre, Birmingham.

Kaplan, R. S. (1983), "Measuring manufacturing performance: a new challenge for managerial accounting research", *The Accounting Review*, pp. 686-705.

Kaplan, R. S. (1984), "The evolution of management accounting", *The Accounting Review*, pp. 390-418.

Kaplan, R. S. (1986), "The role for empirical research in management accounting", *Accounting, Organizations and Society*, pp. 429-452.

Keating, P. J. (1995), "A framework for classifying and evaluating the theoretical contributions of case research in management accounting", *Journal of Management Accounting Research*, Vol. 7, Fall, pp. 67-86.

Laughlin, R. (1995), "Methodological themes: empirical research in accounting: alternative approaches and a case for 'middle-range' thinking", *Accounting, Auditing & Accountability Journal*, Vol. 8, No. 1, pp. 63-87.

Lightbody, M. (2000), "Storing and shielding: financial management behaviour in a church organization", *Accounting, Auditing & Accountability Journal*, Vol. 13, No. 4, pp. 418-560.

Lye, J., Perera, H. and Rahman, A. (2005), "The evolution of accruals-based Crown (government) financial statements in New Zealand", *Accounting, Auditing & Accountability Journal*, Vol. 18, No. 6, pp. 784-815.

Macintosh, N. B. and Scapens, R. (1990), "Structuration theory in management accounting", *Accounting, Organizations and Society*, pp. 455-477.

Martin, P. Y. and Turner, B. A. (1986), "Grounded theory and organizational research", *The Journal of Applied Behavioural Science*, Vol. 22, No. 2, pp. 141-157.

Martin, P. Y. (1984), "Trade unions, conflict, and the nature of work in residential service organizations", *Organization Studies*, Vol. 5, pp. 169-185.

McKinnon, J. (1988), "Reliability and validity in field research: Some strategies and tactics", *Accounting, Auditing & Accountability Journal*, Vol. 1, No. 1, pp. 34-54.

Mead, G. H. (1934), *Mind, Self and Society*, The University of Chicago Press, Chicago, Illinois.

Morgan, G. and Smircich, L. (1980), "The case for qualitative research", *Academy of Management Review*, Vol. 5, No. 4, pp. 491-500.

Muhr, T. (1992), *ATLAS/ti User Manual: Beta Version 0.94c*, Berlin Technical University, Berlin.

Norris, G. (2002), "Chalk and cheese: grounded theory case studies of the introduction and usage of activity-based information in two British banks", *British Accounting Review*, Vol. 34, pp. 223-255.

Parker, L. D. (1994), "The case for field studies in management accounting: towards informed policy and practice in Asia", *Accounting and Business Review*, Vol. 1, No. 2, pp. 211-231.

Parker, L. D. (2001), "Reactive planning in a Christian bureaucracy", *Management Accounting Research*, Vol. 12, pp. 321-356.

Parker, L. D. (2002), "Budgetary incrementalism in a Christian bureaucracy", *Management Accounting Research*, Vol. 13, pp. 71-100.

Parker, L. D. and Roffey, B. H. (1997), "Back to the drawing board: revisiting grounded theory and the everyday accountant's and manager's reality", *Accounting, Auditing & Accountability Journal*, Vol. 10, No. 2, pp. 212-247.

Pasmore, W. and Friedlander, F. (1982), "An action-research program for increasing employee involvement in problem solving", *Administrative Science Quarterly*, Vol. 27, pp. 343-362.

Patton, M. Q. (1990), *Qualitative Evaluation and Research Methods*, 2nd edition, Sage Publications Inc., Newbury Park, California.

Perera, M. H. B. (1994), "Culture and international accounting: some thoughts on research issues and prospects", *Advances in International Accounting*, Vol. 7, pp. 267-285.

Reeves, T. K. and Turner, B. A. (1972), "A theory of organization in batch production factories", *Administrative Science Quarterly*, Vol. 17, pp. 81-98.

Richards, T., Richards, L., McGalliard, J. and Sharrock, B. (1992), *NUD*IST 2.3: Users Manual*, Replee Pty/La Trobe University, La Trobe, Australia.

Riley, J. N. and Sermsri, S. (1974), *The Variegated Thai Medical System as a Context for Birth Control Services*, Working Paper, No.6, Bangkok: Institute for Population and Social Research, Mahidol University.

Rothschild-Whitt, J. (1979), "The collectivist organization: an alternative to rational bureaucratic models", *American Sociological Review*, Vol. 44, pp. 509-527.

Sandelowski, M. (1986), "The problem of rigor in qualitative research", *Advances in Nursing Science*, April, pp. 27-37.

Scapens, R.W. (1990), "Researching management accounting practice: the role of case study methods", *British Accounting Review*, Vol. 22, pp. 259-281.

Slagmulder, R. (1997), "Using management control systems to achieve alignment between strategic investment decisions and strategy", *Management Accounting Research*, Vol. 8, pp. 103-139.

Stevenson-Smith, G. (2004), "Assessment strategies: what is being measured in student course evaluations?", *Accounting Education*, Vol. 13, No. 1, pp. 3-28.

Strauss, A. (1978), *Negotiations: Varieties, Contexts Processes and Social Order*, Jossey-Bass, San Francisco.

Strauss, A. (1987), *Qualitative Analysis for Social Scientists*, Cambridge University Press, New York.

Strauss, A. (1991), *Creating Sociological Awareness*, Transaction, New Brunswick, New Jersey.

Strauss, A. and Corbin, J. (1990), *Basics of Qualitative Research: Grounded Theory Procedures and Techniques*, Sage Publications Ltd, Newbury Park, California.

Strauss, A. and Corbin, J. (1994), "Grounded theory methodology: an overview", in Denzin, N. K. and Lincoln, Y. S. (Eds.), *Handbook of Qualitative Research*, Sage Publications Ltd, Thousand Oaks, California.

Strauss, A. and Corbin, J. (1998), *Basics of Qualitative Research: Techniques and Procedures for Developing Grounded Theory*, Sage Publications Ltd, Thousand Oaks, California.

Strauss, A., Bucher, R., Ehelich, D., Sabshin, M. and Schatzman, L. (1964), *Psychiatric Ideologies and Institutions*, Free Press, New York.

Strauss, A., Bucher, R., Ehelich, D., Sabshin, M. and Schatzman, L. (1963), "The hospital and its negotiated order", in Freidson, E. (Ed.), *The Hospital in Modern Society*, Free Press, New York, pp. 147-169.

Tinker, A. M. (1980), "Towards a political economy of accounting: an empirical illustration of the Cambridge controversies", *Accounting, Organizations and Society*, Vol. 147, pp. 147-160.

Tomkins, C. and Groves, R. (1983), "The everyday accountant and researching his reality", *Accounting, Organizations and Society*, Vol. 8, No. 4, pp. 361-374.

Turner, B. A. (1971), *Exploring the Industrial Sub-Culture*, Macmillan, London.

Turner, B. A. (1983), "The use of grounded theory for the qualitative analysis of organisational behaviour", *Journal of Management Studies*, Vol. 20, pp. 333-348.

Walton, J. A. (1989), *The Night Time Experience of Elderly Hospitalised Adults and the Nurse who care for them*. unpublished manuscript, Massey University, Palmerston North.

9

LEGITIMACY THEORY

Craig Deegan
RMIT University, Australia

Abstract: Legitimacy theory is theory that, in the last decade, has become increasingly used by accounting researchers, particularly researchers working in the area of social and environmental accounting. This chapter explores the notion of 'organisational legitimacy' and emphasises that organisational legitimacy can be considered as a resource upon which many organisations are dependent for their survival. The fundamentals of legitimacy theory, together with an overview of some of its limitations are presented. The chapter emphasises that legitimacy theory is derived from political economy theory and therefore accepts that an organisation is part of a broader social system – a system in which the organisation both impacts, and is impacted by, the society in which it operates. The central concept of a 'social contract' is explored, and an overview is provided of the strategies that organisations can adopt to attain and retain a state of legitimacy. Central to these strategies is the role of corporate disclosure. Examples of empirical research that has adopted legitimacy theory are provided.

Keywords: legitimacy; legitimation; social contract; community expectations; corporate disclosure.

1.   Introduction and Overview

This chapter provides an overview of legitimacy theory – a theory that, in recent years, has increasingly been embraced by researchers, particularly researchers working within the broad area of social and environmental accounting. It is a theory which has broad application to various corporate strategies, particularly strategies that involve the public disclosure of information about an organisation. For example, the theory has been used to explain voluntary disclosures that are made within corporate annual reports or other stand-alone reports such as corporate sustainability reports. As this chapter will demonstrate, legitimacy theory is a theory that gives explicit consideration to the expectations of society (as embodied in what we will refer to as the 'social contract' between the organisation and the society with which it interacts), and whether an organisation appears to be complying with the expectations of the societies within which it operates. As we will explain, a failure to comply with community expectations can, pursuant to legitimacy theory, be predicted to have implications for the ongoing survival of an organisation. Where organisational legitimacy is threatened, evidence indicates that the strategic disclosure of information is one strategy organisations often use in an effort to re-establish organisational legitimacy.

The chapter will explore a number of issues. We will start by considering the nature of 'organisational legitimacy' – that is, what is it? As we will explain, organisation legitimacy can be considered as a 'resource' upon which an organisation can be dependent for its survival. Having considered 'organisation legitimacy' we will then describe the basics of legitimacy theory. As we will explain, legitimacy theory is a *positive theory* which explicitly considers the organisation as part of the broader social system. We will also see that Legitimacy Theory is a theory that has a degree of overlap with a number of other theories, notably stakeholder theory and institutional theory.

Central to legitimacy theory is the notion of a 'social contract'. The following section of this chapter will describe the 'social contract' and will show that the social contract is a concept which has been referred to by various philosophers over hundreds of years.

We will then consider which members of society might confer 'legitimacy' upon an organisation and we will also consider whether all organisations need legitimacy. Discussion will then be provided about what strategies organisations might adopt when their legitimacy is threatened. The penultimate section of this chapter will provide an overview of some empirical studies that have applied legitimacy theory to explain corporate disclosure strategies, and the final section will provide some concluding comments.

To date a number of commentaries of legitimacy theory have been published. The material appearing in this chapter relies in large part on material appearing in Deegan (2002), Deegan (2005), Deegan and Unerman (2006) and Deegan (2006).

2.   What is Organisational Legitimacy?

We cannot discuss legitimacy theory without first explaining what organisational legitimacy is. From an organisation's perspective, *legitimacy* has been defined by Lindblom (1994, p. 2) as:

> *a condition or status which exists when an entity's value system is congruent with the value system of the larger social system of which the entity is a part. When a disparity, actual or potential, exists between the two value systems, there is a threat to the entity's legitimacy.*

Legitimacy is time and place dependent. As Suchman (1995, p. 574) states:

> *Legitimacy is a generalised perception or assumption that the actions of an entity are desirable, proper, or appropriate within some socially constructed system of norms, values, beliefs, and definitions.*

Consistent with the above definitions, what might be considered legitimate at one point in time might not be considered legitimate at a future point in time because of changing community attitudes. As an example, within Australia approximately 30 years ago there were many retail stores that sold clothes that were made from the fur of animals. With changing community attitudes towards the wearing of animal skins, and in particular, the treatment of animals from which the furs and skins were sourced, the demand for fur coats with Australia declined. Much of the changing community attitudes were driven by various media campaigns run by animal welfare organisations. Many stores closed because of changing community attitudes and the resultant lack of demand for their goods. Legitimacy is also 'place dependent' such that what might be construed as appropriate business practices in one society (for example, within one country) might not be acceptable in another. Hence, we need to be careful when discussing 'legitimate behaviour' and 'legitimacy'. It can only be understood within the context of the particular time and the particular place.

As community expectations change, legitimacy theory would suggest that organisations must also adapt and change or else their survival will be threatened. Their survival would be threatened because, pursuant to legitimacy theory, if a community questions the legitimacy of an organisation then that organisation will in turn have difficulty attracting capital, employees, customers, and so forth. An effective manager would be one that is able to anticipate changing community expectations and preferences. In relation to the dynamics associated with changing expectations, Lindblom (1994, p. 3) states:

Legitimacy is dynamic in that the relevant publics continuously evaluate corporate output, methods, and goals against an ever evolving expectation. The legitimacy gap will fluctuate without any changes in action on the part of the corporation. Indeed, as expectations of the relevant publics change the corporation must make changes or the legitimacy gap will grow as the level of conflict increases and the levels of positive and passive support decreases.

The term 'legitimacy gap' – as used in the above quote – is a term that has been utilised by many researchers to describe the situation where there appears to be a lack of correspondence (or a 'gap') between how society believes an organisation *should* act and how it is *perceived* that the organisation has acted (remember, it is perceptions of behaviour that are important in creating legitimacy). In relation to how legitimacy gaps arise, Sethi (1978) describes two major sources of the gaps. Firstly, societal expectations might change, and this will lead to a gap arising even though the organisation is operating in the same manner as it always had. The second major source of a legitimacy gap, according to Sethi (1978), occurs when previously unknown information becomes known about the organisation – perhaps through disclosure being made within the news media. For many issues, it is believed that the media can be extremely influential in forming or shaping the opinions of the public. In relation to the release of previously unknown information about an organisation, Nasi *et al.* (1997, p. 301) make an interesting reference to "organisational shadows". They state:

> *The potential body of information about the corporation that is unavailable to the public – the corporate shadow (Bowles, 1991) – stands as a constant potential threat to a corporation's legitimacy. When part of the organisational shadow is revealed, either accidentally or through the activities of an activist group or a journalist, a legitimacy gap may be created.*

Consistent with what has already been discussed, legitimacy itself can be threatened even when an organisation's performance is not deviating from society's expectations. This might be because the organisation has failed to make disclosures that show it is complying with society's expectations, which in themselves, might be changing across time. That is, legitimacy is assumed to be influenced by disclosures of information, and not simply by (undisclosed) changes in corporate actions. If society's expectations about performance change, then an organisation will need to show that what it is doing is also changing (or perhaps it will need to explicitly communicate and justify why its operations have *not* changed). Legitimising disclosures will vary, depending upon the expectations of the respective communities involved. These expectations will change, and hence it would be anticipated that the organisation's disclosures will also change across time. These disclosures might be responsive (changing as community expectations change) or they might be made in an attempt to shape or change community expectations.

Whilst there are many published studies that support a view that particular disclosures will be made by organisations to enhance their legitimacy – particularly at the time of a social or environmental crisis (for example, Patten, 1992; Deegan *et al.*, 2002) – there is a general lack of research evidence that investigates whether the disclosures *actually* work in terms of changing the perceived legitimacy of the organisation. That is, there is a great deal of research which looks for a disclosure reaction around the time of legitimacy threatening events but there is a general lack of evidence about how effective particular forms of disclosure are in terms of assisting an organisation to gain, maintain or restore corporate legitimacy. That is, do the disclosures actually work in terms of doing what they are intended to do (bolster the legitimacy of the organisation)? This is clearly an area for future research.

Returning to the 'legitimacy gap' discussed above, O'Donovan (2002) provides a useful depiction of the legitimacy gap. His depiction is reproduced in Figure 1 below. In explaining the diagram, O'Donovan states:

> *The area marked X [in Figure 1] represents congruence between corporate activity and society's expectations of the corporation and its activities, based on social values and norms. Areas Y and Z represent incongruence between a corporation's actions and society's perceptions of what these actions should be. These areas represent "illegitimacy" or legitimacy gaps (Sethi, 1978). The aim of the corporation is to be legitimate, to ensure area X is as large as possible, thereby reducing the legitimacy*

gap. A number of legitimation tactics and disclosure approaches may be adopted to reduce the legitimacy gap.

Figure 1
Issues/Events and Corporate Legitimacy

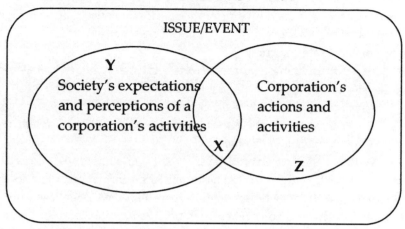

The Figure provided above is clearly quite simplistic, but this in a sense reflects the nature of the theory. For example, the theory has not developed to a degree that allows us to provide any measure or metric of the 'legitimacy gap' nor to provide any guidance about how significant a 'legitimacy gap' must be before an organisation's survival is threatened. Nevertheless, it is still argued by many researchers (see Deegan, 2002) that regardless of the apparent simplicity of the theory it does provide useful explanations of corporate disclosure behaviour.

Following on from the above discussion, organisational legitimacy is considered to be a resource upon which an entity relies for its survival. Because legitimacy is based on community perceptions of an organisation's operations, legitimacy is considered to be a resource that can be influenced (for example, gained, maintained or repaired) or manipulated by way of corporate disclosure practices. Again, for an organisation seeking to be legitimate it is not the *actual* conduct of the organisation which is important, it is what society collectively knows or *perceives* about the organisation's conduct that shapes legitimacy. As Suchman (1995, p. 574) states:

> *An organisation may diverge dramatically from societal norms yet retain legitimacy because the divergence goes unnoticed. Legitimacy is socially constructed in that it reflects a congruence between the behaviours of the legitimated entity and the shared (or assumed shared) beliefs of some social group; thus legitimacy is dependent on a collective audience, yet independent of particular observers.*

The concept of legitimacy – which we have now discussed in some depth – is central to legitimacy theory – but what 'sort' of theory is legitimacy theory. We will now consider this issue.

3.   What Sort of a Theory is Legitimacy Theory?

Theories are often described as either *positive theories* or *normative theories* (see Deegan, 2006 for a detailed explanation of the difference between normative and positive theories). Legitimacy theory is a *positive theory* as it seeks to describe or explain corporate behaviour (in terms of efforts made to appear legitimate), rather than prescribing how organisations should behave (which is the role of a normative theory of corporate conduct).

Apart from being a *positive theory*, legitimacy theory has also been described as a *systems-based theory*. According to Gray *et al.* (1996, p. 45):

> a systems-oriented view of the organisation and society ... permits us to focus on the role of information and disclosure in the relationship(s) between organisations, the State, individuals and groups.

Within a *systems-oriented perspective* (also sometimes referred to as an *open-systems perspective*), the entity is assumed to be influenced by, and in turn, to have influence upon the society in which it operates. A systems-based perspective can be contrasted with other theoretical perspectives which tend to be more 'closed' in orientation. For example, Positive Accounting Theory (Watts and Zimmerman, 1986) – which is another example of a positive theory – typically considers the relationships between only three groups, these being managers (agents), owners (principals), and debt holders, and it generally ignores other stakeholder groups.

Within a broader systems-oriented perspective, the perceptions of the organisation, as held by other parties within that social system, are of importance to the survival of the organisation. Commenting on the use of open-systems theorising Suchman (1995, p. 571) states:

> Open-system theories have reconceptualised organisational boundaries as porous and problematic, and institutional theories (Powell and DiMaggio, 1991) have stressed that many dynamics in the organisational environment stem not from technological or material imperatives, but rather, from cultural norms, symbols, beliefs and rituals. Corporate disclosure policies are considered to represent one important means by which management can influence external perceptions about their organisation. At the core of this intellectual transformation lies the concept of organisational legitimacy.

Legitimacy theory (which we have so far described as a positive, systems-based theory) originates from another theory, this being political economy theory. According to Deegan (2006):

> The 'political economy' itself has been defined by Gray et al. (1996, p. 47) as 'the social, political and economic framework within which human life takes place'. Political economy theory explicitly recognises the power conflicts that exist within society and the various struggles that occur between various groups within society. The perspective embraced in political economy theory, and also legitimacy theory, is that society, politics and economics are inseparable and economic issues cannot meaningfully be investigated in the absence of considerations about the political,

social and institutional framework in which the economic activity takes place. It is argued that by considering the political economy a researcher is better able to consider broader (societal) issues which impact how an organisation operates, and what information it elects to disclose.

Following on from the above point, Guthrie and Parker (1989) explain the relevance of accounting and related disclosures within a political economy perspective. They state (1989, p. 166):

The political economy perspective perceives accounting reports as social, political, and economic documents. They serve as a tool for constructing, sustaining, and legitimising economic and political arrangements, institutions, and ideological themes which contribute to the corporation's private interests. Disclosures have the capacity to transmit social, political, and economic meanings for a pluralistic set of report recipients.

Consistent with the view that organisations are part of a broader social system, the perspectives provided by legitimacy theory (which, as stated, build on foundations provided by political economy theory) indicate that organisations are not considered to have any inherent right to resources, or in fact, to exist. Organisations exist to the extent that the particular society considers that they are *legitimate*, and if this is the case, the society 'confers' upon the organisation the 'state' of *legitimacy*. Relying upon the concept of a 'social contract' – which we will describe shortly – Mathews (1993, p. 26) states:

The social contract would exist between corporations (usually limited companies) and individual members of society. Society (as a collection of individuals) provides corporations with their legal standing and attributes and the authority to own and use natural resources and to hire employees. Organisations draw on community resources and output both goods and services and waste products to the general environment. The organisation has no inherent rights to these benefits, and in order to allow their existence, society would expect the benefits to exceed the costs to society.

Whilst legitimacy theory is considered to derive from political economy theory, as we have indicated above, political economy theory itself has two broad branches. Legitimacy theory derives from one of these branches. As Deegan (2006) states:

Political Economy Theory has been divided (perhaps somewhat simplistically, but nevertheless usefully) into two broad streams which Gray, Owen and Adams (1996, p. 47) have labelled 'classical' and 'bourgeois' political economy. Classical political economy is related to the works of philosophers such as Karl Marx, and explicitly places 'sectional (class) interests, structural conflict, inequity, and the role of the State at the heart of the analysis' (Gray, et al., 1996, p. 47). This can be contrasted with 'bourgeois' political economy theory which, according to Gray, Kouhy and Lavers (1995, p. 53), largely ignores these elements and, as a result, is content to perceive the world as essentially pluralistic.

Classical political economy would tend to explain corporate disclosures as being a tool by which powerful individuals (perhaps those in control of capital) to maintain their own 'favoured' positions (through targeted information disclosures) to the detriment of those individuals without power. Classical political economy focuses on the structural conflicts within society. Researchers working within the critical perspective of accounting (see Deegan, 2006 for an overview of the critical perspective of accounting) – which is often informed by a Marxist perspective – often embrace the 'classical' branch of political economy theory.

By contrast, legitimacy theory – which is embedded in the 'bourgeois' branch of political economy theory – does not consider or question structural or class-based conflicts within society. It assumes that the views of a reasonably unified and pluralistic society shape the activities of organisations. A pluralistic perspective assumes that many classes of stakeholders have the power to influence various decisions by corporations, government and other entities. Within this perspective, accounting is not considered to be put in place to favour specific interests (sometimes referred to as 'elites'). By using 'society' as the topic of focus rather than *subgroups* within society, theories such as Legitimacy Theory ignore 'struggles and inequities within society' (Puxty, 1991). It is the failure to consider class struggles that has fuelled criticisms from many researchers working within the 'critical perspective of accounting'.

Another issue to consider when discussing legitimacy theory is whether the theory can be considered as a discrete, independent theory. Consistent with Gray *et al.* (1995), it should be acknowledged that there is much overlap between some other theories and legitimacy theory and to treat legitimacy theory and these others as sharply discrete theories would be wrong. For example, in relation to the overlap between legitimacy theory and stakeholder theory, Deegan and Blomquist (2005) state:

> Both theories conceptualise the organisation as part of a broader social system wherein the organisation impacts, and is impacted by, other groups within society. Whilst legitimacy theory discusses the expectations of society in general (as encapsulated within the 'social contract'), stakeholder theory provides a more refined resolution by referring to particular groups within society (stakeholder groups). Essentially, stakeholder theory accepts that because different stakeholder groups will have different views about how an organisation should conduct its operation, there will be various social contracts 'negotiated' with different stakeholder groups, rather than one contract with society in general. Whilst implied within legitimacy theory, stakeholder theory explicitly refers to issues of stakeholder power, and how a stakeholder's relative power impacts their ability to 'coerce' the organisation into complying with the stakeholder's expectations.

Legitimacy theory also has much overlap with Institutional Theory. As Deegan (2006) states:

Institutional Theory provides an explanation of how mechanisms through which organisations may seek to align perceptions of their practices and characteristics with social and cultural values (in order to gain or retain legitimacy) become institutionalised in particular organisations. Such mechanisms could include those proposed by both Stakeholder Theory and/or Legitimacy Theory, but could conceivably also encompass a broader range of legitimating mechanisms. This is why these three theoretical perspectives should be seen as complementary rather than competing.

Whilst legitimacy theory discusses how particular disclosure strategies might be undertaken to gain, maintain, or regain legitimacy, institutional theory explores how – at a broader level – particular organisational forms might be adopted in order to bring legitimacy to an organisation. *Institutional Theory* has been developed within the management academic literature (more specifically, in organisational theory) since the late 1970s, by researchers such as Meyer and Rowan (1977), DiMaggio and Powell (1983), Powell and DiMaggio (1991), and Zucker (1977, 1987). A central tenet of Institutional Theory is that there are various forces operating within society that cause organisational forms to become similar. At a broad level, a failure to comply with expectations about how an organisation should be formed can of itself create legitimacy problems for an organisation. Organisations that deviate from being of a form that has become 'normal' or expected will potentially have problems in gaining or retaining legitimacy. As Dillard, Rigsby and Goodman (2004, p. 509) state:

By designing a formal structure that adheres to the norms and behaviour expectations in the extant environment, an organization demonstrates that it is acting on collectively valued purposes in a proper and adequate manner.

Because other chapters of this book are devoted to stakeholder theory and institutional theory no further discussion of these theories will be provided in this chapter. Nevertheless, it is again emphasised that these theories are usefully considered as overlapping and not sharply separate. Indeed, a number of researchers have used a joint consideration of legitimacy theory, stakeholder theory and institutional theory to provide an explanation of particular corporate activities, rather than relying solely on one of the theories for explanation. It is the view of the author of this chapter that the non-discrete nature of legitimacy theory does not invalidate it as a theory, but it should perhaps be acknowledged that the many 'overlaps' that legitimacy theory has with other theories (such as stakeholder theory and institutional theory) has caused some other researchers to question whether a 'valid' theory can have so many overlaps. This is a philosophical issue which we will not consider further in this chapter.

4.   The Relevance of the Notion of a 'Social Contract"

The notion of a 'social contract' is central to legitimacy theory. The social contract is used to describe the set of expectations a society holds about how an organisation should conduct its operations. Organisations are expected to 'comply' with the terms (expectations) embodied within the social contract. Different managers will have different perspectives about how the community expects the organisation to behave and hence they will have different perceptions about the 'terms' or the contents of an organisation's social contract.

As Deegan (2006) indicates, the theoretical construct of the social contract is not new, having been discussed by philosophers such as Thomas Hobbes (1588 – 1679), John Locke (1632 – 1704), and Jean-Jacques Rousseau (1712 – 1778). However, it is only recently that this concept, which was used in philosophy and politics literatures, has been embraced within accounting research. Shocker and Sethi (1974, p. 67) provide a useful discussion of the social contract. They state:

Any social institution – and business is no exception – operates in society via a social contract, expressed or implied, whereby its survival and growth are based on:

(1)   the delivery of some socially desirable ends to society in general, and

(2)   the distribution of economic, social, or political benefits to groups from which it derives its power.

In a dynamic society, neither the sources of institutional power nor the needs for its services are permanent. Therefore, an institution must constantly meet the twin tests of legitimacy and relevance by demonstrating that society requires its services and that the groups benefiting from its rewards have society's approval.

Pursuant to legitimacy theory, and as already noted in this chapter, there are negative implications for an organisation that is considered to have breached its social contract. As Deegan (2006) states:

Where society is not satisfied that the organisation is operating in an acceptable, or legitimate manner, then society will effectively revoke the organisation's 'contract' to continue its operations. This might be evidenced through, for example, consumers reducing or eliminating the demand for the products of the business, factor suppliers eliminating the supply of labour and financial capital to the business, or constituents lobbying government for increased taxes, fines or laws to prohibit those actions which do not conform with the expectations of the community.

The social contract is considered to be made up of numerous terms (or clauses) – some explicit and some implicit. As Deegan (2006) states:

Gray, Owen and Adams (1996) suggest that legal requirements provide the explicit terms of the contract, while other non-legislated societal expectations embody the implicit terms of the contract. That is, there is an imperfect correlation between the law and societal norms (as reflected by the social contract) and according to Dowling and Pfeffer (1975), there are three broad reasons for the difference. Firstly, even though laws are reflective of societal norms and values, legal systems are slow to adapt to changes in the norms and values in society. Secondly, legal systems often strive for consistency whereas societal norms and expectation can be contradictory. Thirdly, it is suggested that whilst society may not be accepting of certain behaviours, it may not be willing or structured enough to have those behavioural restrictions codified within law. It is in relation to the composition of the implicit terms of the 'contract' that we can expect managers' perceptions to vary greatly.

Again it is emphasised that different managers will have different perceptions about the terms of the social contract and hence will adopt different strategies to ensure that organisation's operations are acceptable to various stakeholder groups. As we have already indicated, a legitimacy gap is deemed to arise when an organisation breaches its social contract, and the severity of the gap will in turn influence the extent to which the survival of the organisation is threatened, and the nature of remedial action required.

5. Who Confers Legitimacy, and Do All Entities Need It?

Proponents of legitimacy theory often talk about 'society', and the need for compliance with the expectations of society (as embodied within the *social contract*). However, this provides poor resolution given that *society* is clearly made up of various groups having unequal power or ability to influence the activities of other groups. That is, it is unrealistic to consider that society is truly pluralistic (this concept was described earlier in this chapter). Stakeholder theory provides some assistance because it explicitly considers differences in the power of respective stakeholder groups. Hence, in practice, researchers applying legitimacy theory to explain corporate disclosure practices also tend to incorporate (or 'borrow') some insights provided from the *managerial branch* of stakeholder theory (as Deegan, 2006 explains, stakeholder theory can be broken into two branches – these being the *ethical branch* and the *managerial branch* of stakeholder theory). In practice it is to be expected that organisations will have a series of social contracts with various stakeholder groups and that the importance of compliance with particular 'contracts' will in part be dependent upon the 'power' of the respective stakeholder groups. Whilst we will not pursue the issue of stakeholder power in detail (it is covered in Chapter 11 of this book), authors such as Deegan (2006), Roberts (1992), and Ullman (1985) suggest that stakeholder power is positively related to how important the resources of the stakeholder are to the ongoing survival and success of the organisation. As Roberts (1992, p. 598) states:

A major role of corporate management is to assess the importance of meeting stakeholder demands in order to achieve the strategic objectives of the firm. As the level of stakeholder power increases, the importance of meeting stakeholder demands increases also.

In relation to maintaining 'legitimacy' and the issue of whether all organisations require legitimacy to be conferred by society, the greater the extent to which the organisation trades on its level of legitimacy the more crucial it will be for that organisation to ensure that it does not deviate from the high standards that it has established and promoted. For example, compare an armaments manufacturer with, say, The Body Shop. The products of armaments manufacturers are designed to kill – such an organisation arguably has less to worry about in terms of its legitimacy than The Body Shop. By contrast, an organisation such as The Body Shop trades on its reputation for caring about the environment, society, and the welfare of animals. Hence we might argue that if there is a breach of its stated responsibilities and if this breach is found out by the media for example, that one of its products was treated on animals then this could be extremely costly to the organisation. It has a lot of 'investment in legitimacy' to lose. Indeed, a great deal of its market value will be related to the esteem with which the community holds the organisation (which would have been developed in part by costly advertising-style promotion undertaken by the organisation – the value of which could be slashed by a legitimacy threatening event).

Hence, in summarising the above short section, legitimacy might be conferred by different stakeholder groups – with some deemed more important than others – and not all entities will necessarily be dependent upon maintaining high levels of organisational legitimacy.

6. If Legitimacy is Threatened, What Strategies Might an organisation Adopt?

Central to much of the research undertaken under the banner of legitimacy theory is the role of public disclosures of information to support (or create or regain) organisational legitimacy. As we have already emphasised, legitimacy can be considered to be a resource upon which most organisations rely upon – to various degrees – for their survival. If the managers of an organisation perceive that the organisation's legitimacy is threatened to the extent that this is going to impede the success of the organisation, then legitimacy theory would suggest that remedial actions – typically reliant upon disclosure – will be undertaken.

In considering organisational strategies for maintaining or creating congruence between the social values implied by an organisation's operations, and the values embraced by society, we can apply the insights provided by Dowling and Pfeffer (1975). Dowling and Pfeffer outline the means by which an organisation, when faced with legitimacy threats, may legitimate its activities (p. 127). Tactics might include:

- The organisation can adapt its output, goals and methods of operation to conform to prevailing definitions of legitimacy;
- The organisation can attempt, through communication, to alter the definition of social legitimacy so that it conforms to the organisation's present practices, output and values; and/or
- The organisation can attempt through communication to become identified with symbols, values or institutions which have a strong base of legitimacy.

Consistent with Dowling and Pfeffer's strategy of 'communication', Lindblom (1994) proposes that an organisation can adopt a number of strategies where it perceives that its legitimacy is in question because its actions (or operations) are at variance with society's expectations and values – that is, its actions are not in accordance with the 'social contract'. Lindblom (1994) identifies four courses of action (there is some overlap with Dowling and Pfeffer) that an organisation can take. The organisation can seek to:

1.   educate and inform its 'relevant publics' about (actual) changes in the organisation's performance and activities which bring the activities and performance more into line with society's values and expectations;
2.   change the perceptions that 'relevant publics' have of the organisation's performance and activities – but not change the organisation's actual behaviour (while using disclosures in corporate reports to falsely indicate that the performance and activities have changed);
3.   manipulate perception by deflecting attention from the issue of concern onto other related issues through an appeal to, for example, emotive symbols, thus seeking to demonstrate how the organisation has fulfilled social expectations in other areas of its activities; or
4.   change external expectations of its performance, possibly by demonstrating that specific societal expectations are unreasonable.

According to Lindblom, and Dowling and Pfeffer, the public disclosure of information in such places as annual reports can be used by an organisation to implement each of the above strategies.

In considering the various proposed legitimising techniques identified above we can see that the techniques might be symbolic (and not actually reflect any real change in underlying activities), or they might be substantive (and reflect actual change in corporate activities), or they might be a mixture of both. As Deegan (2006) states:

> According to Ashsforth and Gibbs (1990), it is not necessary for corporations to use either substantive or symbolic management techniques exclusively and they may adopt a mix of substantive and/or symbolic legitimating techniques which they apply with varying levels of intensity. Whatever one of the above strategies is adopted, they will rely upon disclosure if they are to be successful.

To this point we have not differentiated between tactics used to gain legitimacy, maintain legitimacy, or regain legitimacy if it is lost. We have simply said that disclosure is important for assisting an organisation to *have* legitimacy. But as authors such as Suchman (1995) and O'Donovan (2002) indicate, legitimation strategies might differ depending upon whether they are used to either gain, maintain, or repair legitimacy. However, to date, it is not terribly clear from the theory how the strategies will differ. Deegan (2006) states:

> Whilst researchers have proposed that legitimation tactics might differ depending upon whether the entity is trying to gain, maintain, or repair legitimacy, the theoretical development in this area remains weak. Although the literature provides some general commentary, there is a lack of guidance about the relative effectives of legitimation strategies with regards to either gaining, maintaining, or regaining legitimacy. In terms of the general commentary provided within the literature,

gaining legitimacy occurs when an organisation moves into a new area of operations in which it has no past reputation. In such a situation the organisations suffers from the *"liability of newness"* (Ashforth and Gibbs, 1990) *and it needs to proactively engage in activities to win acceptance. This may involve actively promulgating new explanations of social reality in order to garner community* support (Suchman, 1995; Ashforth and Gibbs, 1990).

The task of *maintaining* legitimacy is typically considered easier than gaining or repairing legitimacy (O'Donovan, 2002; Ashforth and Gibbs, 1990). One of the 'tricks' in maintaining legitimacy is to be able to anticipate changing community perceptions. According to Suchman (1995, p. 594), strategies for maintaining legitimacy fall into two groups – perceiving future changes and protecting past accomplishments. In relation to monitoring changing community perceptions, Suchman (1995, p. 595) states:

> *Managers must guard against becoming so enamored with their own legitimating myths that they lose sight of external developments that might bring those myths into question. With advanced warning, managers can engage in pre-emptive conformity, selection, or manipulation, keeping the organisation and its environment in close alignment; without such warning, managers will find themselves constantly struggling to regain lost ground. In general, perceptual strategies involve monitoring the cultural environment and assimilating elements of that environment into organizational decision processes, usually by employing boundary-spanning personnel as bridges across which the organization can learn audience values, beliefs, and reaction.*

In relation to protecting past (legitimacy enhancing) accomplishments, Suchman (1995, p. 595) states:

> *In addition to guarding against unforseen challenges, organizations may seek to buttress the legitimacy they have already acquired. In particular, organizations can enhance their security by converting legitimacy from episodic to continual forms. To a large extent this boils down to (a) policing internal operations to prevent miscues, (b) curtailing highly visible legitimation efforts in favour of more subtle techniques, and (c) developing a defensive stockpile of supportive beliefs, attitudes and accounts.*

In considering *repairing* legitimacy, Suchman (1995, p. 597) suggests that related legitimation techniques tend to be reactive responses to often unforseen crises. In many respects, repairing and gaining legitimacy are similar. As O'Donovan (2002, p. 350) states:

> *Repairing legitimacy has been related to different levels of crisis management (Davidson, 1991; Elsbach and Sutton, 1992). The task of repairing legitimacy is, in some ways, similar to gaining legitimacy. If a crisis is evolving proactive strategies may need to be adopted, as has been the case for the tobacco industry during the past two decades (Pava and Krausz, 1997). Generally, however, the main difference is that strategies for repairing legitimacy are reactive, usually to an unforseen and*

immediate crisis, whereas techniques to gain legitimacy are usually ex ante, proactive and not normally related to crisis.

In concluding this brief discussion on the differences between gaining, maintaining and regaining legitimacy we again emphasise that our theoretical development in the area of explaining legitimising techniques has not developed sufficiently to link specific legitimation techniques with these particular phases of legitimation. This lack of development clearly provides opportunities for future research. Most of the proposed legitimation techniques appear to relate to regaining legitimacy in the light of particular crises – something that has tended to be the focus of many researchers working within the social and environmental accounting area (and who embrace legitimacy theory).

We will now turn our attention to some empirical studies that have utilised legitimacy theory. As indicated earlier, in the accounting area most studies that have adopted legitimacy theory have been undertaken in areas pertaining to social and environmental accounting issues. This in itself is an interesting observation and raises questions about why legitimacy theory has not been embraced more broadly in the academic accounting research community, particularly perhaps by those individuals researching financial accounting disclosures.

7. Empirical Tests of Legitimacy Theory

Deegan (2006) provides a reasonably detailed overview of a number of studies that have utilised legitimacy theory. Given the availability of this information, only a limited number of studies will be referred to in this section.

One of the earliest studies utilising legitimacy theory was conducted by Hogner (1982). It was a longitudinal study of corporate social reporting conducted in the US. The study of US Steel Corporation's disclosures showed that the extent of social disclosures varied from year to year with the variation appearing to represent a response to society's changing expectations of corporate behaviour.

Another highly cited study is Patten (1992) which focused on the change in the extent of environmental disclosures made by North American oil companies before and after the *Exxon Valdez* incident in Alaska in 1989. Patten's results indicate that there were increased environmental disclosures by the petroleum companies for the post-1989 period, consistent with a legitimation perspective. This disclosure reaction took place across the industry, even though the incident itself was directly related to one oil company.

In an Australian study, Deegan and Rankin (1996) utilised Legitimacy Theory to try to explain systematic changes in corporate annual report environmental disclosure policies around the time of proven environmental prosecutions (which were deemed to be legitimacy threatening events). Deegan and Rankin found that prosecuted firms disclosed significantly more environmental information (of a favourable nature) in the year of prosecution than any other year in the sample period, and the prosecuted firms also disclosed more environmental information, relative to non-prosecuted firms. The authors concluded that the public disclosure of proven environmental prosecutions has an impact on the disclosure policies of firms involved.

Gray, Kouhy and Lavers (1995) performed a longitudinal review of UK corporate social and environmental disclosures for the period 1979 to 1991. They make specific reference to the strategies suggested by Lindblom (1994) – as discussed earlier in this chapter. After considering the extent and types of corporate disclosures, they stated (p. 65):

> The tone, orientation and focus of the environmental disclosures accord closely with Lindblom's first, second and third legitimation strategies. A significant minority of companies found it necessary to 'change their actual performance' with respect to environmental interactions (Lindblom's first strategy) and use corporate social reporting to inform their 'relevant publics' about this. Similarly, companies' environmental disclosure has also been an attempt, first, to change perceptions of environmental performance – to alter perceptions of whether certain industries were 'dirty' and 'irresponsible' (Lindblom's second strategy) and, second, as Lindblom notes, to distract attention from the central environmental issues (the third legitimation strategy). Increasingly, companies are being required to demonstrate a satisfactory performance within the environmental domain. Corporate social reporting would appear to be one on the mechanisms by which the organisations satisfy (and manipulate) that requirement.

Deegan, Rankin and Tobin (2002) undertook a longitudinal study examining disclosures about social and environmental issues in the annual reports of BHP (now BHP Billiton), over the period 1983 to 1997. Their study demonstrated positive correlations between media attention for certain social and environmental issues (which was taken as a proxy for social concerns with these issues) and the volume of disclosures on these issues.

Many of the available research papers, including those briefly discussed above explain legitimising strategies at a corporate level. Nevertheless, there have been a number of studies that show that legitimising strategies might also occur at an industry level. If an entire industry has a crisis of legitimacy it might be efficient for a centralised industry body to undertake activities that bring some legitimacy to the industry as a whole. For example, Deegan and Blomquist (2006) provided evidence that the Australian minerals industry developed an industry-wide environmental management code so as to bring legitimacy to the industry generally. At the time of the development of the Code the industry was suffering numerous legitimacy problems because of various environmental catastrophes and various accidents that had injured and killed people. According to Deegan and Blomquist the Australian minerals industry tried to associate itself with a 'symbol' of legitimacy, this being the Code of Environmental Management. Having a code of environmental management could arguably be seen as a symbolic commitment to improved environmental performance by the industry body that developed the

Code, and by those companies who subsequently committed to it. The existence of the Code and the number and names of signatories was publicised in a widespread manner by the industry body. Individual companies also typically highlighted – in such places as their annual reports – that they were signatories to the code.

Whilst there are a large number of studies that support the tenets of legitimacy theory – including those discussed above – it should be acknowledged in the interests of a balanced discussion that there have nevertheless been a number of published studies that have not provided strong support for legitimacy theory. For example, in research that involved interviews with senior executives from large Irish companies, O'Dwyer (2002) found that the social and environmental disclosure policies only sometimes appeared to be motivated by legitimacy-related factors. Campbell (2000) reviewed the social disclosures of the UK organisations Marks and Spencer. Rather than finding that legitimacy theory provided explanations for the social disclosure practices of Marks and Spencer, Campbell found that individual traits, such as the identity of the chairman, seemed to provide better explanation of the corporate disclosure policies. Similarly, Guthrie and Parker failed to find overwhelming support for legitimacy theory.

Guthrie and Parker sought to match the disclosure practices of BHP Ltd across the period from 1885 to 1985 with a historical account of major events relating to BHP Ltd. The disclosures they reviewed were classified into environment, energy, human resources, products, and community involvement. The argument was that if corporate disclosure policies are reactive to major social and environmental events, then there should be correspondence between peaks of disclosure, and events which are significant in BHP Ltd's history. Apart from the environmental disclosures, Guthrie and Parker were unable to provide evidence to support legitimacy theory (however, and by their own admission, their data may have excluded a number of significant legitimacy threatening events or activities).

Hence, whilst the number of studies supporting legitimacy theory seem to outweigh those that do not support legitimacy theory, it nevertheless needs to be acknowledged that empirical support for legitimacy theory is not universal. However, given that theories such as legitimacy theory are used to explain human behaviour (such as the decision by managers to disclose information) it is unrealistic to expect any such theory to have perfect predictive or explanatory ability – humans are not perfectly predictable.

In concluding this brief section on empirical studies we can summarise by saying that, with some exceptions, there tends to be widespread support for the central tenets of legitimacy theory – that organisations will make use of public disclosures as a means of bringing legitimacy to their organisation when events occur that have the potential to undermine the legitimacy of the organisation. But we can perhaps ponder whether is it a 'good thing' that corporations can win back support by 'simply' making particular strategic disclosures. Whilst we will not go into this issue in depth because of constraints of space it is interesting to reflect on the comments of Deegan, Rankin and Tobin (2002). They state:

> *Legitimising disclosures mean that the organisation is responding to particular concerns that have arisen in relation to their operations. The implication is that unless concerns are aroused (and importantly, the managers perceive the existence of such concerns) then unregulated disclosures could be quite minimal. Disclosure decisions driven by the desire to be legitimate are not the same as disclosure policies driven by a management view that the community has a right-to-know about certain aspects of an organisation's operations. One motivation relates to survival, whereas the other motivation relates to responsibility. Arguably, companies that simply react to community concerns are not truly embracing a notion of accountability. Studies providing results consistent with Legitimacy Theory (and there are many of them) leave us with a view that unless specific concerns are raised then no accountability appears to be due. Unless community concern happens to be raised (perhaps as a result of a major social or environmental incident which attracts media attention), there will be little or no corporate disclosure.*

Taking the above position even further, Puxty (1991, p. 39) states:

> *I do not accept that I see legitimation as innocuous. It seems to me that the legitimation can be very harmful indeed, insofar as it acts as a barrier to enlightenment and hence progress.*

Hence, we can really question whether legitimisation strategies are really in the broader interests of the community. As indicated above, this might mean that companies potentially causing harm to the environment and society can 'buy time' by adopting disclosure strategies that legitimise their ongoing existence.

8. Concluding Comments

Legitimacy theory is being increasingly used by accounting researchers and there are no signs that its use is diminishing. Indeed, its use appears to be increasing. Nevertheless, there is a need for the theory to develop further if it is to remain relevant as there are many issues that remain unresolved. For example:

- There is currently little research to indicate how managers determine the terms of their 'social contract';
- There is a lack of clear evidence that tells us what disclosure strategies are most effective in either changing community expectations about 'appropriate' business practices, and/or changing community perceptions about the legitimacy of an organisation;
- Legitimacy theory tends to lack resolution by concentrating on contracts with 'society', rather than particular segments of society. We have little information on who are the most important parties in terms of conferring corporate legitimacy.
- There is little to guide us on the differences in strategies necessary to gain, maintain, or regain legitimacy.

With limitations such as these in mind there are certainly many opportunities for researchers who seek to adopt and hopefully refine legitimacy theory.

References

Ashforth, B. and Gibbs, B. (1990), "The double edge of legitimization", *Organization Science*, Vol. 1, pp. 177-194.

Bowles, M., (1991), "The Organization Shadow", Organization Studies, 12, pp. 387 - 404.

Campbell, D. (2000), "Legitimacy theory or managerial: construction? Corporate social disclosure in Marks and Spencer Plc corporate reports, 1969–1997", *Accounting Forum*, Vol. 24, No. 1, pp. 80-100.

Davidson, D. Kirk, (1991) "Legitimacy: How Important is it for Tobacco Strategies?', *Business & the Contemporary World*, Autumn, pp. 50-58.

Deegan, C. (2002), "The legitimising effect of social and environmental disclosures – a theoretical foundation", *Accounting, Auditing & Accountability Journal*, Vol. 15, No. 3, pp. 282-311.

Deegan, C., (2005), Australian Financial Accounting, McGraw-Hill, Sydney.

Deegan, C. (2006), *Financial Accounting Theory*, 2nd edition, McGraw Hill Book Company, Sydney.

Deegan, C. and Blomquist, C. (2006), "Stakeholder influence on corporate reporting: an exploration of the interaction between WWF-Australia and the Australian Minerals Industry", *Accounting, Organizations and Society*, forthcoming.

Deegan, C. and Rankin, M. (1996), "Do Australian companies report environmental news objectively? An analysis of environmental disclosures by firms prosecuted successfully by the environmental protection authority", *Accounting, Auditing & Accountability Journal*, Vol. 9 , No. 2, pp. 52-69.

Deegan, C., Rankin, M. and Tobin, J. (2002), "An examination of the corporate social and environmental disclosures of BHP from 1983–1997", *Accounting, Auditing & Accountability Journal*, Vol. 15, No. 3, pp. 312-343.

Deegan, C. and Unerman, J. (2006), *Financial Accounting Theory*: European edition, McGraw Hill, London, UK.

Dillard, J. F., Rigsby, J. T. and Goodman, C. (2004), "The making and remaking of organization context: Duality and the institutionalization process", *Accounting, Auditing & Accountability Journal*, Vol. 17, No. 4, pp. 506-542.

DiMaggio, P. J. and Powell, W. W. (1983), "The iron cage revisited: institutional isomorphism and collective rationality in organizational fields", *American Sociological Review*, Vol. 48, pp. 146-160.

Dowling, J. and Pfeffer, J. (1975), "Organisational legitimacy: social values and organisational behavior", *Pacific Sociological Review*, Vol. 18, No. 1, pp. 122-136.

Elsbach, K, & Sutton, R.I., (1992) "Acquiring organisational legitimacy through illegitimate actions: A marriage of institutional and impression management theories", *Academy of Management Journal*, Vol.35, pp.699-738.

Gray, R., Kouhy, R. and Lavers, S. (1995), "Corporate social and environmental reporting: a review of the literature and a longitudinal study of UK disclosure", *Accounting, Auditing & Accountability Journal*, Vol. 8, No. 2, pp. 47-77.

Gray, R., Owen, D. and Adams, C. (1996), *Accounting and Accountability: Changes and Challenges in Corporate Social and Environmental Reporting*, Prentice-Hall, London.

Guthrie, J. and Parker, L. (1989), "Corporate social reporting: a rebuttal of legitimacy theory", *Accounting and Business Research*, Vol. 9, No. 76, pp. 343-352.

Guthrie, J. and Parker, L. (1990), "Corporate social disclosure practice: a comparative international analysis", *Advances in Public Interest Accounting*, Vol. 3, pp. 159-175.

Hogner, R. H. (1982), "Corporate social reporting: eight decades of development at US steel", *Research in Corporate Performance and Policy*, Vol. 4, pp. 243-250.

Lindblom, C. K. (1994), "The implications of organisational legitimacy for corporate social performance and disclosure", *Critical Perspectives on Accounting Conference*, New York.

Mathews, M. R. (1993), *Socially Responsible Accounting*, Chapman and Hall, London.

Meyer, J. W. and Rowan, B. (1977), "Institutionalised organizations: formal structure as myth and ceremony", *American Journal of Sociology*, Vol. 83, pp. 340-363.

Nasi, J., Nasi, S., Phillips, N. and Zyglidopoulos, S. (1997), "The evolution of corporate social responsiveness – an exploratory study of Finnish and Canadian forestry companies", *Business & Society*, Vol. 38, No. 3, pp. 296-321.

O'Donovan, G. (2002), "Environmental disclosures in the annual report: extending the applicability and predictive power of legitimacy theory", *Accounting, Auditing & Accountability Journal*, Vol. 15, No. 3, pp. 344-371.

O'Dwyer, B. (2002), "Managerial perceptions of corporate social disclosure: an Irish story", *Accounting, Auditing & Accountability Journal*, Vol. 15, No. 3, pp. 406 - 436.

Patten, D. M. (1992), "Intra-industry environmental disclosures in response to the Alaskan oil spill: a note on legitimacy theory", *Accounting, Organizations and Society*, Vol. 15, No. 5, pp. 471-475.

Pava, Moses L. & Krausz, Joshua, (1997) Criteria for Evaluating the Legitimacy of Corporate Social Responsibility, *Journal of Business Ethics*, Vol. 16, pp. 337-347.

Powell, W. W. and DiMaggio, P. J. (Eds.) (1991), *The New Institutionalism in Organizational Analysis*, University of Chicago Press, Chicago, Illinois.

Puxty, A. (1991), "Social accountability and universal pragmatics", *Advances in Public Interest Accounting*, Vol. 4, pp. 35-46.

Roberts, R. (1992), "Determinants of corporate social responsibility disclosure: an application of stakeholder theory", *Accounting, Organizations and Society*, Vol. 17, No. 6, pp. 595-612.

Sethi, S. P. (1978), "Advocacy advertising – the American experience", *California Management Review*, Vol. 11, pp. 55-67.

Shocker, A. D. and Sethi, S. P. (1974), "An approach to incorporating social preferences in developing corporate action strategies", in Sethi, S .P. (Ed.), *The Unstable Ground: Corporate Social Policy in a Dynamic Society*, Melville, California, pp. 67-80.

Suchman, M. C. (1995), "Managing legitimacy: strategic and institutional approaches", *Academy of Management Review*, Vol. 20, No. 3, pp. 571-610.

Ullman, A. (1985), "Data in search of a theory: a critical examination of the relationships among social performance, social disclosure, and economic performance of US firms", *Academy of Management review*, Vol. 10, No. 3, pp. 540-557.

Watts, R. L. and Zimmerman, J. L. (1986), *Positive Accounting Theory*, Prentice-Hall Inc., Englewood Cliffs, New Jersey.

Zucker, L. G. (1977), "The role of institutionalization in cultural persistence", *American Sociological Review*, Vol. 42, pp. 726-743.

Zucker, L. G. (1987), "Institutional theories of organizations", *Annual Review of Sociology*, Vol. 13, pp. 443-464.

10

INSTITUTIONAL THEORY

Jodie Moll
University of Manchester, UK

John Burns
University of Dundee, UK

Maria Major
ISCTE – Business School, Portugal

Abstract: Accounting is shaped by its institutional context; its form and role is determined by the organisational environment and it also helps to shape this environment. Institutional theory has become a popular choice for accounting studies that seek to understand why and how accounting becomes what it is, or is not. We describe this theory in this chapter. In order to do this, we distinguish between the three branches of the theory that have exerted the most influence: (1) old institutional economics, (2) new institutional economics, and (3) new institutional sociology. We also provide a review of extant accounting research concentrating on those studies that have adopted both 'old' and 'new' approaches.

Keywords: Institutional theory; legitimacy; organisational change; strategic response.

1.   Introduction

This chapter will concern itself with institutional theory. Our intent is to sketch out the underpinning assumptions of institutional theories and map out its various strands. Furthermore, in order to help students to understand which strands of institutional theory might prove to be relevant and useful for helping to make sense of their research findings, we provide a literature review of its use within the accounting discipline.

The chapter is set out in three sections. First, we outline three institutional approaches that, to date, have probably had most influence on accounting research. In the second section we review extant accounting research that has been informed by institutional explanations, with particular focus on those works that have adopted 'new' institutional sociology and both 'old' and 'new' institutional economics. Finally, the third section is dedicated to consideration of providing a future research agenda for institutional research in accounting, including some discussion of current and recent criticisms directed at institutional theory.

2. Variants of Institutional Theory

Multiple theories (and sub-theories) comprise institutionalism, spanning numerous scholarly disciplines. This section attempts to explain briefly what respective institutional approaches entail, their intellectual roots and key methodological underpinnings. However, we focus on four particular strands of institutionalism, namely: (1) old institutional economics; (2) new institutional economics, and (3) new institutional sociology. More general surveys are available for those wishing to pursue the wider plethora of institutional approaches available across disciplines (DiMaggio and Powell, 1991; Maki *et al.*, 1993; Lowndes, 1996; Scott, 2001). But, importantly, we concentrate (albeit briefly) on those branches that to date have exerted most influence on accounting research. In so doing, three caveats ought to be stated, namely that: (1) the three institutional approaches highlighted below comprise either economic or sociological theories, not 'accounting theory' as such; (2) while there are indeed key differences between them, all three approaches share a concern that 'institutions matter', although there are differences in respective definitions of an institution; and (3) there are no implicit signals in the ordering by which the three approaches are presented.

2.1. Old Institutional Economics

The origins of old institutional economics (OIE) date back over one hundred years ago to the seminal works of Thorstein Veblen (e.g. Veblen, 1898, 1899). OIE also emerged out of opposition to the dominant theorising in its (economics) discipline at the time (Hodgson, 1988; Rutherford, 1995). It thus rejected neo-classical economic theorising that placed emphasis on assumptions pertaining to rationality, optimisation and market-equilibria, and proposed a holistic and interdisciplinary approach that also drew inspiration from sociology, politics and law (Wilber and Harrison, 1978).

Earliest OIE works predominantly explored institutions at the society (or macro-economy) level. A typical definition of institutions would that be of 'settled habits of thought common to the generality of men' (Veblen, 1919, p. 239), or Hamilton's oft-cited definition of institutions as: '[....] a way of thought or action of some prevalence and permanence, which is embedded in the habits of a group or the customs of a people' (1932, p. 84).

Ever since its origins OIE scholars have attempted to conceptualise economic processes that encompass both stability *and* change, rather than comparative analyses of optimal states of rest. Thus, OIE theory would generally consider why/how particular behaviours or structures emerge, sustain and/or change over time rather than merely what structures exists at any given point in time. Indeed, it is this focus on the processes of change that underpins most accounting works that have recently adopted OIE theory.[27]

OIE rejects assumptions of rational-optimising individuals on the grounds that, in order to capture the cumulative path(s) of economic life, individuals' tastes and preferences (and, by implication, their choice- and decision-making) cannot be taken as given or exogenous. Rather, OIE theorists argue that tastes and preferences must be analysed in their own right. Moreover, analysis must account for the multiplicity of influences that shape (and/or re-shape) tastes and preferences through time. Importantly, these influences are of an institutional nature and might include (at various levels) rules, habits, routines, norms and taken-for-granted assumptions (Hodgson, 1988). In addition, OIE particularly stresses the importance of power and politics, learning and (technological) innovation for shaping cumulative processes over time.

Only in fairly recent times have OIE theorists begun to focus more directly on institutional phenomena within organisations. A notable contribution, in this respect, was Richard Nelson and Sydney Winter's (1982) classic book, *An Evolutionary Theory of Economic Change*. Though they themselves would unlikely profess to be OIE theorists as such, their ideas and concepts have since been used to significant effect by prominent OIE scholars (e.g. Hodgson, 1988; Vromen, 1995). In a nutshell, Nelson and Winter highlight the habitual and routinised nature of business practices (including accounting practices – 1982, p. 482), and conceptualise how such routines, over time, underpin a firm's know-how, 'passing on' (mainly tacit) knowledge. Further, such routines they argue can eventually comprise generally accepted ways of thinking and doing (i.e. institutions).

2.2. *New Institutional Economics*

Whereas OIE experienced a lull in its popularity during the mid- and post-war years, there was renewed interest in institutions amongst economists from the 1960s onwards (Hodgson, 1988). However, such renewed interest differed to its 'older' contemporaries. First, there was no uniform paradigm but rather a mesh of different theories (and sub-theories), which collectively came to be labelled new institutional economics (NIE) (Langlois, 1986). Second, the emergence of NIE emerged out of a growing belief at that time amongst economists that institutions should indeed be studied but *within* the neo-classical economics framework. One NIE scholar, Oliver Williamson, who has been credited with much of its early development cited the objectives of this particular strand on institutional theory to be a 'micro-analytical approach to the study of economic organisation' (1985, p. 1). Much of the emerging NIE contribution indeed represented an attempt to open up the 'black-box' of

---

[27] E.g. Ahmed and Scapens (2000, 2003); Burns and Scapens (2000); Burns (2000); Burns and Baldvinsdottir (2005); Caccia and Steccolini (2006); Dietrich (2001); Johansson and Baldvinsdottir (2003); Scapens (1994); Scapens and Jazayeri (2003); Siti-Nabiha and Scapens (2005); Soin *et al.* (2002).

organisations through studies of the institutional environment (i.e., rules and regulations) and institutional arrangements (i.e. governance and other structures within organisations – including accounting systems).

In a nutshell, NIE advocates seek to explain the existence or appearance of some institutions, and the non-existence or disappearance of others. Langlois (1986) made the first serious attempt to group together particular (sub-) theories under one (NIE) umbrella. A detailed discussion of the various sub-branches is beyond the remit of this chapter, but it is worthwhile to note the 'transaction cost economics' strand (Coase, 1937; Williamson, 1975, 1985) that has probably had the most influence on extant accounting research.

A typical definition for an institution in NIE theory would be that of North who stated that: 'Institutions, composed of rules, norms of behaviour, and the way they are enforced, provide the opportunity set in an economy which determines the kind of purposive activity embodied in organisations (firms, trade unions, political bodies, and so forth) that will come into existence' (1993, p. 242). NIE assumes rational-optimising behaviour, although particular sub-theories allow for some relaxation – for instance, many NIE theories incorporate 'bounded rationality' (Simon, 1976) into their work, thereby allowing for an explanation of institutions in the context of cognitive limits, incomplete information and/or difficulties in monitoring and enforcing agreements. Institutions, according to the NIE approach, essentially exist where their benefits exceed the costs involved in creating and maintaining them. Thus, most of the extant NIE-informed accounting literature[28] describes the existence of accounting configurations in cost-minimising/efficiency terms.

2.3. New Institutional Sociology

New institutional sociology (NIS) emerged out of opposition towards the dominant rational-actor perspectives in its discipline at the time, although nowadays NIS is generally viewed as mainstream in its sociological field (Scott, 2001). Sociology boasts numerous institutional approaches (DiMaggio and Powell, 1991; Scott, 2001), but it is the branch within organisational studies (hence, with immediate and direct attention to organisations, their systems and practices), which has probably had most influence on recent accounting research.

A starting point for most NIS-informed-studies is an assumption that intra-organisational structures and procedures, including accounting, are largely shaped by external factors rather than cost-minimising objectives. Thus, organisations which operate in similar environmental settings are assumed to be subject to comparable demands towards what is generally deemed as being appropriate behaviour, including its choice and design of internal structures and procedures

---

[28] For example, Spicer and Ballew (1983); Johnson (1983); Flamholtz (1983); Tiessen and Waterhouse (1983); Spicer (1988); Colbert and Spicer (1995); Zimmerman (1997); Walker (1998), ter Bogt and van Helden (2000).

(Meyer and Rowan, 1977; DiMaggio and Powell, 1983; Meyer and Scott, 1983). For instance, internal structures and procedures will reflect the rules, procedures, myths and norms that are prevalent and generally perceived to be 'right' within society (Meyer, Scott and Deal, 1983). And, by introducing and maintaining such phenomena, an organisation is said to confer legitimacy upon itself. Thus, scholars have used NIS insight to explain how the adoption of particular accounting systems can be understood in terms of a need to conform to external pressures as opposed to an overriding (rational-optimising) drive for increased internal efficiency.[29]

Importantly, it is the external rules, procedures, myths and/or norms that define an institution in NIS theory: 'Institutions consist of cognitive, normative, and regulative structures and activities that provide stability and meaning to social behaviour. Institutions are transported by various carriers – cultures, structures, and routines – and they operate at multiple levels of jurisdiction' (Scott, 1995, p. 33).

Institutions might result from human activity, and are deemed to influence human activity, but do not necessarily emerge from conscious human design (DiMaggio and Powell, 1991, p. 8). Moreover, in practice, actual organisational structures and procedures need not necessarily comply with their external expectations or imagery. This (intentional and/or unintentional) separation between external image and actual structures and procedures has been referred to as 'de-coupling' (Weick, 1976; Meyer and Rowan, 1977; Meyer and Scott, 1992). Thus, most NIS scholars argue that institutions 'rationalize rather than make rational' (Carruthers, 1995, p. 316). And, accordingly, some accounting researchers have studied how firms intentionally de-couple between external appearances (i.e. the technical) and actual structures and procedures of accounting (the institutional).

Congruence between organisational arrangements and impinging (society-level) institutions is explained through a process by which external institutions permeate internal structures and procedures, called 'isomorphism' (DiMaggio and Powell, 1983). Two components of isomorphism are offered, namely: (1) competitive isomorphism and (2) institutional isomorphism. The former defines how competitive forces drive organisations towards adopting least-cost, efficient structures and practices. However, most NIS advocates de-emphasise (1), and stress (2) which portrays such permeation (i.e. from environment-to-organisation) as a predominantly cultural and political process.

Institutional isomorphism is then broken down further into three sub-categories (DiMaggio and Powell, 1983), as follows:

---

[29]   E.g. Abernethy and Chua (1996); Carmona *et al.* (1997, 1998); Carmona and Macias (2001); Carmona and Danoso (2004); Carruthers (1995); Covaleski and Dirsmith (1988a, 1988b, 1995); Covaleski *et al.* (1993, 1996); Euske and Riccaboni (1999); Granlund and Lukka (1998); Collier (2001); Lapsley (1994); Modell (2001, 2002, 2003, 2005); Pettersen (1995, 1999); Major and Hopper, 2004.

1. Coercive isomorphism – whereby impinging external factors (e.g. government policy, regulation, supplier relationships) exert force on organisations to adopt specific internal structures and procedures.
2. Mimetic isomorphism – whereby organisations emulate the internal structures and procedures adopted by other organisations.
3. Normative isomorphism – whereby organisations adopt the structures and procedures advocated by particular dominant professions, professional bodies and/or consultants.

This typically 'macro' focus which has dominated the new institutional approach has recently been subject to much criticism. Consequently, many current sociological institutionalists have called for a more complete account for understanding the emergence, persistence and abandonment of institutions. Specifically, it has been argued that the theory requires greater integration with 'micro' explanations and acknowledgment of the interactive nature of institutional processes, incorporating the intra-organisational processes and the interests and generative capacity of actors into the perspective. Influential efforts to close the micro/macro gap include Greenwood and Hinings (1996), Selznick (1996), Hirsch and Lounsbury (1997). Several accounting studies, including Collier (2001), Modell (2003; 2006) and Burns (2000) have also attempted to provide a more integrative and explanatory framework drawing on literatures such as Hardy's power mobilisation (1996), negotiated order literature (Basu, 1999; Phillips *et al.*, 2000) and goal direct perspectives (Hyndman and Eden, 2000; Thompson, 1995).

Finally, it is worth noting that NIS and OIE approaches both offer a wide range of applicability for understanding the practice of accounting in organisations and share several traits in common. For instance, both draw on a broad variety of insight from cognitive science, cultural studies, psychology and anthropology, and both draw attention to multiple levels of analyses ranging from the individual organisation to society (Scott, 2001). Importantly, this contrasts sharply to 'new' institutional economics which premises itself entirely in the neoclassical economics paradigm.

3. Institutional Research in Accounting

Up to this point, our focus has been a general explanation of the various guises of institutional theory. As mentioned above, in this section we review institutional research in the accounting discipline to capture how such theory has previously been applied, to try and consolidate existing arguments and further contribute to our understanding of the multiple roles of accounting in society. However, some clarification is needed. First, the review of accounting studies in this section is meant only to be illustrative of the use of institutional theory and is not exhaustive. Second, by way of attempting to present the following in an uncomplicated manner, we categorise published research according to its theoretical contributions.[30]

3.1. The Influence of 'Macro' Institutional Forces on Organisational Accounting Systems

One strand of institutional accounting research has focused on the manner by which institutional forces can influence intra-organisational practices – that is, a process by which society (or macro) level factors impinge on (micro level) organisational behaviour. For instance, Hussain and Hoque (2002) studied factors affecting the design and use of non-financial performance measurement systems in four Japanese banks. Through multiple case studies, they identified economic constraints as the most likely external/macro pressures for influencing the design and use of performance measurement systems, while other less prominent factors were identified as being the regulatory control of Central Bank, accounting standards and financial legislation, management strategy, bank size, competition and the emulation of 'best practice'. Similarly, Hussain and Gunasekaran (2002) studied the relationship between extra-institutional factors and the non-financial performance of banks and financial institutions. Their study highlighted a range of institutional (coercive, normative and mimetic) factors that impacted non-financial performance in the banking and finance industries – e.g. Central Bank association, management competency, strategic orientation and best practice emulation.

In a relatively recent study of a UK police constabulary, Collier (2001) explicitly focuses on the dynamics (most notably political and cultural factors) that shape *how* external 'rationalised' phenomena actually became implicated in their choice of new management accounting systems. Whereas, ter Bogt and van Helden (2000) used institutional theory to explore gaps between formally designed accounting systems change and *actual* accounting change in Dutch government organisations. The Netherland government's intentions for redesigned accounting systems were not so much underpinned by pressing financial-related concerns, and ter Bogt and van Helden noted only moderate internal pressures for change. Thus, they argued, a gap emerged between the intention of formal change and the actual change that occurred, particularly as management demonstrated a lack of commitment towards the formal goals.

In the research area of financial reporting and standards setting, Mezias and Scarselletta (1994) used institutional theory to examine the decision processes of a public policy task force that was involved in establishing financial reporting standards. Their purpose was to identify the institutional factors that might affect the task force's decisions, and professional accounting bodies were evidenced to exert an important influence on the types of decisions that were made.

---

[30] Although some scholars may choose to classify several studies in two or more of these categories, we have elected to categorise individual research in a category that we felt most closely represents the purpose and contribution of the study.

Collectively such studies seek to demonstrate how the institutional environment rather than purely technical dimensions influence an organisation. It would also appear from such contributions that a principal source for moulding accounting systems and accounting standards are the institutionalised beliefs and rules embedded in the requirements of governments, professional associations, and of general public opinion. Notwithstanding, given the multiple and often contradictory institutional demands that individual organisations face, they will frequently need to be selective in their response to the wider institutional environment.

3.2.   *The Structuration of the Organisational Field*

A key tenet of many institutional theories is that organisations affect their environments, and the construction and potency of institutions depends to a large extent on organisations within the institutional field (Kondra and Hinings, 1998). Thus, there is said to be duality between organisations and their institutional environments. For instance, nation-states and the accounting professions have been identified as playing key roles at shaping an organisation's institutional environment – i.e. the nation-state is thought to 'create rationalized structural frameworks' whereas the profession is thought to 'create rationalized cultural systems' (Scott, 1991, p. 172). More recently, such international organisations as the OECD and IMF have also been identified as playing a key role in shaping the broader institutional environment. There are several notable studies that attend to this view, and thus improve our understanding of how institutional environments are shaped.

One of the most commonly cited accounting cases informed by institutional theory is that of Ansari and Euske (1987). Comparing institutional theory, technical rational and socio-political perspectives, Ansari and Euske provided explanations for the extent to which cost accounting data is used by military repair facilities in the US. In particular, they noted strong case evidence of socio-political and institutional pressures shaping the information use in the organisations studied. They demonstrated how the US Department of Defence de-coupled its formal statement of accounting systems to the outside world from the actual systems and practices in use. Introduction of a new costing system, they developed, was primarily driven by a desire to outwardly demonstrate 'rationality' (especially to the US Congress) with respect to their internal control mechanisms. Whereas, the authors argued, the new accounting systems were neither rational nor did they contribute towards efficiency-improvement.

Using institutional theory, Carpenter and Dirsmith (1993) examined the role of statistical sampling for improvement in the efficiency and effectiveness of independent audits. Their study focused more broadly on the role of group-interests in the process of institutionalisation and, more specifically, on how the accounting profession drove institutionalisation of statistical sampling to divert pressures from complex organisational environments, client companies' size, and unwillingness of clients to pay for complete examination and verification of complete accounting records. In so doing, Carpenter and Dirsmith demonstrated how audit shifted from fraud detection to expressing an opinion of fairness in financial statements.

Carpenter and Feroz (1992, 2001) investigated the New York State government's decision to adopt generally accepted accounting principles (GAAP) in external financial reporting which, they argued, was largely due to an intention to legitimate their financial management practices but was also strongly influenced by the interplay of power relations and intra-organisational politics.

A later study by the same authors (Carpenter and Feroz, 2001) investigated the deliberations of four US State governments (i.e. New York, Michigan, Ohio and Delaware) to either adopt or reject GAAP in their external reports. Resource dependency was cited as strongly impacting the respective State governments' decisions to accept GAAP. And, conversely, decisions to resist GAAP were argued to be driven by a lack of socialisation of accounting bureaucrats in the accounting professions to promote GAAP adoption.

Bergevarn, Mellemvik and Olson (1995) explored municipal accounting in Sweden and Norway in a bid to understand better how accounting has become 'a taken for granted' construction in the new public sector in these two countries. In particular, the study undertaken set out to understand how accounting had become institutionalised and to identify the type of legitimacy that underpinned the institutionalisation. Bergevarn *et al.* found that the institutionalisation processes differed between the two countries; in Norway the development of municipal accounting was linked to the State and in Sweden the development of municipal accounting was not found to have a principal actor shaping its development. Such findings are inconsistent with the traditional institutional theories, which purport that there should be some consistency between the institutionalisation processes in these countries given their similarities.

Covaleski and Dirsmith (1988a) attempted to understand the evolution of a US university's accounting system, in particular, the role of the State government's budget allocation processes. They reported that accounting had been used to demonstrate to the (Wisconsin) State government that technically 'rational' budget techniques were being used in the university and, thus, that the budget was being used as a means to legitimate its operations to external constituents. Later, the University responded to State budget cuts by changing its financial requests from traditional quantitative budget statements to qualitative statements that comprised three budget categories and sought to highlight the effect of non-funding for the university. In other words, the university was attempting to manipulate its resource environment; however, to maintain control the State government combined the three categories into a single category.

Finally, Modell (2003) conducted a study which traced the development of performance measurement practices to requirements of the Swedish ministry for education and science to address two research questions, namely: (1) how do the goal-directed and process-orientated, NIS approaches, respectively, explain the emergence of PM practices at the macro level of organisational fields; and, (2) how can the evolution of loosely-coupled performance measurement practices at the macro level of organisational fields be explained? From a theoretical viewpoint, he found strong support for NIS explanations noting a loose coupling between many of the PIs developed. The loose coordination of these goals provided a stabilising role, reducing the likelihood of potential conflict between multiple constituents by providing multiple images of the organisational performance. The study also contributed to the more general NIS literature, by demonstrating that loose coupling may occur as a result of the passivity of centrally located actors as well as from pro-active resistance.

3.3. Legitimacy and Organisations

Much institutional thought, particularly NIS, is built on the premise that organisations adhere to wider societal values in order to achieve legitimacy, whereby such values govern the 'appropriateness' of organisational work arrangements and practices. And, as such, a great deal of research to date has focused on the legitimating attributes of accounting systems. For instance, several studies have highlighted how various professional accounting bodies have developed officially-sanctioned ways of developing their formal systems, including their accounting systems (Bealing, 1994; Fogarty, 1992; Fogarty et al., 1997).

Abernethy and Chua (1996) drew on institutional theory to explore the design and operation of management control systems. Their study illustrated how accounting controls operate as part of an organisational control 'mix', the choice for which is influenced by an organisation's operating environment. Abernathy and Chua engaged in a longitudinal field study at an Australian teaching hospital, and revealed that the control systems were primarily used to rationalise and supplement other visible elements of the control package rather than necessarily for planning or control purposes.

Covaleski, Dirsmith and Michelman's (1993) study of case mix accounting systems in US hospitals also portrayed the use of such systems beyond an argument of rationality in structural properties. They suggested that the adoption of 'case-mix' accounting systems had much to do with demonstrating conformity to external institutionalised expectations, particularly those of the US federal government. Individual hospital departments, they continued, that operated with high visibility would more likely be allocated a larger proportion of internally-allocated resources in return for providing external imagery that would legitimate the hospital organisation. And, in so doing, such allocations would reinforce internal power relations.

Institutional theory has also been used in recent years to understand accounting practices in under-developed economies, where the general assumption is that western rules and procedures are employed to portray traits of 'modernisation', irrespective of whether local circumstances necessitate them

(Meyer and Rowan, 1977; Scott, 2001). Hoque and Hopper (1994) used institutional theory to examine the external factors that influenced management control systems in a Bangladesh jute mill. Their results highlighted that the jute mill under investigation had minimal authority over its activities and, in this respect, its control systems were fashioned to a large extent to legitimate the organisation rather than to improve controls.

Alam (1997) drew on institutional theory to examine the technical and symbolic roles of budgeting in two state-owned Bangladeshi organisations. This study highlighted significant differences between respective departmental strategies, correlated to the varied level(s) of environmental uncertainty. One (jute-producer) organisation, characterised by high uncertainty, was observed to use budgets in a manner that buffered their activities from external authorities. Whereas, a different (sugar cane) organisation that operated in more moderate conditions was observed to prepare budgets primarily for the purpose of feeding into its decision-making process. The latter organisation was able to maintain a level of externally-oriented formality while also satisfying internal requirements.

Finally, some studies have suggested that compliance without due regard for the local technical requirements stands little chance of improving management. For instance, a recent study by Rahaman, Lawrence and Roper (2004) suggested that although the Ghana River Authority complied with the World Bank's pressure to improve their operations in light of past records, such compliance had little impact on the management of its social environment, nor in terms of promoting integration with the general public of Ghana.

3.4. The Role of Agency and Power in Institutional Analysis

As suggested previously, the institutional environment is characterised by a range of different authorities, each with their own expectations about what are appropriate ways to operate. The multiple and often conflicting expectations affecting an organisation is suggestive that organisations are not passive in their choice of work arrangements and practices. On the contrary, it implies that it is required to make strategic choices in response to the various institutional pressures (Oliver 1991; Scott, 1991). Furthermore, to be implemented effectively in the organisation, any choice must be backed with sanctioning power. A growing number of researchers have recognised this possibility of strategic action by organisations and have investigated accounting change implementation framed by such a perspective.

The impact of legitimacy dimensions on strategic organisational choices is illustrated by Basu, Dirsmith and Gupta's (1999) study of the US General Accounting Office's audit report process. In this study, the authors suggested a number of complex and interwoven dynamics of the images portrayed to external parties (e.g. Congress, the press and federal agencies) and hypothesised that such images were especially important for sustaining legitimacy in terms of funding dependence. Importantly, Basu et al.'s case study provided evidence to suggest that organisations can manage their relationships with external constituents, both 'disconnecting' and 'connection-strengthening', and actively controlling the degrees of interest by coupling between organisational image and actual operations.

Covaleski and Dirsmith (1988a, 1988b) examined biennial negotiations between the University of Wisconsin and the State of Wisconsin, and noted that budgets were prone to modification during periods of organisational decline. The study also highlighted proactive agents who created and spread (or institutionalised) expectations with respect to organisational policy and operations.

In his study of a small UK chemicals manufacturer, Burns (2000) used institutional theory to tease out the complex and dynamic characteristics of accounting change over time. In particular, his study illustrated how the implementation of new accounting procedures is likely to be less problematic when such change is compatible with existing intra-organisational rules, routines and settled ways of thinking and doing (Burns and Scapens, 2000). However, in situations where this does not apply, Burns further identified power and political mobilisation (Hardy, 1996) as being important for the eventual direction and outcome of change implementation. Thus, Burns' study posits a range of strategic choice limited by institutional rules.

More recently, Modell (2002) explored the influence of institutional factors on organisational cost allocation procedures, arguing that traditional rational-choice explanations for why organisations adopt particular cost allocation procedures offer only a partial view of why a particular technique is selected. Further, Modell develops a framework that gives explicit attention to the interactions between intra-organisational power relationships, speed of change-adoption, market competition and technological complexity.

In keeping with the notion that institutions are the social product of both organisations and individual actors, some scholars have combined insights of institutional theory and structuration theory (Giddens, 1984) to examine the role of agency in the choice process. Such combination of theoretical insight attempts to provide conceptualisation of the processes of accounting change, acknowledging external and intra-organisational relationships that both constrain and/or enable organisational choice (Burns and Scapens, 2000). Granlund (2001), for instance, explored why accounting systems can sometimes prove to be difficult to change despite significant operating and environmental pressures for change, and citing organisational routine, conservative organisational cultures and failure to legitimate change intentions as being key resistors to change (or guardians of stability, depending on the context).

Finally, Seal (1999) used institutional theory to explore accounting within UK local governments. More specifically, he studied the implementation of compulsory competitive tendering (CCT) in a local government, and explained how local governments had resisted central government's attempt to introduce widespread CCT. Such resistance, he observed, was underpinned by a belief that private contractors would be more expensive than internal providers, and that individual local authorities were better suited than central government to determine effective forms of CCT for their entity.

3.5. Accounting as Efficient Configurations

Due to its strict rooting in the neo-classical economics paradigm, an NIE perspective of accounting is narrower and more specific than NIS or OIE perspectives. Most NIE-informed accounting literature describes the existence of particular accounting configurations in cost-minimising or efficiency terms. For example, Spicer and Ballew (1983), Spicer (1988), and Colbert and Spicer (1995) explain particular 'general accounting themes' (e.g. performance evaluation and control, responsibility accounting and transfer pricing) in terms of optimising choices between alternative arrangements, under given transacting conditions. Spicer (1988) and Colbert and Spicer (1995), in particular, argued that transfer-pricing systems are a function of 'transacting conditions' – in particular, asset specificity, the frequency and volume of a firm's transactions and the level of uncertainty and complexity. Baiman (1982, 1990) explored the implications of agency theory (also defined by Langlois, 1989, as part of the NIE grouping) for accounting research and practice. Other scholars have illustrated that NIE theories (in particular the strands of public choice, agency and transaction costs) have constituted dominant paradigms for governments involved in reforming public sector management (Lapsley and Pallot, 2000 – cf. Boston et al., 1996).

The 'markets and hierarchies' (M and H) strand of NIE (Williamson, 1975, 1985), a derivative of transaction cost economics, has influenced management accounting historians in their attempt to explain changes over time of accounting systems and practices in common use. For example, Johnson (1981, 1983) shed light on the birth of, and changes in, western European management accounting since the nineteenth century. His argument was that, by 1800, the transaction costs of undertaking business in market settings (with many individual operators) had become so great that merchant-entrepreneurs began to economise by gathering together all the operators in one factory. This represented the birth of manufacturing firms. Moreover, argued Johnson, with the emergence and growth of firms, there was decline in useful market information (e.g. prices) that is necessary for measuring productivity and profitability. This scarcity, in turn, catalysed the emergence of management accounting. So, in summary, Johnson's argument was that changes in the prevailing market (transacting) conditions led to the emergence of new (lower-cost) modes of organisation which, in turn, incited new sources of information including management accounting.

Zimmerman's (1997) text-book also adopts NIE theory in presenting a 'general framework' of management accounting, by which he relates both conventional and 'new' management accounting practices specifically to the markets and hierarchies approach. More specifically, Zimmerman conceptualises how management accounting typically becomes located in general 'organisational design problems' (see, also, Walker, 1998); and, explains how organisations inevitably face a (cost efficiency-driven) 'trade-off dilemma' between designing management accounting for decision making purposes and designing for control. Critically, Zimmerman adds also that the design of (and, by implication, changes in) an organisation's management accounting is driven by the optimisation (cost-minimisation) of such trade-offs.

Some scholars have used NIE theory to explore possible ways that firms might adjust their accounting configurations in response to changes in transactional conditions (Colbert and Spicer, 1995). And, some (e.g. Spicer and Ballew, 1983) have explored ways that organisations might overcome the internal problems of bounded rationality and/or opportunist behaviour (which, it is held, might hinder optimisation). However, we should probably highlight that most NIE theories conceptualise accounting change with reference to cost-minimising shifts from one 'optimal' configuration (or equilibrium) to another. Primary focus is thus on the instantaneous outcome of change, and any notion of the process or dynamics of change is implied only through a description of what actually exists. This is an important point as, at least methodologically, it sets the NIE approach apart from OIE.

4. A Future Research Agenda for Understanding Accounting as an Institutional Practice

The studies documented in the previous section suggest the use of institutional theories has been widespread by accounting scholars in audit, and financial and management accounting fields. A review of accounting studies is also suggestive that public sector accounting researchers have probably paid more attention to institutional theory than others have. It has commonly been used as the theoretical framework to understand public sector accounting transformation; in particular, the way in which private sector technologies are diffused in the public sector and the influence of multiple agents in this role. This focus is understandable because public sector entities are required to demonstrate accountability and in this regard accounting is seen as one way in which public sector entities can legitimise their operations. Thus, it has become the object of public sector institutional practices. It is also consistent with early neo-institutionalists inclinations to associate technical features with for-profit firms and institutional forces with non-profit or government agencies (DiMaggio and Powell, 1991). Furthermore, in the private sector, it was believed that institutional theories were inept for explaining organisational choice, because market forces would prevail (Meyer, 1977; Powell, 1991; Scott 2001; Scott and Christensen, 1995; Major and Hopper, 2004) and this may help to explain why accounting scholars have been more reluctant to use it as a theoretical lens to explore accounting in the private sector.

The accounting studies summarised in this chapter are important in a number of respects. Collectively, they help to improve our understanding of the institutional environment, by identifying the wide range of bodies actively involved in shaping the institutional environment. Second, understanding the mechanisms used to manipulate the organisational environment and the extent to which they are effective is important for strategically managing organisational responses. Third, and perhaps most importantly, the studies document the institutionalisation of accounting rules and routines in organisational life.

From a methodological point of view, many of the studies reviewed in this chapter involved qualitative methods. Since institutional theory focuses on understanding context specific accounting practices, this methodology is particularly apt. Immersion within the field is necessary to allow the researcher(s) to build up a better understanding of the institutional sector including: (1) the meanings of events and activities to the people involved in them; (2) the influence of physical and social context on these event and activities; and (3) the process by which accounting practices are produced, experienced, and abandoned (see Greenwood and Hinings, 1996; Maxwell, 2005). Furthermore, questionnaire based research approaches are unsuitable since many concepts underpinning institutional explanations are difficult to measure. The processual nature of the institutional process also indicates the need for a longitudinal approach to be adopted (see, for instance, Burns, 2000). As Scott (1995, p. xx) points out:

> *Regulations, norms and cognitive systems do not appear instantaneously but develop over time; the diffusion of common activity patterns and structures through time is viewed as important evidence for the developing strength of an institutional pattern.*

The case nature of much of the research utilising institutional theory also suggests there is still a great deal to be learned about accounting as institutionalised rules and routines. Further studies, including multiple cases, need to be carried out to improve our understanding about the processes leading (or not?) to the institutionalisation of accounting, and how accounting continues to shape the business environment. Such topics are especially pertinent given the major corporate collapses of recent years. Why now, for instance, have accounting systems been given so much prominence in how organisations run – especially in the context of the Enron and World.com debacles? Institutional theory, for instance, suggests that the use of accounting displays responsibility – but the recent corporate collapses suggest otherwise. In similar vein, how do organisations manage to confer legitimacy when their accounting systems report poor performance – despite the importation of socially legitimated ways of managing the organisation?

A third line of inquiry is the relationship between accounting and improvements in organisational efficiency. Given its close association with efficiency, do institutionally driven choices have any impact on the efficiency of an organisation (DiMaggio and Powell, 1991)? In the case of for-profit firms it is also important that when an organisation spends significant resources implementing legitimised accounting practices that the legitimacy attributed to the technique is capable of increasing the revenue for that organisation (DiMaggio and Powell, 1991). Whether this factors into the organisational response decisions remains unclear. Finally, the de-institutionalisation processes leading to the replacement of accounting practices remains a mystery, with most studies to date focusing on the institutionalisation rather than the de-institutionalisation of accounting processes.

From a theoretical perspective, there is also potential for further theoretical development to bridge the gaps between the 'old' and 'new' frameworks, and thus advance our understanding of the interactions between the wider social, environmental and political pressures for change and organisational behaviours – including the choices that organisations make in response to these pressures and the processes required to institutionalise change (Dillard *et al.*, 2004; Burns and Baldvinsdottir, 2005; Modell, 2005). Furthermore, in attempting to understand better the dynamics and process of institutional change over time, incorporating stability *and* transformational agency, numerous scholars have called for more longitudinal studies of accounting change (Burns, 2000; Scapens and Jazayeri, 2003).

The variety amongst institutional theories may suggest theoretical richness, but some theorists argue for a need to link all the contributions into a more compact theoretical body of findings that enable researchers to understand social phenomena (Oliver, 1992; DiMaggio and Powell, 1991). In so doing, there have particularly been claims amongst scholars that future institutionalist research should aim to: (1) consider both efficiency and legitimating arguments from the same framework rather than over-emphasis on just one element (Scott, 2001) which may, in turn, allow for more institutional studies of private sector organisations; (2) attend more directly to the dynamics of power, politics and transformational agency (Seo and Creed, 2002); and (3) develop our theorisation of processes and institutional change – i.e. how institutions are created, transformed and extinguished (Dacin *et al.*, 2002).

5.   Concluding Remarks

Over the last two decades, it would appear that a significant number of scholars have adopted institutional theory to conceptualise and understand accounting practice. The recent volume of such works perhaps indicates a growing credibility amongst accounting scholars.

However, institutional theory is a vast and mixed lot, joined by a common premise that 'institutions matter'. There are differences in respective definitions of an 'institution', and adoption of one (or a combination of) approaches means that researchers inherit particular theoretical assumptions, primary foci, and level(s) of analyses. These, in turn, will likely direct us to different aspects of the research subject (including different interpretations of the same subject). Moreover, end-contributions can differ too.

Thus, in a much summarised form, our chapter has attempted to map out the three main institutional theories that, to date, have probably had the most impact on accounting research. We hope this is a useful starting point to help students to identify which strands of institutional theory might prove relevant and useful in their research endeavours. In addition, we have attempted to highlight areas for future theoretical development, the pursuit of which we now invite our contemporaries to continue to engage in.

References

Abernethy, M. A. and Chua, W. F. (1996), "A field study of control system 'redesign': the impact of institutional processes on strategic choice", *Contemporary Accounting Research*, Vol. 13, pp. 569-606.

Ahmed, M. N. and Scapens, R. W. (2000), "Cost allocation in Britain: towards an institutional analysis", *European Accounting Review*, Vol. 9, No. 2, pp. 159-204.

Ahmed, M. N. and Scapens, R. (2003), "The Evolution of cost-based pricing rules in Britain: an institutionalist perspective", *Review of Political Economy*, Vol. 15, No. 2, pp. 173-192.

Alam, M. (1997), "Budgetary process in uncertain contexts: a study of state-owned enterprises in Bangladesh", *Management Accounting Research*, Vol. 8, pp. 147-167.

Ansari, S. and Euske, K. J. (1987), "Rational, rationalizing, and reifying uses of accounting data in organizations", *Accounting, Organizations and Society*, Vol. 12, No. 6, pp. 549-570.

Baiman, S. (1982), "Agency research in managerial accounting: a survey", *Journal of Accounting Literature*, Vol. 1, pp. 154-213.

Baiman, S. (1990), "Agency research in managerial accounting: a second look", *Accounting, Organizations and Society*, Vol. 15, No. 4, pp. 341-371.

Basu, O. N., Dirsmith, M. and Gupta, P. P. (1999), "The coupling of the symbolic and the technical in an institutionalized context: the negotiated order of the GAO's audit reporting process", *American Sociological Review*, Vol. 64, pp. 506-526.

Bealing Jr., W. E. (1994), "Actions speak louder than words: an institutional perspective on the securities and exchange commission", *Accounting, Organisations and Society*, Vol. 19, pp. 555-567.

Bergevarn, L.-E., Mellemvik, F. and Olson, O. (1995), "Institutionalization of municipal accounting – a comparative study between Sweden and Norway", *Scandinavian Journal of Management*, Vol. 11, pp. 25-41.

Boston, J., Martin, J., Pallot, J. and Walsh, P. (1996), *Public Management: The New Zealand Model*, Oxford University Press, Oxford.

Burns, J. (2000), "The dynamics of accounting change: inter-play between new practices, routines, institutions, power and politics", *Accounting, Auditing and Accountability Journal*, Vol. 13, No. 5, pp. 566-596.

Burns, J. and Baldvinsdottir, G. (2005), "An institutional perspective of accountants' new roles – the interplay of contradictions and praxis", *European Accounting Review*, Vol. 14, No. 4, pp. 725-757.

Burns, J. and Scapens, R. (2000), "Conceptualising management accounting change: an institutional framework", *Management Accounting Research*, Vol. 11, pp. 3-25.

Caccia, L. and Steccolini, I. (2006), "Accounting change in Italian local governments: what's beyond managerial fashion?", *Critical Perspectives on Accounting*, Vol. 17, No. 2/3, pp. 154-174.

Carmona, S., Ezzamel, M. and Gutierrez, F. (1997), "Control and cost accounting practices in the Spanish royal tobacco factory", *Accounting, Organizations and Society*, Vol. 22, No. 5, pp. 411-446.

Carmona, S., Ezzamel, M. and Gutierrez, F. (1998), "Towards an institutional analysis of accounting change in the royal tobacco factory of Seville," *The Accounting Historians Journal*, Vol. 25, No. 1, pp. 115-147.

Carmona, S. and Donoso, R. (2004), "Cost accounting in early regulated markets: the case of the Royal Soap Factory of Seville (1525-1692)", *Journal of Accounting and Public Policy*, Vol. 23, No. 2, pp. 129-157.

Carmona, S. and Macias, M. (2001), "Institutional pressures, monopolistic conditions and the implementation of early cost management practices: the case of the royal tobacco factory of Seville (1820-1887)", *Abacus*, Vol. 37, pp. 139-165.

Carpenter, B. and Dirsmith, M. (1993), "Sampling and the abstraction of knowledge in the auditing profession: an extended institutional theory perspective", *Accounting, Organisations and Society*, Vol. 18, pp. 41-63.

Carpenter, V. L. and Feroz, E. H. (1992), "GAAP as a symbol of legitimacy: New York state's decision to adopt generally accepted accounting principles", *Accounting, Organisations and Society*, Vol. 17, pp. 613-643.

Carpenter, V. L. and Feroz, E. H. (2001), "Institutional theory and accounting rule choice: an analysis of four US state governments' decisions to adopt generally accepted accounting principles", *Accounting, Organisations and Society*, Vol. 26, pp. 565-596.

Carruthers, B. G. (1995), "Accounting, ambiguity, and the new institutionalism", *Accounting, Organisations and Society*, Vol. 20, pp. 313-328.

Coase, R. (1937), "The nature of the firm", *Economica*, Vol. 4, pp. 386-405.

Colbert, G. and Spicer, B. (1995), "A multi-case investigation of a theory of the transfer pricing process", *Accounting, Organisations and Society*, Vol. 20, No. 6, pp. 423-456.

Collier, P. M. (2001), "The power of accounting: a field study of local financial management in a police force", *Management Accounting Research*, Vol. 12, No. 4, pp. 465-486.

Covaleski, M. A. and Dirsmith, M. W. (1988a), "An institutional perspective on the rise, social transformation, and fall of a university budget category", *Administrative Science Quarterly*, Vol. 33, pp. 562-587.

Covaleski, M. A. and Dirsmith, M. W. (1988b), "The use of budgetary symbols in the political arena: an historically informed field study", *Accounting, Organisations and Society*, Vol. 13, pp. 1-24.

Covaleski, M. A. and Dirsmith, M. W. (1995), "The preservation and use of public resources: transforming the immoral into the merely factual", *Accounting, Organizations and Society*, Vol. 20, No. 2/3, pp. 147-173.

Covaleski, M. A., Dirsmith, M. W. and Michelman, J. E. (1993), "An institutional theory perspective on the DRG framework, case-mix accounting systems and health-care organisations", *Accounting, Organisations and Society*, Vol. 18, pp. 65-80.

Covaleski, M. A., Dirsmith, M. W. and Samuel, S. (1996), "Managerial accounting research: the contributions of organizational and sociological theories", *Journal of Management Accounting Research,* Vol. 8, pp. 1-35.

Dacin, M. T., Goodstein, J. and Scott, W. R. (2002), "Institutional theory and institutional change: introduction to the special research forum", *Academy of Management Journal,* Vol. 45, No. 1, pp. 45-56.

Dietrich, M. (2001), "Accounting for the economics of the firm", *Management Accounting Research,* Vol. 12, No. 1, pp. 3-20.

Dillard, J., Rigsby, J. T. and Goodman, C. (2004), "The making and remaking of organization context: duality and the institutionalization process", *Accounting, Auditing and Accountability Journal,* Vol. 17, No. 4, pp. 506-542.

DiMaggio, P. and Powell, W. (1983), "The iron cage revisited: institutional isomorphism and collective rationality in organisational fields', *American Sociological Review,* Vol. 48, pp. 147-160.

DiMaggio, P. and Powell, W. (1991), "Introduction", in Powell, W. and DiMaggio, P. (Eds.), *The New Institutionalism in Organisational Analysis,* The University of Chicago Press, London, pp. 1-38.

Euske, K. J. and Riccaboni, A. (1999), "Stability to profitability: managing interdependencies to meet a new environment", *Accounting, Organizations and Society,* Vol. 24, No. 5/6, pp. 463-481.

Flamholtz, D. (1983), "The markets and hierarchies framework: a critique of the model's applicability to accounting and economic development", *Accounting, Organisations and Society,* Vol. 8, No. 3/4, pp. 147-151.

Fogarty, T. J. (1992), "Financial accounting standard setting as an institutionalized action field: constraints, opportunities and dilemmas", *Journal of Accounting and Public Policy,* Vol. 11, pp. 331-355.

Fogarty, T. J., Zucca, L. J., Meonske, N. and Kirch, D. P. (1997), "Proactive practice review: a critical case study of accounting regulation that never was", *Critical Perspectives on Accounting,* Vol. 8, pp. 167-187.

Giddens, A. (1984), *The Constitution of Society: Introduction of the Theory of Structuration,* University of California Press, Berkeley.

Granlund, M. (2001), "Towards explaining stability in and around management accounting systems", *Management Accounting Research,* Vol. 12, pp. 141-166.

Granlund, M. and Lukka, K. (1998), "Towards increasing business orientation: Finnish management accountants in a changing cultural context", *Management Accounting Research,* Vol. 9, No. 2, pp. 185-211.

Greenwood, R. and Hinings, B. (1996), "Understanding radical organizational change: bringing together the old and new institutionalism", *Academy of Management Review,* Vol. 21, No. 4, pp. 1022-1054.

Hamilton, W. (1932), "Institution", in Seligman, E. and Johnson, A. (Eds.), *Encyclopaedia of the Social Sciences* Vol. 8, pp. 84-89.

Hardy, C. (1996), "Understanding power: bringing about strategic change", *British Journal of Management,* Vol. 7 (Special Issue), pp. 3-16.

Hirsch, P. M. and Lounsbury, M. (1997), "Ending the family quarrel: toward a reconciliation of 'old' and 'new' institutionalisms", *American Behavioural Scientist,* Vol. 40, pp. 406-418.

Hodgson, G. M. (1988), *Economics and Institutions: A Manifesto for a Modern Institutional Economics,* Polity Press, Cambridge.

Hoque, Z. and Hopper, T. (1994), "Rationality, accounting and politics: a case study of management control in a Bangladeshi jute mill", *Management Accounting Research,* Vol. 5, No. 1, pp. 5-30.

Hussain, M. and Gunasekaran, A. (2002), "An institutional perspective of non-financial management accounting measures: a review of the financial services industry", *Managerial Auditing Journal,* Vol. 17, pp. 518-536.

Hussain, M. and Hoque, Z. (2002), "Understanding non-financial performance measurement practices in Japanese banks: a new institutional sociology perspective", *Accounting, Auditing and Accountability Journal,* Vol. 15, pp. 162-183.

Hyndman, N. and Eden, R. (2000), "A study of the coordination of mission, objectives and targets in U.K. executive agencies", *Management Accounting Research,* Vol. 11, pp. 175-191.

Johansson, I.-L. and Baldvinsdottir, G. (2003), "Accounting for trust: some empirical evidence", *Management Accounting Research,* Vol. 14, No. 3, pp. 219-234.

Johnson, H. T. (1981), "Toward a new understanding of nineteenth-century cost accounting", *The Accounting Review,* July, pp. 510-518.

Johnson, H. (1983), "The search for gain in markets and firms: a review of the emergence of management accounting systems", *Accounting, Organisations and Society,* Vol. 8, No. 2/3, pp. 139-146.

Kondra, A. Z. and Hinings, C. R. (1998), "Organizational diversity and change in institutional theory", *Organization Studies,* Vol. 19, No. 5, pp. 743-767.

Langlois, R. (1986), *Economics as a Process: Essays in the New Institutional Economics,* Cambridge University Press, Cambridge.

Langlois, R. (Ed.) (1989), *Economics as a Process: Essays in the New Institutional Economics,* Cambridge University Press, New York.

Lapsley, I. (1994), "Responsibility accounting revived? Market reforms and budgetary control in health care", *Management Accounting Research,* Vol. 5, No. 3/4, pp. 337-352.

Lapsley, I. and Pallot, J. (2000), "Accounting, management and organisational change: a comparative study of local government", *Management Accounting Research,* Vol. 11, pp. 213-229.

Lowndes, V. (1996), "Varieties of new institutionalism: a critical appraisal", *Public Administration,* Vol. 74, pp. 181-197.

Major, M. and Hopper, T. (2004), "Extending new institutional theory: regulation and activity-based costing in Portuguese telecommunications", *Paper presented at the 4th Asia-Pacific Interdisciplinary Research on Accounting Conference,* Singapore, 4-6 July 2004.

Maki, U., Gustafsson, B. and Knudsen, C. (Eds.) (1993), *Rationality, Institutions and Economic Methodology,* Routledge, London.

Maxwell, J. A. (2005), *Qualitative Research Design: An Interactive Approach* (Vol. 41), Sage Publications, Thousand Oaks, CA.

Meyer, J. W. (1977), "The effects of education as an institution", *American Journal of Sociology*, Vol. 83, pp. 55-77.

Meyer, J. and Rowan, B. (1977), "Institutionalized organisations: formal structure as myth and ceremony", *American Journal of Sociology*, Vol. 83, pp. 340-363.

Meyer, J. and Scott, W. R. (1983), *Organisational Environments: Ritual and Rationality*, Sage, London.

Meyer, J. and Scott, W. R. (1992), "Centralisation and the legitimacy problems of local government", in Meyer, J. and Scott, W. R. (Eds.), *Organisational Environments: Ritual and Rationality*, Sage, London, pp. 199-216.

Meyer, J., Scott, W. and Deal, T. (1983), "Institutional and technical sources of organisation structure: explaining the structure of educational organisation", in Meyer, J. W. and Scott, W. R. (Eds.), *Organisational Environments*, Russell Sage, New York, pp. 45-67.

Mezias, S. J. and Scarselletta, M. (1994), "Resolving financial reporting problems: an institutional analysis of the process", *Administrative Science Quarterly*, Vol. 39, No. 4, pp. 654-678.

Modell, S. (2001), "Performance measurement and institutional processes: a study of managerial responses to public sector reform", *Management Accounting Research*, Vol. 12, pp. 437-464.

Modell, S. (2002), "Institutional perspectives on cost allocations: integration and extension", *European Accounting Review*, Vol. 11, pp. 653-679.

Modell, S. (2003), "Goals versus institutions: the development of performance measurement in the Swedish university sector", *Management Accounting Research*, Vol. 14, pp. 333-359.

Modell, S. (2005), "Students as consumers? An institutional field-level analysis of the construction of performance measurement practices", *Accounting, Auditing and Accountability Journal*, Vol. 18, No. 4, pp. 537-563.

Modell, S. (2006), "Institutional and negotiated order perspectives on cost allocations: the case of the Swedish university sector", *European Accounting Review*, forthcoming.

Nelson, R. R. and Winter, S. G. (1982), *An Evolutionary Theory of Economic Change*, Belknap Press of Harvard University Press, Cambridge, Mass.

North, D. (1993), "Institutions and economic performance", in Maki, U., Gustafsson, B. and Knudsen, C. (Eds.), *Rationality, Institutions and Economic Methodology*, Routledge, London, pp. 242-261.

Oliver, C. (1991), "Strategic responses to institutional processes", *Academy of Management Review*, Vol. 16, pp. 145-179.

Oliver, C. (1992), "The antecedents of deinstitutionalization", *Organization Studies*, Vol. 13, No. 4, pp. 563-588.

Pettersen, I. J. (1995), "Budgetary control of hospitals – rituals, rhetorics and rationalized myths?", *Financial Accountability and Management*, Vol. 11, pp. 207-221.

Pettersen, I. J. (1999), "Accountable management reforms: why the Norwegian hospital reform experiment got lost in implementation", *Financial Accountability and Management*, Vol. 15, pp. 377-396.

Phillips, N., Lawrence, T. B. and Hardy, C. (2000), "Inter-organizational collaboration and the dynamics of institutional fields", *Journal of Management Studies*, Vol. 37, pp. 23-43.

Powell, W. W. (1991), "Expanding the scope of institutional analysis", in Powell, W. W. and DiMaggio, P. J. (Eds.), *The New Institutionalism in Organisational Analysis*, The University of Chicago Press, Chicago, pp. 183-203.

Rahaman, A. S., Lawrence, S. and Roper, J. (2004), "Social and environmental reporting at the era: institutionalised legitimacy or legitimation crisis?", *Critical Perspectives on Accounting*, Vol. 15, pp. 35-56.

Rutherford, M. (1995), "The old and new institutionalism: can bridges be built?", *Journal of Economic Issues*, Vol. 29, No. 2, pp. 443-451.

Scapens, R. W. (1994), "Never mind the gap: towards an institutional perspective on management accounting practice", *Management Accounting Research*, Vol. 5, No. 3/4, pp. 301-321.

Scapens, B. and Jazayeri, M. (2003), "ERP systems and management accounting change: opportunities or impacts? A research note", *European Accounting Review*, Vol. 12, No. 1, pp. 201-233.

Scott, W. R. (1991), "Unpacking institutional arguments", in Powell, W. W. and DiMaggio, P. J. (Eds.), *The New Institutionalism in Organizational Analysis*, The University of Chicago Press, Chicago, pp. 164-182.

Scott, W. (1995), *Institutions and Organisations*, Sage Publishing, London.

Scott, W. (2001), *Institutions and Organisations*, 2nd edition, Sage Publishing, London.

Scott, W. R. and Christensen, S. (1995), *The Institutional Construction of Organizations: International and Longitudinal Studies*, Sage, Thousand Oaks, CA.

Seal, W. (1999), "Accounting and competitive tendering in the UK local government: an institutionalist interpretation of the new public management", *Financial Accountability and Management*, Vol. 15, pp. 309-327.

Selznick, P. (1996), "Institutionalism 'old' and 'new'", *Administrative Science Quarterly*, Vol. 41, No. 2, pp. 270-277.

Seo, M.-G. and Creed, W. E. D. (2002), "Institutional contradictions, praxis, and institutional change: a dialectical perspective", *Academy of Management Review*, Vol. 27, No. 2, pp. 222-247.

Simon, H. (1976), "From substantive to procedural rationality", in Latsis, S. (Ed.), *Method and Appraisal in Economics*, Cambridge University Press, Cambridge.

Siti-Nabiha, K. A. and Scapens, W. R. (2005), "Stability and change: an institutionalist study of management accounting change", *Accounting, Auditing and Accountability Journal*, Vol. 18, No. 1, pp. 44-73.

Soin, K., Seal, W. and Cullen, J. (2002), "ABC and organisational change: an institutional perspective", *Management Accounting Research*, Vol. 13, pp. 249-271.

Spicer, B. (1988), "Towards an organisational theory of the transfer pricing process", *Accounting, Organisations and Society*, Vol. 13, No. 3, pp. 303-322.

Spicer, B. and Ballew, V. (1983), "Management accounting systems and the economics of internal organisation", *Accounting, Organisations and Society*, Vol. 8, No. 1, pp. 73-96.

ter Bogt, H. J. and Jan van Helden, G. (2000), "Accounting change in Dutch government: exploring the gap between expectations and realizations", *Management Accounting Research*, Vol. 11, pp. 263-279.

Thompson, G. D. (1995), "Problems with service performance reporting: the case of public art galleries", *Financial Accountability and Management*, Vol. 11, pp. 337-350.

Tiessen, P. and Waterhouse, J. H. (1983), "Towards a descriptive theory of management accounting", *Accounting, Organisations and Society*, Vol. 8, No. 3/4, pp. 251-267.

Veblen, T. (1898), "Why is economics not an evolutionary science?", *Quarterly Journal of Economics*, Vol. 12, pp. 373-397.

Veblen, T. (1899), *The Theory of the Leisure Class*, Macmillan, New York.

Veblen, T. (1919), *The Place of Science in Modern Civilization and Other Essays*, Huebsch, New York.

Vromen J. J. (1995), *Economic Evolution: An Inquiry into the Foundations of New Institutional Economics*, Routledge, London.

Walker, M. (1998), "Management accounting and the economics of internal organisation", *Management Accounting Research*, Vol. 9, No. 1, pp. 21-30.

Weick, K. (1976), "Educational organisations as loosely coupled systems", *Administrative Science Quarterly*, March, pp. 1-19.

Wilber, C., and Harrison, R. (1978), "The methodological basis of institutional economics: pattern model, storytelling and holism", *Journal of Economic Issues*, Vol. 12, No. 1, pp. 61-89.

Williamson, O. (1975), *Markets and Hierarchies: Analysis and Anti-Trust Implications. A Study in the Economics of Internal Organisation*, Free Press, New York.

Williamson, O. (1985), *The Economic Institutions of Capitalism: Firms, Markets, Relational Contracting*, New York: The Free Press.

Zimmerman, J. (1997), *Accounting for Decision Management and Control*, 2nd edition, Richard D Irwin, Chicago III.

11

STAKEHOLDER THEORY

Manzurul Alam
Monash University, Australia

Abstract: This chapter discusses the relevance of stakeholder theory in accounting research as an alternative approach to the shareholder theory. As the supremacy of shareholder value maximisation can be questioned in terms of its relevance in contemporary circumstances, a stakeholder perspective has been seen as an appropriate mode for accounting research to progress. This chapter highlights that the success of modern business depends on sustainability which can be achieved by considering the needs of its stakeholders. It concludes with a call for a wider accounting and performance measurement systems for reporting the effects of organisational performance.

Keywords: Shareholder theory, stakeholder theory, legitimacy, accounting reporting and performance evaluation.

1. Introduction

In recent years the debate over whether the corporation should be designed and held accountable for shareholder wealth maximisation or for meeting the goals of multiple stakeholders has intensified (Shankman, 1999). These two theoretical positions (i.e. shareholder vs stakeholder theories) have been recognised as 'two polar opposites' in management literature. The shareholder theory of the firm has been widely accepted in finance and accounting areas with its focus on the shareholder primacy (Friedman, 1970). Such a perspective argues that its application will result in increased wealth and a better allocation of resources in the society (Quinn and Jones, 1995). Often, economic theories, such as, efficient market theory, are put forward to enhance a win-win situation where everybody benefits when businesses implement correct strategies. The shareholder perspective has come under scrutiny as supporters of stakeholder theory often views such a perspective as restrictive, not least, as it focuses only on shareholders and ignores or mistreats other stakeholders. The actual operation of market efficiency in real world has been questioned and argued for wider business responsibilities (Carroll, 1993; Clarkson, 1995). The recent corporate collapses have further fuelled such debate where each group has put forward its own arguments on organisational objectives and governance structure.

The most common distinction between these theories rests mainly on two issues, i.e. property rights and business objectives. The justification for shareholder perspectives has been grounded in property rights concepts enforced by contracts and managers are seen as agents of shareholders (Fligstein, 1990). Under such concepts, the shareholders have rights to determine how their capital and properties are used as an owner. Such views were expressed by Friedman (1970) when he suggested that a firm should have only one objective and that is to maximise the return to shareholders. Other researchers have suggested a variety of goals to broaden the scope of business objectives. Ansoff (1965) argued to separate 'economic' and 'social' objectives where 'economic' objective remains the central focus. Drucker (1965) on the other hand tried to increase the objectives and suggested eight common objectives (market standing, innovation, productivity, financial and physical resources, profitability, manager performance and development, worker performance and attitude, public responsibility). Critics of property rights observe that such rights are socially constructed and should not be seen as ultimate rights over other forms of rights, such as, human rights (Etzioni, 1998; Donaldson and Preston, 1995). Moreover, property rights are seen to restrict distributive justice in the society. Seen from stakeholder perspectives, the business objectives can be extended to include stakeholder objectives (Clarkson, 1995; Mitchell, et al., 1997; Freeman, 1984). More radical views within the stakeholder perspective may view business organisations as social institutions and as such, concentrate on social objectives.

Accounting research has provided importance to the maintenance of capital and income to maximise shareholders' wealth. Such a focus is often criticised as narrow and restrictive (Gray, et al., 1988). If we follow a stakeholder perspective (Freeman, 1984), a wider conception of performance is needed as we cannot maximise the long term value of the organisation without maintaining good relation with its stakeholders. The aim of this paper is to review the stakeholder framework as a formidable framework for accounting research. The paper also points out how accounting research can benefit by adopting a stakeholder approach.

The paper is organised as follows: The next section identifies the theoretical arguments of stakeholder theory. Section three will introduce different modes of stakeholder theories including stakeholder identification process and stakeholder accountabilities. The following section will highlight accounting research within stakeholder theory followed by a section on corporate governance. The conclusion section highlights several research opportunities from stakeholder perspectives.

2. Basis of Stakeholder Theory

As business organisations are social institutions they can affect a society in many ways (Buchholz, 1993). While certain aspects of their operation may bring some positive outcomes, such as generating employment and economic development, there are also externalities that can be created by the operation of business. Such externalities can come in many forms, such as pollutions and emissions, and these can affect the quality of life in the society. Apart from pursuing a profit maximising objective, organisations need to be responsible for their activities in the society. As such, continued operation and success of business activities are dependent on compliance of societal expectations and gaining support for continued existence in the society. Different theoretical positions can be put forward to explore business and societal relationship.

Social contract theorists argue that the basis of organisational existence can be explained by the implicit boundaries of social expectation. An organisation gains legitimacy as long as its activities are guided by social expectations. Legitimacy is ingrained within the theoretical notions of social contract between the organisation and the society (Deegan, 2002). Society expects certain behaviour of a business and consequently such expectations are needed to be given proper consideration for its continued operation. Companies with poor stakeholder performance may find it difficult to acquire necessary support and resources for its operation. Another aspect of social legitimacy comes from maintaining a congruency between social expectations and company performance. However, we would expect that such expectations are likely to change over time and a major role of corporate management is to monitor such changes so that they can correspondently change their operation and reporting activities. Seen from social contract and legitimacy perspectives, the role of management needs to be broadened to satisfy special obligations to other stakeholders than just merely aiming to maximise the wealth of shareholders. Similarly, ethical theories argue for better distribution of resources as these theories see shareholder profit maximisation inappropriately privileges providers of capital at the cost of social welfare.

The social legitimacy of business has also been supported by institutional theorists (Scott, 1987; Scott and Meyer, 1983; Zucker, 1987). Within institutional theories the new institutional theory adopts a broader perspective by including external and internal organisational contexts (DiMaggio and Powell, 1991; Scott, 1987) as compared to the old institutional theory which focuses on the issues of coalition and competing values in organisation (Burns and Scapens, 2000). The new institutional theory is more relevant to understand stakeholder theory as it focuses on ways in which an organisation intersects and interacts with its cultural and social environment. Organisations are situated in an environment which is comprised of cultural and historical forces within which activities are undertaken. In order to legitimise their existence, organisations adopt certain systems, policies and procedures by imitation and copy one another to demonstrate conformity with institutional practices (DiMaggio and Powell, 1991). Even though there are similarities between institutional and stakeholder theories as both focus on gaining societal acceptance and legitimacy, there are significant differences, not least, the institutional theory mainly demonstrates organisational strategies to cope with its significant environment. The stakeholder theory focuses more from stakeholder view of the organisation. While the basis of stakeholder theory is supported by social contract, legitimacy, ethical, and institutional theories, the discussion in the stakeholder theory centres around who is a stakeholder, what stakes they pursue, and how management can undertake strategies to prioritise these stakeholders. The next section deals with these issues.

3. Stakeholder Theories of the Firm

Stakeholder theory challenges the neoclassical economic theory of the firm by upholding the interest of all stakeholders rather than just shareholders. While the stakeholder concept first appeared within the Stanford Research Institute in 1963, an earlier version of such concept can be traced in Scandinavia (Nasi, 1995). During its formative period, the stakeholder theory had to fight for survival and to emerge as a separate theory of the firm. Numerous questions were raised on how to define a stakeholder, how to reconcile their differences, and how to define organisational objectives from a stakeholder perspective (Argenti, 1993; Sternberg, 1997). Argenti (1993) criticised the stakeholder theory on the grounds that such a theory would lead to inefficiency and sub-optimality generally because of conflicts among stakeholders. Instead he suggested that all such multi-purpose organisations should be transformed into single purpose organisations and all stakeholder apart from shareholder should be categorised into 'interest groups' who may have interests in an organisation but have no claim other than specified under the law. While addressing these criticisms, the stakeholder theorists stated that such a theory can be justified on descriptive accuracy, instrumental power, and normative validity (Donaldson and Preston, 1995). We shall address some of these issues later in this section.

There are numerous definitions of what constitute a stakeholder and such definitions come in various forms and flavours. The classical definition was provided by Freeman (1984) from a strategic management point of view to include any group who can affect or is affected by the achievement of organisational activities. While this definition has gained some acceptance, the question remains who is, and who is not a stakeholder. In most cases, the differences depend on the scholarly positions adopted by different researchers. While the instrumental track of stakeholder approach deals with issues such as implications of organisational decision making, interaction, interdependencies, and risk factors, the normative track generally takes a wider definition (Cohen, 1995).

Rather than viewing a unified stakeholder theory, we can see two separate strands of views exist within the literature. There are some who take an instrumental approach and see such concepts as a way to improve organisational performance (Jones, 1995). Instrumental theory may be seen in contrast to neoclassical economic theory as it argues for mutual trust and co-operation for superior results rather than an opportunistic behaviour. Donaldson and Preston (1995) points out that there is no compelling evidence to support that the instrumental stakeholder perspective will lead to a superior business performance. In contrast to instrumental perspectives, the normative stakeholder theory deals with the reasons for promoting stakeholder interests even in the absence of any obvious benefit. Normative theories also assume that each stakeholder has an intrinsic value regardless of his/her actual power and try to argue for human decency rather than commercial success. The following table summarises a few stakeholder models which are commonly referred within the stakeholder literature and such a list is by no means a comprehensive identification of all stakeholder theories.

Table 1
Commonly cited stakeholder models

Stakeholder Models	Promoters	Features
Stakeholder Strategic Management Matrix Model	Freeman (1984)	Stakeholder management on the basis of a four cell Matrix. Stakeholders are priortised on the basis of co-operation and their relative competitive threats
Stakeholder-Agency Theory	Hill and Jones (1992)	Managers have agency responsibility to all major stakeholders, not just shareholders. Acknowledges power differences between different stakeholders.
Feminist Stakeholder Theory	Burton and Dunn (1996)	Stakeholder management on the basis of relationship, quality, care, and need.
Stakeholder Salience Model	Mitchell et al. (1997)	Stakeholder prioritisation on the basis of legitimacy, power and urgency.

Apart from the Feminist stakeholder theory, the other three models (Stakeholder Strategic Matrix, Stakeholder-Agency, Stakeholder Salience models) can be categorised as instrumental branch of stakeholder theory. These theories focus on management strategies to manage stakeholders for attaining organisational objectives. The stakeholder theory is based on care and services to the most disadvantaged stakeholders (Burton and Dunn, 1996).

4. Stakeholder Identification and Prioritisation

Several attempts were made to identify and distinguish stakeholder groups (Freeman, 1984; Clarkson, 1995; Donaldson and Preston, 1995; Mitroff, 1983). The basis question remains as to how we can manage different stakeholders with different needs and demands, does stakeholder theory provide a clear guideline to deal with numerous stakeholders. As the organisation is unlikely to satisfy and protect all stakeholders equally, a strategic response is required to balance and prioritise the demands made by different stakeholders. Stakeholder theorists suggest that companies manage such relationship based on different factors such as, nature of task environment, the salience of stakeholder groups and the value of decision makers that determine the shareholder ranking process (Donaldson and Preston, 1995; Clarkson, 1995).

Clarkson (1995) attempted to rank stakeholders into two categories, i.e. primary and secondary stakeholders. Primary stakeholders are given priority as their support is considered to be vital for the organisation to survive. Such primary stakeholders comprise shareholders, employees, customers, suppliers, lenders, as well as government and communities. The secondary stakeholders are not attached to the organisation on a transactional basis and are not considered to be critical for the survival of the organisation. Included in this group are the environmentalists, media, and consumer advocates. Mitchell *et al.* (1997) tried to produce a comprehensive model to prioritise stakeholders on several key dimensions, such as power, legitimacy, and urgency perspectives. Their theory is helpful in prioritising the main categories of stakeholders. The notions of power can be seen in terms of authority and possession of significant resources by the stakeholders. Stakeholder claims get prioritised if these claims have legitimacy and are perceived to be significant by stakeholders. Mitchell *et al.* (1997) classified stakeholders based on salience into eight different categories from lowest to highest priority groups (non-stakeholder, dormant, discretionary, demanding, dominant, dangerous, dependent and definitive stakeholders). While non-stakeholders have insignificant power, legitimacy, and urgency, other stakeholders are prioritised based on the relative strengths of power, legitimacy and urgency.

While the dormant stakeholders possess power without legitimacy or urgency, the discretionary stakeholders have legitimacy without power and urgency. The demanding stakeholders can make urgent claims but do not possess any power or legitimacy to follow it up effectively. At the next level, the dominant stakeholders have both power and legitimacy and when they are able to mobilise urgent claims they can become definite stakeholders. The dangerous stakeholders have power and urgency but their claims are not viewed as legitimate. The claims of dependent stakeholders are legitimate and urgent but they lack power. At the highest level, the demands of definitive stakeholder are prioritised ahead of other stakeholders as they have urgent legitimate claims with power to back it up.

Figure 1
Stakeholder Typology and Salience Rankings (Mitchell *et al.*, 1997)

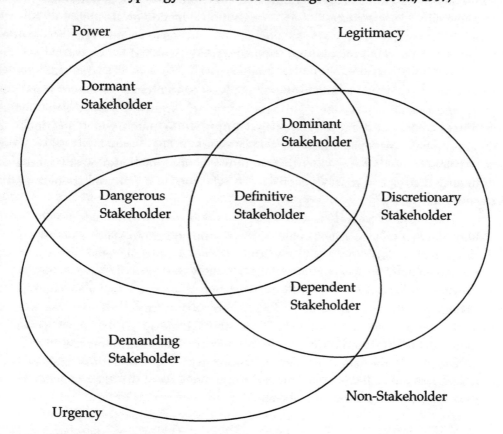

5. Stakeholder Accountability

The concept of accountability requires that organisations are accountable for their activities. Within a wider literature, accountability has been defined from a narrow sense of explaining managerial conduct in discharging different types of managerial responsibilities by providing detailed information on their activities. Jones (1977) states that 'accountability implies a liability to explain to someone else, who has authority to assess the account, and allocate praise or censure'. Stewart (1984) suggested a ladder of accountability ranging from probity and legality to process, performance, programme, and policy accountability. Laughlin (1990) describes accountability in a similar fashion in terms of contractual and communal accountabilities. While 'contractual' implies formal procedures to discharge accountabilities similar to probity and legal accountabilities in Stewart's ladder, communal accountabilities are much broader and less structured which is again similar to policy accountabilities.

Stakeholder accountability with its wider focus as compared to shareholder accountability attempts to identify different stakeholders to whom it may have some responsibility. As the success of an organisation depends on its ability to balance conflicting demands from various stakeholders, it needs to be answerable to a wider group of stakeholder. Werhane and Freeman (1997) identified three possible reasons for stakeholder accountability, i.e. interest-based, right-based, and duty based accountabilities. While an interest-based analysis concentrates on the consequences of organisational actions, the right-based approach argues for fair distribution of resources and opportunities. Duty-based approach is much wider and looks at organisational responsibilities to stakeholders. The scope of stakeholder accountability needs to be wider than commercial accountability (mostly measured in financial terms and assesses profitability, efficiency and financial strength of the organisation).

The question remains as to whether the organisation will be accountable to all stakeholders equally or it will selectively respond to certain stakeholders who are deemed to be significant and powerful. From an ethical sense the corporate management need to pay attention to all, especially the disadvantaged stakeholders. However, as discussed earlier, the organisation does not usually respond to all stakeholders equally. It is the role of managers to balance stakeholder demands so that it can achieve organisational objectives. In reality, the most powerful stakeholders who have control over resources get more priority compared to other stakeholders. As the nature of such relationship changes over time, management needs to assess stakeholder needs on a continuous basis so that they can conform to the changing needs of respective stakeholders.

6. Accounting under Stakeholder Perspectives

Accounting from stakeholder perspective is concerned with a wider conception of organisational performance and reporting, not purely to shareholders, but to a broad range of stakeholders that make up the society. Such a perspective promotes financial, social and environmental information to be disclosed so that different stakeholders can be informed about the effects of organisational operation. Stakeholder approach can be used to widen the scope of accountability (Gray et al., 1997). As a result, separate theories (such as, social and environmental accounting) and reporting guidelines emerged in accounting to include social environmental aspects of organisational performance (Owen et al., 2000; Gray et al., 1988) and the relevance of stakeholder concept is recognised in accounting literature (Gray et al., 1997). Social accounting informs organisational performance on social issues, such as, employment, health and safety, effects of organisational operation to the community. Environment accounting, on the other hand, measures and reports on environmental effects of organisational activities. The Corporate Report (ASSC, 1975) also suggested that corporations should publish further reports to other constituents and 'seek to satisfy, as far as possible, the information needs of users'.

In addition, we can argue that all companies should produce a 'true and fair' financial statement (s. 297 of the Corporation Law). There is some controversy in accounting literature as to what constitutes 'true and fair view' financial statements but we can apply such concepts to suggest wider reporting requirements to represent multi-facet organisational performance.

While stakeholder accounting has gained prominence in the form of social and environment accounting, different reporting guidelines were introduced. Such disclosures can be made either as part of regular accounting reports or as separate disclosures. There are some accounting standards specifically directed towards certain industries and others look at specific areas of organisational activities. The UIG issued Abstract 4 'Disclosure of Accounting Policies for Restoration Obligations in the Extractive Industries' and another requirement for the public reporting of environmentally related information is found at s. 299(1) (f) of the Corporation Law. However, most of these disclosures which are prepared by companies for discharging their stakeholder accountabilities are voluntary in nature and, as such, unregulated. Global Reporting Initiative (GRI) is considered to be a comprehensive guideline apart from SA8000 and AccountAbility1000 (AccountAbility, 2003). GRI is a multi-stakeholder approach for reporting economic, environmental and social dimensions of organisational activities. These guidelines remain voluntary for the organisations to adopt and provide a conceptual framework for developing specific recommendations. SA800 prescribes a set of codes and standards in an effort to bring accountabilities at the factory level. The AccountAbility1000 specifies a process based on ethical principles for reporting organisational performance. It also sets a standard-setting process where different stakeholder groups can be involved. As part of the reporting process, AccountAbility 1000 assists organisations to define goals and targets, measures progress, and establishes a feedback mechanism.

Accounting research has progressed in the areas of social and environmental reporting which are also closely related to stakeholder accountability. As these reportings are largely voluntary, research questions were mainly directed towards issues such as, motivation behind such disclosures (Guthrie and Parker, 1989), disclosure practices with the increase of voluntary group membership (Deegan and Gordon, 1996), self-laudatory behaviour with little negative information (Deegan and Gordon, 1996). Accounting researchers generally tend to view that accounting disclosure can be used as a legitimisation tool to convince the stakeholder that the business is doing the right things and pursuing right objectives as perceived by the society (Meyer and Rowan, 1983).

7.   Performance Reporting from Stakeholder Perspectives

Financial performance evaluation and reporting have long been used to help evaluate the relative success of business activities. Such a measure of performance was viewed as an all inclusive measure of business operation. However, there are many aspects of performance in addition to financial performance of a business including the social and environmental aspects. As such, performance evaluation is often seen to have limited focus given that it ignores the contribution made by different stakeholders. Various calls have been made for expanding the scope of performance measurement and reporting beyond financial measures of performance (Mathew, 1993, Gray, *et al.*, 1997). With the introduction of voluntary reporting guidelines companies are now producing various type of reporting, such as, value added reporting, employee reporting, triple bottom line reporting, social and environmental reporting.

Even though the value added statement remains within the broader perspective of financial performance evaluation from shareholder perspective, it puts performance into 'proper perspectives'. Burchell *et al.* (1985) suggests that the value added statement serves two purposes. Firstly, such a statement broadens the scope of performance on which efficiency and productivity measures can be undertaken to improve the overall performance. Secondly, the value added statements reveal something of a social character of organisational operation. It shows the contribution made by different stakeholders. Value is seen in terms of increase in wealth generation. Such a statement can be of limited use to different stakeholders for several reasons as it fails to highlight the social and environment dimensions of organisational operation.

Apart from value added statements, the other performance measure that comes close to multi-dimensional measurement is the Balanced Scorecard (BSC). The BSC (Kaplan and Norton, 1992) measures performance in four different perspectives and these are financial, customer, internal business, and learning and growth perspectives. Kaplan and Norton (1992) claim such a performance measurement system balances short and long term organisations performance and competing needs of the organisation. Even though BSC is a multi-dimensional measurement and reporting approach it is more explicitly geared towards shareholder value maximisation.

Triple Bottom Line (TBL) reporting has become prominent in recent years for monitoring and reporting social, economic and environmental performance of organisational activities (Brown *et al.*, 2005; Deegan, 1999). The TBL reporting can be considered a holistic approach to engage stakeholders as it communicates social, environmental, and financial information beyond the domains of financial performance. The TBL framework needs to be intertwined with business operation as can lead to the development of practical and achievable goals. Once the TBL reporting is operational, it can identify the weaknesses and gaps in social and environmental practices for future improvements.

As the name suggests, the TBL has three components. The environmental aspects of TBL reporting measure environment effects of organisational activities. Environment effects on air, water, natural resources, and human health are measured and reported. The social side of TBL reporting deals with social effects such as, equality, treatment of minorities, health and safety issues of employees, social contribution and costs, and public concerns. Most of this information can be provided either in financial terms or in narrative statements to satisfy different stakeholders who are interested in the social side of business operation. The financial component discloses financial performance through conventional reporting, such as a statement of changes in financial position, and the balance sheet. Through such multi-dimensional measurement and reporting companies reach different stakeholders to show their contribution and commitment for sustainable development. It also recognises the legitimacy of stakeholders 'right to know' and thus creates a platform for a dialogue where different stakeholders can be involved with the business. Even though TBL styled reporting measures and reports on multi-dimensional aspects of organisational activities, there is lack of empirical evidence to show that such reporting enhances accountability. Controversy remains as to how integration between the three components can be made, how multi-task incentive problems can be solved and how a proper balance these three components can be maintained (Norman and MacDonald (2004)).

While it is generally recognised that a stakeholder approach to reporting and performance evaluation can be useful for the organisation, it is important to see how the basic structure of the organisation can support such relationship from organisational governance perspective. Such an evaluation is much broader as it involves organisational structure and internal processes in line with stakeholder engagement. The next section deals with governances issues from stakeholder perspectives.

8. Organisational Governance from Stakeholder Perspectives

In a profit maximising firm the shareholder supply the capital and bear the risk. As such, the firm remains accountable to its shareholders through its management structure for maximising shareholders wealth. The shareholders are the residual claimants through property right ownership on the assets of the firm. Other parties who contribute towards organisational success are compensated on the basis of agreements (employees are compensated through salary and other entitlements, other suppliers of capital through return of their capital with interests). The accountability relationship towards shareholders is termed as 'fiduciary duty' and such duties are carried out by managers in an agent-principal relationship. The governance issues from a shareholder perspective looks at designing proper mechanisms for controlling managers (agents) so that they act in the interests of shareholders (principal). Such an agency relationship has come under serious scrutiny as it is evident that principal and agents have conflicting interests. Donaldson and Preston (1995) observe that 'the conventional model of the corporation, in both legal and managerial forms, has failed to discipline self-serving managerial behaviour'.

The recent corporate scandals in 2001 and 2002 involving some leading companies, such as Enron, WorldCom, has fuelled the debate concerning different models of corporate governance. It is evident that the existing model of corporate governance can lead to serious consequences. Soon after these corporate collapses, authorities were quick to blame the deficiencies of existing shareholder-based corporate governance and opted for quick solutions in form of better regulations and restrictions on managers. However, it can argue here that when 'Enron' collapsed, it was not only the shareholders but every one of the stakeholders suffered.

The 'Enron' case suggests that we need a better corporate governance structure to ensure that the managers act not only in the shareholders but also other stakeholders as each of the stakeholders has a legitimate or moral right to claim on the value created by the firm. Instead of pursuing a single fiduciary role the stakeholder theory suggests that managers should promote multi-fiduciary roles to protect the interests of stakeholders. Such a governance structure can be devised by mobilising stakeholder commitment and reconciling the differences between different stakeholders.

9.   Conclusion

This chapter has argued for a case for pursuing accounting research from stakeholder perspectives. While it is obvious that there are different versions of stakeholder theory the most fundamental question centres around two issues: (a) what is purpose of the firm, and (b) how accounting and reporting systems can be designed? Stakeholder perspective helps us to broaden our understanding of how different stakeholders can contribute to the success of the organisation. The core of stakeholder theory encourages us to see the value created by different stakeholders who voluntarily come together and support organisational activities. Accounting research can play a significant role in measuring and reporting different aspects of organisational activities, especially considering the corporate social and environment performance of organisation to different stakeholder groups. Accounting research from stakeholder perspectives is still at an early stage and more work needs to be done before introducing a well-balanced reporting and accountability structure.

Accounting research from stakeholder perspectives has grown over the years and raised different issues from social and environmental perspectives. Several new ideas and controversies have attracted many new researchers to investigate different aspects of business reporting and accountability issues from stakeholder perspective. The following kinds of research can be undertaken from an accounting perspective:

(a)   more interdisciplinary research is needed involving different aspects of organisational activities and their connection with accounting and reporting, performance evaluation, and corporate governance;

(b)   more research needs to undertaken on how organisations identify their stakeholders and how they devise their performance reports;

(c) research can also be undertaken to locate the changes in reporting and accountability measures along with the changes in stakeholder demands;

(d) accounting research can concentrate on understanding organisational goals and seeing how managers take mutually advantageous opportunities (e.g. cost reductions throughout the supply chain), and possibly to avert conflict (e.g. communication with dissatisfied stakeholders or activists);

(e) stakeholder research can also help resolve some paradoxes and dilemmas of public sector where partnership and alliances are concerned. The concept of 'public sector bargains' (Hood, 2000) has relevance for greater accountability to different stakeholders;

f) research can concentrate on analysing the effect of relationships with stakeholder groups and different aspects of organisational activities. It would be interesting to investigate how organisations design their organisational processes, including measurement and reporting in relation to stakeholder management to address stakeholder concerns;

(g) a composite index can be used for evaluating the performance of management across all dimensions. Several issues need to be resolved, such as, how to balance different objectives and how to design an index and how to trade-off between stakeholders? Accounting research can be undertaken to introduce a performance reporting system which is wider than mere measurement of financial performance.

There are enormous research potentials for investigating accounting from stakeholder perspectives and such a prospect is a promising one. This chapter has highlighted the elements of stakeholder theory and accounting research which definitely open a new dimension for accounting research.

References

AccountAbility, (2003), *AA1000 Assurance Standard*, Institute of Social and Ethical AccountAbility, London, UK.

Ansoff, I. (1965), *Corporate Strategy*, McGraw Hill, New York, NY.

Argenti, J. (1993), *Your Organisation: What Is It For?*, McGraw-Hill, London.

Brown, D., Dillard, J. and Marshall, S. (2005), *Triple Bottom Line: A Business Metaphor for a Social Construct*, paper presented at Critical Perspectives on Accounting, New York.

Buchholz, R. A. (1993), *Principles of Environmental Management: The Greening of Business*, Prentice Hall, Englewood Cliffs, NJ.

Burchell, S., Clubb, C. and Hopwood, A. (1985), Accounting in its social context: Towards a history of value added in the United Kingdom *Accounting, Organizations and Society*, Vol. 10, No. 4, pp. *381-413*

Burns, J. and Scapens, R. W. (2000), "Conceptualizing management accounting change: an institutional framework", *Management Accounting Research*, Vol. 11, pp. 3-25.

Burton, B. K. and Dunn, C. P. (1996), "Feminist ethics as moral grounding for stakeholder theory", forthcoming in *Business Ethics Quarterly*, Vol. 6, No. 2.

Carroll, A. (1993), *Business and Society: Ethics and Stakeholder Management*, South-Western Publishing, Cincinnati.

Clarkson, M. (1995), "A stakeholder framework for analyzing and evaluating corporate social performance", *Academy of Management Review*, Vol. 20, pp. 65-91.

Cohen, S. (1995), "Stakeholders and consent", *Business & Professional Ethics Journal*, Vol. 14, No. 1, pp. 3-14.

Deegan, C. (1999), "Triple bottom line reporting: a new reporting approach for the sustainable organisation', *CA Charter*, April, Vol. 70, No. 3, pp. 38-40.

Deegan, C. (2002), "The legitimising effect of social and environmental disclosures – a theoretical foundation", *Accounting, Auditing & Accountability Journal*, Vol. 15, No. 3, pp. 282-311.

Deegan, C. and Gordon, B. (1996), "A study of the environmental disclosure policies of Australian corporations", *Accounting and Business Research*, Vol. 26, No. 3, p187-199,

DiMaggio, P. J. and Powell, W. (1991), 'Introduction', *The New Institutionalism in Organisational Analysis*, University of Chicago Press, Chicago, IL.

Donaldson, T. and Preston, L. E. (1995), "The stakeholder theory of the corporation: concepts, evidence, and implications", *Academy of Management Review*, Vol. 20, pp. 65-91.

Drucker, P. (1965), *The Practice of Management*, Mercury Books, London.

Etzioni, A. (1998), "A communitarian note on stakeholder theory", *Business Ethics Quarterly*, Vol. 8, No. 4, pp. 679-691.

Fligstein, N. (1990), *The Transformation of Corporate Control*, Harvard University Press, Cambridge, MA.

Freeman. R. E. (1984), *Strategic Management: A Stakeholder Approach*, Pitman Publishing Inc., Marshfield, Massachusetts, USA.

Friedman, M. (1970), "The social responsibility of business is to increase its profits", *New York Times Magazine*.

Guthrie, J. and Parker, L. (1989), "Corporate social reporting: a rebuttal of legitimacy theory", *Accounting and Business Research*, Vol. 19, No. 76, 343 (10 pages)

Gray, R., Dey, C., Owen, D., Evans, R. and Zadek, S. (1997), "Struggling with the praxis of social accounting: stakeholders, accountability, audits and procedures", *Accounting, Auditing & Accountability Journal*, Vol. 10, No. 3, pp. 325-364.

Gray, R., Owen, D. and Maunders, K. (1988), "Corporate social reporting: emerging trends in accountability and the social contract", *Accounting, Auditing & Accountability Journal*, Vol. 1, No. 1, pp. 6-20.

Hill, C. W. L. and Jones, T. M. (1992), "Stakeholder-agency theory", *Journal of Management Studies*, Vol. 29, No. 2 p131, 24p.

Hood, C. (2000), "Paradoxes of public-sector managerialism, old public management and public service bargains", *International Public Management Journal*, Vol. 3, No. 1, pp. 1-22.

Jones, T. M. (1995), "Instrumental stakeholder theory: a synthesis of ethics and economics", *Academy of Management Review*, Vol. 20, pp. 404-437.

Jones, G. W. (1977), "Responsibility in government", London School of Economics.

Kaplan, R. S. and Norton, D. P. (1992), "The balanced scorecard – measures that drive performance", *Harvard Business Review*, Vol. 70 Issue 1, p71-79, January-February.

Laughlin, R. (1990), "A model of Financial Accountability and the Church of England", *Financial Accountability & Management*, Oxford, Summer 1990, Vol. 6, No. 2; p. 93.

Mathew, M. R. (1993), *Socially Responsible Accounting*, Chapman and Hall, London.

Meyer, J. W. and Rowan, B. (1983), "The structure of educational organisations", in Meyer, J.W. and Scott, W.R. (Eds.), *Organisational Environment: Ritual and Rationality*, Sage, Beverly Hills, pp. 71-98.

Mitchell, R. K., Agle, B. R. and Wood, D. J. (1997), "Toward a theory of stakeholder identification and salience", *Academy of Management Review*, Vol. 22, No. 4, pp. 853-866.

Mitroff, Ian I. (1983), *Stakeholders of the Organizational Mind*, Jossey-Bass, San Francisco.

Näsi, J. (Ed.) (1995), *Understanding Stakeholder Theory*, Helsinki, Finland.

Norman, W. and MacDonald, C. (2004), "Getting to the bottom of 'triple bottom line'", *Business Ethics Quarterly*, Vol. 14 Issue 2, p243-262.

Owen, D. L. Swift, T. A; Humphrey, C. and Bowerman, M. (2000), "The new social audits: accountability, managerial capture or the agenda of social champions?", *European Accounting Review*, May, Vol. 9, No. 1, pp. 81-98.

Quinn, D. P. and Jones, T. M. (1995), "An agent morality view of business policy", *Academy of Management Review*, Vol. 20, No. 1, pp. 22-42.

Scott, W. and Meyer, J. W. (1983), "The organisation of societal sector", in Meyer, J. W. and Scott, W. R. (Eds.), *Organisational Environment: Ritual and Rationality*, Sage, Beverly Hills, pp. 129-154.

Scott, W. R. (1987), "The adolescence of institutional theory", *Administrative Science Quarterly*, Vol. 32, pp. 493-511.

Shankman, N. A. (1999), "Reframing the debate between agency and stakeholder theories of the firm", *Journal of Business Ethics*, Vol. 19, No. 4, pp. 319-334.

Sternberg, E. (1997), "The defects of stakeholder theory", *Corporate Governance: An International Review*, January, Vol. 5, No. 1, pp. 3-10.

Stewart, J. (1984), "The role of information in public accountability", in Hopwood, A. and Tomkins, C. (Eds.), *Issues in Public Sector Accounting*, Philip Allan Publishers Limited, Oxford.

Werhane, P. and Freeman, R. E. (1997), *The Blackwell Encyclopaedic Dictionary of Business Ethics*, Blackwell Publishing Ltd, Oxford.

Zucker, L. G. (Ed.) (1987), *Institutional Patterns and Organizations*, Ballinger, Cambridge, MA, pp. 3-22.

12

INTERPRETING MANAGEMENT ACCOUNTING SYSTEMS WITHIN PROCESSES OF ORGANISATIONAL CHANGE

Cristiano Busco

Università di Siena, Italy

Abstract: The objective of this chapter is to offer a snapshot of some of the recent attempts to conceptualise management accounting systems within its organisational context. Such systems both comprise and extend the traditional financial measurement systems and, as such, raise questions about the 'broadened' role of management accounting within processes of organisational change and transformation. The chapter surveys different streams of 'alternative' management accounting research as identified within recent reviews, and focuses on interpretive perspectives influenced by the work of Latour, Foucault and Giddens. Moreover, as the chapter addresses cognitive vs behavioural dimensions of change, an institutional framework for interpreting the linkages between management accounting systems and organisational change is presented. In so doing, the intensity of processes of change is discussed by looking at the evolutionary vs revolutionary patterns.

Keywords: Management accounting; Organisational change; Structuration theory; Institutional theory; Routines.

1. Introduction

The last few decades have witnessed major transformations in organisational processes, with considerable re-engineering according to diverse operational and business philosophies. In the face of increasing market uncertainty and complexity, there have been continuous efforts to secure competitive advantage through strategic innovations in both product and process technology. This process continues today, and it could be argued that the continuous alignment of business processes with corporate strategies is the main challenge facing 'world class corporations' in the new millennium.

In the process of adapting to the uncertain business environment, organisational resources and processes have to be organised and monitored to achieve the goals individuated by the corporate vision of the business. As such, organisational leaders must translate their broad vision and their strategies into specific goals (and associated performance measures) and communicate them throughout the organisation. For this purpose, they are increasingly relying on new initiatives of organisational transformation, driven by 'holistic' (i.e. comprehensive, organisation-wide) performance measurement systems.

Such systems both comprise and extend the traditional financial measurement systems and, as such, raise questions about the 'broadened' role of management accounting within processes of organisational transformation (see, among others, Scapens, 1994, 1999; Burns and Vaivio, 2001; Quattrone and Hopper, 2001; Busco *et al.*, 2006). From such a perspective, management accounting systems play a key role in binding the dimensions of change, as they have the potential to organise, monitor and manage the alignment of *macro* corporate strategies (usually financially driven and customer oriented) with *micro* business processes (which need to be constantly re-engineered to promote organisational learning and growth).

The large number of field studies that have recently attempted to illustrate the processes of management accounting change within their complex corporate settings has enhanced interest in possible theoretical understandings of these organisational dynamics. Even if the implication of accounting practices within processes of organisational change does not seem to be in question (see Macintosh and Scapens, 1990; Dent, 1991; Burns and Scapens, 2000; McNamara *et al.*, 2004; Bhimani and Roberts, 2004), what is still far from clear is our understanding of the modalities through which such a linkage is accomplished during day-to-day corporate life. The objective of this chapter is to offer a snapshot of some of the recent attempts to conceptualise management accounting change within its organisational context.

The chapter is structured as follows. Section two focuses on some key research issues that have recently featured the study of management accounting systems in their social and cultural context. Within this section, the impacts of environmental, organisational and technological transformations on researching management accounting change are also discussed. Next, section three surveys the different streams of 'alternative' management accounting research as identified within a recent review. In so doing, we focus our attention on the perspectives influenced by the work of Latour, Foucault and Giddens. Then, within section four we focus our analysis on the cognitive vs behavioural dimensions of change, as an institutional framework for interpreting the linkages between management accounting systems and organisational change is presented. In so doing, we explore the intensity (pace) of the processes of change by looking at the evolutionary vs revolutionary patterns. The chapter ends with some final remarks.

2. Exploring Management Accounting Change in its Organisational Context

Over the past 25 years academics and professional accountants world-wide have been debating the relevance, nature and roles of management accounting systems within their organisational contexts (Ashton *et al.*, 1995). In the course of this debate there have been numerous interesting contributions providing evidence to illustrate and/or support different views (Kaplan, 1984; Roberts and Scapens, 1985; Johnson and Kaplan, 1987; Bromwich and Bhimani, 1989, 1994; Ezzamel *et al.*, 1993, 1996; Drury *et al.*, 1993; Scapens *et al.*, 1996; Shields, 1997; Burns and Vaivio, 2001; Baxter and Chua, 2003). As emphasised by Chua (1988), the heterogeneity of the areas on which management accounting research has relied, suggests that this branch of accounting is a 'derived subject' whose understanding involves insights from numerous social science disciplines.

Despite a widespread agreement which defines management accounting as a system tailored to provide 'information that assists managers in fulfilling *goals* of the organisation' (Horngren *et al.*, 1994, p. 4; see also Kaplan and Atkinson, 1998; Barfield *et al.*, 1991), there are many conceptualisations of the role which systems of measurement and accountability play within the corporate realm. While the traditional view which emerged in the 1960s considers these systems to be objects which economically ensure effective and efficient use of resources (Anthony *et al.*, 1992), during the 1980s, there have been many calls to expand management accounting research beyond the technical focus represented by the established 'conventional wisdom' (Hopper and Powell, 1985; Hopwood, 1987; Macintosh and Scapens, 1990). In particular, these perspectives have led a wide range of scholars to search for much deeper perspectives, explaining management accounting practices as social, cultural and political phenomena (Cooper, 1980; Tinker, 1980). Debating about the need to understand accounting practices in their organisational context, Roberts and Scapens (1985, p. 443) point out two broad sets of concerns:

> ... First, by concentrating on accounting practice we sought to remedy what we saw as the rather piecemeal and overly technical character of much contemporary accounting research. A great deal of accounting research focuses rather narrowly on particular elements of accounting systems – budgeting, investment, inflation accounting, etc., often with an implicit concern to improve the efficiency of these systems ... . Our second broad concern was to locate accounting within its 'organisational context' [Hopwood, 1983]. In general, academic accountants have adopted a rather accounting-centric approach to research. Accounting has been treated as if it were a functionally autonomous sphere of practice, and consequently there has been a corresponding neglect of the relationships between accounting and other functional areas within organisations ... .

The debate over processes of management accounting change within the broad organisational context in which they occur heightened during the late 1980s, especially after the publication of Johnson and Kaplan's *Relevance Lost* in 1987. In their seminal work, Johnson and Kaplan questioned the relevance of contemporary management accounting practice. In particular, they wonder whether there has been sufficient change in management accounting techniques to meet the changing business environment, and to fulfill the increasing internal demands for information.

In light of the considerable environmental, organisational and technological transformations which took place over the second part of the twentieth century, Johnson and Kaplan claimed that management accounting had lost its relevance, and as a result, it was failing to support business managers with the key information they need to perform their tasks. Basically, due to the considerable technological and financial constraints, Johnson and Kaplan's explanation for the relevance lost was that companies had generally opted for internal information systems which were mainly designed to meet the compulsory requirements of external financial reporting. For this reason, they call for new *advanced* management accounting techniques to be developed and implemented.

As suggested by Burns *et al.* (2003), the debate over the changing nature of management accounting has been supported by a wide array of research, whose findings are not uniform and, sometimes, contradictory. Therefore, when surveying the literature of the 1990s, it is not surprising to find several contributions – particularly those written by leading American accounting scholars – addressing the issue of management accounting change by describing the successful introduction of new accounting techniques, such as activity-based cost management, strategic management accounting and the balanced-scorecard to name only a few (see, among others, Horngren *et al.*, 1994; Kaplan and Atkinson, 1998).

In the UK, questionnaire surveys and case studies have been used to confirm (Drury *et al.*, 1993; Friedman and Lyne, 1995) or challenge (Scapens, 1994; Loft, 1995; Scapens *et al.*, 1996) Johnson and Kaplan's *manifesto*. Among the others, Scapens *et al.* (1996) commented on the supposed pre-eminence of external financial reporting over management accounting: in particular, they argued that, due to advances in information technology, there are enough 'buffers' placed between the two such that both demands for information can be simultaneously met. The argument put forward is that management accounting practices are definitely changing. However, rather than new management accounting systems or techniques, change often entails the manner in which traditional and/or new techniques are actually being used (Burns and Baldvinsdottir, 1999; Burns *et al.*, 2003).

Many of the studies seeking to explain the behavioural implications of accounting practices are often informed by the insights of social science theories. Portraying themselves as 'non-mainstream', such contributions are often characterised by a 'non-positivist' language and, for this reason, labelled as 'alternative' management accounting research (Ashton *et al.*, 1995; Ryan *et al.*, 2002). Recently, Baxter and Chua (2003) debated the nature of management accounting change by pointing to the role of *alternative research*[31] in attesting 'the improbability of purposeful and predictable change' (p. 105). In particular, they argue that 'there is little empirical evidence that a self-enlightened, well-engineered and progressive path characterises the development of management accounting technologies' (2003, p. 105). Insights from Baxter and Chua's review are offered in the following section, where we take a closer look at those research perspectives influenced by the work of Latour, Foucault and Giddens.

3.   Insights From 'Alternative' Management Accounting Research

Baxter and Chua build their argument in light of the contents of several studies which have appeared in the journal *Accounting, Organizations and Society* since its inception in 1976 until 1999. They confined their attention to those contributions 'that mobilise a 'non-positivist' language to typify management accounting practice' (2003, p. 97). In particular, they decided to 'focus on research that draws on non-positivistic strands of social theory; thus choosing to review research that reflects the interpretive, critical and post modern turns that have occurred more widely throughout the social sciences of the period ... . Accounting is a discipline of the social and it seemed important to us to understand it in the context of a broader set of discourses from the social sciences' (2003, p. 98). In so doing, they draw on studies such as:

- Chua (1995) and Preston *et al.* (1992) to account for the difficult, slow and contested path which characterised the implementation of DRGs-based costing within the health sector;

- Ezzamel and Bourn (1990); Czarniawska-Joerges (1988); Jönsson (1982); Boland and Pondy (1983, 1986) to illustrate the problems that specific organisations experienced in adapting management accounting systems to the changing environmental contexts;

- Hedberg and Jönsson (1978); Cooper *et al.* (1981); Roberts and Scapens (1985); Covaleski and Dirsmith (1983, 1988); Roberts (1990); Dent (1991), and Covaleski *et al.* (1993) to portray accounting practice as part of the institutionalised repertoire of organisations and, for this reason, facilitating stability rather than change.

'Yet', as Baxter and Chua recognise, 'management accounting change does occur, despite these factors that seem to stand in opposition to it' (2003, p. 106). Accordingly, they list some studies which have offered insights into management accounting change (among others, Hopwood, 1987; Miller, 1991; Ahrens, 1996, 1997; Vaivio, 1999). However, commenting on the nature of processes of accounting change, Baxter and Chua (2003, p. 106-107) argue that:

---

[31]   A review of this literature is offered later in the chapter. For the moment, alternative *management accounting research* suggests 'non-mainstream' and 'non-positivist' studies, often informed by the insights of social science theorists.

> *... there is little or no sense of any technical elegance or excellence propelling management accounting change. As such, we are left with a sense of what accounting change is not. Accounting change is not linear, predictable, controllable, exclusively technical or well-behaved.*

Baxter and Chua portray management accounting systems as 'a highly situated phenomena' (2003, p. 108). They suggest how such practices are limited by:
- historical conditions that are specific to given times and places;
- local meanings and values;
- local rationalities found in particular organisational settings;
- the individual habitudes of organisational participants.

In their review, Baxter and Chua identify seven different streams of alternative management accounting research. Responding to the calls for more studies on *Accounting in Action* (Hopwood, 1978; Burchell *et al.*, 1980), such streams can be synthesised as follow:

(1)   *a non-rational design school:* presented as one of the earliest streams of alternative management accounting research to appear in the journal, this perspective 'questions presumptions of rationality in organisational choice – that is, an elaboration of clear, consistent and transitive goals; comprehensive searches for feasible alternatives to problems; a consideration of these alternatives in terms of costs and benefits; and optimised decision strategies' (Baxter and Chua, 2003, p. 98). Among others, examples of this research are Hedberg and Jönsson (1978), Boland (1979, 1981) and Cooper *et al.* (1981). Overall, according to Baxter and Chua, 'research from the non-rational design school helps us to appreciate the problematic construction of management accounting information systems and their constitutive/constraining role in organisational sense-making – a characterisation that is quite distinct from ideas about the sensible allocation of resources that underscores other accounts of management accounting information systems and their use' (2003, p. 99);

(2)   *the naturalistic research:* Baxter and Chua introduce this school as describing management accounting practice 'in situ', that is, in its everyday organisational context. They suggest that there is little that is cumulative within the naturalistic research perspective, i.e. each study addresses a unique aspect of management accounting practice: 'from these studies ... we learn that management accounting technologies are enacted quite differently from one organisation to another; conveying local values, meanings and nuances'. Examples of this research include Boland and Pondy (1983, 1986), Berry *et. al.* (1984), Dent (1991), Ahrens (1997), Mouritsen (1999) and Vaivio (1999);

(3)   *the radical alternative:* this approach is characterised by the attempt to demonstrate how organisational practices, such as management accounting, can be implicated in the creation and maintenance of an unequal society: 'the radical alternative mobilises research to provide a platform for critique,

change and improvement within organisations, in particular, and society, in general' (2003, p. 100). According to Baxter and Chua, within the radical perspective researchers do so in two ways: 'first, they mobilise its critical rhetoric in discussions about management accounting .... Second, they use its radical theories to orientate empirical investigations of management accounting practice' (2003, p. 100). Examples of this research include Armstrong (1987), Hopper *et. al.* (1987), Laughlin (1987), Hopper and Armstrong (1991) and Arnold (1998);

(4) *institutional theory:* the contributions included within this category have been influenced mostly by the institutional approaches that have emerged within organisation theory and sociology, where 'there has been an explicit movement towards cognitive and cultural explanations of institutions, focusing on the meaning and accomplishment of various rules that structure behaviour in organisations and society' (2003, p. 100). In particular, drawing on the work of Meyer and Rowan (1977) as well as Powell and DiMaggio (1991), contributions such as Covaleski and Dirsmith (1983, 1988) and Covaleski *et al.* (1993) portray management accounting practices 'as "rational myths" that confer social legitimacy upon organisational participants and their actions' (Baxter and Chua, 2003, p. 100);

(5) *the Latourian approach:* the scholars which rely on the work of Latour (1987, 1993) aim to demonstrate that accounting numbers and information are constructed to accommodate different interests within the organisation. In particular, 'it is argued that management accounting numbers are 'fabrications' or inscriptions 'built' to take on the appearance of 'facts'' (Baxter and Chua, 2003, p. 102). Therefore, contributions such as Miller (1991), Chua (1995) and Ogden (1997) are identified as discussing how 'the mundaneness of management accounting numbers facilitates the embedding of partisan values into daily routines and organisational functioning' (2003, p. 102).

More recently, Quattrone and Hopper (2001) mobilised Latour's sociology of translation and social constructivism to problematise what they call a *modernist construction of change*. Taking an epistemological perspective on change, they suggest that 'modernist beliefs' take-for-granted what constitutes change and avoid to engage with its definition. In so doing, they challenge theories and studies informed by both individualism and contextualism:

> *Studies based on individuals' rational choice imply that change flows from purposive actions in accordance with an objective, external reality whereas contextualism argues that change results from institutional pressures, isomorphisms and routines. But both depict change as the passage of an entity, whether an organization or accounting practice, from one identifiable and unique status to another. Despite their differences over whether reality is independent, concrete and external, or socially constructed, both assume that actors (or researchers) can identify a reality to trace the scale and the direction*

of changes. This reflects modernist beliefs that organizational space and time are unique and linear (2001, p. 403).

Along these lines, Quattrone and Hopper (2001) rejects linear and purposive conceptions of knowledge, action and rationality, redefining these with the notions of 'enaction', poly-rationality and praxis. Accordingly, abstract and institutionalised forms of knowledge, action and rationality have little influence upon behaviour in organisation since actors attribute meaning through enaction and everyday praxis in a context of poly-rationality. For these reasons, Quattrone and Hopper introduce the concepts of 'drift' and 'a-centred organizations' as proxies for conventional definitions of change and organization. Therefore, *drift* resembles incomplete attempts at organising rather than a move from and to a tangible, definable and reified objects. This make the organisation *a-centred*: multiple centres and points of view attempts to order events, but each attempt is incomplete and unable to centre the organisation in itself.

Such a perspective has major implications for the study of how and why accounting information is produced and its effects on organisational drift, within the context of dynamic and evolutionary fabrications of knowledge in organisations. In particular, suggest Quattrone and Hopper:

Accounting knowledge needs to be treated as a co-production of different points of view across multiple organizational worlds, times and spaces, rather than a static and centred performance measurement activity for predetermined ends (2001, p. 403);

(6) *the Foucauldian approach;* the work of Foucault (1972, 1977) has deeply influenced the emergence of the so-called 'new history' of management accounting. In particular, 'following Foucault's theme of 'archaeology', new histories outline and examine the conditions of possibility that enable particular management accounting technologies to emerge at given times and places' (Baxter and Chua, 2003, p. 101; see also Hopwood (1987) and Miller and O'Leary (1993)). According to Loft: 'Foucault's method for doing historical research involves the detailed study of archives. In this, there are some commonalities with the neoclassical approach, but whilst the neoclassicists emphasise the development of techniques to measure product costs, Foucauldians emphasise the development of techniques for measuring human performance – the origins of accounting as a disciplinary technique' (1995, p.42).

A key contribution within the Foucauldian perspective is offered by Miller and O'Leary's (1987, 1994) studies on the history of budgeting and standard costing during the first three decades of the twentieth century. Within these contributions standard costing and budgeting are portrayed as practices that facilitate the emergence of the 'governable person' within organisations. Miller and O'Leary explore these practices at the level of the governance of economic life which, they argue, should be understood in a dual sense as an ensemble of 'rationalities' and 'technologies'. By *rationalities* they mean 'the changing vocabularies or discursive fields through which collective meaning is given to the ideals that set out the objects and objectives of government', while *technologies* stand for 'all those calculations, techniques, apparatuses, documents and numerous other devices for acting upon the individuals, entities and activities in conformity with a particular set of ideals' (1994, p. 99).

Considered in this dual sense, the governance of economic life within organisations consists in acting upon individuals in order to ally them with the objectives fixed by management. Accordingly, standard costing and budgeting should be considered as 'technologies of governance', through which the exercise of power in advanced industrial societies has shifted. These techniques provided a new way of acting that facilitated the monitoring of individuals' (in)efficiencies, i.e. making them accountable by reference to prescribed standards.

By drawing on Foucault's insights, Miller and O'Leary describe accounting (costing) as a technology of governance to direct workers *at a distance*. In particular, they emphasise how the relevance of accounting has historically extended far beyond the conventional views of its role and essence. Therefore, as argued by Hopwood and Miller (1994, p. 20), 'if we are to understand fully how particular ways of accounting have emerged, and why such significance has accorded them, we have to move beyond the boundaries of the organisation and examine the social and institutional practice of accounting'. Accounting is no longer to be regarded as a neutral subject that objectively reports economics event or facts. Accounting practices and rationales are shifting to higher relevance, in that they can be seen as a system for acting upon individuals while 'shaping their beliefs and behaviour in directions deemed desirable' (Miller and O'Leary, 1994, p. 99);

(7) *structuration theory:* relying on the insights of Giddens' theory of structuration (1984), the contributions classified under this label interpret accounting systems as ways of regularising organisational processes across time and space. In doing so, situations of stability and change are conceptualised as the product of the recursive relationship between *agency*, i.e. individuals' capability to make choices, and the reproduction of *social structures*. One of the building blocks of structuration theory is represented by the need for ontological security which characterise agency. Such a sense of safety is provided by routinised behaviour. Consequently, as noted by Baxter and Chua (2003, p. 100), since 'the routinised nature of much of human behaviour accounts for the replication of given structures across space and time', social structures 'can maintain their saliency in structuring behaviour long after the face-to-face interactions (or 'co-presence') necessary to constitute such regularised practices have ceased'. Organisational rules and routines become

crucial in specific circumstances, when face-to-face contact is not always possible. Accordingly, within particular organisations such as multinational or global corporations, management accounting systems 'become a way of supplementing local meanings and norms by imposing discipline on the work of dispersed organisational participants' (Baxter and Chua, 2003, p. 101). Building on the contributions of Roberts and Scapens (1985), Macintosh and Scapens (1990) interpret management accounting systems in light of Giddens' structuration theory (see also Seal *et al.*, 2004; Busco *et al.*, 2006). In particular, drawing on Giddens' key concepts of *duality of structure* and *structuration*[32], they portray structuration theory as indicating 'the ways in which accounting is involved in the institutionalization of social relations' (p. 474). In so doing, they argue that:

> *management accounting systems represent modalities of structuration in the three dimensions of signification, legitimation and domination* (1990, p. 462).

Importantly, although separable analytically, the three dimensions of structure proposed by Giddens are, in practice, inextricably linked. As explained by Macintosh and Scapens, these dimensions can be drawn upon in interpreting the nature and the role of accounting practices:

> *command over the management accounting process, for example, is a resource which can be used in the exercise of power in organisations. Drawing on the domination structure certain organisational participants hold others accountable for particular activities. Management accounting is a key element in the process of accountability. However, the notion of accountability in management accounting terms makes sense only in the context of the signification and legitimation involved in management accounting practices. Organizational participants make sense of actions and events by drawing upon meanings embedded in management accounting concepts and theories. Furthermore, management accounting gives legitimacy to certain actions of organizational participants* (1990, p. 457).

Therefore, according to Macintosh and Scapens, management accounting practices are deeply implicated in the signification, legitimation and domination structures which characterise the socially constructed organisational reality. Importantly, they conceptualise these systems as 'modalities of structuration', i.e. which have a pivotal role in the recursive relationship between agency and structure.

---

[32] Giddens' theoretical contribution, as well as its use by management accounting scholars, represents one of the main pillars of this contribution. For this reason the building blocks of the theory of structuration are presented and discussed in detail in Chapter Three and Four.

In particular, individuals have the potential to draw on accounting practices as *interpretative schemes* for communicating meanings and understandings within the *signification* structure.

Management accounting provides managers with a means of understanding the activities of their organization and allows them to communicate meaningfully about those activities. As such, a management accounting system is an interpretative scheme which mediates between the signification structure and social interaction in the form of communication between managers. The signification structure in this case comprises the shared rules, concepts, and theories which are drawn upon to make sense of organisational activities (1990, p. 460).

Looking at the *legitimation* structure, Macintosh and Scapens (1990) propose that accounting systems participate in the institutionalisation of the reciprocal rights and obligation of social actors. In so doing, they argue how management accounting systems 'embody norms of organizational activity and provide the *moral underpinnings* for the signification structure and the financial discourse' (p. 460; emphasis added). And again:

They legitimate the rights of some participants to hold others accountable in financial terms for their actions. They communicate a set of values and ideals about what is approved and what is disapproved, and what rewards and penalties can be utilized. As such, management accounting systems are not an objective and neutral means of conveying economic meanings to decision makers. They are deeply implicated in the reproduction of values, and are a medium through which the legitimation structure can be drawn upon in social interaction within organisations (p. 460).

The third dimension of structure, i.e. *domination*, is strongly related to the concept of *power*. While in a broad sense power is considered as 'the ability to get things done and to make a difference in the world' (Macintosh and Scapens, 1990, p. 461), its narrow meaning simply implies domination. Roberts and Scapens (1985) pointed out that, within structuration theory, agency is conceptualised as being involved with power in both the broad and narrow sense. In particular, it is important to emphasise the role of 'resources' as facilities through which individuals draw upon the domination structure in the exercise of power.

Asserting that, in particular space-time locations, the capacity to exercise power may be related to asymmetries in the distribution of resources, Giddens distinguishes two types of resources: *authoritative resources*, deriving from the co-ordination of the activity of social actors, and *allocative resources*, which arise from the control of material products or aspects of the material world. As Macintosh and Scapens suggest, 'both types of resources facilitate the transformative capacity of human action (power in the broad sense), while at the same time providing the medium for domination (power in the narrow sense)' (1990, p. 461). In this sense, management accounting systems are conceptualised as socially constructed resources which can be drawn upon in the exercise of power in both senses.

This section outlined the extensive literature which constitutes 'alternative' research in management accounting. Next, we rely on the institutional perspective developed by Barley and Tolbert (1997) and Burns and Scapens (2000) to illustrate a possible conceptualisation of management accounting and its processes of change. According to this perspective, management accounting systems can be interpreted as a set of rules (the formalised statements of procedures) and routines (the practices habitually in use) that act as repositories and carriers of organisational and individual knowledge. Therefore, it is important to recognise that management accounting systems can facilitate processes of organisational change, but they can also prevent the questioning of existing knowledge and cultural assumptions (Hopwood, 1987; Argyris, 1990; Dent, 1991). A discussion of the role of management accounting systems within evolutionary vs revolutionary processes of change, as well as their cognitive vs behavioural implications is provided below.

4. Interpreting Management Accounting Change: An Institutional Model

The literature on organisational change has in recent years offered some notable studies of the cognitive and cultural (Willmott, 1987; Pettigrew, 1987), as well as the behavioural and structural dimensions of change (Barley and Tolbert, 1997). Drawing on a wide range of disciplines, many researchers have abandoned the earlier context-free descriptions of change, and started to explore its processual dynamics (Laughlin, 1991, p. 209), and various *models* or *pathways* for understanding and classifying organisational change have been developed. In particular, single-loop and double-loop learning (Argyris and Schon, 1978), morphostasis and morphogenesis (Robb, 1988), first-order and second-order change (Bartunek and Moch, 1987), evolutionary and revolutionary change (Nelson and Winter, 1982) and re-orientation and colonisation (Laughlin, 1991) are some of the labels which have been attached to classifications of individual and/or collective reactions to environmental disturbances.

Nevertheless, researchers have paid relatively little attention to the reasons why particular pathways are followed, or why a particular kick (Morgan, 1986, p. 249), environmental impetus (Bartunek, 1984, p. 356), jolt (Laughlin, 1991, p. 209), or stimulus (Harris, 1994, p. 311) preserves, rather than changes, the organisational order. Furthermore, there are few holistic studies linking the cognitive dynamics, which characterise organisational culture, and the behavioural and structural modalities through which culture is reproduced. Therefore, by relying on Giddens' theory of the subject, change could be conceptualised as the *ongoing process of cognitive and behavioural definition and re-definition which influences agents' motivation for action*. This is consistent with Giddens's conceptualisation of knowledge, which is stored both as memory traces and within routinised pattern of behaviour. In this sense, change may be conceptualised as a continuous re-examination, although at different cognitive levels[33], of the stored knowledge which provides agents with a sense of psychological safety (Giddens, 1984; Schein, 1992). Therefore, since change impacts not only on behaviour, but also on the agent's psychological make-up, although the consequences of change may be deciphered through the observation of its overt manifestations, an interpretation of the way in which it comes about may be extremely complicated.

Consequently, while recognising that the process of change is continuous, and involves inertial forces resulting from the routinised practices and patterns of behaviour which provide continuity over time (Nelson and Winter, 1982), the models or pathways cited above represent contingent dynamics depending on the depth and intensity to which the cognitive, regulative and normative structures are impacted by endogenous and/or exogenous disturbances. In particular, drawing on Nelson and Winter (1982), could be described as *revolutionary* those episodes which have a significant impact on the existing routines and institutions (see also Burns and Scapens, 2000). Thus, while often (but not always[34]) caused by major external events, such as economic shocks, ownership change and technological innovations, revolutionary change needs to be understood as involving radical disruptions to the institutionalised values and patterns of behaviour which characterise the existing organisational context and culture.

Described as 'circumstances of radical disjuncture of an unpredictable kind which affect substantial numbers of individuals, [or] situations that threaten or destroy the certitudes of institutionalized routines' (Giddens, 1984, p. 61), *critical situations* threaten the agent's sense of psychological safety which is embedded within the routinised patterns of behaviour. When (in such critical situations) these routines are unfrozen, anxieties arise and individuals tend to question their taken-for-granted assumptions, and it is then that *'revolutionary'* episodes of change occur (Schein, 1992).

In contrast to revolutionary change, in which the taken-for-granted assumptions are questioned fundamentally, *'evolutionary'* change is incremental and involves only minor and, sometimes, unconscious adjustment to the taken-for-granted assumptions (see Burns and Scapens, 2000). As such, the potential for evolutionary change is constrained and also enabled by the underlying routines and institutions encoded within organisational position-practices. Thus, by defining change as an ongoing process of cognitive and behavioural redefinition, which affects agents' motivation for action, the dichotomy between evolutionary and revolutionary change may be, at least partially, abandoned. Since the revolutionary/evolutionary distinction is grounded in the extent of the actors' consciousness/unconsciousness, they can be conceptualised as the *contingent*

---

[33] It is fundamental to recognise that change may occur at different cognitive levels. As described later, this will help us to understand how 'evolutionary' processes of change are interrupted by 'revolutionary' episodes.

[34] See Schein (1992).

momentum of the same ongoing process, which differ only in *intensity*. Whereas the processes which are characterised as evolutionary can be described as path dependent mutation, imitation, emulation and/or adaptation of existing routines, revolutionary change, involving sudden disruptions which can be regarded as *points of discontinuity*. Nevertheless, this discontinuity does not refer to the process of change *per se*, which can still be conceptualised as continuous and uninterrupted, but to its cognitive and behavioural consequences. By dissolving the constraining and enabling abilities of existing routines (at the behavioural level) and institutions (at the cognitive level) such discontinuity involves major individual/collective repositioning. The nature of the evolutionary/revolutionary distinction is further explored in the following pages.

Evolutionary processes of change – The empirical investigation and interpretation of processes of change and institutionalisation is a difficult task. Consequently, in order to decipher the duality of social interaction and taken-for-granted assumptions, we must focus on the organisational processes through which it occurs (Laughlin, 1991). As suggested by Barley and Tolbert (1997, p. 100): 'research on these processes requires a conceptual framework that specifies the relations between interactional episodes and institutional principles'. To overcome the static approach of Giddens' structuration theory, Barley and Tolbert argued that whereas the cognitive assumptions which characterise organisational culture enable and constrain situated interaction synchronically (i.e. at a specific point in time), the ongoing enactment of specific patterns of behaviour allows organisational participants to produce and reproduce these assumptions diachronically (i.e. through their cumulative influence over time). This time dimension is represented in Figure 1 by the thick and bold horizontal lines/arrows at the top and at the bottom, which represent the realms of institutionalised culture and organisational interactions. The connection between these two realms is provided by formalised statements of procedures (rules), the network of social positions (roles) and practices habitually in use (routines) – it is here that management accounting systems (MAS)[35] perform a pivotal role (see Busco *et al.*, 2006).

Drawing from Barley and Tolbert (1997) and Burns and Scapens (2000), the evolutionary path in Figure 1 is represented by four moments of change: encoding, enacting, reproducing and institutionalisation.[36] The first moment (*arrow a*) concerns the 'encoding' of institutionalised, i.e. taken-for-granted, cognitive assumptions within localised behavioural regularities. As such, the rules, roles and routines (which characterise MAS) are informed by the values and beliefs embodied in these institutions. Although this process of encoding involves all the dimensions of

---

[35] Along with other organisational systems.

[36] It is important to recognise that these separate 'moments' are used for analytical purposes only and that, as processes of change are continuous, they will be difficult to distinguish empirically.

structure, it generally relies upon the employment of specific resources of power drawn from the institutionalised structures of domination (see Burns and Scapens, 2000).

Figure 1

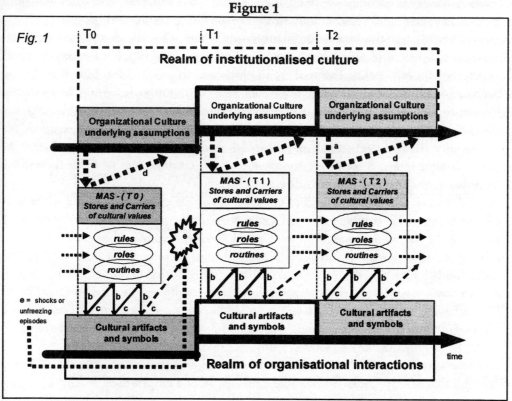

The second moment (*arrow b*) refers to the 'enactment', through the day-to-day activities performed by specific organisational participants, of the patterns of behaviour which are informed by the encoded cognitive assumptions. As such, it is through the enactment of the organisational rules, roles and routines that the essence of organisational culture becomes instantiated in organisational interactions. Although this enactment sometimes involves conscious choice, it is generally the outcome of reflexive monitoring informed by the agents' tacit knowledge. It is through this reflexive monitoring that the third moment (*arrow c*) takes place – i.e. the 'reproduction' of the routinised activities. It is through such a recursive process of enacting and reproduction that MAS, conceptualised as both *repositories* (Giddens, 1984) and *carriers* (Jepperson, 1991; Scott, 1995) of organisational culture, evolve across time and space.

Finally, the fourth moment (*arrow d*) involves a dissociation of values and assumptions from the repositories and localised situations in which they were created – i.e. they become 'institutionalised'.[37] In this sense, they undergo a deep

---

[37] As Burns and Scapens suggest, such taken-for-granted assumptions are more abstract than the rules, roles and routines in which they are stored. For this reason, dotted lines are used

cognitive transformation to become the shared taken-for-granted assumptions, or institutions, which provide the unquestioned (i.e. trusted) basis for social interaction. They become 'so taken for granted that someone who does not hold them is viewed as crazy and automatically dismissed' (Schein, 1991, p. 16).

In relation to the process of institutionalisation, it should be remembered that organisational culture and knowledge is *validated* (i.e. tested), both externally and internally (Schein, 1992). External validation usually occurs through monitoring successful task accomplishment, while internal validation arises from the potential to reduce *anxiety* in situations of 'meaninglessness' and unpredictability (Schein, 1991). It is through such processes that organisational knowledge and culture gets its stability. Thus, when it proves successful, and provides agents with a sense of psychological safety, a feeling of *trust* emerges which preserves its institutionalised features across time and space (Giddens, 1984).

Revolutionary change (cognitive and behavioural discontinuity) – A recognition of the ongoing and cumulative evolutionary path is crucial for understanding processes of change in organisations. One of the key features of agency is that, by relying on their self-reflective abilities and mutual stocks of knowledge, the individuals have the *potential* to make a difference during the ongoing process of day-to-day organisational interaction, either enabling or resisting change. Nevertheless, in specific circumstances, major episodes of disruption can create a discontinuity in the path-dependent process, and give rise to revolutionary change.

By relying on Lewin's contribution (1951), Schein (2003) argues for a tied relationship between radical processes of change and phases of stability. 'Change and stability are two sides of the same coin' (p. 34), he emphasises. Additionally, he describes three different stages which need to be carefully analysed when interpreting processes of profound change. These phases are the following: (1) unfreezing, (2) changing through cognitive redefinition, and (3) refreezing. According to Schein, 'no change will occur unless the system is unfrozen, and no change will last unless the system is refrozen. Most change theories tend to focus only on the middle stage and then cannot account for inability to produce change in the first place, or inability to maintain the changes that have been achieved' (2003, p. 36).

Schein describes the phase of unfreezing as *the creation of a motivation to change*. Such motivation to change can be stimulated by changing the set of forces which act on the system, such that:

(1)   the present state is disconfirmed to some extent;

---

for arrows *a* and *d*. However, through the enabling and constraining processes of social interactions period by period, they bind time in situated contexts of co-presence. Hence, there are several *b* and *c* arrows for each pair of *a* and *d* arrows. Finally, the phases of encoding and institutionalisation represent ongoing processes, rather than single identifiable movements. This explains the broad lines used for arrows *a* and *d*.

(2)   survival anxiety or guilt is created because of failure to achieve the planned goals or to meet the standards;

(3)   a certain amount of psychological safety is generated to overcome the defensive mechanisms, such as the learning anxiety or the defensive routines, which may eventually prevent change (Schein, 2003).

In such episodes of disruption, the institutionalised (cognitive) stocks of knowledge will no longer help organisational participants, who must now assemble new rationales and resources, thereby leading to a collective questioning of the existing rules, roles and routines. As such, the existing institutions remain consciously locked into a past temporal frame, and thereby they lose their ability substantially to shape current behaviour (see 'e' in Figure 1). The disruptive consequences of such episodes for the ongoing dynamics of organisational culture explain the sudden slippage of the two longitudinal arrows in Figure 1 and the return to a 'white' background.[38] Importantly, according to Schein:

> the essence of an effective unfreezing process is a balancing of enough disconfirmation to arouse an optimal level of anxiety or guilt, without arousing so much learning anxiety as to cause denial, repression, projection, or some other defense mechanism. Most analysis of unfreezing limit themselves to disconfirmation and the creation of pain, and fail to note that unless the pain is connected to something the members of the system care about, and unless they feel safe enough to do something about it, they have not really been unfrozen at all (2003, p. 36).

5.   Final remarks

As described in this chapter, over the last two decades or so alternative management accounting research has expanded significantly, while accounting began to be understood and interpreted as a situated, context-dependent practice. In parallel, motivated by the quest for rich descriptions of accounting in action, the literature has seen a considerable growth in both field-work and case studies on management accounting change. As suggested by Roberts and Scapens (1985, p. 444; emphasis added), 'the only way to understand accounting practice is through an understanding of the *organisational reality which is the context of accounting,* and *which is the reality that the accounting systems are designed to account for'.* Drawing on these considerations, and avoiding focussing exclusively on the micro-processes of management accounting change *per se,* this chapter has offered a snapshot of those studies which attempted to provide an understanding of the *role* played by management accounting systems within the wider processes of organisational order construction.

---

[38]   The white background reflects the relative absence of 'history' in the ongoing, path-dependent, cumulative evolutionary process. The revolutionary change, to some extent, wipes the slate clean.

In so doing, after having surveyed the recent research debate on the nature of the process of management accounting change in its social and cultural context, we focussed on the different streams of 'alternative' management accounting research as identified within a recent review by Baxter and Chua (2003). In particular, we emphasised the perspectives influenced by the work of Latour, Foucault and Giddens. Finally, we built on recent attempts to provide holistic explanations for the complex phenomena of management accounting change (Burns and Scapens, 2000) and the recognition of the crucial role played by shared institutionalised values and taken-for-granted assumptions within the ongoing processes of organisational transformation to sketch a possible framework for interpreting the linkages between management accounting systems and organisational change.

References

Ahrens, T. (1996), "Styles of accountability", *Accounting, Organizations and Society*, Vol. 21, pp. 139-173.

Ahrens, T. (1997), "Talking accounting: an ethnography of management knowledge in British and German brewers", *Accounting, Organizations and Society*, Vol. 22, pp. 617-637.

Anthony, R. N., Dearden, J. and Govindarajan, V. (1992), *Management Control Systems*, Homewood: Irwin.

Argyris, C. (1990), "The dilemma of implementing controls: the case of managerial accounting", *Accounting, Organisations and Society*, Vol. 15, pp. 503-512.

Argyris, C. and Schon, D. (1978), *Organizational Learning: Theory of Action Perspective*, Addison-Wesley, Reading, Mass.

Armstrong, P. (1987), "The rise of accounting controls in British capitalist enterprises", *Accounting, Organizations and Society*, Vol. 12, pp. 415-436.

Arnold, P. J. (1998), "The limits of postmodernism in accounting history: the Decatur experience", *Accounting, Organizations and Society*, Vol. 23, pp. 665-684.

Ashton, D., Hopper, T. and Scapens, R. W. (1995), "The changing nature of issues in management accounting", in Ashton, D., Hopper, T. and Scapens, R. W. (Eds.), *Issues in Management Accounting*, Prentice Hall, London.

Barfield, J. T., Rainborn, C. A. and Dalton, M. A. (1991), *Cost Accounting. Traditions and Innovations*, West Publishing Company, St. Paul.

Barley, S. R. and Tolbert, P. S. (1997), "Institutionalization and structuration: studying the links between action and institution", *Organization Studies*, Vol. 18, pp. 93-117.

Bartunek, J. M. (1984), "Changing interpretive schemes and organizational restructuring: the example of a religious order", *Administrative Science Quarterly*, Vol. 29, pp. 355-372.

Bartunek, J.M., Moch, M.K. (1987), "First Order, Second Order, and Third Order Change and Organization Development Interventions: A Cognitive Approach,", Journal of Applied Behavioral Science, Vol. 23 No.4, pp.483-500.

Baxter, J. and Chua, W. F. (2003), "Alternative management accounting research: whence or whither", *Accounting, Organizations and Society*, Vol. 28, pp. 97-126.

Berry, A.J., Caps, T., Cooper, D., Ferguson, P., Hopper, T. and Low, E.A. (1984), "Management control in an area of the NCB: rationales of accounting practices in a public enterprise", *Accounting, Organizations and Society*, Vol. 10, pp. 3-28.

Bhimani, A. and Roberts, H. (2004), "Management accounting and knowledge management: in search of intelligibility", *Management Accounting Research*, Vol. 15, pp. 1-4.

Boland, R. J. (1979), "Control, causality and information system requirements", *Accounting, Organizations and Society*, Vol. 4, pp. 259-272.

Boland, R. J. (1981), "A study in system design: C. West Churchman and Chris Argyris", *Accounting, Organizations and Society*, Vol. 6, pp. 109-118.

Boland, R. J. and Pondy, L. R. (1986), "The micro dynamics of a budget-cutting process: modes, models and structure", *Accounting, Organizations and Society*, Vol. 11, pp. 403-422.

Boland, R. J. and Pondy, L. R. (1983), "Accounting in organizations: a union of natural and rational perspectives", *Accounting, Organizations and Society*, Vol. 8, pp. 223-234.

Bromwich, M. and Bhimani, A. (1994), *Management Accounting: Pathways to Progress*, CIMA, London.

Bromwich, M. and Bhimani, A. (1989), *Management Accounting: Evolution Not Revolution*, CIMA, London.

Burchell, S., Clubb, C., Hopwood, A., Hughes, J. and Nahapiet, J. (1980), "The roles of accounting in organizations and society", *Accounting, Organizations and Society*, Vol. 5, pp. 5-27.

Burns, J. and Baldvinsdottir, G. (1999), "Hybrid accountants: where do they belong and what are they expected to do?", paper presented at the *Conference on Management Accounting Change – A European Perspective*, Manchester, 14-17 April 1999.

Burns, J. and Scapens, R. W. (2000), "Conceptualising management accounting change: an institutional framework", *Management Accounting Research*, Vol. 11, pp. 3-25.

Burns, J. and Vaivio, J. (2001), "Management accounting change", *Management Accounting Research*, Vol. 12, pp. 389-402.

Burns, J., Ezzamel, M. and Scapens, R. W. (2003), *The Challenge of Management Accounting Change: Behavioural and Cultural Aspects of Change Management*, CIMA publications, London.

Busco, C., Riccaboni, A. and Scapens, R. W. (2006), (forthcoming), "Trust for accounting and accounting for trust", *Management Accounting Research*, Vol. 17.

Chua, W. F. (1988), "Interpretive sociology and management accounting research – a critical review", *Accounting, Auditing and Accountability Journal*, pp. 59-77.

Chua, W. F. (1995), "Experts, networks and inscriptions in the fabrication of accounting images: a story of the representation of three public hospitals", *Accounting, Organizations, and Society*, Vol. 20, pp. 111-145.

Cooper, D. J. (1980), "Discussion of 'Towards a political economy of accounting'", *Accounting, Organizations and Society*, Vol. 5, pp. 269-286.

Cooper, D. J., Hayes, D. and Wolf, F. (1981), "Accounting in organized anarchies: understanding and designing accounting systems in ambiguous situation", *Accounting, Organizations and Society*, Vol. 6, pp. 175-191.

Covaleski, M. A. and Dirsmith, M. W. (1983), "Budgeting as a means for control and loose coupling", *Accounting, Organizations and Society*, Vol. 8, pp. 323-340.

Covaleski, M. and Dirsmith, M. (1988), "The use of budgetary symbols in the political arena: an historically informed field study", *Accounting, Organisations and Society*, Vol. 13, pp. 1-24.

Covaleski, M., Dirsmith, M. and Michelman, J. (1993), "An institutional theory perspective on the DRG framework, case-mix accounting systems and health care organizations", *Accounting, Organizations and Society*, Vol. 18, pp. 65-80.

Czarniawska-Joerges, B. (1988), "Dynamics of organizational control: the case of Berol Kemi AB", *Accounting, Organizations and Society*, Vol. 13, pp. 415-430.

Dent, J. F. (1991), "Accounting and organisational cultures: a field study of the emergence of a new organizational reality", *Accounting, Organizations and Society*, Vol. 16, pp. 705-732.

Drury, C., Braund, S., Osbourne, P. and Tayles, M. (1993), *A Survey of Management Accounting Practices in UK Manufacturing Companies*, Chartered Association of Certified Accountants, London.

Ezzamel, M. and Bourn, M. (1990), "The roles of accounting information systems in an organization experiencing financial crisis", *Accounting, Organizations and Society*, Vol. 15, pp. 399-424.

Ezzamel, M., Lilley, S. and Willmott, H. (1993), *Changes in Management Practices in UK Companies*, CIMA Research Report, London.

Ezzamel, M., Lilley, S. and Willmott, H. (1996), "The view from the top: senior executives' perceptions of changing management practices in UK companies", *British Journal of Management*, Vol. 7, pp. 155-168.

Foucault, M. (1972), *The archaeology of knowledge*, Tavistock Publications, London.

Foucault, M. (1977), *Discipline and punish: the birth of the prison*, Peregrine Books, Middlesex.

Friedman, A. and Lyne, S. (1995), *Implementing Activity-Based Techniques*, CIMA Publishing, London.

Giddens, A. (1984), *The Constitution of Society*, Polity Press, Cambridge.

Harris, S. G. (1994), "Organisational culture and individual sensemaking: a schema-based perspective", *Organization Science*, Vol. 5, pp. 309-320.

Hedberg, B. and Jönsson, S. (1978), "Designing semi-confusing information systems for organizations in changing environments", *Accounting, Organizations and Society*, Vol. 3, pp. 47-64.

Hopper, T. and Armstrong, P. (1991), "Cost accounting, controlling labour and the rise of conglomerates", *Accounting, Organizations and Society*, Vol. 16, pp. 405-438.

Hopper, T. and Powell, A. (1985), "Making sense of research into the organisational and social aspects of management accounting: a review of its underlying assumptions", *Journal of Management Studies*, pp. 429-465.

Hopper, T., Storey, J. and Willmott, H. (1987), "Accounting for accounting: towards the development of a dialectical view", *Accounting, Organizations and Society*, Vol. 12, pp. 437-456.

Hopwood, A. G. (1983), "On trying to study accounting in the contexts in which it operates", *Accounting, Organisations and Society*, Vol. 8, pp. 287-305.

Hopwood, A.G. (1978), "Towards an organisational perspective for the study of accounting and information systems", *Accounting, Organizations and Society*, Vol. 3, No. 1, pp. 3-14.

Hopwood, A.G. (1987), "Archaeology of accounting systems", *Accounting, Organisations and Society*, Vol. 12, pp. 207-234.

Horngren, C. T., Foster, G. and Datar, S. M. (1994), *Cost Accounting. A Managerial Emphasis*, Prentice Hall, New Jersey.

Jepperson, R. L. (1991), "Institutions, institutional effects, and institutionalizations", in Powell, W. and DiMaggio, P. J. (Eds.), *The New Institutionalism in Organisational Analysis*, University of Chicago Press, Chicago, pp. 143-163.

Johnson T. and Kaplan, R. S. (1987), *Relevance Lost: The Rise and Fall of Management Accounting*, Harvard University Press, Boston, Mass.

Jönsson, S. (1982), "Budgeting behavior in local government – a case study over 3 years", *Accounting, Organizations and Society*, Vol. 3, pp. 287–304.

Kaplan, R. S. and Atkinson, A. A. (1998,) *Advanced Management Accounting*, 3rd edition, Prentice Hall, New Jersey.

Kaplan, R. S. (1984), "The evolution of management accounting", *The Accounting Review*, Vol. 9, pp. 390-418.

Latour, B. (1987), *Science in Action*, Harvard University Press, Cambridge, MA.

Latour, B. (1993), *We Have Never Been Modern*, Prentice, Essex.

Laughlin, R. C. (1987), "Accounting systems in organisational contexts: a case for critical theory", *Accounting, Organizations and Society*, Vol. 12, pp. 479-502.

Laughlin, R. C. (1991), "Environmental disturbances and organizational transitions and transformations: some alternative models", *Organisational Studies*, Vol. 12, pp. 209-232.

Lewin, K. (1951), *Field Theory in Social Science; Selected Theoretical Papers*, Cartwright, D. (Ed.), Harper & Row, New York.

Loft, A. (1995), "The history of management accounting: relevance found", in Ashton, D et al. (Ed.), *Issues in Management Accounting*, Prentice-Hall, London, pp. 21-44.

Macintosh, N. and Scapens, R.W. (1990), "Structuration theory in management accounting", *Accounting, Organizations and Society*, Vol. 15, pp. 455-477.

McNamara, C., Baxter, J. and Chua, W.F. (2004), "Making and managing organisational knowledge(s)", *Management Accounting Research*, Vol. 15, pp. 53-76.

Meyer, J. W. and Rowan, B. (1977), "Institutionalized organizations: formal structure as myth and ceremony", *American Journal of Sociology*, Vol. 83, pp. 340-363.

Miller, P. (1991), "Accounting innovation beyond the enterprise: problematizing investment decisions and programming economic growth in the UK in the 1960s", *Accounting, Organizations and Society*, Vol. 16, pp. 733-762.

Miller, P. and O'Leary, T. (1987), "The construction of the governable person", *Accounting, Organisations and Society*, Vol. 12, pp. 235-265.

Miller, P. and O'Leary, T. (1993), "Accounting, 'economic citizenship' and the spatial recording of manufacture", *Accounting, Organizations and Society*, Vol. 19, pp. 15-43.

Miller, P. and O'Leary, T. (1994), "Governing the calculable person", in Hopwood, A. and Miller, P. (Eds.), *Accounting as a Social and Institutional Practice*, Cambridge University Press, Cambridge.

Morgan, G. (1986), *Images of Organisation*, Sage, Beverly Hills.

Mouritsen, J. (1999), "The flexible firm: strategies for a subcontractor's management control", *Accounting, Organizations and Society*, Vol. 24, pp. 31-55.

Nelson, R. R. and Winter, S. G. (1982), *An Evolutionary Theory of Economic Change*, Harvard University Press, Boston.

Ogden, S. (1997), "Accounting for organizational performance: the construction of the customer in the privatized water industry", *Accounting, Organizations and Society*, Vol. 22, pp. 529-556.

Pettigrew, A. M. (1987), "Context and action in the transformation of the firm", *Journal of Management Studies*, Vol. 24, pp. 649-670.

Powell, W. W. and DiMaggio, P. J. (1991), *The New Institutionalism in Organizational Analysis*, (Eds.), the University of Chicago Press, Chicago.

Preston, A., Cooper, D. and Coombs, R., (1992), "Fabricating budgets: a study of the production of management budgeting in the National Health Service", *Accounting, Organizations and Society*, Vol. 17, pp. 561-593.

Quattrone, P. and Hopper, T., (2001), "What does organizational change mean? Speculation on a taken for granted category", *Management Accounting Research*, Vol. 12, pp. 403-435.

Robb, F. F. (1988), "Morphostasis and morphogenesis: contexts of participative design inquiry in the design of systems of learning and human development", unpublished discussion paper, University of Edinburgh.

Roberts, J. (1990), "Strategy and accounting in a UK conglomerate", *Accounting, Organizations and Society*, Vol. 15, pp. 107-126.

Roberts, J. and Scapens, R. W. (1985), "Accounting systems and systems of accountability – understanding accounting practices in their organizational context", *Accounting, Organizations and Society*, Vol. 10, pp. 443-456.

Ryan, R. J., Scapens, R. W. and Theobald, M. (2002), *Research Method and Methodology in Finance and Accounting*, 2nd edition, Thomson.

Scapens, R. W. (1994), "Never mind the gap: towards an institutional perspective on management accounting practice", *Management Accounting Research*, Vol. 5, pp. 301-321.

Scapens, R. W. (1999), "Broadening the scope of management accounting: from a micro-economic to a broader business perspective", *Maanblad Voor Accountancy en Bedrijfseconomie*, December, pp. 641-651.

Scapens, R. W., Turley, S., Burns, J., Joseph, N., Lewis, L. and Southworth, A. (1996), *External Reporting and Management Decisions: A Study of their Interrelationship in UK Companies*, CIMA, London.

Schein, E. H. (2003), "Models and tools for stability and change in human systems", *Reflections. The Sol Journal on Knowledge, Learning and Change*, Vol. 4, Issue 2, pp. 34-46.

Schein, E. H. (1991), "What is culture?", in Frost, P. J., Larry, F. M., Louis, M. R., Lundberg, C. C. and Martin, J., *Reframing Organizational Culture*, Sage Publications: Thousands Oaks, California.

Schein, E. H. (1992), *Organizational Culture and Leadership*, 2nd edition, Jossey-Bass Publishers, San Francisco.

Scott, W. R. (1995), *Institutions and Organizations*, Sage Publications, London.

Seal, W., Berry, A. and Cullen, J. (2004), "Disembedding the supply chain: institutionalized reflexivity and inter-firm accounting", *Accounting, Organizations and Society*, Vol. 29, No.1, pp. 73-92.

Shields, M. D. (1997), "Research in management accounting by North Americans in the 1990s", *Journal of Management Accounting Research*, Vol. 9, pp. 3-61.

Tinker, A.M. (1980), "Towards a political economy of accounting: an empirical illustration of the Cambridge controversies", *Accounting, Organizations and Society*, Vol. 5, pp. 147-160.

Vaivio, J. (1999), "Examining 'the quantified customer'", *Accounting, Organizations and Society*, Vol. 24, pp. 689-715.

Willmott, H. (1987), "Studying managerial work: A critique and a proposal", *Journal of Management Studies*, Vol. 24, pp. 249-270.

13

CRITICAL THEORY

Robin Roslender
Heriot-Watt University, UK

Abstract: Critical Theory has become an increasingly important source of insights for accounting researchers associated with the critical accounting project. Although the Critical Theory perspective is only one of many ways of seeing associated with the task of promoting greater awareness among all those involved in accounting as to the conditions and consequences of their practices, it exhibits a number of features that identify it as the most appealing. Of particular significance are its twin underpinnings in social theory and social philosophy, a characteristic it shares with the tradition of Marxist thought from which it originated. This ensures that the Critical Theory perspective has the capacity to provide penetrating critiques of accounting practices. Beyond this, the Critical Theory perspective has a defining affinity with interventionist politics, which in recent times has informed calls for the development of a mode of enabling accounting designed to deliver social betterment.

Keywords: Critical accounting project; emancipatory intent; enabling accounting; Habermas; philosophy of praxis.

1. Introduction

In this chapter the merits of Critical Theory as a theoretical perspective or 'way of seeing' informing research in accounting are considered. Critical Theory has become increasingly influential in accounting research during the past twenty years as a core element of the critical accounting project. The principal objective of this project is to promote greater levels of self-awareness among all of those engaged in accounting regarding the conditions and consequences of their various practices. In order to accomplish this, the critical accounting project challenges the manner in which accounting has conventionally privileged technical issues and knowledges over those demonstrating that the accounting is not created in a social vacuum and as a result of which much of it may be highly contestable. The emergence of a complementary set of critical insights is now widely recognised as a sign of accounting's maturity as an academic discipline, as well as providing a basis for developing accounting as a set of socially responsible practices.

At the outset it is important to affirm that Critical Theory is only one of many ways of seeing informing the critical accounting project. Critical Theory attracted the attention of accounting researchers at the same time as two other perspectives that share its Marxist origins: political economy and labour process theory. Not all of those who have embraced the Critical Theory perspective have emphasised what, for this author, is its defining characteristic: its links with an interventionist mode of revolutionary politics. It is this view of the Critical Theory perspective that is commended in the following pages. This should not be taken to signify that other views of the Critical Theory perspective lack merit, however. Similarly, there are a number of theoretical perspectives commonly associated with the critical accounting project that are clearly some distance removed from such a position. This does not preclude them from offering insights that their more politicised critical accounting colleagues find instructive, particularly when incorporated within their own analyses. The tensions that result from these various differences ensure that the critical accounting project promises to continue generating a stream of valuable insights to the benefit of both accounting and the broader society.

This chapter is structured as follows. In the next section, the origins of the Critical Theory tradition are briefly documented. In section three, Jurgen Habermas' work on the relationship between knowledge and interests is discussed as a point of departure for understanding the appeal of the Critical Theory perspective. In the fourth section the critical turn in accounting research after the mid 1970s is outlined. The principal contributions to the establishment of a Critical Theory perspective in accounting research are reviewed in section five, drawing attention to the differing views that are evident regarding its interventionist politics affinities. A number of recent contributions that emphasise the enabling potentialities of a more emancipatory conception of Critical Theory are discussed in section six. The chapter concludes with a summary of the seven key things anyone contemplating embracing a Critical Theory perspective should be aware of, together with a brief postscript on suggestions for possible future research.

2. The Critical Theory Tradition

As an intellectual tradition, Critical Theory dates back to the early 1920s. At this time, a number of European intellectuals had become unhappy about the way in which Marxist theory was evolving. All of them had strong sympathies with Marxism, both as mode of analysis, i.e. as a social theory, and as practical political project with its social philosophic foundations. What particularly concerned them was the way in which Marxist theory increasingly focused on economic issues while simultaneously evolving into political structures that departed from their supposed democratic socialist foundations. These 'difficulties' were becoming increasingly evident in the context of the Russian social formation, which to the early advocates of Critical Theory no longer appeared to be an inspiration to workers' movements across the world.

Although the Frankfurt School is probably the best known site for the development of Critical Theory, not least because of Habermas' later associations with it, the contributions of two other scholars were also important. Georg Lukacs' 1923 collection of essays: *History and Class Consciousness*, explored a range of social theoretic and social philosophic issues. Returning to Hegel, whose writings had strongly influenced the 'young' Marx, Lukacs argues for analysing the role of superstructural factors within society, e.g. ideology, literature, art, etc. and their impact on the consciousness of the mass of people. For Lukacs, the challenge for Marxist theory was to fashion a proletarian class consciousness based on a totalising analysis of the structure and processes of capitalist social formations, one which would not degenerate into a new mode of domination.

In parallel, Antonio Gramsci was engaged in rethinking Marxist theory in Italy. A committed activist, Gramsci had been heavily involved in the workers' movement and the development of factory councils before his imprisonment in 1926, which only ended months before his death in 1937. During his incarceration Gramsci formulated his necessarily unsystematic contribution to Critical Theory, subsequently published as the *Prison Notebooks* (Gramsci, 1971). As with Lukacs, Gramsci's writings included contributions to both social theory and social philosophy, again influenced by the work of Hegel. Viewing them as a couple, he advocated the philosophy of praxis, in which 'theory' informs 'practice' and vice versa. In respect of theory, Gramsci also commended the study of superstructural factors in an attempt to understand the prevailing ideological dominance or hegemony of ruling class ideas. For Gramsci it is through the successful reproduction of hegemony that the ruling class is able to secure its political domination of the masses. A detailed knowledge of how hegemony is present in the everyday lives of the working class through institutions such as schools, the family and workplaces is therefore a necessary prerequisite for the development of a revolutionary proletarian class consciousness.

The creation of the Institut fur Sozialforschung at the University of Frankfurt in 1923 was to provide an institutional locus for the group of scholars with whom Critical Theory is most closely associated, the Frankfurt School (Jay, 1973). The first generation of Frankfurt scholars fled Germany in 1933, many finding a permanent home in the USA in 1936. Some, most notably Horkheimer, Adorno and Pollock, returned to Frankfurt in 1950, while others, including Marcuse, Lowenthal and Kirchheimer opted to remain in the USA. Habermas, later joined the Institut as Adorno's assistant in 1956, subsequently being appointed a professor there in 1964. Following appointments elsewhere in Germany, he returned to take the chair in sociology and philosophy in 1982, ensuring a continuing connection between Critical Theory and its Frankfurt School affiliations.

In an essay originally published in 1937, Horkheimer, the Institut's Director, succinctly identified the purpose of 'critical' as opposed to 'traditional' theory:

[C]ritical theory in its concept formation and in all its phases of development very consciously makes its own that concern for the rational organization of human activity which is its task to illumine and legitimate. For this theory is not concerned only with the goals already imposed by existent ways of life, but with men [sic] and all their potentialities (Horkheimer in Connerton, 1976, p. 223).

Critical Theory is intimately wedded to change. More specifically, it is concerned with the promotion of a better society, one in which the prevailing social arrangements serve the interests of the mass of people, whose 'potentialities' are perceived to be constrained by those arrangements already in place. In common with their contemporaries, Lukacs and Gramsci, Horkheimer and his colleagues were persuaded that it was vital to focus attention on the superstructural factors rather than those of an economic nature then privileged by Marxist theory. Consequently, much attention was directed at an array of social phenomena such as rationality, technology, law, the family, language, art, music, literature, the mass media, consumerism, etc., all of which were demonstrated to manifest control implications equally debilitating as any of a more economic nature.

Although collectively committed to formulating a more humanistic corpus of Marxist theory, designed to hasten the transformation to a better social order, the Frankfurt School's direct involvement in the workers' struggle was always limited and declined over time. As Burrell and Morgan (1979) observe, the Frankfurt School were 'theoreticians rather than activists' whose contributions 'moved increasingly towards philosophy and intellectual criticism rather than revolutionary practice' (p. 291). Their preference was for the promotion of greater individual self-awareness based on a process of self-reflection informed by carefully fashioned social critique. Habermas has largely continued this tradition. As a consequence, the philosophy of praxis, articulated in the duality of social theory and social philosophy, comes less to the fore. Instead, the sophistication of the analysis is pronounced, reaching ever greater heights of interdisciplinarity. In line with Marx's own attempts to transcend the trend to discipline-based knowledges, Critical Theory was always envisaged as being interdisciplinary in character, with individual exponents integrating insights from across disciplinary boundaries with their own point(s) of departure. In truth, for many of those involved this was simply a continuation of their own intellectual formation in the classical German tradition.

A strong sociological emphasis is also evident in much of the work of the Frankfurt School. Again this should not be wholly surprising given that in Europe sociology is regarded as a wide-ranging discipline, open to much interpretation and intellectual creativity. Habermas himself is often identified as a sociologist, with a penchant for integrating a vast portfolio of insights in the traditions of grand theorising. Included among these are contributions from systems theory, linguistic philosophy, psychoanalytic theory, cognitive psychology and the philosophy of knowledge. This said, Habermas regards himself as a philosopher whose project is no less than the reconstruction of historical materialism, Marx's own theory or 'philosophy' of history, consistently affirming the integration of social theory and social philosophy throughout his work.

3.   Habermas on Knowledge and Interests

In an academic career now spanning half a century, Habermas has produced an enormous corpus of writings, sustaining an even greater secondary literature on his many contributions to social theory and social philosophy. This said, Habermas (1972) continues to provide a readily accessible introduction to what distinguishes a Critical Theory perspective from alternative ways of seeing. Habermas does so by exploring the relationship between knowledge and human interests. Three types of interests are initially identified: technical, practical, and emancipatory. Each interest is identified with a particular form of 'science': empirical-analytic; historical-hermeneutic; and critical, which in turn give rise to different types of knowledge.

In the case of the empirical-analytical sciences, the objective is the mastery and control of natural processes for the benefit of society's members. For Habermas, the technical interest associated with such positivistic approaches to knowledge is rooted in work or labour. In contrast to this, the practical interest of the historical-hermeneutic sciences is concerned with language rather than with work. As the science of interpretation, hermeneutics entails making sense of what people say and think, and the ways in which this is connected with action. In this way, the historical-hermeneutic sciences differ from the empirical-analytic sciences, thereby providing an appropriate basis for the cultural (social) sciences. Both types of science have in common, however, the goal of producing nomological, i.e. law-like, knowledges, however.

More crucially, for Habermas the capacity of the historical-hermeneutic sciences to transform society is constrained by the way in which interaction is distorted and confused by social structures. As a consequence, people may gain wrong understandings of each other. They can be misled and manipulated, and systematically blinded. A third approach to science is therefore necessary. Habermas terms this third approach 'critical social science', identifying it with the emancipatory interest. Like the practical interest, the emancipatory interest is associated with language, interaction and communication. For Habermas, the purpose of critical social science is to rid language, interaction and communication of distortions, as a precursor to enabling people to participate fully in decision-making processes via the mechanism previously termed the 'ideal speech situation' (Habermas, 1970).

At this juncture there is merit in quoting Habermas at some length on critical social science:

> *The systematic sciences of social action, that is economics, sociology, and political science, have the goal, as do the empirical-analytic sciences, of producing nomological*

knowledge. A critical social science, however, will not remain satisfied with this. It is concerned with going beyond this goal to determine when theoretical statements grasp invariant regularities of social action as such and when they express ideologically frozen relations of dependence that can in principle be transformed. To the extent that this is the case, the critique of ideology, as well, moreover, as psychoanalysis, take into account that information about lawlike connections sets off a process of reflection in the consciousness of those whom the laws are about. Thus the level of unreflected consciousness, which is one of the initial conditions of such laws, can be transformed. Of course, to this end a critically mediated knowledge of laws cannot through reflection alone render a law itself inoperative, but it can render it inapplicable.

The methodological framework that determines the meaning of the validity of critical propositions of this latter category is established by the concept of self-reflection. The latter releases the subject from dependence on hypostatized powers. Self-reflection is determined by an emancipatory cognitive interest. Critically oriented sciences share this interest with philosophy (Habermas, 1972, p. 310).

As the embodiment of critical social science, a Critical Theory perspective is not confined to providing knowledge of that which presently exists. Because of the role played by (class) interests, the prevailing social arrangements result in serious drawbacks for the great majority of those who experience them. Their recognition and understanding of the constraints placed upon them by the prevailing social arrangements and how these might be transformed, for their own betterment, are obscured by ideology, something that neither empirical-analytic nor historical-hermeneutic approaches to knowledge, however sophisticated, are able to transcend. Only a critical social science approach, with its characteristic change orientation, promises such an outcome. A critical social science approach seeks to provide the knowledge required for the democratic communication and interaction required to promote emancipation and the construction of a new set of social arrangements that will serve the interests of the majority of people.

In this way, Critical Theory for Habermas can also be recognised as a theory of communicative action, the phrase that subsequently provides the title of his two volume magnum opus (Habermas, 1984, 1987). Critical Theory seeks to provide a form of knowledge that is questioning of the prevailing social arrangements, i.e. an alternative knowledge. More than this, however, the resulting knowledge will serve as an input into a process of reflection by society's members on the nature of their involvement within the prevailing social arrangements and how this might be changed, for their benefit. Critical Theory is not concerned with the provision of insights for their own sake but for the purpose of informing the transformation of what is into what those who experience it wish it to be, through a process of interaction and reflection. Or put another way, Critical Theory aims to promote self-awareness of both what is and what might be, and how the former might be transformed to install the latter.

4. The Critical Turn in Accounting Research

Critical Theory has become an influential accounting research perspective as a consequence of the promotion of the critical accounting project. The University of Sheffield was arguably the most important site for the emergence of this project. It was here in the mid 1970s that a small group of scholars, most notably Tony Lowe and Tony Tinker, began developing some form of sociology of accounting, as a complement to the longer established history, philosophy and politics of accounting (Roslender and Dillard, 2003). Lowe and Tinker had come to sociology via studies in the management control field, where contingency theory (with its own sociological underpinnings) had recently emerged to extend its predominantly organisational psychology emphases. At this time following a decade of intense debate, many younger sociological scholars were persuaded of the value of developing a critical sociology tradition, which sought not only to understand society, but to change it. Marxist theory, including elements of Critical Theory, was firmly established as central to such a project. Lowe, Tinker and some of their colleagues were attracted to such a sociology since they too were sympathetic to these objectives.

Equally, there was also strong enthusiasm for exploring the merits of the broader sociological tradition or at least those parts that offered an alternative to the hitherto dominant functionalist paradigm (Burrell and Morgan, 1979). It was quickly accepted that the emphasis of accounting studies, like accounting practice, was inherently functionalist, exhibiting little interest in questioning its own development or purpose. In what Burrell and Morgan identify as interpretive modes of sociological analysis lay the means of understanding how accounting was constructed and reconstructed, through the actions of human agency. Like education, the family, deviance or the professions, accounting was to be recognised as a social construction, given meaning by those involved in this process. It was not a given that reflected an underlying consensus nor was it static. It had a history, which itself was contested, something that would inevitably persist in its socially constructed future.

The study of management control in the UK National Coal Board published in 1985 by Berry, Capps, Cooper, Ferguson, Hopper and Lowe, provides an influential example of the sociological turn in accounting research. Taking one of the vaguest of accounting themes, it demonstrates how management control is constructed and continually reconstructed in practice, capturing more in twenty or so pages than twenty years of (functionalist) textbook contributions had succeeded in doing. The same paper also exhibits a strong critical edge to it, enhancing its value. By this point, Tinker had relocated to the USA, establishing himself as one of the principal advocates of the political economy perspective in critical accounting research (Tinker, 1980, 1985; Tinker, Merino and Neimark, 1982), together with David Cooper, one of the NCB researchers (Cooper, 1980; Cooper and Sherer, 1984). Political economy can best be understood as modern day successor to the mode of orthodox Marxist analysis that had worried Lukacs, Gramsci and the Frankfurt

School so much in the early 1920s. Definitively politically oriented, latter day political economy had incorporated both sociological insights and some more closely associated with Critical Theory, but ultimately it remained a holistic perspective, with more than a few functionalist traits.

Within Burrell and Morgan's scheme, political economy is identified as an example of a radical structuralist perspective. The same designation applies to labour process theory (Braverman, 1974), with Hopper its principal protagonist in accounting research soon to be joined by the sociologist Armstrong (1984, 1985, 1987) and organisational analyst Willmott (Hopper, Storey and Willmott, 1987). Labour process theory had rapidly revitalised the sociologies of work and organisations after the mid 1970s, consistent with the broader critical sociology emphasis. Its appeal to an acquisitive group of critical accounting researchers was immediate. It offered a way of seeing that was definitively politically engaged. It was less open to the charge of functionalism. More focused than the political economy perspective, it was soon recognised to be especially insightful when employed to study the context for management accounting practices.

It was into this evolving maelstrom of critical accounting research that insights from the Critical Theory tradition, and particularly those of Habermas, were introduced in the early 1980s. Critical Theory was the third Marxist perspective alongside political economy and labour process theory, a further way of seeing alongside those of an interpretive nature which had also attracted the generic designation 'critical'. In this regard, the term critical signifies the alternative to mainstream or 'functionalist' accounting studies, whether technically or non-technically oriented. The critical mix was soon to be further enriched by another set of insights, those associated with the French scholar, Michel Foucault, which some working with labour process theory had begun to integrate with its founding Marxist principles. In due course, the Foucauldian approach to critical accounting research was to become as varied as the Marxist approach or indeed the interpretive approach, and with no little (often confusing) cross-fertilisation. More significantly, not all Foucauldian work exhibited the political motivations that some would claim for a truly critical accounting project (Roslender and Dillard, 2003). For this reason, it is considered separately in this collection.

5.   Installing a Critical Theory Perspective
The most influential introduction to the contribution that a Critical Theory perspective might make to accounting research was provided by Richard Laughlin, who two decades later remains its key exponent. Laughlin himself was one of the group of Sheffield scholars who had contributed so much to the promotion of critical accounting research. This perhaps explains why he designates Critical Theory as 'a further methodological approach' that anyone interested in pursuing critical accounting research might consider, alongside symbolic interactionism,

structuration theory, 'more traditional Marxian analysis' and a 'model informed by the thinking of Foucault' (Laughlin, 1987, p. 480).

In Laughlin's view, Critical Theory is ideally suited to the study of accounting systems in their organisational contexts on a number of grounds. It provides a means of addressing both the technical and social aspects of accounting. In its concern with language, most evident in the case of Habermas, Laughlin's principal focus, Critical Theory is appropriate to the study of accounting systems, which are themselves organisational language systems. In addition, Critical Theory draws attention to the creative potential of the human agency, which it constantly seeks to unfetter. Laughlin identifies three characteristics of Critical Theory as being particularly attractive: it links theory and practice; it is concerned with critique and the need to promote transformation and a better life; and it has always been addressed to going beyond what is given or is visible. Such a characterisation conveys a strongly political Critical Theory perspective, something a little at odds with Laughlin's description of Habermas' work on the role of language in societal development processes as being 'seemingly less radical' (p. 485).

Following a brief overview of some of Habermas' social theoretic insights (pp. 486-487), Laughlin outlines what he designates as Habermas' methodological approach for understanding and changing accounting in organisational contexts. This involves three stages, the first of which is termed the 'formulation of critical theorems stage'. Here the researchers embrace the task of identifying and understanding the (problematic) issues associated with the operation of an existing accounting system. They begin this process from a state of 'quasi-ignorance', generally aware of the nature and mechanisms associated with accounting systems, and committed to the development of 'better' systems. The latter are not simply technically better. In keeping with the precepts of Critical Theory, they must also contribute to social betterment. The 'processes of enlightenment stage' entails the researchers engaging in discussion with the researched, the organisational participants, in order to establish that the two parties have the same understanding of the prevailing issues. There can be no value in the two parties having different understandings of the same organisational reality. They need to establish a 'justified or grounded' consensus, some form of relativised form of truth, before they can proceed to a more detailed understanding, and in due course the most desirable changes that should be put in place. This is the third 'selection of strategies' stage, in which through further discussion, the researchers and their organisational participant colleagues derive 'strategies which are intended to lead to change and development in the accounting system and the social context and the interrelationships between the two' (p. 489).

Such a methodology is, of course, very unHabermasian, the greater part of Habermas' work being the epitome of high theory. Similarly, although some of the work of the first generation Frankfurt School scholars was heavily empirical, as we observed earlier, it was not informed by such an interventionist model. Yet as

Broadbent, Laughlin and Read (1991) subsequently comment, the discursive processes through which this methodology is enacted necessarily constitute something akin to an ideal speech situation. Consequently, such a methodology should be recognised as an examplar of Habermasian critical social science in action, with its defining emancipatory intentions and motivations.

Laughlin is very aware that, having made the case for this methodology, very obvious practical difficulties need to be confronted before it might be enacted successfully. First, as with any methodological approach, access to particular organisational sites is always problematic. Implicitly, the critical underpinnings of this methodology may accentuate such difficulties. Second, Laughlin stresses that it is important to ensure that the researchers and the researched are able to enact the necessary discursive processes (effectively). He also adds that it is vital that those being researched are able to effect change in due course. Third, because of complexity of the proposed methodology, it is more likely to unravel, as a consequence of which those involved should embrace it in the full knowledge that the actual research experience can only ever strive to meet the ideals set out in the paper. Overlaying all of this are resource issues, a matter raised by Laughlin in the closing paragraphs of his paper.

A second key contribution to the promotion of a Critical Theory perspective in accounting research was offered by Jesse Dillard in 1991. This paper differs from Laughlin's in a number of important ways. First, its focus is on critical social science, Habermas' (1972) third approach to science, rather than Critical Theory itself. The paper includes relatively few references to the work of Habermas and the principal figures in the first generation of Frankfurt School scholars, with Fay (1987) providing Dillard's critical theoretic framework. Second, there is no suggestion that Critical Theory (or critical social science) offers a methodological approach. Instead it is characterised as a powerful way of seeing that promises to reveal disturbing alternative knowledges, which in turn are likely to enhance individual self-awareness and a desire to engage in transformative action. Although never mentioned in the paper, critical social science embodies the philosophy of praxis that was intimately associated with the inception of Critical Theory. Third, the paper incorporates a range of substantive insights drawn from the broad spectrum of radical humanist and radical structuralist approaches, rather than Laughlin's preference for a (Habermasian) focus on the centrality of language, to fashion what Dillard terms a 'more traditional revolutionary-focused critical perspective' (Dillard,1991, p. 14). Finally, these insights are deployed in the analysis of two contributions to the canon of accounting theory: Mattessich's *Accounting and Analytic Methods* and Tinker's *Paper Prophets*, identified as examples of the functionalist and radical structuralist traditions respectively.

Rather than identifying the merits of Critical Theory as a methodology, Dillard's paper is an example of an accounting scholar becoming aware of the conditions and consequences of the practices of accounting and the institution of accountancy from which they emanate. The choice of Fay's perspective as the means of making this journey is consistent with invoking Marx's Eleventh Thesis on Feuerbach at the beginning and end of the paper. For Fay, critical social science, with its roots in Critical Theory, is constituted by ten sub-theories that he arranges into four categories. These are: the theory of false consciousness; the theory of crisis; the theory of education; and the theory of transformative action, each of which Dillard briefly outlines. Fay also conceptualises his perspective in terms of the three Es of enlightenment, empowerment and emancipation. What this means for the individual who embraces the Critical Theory perspective is that initially s/he engages in a process of re-understanding what passes for everyday or commonsense knowledge through a process of critical self-reflection, aided by a stock of alternative insights derived from the Critical Theory tradition. This process of enlightenment has the further consequence of empowering the individual, in the sense of equipping her/him with a more reflective understanding of 'what might be' as well as 'what is'. The third E, that of emancipation, entails the individual engaging in transformative action, in an attempt to contribute to the creation of a better society.

Although the overlap with Laughlin's Critical Theory methodology is readily apparent, the difference between these two founding contributions on the Critical Theory perspective within accounting research is significant, being more than simply one of emphasis. Dillard strongly endorses the 'revolutionary' political character of critical social science, while Laughlin prefers to commend a powerful methodological approach that (also) has an unquestionably radical edge.

In his 1991 paper with Broadbent and Read, Laughlin advances a further interpretation of a Critical Theory perspective. Habermas continues as the principal source of Critical Theory insights for Broadbent *et al.*, which are now predominantly of a social theoretic nature. Of particular interest are Habermas' views on the role of the internal colonisation process within social evolution, as discussed in the *Theory of Communicative Action* (Habermas, 1984, 1987). In section two of the paper, Broadbent *et al.*, initially outline the principal elements of Habermas' thinking before refining and reworking these in an effort to make them less abstract and thereby more relevant to the task of analysing concrete accounting practices, in this instance (then) recent financial and administrative changes in the British National Health Service.

In the introduction to their paper, Broadbent *et al.*, clearly identify the appeal of Habermas' recent contribution to the Critical Theory tradition as the 'ability to both understand and evaluate' (p. 1). Consequently, their own efforts to refine and rework Habermas' social theory are to be regarded as further developing his 'societally-based evaluatory model' (p. 2). It is this notion of evaluation that is new to the debate. It might be argued that by referring to it at this point, what was implicit in Laughlin (1987) is now simply made more explicit – that the discursive process set in train by the enrolment of a Critical Theory methodology in the research process would necessarily give rise to an evaluation by organisational participants and shared with the research team. This is not what Broadbent *et al.*, have in mind, however. It is now the task of the researchers to engage in evaluating developments such as financial and administrative changes in the NHS, with only minimal involvement on the part of the various groups of organisational participants who are implicated in these changes. The latter is argued to be a further necessary practical refinement of Habermas' thinking.

Leaving aside the question of whether this manoeuvre is consistent with the general tenor of Habermas' thinking, what is noticeable about this third formulation of the Critical Theory perspective is that it omits any explicit mention of social transformation. Critical accounting researchers who embrace this perspective are called upon to set about understanding some aspect of accounting or kindred practices as a preface to offering an evaluation thereof. As Broadbent *et al.*, indicate in their introductory comments, although Habermas' own theoretical position is not value-free, the outcomes of any such analyses are not pre-determined. The idea of seeking to change such practices is, therefore, uncoupled from their analysis, a position that, although defensible, is the negation of Marx's Eleventh Thesis on Feuerbach. This uncoupling may not be personally troubling to scholars such as Broadbent, Laughlin and Read, who have consistently sought to expose the damaging implications of a wide range of accounting practices while continually engaging in the policy debate in order to bring about socially beneficial change in the accounting arena. For those not quite so committed to promoting the necessity for social transformation, understanding and evaluation gained through employing refined Habermasian social theory can result in the provision of just another set of insights, which are to be accorded no more credibility than those on offer from competing ways of seeing.

In the same issue of *Critical Perspectives on Accounting*, Arrington and Puxty (1991) published another influential contribution to the Critical Theory perspective in accounting research. In contrast to Broadbent *et al.*'s focus on aspects of Habermas' social theory, Arrington and Puxty's paper offers readers an introduction to some aspects of his social philosophy. While discussing communicative rationality and the notion of ideal speech communities at length, there is no suggestion that Critical Theory furnishes a powerful methodology that accounting researchers might pursue. This said, Arrington and Puxty do not rule out the possibility of empirical enquiry based on 'the abstract, perhaps metatheoretical, approach to accounting' they advance. After Habermas, they designate this approach as 'a kind of "formal pragmatics"' that is necessary as 'an antecedent to *empirical* inquiry' (Arrington and Puxty, 1991, pp. 48-49). The purpose of such enquiries is to contribute to broadening the understanding that accounting researchers have of accounting. Their task is to introduce a number of ideas from Habermas' work, particularly those of interests and rationality, that they believe will facilitate this process.

There is little doubt in the authors' minds that viewing accounting through the lens of Critical Theory will reveal a range of important alternative insights about accounting's less savoury side. In this regard their position is similar to that advanced by Dillard, although his paper is much less abstract than theirs. The formulation of evaluatory models, as in Broadbent *et al.*, does not appear to be part of Arrington and Puxty's project, possibly because like Dillard they seek to link the Critical Theory to an emancipatory attitude. In such an attitude, the theorist (critical accountant) is 'more concerned to critique how existing regimes of accounting create and sustain social pathologies that are injurious to other interests' (p. 38), rather than to work towards continuing to develop a mode of accounting that serves the interest of capital. This said, Arrington and Francis are less forthcoming than Dillard about actual engagement in transformative action, although in their final paragraph they return to the notion of accounting in the public interest. Here, bureaucratic expertises such as accounting would be governed by public argument, i.e. an ideal speech community. This clearly entails something more than individual accountants becoming aware of the conditions and consequences of their practices, and thereby motivated to take transformative action in the interests of promoting a better set of social arrangements.

Finally, a 1992 essay with Power allows Laughlin to codify his thoughts on what a Critical Theory perspective promises accounting researchers. In the authors' words:

> [T]he arguments are suggestive of a conception of accounting in which there is a need both to recover the public dimension of its legitimacy and also to comprehend its possible effects on human subjects. This requires a richer theoretical perspective than dominant instrumental conceptions of accounting provide (Power and Laughlin, 1992, p. 114).

A Critical Theory perspective provides an alternative understanding of accounting to that furnished by traditional or functionalist approaches. Although not the sole source of such alternative understandings, for Power and Laughlin a Critical Theory perspective provides the most insightful observations. The principal reason for this is that a Critical Theory perspective 'occupies what might be described as a "middle" position' (p. 120), something evident in their diagrammatic representation of various approaches to accounting information on p. 118 (see also Laughlin (1995) for a fuller explanation of this). Habermas' recent work on the theory of communication is identified as informing such a Critical Theory perspective. Overall, it is principally the social theory aspects of Habermas' work that Power and Laughlin outline in their essay. As a result, it very difficult to reconcile the emancipatory intent of Critical Theory identified in the quotation at the beginning of this paragraph with their exposition of its potential as an alternative way of seeing.

For those new to the field, it is difficult to identify a Critical Theory perspective's philosophy of praxis antecedents from Power and Laughlin's essay. In addition to provocatively identifying its 'middle' positioning, Power and Laughlin distance Critical Theory from 'radically orientated studies' of a neo-Marxist sort (identifying examples from the political economy and labour process theory perspectives on p. 120). The latter are characterised as being largely dismissive of anything of value in accounting practice or similar capitalist managerial technologies, in opposition to Habermas who they argue (with justification) embraces a much more positive view of the prospects for social evolution. In the absence of any detailed discussion of the social philosophic aspects of Habermas' writing, and their roots within the contributions of his predecessors within the Critical Theory tradition, it is easy for new readers to simply view Habermas as providing the conceptual framework for a valuable critique of the institution of accountancy and its myriad practices. However, as Dillard (1991) had previously reminded us, once we have such an understanding, the necessity is to secure change, i.e. social betterment. It is to these aspects of a Critical Theory perspective that we now turn.

6. Recapturing the Emancipatory Intent

In collaboration with Cooper, Power and Laughlin have recently published a revised version of their 1992 essay (Power, Laughlin and Cooper, 2003). Amongst other things, this affords them an opportunity to identify a further decade or so of accounting research informed by a Critical Theory perspective. The result is a strong affirmation that such a perspective, after Habermas, provides a range of valuable, although often negative insights about accounting, at least when considered alongside more mainstream ways of seeing. As in their previous essay, there is no suggestion that Critical Theory furnishes a methodology in the way that Laughlin (1987) had suggested. The authors leave the issue of the evaluatory qualities of Habermas' contribution, as identified in Broadbent *et al.* (1991), implicit and thereby readily overlooked. The distancing of a Critical Theory perspective from more radical neo-Marxist perspectives, those which represent accounting as a 'fundamentally distorting practice in so far as it represents and promulgates the interests of capital' (p. 138), remains firmly at odds with Dillard's view of a critical social science. The omission of the 1992 observation that Critical Theory occupies a '"middle" position' is interesting, although Laughlin (2004) revisits the subject. Likewise the reaffirmation that:

> Overall, Critical Theory recognizes that the enabling or distorting status of a practice such as accounting is an open empirical question … (Power et al., 2003, p. 138).

Towards the end of their essay, however, the authors make reference to two contributions to the literature that they suggest make 'some useful suggestions' as to what a '"truly" communicative and enabling accounting would look like' (p. 150, cf Power and Laughlin, 1992, p. 132), those of Broadbent (1998) and Broadbent, Ciancanelli, Gallhofer and Haslam (1997). These papers, together with further contributions from Gallhofer and Haslam (1997, 2003) allow us to envisage a Critical Theory perspective that begins to emphasise its original emancipatory credentials.

In their editorial to a special issue of the *Accounting, Auditing and Accountability Journal*, Broadbent *et al.* (1997) begin by setting out unambiguously their aim as being: 'to open up and extend further a debate on how accounting could be mobilized to promote social "betterment" – welfare, justice, emancipation' (p. 265). They view what they term 'enabling accounting' as providing accounting researchers with a means of becoming directly involved in the 'pressing political and professional issues of the day', thereby addressing a perceived lacuna in the critical accounting project. Twenty years of critical accounting research has yielded many crucial theoretical and substantive advances. Nevertheless, the authors take the view that an 'equally sustained debate on accounting's emancipatory potential' appears to be missing. As we have seen in the previous section, although the terms emancipatory and enabling are by no means absent from accounting's founding Critical Theory literature, Dillard's 1991 paper aside, it would not be difficult for less well informed readers to overlook their significance.

Broadbent *et al.*, continue by explicitly linking their concern with developing an enabling accounting with 'our critical theoretical stance'. This in turn is informed by what is described as a 'constructive dimension of postmodern theorizing', namely an 'awareness of the need to recognize the multiplicity of views and voices which abounds in the social world'. Enabling accounting is therefore intimately associated with providing these 'other voices' with a means of articulating their own viewpoints in the accounting arena. This necessitates the assumption of an interventionist stance on the part of critical accounting researchers who might embrace enabling accounting. Unlike some critical researchers, Broadbent *et al.*, are comfortable 'to prescribe accounting interventions' (p. 267). Equally, they reject the suggestion that there is nothing in accounting worth rescuing, describing this as a 'surprisingly blinkered view of the artefact.' (p. 268). In their concluding section, Broadbent *et al.*, identify some ways in which the promotion of an enabling accounting might be advanced. Two are of particular interest: the need to return to asking some fundamental questions about accounting, given the centrality that must now be accorded to other voices; and how accounting might become a more subjective communication for emancipation, within a more open scenario.

In her subsequent paper, Broadbent (1998) seeks to encourage further debate about an enabling accounting or 'how accounting might become a more emancipatory resource in our society' (p. 267). Crucial to any such project is a familiar notion, Habermas' concept of an ideal speech situation, which Broadbent subjects to close scrutiny, particularly from a feminist perspective, at some length and with the intention of operationalising it. Within Habermas' social philosophy an ideal speech situation is just that, an ideal to be aspired to as a means of ensuring the form of communication necessary for a democratic social order. At the concrete level of an enabling accounting, a (reconfigured) ideal speech situation holds out the promise of admitting the views and voices of accounting's many stakeholders. As a consequence of an ideal speech situation's association with the public sphere, it follows that an enabling accounting will necessitate the creation of a much more inclusive discourse, in stark contrast to its traditional exclusivity and consequent lack of transparency.

Broadbent reminds us that however appealing such an approach might be, it is likely to prove extremely difficult to accomplish. Consequently, she observes that perhaps the best we can hope for from the ideal speech situation arrangement is that it 'provides us with a framework which can show us how far we fall from the ideal' (p. 290). Given the feminist foundations of Broadbent's contribution, she is particularly worried about the possibilities for 'opening up the discourse to values informed by the feminine' in the context of a masculine 'accounting logic' in a similarly oriented arena, that of the ideal speech situation (p. 290). The paper ends with a 'speculative' agenda for a more enabling accounting. Initially it will be necessary to avoid prejudging what sort of information might be desirable. For different stakeholders, some of whom are identified: workforces; community groups; environmental groups; younger people; older workers; local and central government; etc. different information sets will be relevant at different times. Of necessity, the form that such accountings will take is likely to depart radically from those we now recognise as accounts. Again, in line with the feminist underpinnings of the paper, an enabling accounting should be characterised by a greater extent of subjectivity as a result of the incorporation of the values of the universal feminine.

The issue that motivates Gallhofer and Haslam (1997) is the necessity to highlight, and thereby enhance, the emerging critique of 'critical' accounting research. They take the view that 'all is not well' in this field, with the result that to some extent 'such research risk[s] at the very least posing obstacles to the promotion of an enabling and emancipatory accounting' (p. 73). Indeed, they wonder if some research designated as 'critical' merits this description, given its lack of a contribution to a meaningful emancipatory project. In first part of the paper, Gallhofer and Haslam outline their own perceptions of the integrity of the critical accounting project to date. 'Foucauldian' accounting studies are suggested to pose problems in these latter regards, as do other contributions that appear to be driven by novel approaches. At the same time, however, they do not wish to disregard the potential contribution of such perspectives, although in Gallhofer and Haslam's view, they may be more valuably deployed in conjunction with other ways of seeing, such as Marxist or German Critical Theory perspectives. There are also strong indications that some of the work in the latter traditions may promote similar worries and concerns from those committed to promoting an enabling accounting approach.

After Bronner (1994), Gallhofer and Haslam argue for a 'Critical Theory with public aims' (p. 81). Their view of an enabling accounting affirms the link with the philosophy of praxis evident at the inception of the Critical Theory tradition:

For us, an important characteristic of an enabling accounting is its ability to act as a force for radical emancipatory social change through making things visible and comprehensible and helping engender dialogue and action towards emancipatory change (Gallhofer and Haslam, 1997, p. 82).

An enabling accounting provides a means of promoting a renewed identification with the repressed and the disempowered. This returns to the notion of other voices invoked in Broadbent *et al.*'s 1997 editorial commentary. Among these are: women; ethnic minorities; indigenous peoples; colonised peoples; the poor; the exploited; the disabled; children; and the aged. These and other excluded groups are to be encouraged to fashion their own enabling accountings alongside conventional accounting, with which they should seek to interact. Implicit here is the necessity for the emergence of a cadre of critical accounting practitioners, operating alongside their professional counterparts. In this light, Gallhofer and Haslam identify the necessity for critical accounting researchers to develop a 'critical and radical pedagogy' which will promote an 'awareness of the significance and benefits of an emancipatory accounting amongst accountants of the future.' (p86). For Gallhofer and Haslam, the promotion of social betterment through the an enabling and emancipatory accounting requires that critical accounting researchers must go some considerable way 'beyond' the practices that many within critical accounting research increasingly seem comfortable with.

Gallhofer and Haslam have recently reaffirmed a commitment to the development of emancipatory accounting. Their 2003 monograph: *Accounting and Emancipation: Some Critical Reflections* contains three lengthy essays on the accounting writings of Jeremy Bentham, the counter accountings evident in the work of a group of nineteenth century radical social activists aligned to labour and a sympathetic critique of the social accounting movement. In their introductory chapter, Gallhofer and Haslam make the case for linking accounting and emancipation, both in the light of their supposed mutual incompatability and, picking up the theme of their 1997 paper, the emergence of the philosophic critique of modernity associated with postmodern and poststructural interventions. The monograph concludes with a short epilogue entitled: 'Accounting, emancipation and praxis today'. This sets the tone for the remaining paragraphs, which emphasise that an emancipatory accounting necessitates 'intervention' in the on-going 'struggle'. Noticeably absent is any direct reference to the substantive (critical) theory that characterised the Critical Theory perspective as it became established within accounting research in the late 1980s and early 1990s. The insights that such a perspective furnishes are perceived by Gallhofer and Haslam to be one element of a much more wide-ranging project:

Critical theoretical and holistic praxis is here the struggle to progress towards the emancipated state. It responds to concerns about how we are to achieve this progress or what is to be done. Locating accounting in praxis thus is to ask what is the role of accounting in progressing emancipation and how can we mobilise it to realise its potential. This involves understanding accounting contextually, going beyond a perception of the practice as static and technical and envisioning progressive emancipatory development. And it involves an envisioning of an emancipatory accounting and a whole range of further interventions in interaction therewith to help engender emancipatory progress, whether implicating more direct challenges to accounting or the more direct opening of possible pathways for accounting's development (Gallhofer and Haslam, 2003, pp. 156-157).

7. In Summary: Seven things you need to know about Critical Theory

From the above pages it should be very evident that Critical Theory is not a narrow theoretical perspective directly comparable with structuration theory, institutional theory, contingency theory, etc. While it came to the attention of accounting researchers at the same time as labour process theory, the two are not comparable for the same reason. The political economy perspective, on the other hand, is similar in that it also constitutes an attempt to develop a meta-theoretical perspective or 'grand narrative' as scholars working in the realms of postmodern social theory pejoratively describe such projects. This is hardly surprising since political economy, as the theoretical framework underpinning nineteenth and early twentieth century Marxist thinking, is what the founders of the Critical Theory tradition sought to reformulate in the course of their own praxis. In many ways Critical Theory and political economy are simply two sides of the same coin, complementing each other in much the same way as do the base and superstructure within the Marxist lexicon.

From the outset, Critical Theory has been an interdisciplinary perspective. Scholars such as Gramsci, Horkheimer, Adorno and Marcuse brought to the grand narrative project their own intellectual formations and resultant disciplinary expertises, which they painstakingly combined in the pursuit of knowledge. Habermas continued this tradition, drawing on ideas and developments across the social sciences and beyond to fashion his own grand theory. This said, because of its twin generic social theoretic and social philosophical emphases, Critical Theory has often been identifiable with the discipline of sociology. Again this is not too surprising given Comte's early designation of sociology as the 'queen of the sciences' and its continuing eclectic character. Critical Theory can perhaps be best understood to be 'theory' of any description that is enrolled to be 'critical' in the sense of Critical Theory. Consequently, there are no limitations on what might be incorporated within Critical Theory. It exists to be formulated and reformulated on an ongoing basis.

This leads us to the third and arguably the defining characteristic of Critical Theory. It provides a way of seeing that exists as a prerequisite for social change. At several points in the previous pages Marx's Eleventh thesis on Feuerbach has been invoked. This tells us that simply interpreting or understanding what we choose to study is not enough. The purpose of the exercise is to turn this learning to the advantage of society, i.e. the promotion of a better society. The presupposition is that there are many things about the existing social arrangements that merit changing. Recalling Horkheimer's founding statement of Critical Theory, 'traditional' theory does not subscribe to this axiom. It is this quality that distinguishes 'critical' theory from traditional theory. This is not to imply that all of those scholars who elect to embrace other ways of seeing are committed to the reproduction of the existing social arrangements, rather that they do not avail themselves of a way of seeing, Critical Theory, that explicitly links understanding and change as the enactment of the philosophy of praxis.

Fourthly, viewed in a slightly different way, Critical Theory makes no pretence of being objective. Those who embrace a Critical Theory perspective do so because they recognise and value its partiality. Critical Theory provides a particular set of insights not available from other perspectives. Equally, these insights are by and large consistent with the beliefs of those who embrace the Critical Theory perspective. Although this might appear to depart significantly from the model that we associate with scientific enquiry, most closely identified with Habermas' empirical-analytic sciences, Critical Theory shares with these and the historical-hermeneutic sciences the characteristic of being a highly rigorous mode of enquiry. While those who embrace a Critical Theory perspective are themselves reasonably assured of what they will uncover in the course of their research, the resulting contributions to the stock of knowledge are required to be as persuasive as any other contributions The Critical Theory perspective is not well served by accusations of slipshod scholarship from those who are uneasy with this invariably uncomfortable message.

The fifth and sixth points relate to the 'theory' vs 'empirics' dichotomy in the context of a Critical Theory perspective. In principle, there is no reason why adopting such a perspective precludes empirical work. Laughlin's 1987 Critical Theory methodology entailed such an arrangement, while some of the Frankfurt School's best known work, e.g. in association with Lazarsfeld, is heavily empirical in nature. As we noted earlier, however, Habermas does not appear to favour this approach. What a systematic set of empirical insights promises (but does not guarantee) is a richer understanding of the issues under enquiry. This may be of particular value in the case of trying to understand aspects of the prevailing social arrangements that the researcher and her/his research subjects are committed to changing, as in the case of Laughlin's Critical Theory methodology. In instances such as these, as well as in the context of promoting other voices, it is in the interests of both parties that the researcher becomes as familiar as s/he is able with the situation that is to be scrutinised and, ideally, changed. Once again, there is merit in seeing the pursuit of systematic insights in the context of rigour rather than the pursuit of the chimera of objectivity.

This said, it is in no sense obligatory that adopting a Critical Theory perspective requires the collection of empirical materials in this way. This is particularly true where the researcher is operating at a higher level, although not necessarily at Habermas' preferred meta-theoretical level. As we have observed earlier, Critical Theory provides a valuable conceptual framework for understanding practices such as accounting. It is clearly possible to use this framework to develop penetrating analyses of accounting that incorporate empirical materials of a less systematic sort. In such instances, empirical materials are used to illustrate more general points and issues, rather than to provide detailed insights. The purpose of theoretical analyses, however, remains the same, i.e. to contribute to the promotion of change that will in turn result in social betterment. The Critical Theory perspective does not seek to generate 'theory' for its own sake. Theory, like any empirical materials, provides a means to an end, that of a better understanding of what presently exists as a basis for ensuring that what might be is similarly enhanced.

Finally, the adoption of a Critical Theory perspective should not be seen as being synonymous with the wholesale rejection of the institution of accountancy and its various practices. Whilst these have been developed to serve the interests of the minority, and in many instances to the great disadvantage of the majority, they may provide a basis on which to construct an alternative set of structures and processes consistent with social betterment. The Critical Theory perspective offers a means of establishing what it might be desirable to retain from what currently exists, while always being informed by the belief that it is possible to build something better, which will serve the interests of a much broader set of stakeholders. It is therefore not a perspective to be embraced lightly or deployed because it promises to furnish an(other) interesting set of insights. As the embodiment of the philosophy of praxis, Critical Theory does not content itself with understanding accounting. By means of intervention, Critical Theory seeks to promote a better fit between accounting and the interests of all of society's various stakeholder groups.

8.   Postscript: Suggestions for Future Research

In the first instance, research using the Critical Theory perspective should be pursued across as broad a spectrum of accounting's sub disciplines as possible. Past experience indicates that all parties will benefit from the attention of researchers armed with this alternative way of seeing. In addition, it is desirable that some attention is given to how it might be possible to establish a cadre of critical accounting practitioners whose role it would be to explore the possible practical application of critical accounting research insights. As we observed earlier, the emergence of such a cadre is implicit in the recent enabling accounting literature. Roslender and Dillard (2003) offers some preliminary thoughts on where such a cadre might focus their attention, identifying liaisons with colleagues, students, accounting professionals, employers, politicians and similar opinion formers. Further consideration should now be given to the mechanics of establishing on-going contact with these and other stakeholders who might not initially be favourable to the message of critical accounting research. Beyond this, and again picking up on a view expressed in the enabling accounting literature, the community of Critical Theory scholars should direct some of its energies to the question of how best to incorporate insights emanating from outside the Critical Theory tradition, thereby continuing a process which is synonymous with its own evolution.

References

Key readings are identified with an asterisk (*)

Armstrong, P. (1985), "Changing management control strategies: the role of competition between accountancy and other organizational professions", *Accounting, Organizations and Society*, Vol. 10, No. 2, pp 129-148.

Armstrong, P. (1986), "Management control strategies and inter-professional competition: the case of accountancy and personnel management", in Knights, D. and Willmott, H. (Eds.), *Managing the Labour Process*, Gower Press, London, pp. 19-43.

Armstrong, P. (1987), "The rise of accounting controls in British capitalist enterprises", *Accounting, Organizations and Society*, Vol. 12, No. 5, pp. 415-436.

Arrington, C. E. and Puxty. A. (1991), "Accounting, interests and rationality: a communicative relation", *Critical Perspectives on Accounting*, Vol. 2, No. 1, pp. 31-58.

Berry, T., Capps, T., Cooper, D., Ferguson, D., Hopper, T. and Lowe, T. (1985), "Management control in an area of the NCB: rationales for accounting practice in a public enterprise", *Accounting, Organizations and Society*, Vol. 10, No. 1, pp. 3-28.

Braverman, H. (1974), *Labor and Monopoly Capital: The Degradation of Work in the Twentieth Century*, Monthly Review Press, New York.

Broadbent, J. (1998), "The gendered nature of 'accounting logic': pointers to an accounting that encompasses multiple values", *Critical Perspectives on Accounting*, Vol. 9, No. 3, pp. 69-98.

Broadbent, J., Laughlin, R. and Read, S. (1991), "Recent financial and administrative changes in the NHS: a critical theory analysis", *Critical Perspectives on Accounting*, Vol. 2, No. 1, pp. 1-29.

Broadbent, J., Ciancanelli, P., Gallhofer, S. and Haslam, J. (1997), "Enabling accounting: the way forward", *Accounting, Auditing and Accountability Journal*, Vol. 10, No. 3, pp. 265-275.

Bronner, (1994), *Of Critical Theory and its Theorists*, Blackwell Press, Oxford.

Burrell, G. and Morgan, G. (1979), *Sociological Paradigms and Organisational Analysis*, Heinemann Books, London.

Connerton, P. (Ed.) (1976), *Critical Sociology*, Penguin Books, Harmondsworth.

Cooper, D. J. (1980), "Discussion of 'Towards a political economy of accounting reports'", *Accounting, Organizations and Society*, Vol. 5, No. 1, pp. 161-166.

Cooper, D. J. and Sherer, M. J. (1984), "The value of corporate accounting reports: arguments for a political economy of accounting", *Accounting, Organizations and Society*, Vol. 9, No. 3/4, pp. 207-232.

*Dillard, J. F. (1991), "Accounting as a critical social science", *Accounting, Auditing and Accountability Journal*, Vol. 4, No. 1, pp. 8-28.

Fay, B. (1987), *Critical Social Science*. Polity Press, Cambridge.

Gallhofer, S. and Haslam, J. (1997), "Beyond accounting: the possibilities of accounting and 'critical' accounting research", *Critical Perspectives on Accounting*, Vol. 8, No. 1/2, pp. 71-95.

*Gallhofer, S. and Haslam, J. (2003), *Accounting and Emancipation: Some Critical Interventions*, Routledge, London.

Gramsci, A. (1971), *Selections from the Prison Notebooks*, in Hoare, Q. and Nowell, G. Smith (Eds.), Lawrence and Wishart, London.

Habermas, J. (1970), "Towards a theory of communicative competence", *Inquiry*, Vol. 13, pp. 360-375.

*Habermas, J. (1972), *Knowledge and Human Interests*, Heinemann Books, London.

Habermas, J. (1984), *The Theory of Communicative Action Vol 1: Reason and the Rationalization of Society*, translated by T. McCarthy, Polity Press, Cambridge.

Habermas, J. (1987), *The Theory of Communicative Action Vol 2: The Critique of Functionalist Reason* , translated by T. McCarthy, Polity Press, Cambridge.

Hopper, T., Storey, J. and Willmott. (1987), "Accounting for accounting: towards the development of a dialectical view", *Accounting, Organizations and Society*, Vol. 12, No. 5, pp. 437-456.

Jay, M. (1973), *The Dialectical Imagination: a History of the Frankfurt School and Institute for Social Research*, Heinemann Books, London.

*Laughlin, R. C. (1987), "Accounting systems in organizational contexts: a case for critical theory", *Accounting, Organizations and Society*, Vol. 12, No. 5, pp. 479-502.

Laughlin, R. C. (1995), "Empirical research in accounting: a case for middle-range thinking", *Accounting, Auditing and Accountability Journal*, Vol. 8, No. 1, pp. 63-87.

Laughlin, R. (2004), "Putting the record straight: a critique of 'Methodology choices and the construction of facts: some implications from the sociology of knowledge'", *Critical Perspectives on Accounting*, Vol. 15, No. 2, pp. 261-277.

Lukacs, G. (1971), *History and Class Consciousness: Studies in Marxist Dialectics*, originally published in 1923, translated by R. Livingstone, Merlin Press, London.

Power, M. and Laughlin, R. C. (1992), "Critical theory and accounting" in Alvesson, M. and Willmott, H. (Eds.), *Critical Theory and Management Studies*, Sage, London.

*Power, M., Laughlin, R. and Cooper, D. J. (2003), "Accounting and critical theory" in Alvesson, M. and Willmott, H. (Eds.), *Studying Management Critically*, Sage, London.

*Roslender, R. and Dillard, J. F. (2003), "Reflections on the interdisciplinary perspectives on accounting project", *Critical Perspectives on Accounting*, Vol. 14, No. 3, pp. 325-351.

Tinker, T. (1980), "Towards a political economy of accounting: an empirical illustration of the Cambridge controversies", *Accounting, Organizations and Society*, Vol. 5, No. 1, pp. 147-160.

Tinker, T. (1985), *Paper Prophets: A Social Critique of Accounting*, Holt Rinehart and Winston, London.

Tinker, A. M., Merino, B. and Neimark, M. D. (1982), "The normative origins of positive theories: ideology and accounting thought", *Accounting, Organizations and Society*, Vol. 7, No. 2, pp.167-200.

14

THE LABOUR PROCESS

Jesse Dillard
Portland State University, USA

Abstract: Why have we not developed the study of the labor process such that it more clearly articulates the forces and processes leading to practicable action programs for improving the human condition? The utopian connection of concept and execution in a classless society based on democratic planning is swept from sight. The scholastic commodification of the lived experience of work and workers has separated the working classes from the intellectual craft worker. Labour process theory provides an enlightening and necessary component in reestablishing ourselves as organic intellectuals decidedly devoted to the utopian goal of a democratically governed society based on justice, equality, and trust.

A critically informed labour process approach to accounting theory and practice recognises that extant accounting control systems are both a medium and outcome of a historically informed capitalist mode of production. Accounting practices arise out of the foundational contradictions and conflicts inherent within the capitalist mode of production. A fundamental tenet of a critically informed labor process approach is its conviction that the prevailing systems and their apparent trajectory are not predetermined and inalterable but are susceptible to emancipatory change. To be effective, labour process studies must consciously strive to be concrete and engaged within the work place, recognize the socially constructed nature of both technical and social circumstances, and keep in the forefront the possibility for emancipatory change.

Keywords: Labour process, enabling accounting, critical accounting, Braverman, labour process theory

1. Introduction

I can still remember the excitement with which I read Harry Braverman's classic time, *Labor and Monopoly Capitalism*.[39] I was beginning a journey from a positivist

---

[39] All references in this chapter are to Braverman (1974) unless otherwise stated.

and managerialist world, originating in and nurtured by deep roots in the blue-collar southern US textile culture, to a different and more complex world. I had watched, with inattention and distorted understanding, exploitation and annihilation. The mill was life and death. It was all powerful, pushed along by some visible or invisible hand that demanded more and more for less and less. People lost their jobs, and therefore, their dignity. Automation increased and finally the mill shut down. The social relations and the outcomes of capitalism for the textile workers in this small southern mill town finally began to take shape for me as Braverman explained the relationship between labour and monopoly capitalism. Braverman took some of Marx and made it real for my then 'today,' a perspective that my trade school education summarily excluded, distorted, and rejected. I had been trained to be part of the visible hand, to valorise efficiency and exploitation of natural and human capital for the benefit of monopoly capital. I have since recognised that even after Braverman, maybe, I still did not have the complete story, but I had been exposed to a good deal of it, in an articulate and powerful way. What Braverman said and how he said it, just made sense. It explained a world I had experienced, where class and wealth distribution were directly related to life opportunities, and the reified world was authoritarian and paternalistic. So for me labour process theory must begin with Braverman and what comes after is considered relative to this Marxist based articulation.

Braverman's work revitalised interest and research in Marx's labour process theory motivating a significant literature evaluating, criticising, refuting, and extending his work. I make no claim to a comprehensive review of this literature. What I propose is an outline of labour process theory, grounded in Braverman's formulation, with an introduction to the literature that has emerged as well as a discussion of the major criticisms that have been raised as to its validity, comprehensiveness, and contemporary applicability. Next, I undertake a selected review of the labour process work in the accounting literature illustrating selected recent applications. The discussion concludes with a summary and suggestions for possible applications for labour process theory in accounting and information systems research.

2. The Labour Process

The labour process is a branch of industrial sociology informed by Marxist theory precipitated in its contemporary form by *Labor and Monopoly Capitalism* authored by Harry Braverman in 1974. The ideas set forth are grounded in, and represent an extension of, Marx's central notions of class and the capitalist labour process. Above all, *the labor process research is a Marxist critique of the labor process as it is manifested under monopoly capitalism*. History and the sociology provide the methodology and context for investigating characteristics and inclinations of the capitalist workplace including the nature of skill, the decline of skilled labour, worker control strategies, and worker resistance (Meiksins, 1994).

Braverman's thesis states that:

The 'mode of production' we see around us, the manner in which labor processes are organized and carried out, is the 'product' of the social relations we know as capitalism. But the shape of our society … is not an instantaneous creation of 'laws' which generate that society on the spot and before our eyes. Every society is a moment in the historical process, and can be grasped only as part of that process. Capitalism, as social form, when it exists in time, space, population, and history, weaves a web of myriad threads; the conditions of its existence form a complex network each of which presupposes many others (Braverman, 1974, pp. 21-22).

Labour process is about the control of labour power. Labour power is the human's ability to perform work. 'For humans in society, labour power is a special category, separate and inexchangeable with any other, *simply because it is human*. Only one who is the *master of the labor of others* will confuse labour power with any other agency for performing a task, because to him, steam, horse, water, or human muscle which turn his mill are viewed as equivalents, as 'factors of production' (Braverman, p. 51).[40]

The labour process is predicated on the conditions whereby the worker sales his or her labour power to the employee. The exchange of labor power represents the unique characteristic of capitalist production.[41] Braverman (p. 52) identifies three conditions for capitalist production that become generalised through society and as such establish the fundamental social relationships. First, because workers are separated from the means of production, they can gain access only by selling their labour power to those who control these means of production. Second, legal constraints (slavery, serfdom) to the disposition of a worker's labour power are removed. Third, the worker is employed by the capitalist to expand the capital stock of the capitalist. The worker enters into such an agreement because she has no other alternative means of livelihood. Because of the political and social relationships, the drive toward the accumulation of capital controls and constructs the labour process. 'It thus becomes essential for the capitalist that control over the labour process pass from the hands of the worker into his own. This transition presents itself in history as the *progressive alienation of the process of production* from the worker; to the capitalist, it presents itself as the problem of *management*' (Braverman, p. 58).

An analysis of the labour process separates the production process into its elemental features, providing the basis for the specialisation of labour. In doing so, Braverman (p. 82) argues that general knowledge of the production process is 'a positive barrier to the functioning of the capitalist mode of production'. Thus, it follows that 'the capitalistic mode of production systematically destroys all-around skills where they exist, and brings into being skills and occupations that correspond

---

[40] Italics in the original quotation unless otherwise noted.
[41] Exchange relations, commodities, and money are also necessary, but Braverman argues that the exchange of labour power is uniquely central to capitalist modes of production.

to its needs'. The capitalist labour process results in the commodification of labour power such that it can be bought and sold in the market place. For Braverman, scientific management represents the quintessential means of capitalist control of the labour process as it separates mind and hand. No occupation or organisational process is exempt. 'While the social division of labor subdivides *society*, the detailed division of labor subdivides *humans*, and while the subdivision of society may enhance the individual and the species, the subdivision of the individual, when carried on without regard to human capabilities and needs, is a crime against the person and against humanity' (Braverman, p. 73).

As capital more completely subsumes the labour process, the possibility of all other forms of gaining a livelihood become impossible. The control of humans over the labour process becomes the control of the labour process over humans. However, the degenerate forms of work demanded of the capitalistic mode of production also give rise to worker resistance. Resistance and change require capital's continual and escalating vigilance.

The transformation of working humanity into a 'labour force', a 'factor of production', an instrument of capital, is an incessant and unending process. The condition is repugnant to the victims, whether their pay is high or low, because it violates human conditions of work. Since the workers are not destroyed as human beings but simply utilised in inhuman ways, their critical, intelligent, conceptual faculties, no matter how deadened or diminished, always remain in some degree a threat to capital. Moreover, the capitalist mode of production is continually extended to new areas of work, including those freshly created by technological advances and the shift of capital to new industries and/or different geographical locations. This mode of production is, in addition, continually being refined and perfected, imposing unceasing pressure upon the workers.

At the same time, the habituation of workers to the capitalist mode of production must be renewed with each generation. Even though a human being grows up under capitalism, she is not formed within the matrix of work life but injected into it from the outside after a prolonged period of adolescence during which the individual is held in reserve. The necessity for adjusting the worker to work in its capitalist form, for overcoming natural resistance intensified by swiftly changing technology, antagonistic social relations, and the succession of the generations, does not end with the 'scientific organization of labor,' but becomes a permanent feature of capitalist society. (Braverman, pp. 139-140). The somewhat nebulous panacea offered by Braverman is to return control over the labour process back to those who carry it out, though the means by which this is to be done are not well articulated or developed.

In the next section, I consider some of the criticisms and extensions associated with contemporary labour process theory. These criticisms and extensions generally have been developed within the sociology and social theory literature and point to attempts at, and possibilities for, modification and expansion of Braverman's initial articulation. For the most part, the work is sympathetic to labour process theory and is directed toward strengthening this field of study even if the critics have major concerns with Braverman's initial formulations. As a result of these critiques and debates, labour process theory has been significantly developed and improved.

3. Current Critique

According to Michael Burawoy (1996), *Labor and Monopoly Capital* has become conventional wisdom. Braverman brings together stratification theory and industrial sociology, shifting attention to structure and history away from adaptation and ahistoricalism. In a simple and comprehensible way, Braverman articulates the 'deskilling hypothesis' whereby capitalist modes of production continually degrade work by accentuating the division of labour, especially the separation of manual from mental labour. However, while sympathetic with the arguments, Burawoy claims that this idea is unoriginal and that its resurgence based on Braverman's work may be more a matter of timing than the originality and force of the ideas set forth. In the late 1960s and early 1970s, Marxist critique was again gaining sway as a reaction to functionalism. Braverman's work provided a basis for objectivist theories of class structure where '*a dynamic hierarchy based on work replaced a fixed hierarchy based on status*' (Burawoy, 1996, p. 297) refocused attention on how management organised and imposed work process in order to satisfy the ever increasing productivity requirements.

3.1. Contemporary Criticism

Critical reviews of Braverman's conceptualisation of the labour process (e.g. Burawoy, 1996; Meiksins, 1994; Noon and Blyton, 1997; Spencer, 2000) suggest several major areas of dispute[42] that have given rise to, and are the result of, a significant number of research studies and debates resulting in extensions and proposed revisions to labour process theory. Examples include the edited collections found in Burawoy and Skocpol (1982), Wood (1982), Knights, *et al.* (1985), Knights and Willmott (1990), and Wardell, Steiger, and Meiksins (1999) as well as works by Burawoy (1979, 1985), Friedman (1977), Thompson (1983), Littler (1990), and Knights and Willmott (1986, 1986a, 1987, 1992).

One major criticism is that Braverman's conceptualisation of skill and its role and presence in the work place are too narrowly formulated. (See Spenner, 1983; Steinberg, 1990; Samuel, 1977; Penn, 1984; Hirschorn, 1984; Zuboff, 1988; Wright and Singlemann, 1982; Rumberger, 1981; Kusterer, 1978; Elger, 1982; Meiksins, 1987; Edwards, 1979; Burawoy, 1985; Thompson, 1990; Cohen, 1987). A second major criticism is that management and its motivations and processes are under-theorised (e.g. Littler, 1982; Zimbalist, 1977; Shaiken, 1994; Garson, 1988; Friedman, 1977; Edwards, 1979; Stark, 1980; Meiksins, 1984; Piore and Sabel, 1984; Smith, 1990; Kelly, 1985, and Wardell, 1990). The agency of managers is circumscribed by depicting

---

42   These are not necessarily intended to be mutually exclusive categories.

their primary role and motivation as translators of marketing pressures. In this regard, production and control technology presumes mass production, which may not apply to more recent manufacturing work design strategies or adequately address service sector work organisation. In Braverman's conceptualisation, scientific management provides the primary technique employed by management in reformulating the labour process.

Braverman's view tends to be somewhat narrow and parochial. The decidedly Marxist perspective represents a limiting ideological base. By considering only western industrialised contexts, the perspective is geographically constrained. Race and gender do not enter into Braverman's domain of analysis (see Beechey, 1982; Littler, 1982; West, 1990; Cochburn, 1983).

As it is a reaction to what he perceived to be the prevailing subjectivist bias, Braverman's perception of the workplace and its occupants is overly objectivist (Zimbalist, 1977; Elger, 1982; Salaman, 1986; Willmott, 1990) and the possibilities of, and the means for, worker resistance are not adequately addressed (Zimbalist, 1977; Salaman, 1986; Burawoy, 1979, 1985; Clawson and Fantasia, 1983). According to Burawoy (1996), Braverman depicts workers as neither rational nor irrational thus relieved of all subjectivity. They became objects of labour, appendages of machines, another instrument of production, and executors of managerial conceptions. The exchanges among Storey (1985, 1989), Friedman (1987, 1989, 1990, 2004), Willmott (1990), and O'Doherty and Willmott (2001) with respect to this issue and its proper formulation within labour process theory provide an example of the current labour process debates. A central dimension is the appropriateness and applicability of post modern/post structuralist perspectives in understanding and developing labour process theory, and the extent of its applicability to the 'new workplace'.

3.2. Applications in the New Workplace

Sewell's (1998)[43] work on teams[44] is an example of building on the fundamental capitalist tenets and applying labour process theory to address new workplace strategies and techniques. Two media of control are considered: horizontal (peer/team members) and vertical (surveillance). Consistent with previous suggestions (e.g. Knights, 1990; Willmott, 1990), Sewell appropriates Foucault's ideas concerning surveillance in developing a more complete and up-to-date model of work discipline. In doing so, Sewell recognises the criticality of considering electronic means and mediums in the analyses of the labour process within the current workplace.[45] The horizontal dimension illustrates how purported

---

[43] The discussion is based on the empirical work by Sewell and Wilkinson (1992a, 1992b, 1993).

[44] Also, see Barker (1993) and McKinlay and Taylor (1996).

[45] See, for example, Garson, 1988; Carayon, 1993; Kallman, 1993; Poster, 1990; Lyon, 1993, 1994; Zuboff, 1988; Robins and Webster, 1988; Robey, 1981.

mechanisms for increasing worker autonomy are ultimately the consequence of the capitalist demands for profit and increased productivity.

Sewell (1998) attests to the validity of Braverman's core tenets of analysis while expanding and updating it in considering the implications of alternative work place design techniques using teams. First, current work place design techniques (re-engineering, total quality management, organisational learning, working in teams, lean production, flexible specialisation, and downsizing) are based on, controlled by, and result in capitalist modes of production. Second, the drive to constantly reconstruct the workplace is capital's response to the necessity of reducing worker resistance and increasing productivity. Third, while worker empowerment initiatives may appear to be inconsistent with scientific management driven worker deskilling, 'they do not represent an annulment of the enduring imperatives of capitalism' (p. 400) and, in fact, represent more effective means of increasing productivity and profits.

The capitalist modes of production may change as a result of changing technological, cultural, and political forces, but the underlying demands of the capitalist economic system remain the same, though camouflaged in different uniforms. The validity of a labour process is not subject to debate. Generally, the criticisms are directed toward strengthening the case for adopting a labour process perspective. By criticising Braverman's formulations, its weaknesses can be identified and remedied, and more importantly, labour process theory can evolve as the work context evolves under the pressures of global capitalism. Labour process theory can be modified and expanded to study the ever changing domain of the capitalist modes of production. Work such as that exemplified by Sewell (1998) reinforces the proposition that the tenets of the configuration of capitalistic modes of production represent a response to the capitalists demands for growth and wealth accumulation through the divorce of manual and mental work through deskilling. Sewell's work also indicates the propensity for workers to resist these impositions. Next, I consider applications of labour process theory in the accounting literature.

4.   Applications in the Accounting Literature

Following from the fundamental antagonisms of capitalism, power derives from control over the mode of production. The control systems are devices predicated on maintaining that power by responding to the demands of the capitalist modes of control. Management accounting is recognised as an interested administrative technology directed toward maintaining the vested interests of capital. This administrative technology does not arise out of technical and organisational progress but emerges in response to crises and opportunities associated with the unfolding of the contradictory logic of the capitalist mode of production. The deviance toward which the management accounting controls are directed are seen, not as malfunctions of either individual or organisational design, but as the result of class conflicts that lead to deviance in response to the demands for growth and wealth accumulation. These dimensions represent a research program following from the insights gained through the application of labour process theory.

4.1. Initial Applications

Understandably lagging a bit behind the sociological literature, accounting research evidences a flurry of work proposing and applying labour process theory in investigating how accounting systems and controls are both the medium and outcome of capitalist modes of production. The leading initial proponents of labour process theory in accounting research are Trevor Hopper and Peter Armstrong. The leading early works include Hopper and Powell (1985), Hopper, Storey and Willmott (1987), Hopper, Cooper, Lowe, Capps and Mouritsen (1986), and Armstrong (1985, 1986, 1987, 1989). Other notable work included Knights and Collinson (1987), Neimark and Tinker (1986, 1987). Hopper and Armstrong (1991) is arguably one of the last major labour process paper published in accounting as part of this initial flurry of initial activity. At this point, the postmodern/post structuralist begins to hold sway (Roslender and Dillard, 2003).

These early studies undertook a Marxist critique of the labour management relationships and the implications of, and for, accounting as a means of control. Hopper, *et al.* (1987) consider the conventional and naturalistic approaches to management accounting in order to identify their deficiencies and move beyond them. These authors propose what they term a 'critical perspective' grounded primarily in labour process theory that addresses some of the deficiencies of the alternative approaches. The traditional approaches generally assume that the good of all is dependent upon what is good for the capitalists. The labour process approach recognises the partiality of such a position and explicitly acknowledges the relationship between the formal organisational goals, formulated in the interests of the owners/capitalist, and how workers may resist the implementation of these goals. The traditional approaches do not adequately consider the context, such as class structure and state regulations, in considering how and why management control systems take the form that they do. The traditional approaches cannot explain compliance and conflict while the labour process perspective theorises the fundamental antagonism between capital and labour manifest as worker resistance.

4.2. Subsequent Applications

The work grounded in the Marxist tradition has continued to be developed over the years, though at a relatively slower rate as the contentious issues and apparent shortcomings of Braverman's formulation have become more clearly articulated and more widely discussed, and as the alternative literature is moving more toward a postmodern/post structuralist critique. Notable recent work includes that of Townley (1995), Armstrong, *et al.* (1996), Roslender (1996), McLean (1996), Arnold (1998, 1999), Mouritsen (1999), Cooper and Taylor (2000), Uddin and Hopper (2001), Armstrong (2002), Saravanamuthu and Tinker (2003), and Major and Hopper (2005).

By the early 1990s, the labour process, as also more generally Marxist based critique, was being overtaken by the wave of poststructuralist/postmodernist inspired research (Roslender and Dillard, 2003). This new genre follows a more general Foucauldian trend in alternative accounting research that began with Burchell *et al.* (1985). The work place was now being framed as, and viewed through, a Foucauldian lens. Significant early works in this area include Hoskin and Macve (1986), Loft (1985), and Miller and O'Leary (1987). In response to Braverman's alleged 'subjectivity' problems, two noted labour process scholars, David Knights (1990) and Hugh Willmott (1990) explicitly called for incorporating Foucauldian analysis into labour process analyses. Examples of heeding this call include Miller and O'Leary (1993, 1994), Ezzamel and Willmott (1998), and Ezzamel *et al.* (2004). Foucauldian scholarship necessarily breaks with the tenets of a Marxist critique. Thus, the evaluation of the capitalist work place loses its political dimension, and the program for change is buried in a muddle of discursive formations and hyper reality.

Presently, Marxist scholarship may have been eclipsed by postmodern or poststructuralist ideology as the alternative perspective of preference. However, the applicability of the ideas is continually illustrated in important areas such as gender (e.g. Cooper and Taylor, 2000), work in developing countries (Uddin and Hopper, 2001), application of new management techniques (Armstrong, 2002), and managers as labour subjected to the demands of the capitalist modes of production (Saravanamuthu and Tinker, 2003).

4.3. *The Labour Process and Gender*

Cooper and Taylor (2000) take an orthodox route through history and sociology in analysing the workplace practices and process of non-professionally qualified accountants in accounting roles, a much neglected subject group within the accounting literature. Following Braverman's historical analysis, accounting clerks' work is analysed from the mid nineteenth century until 1996. Using this analysis, the authors show that the technology of scientific management is used in both deskilling and reducing work life autonomy of accounting clerks. As a result, wages, work life quality, and job security have declined. Deskilling and loss of real income are documented. Further, as the degradation progresses, the composition of the workforce shifts from predominately male to predominately female indicating the validity of the labour process analysis. Cooper and Taylor sum up the implications of their analysis with the follow quote from Braverman.

> *The progressive elimination of thought from the work of the office worker thus takes the form, at first, of reducing mental labour to a repetitious performance of the same small set of functions. The work is still performed in the brain, but the brain is used as the equivalent of the hand of the detail worker in production, grasping and releasing a single piece of 'data' over and over again. The next step is the elimination of the thought process completely – or at least insofar as it is ever removed from human labor – and the increase of clerical categories in which nothing but manual labour is performed* (Braverman, 1974, p. 319).

4.4. The Labour Process in Developing Countries

Uddin and Hopper (2001) apply labour process theory in studying the workplace conditions within a soap factory in Bangladeshi. Burawoy's (1979, 1985) work provides the primary theoretical basis for their analysis. The authors undertake an intensive case analysis attaining data from interviews, participant observation, internal document analysis, and publicly available information. While both Braverman and Burawoy's ideas are fundamentally grounded in a Marxist critique of the capitalist forms of production, Braverman proposes deskilling as the primary means of control over the labour process. Taking a slightly different perspective, Burawoy proposes that the diversion of management-labour conflict obscures the presence and distribution of surplus value, reducing labour's resistance to management's control.

Uddin and Hopper investigate control, coercion, and consent. Internal labour markets, the presence and efficacy of labour representation (unions) and collective bargaining, and gaming behaviour of both workers and first line management obscures and dissipates the labour-management conflict facilitating the appropriation of surplus value by management. The authors conclude that:

> Management need not synchronize positive employee attitudes with behaviour: subjectivity is irrelevant to effort ... capital could impose its ends without legitimation and consent. Management directly and explicitly stripped out labour costs regardless of whether labour had attitudes of cooperation or their self-identity was threatened ... . [T]here is a danger that an undue preoccupation with subjectivity can deflect attention from the importance of materialistic and institutional factors (Uddin and Hopper, 2001, p. 667).

Within the Bangladeshi soap factory, worker subjectivity is of little consequence, a position more in line with Braverman than with Burawoy and other critics.

With respect to accounting systems, regimes of control define the parameters of the accounting system. For example, hegemonic and market based control regimes were transformed into political hegemony and political despotism. Under private ownership within the market based control regime, it appears that within the company studied, the primary tenets of labour process theory describe the dynamics of management-labour relations that create and are created by the emerging forms of despotism and coercive controls.

4.5. The Labour Process as the Hidden Driver for Modern Administrative Technology

Armstrong's (2002) work represents an indirect application of labour process theory in exploring the implications of 'innovations' in modern administrative technology. Specifically, the author considers and critiques the application of Activity Based Management/Activity Based Costing (ABM) to staff functions, using an example from the purchasing function. Though not explicitly stated, Armstrong employs a labour process lens to assess the surreptitious application of scientific management (a productivists mindset) to non-production functions within the modern work organization. ABM represents a set of techniques for doing so.

The labour process theory constructs such as deskilling, standardisation of tasks, and object costing are imbedded within the ABM rhetoric and processes, though they are not explicitly articulated as such. What ABM facilitates by its totalising conceptualisations is the application for these disciplinary concepts to not only the production processes but also to 'intellectual' work, which has been traditionally unaffected. Performance specification shifts from being framed in the culture of the actor or professional to being framed by, and within, the culture of the monitor.[46] Armstrong argues that by using ABM, management accounting can now claim to have the capability to construct 'regimes of accountability' (p. 103) for all organisational functions. All acts are presumed to be specifiable and repeatable and to be associated with a product or a process. If the activity cannot be specified as such, then it is a candidate for elimination. Armstrong considers both the truth claims and the social consequences of ABM in light of the tenets of labour process theory. He goes on to show how such a productivist perspective is clearly 'flawed and myopic' and might actually be detrimental to capitalist objectives because the technique cannot embrace non-routine work.

4.6. Subordinate Management and the Labour Process

Saravanamuthu and Tinker (2003) investigate the capitalist labour process in three sub-units of an Australian firm involved in the automotive and parts manufacturing industry. Following Marx, they associate subordinate management as a component of labour. Following Braverman, Friedman, Burawoy and others, they apply labour process theory in exploring the politics of management. As the ever present demands of capital require subordinate management's control and exploitation of the labour process, the dynamic and ongoing tension between management's social and economic responsibilities renders accounting performance representations contestable. An analysis of the different subunits reveals different levels of power and influence exercised by labour, which required different approaches on the part of management to control the labour process. These local differences do not indicate a cessation of the fundamental capital-labour conflicts but do point out the criticality of context in their manifestations.

Saravanamuthu and Tinker (2003) conclude that although ideology articulated as economic citizenship may have superseded more technocratic modes (e.g. scientific management) as the primary means for controlling the labour process under certain circumstances, the means of control employed reflect management's response to the demands of capital. Accounting represents the primary means by which capital holds management accountable as well as the historical relationship between the competing needs of labour and management. Saravanamuthu and Tinker's (2003) work suggests that accounting systems evolve out of 'management's

---

[46] As has been the experience of the craftsman in an earlier time.

discriminate accommodation of worker autonomy in labour strategies' (p. 55), a situation not unrelated to Friedman's (1977) responsible autonomy. Such strategies do not indicate the remission of the fundamental capital-labour contradictions, they only succeed in obscuring them.

5. Future Research Considerations

Future research efforts must build on both the foundations of the labour process theory as well as develop and extend it in responding to its critics. Labour process theory research is one central topic area within the critical accounting project as set out by Roslender and Dillard (2003) and represents an integral component in the development of an enabling accounting (e.g. Broadbent, *et al.*, 1997). Following from our understanding of, and previous research pertaining to, the labour process, work in the area should be directed toward identifying what groups are experiencing the debilitating effects of the capitalist labour process. We must consider workers upon whom accounting and accountants act, managers who implement and are subjected to the structural demands, and certified and uncertified accounting professionals both within and outside of corporations.

Labour process theory provides theory and guidance in explaining and evaluating the work environment, predicting its future evolution, and providing guidance in overcoming the detrimental effects. Traditional indicators have been real and relative trends in compensation. Future work needs to also include analyses of ethnic and gender trends within the work place and as part of the compensation analysis. One indication is the extent to which tasks are being fragmented. Traditional labour process research must continue to focus on specialisation, task flexibility, routinisation, and standardisation as the primary means by which work is deconstructed and deskilled. In addition, we must also consider the effects of alternative organisational arrangements such as flexible production and integrated work teams on the labour process. Related to the new organisation forms, research is needed that considers the differentiation between social integrative structures facilitating coordination and focus and those structures designed and implemented for control and surveillance. The propensity for self management through these new organisational forms and interpersonal relationships should be integrated into the study of the current capitalist modes of production. As part of the evolving work place, we must consider at what level members of management move from being the controlled to being the controllers. Insight in this, and other issues, requires an analysis of the locus, distribution, and implementation of power within the work environment.

Another fruitful area for future research is the use of labour process theory in conjunction with other theories of work management within organisational hierarchies. The work of Major and Hopper (2004, 2005) provide an example where labour process theory can be used in conjunction with more functional formulations. At a macro level, these authors employ new institutional theory in explaining the motivation and process by which new management techniques (activity based costing, in this case) for better controlling the labour process are implemented. On a more micro level, labour process theory is combined with technical, factor, and process approaches to provide a more complete, though not necessarily theoretically consistent[47], explanation of actions related to control systems and management programs found within work organisations. However, in doing so one must not lose sight of the structural demands of the extant capitalistic system that ultimately motivate the actions of management even though the alternative approaches do not make this relationship explicit (Armstrong, 2002).

The researcher must be cautioned that, as with any well developed literature, there are significant expectations associated with entering the labour process debate. One must evidence awareness of the issues and the arguments that have been set forth as well as their refutations. The major issues are briefly reviewed. First, the level of worker subjectivity and resistance must be addressed. The extant literature suggests that both structural imperatives as well as contextual variables must be considered. Second, Braverman's conceptualisation of skill, and its role in the workplace, is too narrowly formulated. Specifically, there is too much emphasis on the 'deskilling hypothesis'. The ideas concerning deskilling were initially predicated on mass production as the form of work organisation and scientific management as the primary technique for controlling the labour process. As alternative techniques are implemented, the analytical parameters may need to be expanded. Third, management and its motivations and processes are under-theorised. The primary role of management is to respond to market pressures using the control techniques yielding a restrictive conceptualisation of management agency. Fourth, the Marxist ideology underpinning the theory provides a limited and outmoded ideological base. Fifth, restricting the historical analysis to western industrial development constrains the geographical and cultural applicability of the theory. Sixth, race and gender issues are not recognised as critical dimensions in control of the labour process and the effects thereon are not recognised as consequences of control of the labour process. Further research must consider each of these issues carefully in applying labour process theory in studying management and accounting control regimes.

6. Closing Comments

After writing this chapter, I returned to my roots in upstate South Carolina, once the self-proclaimed textile capital of the world. I drove down by the mill. It was abandoned, boarded, and broken. The bridge was washed away. The parking lot was overgrown. There was an eerie, ghostlike quietness where organised bedlam

---

[47] Major and Hopper (2005) do not attempt to reconcile or integrate these alternative theoretical perspectives arguing that to do so 'would render violence to the findings and assumptions of each approach' (p. 212) and that the validity of such eclectic approaches should be appraised based on the utility derived by the reader.

had once reigned, three shifts of it. About the only positive change was the river that ran through. It no longer reeked of printer's dye and chloride.

I thought of the people who had populated this place and of the social structures that hallowed and hollowed them. I recalled the schools that were to train the disciplined worker, and the churches that were to sustain the disciplined worker. I wondered how those who lost their jobs sustained themselves. I thought about the criticisms of Braverman's ideas, especially those related to subjectivity and resistance. It became painfully clear that no amount of agency or resistance would have affected the outcome. Capital chases after cheap labour, and, presently, the standard of living in Asia seems more conducive to textile industry profits. I also wondered if one of the reasons for the flight offshore was that the jobs had become deskilled to the point where little, if any, education or training was necessary to carry them out. As such, labour has become a fungible commodity, allowing the cost to be driven to subsistence levels or below.

Not only do those who control the means of production control the labour process, they also dictate the location in which the production processes are carried out. As illustrated by Uddin and Hopper (2001), the process is repeated yet again in another location. The worker's task will be deskilled, and the workers will be exploited. The mechanisms may be different. The technologies more advanced. The modes of organisation more refined, but the effect will be the same. The cost of production will be reduced by driving down labour costs through control and manipulation of the labour process. The structural imperatives of capitalism are relentless and we must be ever mindful of them as we attempt to better understand and enhance the labour process.

Why have we not developed the study of the labour process such that it more clearly articulates the forces and processes leading to practicable action programs for improving the human condition? Burawoy (1996) proposes that the critique of the labour process energised by Braverman in 1974 has been absorbed into the amorphous body of social science. Scientific rigour overrules critique. We lose sight of 'The Degradation of Work in the Twentieth Century'. The utopian connection of concept and execution in a classless society based on democratic planning is swept from sight. 'Structure dissolves into a linguistic construction, and history reduces to narrative. Experience becomes discourse, oppression becomes talk about talk' (Burawoy, 1996, p. 299). This scholastic commodification of the lived experience of work and workers has separated the working classes from the intellectual craft worker. Labour process theory provides an enlightening and necessary component in re-establishing ourselves as organic intellectuals decidedly devoted to the utopian goal of a democratically governed society based on justice, equality, and trust.

Specifically, a critically informed labour process approach to accounting theory and practice recognises that extant accounting control systems are both a medium and outcome of a historically informed capitalist mode of production. Accounting practices arise out of the foundational contradictions and conflicts inherent within the capitalist mode of production. A fundamental tenet of a critically informed labour process approach is its conviction that the prevailing systems and their apparent trajectory are not predetermined and inalterable but are susceptible to emancipatory change. To be effective, labour process studies must consciously strive to be concrete and engaged within the work place, recognise the socially constructed nature of both technical and social circumstances, and keep in the forefront the possibility for emancipatory change.

References

Armstrong, P. (1985), "Changing management control strategies: the role of competition between accountancy and other organizational professions", *Accounting, Organizations and Society*, pp. 129-148.

Armstrong, P. (1986), "Management control strategies and inter-professional competition: the case of accountancy and personnel management", in Knights, D. and Willmott, H. (Eds.), *Managing the Labor Process*, Vol. 10, No. 2, pp. 19-43, Gower, London.

Armstrong, P. (1987), "The rise of accounting controls in British capitalist enterprises", *Accounting, Organizations and Society*, Vol. 12, No. 5, pp. 415-436.

Armstrong, P. (1989), Management, labour process and agency", *Work, Employment and Society*, Vol. 3, No. 3, pp. 307-322.

Armstrong, P. (2002), "The cost of activity-based management", *Accounting, Organizations and Society*, Vol. 27, pp. 99-120.

Armstrong, P., Marginson, P., Edwards, P. and Purcell, J. (1996), "Budgetary control and the labour force: findings from a survey of large British companies", *Management Accounting Research*, Vol. 7, No. 1, pp. 1-23.

Arnold, P. (1998), "The limits of postmodernism in accounting history: the Decatur experience", *Accounting, Organizations and Society*, Vol. 23, No. 7, pp. 665-684.

Arnold, P. (1999), "From the union hall: a labor critique of the new manufacturing and accounting regimes", *Critical Perspectives on Accounting*, Vol. 10, No. 3, pp. 399-424.

Barker, J. (1993), "Tightening the iron cage: concertive control of self managing teams", *Administrative Science Quarterly*, Vol. 38, pp. 408-437.

Beechey, V. (1982), "The sexual division of labor and the labor process: a critical assessment of Braverman", in Wood, S. (Ed.), *Skilling, Deskilling and the Labor Process*, Hutchinson, London, pp. 54-73.

Braverman, H. (1974), *Labor and Monopoly Capital: The Degradation of Work in the Twentieth Century*, Monthly Review Press, NY.

Broadbent, J., Ciancanelli, P., Gallhofer, S. and Haslam, J. (1997), "Enabling accounting: the way forward?", *Accounting, Auditing and Accountability Journal*, pp. 265-275.

Burawoy, M. (1979), *Manufacturing Consent: Changes in the Labour Process Under Monopoly Capitalism*, University of Chicago Press, Chicago.

Burawoy, M. (1985), *The Politics of Production*, Verso Books, London.

Burawoy, M. (1996), "A classic of its time", *Contemporary Sociology*, Vol. 25, Vol. 3, pp. 296-299.

Burawoy, M. and Skocpol, T. (Eds.) (1982), "Marxist inquires: studies of labor, class, and states", *The American Journal of Sociology*, Vol. 88 (Supplement).

Burchell, S., Clubb, C. and Hopwood, A. (1985), "Accounting in its social context: towards a history of value added in the United Kingdom", *Accounting, Organizations and Society*, Vol. 10, No. 4, pp. 381-414.

Carayon, P. (1993), "The effect of electronic performance monitoring on job design and worker stress: review or the literature and conceptual model", *Human Factors*, Vol. 26, pp. 385-395.

Clawson, D. and Fantasia, R. (1983), "Review essay: beyond Burawoy: the dialectics of conflict and consent on the shop floor", *Theory and Society*, Vol. 12, No. 3, pp. 671-680.

Cockburn, C. (1983), *Brothers: Male Dominance and Technological Change*, Pluto Press, London.

Cohen, S. (1987), "A labor process to nowhere?", *New Left Review*, Vol. 165, pp. 34-50.

Cooper, C. and Taylor, P. (2000), "From Taylorism to Ms Taylor: the transformation of the accounting craft", *Accounting, Organizations and Society*, Vol. 25, No. 6, pp. 555-578.

Edwards, R. (1979), *Contested Terrain*, Basic Books, New York.

Elger, T. (1982), "Braverman, capital accumulation and deskilling", in Wood, S. (Ed.), *The Degradation of Work: Skill, Deskilling and the Labor Process*, Hutchinson, London, pp. 23-53.

Ezzamel, M. and Willmott, H. (1998), "Accounting for teamwork: a critical study of group-based systems of organizational control", *Administrative Science Quarterly*, Vol. 43, pp. 358-396.

Ezzamel, M., Willmott, H. and Worthington, F. (2004), "Accounting and management-labour relations: the politics of production in the 'factory with a problem'", *Accounting, Organizations, and Society*, Vol. 29, No. 3/4, pp. 269–302.

Friedman, A. (1977), *Industry and Labour*, Macmillan, London.

Friedman, A. (1987), "The means of management control and labour process theory: a critical note on Storey", *Sociology*, Vol. 21, pp. 287-294.

Friedman, A. (1989), *Computer Systems Development: History, Organization and Implementation*, Wiley, London.

Friedman, A. (1990), "Managerial strategies, activities, techniques and technology: towards a complex theory of the labour process", in Knights, D. and Willmott, H. (Eds.), *Labour Process Theory*, Macmillan, London, pp. 177-208.

Friedman, A. (2004), "Strawmanning and the labor process", *Sociology*, Vol. 38, No. 3, pp. 573-591.

Garson, B. (1988), *The Electronic Sweatshop: How Computers are Transforming the Office of the Future into the Factory of the Past*, Simon and Schuster, New York.

Hirschorn, L. (1984), *Beyond Mechanization*, MIT Press, Cambridge, MA.

Hopper, T. and Armstrong, P. (1991), "Cost accounting, controlling labour and the rise of conglomerates", *Accounting, Organizations and Society*, Vol. 16, No. 5/6, pp. 405-438.

Hopper, T. and Powell, A. (1985), "Making sense of research into the organizational and social aspects of management accounting: a review of its underlying assumptions", *Journal of Management Studies*, Vol. 22, No. 5, pp. 429-465.

Hopper, T., Storey, J. and Willmott, H. (1987), "Accounting for accounting: towards the development of a dialectical view", *Accounting, Organizations, and Society*, Vol. 12, No. 5, pp. 437-456.

Hopper, T., Cooper, D., Lowe, T., Capps, T. and Mouritsen, J. (1986), "Management control and worker resistance in the National Coal Board: financial controls in the labour process", in Knights, D. and Willmott, H. C. (Eds.), *Managing the Labour Process*, Gower, London.

Hoskin, K. and Macve, R. (1986), "Accounting and the examination: a genealogy of disciplinary power", *Accounting, Organizations and Society*, Vol. 11, No. 2, pp. 105-136.

Kallman, E. (1993), *The Wisdom of Teams: Creating High-Performance Organization*, Harvard Business School Press, Boston.

Kelly, J. (1985), "Management's redesign of work: labor process, labor markets, and product markets", in Knights, D. *et al.*, *Job Redesign*, Gower, Aldershot.

Knights, D. (1990), "Subjectivity, power and the labour process analysis", in Knights, D. and Willmott, H. (Eds.), *Labour Process Theory*, Macmillan, London: pp. 297–335.

Knights, D. and Collinson, D. (1987), "Disciplining the shopfloor: a comparison of the disciplinary effect of managerial psychology and financial accounting", *Accounting, Organizations and Society*, Vol. 12, No. 5, pp. 457-478.

Knights, D., Collinson, D. and Willmott, H. (1985), *Job Redesign*, Gower, Aldershot.

Knights, D. and Willmott, H. (Eds.) (1990), *Labour Process Theory*, Macmillan, London.

Kusterer, K. (1978), *Know-How on the Job: The Important Working Knowledge of 'Unskilled Workers'*, Westview Press, Boulder.

Littler, C. (1982), *The Development of the Labor Process in Capitalistic Societies*, Heineman, London.

Littler, C. (1990), "The labor process debates: a theoretical review, 1974-1988", in Knights, D. and Willmott, H. (Eds.), *Labour Process Theory*, Macmillan, London, pp. 46-94.

Loft, A. (1985), "Towards a critical understanding of accounting: the case of cost accounting in the UK 1914-1925", *Proceedings of the Interdisciplinary Perspectives on Accounting Conference*, Manchester, July 1985.

Lyon, D. (1993), "An electronic panopticon?: a sociological critique of surveillance theory", *Sociological Review*, Vol. 41, p. 653-678.

Lyon, D. (1994), *The Electronic Eye: The Rise of Surveillance Society*, Polity, Cambridge, UK.

Major, M. and Hopper, T. (2004), "Extending new institutional theory: regulation and activity-based costing in Portuguese telecommunications", paper presented at the Fourth Asia Pacific Interdisciplinary Research in Accounting Conference, Singapore, 4–6 July 2004.

Major, M. and Hopper, T. (2005), "Managers divided: implementing ABC in a Portuguese telecommunications company", *Management Accounting Research*, Vol. 16, No. 2, p. 205-229.

McKinley, A. and Taylor, P. (1996), "Power, surveillance and resistance: inside the 'factory of the future'", in Ackers, P., Smith, C. and Smith, P. (Eds.), *The New Workplace and Trade Unionism*, Routledge, London, pp. 279-300.

McLean, T. (1996), "Bureaucratic and craft administration of the production process: the formation of accounting and non-accounting control arrangements", *Management Accounting Research*, Vol. 7, No. 1, pp. 119-134.

Meiksins, P. (1994), "Labor and monopoly capital for the 1990s: a review an critique of the labor process debate", *Monthly Review*, Vol. 46, No. 6, pp. 45-59.

Meiksins, P. (1987), "New classes and old theories: the impasse of contemporary class analysis", in Levine, R. and Lembcke, J. (Eds.), *Recapturing Marxism: An Appraisal of Recent Trends in Sociological Theory*, Praeger Publishers, New York, pp. 37-63.

Meiksins, P. (1984), "Scientific management and class relations: a dissenting view", *Theory and Society*, Vol. 13, pp. 177-209.

Miller, P. and O'Leary, T. (1987), "Accounting and the construction of the governable person", *Accounting, Organizations and Society*, Vol. 12, No. 3, pp. 235-265.

Miller, P. and O'Leary, T. (1993), "Accounting expertise and the politics of the product: economic citizenship and modes of corporate governance", *Accounting, Organizations and Society*, Vol. 18, No. 2/3, pp. 187-206.

Miller, P. and O'Leary, T. (1994), "Accounting, 'economic citizenship' and the spatial reordering of manufacturing", *Accounting, Organizations and Society*, Vol. 19, No. 1, pp. 235-265.

Mouritsen, J. (1999), "The flexible firm: strategies for a subcontractor's management control", *Accounting, Organizations and Society*, Vol. 24, No. 1, pp. 31-55.

Neimark M. and Tinker, T. (1986), "The social construction of management control systems:", *Accounting, Organizations and Society*, Vol. 12, No. 1, pp. 369-395.

Neimark M. and Tinker, T. (1987), "The role of annual reports in gender and class contradictions at General Motors: 1917-1976", *Accounting, Organizations and Society*, Vol. 12, No. 1, pp. 71-88.

Noon, M. and Blyton, P. (1997), *The Realities of Work*, Macmillian, London.

O'Doherty, D. and Willmott, H. (2001), "Debating labour process theory: the issue of subjectivity and the relevance of poststructuralism", *Sociology*, Vol. 35, pp. 457-476.

Penn, R. (1984), *Skilled Workers in the Class Structure*, Cambridge University Press, Cambridge.

Piore, M. and Sabel, C. (1984), *The Second Industrial Divide*, Basic Books, New York.

Poster, M. (1990), *The Mode of Information: Poststructuralism and Social Context*, Polity Press, Cambridge, UK.

Robey, D. (1981), "Computer information systems and organization structure", *Communications of the ACM*, Vol. 24, pp. 679-687.

Robins, K. and Webster, F. (1988), "Cybernetic capitalism: information, technology, everyday life", in Mosco, V. and Wasko, J. (Eds.), *The Political Economy of Information*, University of Wisconsin Press, Madison, pp. 44-75.

Roslender, R. (1996), "Critical accounting and the labour of accountants", *Critical Perspectives on Accounting*, Vol. 7, pp. 461-484.

Roslender, R. and Dillard, J. (2003), "Reflection on the interdisciplinary perspectives on accounting project", *Critical Perspectives on Accounting*, Vol. 14, pp. 325-351.

Rumberger, R. (1981), "The changing skill requirements of jobs in the US economy", *Industrial and Labor Relations Review*, Vol. 34, No. 4, pp. 578-590.

Salaman, G. (1986), *Working*, Tavistock, London.

Samuel, R. (1977), "The workshop of the world: steam power and hand technology in mid-Victorian Britain", *History Workshop Journal*, Vol. 3, pp. 6-72.

Saravanamuthu, K. and Tinker, T. (2003), "Politics of managing the dialect of control", *Accounting, Organizations, and Society*, Vol. 28, No. 1, pp. 37-64.

Sewell, G. (1998), "The discipline of teams: the control of team-based industrial work through electronic and peer surveillance", *Administrative Science Quarterly*, Vol. 43, pp. 397-428.

Sewell, G. and Wilkinson, G. (1992a), "Someone to watch over me: surveillance, discipline and the just-in-time labour process", *Sociology*, Vol. 26, pp. 271-289.

Sewell, G. and Wilkinson, G. (1992b), "Empowerment or emasculation: shop floor surveillance in a total quality organization", in Blyton, P. and Turnbull, P. (Eds.), *Reassessing Human Resource Management*, Sage, London, pp. 97-115.

Sewell, G. and Wilkinson, G. (1993), "Human resources management in 'surveillance' companies", in Clark, J. (Ed.), *Human Resource Management and Technical Change*, Sage, London, pp. 137-154.

Shaiken, H. (1994), *Work Transformation*, Lexington Books, Lexington, MA.

Smith, V. (1990), *Managing in the Corporate Interest*, University of California Press, Berkeley.

Spencer, D. (2000), "Braverman and the contribution of labour process analysis to the critique of capitalist production – twenty-five years on", *Work, Employment and Society* Vol. 14, pp. 223-243.

Spenner, K. (1983), "Deciphering Prometheus: temporal change in the sill level of work", *American Sociological Review*, Vol. 48, pp. 824-837.

Stark, D. (1980), "Class struggle and the transformation of the labor process", *Theory and Society* Vol. 9, pp. 89-130.

Steinberg, R. (1990), "The social construction of skill", *Work and Occupations*, Vol. 17, pp. 449-482.

Storey, J. (1985), "The means of management control", *Sociology*, Vol. 19, pp. 193-211.

Storey, J. (1989), "The means of management control: a reply to Friedman", *Sociology* Vol. 23, pp. 119-124.

Townley, B. (1995), "Managing by the numbers: accounting, personnel management and the creation of a mathesis", *Critical Perspectives on Accounting*, Vol. 6, No. 6, pp. 555-575.

Thompson, P. (1983), *The Nature of Work: An Introduction to Debates on Labour Process*, Macmillan, London.

Thompson, P. (1990), "Crawling from the wreckage: the labor process and the politics of production", in Knights, D. and Willmott, H. (Eds.), *Labour Process Theory*, Macmillan, London, pp. 95-124.

Uddin, S. and Hopper, T. (2001), "A Bangladesh soap opera: privatisation, accounting, and regimes of control in a less developed country", *Accounting, Organizations, and Society*, Vol. 26, pp. 643-672.

Wardell, M. (1990), "Labor and the Labor Process", in Knights, D. and Willmott, H. (Eds.), *Labour Process Theory*, Macmillan, London, pp. 153-176.

Wardell, M., Steiger, T. and Meiksins, P. (Eds.) (1999), *Rethinking the Labor Process*, State University of New York Press, Albany.

West, J. (1990), "Gender and the labor process: a reassessment", in Knights, D. and Willmott, H. (Eds.), *Labour Process Theory*, Macmillan, London, pp. 244-273.

Willmott, H. (1990), "Subjectivity and the dialectics of Praxis: opening up the core of labour process analysis", in Knights, D. and Willmott, H. (Eds.), *Labour Process Theory*, London: Macmillan, pp. 336-378.

Wood, S. (Ed.) (1982), *The Degradation of Work: Skill, Deskilling and the Labor Process*, Hutchinson, London.

Wright, E. and Singlemann, J. (1982), "Proletarianization and the changing American class structure", in Burawoy, M. and Skocpol, T. (Eds.), "Marxist Inquiries: Studies of Labor, Class and States", *American Journal of Sociology*, Vol. 88, Supplement, pp. 179-209.

Zimbalist, A. (Ed.) (1977), *Case Studies on the Labor Process*, Monthly Review Press, New York.

Zuboff, S. (1988), *In the Age of the Smart Machine*, Basic Books, New York.

15

GANDHIAN–*VEDIC* PARADIGM: THEORISING SUSTAINABLE DEVELOPMENT

Kala Saravanamuthu
University of New England, Australia

Abstract: This chapter draws on Gandhi's interpretation of the *Vedic* philosophy of living in harmony with Nature in proposing an alternative to the dominant paradigm of economic growth, which is based on the logic of control. The implications of Gandhi's principles of *satyagraha* (that is, assertive search for truth through dialogue) and *swaraj* (freedom) are applied in formulating a discursive accountability framework that engages dialectically with the individual and structure through the psychology of fear-reflectivity. It advocates reform in the interest of sustainable development by transcending the logic of control's fragmentation of time and space. The Gandhian-*Vedic* paradigm enables radical reforms to consumption patterns and production methods by tailoring accountability to local circumstances, and reducing the dichotomisation of means from ends.

Keywords: Gandhi, *Vedic*, sustainability, fragmentation, dialectic, accountability.

1. Introduction

There have been repeated calls for a paradigm shift to discourage the perpetuation of industrialisation's logic of control and its growth fetish because unbridled economic growth is turning in on itself as its benefits transform into the hazards of contemporary society (Beck, 1993). The logic of control artificially dichotomises the economic aspects of society from its socio-environmental consequences (following Dickens, 1992; Beck, 1993; Merton, 1965). The hazards of dichotomisation manifest as pollution of the larger natural environment and erosion of ethical values (Hamilton, 2003; Wiggins, Marfo and Anchirinah, 2004; Steinfeld, 2004). Beck (1993) reflects this dilemma in his description of post-industrial society as 'risk society'. The term 'risk' also captures the urgency in society's subsequent search for an alternative paradigm for civilisation.

This chapter responds to the implied search for better accountability (to society) by re-engaging with Gandhi's oft-quoted conviction that economics and social values cannot be dichotomised. It proposes an ethical alternative to the ethos of control:

> *True economics never militates against the highest ethical standard, just as all true ethics to be worth its name must at the same time be also good economics. An economics that inculcates Mammon worship, and enables the strong to amass wealth at the expense of the weak, is a false and dismal science. It spells death. True economics, on the other hand, stands for social justice, it promotes the good of all equally including the weakest, and is indispensable for decent life* (Gandhi in *Harijan*, 9 October 1937, quoted in Gandhi, 2001a, p. 71).

Gandhi's stance has been popularised by theorists such as Schumacher (1973), Parekh (1991), Dasgupta (1996) and Copley (1987). However, their literature does not immerse itself in the *Vedic* philosophy, which has informed Gandhi's core values. Consequently, it reduces the totality of the Gandhian perspective to a static association between small-scale technology, non-violence and individualism. Further, critics (such as Bhattacharya, V. R., 1969) dismiss Gandhi's ethical aims as wishful utopian ideals. Gandhi has contested this narrow appreciation of his vision for India (and the larger society) towards the end of his life in 1946:

> *I may be taunted with the retort that this is all Utopian and, therefore, not worth a single thought. If Euclid's line, though incapable of being drawn by human agency, has an imperishable value, my picture has its own for mankind to live. Let India live for this true picture, though never realizable in its completeness. We must have a proper picture of what we want, before we can have something approaching it* (Gandhi, 1958-1984, Vol. 85, p. 33, quoted in Dalton, 1993, p. 188).

It is therefore not surprising that Dalton (1993) opens his book on Gandhi's non-violence strategies with this quizzical observation:

> *Gandhi was not primarily a theorist but a reformer and activist. When pressed for a treatise on his philosophy, he protested that 'I am not built for academic writings. Action is my domain'* (Gandhi, 1958-1984, Vol. 83, p. 180). *Yet he was guided by values and ideas that remained remarkably enduring throughout his life* (Dalton, 1993, p. 1).

These enduring values have been informed by *Vedic* principles of living in harmony with the 'whole', that is, the interconnected relationships between humans, animals, the bio-diversity, the eco-system, the landscape and natural forces. These principles are to be applied in context-specific situations.

Nevertheless, because of the seriousness and prevalence of the criticism of utopianism, it will be dealt with more comprehensively here. Such criticisms have even been echoed in a review of an earlier draft of this chapter: it describes the Gandhian-*Vedic* method as 'noble', but questions whether the method is able to 'address [the] modern problem of feeding 6 billion people, providing jobs and economic development, which often brings mankind into conflict with nature and natural forces' (anonymous reviewer). This criticism essentially conflates the Gandhian approach with an anti-technology, and backward looking stance because of Gandhi's strategy of rural economics and small-scale technology for the Indian sub-continent. It is convenient and simplistic to label the Gandhian method as a failed attempt to freeze development in romantic notions of a time past (Pathak, 1969; cf. Palshikar, 1969). It is argued here that Gandhi's strategies for India merely reflect the harsh reality that confronted him: namely, that India's largely poverty-stricken population had been very much dependent on an agrarian economy.

> *We are inheritors of a rural civilization. The vastness of our country, the vastness of the population, the situation and the climate of the country have, in my opinion, destined it for a rural civilization. To uproot it and substitute it for an urban civilization seems to me an impossibility, unless we are prepared by some drastic means to reduce the population from three hundred million to three or say even thirty. I can therefore suggest remedies on the assumption that we must perpetuate the present rural civilization and endeavour to rid it of its acknowledged defects.* (Gandhi in *Young India*, 7 November 1929, quoted in Gandhi, 2001a, p. 153).

Nehru moved away from this approach when he sought to emulate Europe's rapid economic growth through industrialisation (Nanda, 1979). Historians reveal that it was only towards the end of his life – as he became increasingly frustrated by the failure of his efforts – did Nehru appreciate the advantages of Gandhi's strategy of developing by meeting the needs of the poor and underprivileged (Brown, 2003; Mishra, 2003).

At this juncture it is useful to ask whether the Gandhian-*Vedic* approach is one that should be (culturally) confined to the Indian sub-continent, or whether it has universal relevance. The Gandhian method should not be conflated with the strategies of small-scale technology and rural development because it assertively searches for truth by employing moral and political means to engage interested parties in reasoned dialogue (or *satyagraha*: Parekh, 1991). There has been much wider acknowledgement of its principles of engaging one's opponent in constructive dialogue: history has shown that the black-rights movement in the US (led by Martin Luther King) drew on *satyagrahic* methods in bringing about reform. Similarly, the networked members around the globe are working co-operatively in identifying more sustainable lifestyles by engaging the local community, consumers, competitors, regulators, financiers as well as the state through a myriad of strategies aimed at constructive dialogue as a means of facilitating reform (Carley and Christie, 2000; Mazmanian and Kraft, 2001). These strategies mirror Gandhi's *satyagrahic* method, which empowers the weaker (by refusing to consent to the hegemony of exploitation) whilst discursively engaging with those in positions of power. Gandhi through his political activism came to appreciate the three levels of societal dialogue (which critical discourse analysts now label as macro, meso and micro levels of discourse analysis) and the need to dialogically engage all three levels to facilitate reform: van Dijk (1998) explains that discourse and verbal interaction belong to the micro-level of social order; the macro refers to power, dominance and inequity between social groups; the meso-level is posited between the previous two levels. These levels may be bridged (or linked) in several ways: an approach is through personal and social cognition (elaborated later), which is central to the *satyagrahic* approach of dialogically bringing various interests groups together. Cognition is thus the 'crucial interface ... between personal and the social, hence between the individual discourse and social structure' (van Dijk, 1998, p. 4 of 51). Therefore the *Vedic* connection does not confine the Gandhian method to the Indian sub-continent because its philosophy is concerned with understanding human existence as an integral part of a larger and interconnected whole. Further, the reformist interpretation of the *Vedic* literature adopted here contests the notion of an all-supreme 'god' and it instead holds humans responsible for their actions (developed later).

Having highlighted the relevance of the Gandhian-*Vedic* paradigm, it is only reasonable to subject the earlier criticisms of Gandhism to scrutiny as well: any argument that favours maintaining the status quo (of globalised market economics) simply because reforms could threaten the world's capacity to feed itself, provide jobs and economic 'development' presumes that there is no risk involved in continuing along the path of market economics. Such rationale is blind (and deaf) to the plight of the small island-nations that are in danger of being inundated by the rising sea level (due to global warming which is caused in part by the collateral damage of the unprecedented and much desired economic 'development'). It has also resulted in the higher incidence of droughts that has led to devastating famines. These 'natural' catastrophes hit the poorer nations (such as Niger in Africa) the hardest. Pouring more aid into these countries is not the answer. Further, donor nations are less forthcoming with aid: the UN has disclosed that the world had been galvanised into providing aid to Niger only when pictures of starving people and children were televised across the world. The world did not respond to the UN's earlier warnings that such a disaster had been imminent when Niger's agriculture had been devastated by drought and locust plague (*SBS News*, 2005). Similarly, but on a less spectacular scale, farmers in developed countries have admitted that they are less able to grow the crops that they used to cultivate a few years before because of the increasing salinity of the soil (Saravanamuthu, 2004). Farmers in developing countries such as China have not been spared either: China is contemplating switching from large-scale cultivation of wheat to labour intensive crops like vegetables because its waterways are polluted (O'Sullivan in *Bush Telegraph*, 2005). Farming communities everywhere are at the front-line of socio-environmental degradation: the primary asset that farmers depend on (namely the land) is wasting away through the continued application of conventional agricultural methods that are based on Beck's (1993) logic of control. The desperation is reflected in a farmer's definition of sustainability: 'it is about slowing down the rate at which the window is closing' (Saravanamuthu, 2004).

In terms of scope, the Gandhian-*Vedic* paradigm is directed at accountability within networked communities: these communities have banded together in addressing the repercussions of Beck's (1993) risk society whilst engaging with the contradictions in societal structures (Carley and Christie, 2000; Mazmanian and Kraft, 2001). It is suggested that as the pressures of risk society increases, the sustainability ethos will permeate outwards from these networked pockets to the rest of society. Thus, it is only a matter of time before the implications of risk society catches up with the manufacturing world, as well as the state: it will reveal the unsustainable nature of the (much touted) employment opportunities generated by market economics. As it stands, the two developed nations which refused to sign the Kyoto Protocol on reducing greenhouse gas emissions (namely Australia and the US[48]), have now conceded that, 'there is a threat from climate change' (Shanahan, 2005, p. 1): so much so that Australia's Howard government has:

> ... joined the US, China, India and South Korea in a secret regional pact on greenhouse gas emissions to replace the controversial Kyoto climate protocol. The alliance, which is yet to be announced, will bring together nations that together account for more than 40% of the world's greenhouse gas emissions (Shanahan, 2005, p. 1).

The change of heart coincides with an Australian government research agency's (Commonwealth Scientific and Industrial Research Organisation) report, which had warned that:

> ... climate change was inevitable and Australia should expect higher temperatures, more droughts, severe cyclones and storm surges in the next 30-50 years. In Australia the CSIRO predicts temperatures could rise between 1C and 6C by 2070. Average global temperatures have already risen 0.6C in the past 100 years as a result of accumulated greenhouse gases.

This shift in attitude is admittedly not a complete change in mindset as the new alliance (which seeks to complement the Kyoto protocol) continues to implicitly prioritise 'the Australian economy ... and coal exports' whilst 'moving more and more towards renewable (energy) such as solar and wind' (Shanahan, 2005, p. 1). It is a similar situation in Bush's US. The agreement has not set any emission targets nor is it binding on its members. It relies on technological innovations over the next 30 years to reform production methods, but does not attempt to rein in consumption. Nevertheless, the mere recognition that global warming is attributed to societal choices is in itself a manifestation of the cultural change that will continue

---

[48] An article in the CSIRO newsletter, ECOS, discloses that a research carried out by The Australia Institute has disclosed that Australians stand at 27% of greenhouse gas emission per capita in 2001. The USA stands at 21%, with Germany, Russian and the UK each hovering at about the 11% mark, and Japan at 10%. The author of the report, Turton, argues that Australia's smaller population does not make it a non-major greenhouse polluter in absolute terms: 'Our [that is, Australia's] total emissions exceed those of major European economies such as France and Italy (each with three times Australia's population) and are only 20% lower than those of the UK' (Turton, 2004, p. 6).

to spread in risk society as it runs out of soft options. It means that the business-as-usual mentality, which dismisses (Gandhian-*Vedic*) reforms as utopian on grounds that social and environmental reforms threaten jobs and 'prosperity', cannot continue to be legitimised. In other words, the Keynesian excuse for maintaining the status quo (below) should begin to give way to radical reform of consumption patterns and production methods as recommended by the Economic and Social Research Council (2000):

> For at least another hundred years we must pretend to ourselves and to everyone that fair is foul and foul is fair; for foul is useful and fair is not. Avarice and usury and precaution must be our gods for a little longer still. For only they can lead us out of the tunnel of economic necessity into daylight (Keynes, 1930, quoted in Schumacher, 1973, p. 22).

1.1.   Gandhi and the Advaitic Vedic Philosophy

A deeper understanding of Gandhi, his values and his strategies (that combine deductive and inductive methods of inquiry) requires an appreciation of the *Vedic* philosophy that shaped his psyche, which ironically led him to reform the orthodox interpretation of the Hindu philosophy from within. The traditional interpretation had conflated spirituality with personal salvation and had resulted in an unhealthy obsession with 'me and my life after death'. Gandhi is not the first person to reform this narrow interpretation of the *Vedas*: Vivekananda, an *Advaitic Vedic*[49] reformer who died in 1902, had initiated a radical re-orientation by advocating personal development through service and responsibility for the other. Vivekananda has also made the *Vedic* literature (which is documented in *Sanskrit*) more accessible through a series of lectures delivered in English in the US, UK and India (see the eight volumes of Vivekananda, 1992). Gandhi has further advanced Vivekananda's reformist cause through his ethico-political activism in the interest of humanity and Nature. He incorporates aspects of the politico-social literature of Tolstoy and Ruskin, as well as developments in health science, economics and education into his *Vedic*-based strategy of *satyagraha* (that is, assertive resistance and discursive engagement) and his goal of *swaraj* (or self-rule). The Gandhian-*Vedic* method is shaped by the *Advaitic Vedic* epistemology of knowledge, *Satchitaananda*: that is, Existence – Knowledge – Realisation (Gandhi, 1935, in Gandhi, 1993b, pp. 33-34; Gandhi, 2001b). It depicts the path of human evolution as a journey of acquiring knowledge about the interconnected relationships between elements of the 'whole'. The assimilation of contemporary knowledge into the *Vedanta* also ensures the

---

[49]   There are two schools within the *Vedic* tradition: *Advaitism* and *Dvaitism*. The former is grounded in the concept of 'oneness' or the union of subject and object (or the spiritual oneness of all beings: Dalton, 1993), whereas *Dvaitism* is premised on a dualist interpretation (Gandhi, 1926, 'Advaitism and God', *Young India* quoted in Gandhi, 1987, p. 79-81).

continued relevance of the following *Vedic* concepts to risk society: *ahimsa*, spiritual freedom, interconnected relationship between parts that constitute the whole, *karmic* law and *dharma* (these concepts are explained later).

The *Vedic* literature is 'old' in the sense that the *Vedas* themselves have been traced back to at least 5,000 B.C. (Vivekananda, 1992a, pp. 446-480). Despite this, the Gandhian-*Vedic* paradigm developed here is 'newer' because Gandhi and his fellow reformers (namely, Vivekananda and Krishnamurti) have transformed it from within by assimilating accumulated knowledge about human-nature interconnectedness into its fundamental tenets. The inherent learning embedded in the Gandhian approach makes a mockery of any attempt to concretise truth as an absolute and static concept. Gandhi's autobiography (titled, '*The story of my experiments with truth*') contains this caution:

> I hope ... that no one will regard the advice interspersed in the following chapters as authoritative. The experiments narrated should be regarded as illustrations, in the light of which every one may carry on his own experiments according to his own inclinations and capacity ... . My purpose is to describe experiments in the science of Satyagraha ... . (Gandhi, 1993a, p. xxiv).

Gandhi's critics appear to have ignored this important caveat: see Parekh (1991), Dasgupta (1996), Bhattacharya, V. R. (1969). His search is dialectically shaped by contradictions that are embedded within the individual and social structures (following Vivekananda, 1992b, p. 309):

> I would like to say to the diligent reader of my writings ... that I am not at all concerned with appearing to be consistent. In my search after the Truth I have discarded many ideas and learnt many new things ... . What I am concerned with is my readiness to obey the call of Truth, my God, from moment to moment, and therefore, when anybody finds any inconsistency between any two writings of mine, if he has still faith in my sanity, he would do well to choose the later of the two on the same subject (Gandhi in *Harijan*, 29 April, p. 2, quoted in Gandhi, 1987, p. iii).

Gandhi's *satyagrahic* method (that informs his search for truth) provides an ethico-experimental means of engaging with:

(a)   the tension caused by contradictions inherent in social relationships; and

(b)   confusion over the meaning and implications of 21st century sustainability. The confusion emanates from the ambiguity surrounding the nature of the relationship between culture and nature. It is aggravated by the use of the sustainability rhetoric to obscure the perpetuation of business-as-usual practices (or 'greenwash' tactics: Tokar, 1997; also Birkin, Edwards and Woodward, 2005).

The Gandhian-*Vedic* framework acknowledges and embraces ambiguity about the relationships among elements of the whole. It proceeds on the *karmic* premise that every action generates knock-on consequences because elements of the whole are interconnected to each other. Even though it does not set out a specific definition of the whole, it does not try to eliminate the (underlying) ambiguity through questionable presumptions either. Rational frameworks (which disseminate industrialisation's logic of control through the vocabulary of efficiency and productivity) conjure up illusions of stable environments, which may be manipulated in the pursuit of higher profits: the consequences of these manipulations are dismissed as 'externalities' (cf. Luhmann, 2005, which will be integrated into the second half of this chapter). The rational logic also conceptualises actors as individuals who always make decisions that maximise benefits (cf. Simon, 1957). These actors also appear to be immune from the psychology of fear that occurs when individuals engage with the unknown or unfamiliar (see Renn *et al.*, 2001 for critique of rational models).

In contrast, the Gandhian-*Vedic* framework provides a socio-economic context in which the individual's interaction with the structure is articulated through the psychology of fear-reflectivity. The engagement itself is conceptualised in terms of the dialectic between personal-structural contradictions (also Mahadevan, 1969): discourse theorists theorise it as the cognitive interface between individual discourse and social structure (van Dijk, 1998). This dialectical movement forms the theoretical foundation for Gandhi's goal of *swaraj* that is attained through his strategy of *satyagraha*. The Gandhian-*Vedic* paradigm formulated here will be articulated as an accountability framework that explains how the contemporary risk discourse may be more effectively socialised (to ensure greater acceptance of its message): risk management tools have been advocated as a means of grappling with ambiguity surrounding sustainability (see Power, 2003; Cohen, 2001).

1.2. Gandhian-Vedic Versus Judeo-Christianity Theorisations

The Gandhian-*Vedic* approach integrates social, ecological and economic aspects of development. It presents an alternative to the Judeo-Christian notion of creation, which dichotomises culture from nature. The Judeo-Christian notion of creation manifests as the presumption of human dominion over nature, which in turn constructs a reality that sits uncomfortably with the high levels of degradation confronting risk society (following White, 1967; Dickens, 1999; Beck, 1993; Birkin 1996). Although the Church's influence waned with the rise of rationalist Enlightenment values, Mebratu (1998) notes that Christian theology has been called to account again in the environmentalist literature:

> *The rise of environmentalism opened the new door of criticism toward the traditional religions. The Judeo-Christian religious traditions were specifically singled out by environmental groups as one of the major instruments enhancing the destruction of the natural environment through teaching man's domination over nature. It is against this backdrop that a new breed of theologians known as ecotheologians have started to emerge. Ecotheologians have sought to reinterpret old traditions: finding and stressing passages in classic texts to help us face the current crisis* (Mebratu, 1998, p. 508).

One such ecotheological effort is the Church of England's (Mission and Public Affairs Council, 2005) attempt to re-examine the meaning and implications of the

Christian teaching. It has released a 'Christian vision for a sustainable future' which acknowledges that:

> ... historically, Christians have been partly to blame because of the way they have interpreted their tradition. Within Christian teaching however, there are insights that can undo some of the damage of the past (Mission and Public Affairs Council, 2005, p. x).

Starting with the premise that 'God created the universe: humans can only hope to adapt to it', the Church of England's current thesis puts forward a more environmentally friendly interpretation of how humans exercise 'dominion under God' (Mission and Public Affairs Council, 2005, p. 16). It refers to an interconnected relationship between all beings (or 'unbreakable kinship of all God's creatures', p. 19) within the sacrament of creation and dominion implied in the *Genesis*:

> And God blessed them and God said to them, 'Be fruitful and multiply, and fill the earth and subdue it; and have dominion over the fish of the sea and over the birds of the air and over every thing that moves upon the earth' (*Genesis* 1.28 quoted in Mission and Public Affairs Council, 2005, p. 25).

However, the Church's attempt to theorise a sustainable connection between its biblical teachings and the environment falls short again because it portrays human stewardship for the environment as a benevolent act by a responsible servant of God (who bears God's likeness unlike other creatures). The problems that emanate from a notion of an all-knowing god will be raised later in the chapter through the critique of Hegel's dialectic. For now, it is sufficient to point out that the notion of benevolence implies that (human) care for the environment is an altruistic act: in other words, it is an optional (although) responsible and moral behaviour for the human race because humans remain distinct from other aspects of planetary life (which do not resemble God).

Gandhian economics is underpinned by the *Advaitic Vedic* philosophy, which is constructed on the presumption that all forms of life have been 'projected' from a mass of energy, and that has subsequently evolved over time (explained later). Consequently it does not entertain the possibility of dichotomy between the (human) self and the other: the act of caring for the other is not altruistic or optional. Because the *Advaitic Vedic* method is founded on the premise that humans are an integral part of the whole (which in turn is made up of humans and nature), it encourages behaviours that acknowledge this holistic essence of human-nature relations. It actively promotes perceptions that minimise the fragmentation of time and space. This is in opposition to the Christian retheorisation above, which retains traces of the separatedness of humans from nature within an interconnected whole: this dichotomy enables Christians to exercise dominion over nature within the three-fold role of humanity, namely, as prophets, priests and kings[50] (Mission and

---

[50] The Mission and Public Affairs Council (2005) re-theorisation of the Biblical text argues that 'misguided anthropocentrism' has had 'unfortunate effects both on the earth and on

Public Affairs Council, 2005, pp. 21-26). Therefore, despite the concerted effort to clarify the notion of human dominion over nature, White's (1967) stance that Judeo-Christianity has reinforced the notion of dichotomy will be followed henceforth.

To summarise, the Gandhian-*Vedic* paradigm developed here proposes an alternative approach to societal progress. It is used to counter the unacceptably high levels of socio-environmental degradation, which has resulted from the perpetuation of industrialisation's logic of control (following Beck, 1993). The Gandhian-*Vedic* method is teased out from the theory of *swaraj-satyagraha*. Its response to the sustainability challenge dovetails into the larger paradigm of ethical societal development (Spoor, 2004; Balisacan and Fuwa, 2004) because it engages with the causes of poverty and ecological exploitation in the face of unprecedented levels of economic prosperity (among the 'have-mores'[51]). Gandhi (following earlier reformers such as Vivekananda and C.R. Das) has retained social equality (or *sarvodaya*) as a central plank in his attempts to overcome the hazards of civilisation. He accordingly elevates service to the other beyond altruism/benevolence:

> *I recognize no God except the God that is found in the hearts of the dumb millions ... and I worship the God that is Truth or Truth which is God through the service of these millions* (Gandhi, quoted in Tendulkar, 1960, p. 58).

---

humanity itself' (p. 21). It draws from the Bible to assert that the proper place for humanity is to be found in the three roles as prophets, priests and kings.

'A **prophet** is a seer: one who perceives things as they truly are, that is, shown by God, and who speaks of what he or she sees' (p. 21). Consequently the prophet 'sees to the inner essence of each and every thing, and stands witness to its reality. He sees the *logos* of God, which made the thing come to be ... ' (p. 22).

The **priest** plays a more active role because the priest 'standing between earth and heaven ... can bring God's blessing on all the earth, by caring for it as God's steward, not its master' (pp. 23-24). It is argued here that even the servant (as agent) of god 'taking care' of the rest of God's creation sets humanity apart from it (in opposition to the *Vedic* assertion that humans as an integral part of the whole have to behave in harmony with the whole or face the consequences of risk society as the whole hovers out of balance). The Christian dichotomy is more obvious in the third role of humanity, that of **kingship**. Whilst the 'servant-king' (p. 24) is expected to 'defend the rights of the poor and disadvantaged' (p. 24), kingship 'also implies dominion' (p. 25).

However it is argued, 'A wrong understanding of human dominion over the earth has had devastating consequences. What might the proper meaning of the verse [that is, Genesis 1.28 about filling the earth and subduing it, etc. quoted earlier in the text] ... . According to Romans 8, Christians are the key to the salvation of the earth' (p. 25) through the role that Adam was called to fulfill and failed, namely to till and keep the garden. Therefore, 'Dominion is an exercise of vicegerency: lordship under God. The biblical term for humanity's relationship with creation is 'steward'. A steward is a servant who relates to God, on whose behalf s/he exercises dominion. S/he is also called to render an account to God of his/her stewardship of tilling and keeping' (p. 26).

[51] This cynical term is borrowed from none other President George W. Bush who described the extremely wealthy as 'have-mores' (source: Michael Moore's movie, *Fahrenheit 9/11*).

Therefore, the Gandhian-*Vedic* method (compared to reconfigurations of Judeo-Christian paradigms) would be more likely to minimise Beck's (1993) risks of civilisation because the *Vedic* theorisation of the origin of life ensures that it does not dichotomise humans and nature. The *Vedic* connection to Gandhi's method of engagement is further elucidated in the following section. It favours changing human mindsets about self-centred progress in the favour of responsibility for the other. Therefore, it reforms both the individual and structure.

The rest of this chapter is structured as follows: section two explains the *Advaitic Vedic* connection to Gandhi's *satyagraha* and *swaraj*. Section three illustrates the theoretical implications of the Gandhian-*Vedic* sense of responsibility to the other in relatively recent areas of social research, namely gender and animal welfare issues. Section four teases out the principles of *satyagraha* and *swaraj* that are relevant to the sustainability debate, whilst section five develops the Gandhian-*Vedic* framework of accountability before concluding.

2. Theory of Swaraj and Satyagraha: The Advaitic Vedic Connection

The Gandhian-*Vedic* paradigm will be constructed on the dialectical movement that connects the contradictions embedded in **societal norms** with the psychology of (fear-reflectivity of) an **individual** actor. This section will articulate the dialectical movement through the theory underpinning Gandhi's goal of *swaraj*, and his *satyagrahic* means of achieving it. *Swaraj* has been expanded from a national self-rule to include personal self-discipline. *Satyagraha* refers to the power of truth that shapes an individual's journey in realising the interconnected nature of relationships that constitute the whole:

> *Gandhi's contribution lies not only in his idea of freedom as swaraj but as well in his unique conception of the power of satyagraha and the connections he forged between them* (Dalton, 1993, p. 76).

Satyagraha and *swaraj* are rooted in several inter-related *Advaitic Vedic* concepts, which will be explained (below), before being incorporated into the Gandhian-*Vedic* paradigm that facilitates greater socio-ecological accountability:

1. *Ahimsa* which is simplistically referred to as 'love';
2. **Freedom** that binds internal personal development (spirituality) and external (such as national) liberation;
3. **Responsibility for the other** by experimenting with a truth that embraces values of *ahimsa* and freedom (Gandhi, 1958-1984, Vol. 10, pp. 46, 64, quoted in Dalton, 1993, p. 25).

2.1. Ahimsa and the Sustainable Ethos

The Gandhian-*Vedic* logic of responsibility is derived from the concept of *ahimsa*, which refers to the ambiguous but undeniable relationship that binds people, animals, vegetation, and all forms of matter together. It is an 'undeniable' relationship even though scientists admit that their knowledge about these relationships is far from complete: they are still in the dark about the variety of organisms that exist in the soil alone (Heywood, 1995; Ehrlich, Ehrlich and Holdren, 1977). Nevertheless, ecologists acknowledge that the health of ecological systems is easily disrupted by human activities (Ehrlich, 1968), which in turn jeopardises human existence itself (Ehrlich and Ehrlich, 1970).

The *Vedanta* theorises this relationship as a flow of energy that manifests as various forms of matter (and beings): the known and unknown manifestations of this energy is another way of describing the 'whole'. This whole is personified in terms of the following transformations of energy: from creation (*Brahman*) to sustenance (*Vishnu*) to destruction (*Shiva*), which in turn sows the seeds of (re)creation. The term 'creation' does not adequately convey the *Advaitic Vedic* meaning of an energy flow that is constantly transforming within a unified whole. Vivekananda (1992a) uses the term 'projection' from a pre-existing mass of energy in place of 'creation' because he argues that that something cannot be created out of nothing[52]:

> *All matter throughout the universe is the outcome of one primal matter called Akasha; and all force, whether gravitational, attraction or repulsion, or life, is the outcome of one primal force called Prana. Prana acting on Akasha is creating or projecting the universe. At the beginning of a cycle, Akasha is motionless, unmanifested. Then Prana begins to act, more and more, creating grosser and grosser forms out of Akasha – plants, animals, men, stars, and so on. After an incalculable time, this evolution ceases and involution begins, everything being resolved back through finer and finer forms into the original Akasha and Prana, when a new cycle follows. Now there is something beyond Akasha and Prana. Both can be resolved into a third thing called Mahat – the Cosmic Mind. This Cosmic Mind does not create Akasha and Prana, but changes itself into them ... . According to ... Sankhya psychology, [for] perception [to occur], the mind or Manas must ... attach itself to the [sensory] organ ... . [The resulting] sensation must be carried to the intellect or Buddhi – the determinative, reactive state of the mind. When reaction comes from the Buddhi [it takes the form of an external reaction, egoism and will power. However, all of these projections are taking place on] something that is stationary – relatively to the body and mind – that is, on what is called the Soul or Purusha or Atman* (Vivekananda, 1992a, pp. 359-361).

The term *Sankhya* has been introduced in the preceding quotation: it refers to the dualist interpretation of the *Vedas* (Vivekananda, 1992a, footnote on pp. 361-362). The term 'dualist' has a specific connotation that is used to differentiate the *Advaitic* from the *Dvaitic* interpretations of the *Vedas* (also see endnote 2). The *Advaitic Vedic* assertions about interconnected relationships are based on the *Sankhya* psychology: both interpretations are based on the assumption of an infinite soul. However, the

---

[52] The First and Second Laws of Thermodynamics support these *Vedic* assertions: the First law asserts that energy may be transformed but not destroyed or created, whilst the Second states that some energy is transformed into an unavailable or less available form.

Sankhya asserts that there are many souls, whilst the *Advaitic Vedanta* asserts that there is only one soul and it is projected in many forms (Vivekananda, 1992a, pp. 363-364). The *Advaitic Vedanta* uses the ongoing transformation of the flow of energy (namely, *Brahman-Vishnu-Shiva-Brahman*) to reinforce its presumption of equality among all constituent elements of nature (including humans). Therefore, humans are neither superior, nor inferior, to others: the iron law of *karma*, which asserts that every action has a consequence, governs *Advaitic Vedic* relationships.[53] Ideally, any action has to be considered in light of its impending consequence on the interconnected chain of relationships (Vivekananda, 1992a, 'The *Vedanta* philosophy', pp. 357-365). Gandhi is unequivocal about its implications:

> *They say, 'means are after all means'. I would say, 'means are after all everything'. As the means so the end. There is no wall of separation between the means and the end …. Realization of the goal is in exact proportion to that of the means. This is a proposition that admits no exception* (Gandhi in *Young India*, 17 July 1924, quoted in Gandhi, 2001a, p. 65).

Here the *Purusha* (see quotation before the last one from Vivekananda, 1992a, pp. 359-361) is treated as the unit of energy that connects the individual to the rest of the whole. The purpose of Gandhi's (1993a) journey of experimenting with truth is to realise the essence of this inner *Purusha* as a means of normalising behaviours that embrace responsibility for the other. The *Bhagavadgita*[54] personifies the destination of this journey as the (re)absorption into the ethos of *Brahman* (the source of projection of energy):

> *When he realises the whole variety of beings as resting in the One, and is an evolution from that One alone, then he becomes Brahman* (Chidbavananda, 1991, Chp. XIII, verse 30, p. 712).

Nevertheless, this *karmic* interconnectedness is often not reflected in human perceptions and behaviour. People are more often than not swayed by narrow self-centred goals such as the lop-sided economic benefits that are secured at the expense of the whole. Such outcomes disregard the whole: these realities fragment spatio-temporal dimensions of the whole instead (Vivekananda, 1992b, pp. 130-143: Krishnamurti, 1994). The *Vedanta* explains such myopic behaviour in terms of *Maya*:

---

[53] *Karmic* law is popularly associated with reincarnation. Gandhi explains the connection: 'Hinduism believes in the oneness not of merely all human life but in the oneness of all that lives. Its worship of the cow is, in my opinion, its unique contribution to the evolution of humanitarianism. It is a practical application of the belief in the oneness and, therefore, sacredness, of all life. The great belief in transmigration is a direct consequence of that belief' (Gandhi in *Young India*, 20 October 1927, quoted in Gandhi, 2001a, p. 255).

[54] The *Vedas* are divided into the *Upanishads* (the philosophy) and the rituals (hymns etc). The *Upanishads* comprise of more than a hundred *Sanskrit* books on the principles of life. They are 'condensed shorthand sketches' providing very little background information. The *Bhagavadgita* provides a condensed and systematic commentary on the *Upanishads* (Vivekananda, 1992a, pp. 446-480).

the term refers to lived experiences in which projections (of the all-pervasive energy) are perceived as separate and distinct realities. This fragmented view of actuality obscures the underlying interconnectedness between all beings.

> *We are all one, and the cause of evil is the perception of duality. As soon as I begin to feel that I am separate from this universe, then first comes fear, and then comes misery … . According to the Advaita philosophy, then, this differentiation of matter, these phenomena are … for a time, hiding the real nature of man … . In the lowest worm, as well as in the highest human being, the same divine nature is present … . Behind everything the same divinity is existing, and out of this comes the basis of morality. Do not injure the other [or ahimsa] … . In injuring another, I am injuring myself; in loving another, I am loving myself. From this also springs the principle of Advaita morality which has been summed up in one word – self-abnegation. The Advaitist says, this little personalised self, which makes me different from all other beings, brings hatred and jealousy and misery … . When this idea has been got rid of, all struggle will cease … and the veil of ignorance will fall … and [man] will feel that he is one with nature* (Vivekananda, 1992a, pp. 364-365).

Thus the *Vedanta* articulates the consequences of the individual's engagement with structural contradictions in terms of the impact of social contradictions on perceptions of actuality (or *Maya*): that is, the structure and individual are connected through the psychology of fear-reflectivity, which is explained in sub-section (2) below.

2.2. Internal (Spiritual) and External Freedom From Circular Dialectics of Social Contradictions

The Gandhian-*Vedic* notion of freedom refers to emancipation from the circular dialectic of social contradictions, which occurs as the individual engages with the structure. Dialectical outcomes cannot be ascertained beforehand because they are shaped by the contradictions in social, political and economic forces.[55] Circular dialectics refers to a situation in which one set of social contradictions is replaced by another set. It explains why an individual (who has consented to exploitative norms of risk society) is trapped on the treadmill of alienation and exploitation. In practical terms, it explains that an individual who consents to social norms, which emanate from the logic of control (such as blatant consumerism or reliance on fossil fuel energy to raise the 'standard' of living), creates a rod for her/his own back:

---

[55] Craib (1997, p. 39-41) identifies the following elements as constituting the dialectical method: firstly, it refers to the notion of the whole or totality which is an inclusive way of constructing knowledge (following Marx's two moments of thinking in *Grundisse*), secondly, a Hegelian influence of having a multi-causal model of analysis where social reality is constructed from may causes, 'none of which we understand properly until we find its place in the whole process' (Craib, 1997, p. 40), and thirdly, the connected concept of contradiction and movement which asserts that society is a combination of contradictory elements that are in a permanent process of change. Thus, contradiction, conflict and change are a normal part of societal progress.

consequences of the exploitative ethos manifest as socio-environmental degradation (see Beck, 1993). Band-aid fixes to degradation merely suppress the symptoms of the risk society without eliminating the underlying causes of unsustainable practices: an example is the Australian government's proposal to compress and store greenhouse gases underground instead of reducing reliance on fossil fuel in the first place. It results in a new set of contradictions that replace the previous set. Consequently, the Economic and Social Research Council (ESRC, 2000) asserts that sustainable development cannot occur unless there are radical changes to consumption patterns and production methods. In other words, the vision of a sustainable future will continue to be used to excuse business-as-usual practices unless the logic of control is acknowledged as contributing (even partially) to the hazards of civilisation.

Reform in the interest of sustainability as advocated by ESRC involves engaging with both the individual and structure (following Tinker and Gray, 2003). Gandhian reform involves dislodging the hegemonic influence of economic growth (for itself) from the fragmented self by embarking on a journey of experimenting with notions of truth. It leads to a increasing awareness of one's inner *Purusha*, and hence spiritual (re)connection with the other:

> He whom the sages have been seeking in all places is in our own hearts: the voice that you heard was right, says the Vedanta, but the direction that you gave to the voice was wrong. That ideal of freedom that you perceived was correct, but you projected it outside yourself, and that was your mistake. Bring it nearer and nearer, until you find that it was all the time within you, it was the Self of your own self. That freedom was your own nature, and this Maya [or fragmented lived experiences] never bound you (Vivekananda, 1992b, p. 128).

The individual is an inherent part of the reform process because structural contradictions affect personal contradictions, which in turn shape a person's psychology and cognition. Hence, Gandhi's *swaraj* refers to both freedom from internal contradictions as well as structural ones. The *Vedas* assert that an individual's behaviour is the dialectical outcome of contradictory tendencies (such as greed and selflessness), which naturally co-exist in every person.[56] Krishnamurti (2000, 1983, 1977) links personal contradictions to structural influences through the psychology of fear-reflectivity. Initially an individual's lived experiences leave an impression on her/his mental schema: in other words, a person is mentally conditioned as a result of one's experiences (Krishnamurti, 1969). An individual

---

[56] Ramakrishna's commentary on the nature of human beings in the *Bhagavadgita*: 'Man is born with two tendencies, *Vidya guna* and *Avidya guna* – the noble and the base – dormant in him. The former leads him Godward and the latter makes him earth-bound. In babyhood both the tendencies are in equilibrium ... . If he grows in the life in senses, the scale of worldliness goes down with that base weight. But if he emerges in spirituality, the scale in him of Godliness goes down towards Iswara [the whole] with that holy weight'(Ramakrishna, quoted in Chidbhavananda, 1991, p. 650). The concept of god is explained later.

who faces a new set of circumstances (such as contemporary socio-environmental degradation) may respond either reflectively, or out of fear (Lazarus and Folkman, 1984; Clarke and Kissane, 2002; Wolfenstein, 1957). A reflective response occurs when a person copes with an unfamiliar challenge by modifying her/his mental schema to create a 'what is' reality (Krishnamurti, 1969). It is accompanied by conscious decision to modify one's own behaviour, expectations and values (following ESRC, 2000). Therefore, reflective behaviour is the ability to cope with changing circumstances (Krishnmurti, 1994; Horowitz, 1997). A fear response avoids the challenges that accompany change by resorting to the comfort of familiar 'what was' realities. It effectively shuts out the new reality and perpetuates the logic of exploitation (Krishnamurti, 1994). Behaviour that is dominated by 'what was' perceptions will continue to fragment time and space dimensions of the whole by privileging private interests over the whole (Vivekananda, 1992, a, b).

Therefore *ahimsic* outcomes are **enabled by** 'what is' realities. *Ahimsic* behaviour also **enables** an individual to transcend the fragmented discourses of the self (which is caused by the hegemonic influence of the logic of control) and embrace 'what is' realities.

> *Service [to the other] is not possible unless it is rooted in love or Ahimsa* (Gandhi, in *Young India*, 20 September 1928, quoted in Gandhi, 2001a, p. 63).

In other words, one's responsibility for the other (or spiritual interconnectedness) minimises the likelihood of circular dialectics of social contradictions (following Krishnamurti, 1994, 2000): it reduces the chances that Beck's (1993) hazardous norms of risk society may be perpetuated. (The terms 'hazard, risk and uncertainty' will be assimilated into the *satyagrahic* accountability framework in the second half of this chapter). Spiritual development involves curtailing the human ego by detaching private interests from one's thoughts and actions. Therefore, Gandhi's ideas of non-violence, *satyagraha* and *swaraj* are directed at sacrificing the self, or ego (Gandhi, 1958-1984, Vol. 10, p. 48 quoted in Dalton, 1993, p. 25), because it minimises inner conflicts (or personal contradictions). To summarise, *satyagraha* minimises the frequency of occurrence of circular dialectics of social contradictions in the following manner: it transforms the person who engages with structural contradictions, and in doing so, reforms societal structures (following Dalton, 1993; Bondurant 1964; Iyer, 1973).

> *Not until we have reduced ourselves to nothingness can we conquer the evil in us… . And when a man thus loses himself, he immediately finds himself in the service of all that lives. It becomes his delight and his recreation* (Gandhi in *Young India*, 20 December 1928, quoted in Gandhi, 2001a, p. 64).

> *A life of service must be one of humility… . Inertia must not be mistaken for humility, as it has been in Hinduism. True humility means most strenuous and constant endeavour entirely directed to the service of humanity* (Gandhi in *From Yeravda Mandir*, Ahmedabad: Navajivan Publishing House, 1945, Chp. XII, quoted in Gandhi, 2001a, p. 63).

Furthermore, *satyagraha* argues that oppression cannot continue unless the victims themselves perpetuate 'what was' realities by accepting and embedding the logic of exploitation into their mental psyche (Parekh, 1991):

Control over the mind is alone necessary [for the satyagrahi, or person practising satyagraha] and when that is attained, man is free (Gandhi, 1958-1984, Vol. 10, pp. 50-51, quoted in Dalton, 1993, p. 25).

Satyagraha draws from the *Bhagavadgita*[57] in centralising self-discipline in its assumptions (below) for engendering change:

* Power is ultimately derived from victims;
* Structures of oppression cannot be sustained without the cooperation of the victims; and hence,
* oppression may not be maintained unless its victims accept its rationality (Parekh, 1991, p. 154).

However, *satyagrahic* change does not occur automatically because personal reform takes place[58] against the backdrop of ongoing circular dialectics of social contradictions:

We who are progressing know that the more we progress, the more avenues are open to pain as well as to pleasure. This is Maya ... . Maya is not a theory for the explanation of the world: it is simply a statement of facts as they exist, that the very basis of our being is contradiction, that everywhere we have to move through this tremendous contradiction that wherever there is good, there must also be evil .... [vice versa] ... . Thus the Vedanta philosophy is neither optimistic nor pessimistic. It admits that this world is a mixture of good and evil ... . There will never be a perfectly good or bad world because the very idea is a contradiction in terms ... . The fire that burns the child may cook a good meal for a starving man ... . What then is the use of Vedanta ... [for] doing good work? The answer is, in the first place, we must work for lessening misery, for that is the only way to make ourselves happy ... . In the second place, we must do our part, because that is the only way of getting out of this life of contradiction. Both the forces of good and evil will keep the universe alive for us, until we awake from our dreams and give up this building of mud pies. That

---

57 The term '*yoga*' refers to the journey leading to spiritual interconnectedness with the whole. The *Bhagavadgita* describes this *satyagrahic* goal: 'His mind being harmonized by yoga, he sees himself in all beings and all beings in himself, he sees the same in all' (Chidbavananda, 1991, Chp. VI, Verse 29, p. 390).

58 The emphasis on individual reform in the context of naturally occurring personal contradictions sets the Gandhian-*Vedic* approach apart from the Enlightenment doctrines because the Gandhian-*Vedic* dialectical movement tempers the Enlightenment presumption that beliefs are accepted on the basis of reason alone. Furthermore, unlike the Enlightenment's devaluation of local customs and norms, the *satyagrahic* dialectic of contradictions between individual and structure also accommodates local values because reform cannot occur until and unless people embrace it as a meaningful way of proceeding.

lesson we shall have to learn, and it will take a long, long time to learn it (Vivekananda, 1992d, pp. 60-63).

Currently, the international backdrop is one where profit is secured by fragmenting time and space: its *Maya* is the socialisation of time and space[59] (following Giddens, 1990) and the commodification of nature (following McKibben, 1990). Giddens uses the socialisation of time and space to theorise the movement of globalisation: it is a process through which capitalism's commodification of all aspects of life is embedded in all cultures and generations. The ethos of commodification fragments human perceptions because it prioritises the economic aspects over socio-environmental ones, whilst inducing people onto the treadmill of consumerism (that in turn perpetuates the logic of commodification). Hence *Maya* (in this context) is the perpetuation of social contradictions that thwart reform in the interest of sustainability. *Maya* creates a climate of dependence and fear (of the unknown whole) that further entrenches the average citizen in the logic of fragmentation despite being simultaneously exploited by it. This contemporary situation is not unlike the pervasive, oppressive and strangling fear (of everything from the army, police to unemployment and starvation), which had prevailed in British India (following Nehru, 1959). Thus, Gandhi's legacy to the world is his method of engineering *satyagrahic* change in the face of fear of the concentration of power, and the unknown consequences of resisting the hegemonic logic of control. His *satyagraha* reconnects personal spiritual development to the formation of a networked ethical society:

> *Gandhi broke the hypnotic spell of the British Raj in India. He tried to rid the Indian people of the pervasive, perpetual and paralysing fear with which they were seized. He taught them to say 'no' to their oppressors, both foreign and indigenous. He uplifted the spirit and exalted the dignity of a vast number of people by teaching them to straighten their backs, to raise their eyes, and to face circumstances with a steady gaze* (Mehrotra, 1979, p. 154, quoted in Dalton, 1993, p. 237, footnote 4).

Gandhi extends the concept of *swaraj* from independence for India to psychological liberation from the ethos of subjugation. In doing so, he targets circular dialectics: that is, he enables individuals to step off the treadmill of contradictions and counter-contradictions through *satyagrahic* means of attaining *swaraj*. It involves escalating the tension between opposing parties (through political and moral means) until the point where the common interest between the parties becomes so obvious that they engage in dialogue to resolve the conflict (Dalton, 1993; Parekh, 1991). Bondurant (1964) explains that *satyagraha* is not a zero-sum

---

[59] Time-space distanciation is 'the central concept which Giddens uses to explain both (a) the historical movement from traditional societies to modern ones, and (b) the part played by globalisation in speeding up the movement begun by the modernisation process.' (Source: http://www.sociologyonline.co.uk/global_essays/GlobalGiddens1.htm). His structuration of institutional structures is explained through the reproduction of social activities over time and space.

strategy in the sense that a party does not gain from the loss suffered by the opponent because securing concessions at the expense of the other is an unsustainable quick fix. Instead *satyagraha* 'force[s] warring parties to a point where their common interest becomes [so] clear and compelling' (Dalton 1993, p. 166) that its subsequent 'resolution will elicit the best from all parties' (Dalton 1993, p. 43 following Gandhi, 1948).

The *satyagrahic* process relies on political and moral means to engage the other party in dialogue. Gandhi's trademark norm of non-coercion is essentially *ahimsa*. Non-violence is also an acknowledgment of the non-existence of an absolute truth out there: hence, no one should impose her/his (partial) view on the other because such coercion could trigger the psychology of fear and jeopardise the purpose of reform. Instead truth is relative to the knowledge-based journey into the unknown: *Satchitaananda*. Along the way, *satyagraha* strengthens interpersonal relationships to the point where reflective networked communities are formed without dichotomising societal progress and nature.

2.3. Engendering the Ethos of Responsibility for the Other by Experimenting with Truth

Satyagraha sets the foundation for the ethos of accepting responsibility for the other by applying the 'non-violent use of power in pursuit of truth, the kind of truth that brings self-knowledge, self-awareness, and self-control' (Dalton, 1993, p. 138). It provides a discursive means of grappling with the ambiguous concept of sustainable development: the Gandhian-*Vedic* framework of accountability becomes a 'tool of insistence' (Chatterjee, 1969, p. 85) that increases the tension between 'what is' and 'what was' representations. In other words, it makes the gap between contemporary societal progress and sustainable development so obvious that it cannot be brushed aside any more. In so doing, it facilitates reform through discourse, or the social construction of tools of communication. (Communication as a vehicle of emancipation will be revisited later via Luhmann, 2005.) Gandhi believes that this outcome cannot be achieved through Tolstoy-style passive resistance (or by merely increasing sensitivity to the needs of the other: see Tinker, 1985) because:

> ... in my opinion, it [passive resistance] is not really resistance but a policy of communal suffering (Gandhi, 1958-1984, Vol. 7, p. 67, quoted in Dalton, 1993, p. 14).

Further, the economic aspects of social engagement remain an integral part of the *satyagrahic* method even though the rhetoric of sustainability has been exploited by capital to continue with business-as-usual prioritisation of economic interests (Tokar, 1997, Athanasiou, 1996). Gandhi readily acknowledges that poverty is a hurdle to reform (Gandhi, 1927 in *Young India*, 5 May, in Gandhi, 2001a, p. 52), whilst admitting that large-scale technology has concentrated wealth in the hands of a few by exploiting many (Gandhi, *Young India*, 17 September 1925, in Gandhi, 2001a, p. 119). Consequently, he relies on charkha (or spinning wheel) style reform because it minimises the chances of individuals becoming ensnared in the circular dialectics of social contradictions. The charkha (as a metaphor for sustainable reform) enables people to secure sufficient economic independence that would in turn enable them to make decisions that could free them from the oppression (of imperialism or capitalism) whilst reducing spatio-temporal fragmentation. That is, the long-term fix involves embracing *ahimsic* responsibility for the needs of the other (following Gandhi, 1958-1984, Vol. 28, p. 427 in Dalton, 1993, p. 75). Gandhi uses the term 'love' or godly values to signify the conscious attempt to minimise fragmentation through *ahimsic* responsibility (or spiritual development):

> *Man's ultimate aim is the realization of God, and all his activities, social, political, religious, have to be guided by the ultimate aim of the vision of God. The immediate service of all human beings becomes a necessary part of the endeavour, simply because the only way to find God is to see Him in His creation and be one with it. This can only be done by service to all. I am a part and parcel of the whole, and I cannot find Him apart from the rest of humanity* (Gandhi, *Harijan*, 29 August 1936, quoted in Gandhi, 1993b, p. 10).

The term 'god' used in a reformist sense by Gandhi and Vivekananda: that is, it is used to contextualise the concepts of truth and interconnected responsibility that Gandhi employs in *swaraj* and *satyagraha*. The reformist interpretation of the concept of "God" aims to free individuals from organised religion's reliance on blind faith to thwart reform in the interest of the poor, weak and voiceless because of its potential to undermine the authority of organised religion. Gandhi uses "God" to personify desirable moral-ethical values:

> *To me God is Truth and Love; God is ethics and morality; God is fearlessness. God is the source of Light and Life and yet He is above all of these. God is conscience. He is even the atheism of the atheist. He is the searcher of hearts. He transcends speech and reason. He knows us and our hearts better than we do ourselves* ... (Gandhi, 1925, 'God Alone is', *Young India*, quoted in Gandhi, 1995, pp. 9-10).

His predecessor, Vivekananda, is much more direct in his explanation of the origin and subsequent use of the term:

> *... the stumbling block to mutual understanding ... is the word 'God', for that word embraces all possible ambiguities of thought, and is used oppressively to bandage the clear eyes of Freedom ... I have been asked many times, 'Why do you use that old word God?' Because it is the best word for our purpose ... because all the hopes, aspirations, and happiness of humanity have been centred in that word. It is impossible to change the word. Words like these were first coined by great saints, who realised their import and understood their meaning. But as they become current in society, ignorant people take these words, and the result is, they lose their spirit and glory. The word God has been used from time immemorial, and the idea of this cosmic intelligence, and all that is great and holy is associated with it. If we reject it, each man will offer a different word, and the result will be a confusion of tongue, a new tower of Babel. Use the old word, only use it in the true spirit, cleanse it of*

superstition, and realise fully what this great ancient word means … these words are associated with … all that is highest and best, all that is rational, all that is lovable, all that is great and grand in human nature (Vivekananda, quoted in Rolland, 1988, pp. 261-262).

… it is the sum total of intelligence manifested in the universe … all the forms of cosmic energy, such as matter, thought, force, intelligence, and so forth, are simply the manifestation of that cosmic intelligence (Vivekananda, Lecture on, 'Jnana-Yoga. The cosmos: the macrocosm'. Delivered in New York on 19 January 1896, quoted in Rolland, 1988, p. 262).

Because the *Vedas* have been associated with religious rituals (that have historically been used by the priest class to exploit the masses in India), Vivekananda argues that religious knowledge should be subjected to the same methods of investigation as science and secular knowledge:

If a religion is destroyed by such investigation it was nothing but a useless and unworthy superstition; the sooner it disappeared the better … . All that is dross would be taken away: but the essential parts would emerge triumphant for such investigation (Vivekananda, quoted in Rolland, 1988, pp. 236).

Gandhian ethico-economics is an *ahimsic* approach to sustainable living: it intrinsically embraces social, ecological, environmental and economic aspects of planetary existence by pushing the frontier of knowledge through ethical experimentation. It is based on the *Advaitic Vedic* journey of spiritual development based on the *Vedic* epistemology of knowledge, or *Satchitaananda*, (which means, 'Existence-Knowledge-Realisation').

Experience is the only source of knowledge (Vivekananda, 'Religion and science', 1992c, p. 81).

No one of these Yogas [Vedic paths to self-realisation and freedom] gives up reason … or asks you to deliver your reason into the hands of priests of any type whatsoever … . Each one of them tell you to cling to your reason, to hold fast to it. [There are three] instruments of knowledge … . The first is instinct … most highly developed in animals; this is the lowest instrument of knowledge. What is the second instrument of knowledge? Reasoning … [it is] most highly developed in man … . Yet even reason is still insufficient. Reason can go only a little way and then it stops, it cannot go any further; and if you try to push it the result is helpless confusion, reason itself becomes unreasonable. Logic becomes an argument in a circle … . Therefore there must be an instrument that takes us beyond, and that instrument is called inspiration (Vivekananda, 1992b, 'The ideal of a universal religion', p. 389).

Gandhi's experiments with truth (in engaging with the British imperialism) have shed more light on Vivekananda's third instrument of knowledge: inspiration. He has developed the concept of *satyagraha* to prompt the adversary into engaging in constructive dialogue to resolve any differences. *Satyagrahic* dialogue with the other inspires an ethical inspiration because (partisan) reason *per se* is limited by perceptions that fragment time and space (Vivekananda, 1992d, p. 51). *Satyagraha* enables the individual to transcend the fragmentation of time and space, which is inherent in conventional realities, by extending thought beyond existing ('what was') boundaries of knowledge. It is not based on rational argument in an asocial sense: it is intended to facilitate public acceptance of reform of both individual values and structural ones.

Gandhi's *satyagraha* is based on the dialectic between the contradictions that occur naturally within an individual and, the contradictions that are embedded in societal structures. It is therefore not surprising that the *Vedic* concept of constant transformation of the various manifestations of energy (*Brahman-Vishnu-Shiva-Brahman*) mirrors Hegel's theorisation of transformation and his emphasis on 'becoming' rather than 'being'. The notion of 'becoming' is reflected in Krishnamurti's emphasis on 'what is' realities instead of being (or 'what was' mental schemas). However, Hegel's powerful analytical tool is weakened by his attempt to incorporate the Absolute (which he used as code for the Christian god: Fox, 2005) into his dialectic. The Gandhian-*Vedic* notion of godliness overcomes Hegel's attempts to embrace a panentheistic[60] reality within the dialectic. The Hegelian presumption confuses the dialectical outcomes because it gives rise to the following contradictions: 'Why did God need to create anything if he is complete and perfect? Where does evil come from if God is all-good? Where does Satan get his power from if God is omnipotent?' (Fox, 2005, p. 152). The Gandhian concept of godliness becomes a force that elevates the process of 'becoming' beyond a mechanical process of transformation to one that is partly influenced by human agency.

In summary, the Gandhian-*Vedic* approach is the antithesis of rational actor models. It is based on the dialectical interaction between the individual and structure: thus *satyagraha* becomes a means of minimising the likelihood of circular dialectics of social contradictions as the individual engages with social structures.

3.   Gandhian-*Vedic* Responsibility Illustrated

The various formulations of critical literature have highlighted exploitation in the workplace (namely, the Labour Process literature following Braverman, 1974), gender issues (through the feminist critique) as well as environmental issues (through formulations like Deep Ecology). Here, the implications of *satyagrahic* responsibility (through personal development and structural reform) will be illustrated with regard to gender equality. It will also venture into a relatively new area of critique, namely, animal welfare. In the case of animal welfare, it argues for rights for all creatures (from the multitude of insects that keep the ecosystem ticking over to animals reared for human consumption) that should be respected in animal

---

[60]   Fox (2005) explains that panentheism is based on the view that God permeates into everything. He vividly illustrates this assumption through an example of a sponge that is saturated with water: the water is likened to the Hegelian notion of a God that is in everything without being identical with the sponge.

husbandry practices. This section will illustrate how the Gandhian-*Vedic* paradigm may be used as a method of inquiry and reform.

On gender issues, women have traditionally been treated as second-class citizens in India. As the *Purusha* (that links everyone to the whole) is gender neutral, Gandhi applies the *ahimsic* principle of equality in declaring that:

> Woman is the companion of man, gifted with equal mental capacities. She has the right to participate in every minute detail in the activities of man and she has an equal right of freedom and liberty with him. She is entitled to a supreme place in her own sphere of activity as man is in his. This ought to be the natural condition of things and not as a result only of learning to read and write. By sheer force of vicious custom, even the most ignorant and worthless men have been enjoying a superiority over women which they do not deserve and ought not to have. Many of our movements stop half way because of the conditions of our women. Much of our work does not yield appropriate results; our lot is like that of the penny-wise and pound-foolish trader who does not employ enough capital in his business (Gandhi, 1933, in Speeches and Writings of Mahatma Gandhi, (compiled by Natesan, G. A., Madras, p. 425, quoted in Gandhi, 2001a, p. 225-226).

He rejects the arbitrary imposition of sexual constraints on women, such as the *purdah*, which is prescribed as attire to cover a woman's body, hair, and even face:

> Chastity … cannot be protected by the surrounding wall of the purdah. It must grow from within, and to be worth anything, it must be capable of withstanding every unsought temptation (Gandhi in Young India, 3 February 1927, quoted in Gandhi, 2001a, p. 227).
>
> And why is there all this morbid anxiety about female purity? Have women any say in the matter of male purity? We hear nothing of women's anxiety about men's chastity. Why should men arrogate to themselves the right to regulate female purity? (Gandhi in Young India, 25 November 1926, quoted in Gandhi, 2001a, p. 227).

Animal welfare is seldom theorised in traditional emancipatory theories. Even Marx has failed to appreciate the subtle connection between *ahimsa* and welfare of humanity in general. Marx has misconstrued the way in which the India culture has elevated the status of animals:

> We must not forget that these little communities were contaminated by distinctions of caste and by slavery, that they subjugated man to external circumstances instead of elevating man the sovereign of circumstances, that they transformed a self-developing social state into never changing natural destiny, and thus brought about a brutalizing worship of nature, exhibiting its degradation in the fact that man, the sovereign of nature, fell down on its knees in adoration of Kanuman [sic: 'Hanuman'], the monkey, and Sabbala, the cow (Marx, 1853, p. 5 of 7).

His criticisms are perhaps an indicator of the depth to which Judeo-Christian presumption of human dominion over nature is embedded in western paradigms.

Even Engels (1959, quoted in Dickens, 1992, p. 78) concedes that the logic of control and domination will continue to plague communal oriented paradigms. The *satyagrahic* method adopts a much bolder agenda for reform: it attempts to change mindsets in favour of *ahimsic* care and responsibility for the other including animals. Such concerns are no less central than labour rights. Gandhi vividly articulates the responsibility in animal husbandry:

> *I believe in the protection of the cow in its much larger sense than the popular* (Gandhi, *Young India*, 6 October 1921, quoted in Gandhi, 1987, p. 31).
>
> *The central fact of Hinduism is ... cow protection. Cow protection to me is one of the most wonderful phenomena in human evolution. It takes the human being beyond his species. The cow to me means the entire sub-human world. Man through the cow is enjoined to realize his identity with all that lives. Why the cow was selected for apotheosis is obvious to me. The cow was in India the best companion. She was the giver of plenty. Not only did she give milk, but she also made agriculture possible. The cow is a poem of pity. One reads pity in the gentle animal. She is the mother to millions of Indian mankind. Protection of the cow means protection of the whole dumb creation of God. The ancient seer, whoever he was, began with the cow. The appeal of the lower order of creation is all the more forcible because it is speechless ... . Hindus will not be judged by their ... correct chanting of the mantras, not by their pilgrimages, not by their most punctilious observance of caste rules but by their ability to protect the cow. Whilst professing the religion of cow protection, we have enslaved the cow and her progeny, and have become slaves ourselves* (Gandhi, *Young India*, 6 October 1921, quoted in Gandhi, 1987, p. 33-34).

Gandhi bemoans the fact that Hindus have treated the cow poorly despite paying lip service to its protection (Gandhi in *Young India*, 24 December 1931, quoted in Gandhi, 2001a, p. 245). He turns to the science of livestock husbandry to attain the goals of *ahimsa* and hence attain freedom for all participants (animal and human) from the vicious cycle of circular dialectics (Gandhi in *Harijan*, 31 August 1947, quoted in Gandhi, 2001a, pp. 128-130). It should be noted that his scientific stance is based on compassion and responsibility, instead of the contemporary use of science to maximise economic returns through intensive livestock management. Intensive practices not only dichotomise the (voiceless) other from humanity *per se*, but it also commodifies the animal and farming lifestyle as mere cogs within the machinations of capitalist food production and distribution.

4. The Gandhian-*Vedic* Paradigm: Tools for engaging with the Sustainability Discourse

Gandhi's stance on non-violence reflects his rock solid belief that means cannot be dichotomised from the ends. Consequently, he rejects vulgar party politics in favour of the need for economic and political decentralisation (Haithcox, 1971): the accompanying devolution of power and authority reinforces the central role of the individual in social reform. He argues that reforming the individual from within leads to sustainable external liberation (Gandhi, 1958-1984, Vol. 39, p. 319; Gandhi in *Harijan*, 18 January 1942, quoted in Dalton, 1993, p. 77):

> *There is a causal connection between the purity of the intention of the individual and the extent of effectiveness of non-violent action* (Gandhi, 1958-1984, Vol. 84, p. 47, quoted in Dalton, 1993, p. 45).

Thus *swaraj* incorporates freedom from both personal and structural contradictions through the practise of *satyagraha* (following Gandhi, 1958-1984, Vol. 38, p. 18, cited in Dalton, 1993, p. 7):

> *Let there be no mistake about my conception of Swaraj. It is complete independence of alien control and complete economic independence. So at one end you have political independence, at the other end the economic. It has two other ends. One of them is moral and social, the corresponding end is Dharma, i.e. religion in the highest sense of the term ... . Let us call this the square of Swaraj, which will be out of shape if any of its angles is untrue* (Gandhi in *Harijan*, 2 January 1937, quoted in Bhattacharyya, B., 1969, p. 280).

The three dimensions of Gandhi's square of *swaraj* (namely, politico-economic independence, moral and social aspects of *dharma*) also serve to connect the Gandhian-*Vedic* approach with the sustainability discourse. The challenge facing any attempt to develop sustainability is overcoming the hegemony of control that has led to the emergence of risk society (Beck, 1993). Saravanamuthu (forthcoming) argues that this involves engaging in a discourse that minimises the fragmentation of time and space because it makes people much more conscious of the consequences of their actions. The process of de-fragmenting spatio-temporal representations of actuality whilst engaging with the logic of control (which is embedded in social structures) should be shaped by the *satyagrahic* mode of increasing the tensions between conflicting perspectives. It raises the tension to the point where the common ground becomes so obvious that it makes sense to resolve the conflict in the best possible interest of both parties. The concept of *dharma* reflects the goal of such *satyagrahic* engagement:

> *At universal level, Dharma, know as 'rita', prevails in the law of nature. At global level it is the 'Manav Dharma', which is an expression of humanism and universality, built around a proper understanding of the purpose of life. At social level, Dharma stands for justice and is the entire code of conduct ... . At a personal level, it allows individuals to hold on to their beings by following ethical standards like: fortitude, forgiveness, self-control, non-coveting, purity, control over senses, power of the mind to discriminate between good and bad, learning, truthfulness and absence of anger. It is through the observance of Dharma that man realizes his relevance. Dharma is a way of life, which creates a balance between material and spiritual requirements of people at all levels. Although ... acquisition and enjoyment of material possessions is thought to be necessary, the balancing aspect of Dharma ensures fairness in all dealings and restricts people from going beyond moral and ethical norms. In this way people are free to shape their lives, yet be in conformity with the value system*

(Source: Modi, B. K., President of the Indian Council of Religious leaders, 'Towards a *Dharmic* Society', In SanathanaDharma.com, available at http://www.sanathanadharma.com/articles/dharmic.htm).

In striving for a *dharmic* society, *satyagrahic* accountability has to engage with the circular dialectics of social contradictions (as people consent to the logic of control). However, like Euclid's elusive straight line, it provides a beacon that guides attempts to grapple with the hazards of risk society by exposing the crippling effect of the logic of control on humanity. Gandhi has shown the potential power that may be subsequently unleashed by adopting an inclusive *satyagrahic* strategy: the power of spiritual self-realisation. Increased spiritual awareness leads to greater acceptance of responsibility for the other because it undermines the logic of control and frees the latent political power of the people. It facilitates engagement in 'what is' realities instead of fearing it; rejects the hegemony of the prevailing discourse; and embraces high moral codes that enable reform to occur from within the person (following Dalton, 1993, p. 172; Rudolph and Rudolph, 1983).

Table 1 (below) translates the square of *swaraj* into Gandhian-*Vedic* tools for minimising the fragmentation of time and space in the accountability discourse.

Table 1

Translating *swaraj* into a sustainable template

Dimension	Gandhi's *swaraj*	Gandhian-*Vedic* paradigm for sustainable development
1	Politico-economic independence	Customised accountability
2	Social interconnectedness	Reduce dichotomisation of means-ends
3	Spiritual (moral) development	Increase reflectivity of an individual

The relationship between the *satyagraha-swaraj* and the sustainability requirements of risk society will be discussed briefly below, before putting forward a diagrammatic representation of its implications for accounting's contribution to the sustainability debate.

4.1.   Dimension 1: Customise Accountability

Gandhian freedom refers to both political and economic independence from the yoke of exploitation because:

> he knew well enough that political freedom, devoid of its economic content, was a mere philosophical abstraction (Bhattacharyya, B., 1969, p. 280).

Here Gandhi's politico-economic independence (in the context of his emphases on rural economics and small scale technology to meet India's needs) has been translated into customised accountability. Information used to provide accounts to the other should be tailored to local circumstances: it follows on from the fact that the Gandhian-*Vedic* outcomes are context relevant. Tailoring accountability to cater for local circumstances is another way of embedding the logic of *ahimsa* and personal-external freedom into the construction of feedback. *Ahimsic* responsibility for the other is intended to increase the likelihood that the reform agenda will facilitate a reflective rather than fear response: reflectivity requires individuals to perceive 'what is' realities as a necessary challenge of the 21st century (that frees the individual and society from the hazards of civilisation), instead of seeking refuge in 'what was' hegemonic rhetoric. ESRC (2000) reform has a greater chance of succeeding in a climate of evolving realisation of human interconnectedness with nature. This realisation emerges from various modes of providing accounts of one's actions: from social norms that indicate acceptable behaviour, to formal accountability mechanisms such as the accounting reports for corporate citizens. The key here is to customise the ensuing process of accountability instead of universalising it in a futile attempt to impose a 'one size fits all' governance framework (see Saravanamuthu, 2005a). Customised accountability leads to greater spiritual interconnectedness with local circumstances: it sows the seeds of economic and political freedom, which in turn minimises the likelihood of the circular dialectic of social contradictions.

The aim here is not to attempt to eliminate contradictions altogether because contradictions will remain as long as personal contradictory tendencies exist in humans. The aim is to minimise the likelihood of the dialectical outcome that replaces one set of debilitating contradictions with another. Hence the long-term goal of *satyagraha* and *swaraj* is personal freedom from bondage to 'me and mine'. In the interim, it involves engaging in customised dialogue (with accounting as a medium of communication) to highlight the common ground between competing interest groups and thereby achieve a better resolution.

Because of the delays inherent in the politics of setting financial accounting standards (following Previts and Merino, 1979), customisation may be effected more immediately through reconfiguration of management accounting systems than through the reformulation of external reporting disclosure requirements. Having said that, Elkington's concept of Triple Bottom Line (TBL) reporting appears to be influencing disclosure in financial reports. However, because users of financial statements have traditionally associated 'good' performance with economic indicators (such as profit, or high earnings per share figures), it is possible that these 'what was' mental categories may influence the construction of TBL perceptions: consequently, competing information may be dismissed as supplementary indicators that may be traded-off against higher economic growth rates. Whilst the Gandhian-*Vedic* method acknowledges the significance of the economic dimension in enabling socio-environmental reform, it is not a zero-sum strategy (following Bondurant, 1964). Instead it is based on balancing (for instance) Elkington's social, environmental and economic aspects of living. Section five will develop it by incorporating risk assessments into the provision of accounts.

4.2. Dimension 2: Reduce Dichotomisation Between Means and Ends

Gandhi's social interconnectedness and responsibility for the other extends to nature as well. It means that representations of actuality should minimise the fragmentation of time and space. This results in behaviour where there is greater emphasis on the 'means' to ascertain the 'end', instead of relying on the outcome (of endless economic growth) to justify the means. Its lower dichotomisation of means and ends also contributes towards the customisation of accounts.

4.3. Dimension 3: Increase Reflectivity

As elaborated in an earlier subsection (2: Internal (spiritual) and external freedom from circular dialectics of social contradictions), a person is more likely to respond reflectively to 'what is' challenges of risk society when the person is able to associate her/his reality with the needs of the other. Therefore spiritual interconnectedness increases the chances that the logic of responsibility could replace the hegemonic hold of the control rationale in social norms.

5. Gandhian-Vedic Accountability: The Square of Sustainable Development

The three dimensions (above) have been incorporated into a modified square of *swaraj*. The square also captures cumulative developments on the land (as landholders experiment with better land and water management practices), and the impact of this engagement on the provision of accounts to the larger network of stakeholders. In the case of accountability, it has been recognised that accounting has to follow the literary turn in providing greater depth and variety to representations of actuality (Macintosh and Baker, 2002); that the framework has to enable and engender dialogue between stakeholders (Birkin, 2000, 1996); and that this dialogue could take the form of managing risk as a proxy to definitive measures of performance (Power, 2004, 2003). These developments augur well for the next stage proposed here: that is, applying *satyagrahic* pressure through a social appreciation of risk management tools (following Luhmann, 2005) in insisting on a more ethical path to development.

The formulation of a *satyagrahic* tool of insistence (following Chatterjee, 1969) involves stepping back and pulling the philosophical-practical strands of the Gandhian-*Vedic* paradigm together before teasing out a risk management approach to sustainable development. Figure 1 provides an overview of the implications of each *swaraj* dimension for enhanced accountability to stakeholders. The movement of the shaded circles representing the path society should ideally embark on from the bottom corner (which is risk society that embraces the logic of control) to the top corner of the square (which represents an ethical society constructed on the ethos of responsibility for the other). However, as the movement through personal and structural contradictions is a dialectical one, the direction of the journey of experimenting with truth cannot be ascertained beforehand.

Figure 1
Overview of a three dimensional conceptualisation of the implications of
Gandhi's *swaraj* for sustainability: the representation of actuality to engender the
culture of spiritual interconnectedness with the other

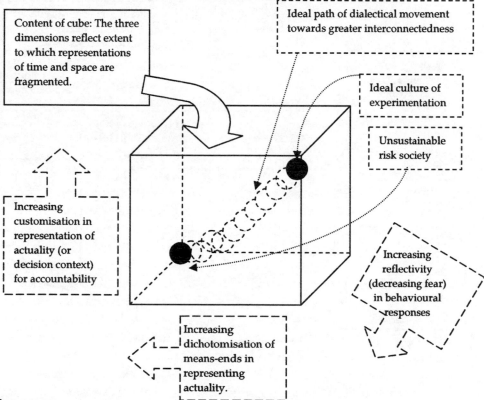

Content of cube: The three dimensions reflect extent to which representations of time and space are fragmented.

Ideal path of dialectical movement towards greater interconnectedness

Ideal culture of experimentation

Unsustainable risk society

Increasing customisation in representation of actuality (or decision context) for accountability

Increasing reflectivity (decreasing fear) in behavioural responses

Increasing dichotomisation of means-ends in representing actuality.

Key:

Height of square box represents degree of customisation in accountability.
Length of square box represents degree of means-end dichotomisation in representing actuality.
Width of square box represents range of reflectivity-fear behavioural response.

Figure 2 (below) adds more detail to the overview square provided in Figure 1.

Figure 2
Detailed three dimensional conceptualisation of the implications of Gandhi's *swaraj* for sustainability: the representation of actuality to engender the culture of spiritual interconnectedness with the other

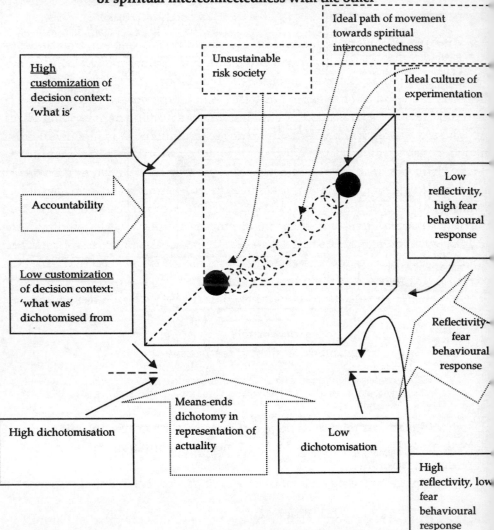

Key:
Height of square box represents degree of customisation in accountability.
Length of square box represents degree of means-end dichotomisation in representing actuality.
Width of square box represents range of reflectivity-fear behavioural response.

The implication of the square of *swaraj* for the construction of accounting information and accountability processes is that information should be tailored to local circumstances in a (broader) risk management context. It means that the account giving process should minimise the dichotomisation of means from ends and re-centre the role of the individual actor in social reform (through the resulting 'what is' representation of actuality).

5.1. Tailoring Information to Local Circumstances within a (Broader) Risk Management Context

Sustainability is commonly referred to as the process of juggling Elkington's social, environmental and economic needs (following Korhonen, 2003). A very down-to-earth definition expressed by a horticulturalist reveals the ambiguity surrounding the meaning of the term: 'sustainability is about slowing down the rate at which the window is closing' (Saravanamuthu, 2004). Therefore the process of customising accountability involves engaging with ambiguity about the meaning (and implications) of the term: it implies firstly, that accounting cannot profess to definitively represent performance (based on a predefined notion of sustainability) as doubts remain over what 'it' (sustainability) signifies in the first place (see Mebratu, 1998). Secondly, certain types of information (economic indicators in particular) have long been associated with 'what was' expectations of 'acceptable' performance. Economistic ('what was') expectations are increasingly criticised in risk society, as there is greater acknowledgement that society has to change its ways. The politics of maintaining the status quo compounds this dilemma (Tokar, 1997): it is not surprising that people are sceptical of the way in which performance indicators are evolving in risk society. However, there is insufficient information about the 'correct' way to proceed.

In this context, tailoring information to local circumstances implies that the information should enable stakeholders to grapple with both the known (that is, accumulated albeit partisan knowledge) and unknown in developing (an evolving) meaning of what it means to be sustainable, whilst experimenting with its implications. It means navigating between risk and uncertainty amidst ambiguity over the meaning and implications of sustainability. Rational theorisations of risk and uncertainty will be socialised in the following subsections by combining aspects of Luhmann's (2005) theory of risk within the Gandhian-*Vedic* context of *karmic* interconnectedness of the whole. *Karmic* law asserts that every action has a consequence within the domain of constant transformation of energy: this is the ambiguous context within which networked groups tease out the meaning and implications of sustainability as they search for sustainable management practices.

5.2. Conventional Risk and Uncertainty

The distinction between risk and uncertainty is attributed to Frank Knight's (1921) theory of profit and entrepreneurship: risk refers to the situation where the probability distribution of a random variable is known, but uncertainty prevails if its distribution is unknown. Even though Bayesian decision theory asserts that a decision maker will seek to maximise the expected value regardless of whether it is attributed to risk or uncertainty, Bewley (2002) argues that Knight's distinction between risk and uncertainty is important because decision makers are averse to the vagueness of probabilities (following Ellsberg, 1961, 1963). It is not simply a question of undertaking an investment on the basis that it has a positive expected value because there is a 'form of aversion to uncertainty which is distinct from the usual risk aversion' (Bewley, 2002, p. 81). This aversion is examined through uncertainty aversion and inertia: that is, Bewley investigates why people choose not to make a decision in situations where probability of loss is ambiguous. Wage rigidity and rigid long-term contracts are outcomes of such non-decisions. He views long-term wage contracts (in opposition to shorter contracts that could take advantage of spot fluctuations) in terms of bargaining costs and vagueness about the relationship between investment and wage levels (following Williamson, 1975, 1985). Consequently, if an employer is able to convince workers that low wages are necessary for the health of the firm, the workers would agree (for a period of time at least) because the costs of bargaining each short term contract would be the same as the cost for the long term one.

Figure 3 shows the rationalist perspective, where the risk and uncertainty are differentiated by the extent to which a probability distribution of a random variable may be ascertained. Ambiguity encapsulates this continuum and moderates the actions of a rational decision maker seeking to maximise the expected value of returns (following Bewley, 2002).

Figure 3
Rationalist view of risk-uncertainty-ambiguity

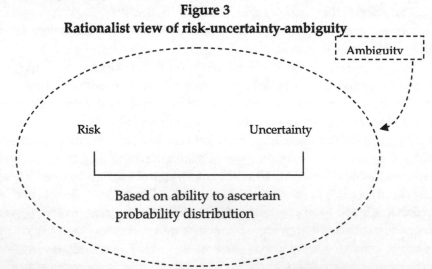

However, even Bewley's modified rationalist explanation is based on contentious assumptions. A core assumption is that the rational decision maker uses reason and all available information to further her/his own interests and values even though its behavioural validity has long been questioned (Simon, 1957). McFadden (1999) reveals that conventional economics presumes that a rational actor (whom he labels 'Chicago man') is one (i) who processes information to create perceptions and beliefs in accordance with Bayesian statistical principles of perception rationality; (ii) whose preferences are consistent and immutable based on preference rationality; and (iii) whose cognitive process is limited to preference maximisation or process rationality. He goes on to demonstrate how Chicago man has become a convenient and widely successful means of influencing instruments of social manipulation even though its construction is inherently false.

Another contentious aspect of rationalist representation of risk-uncertainty is the definition of uncertainty itself: it is the 'imprecision in estimates of future consequences [that are] conditional on present actions' which is in turn based on rigid presumptions[61] (March, 1994, p. 178). Even if these assumptions are put aside, the very definition of uncertainty is at odds with the ethos of sustainability suggested in Beck's (1993) risk society: namely, consequences are not conditional on present actions because a significant part of the hazards are already present. These inherited dangers are the culmination of society's historical adherence to the logic of control. Even though present actions will continue to aggravate the state of degradation, the presence of inherited hazards implies that there may be no overt causal relationship between present actions and these hazards; there is only ambiguity about the risk it poses. Agricultural and landscape management disciplines (which engage in socio-environmental management) acknowledge the ambiguous nature of the task of trying to slow down the rate at which the window is closing on livelihoods (Carley and Christie, 2000; Brunckhorst, 2000; Mazmanian and Kraft, 2001). Hence, the *satyagrahic* mode of providing accounts should engage with risk-uncertainty and ambiguity in facilitating a culture of experimenting with the unknown, instead of shirking from it.

Even though ambiguity is 'related to but distinguishable from uncertainty' (March, 1994, p. 178), rational theories of choice and rule-based theories of identity fulfilment do not provide guidance on dealing with ambiguity. Ambiguity, in the context of limited rationality, describes a situation in which the decision maker is less confident about the truth of the matter at hand, or where the boundaries between aspects of the world cannot be neatly compartmentalised into mutually exhaustive and exclusive situations, or where information may not make the situation any clearer (following March, 1994). Shapira (1995) analyses data on risk and managerial decision making from 700 managers to argue that managers do not behave in accordance to theories of rational choice: it means that distributions of probability outcomes are ignored, and probability theory itself is rejected as managers shy away from chance outcomes. Instead managers are more concerned

---

[61] March (1994) identifies three assumptions that underpin this definition: '(1) that it is possible to specify all the mutually exhaustive and exclusive states of the world that might exist; (2) that although it is not possible to specify precisely which state exists, some state does, in fact, exist; and (3) that the uncertainty about which state exists will be reduced by the unfolding of information over time' (p. 178).

with how things actually work out, which includes the political implications of their decisions. Thus Einhorn and Hogart, (1985) define ambiguity as vagueness in decision-making that results from limited knowledge: their model relies on of anchoring-and-adjustment in which initial estimates provide an anchor, whilst adjustments are made for what might be (the 'what is' reality). Shapira confirms the latter in revealing that managers believe that they are able to control a decision after it has been made: namely, managers believe that they are able to reduce the risk of negative consequences, or avoid responsibility for these repercussions after having chosen to accept the risk. Thus ambiguity under limited rationality has implications for organisational learning and choice (March and Olsen, 1975).

5.3 Luhmann's Sociological Theory of Risk

A counter to the rationalist approach takes the form of Luhmann's (2005) sociological theory of risk. Luhmann argues that the rationalist approach to risk does not assist the decision maker because the paradox inherent in its formulation:

> ... it translates into calculation injunctions the problem of how loss can be averted to the highest possible degree despite exploitation of the options of rationality (Luhmann, 2005, p. 18).

The rest of this sub-section will use Luhmann's theorisation of risk to shed light on how ambiguity may be responsibly accommodated in the provision of accounts (so as to encourage reflective behaviours). Because Luhmann's theory is set in the context of societal communication, it dovetails into the discursive emphasis of *satyagrahic* accountability.

Luhmann's criticism of rationalism in the quotation above has to be understood in the context of his approach to sociology. In their Introduction, Bechmann and Stehr (2005) explain that because Luhmann regards sociology as a theory of society instead of as a science: he uses system theory to reflect society in its totality whilst asserting that there is no such thing as objective observation. He does not regard society as an object of research but uses society as the subject in theorising the process of sociological cognition. Luhmann regards communication as the mechanism that constitutes society. Communication means autopoietic reproduction of knowledge and meaning (following Maturana and Valera, 1992). It implies that society continually transforms itself in the linguistic domain[62]: it highlights the significance of information (including accounting and accountability mechanisms) in sustainability reform. For Luhmann, societal movement occurs

---

[62] In human society subjugated voices challenge 'what was' perceptions of contemporary situations in the linguistic domain (following Maturana and Valera, 1992, chapter 9; Krishnamurti, 1978). Maturana and Valera refer to this unending process of changing perceived realities as 'autopoiesis'. 'Poiesis' means creation or production: it is a means by which society decentres accumulated knowledge that has been constructed on appropriation-oriented lifeworld principles and embraces new norms (following Habermas, 1990). Because 'what is' reality enables individuals to connect with the whole, it is described as the love that binds the whole (Maturana and Valera, 1992, p. 246; 1980).

through the contingencies and complexities of the social that manifest as paradoxes in communication: he relies on systems theory to describe the world through a network of contingent distinctions (or paradoxes).

In other words, Luhmann uses contradictions in language to identify characteristics of a thing. It is a means of establishing the difference between (communication as) a system and its environment. Because he assumes that a system cannot transcend its own boundaries, the 'outside' of the system becomes the 'inside' of the environment. This provides the mechanism for a social world that 'temporalizes, differentiates, and decentralizes all identities' in opposition to classical theories that aim for unity as the ultimate point of reference (Bechmann and Stehr, 2005, p. xiv). Therefore, the desired society does not possess an end point of shared norms and value patterns. Instead society is dialectically shaped by the relational connection between opposites. Observation itself is based on a paradox because any reality (which is constructed on a partial view of the paradox) cannot reflect the whole: these partial realities sustain societal movement. Therefore, information is an outcome of the disappearance-appearance paradox because it is a 'product of decay that disappears by being updated' (p. xxi) over time.

Returning to Luhmann's earlier criticism of rational theories of risk, he moves away from the rationalist's dichotomy of optimal/non-optimal by emphasising its paradoxical nature. Luhmann conceptualises risk as a fluid dynamic that evolves as societal communication shifts from one aspect of the paradox to another. He initially conceptualises risk as the opposite of 'security'.[63] Security has the same impact on the psychology of fear-reflectivity as Krishnamurti's constancy (or rather, the lack of it in a world of transforming manifestations of energy). As the emphasis on security results in the unlikely scenario where all ventures that are deemed risky are shunned, he reconfigures his risk/security model to accommodate circumstances where an estimate of risk may reflect outcomes that one may reasonably expect to achieve. Luhmann argues that:

> ... what remains is an open question of whether one ought to regret preferring the 'safe' variant or not. However, this is a question that will frequently be impossible to answer if the opportunity is not taken up at all, and the risky causal proceeding is not even set in motion. The risk of the one variant nevertheless colours the entire decision making situation (Luhmann, 2005, p. 21).

He extends this broader understanding of uncertainty in his sociological orientation of risk:

> ... what can occur in the future also depends on decisions to be made at present. For we can only speak of risk if we can identify a decision without which the loss could not have occurred. It is not imperative for the concept (although it is a question of definition) whether the decision maker perceives the risk as a consequence of his

---

[63] Luhmann refers to Lopez, L. L., (1987), "Between hope and fear: the psychology of risk", *Advances in Experimental Social Psychology*, Vol. 20, pp. 255-259.

decision or whether it is others who attribute it to him; and it is also irrelevant at what point in time this occurs – whether at the time when the decision is made or only later, when the loss has actually occurred. For the concept as we intend to define it, the only requirement is that the contingent loss be itself caused as a contingency, that is to say it be avoidable (Luhmann, 2005, p. 16).

This leads him to develop, firstly the distinction between risk and danger, and secondly reintroduce the notion of holistic time to bridge the dichotomisation of risk-danger that is implied in rationalist methods. Luhmann acknowledges that Giddens (1990) has explicitly rejected the distinguishing of these terms on grounds that risk is the danger that future loss could occur (and thus does not depend on the consciousness of the decision maker). However, Luhmann asserts that it is necessary to differentiate between the terms to identify whether a loss could occur even though a decision had not been made by a particular individual. Danger is when the loss is not avoidable because it is not within an individual's sphere of control.

Luhmann's risk analysis identifies with the potential effect of hazards on individuals and society (following Renn, 1985): it dovetails nicely into Beck's (1993) reliance on the increased awareness of hazards confronting risk society to motivate individual reflectivity. Luhmann's differentiation of risk and danger reflects the complexities of risk society because it extends the sociological implications beyond the causal effects of identifiable decisions. In short:

... *one is exposed to dangers* (Luhmann, 2005, p. 23).

Figure 4
Luhmann's risk-danger continuum and ambiguity

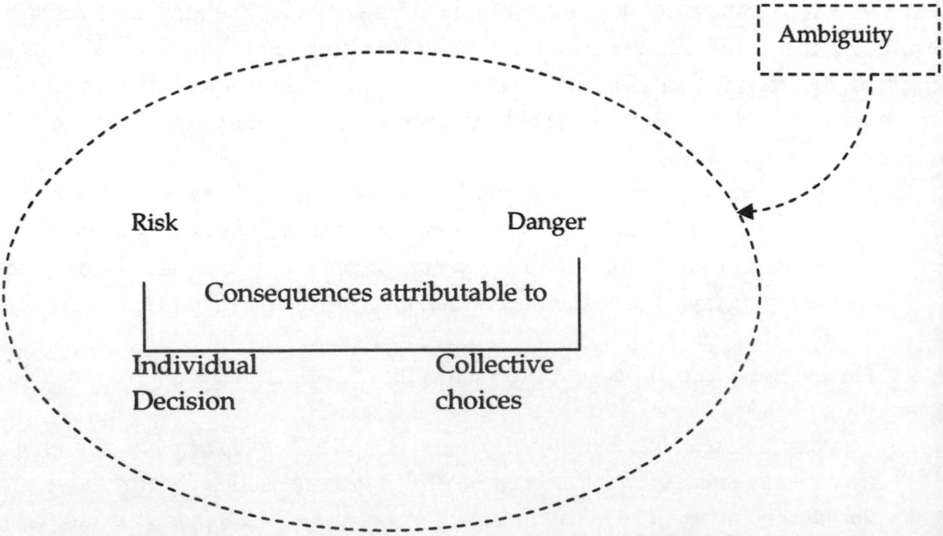

Because dangers are not causally attributed to any single person's actions, the risk-danger continuum becomes a means of theorising ambiguity in risk society. The impact of ambiguity on decisions made by individuals and communities depends on whether risk or danger is prioritised (or 'marked'):

Marking risks then allows dangers to be forgotten, whereas marking dangers allows the profits to be forgotten that could be earned if risky decision[s] are made. In older societies it was thus danger that tended to be marked, whereas modern society has until recently preferred to mark risk, being concerned with optimizing the exploitation of opportunity. The question is whether this will remain the case, or whether the present situation is not characterized by the decision maker and individual affected by the decision each marking the respective other side of one and the same distinction, thus coming into conflict because each party has his own way of seeing things and his own expectations about the way others see them (Luhmann, 2005, pp. 24-25).

The risk-danger approach of engaging with common dangers (such as environmental degradation) sets the stage for the discursive turn in accountability mechanisms (following Macintosh and Baker, 2002; Birkin, 2000, 1996). For instance, the Kyoto Protocol's response to the danger of global warming is to set national emission targets for developed countries (inadequate as they are) to address production methods and consumption patterns, whilst the Bush-Howard alliance addresses production methods alone (without setting emission targets) by relying on technological advances in the next 30 years. The alliance also includes emissions of a few large developing nations: China, India and South Korea. These competing-yet-complementary discourses on climate change represent Luhmann's risk responses in discursive conflict: it mirrors the gap between Krishnamurti's 'what is' and 'what was' realities that becomes the basis of *satyagrahic* engagement to minimise the fragmentation of time and space in social discourse.

5.4   Assimilating Luhmann into the Gandhian-Vedic Paradigm

Luhmann minimises the fragmentation of time by introducing the notion of continuous time to bridge perceptions of risk and danger. Luhmann asserts that the notion of the 'present' only serves to fragment the past and the future, which artificially cocoons the decision-maker from (the dangers of) past actions. Luhmann's temporal insight is assimilated into the Gandhian-*Vedic* method in the following manner: the notion of the present fragments Krishnamurti's 'what is' from 'what was', instead of representing it as a continuous stream of actions and consequences. For instance, global warming is the consequence of collective societal choices about progress it has historically legitimised. It has become a contemporary concern because (*karmic*) consequences have crossed the threshold of ecological sustainability (following Luhmann, 2005, p. 26-28) to the point that it now poses a threat (or danger/hazard) to society. However, accumulated knowledge is unable to specify the threshold of sustainability: this unknown manifests as the conventional boundary of 'uncertainty' and Luhmann's 'danger'. The boundary between the known and the unknown also serves to restrict irresponsible behaviours (that could aggravate these dangers) in the *Satchitaanandaic* journey of experimentation: these behavioural limits become ethical norms for a particular period. These norms change as accumulated knowledge sheds more light on the matter, effectively transforming dangers into risks (following Luhmann, 2005).

Constructing ethical norms from thresholds of sustainability is a way of theorising the actions of the actor into social forces of change. However, it is often asserted that Luhmann theorises the underlying social conflicts in anti-humanist, social constructivist terms; he rejects the humanistic-anthropocentric means of defining society. These aspects of Luhmann's theory appear to be at odds with, and complement, the Gandhian-*Vedic* approach: Gandhi focuses on the individual to bring about reform even though both approaches reject an anthropocentric means of defining society. On the one hand, both approaches theorise movement in society through contradictions (or in Luhmann's terminology, paradoxes or distinctions). The Gandhian-*Vedic* concentrates on the dialectical movement that results from structural-personal contradictions, whilst Luhmann looks at it from the point of view of paradoxes in communication whilst asserting that people belong to the environment of society (instead of assuming that society consists of people: Stehr, N. and Bechmann, G. in Luhmann, 2005, p. xv). On the other hand, Luhmann's societal movement could become locked into a circular logic of paradoxes – to remain forever relative and contingent on the previous transformation. Gandhi (re)centres the individual in societal movement: the individual's reflective[64] behaviour could break the circular dialectics.

> *If the individual ceases to count, what is left of society? Individual freedom alone can make a man voluntarily surrender himself completely to the service of society. If it is wrested from him, he becomes an automaton and society is ruined. No society can possibly be built on a denial of individual freedom* (Gandhi, *Harijan*, 1 February 1942, quoted in Gandhi, 2001a, p. 21).

The power of the *satyagrahic* ethos has been demonstrated in Gandhi's (1993) engagement with British imperialism. Gandhi's discursive method becomes a vehicle of reflective accountability because it targets the individual's psychology of fear-reflectivity and changes the individual from within, whilst transforming public discourse. Therefore, it facilitates a collective formulation of alternative norms by drawing stakeholders together in reflective dialogue: this is why Gandhi succeeded in galvanising the Indian masses against oppression when earlier attempts (by Aurobindo Ghose and the one-time Indian Marxist, Manabendra Nath Roy) had failed. *Satyagraha* strengthens interpersonal relations between competing interests (Dalton, 1993 following Bondurant, 1964) and creates networked communities that are united by reflective agency. Gandhi's method:

> ... *patiently probes and exposes the society's moral defences, asks disturbing questions and unsettles settled convictions without frightening those involved. It also*

---

[64] Beck makes the distinction between 'reflexive' (self-confrontation) and 'reflective' (knowledge) in explaining that when individuals are confronted by the hazards of risk society, it cannot be presumed that they will respond reflectively.

cuts across ideological and party lines, builds up communities of concerned citizens, cultivates and mobilizes new constituencies and gives hope to those paralyzed into inaction by an externally engineered feeling of powerlessness and releases a new moral energy (Parekh, 1991, p. 166).

The Gandhian-*Vedic* method departs from Luhmann's theorisation at this point: it argues that personal-structural contradictions moderate the degree to which social identities are temporalised, differentiated, and decentralised (Bechmann and Stehr, 2005, following Luhmann). In other words, that Gandhian-*Vedic* paradigm views Luhmann's risk-danger decision process as a knowledge-led journey that mirrors its journey of *Satchitaananda*: this journey of searching for truth through knowledge connects (individual) human actions to the (collective) dangers. The Gandhian-*Vedic* method steadfastly retains the individuality of the player who embarks on the *Satchitanandic* journey: it integrates the individual into the collective through the dialectic between personal and structural contradictions. Personal contradictions moderate the effect of rationality: it manifests in a way in which the individual responds to ambiguity. For instance the danger of the repercussions global warming is couched in ambiguity about its meaning and hence implications. It could cause decision-makers to seek refuge in 'what was' mental schemas (which provide illusory security of having control over dangers/hazards): a fear response. Fear responses reduce the chances of radically reforming consumption behaviours and production methods. A *satyagrahic* approach to Luhmann's risk-danger discourse could result in reflective responses that embrace responsibility for danger (or responsibility beyond one's immediate self-interest). Gandhi's experiences will now be used to inform the construction of *satyagrahic* accountability by individuals to members of their networked community, and subsequently (as the sustainability ethos permeates out) to the rest of society.

5.5. Satyagrahic Accountability

The Gandhian-*Vedic* 'whole' extends Luhmann's articulation of the connection between risk and danger to natural systems and forces. Extending responsibility to the other beyond one's immediate sphere of interest also reflects Gandhi's firm belief that means are everything because means cannot be isolated from ends (Gandhi in *Young India*, 17 July 1924, quoted in Gandhi, 2001a, p. 65). It involves reducing the fragmentation of time and space in representations of reality (following Krishnamurti, 1994).

Minimising the fragmentation of time and space in the representation of performance implies that an entity would embrace its responsibility to the other (be it the local community, customers, natural environment, etc.) well beyond its traditional interpretation of property rights. It is hoped that as time goes on the term 'externalities' will become a relic of the 20th century. It has been argued that such change is already here: common law embraces just such an ethos in (re)defining the rights and obligations of landholders (see Saravanamuthu, forthcoming); whilst internationally, there are varying degrees of 'inclusiveness' in financial accounting.

Australia merely requires directors to disclose material Triple Bottom Line consequences, whilst France specifies the multiple performance indicators that should be disclosed.

Nevertheless, it is expected that the most immediate changes will occur in pockets of society where the local communities are confronted with imminent socio-environmental problems (following Carley and Christie, 2000; Saravanamuthu, 2004, 2005b). These networked communities essentially use management accounting information in a discursive manner to engage with structural and personal contradictions, and avoid becoming trapped by the circular dialectical movement. It is expected that their innovative ideas will permeate out to the rest of society.

Case studies of networked communities (carried out by the author: Saravanamuthu, 2004, 2005b) show that spatio-temporal fragmentation in the provision of accounts may be minimised by using the radar plot to represent performance. It essentially locates performance within the broader context of risks and dangers. The radar plot in Figure 5 reflects the risk/danger that emanates from the decision to engage in a particular activity that has been introduced into a natural environment, say a citrus crop. The individual spokes of the radar plot represent different aspects of cultivating citrus. Performance is represented by using the best available knowledge about the whole, including its entomological, atmospheric soil and hydrological impacts (following Ji, 2004). It reduces spatio-temporal fragmentation in the decision situation by juxtaposing conflicting-and-complementary feedback. It translates a variety of measurements into a graduated scale of low to high risk impact, thus granting equal representation to known horticultural consequences whilst highlighting the relative risk of these consequences.

Figure 5
Radar plot diagram of introduced activity

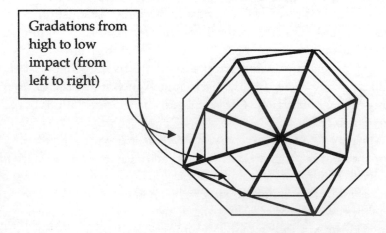

Luhmann's danger (or health of the whole) is portrayed as follows: a situation is only as sustainable as its greatest hazard, or lowest threat to sustainability threshold. It is reflected through the substantive gap analysis of multi-dimensional performance between the radar plots for citrus and native vegetation (that has evolved to survive local conditions and therefore has least impact on the surroundings): Figure 6.

Figure 6
Radar plot for naturally occurring (least impact) activity

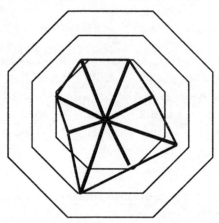

Therefore radar plot (Figures 5 and 6) is a diagrammatic representation of the *satyagrahic* ethos because its equal representation of conflicting-and-complementary feedback increases tension between stakeholders through dialogue, which in turn makes the common interest binding stakeholders all the more apparent. The common interest, for now, is to retard the continued escalation of hazards in risk society. Diagrammatic representation of risk is also advocated in Power's (2004, p. 55) intelligent risk management practice because it counterbalances any partisan assumptions embedded in calculative techniques (that could aggravate spatio-temporal fragmentation).

Incidentally, the Church of England's ecotheological revision of its biblical teachings draws the analogy between its covenant and a spider's web (which is similar in structure to the radar plot). The Church now asserts that:

> *Through God's gracious love, creation is bound by the everlasting covenant to the invisible God, and all creatures are bound to each other in a web of interrelationship ... . The image of the covenant as a spider's web is instructive: each of its strands supports the whole. If just one or two strands of the web are cut, the web may survive, sever enough strands and the whole web falls apart* (Mission and Public Affairs Council, 2005, p. 17).

As critiqued earlier, this newfound Christian holism does not explain why an all-supreme God is bound by the underlying circular dialectics of social contradictions, which causes a highly severed web to fall apart.

6. Conclusion

This chapter puts forward an alternative paradigm to the dominant Judeo-Christian one of human dominion over Nature. It is a means of understanding the hazards of civilisation that the current generation confronts, and which will continue to haunt future generations. Any attempt to redress these mistakes requires changing the way in which society perceives the problem and hence its prescriptions. The solution here is targeted squarely at radical reform of personal perceptions (and lifestyles) as well as structural forces. As Gandhi himself has demonstrated through his life experiences, it is not a quick fix.

Acknowledgement

My sincere thanks to Austin Adams for his assistance in diagrammatically representing the square of *swaraj*, namely Figures 1 and 2; Ian Reeve of Rural Futures (University of New England) for suggesting the radar plot to represent multi-faceted performance. I thank the following for their constructive comments: Bill Kaghan, Boris Brummans, Peter Humphreys and the two anonymous reviewers. I am grateful to the late Swami Shanthananda for explaining the finer points of the *Advaitic Vedic* philosophy.

Glossary of Sanskrit terms commonly used in this chapter

Term	Explanation
Advaitic Vedic	One of two main schools of *Vedic* thought. It is associated with reformist thinking namely teachers such as Vivekananda (19-20th century) and political activist – spiritual aspirant like Gandhi.
Ahimsa	Ethos of interconnectedness that leads to the principle of embracing responsibility for the other.
Bhagavadgita	A central *Vedic* text that contains all the key principles. It is enunciated through a battle scene between warring cousins: the battle scene is a metaphor for the battle of life (in overcoming contradictions).
Brahman-Vishnu-Shiva	The *Vedic* philosophy is founded on the concept of constant transformation of energy. This state of becoming is personified as *Brahman* (creation, or more appropriately projection), *Vishnu* (sustenance), and *Shiva* (destruction, which leads to the cycle beginning all over again).
Dharma	Literally means righteous living. In practical terms it spells out how the laws of nature are connected to the individual going about her/his daily life: reinforces the notion of interconnectedness and that ethical living is an inherent and 'natural' way of living.
Law of Karma	Principle which asserts that every action has a consequence. It reinforces the notion of interconnectedness and *ahimsa*.
Maya	Perceptions or constructed realities that fragment time and space dimensions of the whole. When it is located in the context of the journey of searching for truth, *Maya* becomes 'experiences' through

	which one learns to realise that fragmenting the whole in the private interest results in karmic repercussions that exploit the whole (and hence oneself).
Purusha	In this chapter it is defined as a unit of energy representing the spiritual connection between the individual and the whole.
Sanskrit	The *Vedas* were initially verbally passed down by way of mouth 2000 years before the earliest known documentary evidence that was traced back to 5000 BC – the medium used was Sanskrit. Hence Vivekananda argues that Sanskrit is the *Vedas*.
Satchitaananda	The epistemology of knowledge that translates into Existence-Knowledge-Realisation.
Satyagraha	Term that was coined in during the time of the Gandhi's struggle against British imperialism. It refers to the use of moral and political means to engage the other in constructive dialogue. It involves resisting adherence to the hegemonic influences that lead to the exploitation of the many for the benefit of a few.
Swaraj	Initially used to imply national independence. However, as the Gandhian-Vedic method involves freeing the individual as well, it also denotes personal freedom through spiritual interconnectedness with the other.
Vedic, Vedanta, Vedas	Hindu scriptures that have been traced back to 5,000 BC. See footnote 54 for details.

References

Athanasiou, T. (1996), *Divided Planet: The Ecology of Rich and Poor,* Little, Brown and Company, Boston.

Balisacan, A. M. and Fuwa, N. (2004), "Going beyond crosscountry averages: growth, inequality and poverty reduction in the Philippines", *World Development,* Vol. 32, No. 11, pp. 1891-1907.

Bechmann, G. and Stehr, N. (2005), "Introduction", in Luhmann, N. (Ed.) (2005), *Risk. A Sociological Theory,* Trans. Barrett, R. Aldine Transaction, New Brunswick.

Beck, U. (1993), *Risk Society. Towards a New Modernity,* Trans. Ritter, M. Sage Publications, London.

Bewley, T. F. (2002), "Knightian decision theory. Part I", *Decisions in Economics and Finance,* Vol. 25, pp. 79-110.

Bhattacharyya, B. (1969), "Gandhi's concept of freedom: people's swaraj", in Biswas, S. C. (Ed.), *Gandhi: Theory and Practice. Social Impact and Contemporary Relevance.* Vol II, Indian Institute of Advanced Study, Simla, India, pp. 275-284.

Bhattacharya, V. R. (1969), "Economic thoughts of Gandhi", in Biswas, S. C. (Ed.). *Gandhi: Theory and Practice. Social Impact and Contemporary Relevance,* Vol. II, Indian Institute of Advanced Study, Simla, India, pp. 183-187.

Birkin, F. (1996), "The ecological accountant: from the cogito to thinking like a mountain", *Critical Perspectives on Accounting,* Vol. 7, pp. 231-257.

Birkin, F. (2000), "The art of accounting for science: a prerequisite for sustainable development?", *Critical Perspectives on Accounting*, Vol. 11, pp. 289-309.

Birkin, F., Edwards, P. and Woodward, D. (2005), "Accounting's contribution to a conscious cultural evolution: an end to sustainable development", *Critical Perspectives on Accounting*, Vol. 16, pp. 185-208.

Bondurant, J. (1964), "Satyagraha vs. Duragraha", in Ramachandra, G. (Ed.) *Gandhi: His Relevance for Our Times*, Bharatiya Vidya Bhavan, Bombay.

Braverman, H. (1974), *Labor and Monopoly Capital: the Degradation of Work in the Twentieth Century*, Monthly Review Press, NY.

Brown, J. (2003), *M. Nehru: a Political Life*, Yale University Press, New Haven.

Brunckhorst, D. J. (2000), *Bioregional Planning: Resource Management Beyond the New Millennium*, Harwood Academic, Amsterdam.

Bush Telegraph (2005), Broadcast on 10 August, Radio National, Australian Broadcasting Corporation.

Carley, M. and Christie, I. (2000), *Managing Sustainable Development*, Earthscan Publications Ltd, London.

Chatterjee, M. (1969), "Gandhi-ji's conception of collective action", in Biswas, S. C. (Ed.), *Gandhi: Theory and Practice. Social Impact and Contemporary Relevance*, Vol II, Indian Institute of Advanced Study, Simla, India, pp. 78-86.

Chidbhavananda, S. (trans.), *The Bhagavad Gita*, Sri Ramakrishna Tapovanam (Publication section), Tirupparaitturai, India, 1991.

Clarke, D. M. and Kissane, D. W. (2002), "Demoralization: its phenomenology and importance", *Australian and New Zealand Journal of Psychiatry*, Vol. 36, pp. 733-742.

Cohen, M. J. (Ed). (2001), "Environmental sociology, social theory and risk: an introductory discussion", in *Risk in the Modern Age. Social Theory, Science and Environmental Decision-Making*, Vols. 3-31. Palgrave, Houndmills, UK.

Copley, A. (1987), *Gandhi. Against the Tide*, Basil Blackwell Ltd, Oxford, UK.

Craib, I. (1997), *Classical Social Theory: An Introduction to the Thought of Marx, Weber, Durkheim, and Simmel*, Oxford University Press, Oxford.

Dalton, D. (1993), *Mahatma Gandhi. Nonviolent Power in Action*, Columbia University Press, NY.

Dasgupta, A. K. (1996), *Gandhi's Economic Thought*, Routledge, London.

Dickens, P. (1992), *Society and Nature. Towards a Green Social Theory*, Harvester Wheatsheaf, London.

Economic & Social Research Council (2000), "Summary: What have we learnt about sustainable production and consumption?", in the *Global Environmental Change: Re-thinking the Questions programme*, UK. Available at

http://www.gecko.ac.uk/doc-c/coredoc-c-summary.html accessed on 6/5/01.

Ehrlich, P. (1968), *The Population Bomb*, Ballantine, NY.

Ehrlich, P. and Ehrlich, A. (1970), *Population, Resources, Environment: Issues in Human Ecology*, W. H. Freeman, San Francisco.

Ehrlich, P., Ehrlich, A. and Holdren, J. (1977), *Ecoscience: Population, Resources, Environment,* Freeman & Co., San Francisco.

Einhorn, H. J. and Hogart, R. M. (1985), "Ambiguity and uncertainty in probabilistic inference", *Psychological Review,* Vol. 92, No. 4, pp. 433-461.

Ellsberg, D. (1961), "Risk, ambiguity and the Savage axioms", *The Quarterly Journal of Economics,* Vol. 75, pp. 643-669.

Ellsberg, D. (1963), "Reply", *The Quarterly Journal of Economics,* Vol. 77, pp. 336-342.

Engels, F. (1959), "Socialism: Utopian and scientific", in Feuer, L. (Ed.), *Karl Marx and Friedrich Engels, Basic Writings,* Collins, London.

Fox, M. A. (2005), *The Accessible Hegel,* Humanity Books, NY.

Gandhi, M. K. (1948), *Delhi Diary,* Navajivan Publishing House, Ahmedabad.

Gandhi, M. K. (1958-1984), *The Collected Works of Mahatma Gandhi,* 90 volumes. Delhi: Publications Division, Ministry of Information and Broadcasting, Government of India.

Gandhi, M. K. (1987), *The Essence of Hinduism,* Navajivan Publishing House, Ahmedabad.

Gandhi, M. K. (1993a), *Gandhi: an Autobiography. The Story of My Experiments with Truth.* Trans. Beacon Press, Desai, M. Boston.

Gandhi, M. K. (1993b), *Mohan-Mala (a Gandhian Rosary),* Compiled by Prabhu, R. K., Navajivan Publishing House, Ahmedabad.

Gandhi, M. K. (1995), *Truth is God,* Compiled by Prabhu, R. K. Navajivan Publishing House, Ahmedabad.

Gandhi, M. K. (2001a), *India of My Dreams,* Compiled by Prabhu, R. K. Navajivan Publishing House, Ahmedabad.

Gandhi, M. K. (2001b), *The Message of the Gita,* Navajivan Publishing House, Ahmedabad.

Giddens, A. (1990), *The Consequences of Modernity,* Stanford University Press, Stanford.

Habermas, J. (1990), *Moral Consciousness and Communicative Action,* Trans. Lenhardt, C. and Nicholsen, S. W., Polity Press, Cambridge, England.

Haithcox, J. P. (1971), *Communism and Nationalism in India. M.N. Roy and Comintern Policy 1920-1939,* Princeton University Press, Princeton.

Hamilton, C. (2003), *Growth Fetish,* Allen & Unwin, Crows Nest, NSW.

Heywood, V. (Ed.), (1995), *Global Biodiversity Assessment,* Cambridge University Press, Cambridge, England.

Horowitz, M. J. (1997), *Stress Response Syndromes. PTSD, Grief, and Adjustment Disorders,* Jason Aronson, Northvale, New Jersey.

Iyer, R. N. (1973), *The Moral and Political Thought of Mahatma Gandhi,* Oxford University Press, NY.

Ji, Z. G. (2004), "Use of physical sciences in support of environmental management", *Environmental Management,* Vol. 34, No. 2, pp. 159-169.

Knight, F. H. (1921), *Risk, Uncertainty and Profit,* Houghton Mifflin, Boston.

Krishnamurti, J. (1969), *Freedom from the Known,* Lutyens, M. (Ed.), Harper Collins Publishers, NY.

Krishnamurti, J. (1978), *The Impossible Question*, Penguin Books, Harmondsworth, England.

Krishnamurti, J. (1994), *On Conflict*, Harper, San Francisco.

Krishnamurti, J. (2000), *The Awakening of Intelligence*, Penguin Books, New Delhi.

Korhonen, J. (2003), "Should we measure corporate social responsibility?", *Corporate Social Responsibility and Environmental Management*, Vol. 10, pp. 25-39.

Lazarus, R. S. and Folkman, S. (1984), *Stress, Appraisal and Coping*, Springer, NY.

Luhmann, N. (2005), *Risk. A Sociological Theory*, Trans. Barrett, R. Aldine Transaction, New Brunswick.

Macintosh, N. B. and Baker, C. R. (2002), "A literary theory perspective on accounting: towards heteroglossic accounting reports", *Accounting, Auditing & Accountability Journal*, Vol. 5, No. 2, pp. 184-222.

Mahadevan, T. K. (1969), "An approach to the study of Gandhi", in Biswas, S. C. (Ed.). *Gandhi: Theory and Practice. Social Impact and Contemporary Relevance.* Vol. II, Indian Institute of Advanced Study, Simla, India, pp. 45-61.

March, J. G. (1994), *A Primer on Decision Making. How Decisions Happen*, The Free Press, NY.

March, J. G. and Olsen, J.P. (1975), "The uncertainty of the past: organizational learning under ambiguity", *European Journal of Political Research*, Vol. 3, pp. 147-71.

Marx, K. (1853), "The British Rule in India", Source: MECW Volume 12, p. 125. Written: 10 June 1853. First Published: in New-York Daily Tribune, 25 June 1853. Source: MECW Vol. 12, p. 125. Accessed on 12 June 2004 at http://www.marxists.org/archive/marx/works/1853/06/25.htm.

Maturana, H. R. and Valera, F. J. (1980), *Autopoiesis and Cognition. The Realization of Living,* D. Reidel Publishing Co., Dordrecht, Holland.

Maturana, H. R. and Valera, F. J. (1992), *The Tree of Knowledge. The Biological Roots of Human Understanding*, Shambhala, Boston.

Mazmanian, D. A. and Kraft, M. E. (Eds.), (2001), *Toward Sustainable Communities: Transition and Transformation in Environmental Policy*, MIT Press, Cambridge, Mass.

McFadden, D. (1999), "Rationality for economists?", *Journal of Risk and Uncertainty*, Vol. 19, No.1-3, pp. 73-105.

McKibben, B. (1990), *The End of Nature*, Viking, London.

Mebratu, D. (1998), "Sustainability and sustainable development: historical and conceptual overview", *Environmental Impact Assessment Review*, Vol. 18, pp. 493-520.

Mehrotra, S. R. (1979), *Towards India's Freedom and Partition*, Vikas, New Delhi.

Merton , T. (Ed.). (1965), *Gandhi on Non-Violence. Selected Texts from Mohandas K. Gandhi's Non-Violence in Peace and War*, New Directions, NY.

Mishra, P. (2003), "Rational elitist: a review", *Times Literary Supplement*, 14 December, accessed on 11 November 2004. Available at http://www.powells.com/review/2003_12_14.html

Mission and Public Affairs Council (2005), *Sharing God's Planet. A Christian Vision for a Sustainable Future*, Church House Publishing, London.

Nanda, B. R. (1979), "Gandhi and Jawaharlal Nehru", in Nanda, B. R., Joshi, P. C. and Krishna, R., (Eds.), *Gandhi and Nehru*, Oxford University Press, New Delhi, pp. 1-31.

Nehru, J. (1959), *Discovery of India*, Doubleday, NY.

Palshikar, V. (1969), "Gandhi's economic ideas and their present relevance", in Biswas, S. C. (Ed.), *Gandhi: Theory and Practice. Social Impact and Contemporary Relevance*. Vol II, Indian Institute of Advanced Study, Simla, India, pp. 223-232.

Pathak, D. N. (1969), "Gandhiji: tradition and change. A study in modernisation", in Biswas, S.C. (Ed.), *Gandhi: Theory and Practice. Social Impact and Contemporary Relevance*. Vol II, Indian Institute of Advanced Study, Simla, India, pp. 150-157.

Parekh, B. (1991), *Gandhi's Political Philosophy. A Critical Examination*, Macmillan, Houndsmills.

Power, M. (2003), "Risk management and the responsible organization", in Ericson, R. and Doyle, A. (Eds.), *Risk and Morality*. Toronto University Press, Toronto, pp. 145-164.

Power, M. (2004), *The Risk Management of Everything. Rethinking the Politics of Uncertainty*, Demos, London. Available at www.demos.co.uk

Previts, G. and Merino, B. (1979), *A History of Accounting in America: An Historical Interpretation of the Cultural Significance of Accounting*, A Ronald Press Publication, NY.

Renn, O. (1985), "Risk analysis: scope and limitations", in Otway, H. and Peltu, M. (Eds.), *Regulating Industrial Risks: Science, Hazards and Public Protection*, Butterworths, London, pp. 111-127.

Renn, O., Jaeger, C.C., Rosa, E.A., and Webler, T. (2001), "The rational actor paradigm in risk theories: analysis and critique", in Cohen, M. J. (Ed.), *Risk in the Modern Age. Social Theory, Science and Environmental Decision-Making*, Vol. 3-31. Palgrave, Houndmills, UK.

Rolland, R. (1988), *The Life of Vivekananda and the Universal Gospel*, Trans. Malcolm-Smith, E. F., Advaita Ashrama, Calcutta.

Rudolph, S. and Rudolph, L. (1983), *Gandhi: the Traditional Roots of Charisma*, University of Chicago Press, Chicago.

Saravanamuthu, K. (forthcoming), "Emancipatory accounting and sustainable development: a Gandhian-*Vedic* theorisation of experimenting with truth", *Journal of Sustainable Development*.

Saravanamuthu, K. (2004), "Gandhian-Vedic emancipatory accounting: engendering a spiritual revolution in the interest of sustainable development", *International Conference on Corporate Social Research*, October, University of Nottingham, UK.

Saravanamuthu, K. (2005a), "Corporate Governance: Does any size fit?", *Advances in Public Interest Accounting*, Vol 11.

Saravanamuthu, K. (2005b), "Reflexive modernisation through Gandhi's *satyagrahic* accountability: a search for sustainable practices in the South Australian citrus industry", *Critical Management Studies conference*, 3 to 6 July, University of Cambridge, UK.

SBS News (2005), broadcast on 26 July.

Schumacher, E. F. (1973), *Small is Beautiful: Economics as if People Mattered*, Harper & Row, NY.

Shanahan, D. (2005), "New Asia-Pacific climate plan: Bush and Howard accept greenhouse effect will make things hot", *The Australian*, 27 July, p. 1.

Shapira, Z. (1995), *Risk Taking: A Managerial Perspective*, Russell Sage Foundation, NY.

Simon, H. (1957), *Models of Man: Social and Rational*, John Wiley & Sons, NY.

Spoor, M. (Ed.) (2004), *Globalisation, Poverty and Conflict. A Critical Development Reader*, Kluwer Academic Publishers, Dordrecht.

Steinfeld, E. S. (2004), "China's shallow integration: networked production and the new challenges for later industrialization", *World Development*, Vol. 32, No. 11, pp. 1971-1987.

Tendulkar, D. G. (1960), *Mahatma*, Vol. 5. Government of India Publications Division, Delhi.

Tinker, T. (1985), *Paper Prophets: a Social Critique of Accounting*, Praeger Publishers, NY.

Tinker, T. and Gray, R. (2003), "Beyond a critique of pure reason: from policy to politics to praxis in environmental and social research", *Accounting, Auditing & Accountability Journal*, Vol. 16, No. 5, pp. 727-761.

Tokar, B. (1997), *Earth for Sale: Reclaiming Ecology in the Age of the Corporate Greenwash*, South End Press, Boston, MA.

Turton, H. (2004), "Australia tops the GHG league table", *ECOS*, Issue 120, July-August, p. 6.

Van Dijk, T. A. (1998), "Critical discourse analysis", Second draft for book chapter in Tannen, D., Schiffrin, D. and Hamilton, H. (Eds.) (2001), *Handbook of Discourse Analysis*, Oxford Blackwell, pp. 352-371. Draft accessed in December 2005 at http://www.mfsd.org/debate/vandijk.pdf

Vivekananda, S. (1992a), *The Complete Works of Swami Vivekananda*. Vol. I, Advaita Ashrama, Calcutta.

Vivekananda, S. (1992b), *The Complete Works of Swami Vivekananda*. Vol. II, Advaita Ashrama, Calcutta.

Vivekananda, S. (1992c), *The Complete Works of Swami Vivekananda*. Vol. VI, Advaita Ashrama, Calcutta.

Vivekananda, S. (1992d), "Maya and illusion", in *The Yoga of Knowledge: Jnana Yoga*. Advaita Ashrama, Calcutta, pp. 47-71.

White, L. Jr. (1967), "The historical roots of our ecological crisis", *Science*, Vol. 155, pp. 1203-1207.

Wiggins, S., Marfo, K. and Anchirinah, V. (2004), "Protecting the forest or the people? Environmental policies and livelihoods in the forest margins of southern Ghana", *World Development*, Vol. 32, No. 11, pp. 1939-1955.

Williamson, O. E. (1975), *Markets and Hierarchies: Analysis and Antitrust Implications. A Study in the Economics of Internal Organisation*, The Free Press, NY.

Williamson, O. E. (1985), *The Economic Institutions of Capitalism: Firms, Markets, Relational Contracting*, The Free Press, NY.

Wolfenstein, M. (1957), *Disaster: A Psychological Essay*, Free Press, Glencoe, Ill.

16

POWER AND ACCOUNTING: A GUIDE TO CRITICAL RESEARCH

Danture Wickramasinghe
The University of Manchester, UK

Abstract: This chapter underlies two questions: What is power? How is power related to accounting? Power is defined as influence or control, despite resistance. How power is related to accounting has been seen in a typology of *locations of power* and *levels of analysis*. Two locations of power have been identified: the power *of* accounting and power *over* accounting. The power *of* accounting has been articulated for its ability to generate shared interest among competing groups, to create a powerful language for a managerial discourse, to unfold social and organisational reality through accounting data, and to produce an organisational knowledge for controlling the others. The power *over* accounting has been expressed in terms of its dependence on the power of historically established organisation structures, state politics and crony capitalism, and social cultures and traditions. Along with institutional and organisational levels of analyses, the chapter promotes the use of anti-positivistic methodologies.

Keywords: power of accounting, power over accounting, control, institutional and organisational analysis, legitimacy, resistance.

1.   Introduction

The last 25 years have witnessed accounting research moving from an understanding of accounting as an isolated and neutral technology to an appreciation of accounting as an institutional and social practice (Hopwood & Miller, 1994). An established premise is that the origin of accounting resides in the exercise of social and organisational power rather than a response to the demands for enhancing economic efficiency (Hopper & Armstrong, 1991; Hoskin & Macve, 1988). Studies in accounting have become equivalent to studies on the exercise of power within and beyond organisations. It has been said that power, being embedded in everyday social and organisational life, is fundamental to accounting. It has been revealed that the ways in which accounting holds power (Collier, 2001; Miller & O'Leary, 1987) and that how accounting is embedded in power relations

(Covaleski & Dirsmith, 1986). A considerable body of literature on this has now flourished.

Despite this trend, how accounting and power research could be (and has been) undertaken has gone undocumented. Compared to research on power in organisation theory (Pfeffer, 1980; Mintzberg, 1985; Clegg, 1989; Fincham, 1992) and political sociology (Polsby, 1963; Lukes, 1974), accounting literature remains silent about a review of methods and frameworks by which power research could be undertaken. In an attempt to review this literature, it would be necessary to ask two key questions: What is power? How is power related to accounting? Despite the engagement of addressing almost similar questions in accounting research, a theoretical and methodological review of this body of work has been left unnoticed.

The purpose of this chapter is to review and discuss the theoretical and methodological underpinnings of accounting research on power and to guide researchers interested in this area. The next section presents a review of the broader concept of power. Special attention is drawn to outline the frameworks of power which have been developed in sociology and political theory. This proceeds to categorise the power research in accounting within a typology of *locations of power* and *levels of analysis*. It shows that power can be located either in accounting itself or in other organisational and social apparatus. This creates a dichotomy of power *of* accounting and power *over* accounting. The locations of power can be studied through an analysis, either at the level of the organisation or beyond (or without) it. Later in the chapter, the typology leads to a discussion on the theoretical and methodological underpinnings of *locations of power* and *levels of analysis*. In its elaboration, the chapter draws on numerous theoretical frameworks which have been employed in each of the categories of power research in accounting. This chapter concludes with some implications for future research.

2. What is Power?

In your life, you may have come across situations where some people (or some things) are more powerful than others (other things), so that powerful people influence the behaviour of others to get things done. This influence resembles power. In Weber's (1978) terms, power is one's ability to carry out his/her own will in a social relationship, despite resistance. This ability involves capacity for action, command and control[65]. Sometimes, action itself possesses power for acting, commanding and controlling. This capacity comes from variety of sources. These include authority, distinctive knowledge and skills, ability to manage uncertain situations, access to control of resources, etc.. Establishing authority by setting rules and procedures for action is a common source of power. Exercising power through authority is said to be legitimate where we can see the "hierarchical structure of

---

64   There are a number of sources (see Pfeffer, 1980; Mintzberg, 1985; Clegg, 1989; Fincham, 1992; Pettigrew & McNulty, 1995; Buchanan & Badham, 1999) which define power in organisations. Almost all these reflect a similar idea.

offices and their relations to each other" (Clegg, 1989). Some people exercise power in uncertain situations through their distinctive knowledge, skills and expertise. For example, if there is an uncertainty of breaking down of machines in a factory, then the machine maintenance engineers have more power than the other ordinary workers. Power for controlling resources is another source. When the organisations are arranged as a set of subunits, one subunit possessing essential resources (e.g. knowledge, money, access to top management) would tend to exercise power by influencing the decisions about allocation of resources (Pfeffer & Salancik, 2002). What you have noticed here is that power has to be understood by referring to its sources.

Power creates, and relates to, politics and resistance within and without organisations. When power mobilises through relations, and between people, politics is inevitable. Clegg et al. (2005) define that "the process of mobilizing power is the process of politics" (p. 161). When there is, for example, a new bonus scheme which has been introduced, some groups of people would claim against the new scheme on the grounds that they find some anomalies. This is a common trend in the contemporary world, where the capacity for action is mostly questioned. It is because people live with different cultures with divergent beliefs, language, myths, legends, etc.. Established organisational cultures assimilated with people's cultures tend to question new initiatives in organisations and societies (Pettigrew, 2002). As power mobilises into politics, organisations are prone to enormous contradictions between different groups which produce resistance. Employees, for example, tend to be organised as trade unions and create demands through union actions. Resistance is thus embedded in power relations reacting to initiative enacted by others.

3. Frameworks of Power

The notion of power has attracted a wide spectrum of analyses and reviews in social sciences. Power cannot be understood by referring to a single authority or by providing a universally accepted definition. One best way to proceed is by a review of the debates and teasing out alternative conceptualisations and frameworks. In this section, we shall consider these alternative frameworks, namely early roots of power, single-face of power, two-faces of power, three-faces of power, and circuits of power. The purpose of this review is not to present full accounts of debates. Rather, this is to be a guide for accounting researchers to see the landscape of power concepts from which they might develop a preferred theoretical framework, together with a specific social theory for understanding either power of accounting or power over accounting.

3.1. Early Roots of Power

You may find the works of Lukes (1974), Pfeffer (1980) and Clegg (1989) as excellent summaries and reviews of early contributors, Hobbes (1962) and Machiavelli (1958).

To Hobbes, power is something that can be legislated as an explicit model of order whereby man becomes powerful. This order is constituted by science and monarchy, and with this, man can secure sovereignty. This process is mechanistic, which emphasises motion, causality, agency and action, and generates a discursive framework for understanding what power is. In terms of this conception, power generates from legislation and operates as a discourse. Machiavelli, in contrast, emphasises the practical ways in which power can be secured. These include strategies, deals, negotiations, fraud and conflicts rather than legislation. Here, order can be secured though strategies rather than science and monarchy. This conception is not about what power *is*, as in Hobbes' terms, but what power *does*. To elaborate what actually power *does*, it is important to interpret what actually happens when strategies are adopted, and actions are taken. These two ideas open up two distinct avenues for research. The Hobbes' idea provides us with a prelude for a modern conception of power. Weber's (1978) conception of legal-rational bureaucracy resembles Hobbes' conception of legislation. In contrast, Machiavelli urges us to engage in ethnographic enquiries if we want to define and understand what actually power *does*. This leads to a post-modern turn into power research, as Clegg (1989) observes.

3.2.   Single-Face of Power

Writing in 1957, Robert A. Dahl described power as follows: 'A has power over B to the extent that he can get B to do something that B would not otherwise do' (p. 201). Simply, this conception is about who governs, and it can be tabulated as individual 'successes' and 'defeats' (Lukes, 1974). An understanding of these 'successes' and 'defeats' is an empirical issue: actual behaviour must be studied, especially within a decision-making situation. In this, power can be described, interchangeably, as 'influence' and 'control': 'as the capacity of one actor to do something affecting another actor, which changes the probable pattern of specified future events', as Polsby (1963, pp. 3-4) commented.

Dahl's conception of power represents the single-face framework which focuses on behaviour in decision-making over key important issues. In this, there can be actual observable conflicts of subjective interests, and these interests can be seen in policy preferences reflected in political participation. Power represents the ability to make decisions under such circumstances. It is single-face because it focuses on one object: observable behaviour towards making concrete decisions. In short, single-face framework argues for observable issues and conflicts which can be seen in political agendas and actions. Here, power is manifested in structures (e.g. organisations and societies) rather than in agencies (individuals).

Hardy (1996) follows Dahl's idea of power, through Lukes (1974), to link the notion of power to a managerial context. Here, single-face of power is about influencing decision outcomes through key resources such as information, knowledge, control of money, rewards and sanctions etc.[66] Continuous deployment of 'carrot' and 'stick' would be the main strategy ensuring the desired behavioural outcome. To Hardy, the type of power under such situations is *power of resources*. Resources such as accounting information or control systems would have such power and, in turn, can facilitate the strategies that would ensure desired behaviour. As will be shown later, linking Hardy's ideas to institutional theory, Burns (2000) studied how accounting was instrumental in the mobilisation of power.

3.3. Two-Faces of Power

In response to Dahl, Bachrach and Baratz (1962) introduced the concept of two-faces of power. When there is a decision-making situation (doing things), they have identified, there is a non-decision-making situation (things do not get done) as well. When power is exercised in decision-making, attention is drawn to avoid some other decisions. In other words, decision-making and non-decision-making occur at the same time, or every decision-making situation has implications for what has not yet been decided. Here, power represents coercion, influence, authority, force and manipulation: coercion is to secure compliance by threat of deprivation; influence is to change one's course of action without resorting to a threat of severe deprivation; authority represents procedures which can be made legitimate and reasonable. Under these circumstances, objects of analysis are different to single-face of power in that it involves interpretive understanding of intentional actions, non-decisions, and potential issues.

Under non-decision-making situations, an organisation has to deal with not only existing issues at hand but also ensuing potential issues, not only observable overt conflicts between groups but also hidden covert conflicts, not only policy preferences being revealed in political participation but also policy preferences embedded in sub-political grievances. This demands wider scopes of methodologies to capture the realities of power.

According to Hardy (1996), the type of power in this context is termed as *power of process*. In organisations, dominant groups may use the device of non-decision-making to protect the power status. However, through political actions, such a non-decision-making situation could be extended to normal decision-making situations by which changes could be brought, depending on exiting values and norms being compatible with the new ones. Hardy and Redivo (1994) examined such effects. How new accounting systems can gain such a compatibility is an area being examined in accounting studies (e.g. Burns and Scapens, 2000).

3.3.1. Three-faces of power: This is not a particular framework. Rather, it provides a substantial critique of both the single-face and two-face frameworks. The main authority of this critique is Lukes (1974). He argues that those two views are too individualistic and apolitical because potential issues are kept out of politics, not

---

65 Early studies in management and control (Hickson *et al.*, 1971; Pettigrew, 1973; Pfeffer and Salancik, 1974) examined these types of power relations.

only through decisions (or non-decisions) but also through broader social forces and institutional practices. Lukes shows that conflicts can be latent representing contradictions between the interests of those exercising power and those subject to it. The three-face framework leads us to explore the questions of how structures (resources and rules) as well as agencies (individual actions) influence decisions, and how potential issues can be concealed. This framework adds a sociological flavour to the analysis of power which captures social (classes, castes, religions, etc.) and institutional practices (values, cultures, mores, etc.).

Hardy (1996) terms this as *power of meaning*. People in organisations tend to follow meanings about the *status quo*. A study on a factory closure (Hardy, 1985), a number of justifications such as redundancy compensation and managerial credibility were found which were brought on to the table. These justifications – meanings about the *status quo* – had power to legitimise the closure. Although this type of power reflects enormous complexities, Hardy shows, the strategy of creating meanings would be most effective. Accounting has a vital role to play in the construction of such meanings (Roberts and Scapens, 1985).

3.3.2. Circuits of power: Having focused on the connections of power with relationships, techniques, procedures, knowledge, and environmental contingencies, Clegg (1989) has identified that power can be seen in a circuit. To Clegg, the circuit is meant for understanding the complexity between relationships, their meanings, strategies and outcomes. So, power cannot be theorised in a single concept: different concepts must be grouped into multilayered clusters for identifying distinct but closely related concepts of power. Clegg clusters these concepts as agency, dispositional and facilitative concepts of power. Within these relationships, positive outcomes as well as resistance, controls as well as consensuses, reproduction as well as transformations, facilitations as well as restrictions, empowerment as well as disempowerment, can be identified.

This framework encompasses three arenas of focus: episodic power relations which move through social relations and arenas of struggles reproducing and transforming rules; rules of practices which entail certain rules for operating controls; and domination which acts over the others. It operates at three levels: agency (individual actions), social integration (interacting with social forces), and system integration (technological means of control over all physical and social environment and the resources associated with these controls). Subject to exogenous environmental contingencies and internal relationships between agencies and members, within the circuits of power, rules and their meanings are fixed and new disciplinary practices are introduced.

The circuit contains every systemic ramification of power within an organisation. Hardy's (1996) idea of *power of systems* is similar to this idea of circuits of power. When a system is in place, people unconsciously follow cultures, values, norms, beliefs, etc. which have been established. When managers want to bring about change, they need to break or change this systemic power. To break or change, managers tend to use the powers of resources, processes and meanings. Accounting is embedded in these powers and, perhaps, dominates them. In other words, accounting can mobilise those types of power to change or break the circuits of power, the power of exiting system (Burns, 2000).

4. Power and Accounting

Accounting is one of social, institutional[67] and organisational practices which play a role of calculating, reporting, and controlling organisational apparatuses (Hopwood and Miller, 1994). As a social and institutional practice, accounting can be an enabling force in the configuration of social and organisational orders, or accounting can be embedded in political and cultural ramifications in these orders. With regard to the functioning of accounting as an organisational and institutional practice, there is a fundamental question you may want to explore: Is accounting a source of power or subject to power? If accounting is a source of power, then you might want to investigate how this source of power emerges and operates in an organisational and institutional context. If accounting is subject to the power of other organisational and institutional apparatus, then you might want to examine what they are, and how they interact with accounting. These questions lead us to a typology, as shown in Figure 1. In this, the connection of power with accounting is seen as a dichotomy of power *of* accounting and power *over* accounting,[68] together with two levels of analysis: organisational (internal) and institutional (external).

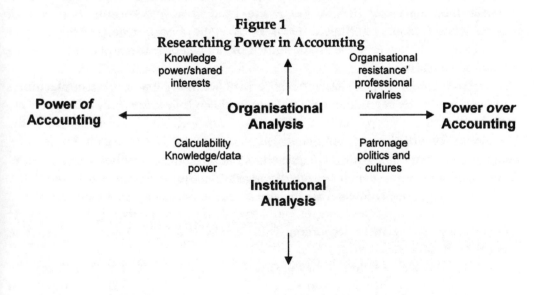

Figure 1
Researching Power in Accounting

---

[67] Institutions mean social, cultural, legal and economic practices prevalent in a society. There are three variants of institutionalism: neoclassical institutional economic, old institutional economic, and new sociological (for more details, see Burns and Scapens, 2000).

[68] In a similar vein, Scapens and Roberts (1993) used the terms 'power to do' and 'power over'.

4.1.   Power of Accounting

Power *of* accounting implies accounting being a holder of power. To hold power, accounting must be a particular resource to be used by decision makers. If this is not successful, then accounting can facilitate a particular political process to be a power of process. Finally, accounting can be powerful to create meanings through a particular language of business. In a sense, power *of* accounting, as a resource, would get diluted through processes and meaning systems. However, if accounting seems to be a power of resource, it can be an enabling practice that overcomes other types of organisational and institutional power. In this, accounting plays a leading role in the configuration of social and organisational apparatuses.

Weber (1978) considered accounting as one of fundamental practices in the formation of capitalism. It is because, Weber argued, accounting is the basis for the development of rational calculations upon which modern enterprises emerged and developed. Accounting's power of calculations operates in two ways, as Weber illustrated. One is *ex-ante* calculations of potential risks and chances of profits, and the other is *ex-post* calculation of actual profits and losses realised. When analysing this importance of accounting as a powerful practice, one can undertake divergent analyses from micro-organisational aspects to macro-institutional aspects (Colignon and Covaleski, 1991). Accounting's superiority has also been highlighted by accounting historians. Sombart (1953) showed that accounting was instrumental in the establishment capitalism. He argued that double-entry book-keeping transformed the world into figures where production and consumption became calculations (Miller and Napier, 1993). Both Weber and Sombart discerned that accounting held power to the establishment of rational practices and capitalist ethos in modern societies.

To Marxist writers, accounting techniques are capable of manufacturing worker consent by reproducing class interest and so-called efficiency (Hopper *et al.*, 1987). Writing on the power of accountants, Armstrong (1987) showed that, in the evolution of British capitalist enterprise, accountants within organisations were capable of competing with other professionals for controlling the labour process, and accountancy profession became prominent in this historical epoch. Similarly, Anderson *et al.* (1997) found that the rise of the accountancy profession in British management was a priesthood of industry. It has been analysed that corporate control and management accounting were a powerful force controlling labour in post-war Britain (Armstrong, 1993).

The Marxist perspective has always been structural, in that they define the roles of accounting in relation to structural changes in the broader socio-political context. There are theoretical stances where structural forces are kept out of the centre of analysis. For example, the Foucauldian approach to power of accounting is that accounting has knowledge power, and this power stems from writing, examination and grading (Hoskin and Macve, 1994). This approach refutes the proposition that accounting calculations are directly linked to the development of capitalism. Agreeing with Yamey (1964), who showed that there is no direct relationship between double-entry book-keeping and the rise of capitalism, Hoskin and Macve illustrated that writing, which developed within schools and universities in the late eighteenth century, gave rise to knowledge which made the individuals disciplined. Disciplinary practices became an integral part of enterprises. Accounting was one of these disciplinary practices through which writing, examination and gradating were executed. Accounting, as Miller and O'Leary (1987) showed, made individuals governable persons. In the name of accounting, performance of individuals was to be calculated, recorded, and graded, and, in this way, accounting performed the power of calculability. It was the calculative ability of accounting which led to the development of capitalist enterprises, not double-entry book-keeping (Miller and Napier, 1993).

Between the structural and post-structural perspectives, there is the structuration theory developed by Anthony Giddens. According to Giddens, there is a social process whereby agent (capacities of individuals) and structure (capacities of systems: rules and resources) interact. In this interaction, regulations and social orders are produced and reproduced. So, the structures are the outcomes of those interactions. There are three analytical layers in this structuration process: signification, domination and legitimation. Signification creates meanings for social interactions, domination produces power, and legitimation provides system morality (Scapens and Roberts, 1993). In this theoretical context, power is related to conflict and resistance only if interests (of capital and labour) do not coincide. If accounting coincides with others' interests, then it can achieve hierarchical controls, otherwise there would be resistance. Roberts and Scapens (1985) termed those two situations as 'power to do' and 'power over', respectively. 'Power to do' can share interests and eliminate resistance, while 'power over' would create conflicts between interests and produce resistance. As long as accounting can signify, dominate and legitimise, it holds power, otherwise it would produce resistance.

Similar explanations can be found in institutional economic theory, which focuses on rules, routines and institutions (Burns and Scapens, 2000). When people in organisations come to exercise their power over the others, they may tend to use accounting initiatives to legitimise the exercise of power. Burns (2000) reported that a product development department of the firm he studied had exercised its power over the colleagues when a new accounting system was introduced. Using Hardy's (1996) framework, Burns found that their power was in a mobilisation process through the new accounting system. Accounting had power to make people powerful for them to mobilise their power over the others. In so doing, rules become routines, and routines become institutionalised. These rules and routines represent new accounting, and they can shape the political behaviour of actors. Here, the routines become institutionalised only if there is the consent of the actors. This would not occur if accounting cannot be an enabling force to change people's previous routines. As with the structuration theory, accounting holds power as long as it can construct institutionalised routines.

4.1.1.   Organisational level analysis: An organisational level analysis on power of accounting seeks the issues of micro-politics and resistance in relation to the roles of accounting. Case study approaches to collecting and analysing data are now an acceptable and popular methodological and epistemological stance for undertaking these types of analyses. Within such analyses, more emphasis is drawn on the functioning of organisation apparatus, including evolution of organisation structure, its control system, its established institutions such as rules and procedures, traditions, cultures, its professional groupings, etc. An analysis can be executed to tease out the power of accounting being a forerunner for most of this apparatus. It does not mean that broader external factors are unimportant. Rather, it is a methodological discipline focusing the analysis on a particular aspect rather than being ambitious to be a 'smart researcher' capturing 'everything'. A number of accounting researchers have turned to be of this category, analysing how power of accounting is visible and illuminated within an organisational setting.

One of the pervasive accounting devices being operated in an organisational context is budgeting. Budgets have power as long as they can get things done. There are a number of examples where budgets were powerful. Focusing on an organisational level analysis, Collier (2001) found that, in a police force, the system of devolved budget became powerful. Despite some resistance developed with an understanding of this system as a distraction from operational policing, managers saw the devolved budget was enabling the administrators to allocate their resources in accordance with local priorities and requirements. In order to explain this accounting initiative theoretically, Collier used Gidden's structuration theory which does not see power as a conflicting phenomenon. In this case, the new accounting initiative soon coincided with the interests of administrators. Administrators came to share the interests between 'those pursuing accountability and those pursuing technical work activity'. Actions of agencies (administrators) and influences of structures (new accounting system) became a shared interest. Accounting had been seen as a powerful structure bringing new rules and procedures into the existing management control system. Devolved budget became a powerful control device enabling the administrators to consider local priorities and requirements. The type of power that accounting had been holding was facilitative, rather than casual or dispositional. Looking from the angels of Hardy's ideas, this is a power of accounting coupled with a political process that has created a particular meaning about the role of devolved budgets.

Regarding the construction of meanings, Christensen (2004) found that accounting was instrumental in making and remaking a discourse. The discourse was for the elimination of Japanese Language Programme and for the retrenchment of the lecturer on 'some' strategic grounds. However, there were no accounting data supporting this discourse. Instead, accounting words such as 'viability', 'on-cost', 'capital contribution', borrowing against future grants' created a powerful language for establishing the above discourse. These accounting words were seen to be powerful in the construction of a particular managerialist ideology. To make sense of this organisational event, Christensen used Foucault's power/knowledge framework. The use of accounting words seemed to be a disciplinary practice. Being enlightened by these accounting words, managers had maintained their power position over the Japanese language programme. What we learn from this is that power of accounting does not rest only on accounting numbers (calculative power of accounting). Power of accounting words also seems to be creating legitimacy for decision making through the construction of organisational discourses. However, the type of power operated in this context had been developed into dispositional rather than a facilitative type.

However, the power accounting cannot be an ultimate organisational outcome. What could be real is that struggle to preserve power, there would be a continuous game. A study by Kurunmaki (1999) illustrated the power of a financial management initiative by which cost centres of a Finnish hospital were transformed into profit centres. The main aim of this programme was to transform the systems of accountability, which was powered by medical and health professionals, into a system signalled by competitive market environment. In this transformation, the power of medical health professionals have transferred into the hands of financial experts, marking a vital role for accounting. However, the continuous struggle for this redistribution of power and control in the Finnish hospitals remains unfinished.[69]

4.1.2.   Institutional Level Analysis: An institutional level analysis on power over accounting considers broader socio-structural factors such as economy, culture, ethnicity, gender, professions, programmes such as privatisation, liberalisation, new public management, or trends such as globalisation, financialisation, digitalisation of production technologies, etc. The functioning of accounting within organisations is not independent of these structural aspects. Sometimes, accounting is instrumental in accommodating these aspects, and at other times, accounting's power becomes subordinated to them. An institutional level analysis seeks the dialectic and historical interplays between organisations and these exogenous factors, programmes and trends. This focus would allow us to address the issue of how accounting can become powerful in the configuration of these factors into a particular social and organisation order.

From such a broader perspective on the power of accounting, Shaoul (1997) illustrated a particular socio-economic reality mirrored by those accounting data. To unfold a set of issues around water privatisation in the UK, Shaoul has used an accounting model which concerned how 'financial surplus is created within a firm

---

[69] The theoretical framework for this analysis was based on French philosopher, Pierre Bourdieu's ideas of 'field' and 'capital'.

and then distributed to the different stakeholders'. The analysis has revealed that the government's claim – privatisation of water would improve industrial performance through the discipline of the market – cannot be substantiated. The value-added model and cash-flow analysis had come to refute assumptions about 'superiority of private ownership', 'public sector inefficiency', and 'stakeholder economy'. This indicated that 'the constructive and enabling power of the accounting model' was able to challenge the ways in which 'existing problems' were defined, and the ways in which 'alternative problems and solutions' can be offered. In this case, the institutional factor was the water privatisation programme and its all government politics and rosy expectations of policy makers. Through its explanatory power, accounting had revealed that the privatisation programme cannot be a tenable public policy.[70]

The power of accounting can also be understood in relation to wider socio-economic and historical transformation of societies. Hooper and Pratt (1993) studied the power of accounting in the development of capitalism in New Zealand. To substantiate the power of accounting in this transformation, the authors used a case study of the development of farming enterprises from the 1920s to 1930s and focused on the mechanisms of change in terms of exercise of power. Following Foucault, Christensen found that the knowledge power of accounting has been supportive in the capital accumulation towards protecting wealth. In capitalism, wealth must be given into the hands of workers for the wealth to work towards making profit and accumulating capital. Thus wealth must be protected, and knowledge power is a protecting mechanism. In New Zealand, the development of capitalism was much related to the use of the power of accounting by which Maori land was acquired, and the Maori community was made to be a commodity. The study had provided detailed rich accounts as to how it happened. Despite why accounting did support in the transformation of the economy cannot be substantiated by employing Foucault,[71] this case study has proved that the Foucauldian approach can be used to understand the power of accounting, not only within a micro-political setting but also within a wider socio-historical context.

4.2. Power over Accounting

Power over accounting means possible failures of accounting or dysfunctional effects of accounting because of the power of non-accounting factors such as organisational cultures, power of other organisational professionals, and usual and unintended events and incidents occurring in the broader social system. This does not mean that accounting is not important at all. There must be situations and conditions against which accounting has to struggle. This is true, as accounting is not the only mechanism of power. When Miller and O'Leary (1987) argue that

---

[70] Because of this power of accounting, media people use public accounting data to criticise government policies and to unveil corporate scandals.

[71] This is because Foucault used to conceal class interest in modern capitalism.

'various technical expertises such as accounting' come together to constitute knowledge power, they really mean that there is other expertise which may run over accounting. The purpose of this section is to highlight how accounting struggles to secure power in the midst of such situations and conditions.

To reinforce this idea of accounting's struggle, we shall consider one such 'non-accounting' force: labour responses to the managerial manipulation of accounting numbers. Despite the argument that accounting is powerful as it reproduces capitalists' interest (Hopper et al., 1987), there are occasions where the validity of accounting numbers is questioned by the labour force. Bougen (1989) provided evidence to argue that managers had to abandon 'accounting explanations' of factory performance, as the workforce wanted to hear 'common sense' explanations. Marking how the explanatory power of accounting is subject to such challenges in an industrial relations context, Bougen et al. (1990) reinforced this phenomenon by producing a case study of the coal industry. They reported that once, accounting was accepted from the 1870s (appearance of accounting), and next, it was rejected from 1911. The rejection was due to a number of reasons. First, accountants who were capable of handling accounting as an economic discourse failed to see how accounting was implicated in a moral (more ethical and human) discourse in which wage negotiations were carried out. Second, mine-workers tended not to see any explanations provided by accounting stories or any equivalent stories as a legitimate explanation about 'standard of life'. Third, as accounting was rejected by mine-workers, there was no chance to validate the usefulness of accounting at all.

In this way, a number of propositions have been advanced to argue for the failures of accounting's power. Despite the fact that accounting is related to organisational power in terms of the use of accounting and control systems in decision-making (Pettigrew, 1972), changing organisational performance (Dornbusch and Scott, 1975), and conferring legitimacy (Meyer and Rowan, 1977), Markus and Pfeffer (1983) showed that accounting's power is diluted in a number of situations. First, resistance to the implementation of new information systems would occur when the existing power distribution is challenged, e.g. the change in location of accounting systems from divisional to corporate level. Second, resistance would occur when the paradigms of accounting are changed, for example, a change from a managerial reporting to an external reporting. Third, resistance would occur when information systems come to impose on organisational functions where there is an inherent culture of making decisions in a different manner, e.g. even though the new systems were expected to quantify everything, it was difficult to quantify clinical judgements expressed by a cardiologist. Such propositions and related observations suggest that accounting's power for influencing and changing is a contestable terrain.

The powerlessness of accounting can be captured by a number of theoretical frameworks. If we want to adopt a broader structural – political economy framework, then we may undertake a broader institutional analysis to see how social and institutional forces reject the importance of accounting. Some structural factors captured by critical accounting research are bureaucracy (Wickramasinghe *et al.*, 2004), ethnicity (Dave, 2005), cultures and traditions (Wickramasinghe and Hopper, 2005), state politics (Uddin and Hopper, 2001), etc. If we take a structuration theory perspective, then we may find how accounting struggles in the construction of a social and organisational order when institutionalised practices are much more powerful than the power of accounting (Scapens and Roberts, 1993). If we take the institutional theory, then we may see how accounting is confronted with other organisational factors making accounting change projects unsuccessful (Markus and Pfeffer, 1983). Whatever the framework you may use, it must guide you to a better focus. With an appropriate framework, you may focus your study either on an organisational or institutional level analysis.

4.2.1. Organisational Level Analysis: An organisational level analysis contemplates how accounting's orthodox functions are questioned, rejected or, at least, differently shaped by other organisational factors such as politics, resistance and culture.

Following Cyert and March (1963), Wildavsky (1965), Pondy (1970), and Pfeffer and Salancik, (1978), Covaleski and Dirsmith (1986) argued that budgeting cannot always be a rational means of achieving organisational objectives. Instead, budgets were implicated in organisational political bargaining, control and power. Through a naturalistic methodology, they studied the effects of a new computerised accounting and budgeting system being implemented. Being clinical workers attending to patients' care, nurse managers were now required to tend a budget. The nursing managers were the main actors who had provided interpretations about the budgeting initiative. Their main concern was that they did not see any positive effect of the new budgeting system on external communication. They urged that budgeting was 'inadequate for reflecting and representing the variety and multifaceted nature of nursing'. They found 'critical attacks' on the system 'in terms of its output being poor, too much, too little, too late, and too inaccurately' (p. 205). As long as the nurses did not enjoy the new budgeting system, responsibility and authority were misaligned; the accountability system was ill-defined; and the resource allocation function was under a flux. However, system implementers hoped that budgeting would operate in a rational manner. This unexpected circumstance had created two political camps: the rational camp of system implementers and the opposing camp of nurse managers. The system was implemented through political processes where actions were symbolically and ritually rationalised and legitimised, rather than just accepting what system implementers wanted. Thus rational budgeting, in this case, has little power in influencing the functioning of an organisational control system.

Scapens and Roberts (1993) did a similar study on resistance to a new accounting system introduced into an engineering division of a large multidivisional company. The new system aimed to improve the quality of management information. The existing system suffered from some 'inconsistencies in the information they were receiving from the unit companies'. To introduce a better system, a project team was assigned. Their task was to implement a new computer-based management information system. However, they were encountering 'increasing level of resistance'. The project manager saw the resistance he encountered as an irrational act. But in terms of structuration theory, the theory they used in this study, is not so irrational. There was a market demand to change the organisation structure (and its accountability system) from a centralised form to a decentralised form. However, this change had not been complete, as old habits of a centralised, functionally-based accountability system were still persistent. In this context, resistance developed as the new initiative came to challenge the existing power position. The structural power had developed throughout organisational history, and the resistance was linked to this context, together with a number of other 'interrelated influences'. Here, structuration theory was a sensitising tool to focus on the exercise of power, especially through the processes of signification, legitimation and domination. The existing power was still dominating the power of accounting until the new system gets legitimised.

4.2.2. Institutional Level Analysis: Here, we focus on external factors which shape internal control systems. We see how the power of accounting becomes 'subservient' to these factors, and how accounting would become 'unimportant'. Two distinct examples are considered: Uddin and Hopper (2001) and Wickramasinghe and Hopper (2005). One thing to note here is that the underlying external factors such as culture and politics can be much more prevalent in developing countries where capitalism has not yet been fully developed. It does not mean, however, that institutional factors can be found only in developing countries!

Uddin and Hopper (2001) considered state politics, political parties, classes, trade unions and external financial institutions as structural factors. The study was based on an intensive case study, and theoretically, it drew on Michael Burawoy's (1985) concept of 'politics of production'.[72] What they found was that power to maintain accounting control was subject to politics of production which was transformed from a colonial despotic regime through a hegemonic regime to the present market-based despotic regime. The paper concentrated on hegemonic and market-based regimes of accounting controls. The hegemonic regime was largely political, in that workers were motivated by political expectations of trade unions and politicians. These politics penetrated through influence on the internal labour market, internal state and gaming behaviour. Thus accounting controls were not important. Instead, accounting acted as a ceremonial practice sending reports to ministries and official authorities. The control system in this regime was hegemonic,

---

[72] It shows that politics at the point of production can develop worker consent through internal markets, states and games.

by which workers enjoyed the influence of politics. Privatisation brought the new market-based regime where politicians tended to abandon exerting political influences. Now, physical forms rather than cost and accounting forms of control came to facilitate coercive pressures upon managers and operators. What eventually happened was that, as the regulatory mechanism was weak, new crony capitalism came to benefit from the enterprise, which the international aid agencies did not expect to happen.

Wickramasinghe and Hopper (2005) have reported how external culture affects internal budgeting system in a factory located in a *Sinhalese* village in Sri Lanka. Theoretically, the paper developed a cultural political economy framework which defines reciprocal relationships between mode of production, culture, state, and politics. Power was exercised not only through formal relationships between state agencies, trade unions and the mill management, but also through informal relationships with village cultures. As a means to achieve internal control, production budgets were prepared. But the targets were determined not only by rational planning and market signals but also by the workers' inspirations stemming from village traditions with which they used to live. These traditions developed and evolved from Kingship regimes of control, and were assimilated with modern trade union and political party influences. Thus power of production budgets was challenged by these combined effects of cultural political economy. Culture and associated politics are more powerful than the attempts of controlling employees through production budgets.

5. Way Forward

It has been observed that accounting is central in the exercise of power within and beyond organisations. You have seen that there is no unitary framework of power in social and human sciences. Given the centrality of power in any social relation, power is a central concept in any social and organisation theory. Assertions and propositions put forward in early roots and one-face of power (power of resources) have provided you with some parameters for defining the notion of power. However, the definition becomes complicated when you have looked through two-faces (power of processes), three-faces (power of meanings) and circuits of power (power of systems). 'Circuits of power' is a combination of all possible power theories. Possibly, it is more ambitious to use this whole framework in a single study, as a deeper analysis always requires a well focused theoretical framework. Instead, circuits of power may help start developing a framework, but a chosen segment of this framework may be more useful for focusing on a particular aspect of your research.

Regarding the power of accounting, there are essential questions to explore. One set of questions is related to the power of accounting: Is accounting a source of power? If so, how does this power emerge and operate in a social and organisational context? Another set of questions is related to the power over accounting: Is accounting subject to other sources of power? If so, what are these forces and how do they affect the functioning of accounting in a social and organisational context? Along with these questions, a typology of 'locations of power' and 'levels of analysis' has been used to organise our review. It must be remembered that the typology is not a theoretical framework of power *per se*. Rather, it categorises the dimensions of power literature with a view to relating those categories to the key questions above. A theory you may use for your piece of research should be a specific one. In the discussion, we have seen how such specific theories are related to power *of* accounting and power *over* accounting.

Attention was drawn to the use of an anti-positivistic case study/qualitative methodology as opposed to positivistic sample/quantitative studies. We have promoted critical rather than prescriptive-functional perspectives[73] on power research in accounting. We did not want to criticise or underestimate the importance of the latter. Instead, we wanted to respect the growing interest in and meaningfulness of the former. Interrelated influences related to power *over* accounting, as Scapens and Roberts (1993) remarked, and multiple meanings attached to the power *of* accounting, as Miller and O'Leary (1987) commented, can be well captured in detail if we adopt anti-positivistic methodologies. We should not be ambitious for generalising our piece of work in hand to all 'times and spaces'. The domain of social sciences, including accounting, has little room for so-called generalisation. Instead, we should be patient enough to understand how power operates in a particular setting.

We wish to conclude this chapter by reiterating the dichotomy of power *of* and power *over*. On the one hand, we have seen that, as accounting is capable of generating shared interest among competing groups, as accounting is smart enough to create a powerful language for a managerial discourse, as accounting is powerful in unfolding social realities by means of publicly available data, and as accounting knowledge is able to transform primitive societies into modern industrial ones, accounting would be a powerful organisational and institutional practice. In this, accounting would dominate other organisational resources, processes and meaning systems. If the organisations are institutionalised with these powers, accounting can be made powerful to break existing systems through which strategic changes can be brought. In research, we need to see how this happens.

On the other hand, we have seen that, as some professional groups would negatively react to new accounting systems, as historically established organisation structures would not be prepared to compromise with ensuing systems of accountability, as state politics and crony capitalism would come to arrest the need of accounting, and as cultures and traditions influence the management to neglect rational accounting data, accounting would not be the most powerful organisational

---

[72] One example of such a piece of research is that by Abernethy and Vagnoni (2004). This is an important study dealing with quantitative data collected from questionnaires.

and institutional practice. In this, other resources, processes and meaning systems would come to occupy in the functioning of management controls in organisations. If you are confronted with such cases, then you may want to see how accounting becomes dysfunctional or unimportant in the face of other organisational and institutional powers which reflect in resources, processes and meaning systems.

References

Abernethy, M. A. and Vagnoni, E. (2004), "Power, organizational design and managerial behaviour", *Accounting, Organizations and Society*, Vol. 29, No. 3/4, pp. 207-225.

Anderson, M., Edwards, J. R. and Mathews, D. (1997), *The Priesthood of Industry: The Rise of the Professional Accountant in British Management*, Oxford University Press, Oxford.

Armstrong, P. (1987), "The rise of accounting controls in British capitalist enterprises", *Accounting, Organizations and Society*, Vol. 12, No. 5, pp. 415-436.

Armstrong, P. (1993), "Professional knowledge and social mobility: postwar changes in the knowledge-base of management accounting", *Work, Employment and Society*, Vol. 7, No. 1, pp. 1-21.

Bachrach, P. and Baratz, M. S. (1962), "Two faces of power", *American Political Science Review*, Vol. 56, No. 4, pp. 947-952.

Bougen, P. D. (1989), "The emergence, roles and consequences of an accounting-industrial relations interactions", *Accounting, Organizations and Society*, Vol. 14, No. 3, pp. 203-234.

Bougen, P. D., Ogden, S. G. and Outram, Q. (1990), "The appearance and disappearance of accounting: wage determination in The U.K. coal industry", *Accounting Organizations and Society*, Vol. 15, No. 3, pp. 149-170.

Buchanan, D. and Badham, R. (1999), *Power Politics and Organizational Change: Winning the Tuff Game*, Sage, London.

Burawoy, M. (1985), *The Politics of Production*, Verso, London.

Burns, J. and Scapens, R. (2000), "Conceptualising management accounting change: an institutional framework", *Management Accounting Research*, Vol. 11, No. 1, pp. 3-25.

Burns, J. (2000), "The dynamics of accounting change: inter-play between new practices, routines, institutions, power and politics", *Accounting, Auditing & Accountability Journal*, Vol. 13, No. 5, pp. 566-596.

Christensen, M. (2004), "Accounting by words not numbers: the handmaiden of power in the academy", *Critical Perspectives on Accounting*, Vol. 15, No. 4/5, pp. 485-512.

Clegg, S. R. (1989), *Frameworks of Power*, Sage, London.

Clegg, S., Kornberger, M. & Pitsis, T. (2005) *Managing and organizations: an introduction to theory and practice*, Sage, London.

Colignon, R. and Covaleski, M. (1991), "A Weberian framework in the study of accounting", *Accounting, Organizations and Society*, Vol. 16, No. 2, pp. 141-157.

Collier, P. M. (2001), "The power of accounting: a field study of local financial management in a police force", *Management Accounting Research*, Vol. 12, No. 4, pp. 465-486.

Covaleski, M. A. and Dirsmith, M. W. (1986), "The budgetary process of power and politics", *Accounting, Organizations and Society*, Vol. 11, No. 3, pp. 193-214.

Cyert, R. M and March, J. G. (1963), *A Behavioural Theory of the Firm*, Prentice Hall, Englewood Cliffs.

Dahl, R. A. (1957), "The Concept of Power", *Behavioural Science*, Vol. 2, No. 3, pp. 201-205.

Dave, S. S. K. (2005), "The politics of accounting, race and ethnicity: a story of a chiefly-based preferencing", *Critical Perspectives on Accounting*, Vol. 16, No. 5, pp. 551-577.

Dornbusch, S. M. and Scott, W. R. (1975), *Evaluation and the Exercise of Authority: A Theory of Control Applied to Diverse Organizations*, Jossey-Bass, San Francisco.

Fincham, R. (1992), "Perspective on power: processual, institutional and internal forms of organizational power", *Journal of Management Studies*, Vol. 29, Fall, pp. 741-759.

Hardy, C. and Redivo, F. (1994), "Power and organizational development: a framework for organizational change", *Journal of General Management*, Vol. 20, No. 1, pp.1-13.

Hardy, C. (1985), *Managing Organizational Closure*, Grower, Aldershot, UK.

Hardy, C. (1996), "Understanding of power: bringing about strategic change", *British Journal of Management*, Special Issue, pp. s3-s16.

Hickson, D. J., Hinings, C. R., Lee, C. A., Schneck, R. E. and Pennings, J. M. (1971), "A strategic contingencies theory of intra-organizational power", *Administrative Science Quarterly*, Vol. 16, No. 2, pp. 216-229.

Hobbes, T. (1962), *Leviathan*, Macmillan, London.

Hooper, K. and Pratt, M. (1993), "The growth of agricultural capitalism and the power of accounting: a New Zealand study", *Critical Perspectives on Accounting*, Vol. 4, No. 3, pp. 247-274.

Hopper, T. M., Storey, J. and Wilmott, H. (1987), "Accounting for accounting: towards the development of a dialectical view", *Accounting, Organizations and Society*, Vol. 12, No. 5, pp. 437-456.

Hopper, T. and Armstrong, P. (1991), "Cost accounting, controlling labour and the rise of conglomerates", *Accounting, Organizations and Society*, Vol. 16, No. 5/6, pp. 405-438.

Hopwood, A. G. and Miller, P. (1994), *Accounting as Social and Institutional Practice*, Cambridge University Press, Cambridge.

Hoskin, K. and Macve, R. (1994), "Writing, examining, disciplining: the genesis of accounting's modern power", in Hopwood, A. G. and Miller, P. (Eds.), *Accounting as Social and Institutional Practice*, Cambridge University Press, Cambridge, pp. 67-97.

Hoskin, K. W. and Macve, R. H. (1988), "The genesis of accountability: the West Point connections", *Accounting, Organizations and Society*, Vol. 13, No. 1, pp. 37-73.

Kurunmaki, L. (1999), "Professional vs. financial capital in the field of health care – struggles for the redistribution of power and control", *Accounting, Organizations and Society*, Vol. 24, No. 2, pp. 95-124.

Lukes, S. (1974), *Power: A Radical View*, Macmillan, London.

Machiavelli, N. (1958), *The Prince*, Everyman, London.

Markus, M. L. and Pfeffer, J. (1983), "Power and the design and implementation of accounting and control systems", *Accounting, Organizations and Society*, Vol. 8, No. 2/3, pp. 205-218.

Meyer, J. and Rowan, B. (1977), "Institutionalized organizations: formal structure as myth and ceremony", *American Journal of Sociology*, Vol. 83, No. 2, pp. 340-363.

Miller, P. and Napier, C. (1993), "Genealogies of calculation", *Accounting, Organizations and Society*, Vol. 18, No. 7/8, pp. 631-647.

Miller, P. and O'Leary, T. (1987), "Accounting and the construction of governable person", *Accounting, Organizations and Society*, Vol. 12, No. 3, pp. 235-265.

Mintzberg, H. (1985), "The organization as a political arena", *Journal of Management Studies*, Vol. 22, No. 2, pp.133-154.

Pettigrew, A. and McNulty, T. (1995), "Power and influence in and around the boardroom", *Human Relations*, Vol. 48, No. 8, pp. 845-874.

Pettigrew, A. (1973), *The Politics of Organizational Decision-Making*, Tavistock, London.

Pettigrew, A. (2002), "Strategy formulation as a political process", in Clegg, S. R. (Ed.), *Central Currents in Organization Studies II: Contemporary Trends*, Sage, London, pp. 43-49.

Pettigrew, A. M. (1972), "Information control as a power resource", *Sociology*, Vol. 6, No. 2, pp. 187-204.

Pfeffer, J. (1980), *Power in organizations*, Pitman, Massachusetts.

Pfeffer, J. and Salancik, G. (1974), "Organizational decision-making as a political process: the case of a university budget", *Administrative Science Quarterly*, Vol. 199, No. 2, pp. 135-151.

Pfeffer, J. and Salancik, G. (1978), *The external control of organizations: a resource dependence perspective*, Harper and Row, New York.

Pfeffer, J. and Salancik, G. (2002), "The bases and uses of power in organizational decision making: the case of a university", in Clegg, S. R. (Ed.), *Central Currents in Organizational Studies II: Contemporary Trends*, Sage, London, pp. 21-42.

Polsby, N. (1963), *Community Power and Political Theory*, Yale University Press, New Haven.

Pondy, L. (1970), "Toward a theory of internal resource-allocation", in Zald, M. (Ed.), *Power in Organizations*, Vanderbilt University, Nashville, pp. 270-311.

Roberts, J. and Scapens, R. (1985), "Accounting systems and systems of accountability-understanding accounting practices in their organizations contexts", *Accounting Organizations and Society*, Vol. 10, No. 4, pp. 443-456.

Scapens, R. W. and Roberts, J. (1993), "Accounting and control: a case study of resistance to accounting change", *Management Accounting Research*, Vol. 4, No. 1, pp.1-32.

Shaoul, J. (1997), "The power of accounting: reflection on water privatization?", *Accounting, Auditing and Accountability Journal*, Vol. 10, No. 3, pp. 382-405.

Sombart, W. (1953), "Medieval and modern commercial enterprise", in Iane, F. C. and Riemersma, J. C. (Eds.), *Enterprise in Secular Change: Readings in Economic History*, Allen and Unwin, London, pp. 24-45.

Uddin, S. and Hopper, T. (2001), "A Bangladesh soap opera: privatization, accounting, and regimes of control in a less developed country", *Accounting, Organizations and Society*, Vol. 26, No. 7/8, pp. 643-672.

Weber, M. (1978), *Economy and Society: An Outline of Interpretive Sociology*, in Roth, G. and Wittich, C. (Eds.), University of California Press, Berkeley.

Wickramasinghe, D. and Hopper, T. (2005), "A cultural political economy of management accounting controls: a case study of textile mill in a traditional Sinhalese village", *Critical Perspectives on Accounting*, Vol. 16, No. 4, pp. 473-503.

Wickramasinghe, D. Hopper, T. and Rathnasiri, C. (2004), "Japanese cost management meets Sri Lankan politics: disappearance and reappearance of bureaucratic management control in a privatised utility", *Accounting, Auditing and Accountability Journal*, Vol. 17, No. 1, pp. 85-120.

Wildavsky, A. (1965), *The Politics of the Budgetary Process*, Little, Brown, Boston.

Yamey, B. S., (1964), "Accounting and the rise of capitalism: further notes on a theme by Sombart", *Journal of Accounting Research*, Vol. 2, No. 2, pp.117-136.

17

CASE STUDIES AND ACTION RESEARCH

Carol Adams
La Trobe University, Australia

Zahirul Hoque
Deakin University, Australia

Patty McNicholas
Monash University, Australia

Abstract: Like other disciplines, the case study has now become a popular strategy in accounting research. This chapter has two purposes. Firstly, it demonstrates why case studies are important and how one can use case study methods to describe and interpret a practical situation. Secondly, it discusses the action research case study methodology which involves the participants in order to both create knowledge and address a specific issue. This chapter explores these two approaches through their assumptions, concepts and perspectives.

Keywords: Case study; action research; accounting research.

1. Introduction

A case is a description of a situation (Easton, 1982). Such a situation can be 'actual' or fictitious. A case may involve individuals, groups, organisations, society, social organisations or nations (Easton, 1982; Yin, 2003). Cases are used for teaching by which students gather knowledge about practical problems or issues. Researchers develop cases using evidence from practice. In so doing, researchers make no use of quantification or tests of predictions or hypotheses. The case study method involves an in-depth investigation of a phenomenon. Like other disciplines, the case study has now become a popular strategy in accounting research. This chapter is about the use of case study methods in accounting research. It provides a brief review of the literature on case study methods in accounting research to highlight the fact that case study method has been used exclusively for 'academic purposes'. This chapter further discusses the action research methodology. It explores both case study and action research approaches through their assumptions, concepts and perspectives.

2.   The Case Study Approach

Morgan and Smircich (1980, p. 491) suggest:

> ... the case for any research method, whether qualitative or quantitative (in any case, a somewhat crude and oversimplified dichotomisation) cannot be considered or presented in the abstract, because the choice and adequacy of a method embodies a variety of assumptions regarding the nature of the knowledge and the methods through which that knowledge can be obtained, as well as a set of root assumptions about the nature of the phenomena to be investigated.

Thus the rationale for a particular research strategy is grounded in the core assumptions regarding ontology, human nature and epistemology (for a review, see Burrell and Morgan, 1979; Morgan, 1980; Morgan and Smircich, 1980; Morgan, 1983). These assumptions provide a rationale as to why research should be conducted in a particular way and how the strategy can be implemented in practice (Morgan, 1983). Morgan and Smircich (1980, p. 494) further commented:

> The social world is a continuous process, created afresh in each encounter of everyday life as individuals impose themselves on their world to establish a realm of meaningful definition.

This suggests that actors develop or create their realities, not only through their own creative activity, but through common experience and interaction with others (see also Tomkins and Grove, 1983; Hopper and Powell, 1985). By adopting this tradition, accounting and control has been viewed as socially constructed and not independent of the social, economic and political aspects of the organisation (Burchell, et al., 1980; Tinker, 1980; Berry, et al., 1985; Hopper, et al., 1986). This emphasises the subjective perspective of organisational actors. Case study methods are useful when 'how' or 'why' questions are being posed, when the researcher has little control over events, and when the focus is on a contemporary phenomenon within some real-life context (Yin, 2003). Others (e.g. Filstead, 1970; Patton, 1987; Whyte, 1988) view 'case-studies' as an intensive examination of a single phenomenon. According to Yin (2003), a case study researcher constructs alternative interpretations until (s)he is satisfied that the representation is a faithful account. This contrasts with the 'hypothetical-deductive approach' that requires the specification of certain variables and the statement of specific hypotheses before data collection begins. Miles and Huberman (1984) and Patton (1987) argue that in contrast to survey methods, case study approaches emphasise the importance of getting close to the practising people and situations to understand personally the realities and minutiae of daily life.

Some accounting scholars (Burchell et al., 1980; Colville, 1981; Tinker, 1980; Willmot, 1983; Cooper, 1983; Cooper and Sherer, 1984; Hopper and Powell, 1985; Chua, 1986) question the adequacies of 'positive' or 'scientific' methods to management accounting research and believe the positive approach to accounting research fails to capture (1) individual differences or variations in perceptions about the real-world practice, (2) how accounting interacts with organisational effectiveness and adaptability and, (3) the importance of subjective and institutional factors in management accounting practice.

These criticisms led some British writers to advocate the use of interpretive approach in the study of management accounting practice (Burchell *et al.*, 1980; Cooper, 1981; Hopper and Powell, 1985; Berry *et al.*, 1985; Hopper *et al.*, 1987). In the United States Robert Kaplan (1983, 1984, 1986) and others have also encouraged field/case studies in the interpretive fashion as a means to learn the accounting and control practices first hand.

It is also claimed by other scholars (for example, Kaplan, 1983; Chua, 1986; Scapens, 1990; Covaleski and Dirsmith, 1990; Ferriera and Merchant, 1992) that an open-ended, intensive case study-based field research in the 'interpretive' tradition can permit a wider and richer understanding of management accounting practice. Several methods including participant observation, content analysis, formal and informal interviews, role plays, experiments, contrived and unobtrusive observations, videotaped behavioural displays, and focus group interviews come under the label of case study research (for a fuller discussion, see Miles and Huberman, 1984; Silverman, 1985). At their best, such techniques can produce richer material and often may help accounting researchers describe, translate, analyse and infer the meanings of events or phenomena occurring in the social world.

Thus a case study approach directs the researcher to go into the field to learn the processes firsthand. Using this approach, the researcher visits the organisation, observes the processes and sometimes even engages personally in those processes as a 'participant observer'. (S)he talks with participants about their experiences and perceptions about the organisation and its management processes. The data from the various sources may then be organised into major themes, categories, and case examples through, say, content analysis (Van Maanen, *et al.*, 1982; Yin, 1984; Eisenhardt, 1989). As Yin (1981, p. 59) noted:

> ... the context is part of the study, there will always be too many 'variables' for the number of observations to be made thus making standard experimental and survey methods irrelevant.

Case study approaches can help one to study accounting in several respects, most notably:

- to deal with multiple sources of evidence, such as document analysis, informants and respondents interviewing, participant observations, observation of management meetings, and questionnaire survey;
- to deal with a detailed description of management and accounting control processes and how the processes affect participants in practice;
- to analyse the strengths and the weaknesses of processes reported by the people interviewed;
- to make sense of the situation in its socio-political context;
- to discover how the experiences, words, feelings, attitudes and value judgment of the participants in the organisation are implicated in the research questions; and

- to capture individual differences or variations in perceptions about the real-world practice.

3. Types of Case Studies

Yin (2003) illustrates the following four types of case studies:

(i) **Exploratory case studies**: An exploratory case study researcher explores a phenomenon where the phenomenon being studied has no clear, single set of outcomes. Exploratory research does not attempt to provide conclusive answers to the phenomena, but it guides a researcher to develop ideas for future research.

(ii) **Descriptive case studies**: A descriptive case study method describes an event in its real-life context. Describing the budget-making process in an organisation is an example of a descriptive type case study. Descriptive research may investigate to seek answers to these types of questions: Who develops the budget? How is the budget developed? What are the contents of the budget? To what extent is the budget being used by managers?

(iii) **Illustrative case studies**: Illustrative case studies illustrate certain phenomena in a descriptive mode.

(iv) **Explanatory or causal case studies**: An explanatory case study not only describes the phenomena, but also explains why or how the phenomenon being studied is happening. Explanatory case studies attempt to seek answers to 'why' questions. For example, using an explanatory case study method, a researcher may wish to understand why the particular organisation has the control system it presently uses, what this is used for, in what specific circumstances, and to what effect.

Case studies should not be confused with other related methods such as ethnography and grounded theory. Ethnography and grounded theory methods do not specify any prior theoretical positions at the outset of an enquiry (for details, see Chapter 9).

Yin (1981, p. 58) suggests that case studies do not imply the use of a particular type of evidence. Case studies can be done by using either qualitative or quantitative evidence or both. Chapter 19 deals with the qualitative research tradition and Chapter 22 deals with the survey design as one of the quantitative techniques.

4. Components of a Case Study

Yin (2003) identifies five components of a case study research design. These are:

(i) **Research questions**: A case study research is appropriate for 'why' and 'how' types questions.

(ii) **Research propositions**: As a case study research poses 'why' and 'how' questions, unlike surveys or experimental studies, it does not start with conventional 'research propositions', unless there is a legitimate reason.

(iii) **Unit of analysis**: A case may be an individual, group, social institution or a nation. Yin (1991) suggests that the unit of analysis is related to the way the researcher defines his/her initial research questions.

(iv)   **Linking data to propositions**: Yin identifies this component as a least concern for a case study because of its lack of propositions. However, a case study researcher may look for 'pattern matching' (Campbell, 1975) where several pieces of information from the same case may be related to some theoretical proposition (Yin, 1991).

(v)   **Criteria for interpreting the findings**: The case study findings can be interpreted using some prior theoretical bases.

5.   Criticisms of Case Study Approaches

Case study approaches, however, have weaknesses. Firstly, case studies are conducted primarily in a single or few organisations embedded in a larger population. Thus, it is difficult to draw boundaries for the area of study with respect to exploring larger systems. Secondly, the interpretation of the social reality raises the problem of his/her bias, as the researcher in this context cannot be regarded as an independent observer. Finally, assurances of confidentiality for gaining access to the organisation raises problems in writing case reports. This may prevent the researcher from checking the validity of evidence through feedback to the subjects (for details, see Scapens, 1990). Other weaknesses of case study methods are: the case study research takes a long time and may result in massive, unreadable documents; and, this strategy provides little basis for generalisation (Halfpenny, 1979; Yin, 1984; Patton, 1987; Miles and Huberman, 1984). Scapens (1990, p. 278), however, comments:

> In comparison with more traditional forms of accounting research, it is important to recognise that case studies are concerned with explanation rather than prediction. Researchers should avoid the temptation of thinking of case studies only in terms of statistical generalisation ... researchers who see generalisations only in this sense will either reject case study methods or not fully exploit their potential.

Despite their weaknesses case study approaches help a researcher gain a deep understanding of the operation of management control systems in organisations. 'Experiments' or 'survey' designs are not appropriate for understanding the phenomena in their contexts.

6.   Action Research

The term 'action research' methodology originates primarily in the work of Kurt Lewin and his colleagues in the mid-1940s (Cady and Caster, 2000; Karmin, 2001). Action research is an approach to research that aims to both take action and create knowledge or theory about that action (Coughlan and Coghlan, 2002). The outcome of combining 'action' with 'research' is to overcome important social and organisational issues together with those practitioners who are experiencing the issues directly (Cunningham, 1993; Cardno and Piggot-Irvine, 1996; Davison, 2001; McKay and Marshall, 2001; Reason and Bradbury, 2001; Naslund, 2002).

7.   Features of Action Research

Action research has some broad characteristics that define it. Firstly, it typically works through a cyclical four-step process of intentionally: planning, taking action, evaluating that action, leading to further planning and so on, thereby promoting skills of inquiry, reflection, problem solving, and action (Rock and Levin, 2002). This cycle can be repeated in the same context until satisfactory outcomes have been achieved (McKay and Marshall, 2001). Figure one sets out the various stages of action research identified in the literature. Secondly, action research is participative. Members of the case study organisation actively participate in the cyclical process, rather than merely being objects of the study (Olesen and Myers, 1999). The actors work together so that the issue may be resolved or the system improved (Reason, 1999). Thirdly, action research is concurrent with action therefore both the researchers and practitioners are able to gain knowledge through participation in the project. Hence this methodology provides a powerful means of improving and enhancing practice, as well as bridging the theory-practice gap, as the action/solutions are the result of the combined efforts, expertise and knowledge of both the practitioners and researchers (Cardno and Piggot-Irvine, 1996). Fourthly, action research is both a sequence of events and an approach to problem solving. As a sequence of events, it comprises cycles of gathering data, feeding data back to the practitioners, analysing the data, planning action, taking action and evaluation, leading to further data gathering and so on. As an approach to problem solving it is an application of fact finding and experimentation to practical problems requiring action and solutions involving the collaboration and co-operation of both the practitioners and researchers, without which projects cannot be successfully undertaken and completed (Clark, 1972; Cardno and Piggot-Irvine, 1996; Avison, Lau *et al.*, 1999; Gronhaug and Olson, 1999; Olesen and Myers, 1999; Davison, 2001; McKay and Marshall, 2001; Sax and Fisher, 2001; Coughlan and Coghlan, 2002; Earl-Slater, 2002). The desired outcome of the action research approach is not just solutions to immediate problems, but also intended and unintended outcomes, as well as making a contribution to knowledge and theory development. As action research is about research *in* action it does not postulate a distinction between theory and action (Coughlan and Coghlan, 2002).

Figure 1
Stages of Action Research

Earl-Slater, 2002 #10	Dickens and Watkins, 1999 #4	Sax and Fisher, 2001 #5	Ziegler, 2001 #9	Adams and McNicholas (2006)
Reconnaissance	Analysing	Targeting an area of collective interest	Identify a topic	Identification of problem
			Recruit practitioner-researchers	

			Review the action research process and invite participants to contribute their insights to the upcoming process	
			Select a problem	
	Fact finding	Collection	Collect and analyse information	Data collection to evaluate and analyse the problem
	reconceptualiz ation			Data analysis and feedback
Planning	Planning	Organising Analysing	Plan activities to address the problem	
		Interpreting data		
Action	Acting (execution)	Taking action	Take action and monitor results	
Reflection and revision	Observing			
	Reflecting		Share lessons learnt	Write up
	Acting again			

Essentially action research requires a real issue of both research and managerial significance upon which the organisation is embarking that has an uncertain outcome. The organisation must also be willing to be the subject of rigorous inquiry thereby enabling the undertaking of a 'live' case study in real time. The researcher has to gain access and be contracted as an action researcher before the study can proceed (Schein, 1999; Gummesson, 2000). A crucial element is to ensure that both the researcher and all the contacts within the organisation have a clear, specific and agreed information of what is to take place (Mumford, 2001). Key members of the organisation must develop an understanding of the context of the action project to determine why the project is necessary and desirable, and what the economic, political, social and technical forces are that are driving the need for action (Coughlan and Coghlan, 2002).

Data may be gathered in a number of ways, depending on the context. Hard or secondary data may consist of operational statistics, financial accounts, marketing reports, environmental reports, as well as detailed examination of the organisations website. Primary data is gathered through participant observations, discussions and interviews (Robson, 1993; Meyer, 2000; Karmin, 2001).

The action researcher collects the data, analyses it and then provides the findings to the organisation which then provides feedback on the findings. The literature supports this approach of sharing information and analysing data collaboratively to facilitate the action research process (Cardno and Piggot-Irvine, 1996; Harris and Harris, 2001; Coughlan and Coghlan, 2002). The rationale for collaboration is that the clients know the organisation best, know what will work and ultimately are the actors who will be required to implement and follow through the actions to be taken. Hence, their involvement in the analysis is critical. The methodology thus allows the researchers to remain focused on the problem and as required, allows the organisation to take immediate remedial action.

8. Criticisms of Action Research

As action research is a form of case study, some of the same criticisms apply. The 'double challenge' of combining action and research potentially may lead to some difficulties of project control. These difficulties may also be compounded by the fact that each project is highly situational, and, to some extent at least, is unique. Therefore it is difficult to outline general laws about how to carry out such projects.

One of the drawbacks of using action research is that it can be *time-consuming*. For example, a project may last for weeks, months or even years and typically requires substantial involvement of organisational staff as well as researchers. However, some researchers argue that the use of this methodology prevents short-term solutions being instigated that could be costly for the organisation in the long-term (Avison, *et al.*, 2001; Mumford, 2001). Effective action research can also involve the complexity of multiple activities occurring during the research process. The nature of participative collaboration can involve political aspects of knowledge production, whereby knowledge gained through people's lived experiences aims to empower them to produce further knowledge and action that will benefit them directly in the short and long term (Reason and Bradbury, 2001; McNicholas and Humphries, 2005; McNicholas and Barrett, 2005).

Another criticism of this methodology is that *it is hard to validate the data gathered and generalise the results* (Baskerville and Wood-Harper, 1996; Mumford, 2001; Coghlan, 2002). The principal threat to validity is the lack of impartiality on the part of the researcher, as the action researcher is engaged in shaping and telling a story. The need to consider the degree, to which the story is a valid representation of what has taken place and how it is understood, rather than a biased interpretation, is paramount (Smith, 1999; McNicholas and Barrett, 2005). As action research is typically context-bound rather than context-free each situation may be unique and not able to be repeated. Such criticism will particularly come from those researchers who evaluate research according to scientific criteria. Thus in some quarters it may be difficult to attract research funding to undertake action research projects. However, this approach has been supported by researchers who argue that if the project is able to resolve the organisation's problem(s), then that research has been found to be credible and valid (Reason and Bradbury, 2001).

Many critics have argued that the close relationship between the researchers and the practitioners can have an impact on the objectivity of the researcher, thereby affecting the research project and its findings. Consequently, it may also be considered to be a *form of consultancy* (Baskerville and Wood-Harper, 1996; McKay and Marshall, 2001) or consulting masquerading as research (Coughlan and Coghlan, 2002). This criticism needs to be taken seriously by researchers. However, Gummesson (2000) argues that four factors clearly differentiate action research and consulting: (i) researchers gather more rigorous documentation than consultants; (ii) researchers require theoretical justifications whereas consultants require empirical justifications; (iii) consultants operate under tighter time and budget constraints; and (iv) consultants operate in a linear fashion of engagement, analysis, action and disengagement, whereas the action research process is cyclical (Baskerville and Wood-Harper, 1996). In reality action research shares these problems with many other methods of undertaking social science research which seeks to make a difference and bring about change both for individuals and within organisations.

9.   Conclusion

This chapter has argued that the study of the complex phenomena, such as management control systems inevitably requires in-depth, detailed field-research. The decision to adopt case study approaches for a study should be made on the basis of its potential to make sense of the everyday in its context. As such, field-research is directed at describing, translating, and analysing actions, events and control procedures in the setting from the perspective of organisational members involved in practice.

Action research provides an opportunity for the researcher to work closely with the participants from the case study organisation to enhance and improve practice. Participative collaboration aims to both develop knowledge and address a practical issue for the organisation.

References

Adams, C. A. and McNicholas, P. (2006), "Making a difference: social and environmental accountability and organisational change", working paper.

Avison, D., Baskerville, R. and Myers, M. (2001), "Controlling action research projects", *Information Technology and People*, Vol. 14, No. 1, pp. 28-45.

Avison, D., Lau, F., Myers, M. and Nielsen, P. (1999), "Action research", *Communication of the ACM*, Vol. 42, No. 1, pp. 94-97.

Baskerville, R. L. and Wood-Harper, A. T. (1996), "A critical perspective on action research as a method for information systems research", *Journal of Information Technology*, Vol. 11, pp. 235-246.

Berry, A.J., Capps, T., Cooper, D. J., Ferguson, P., Hopper, T.M. and Lowe, E.A. (1985), "Management Control in an area of the NCB: Rationales of Accounting Practices in a Public Enterprise", *Accounting, Organizations and Society*, Vol.10, No.1, pp. 3-28.

Burchell, S., Clubb, C., Hopwood, A.G., Hughes, T. and Nahapiet, J.E. 91980), "The Roles of Accounting in Organizations and Society, *Accounting, Organizations and Society*, Vol.5, No.1, pp. 5-28.

Burrell, G. and Morgan, G. (1979), *Sociological Paradigms and Organizational Analysis*, London: Heinemann.

Cady, S. H. and Caster, M. (2000), "A diet for action research: an integrated problem and appreciative focused approach to organisation development", *Organization Development Journal*, Vol. 18, No. 4, pp. 79-93.

Campbell, D.T. (1975), "Degrees of Freedom and the Case Study", *Comparative Political Studies*, Vol.8, pp. 178-193.

Cardno, C. and Piggot-Irvine, E. (1996), "Incorporating action research in school senior management training", *The International Journal of Educational Management*, Vol. 10, No. 5, pp. 19-24.

Chua, W. F. (1986), "Radical Developments in Accounting Thought", *The Accounting Review*, October, pp. 601-632.

Clark, P. A. (1972), *Action Research and Organisational Change*, Harper and Row, London.

Coghlan, D. (2002), "Putting 'research' back into OD and action research: a call to OD practitioners", *Organization Development Journal*, Vol. 20, No. 1, pp. 62-65.

Colville, I. (1981), "Reconstructing Behavioral Accounting", *Accounting, Organizations and Society*, Vol.6, No.2, pp. 119-132.

Cooper, D.J. (1983), Tidiness, Muddle and Things: Commonalities and Divergences in Two Approaches to Management Accounting Research, *Accounting, Organizations and Society* (Vol.8, No. 2/3, 1983) pp. 269-286.

Cooper, D.J. and Sherer, M.J. (1984), "The Value of Accounting Reports: Arguments for a Political Economy of Accounting", *Accounting, Organizations and Society*, Vol.9, NO. 3/4, pp. 207-232.

Coughlan, P. and Coghlan, D. (2002), "Action research for operations management", *International Journal of Operations and Production Management*, Vol. 22, No. 2, pp. 220-240.

Covaleski, M.A. and Dirsmith, M.W. (1990), "Dialectic Tension, Double Reflexity and the Everyday Accounting Researcher: On Using Qualitative Methods", *Accounting, Organizations and Society*, Vol.15, No.6, pp. 543-573.

Cunningham, J. B. (1993), *Action Research and Organisational Development*, Praeger Publishers, USA.

Davison, R. (2001), "GSS and action research in the Hong Kong police", *Information Technology and People*, Vol. 14, No. 1, pp. 60-77.

Dickens, L. and Watkins, K. (1999), "Action research: rethinking Lewin", *Management Learning*, Vol. 30, No. 2, pp. 127-140.

Earl-Slater, A. (2002), "Critical appraisal of clinical trials: the superiority of action research", *British Journal of Clinical Governance*, Vol. 7, No. 2, pp. 132-135.

Easton, G. (1982), *Learning from case Studies*, Prentice Hall International, Englewood Cliffs, New Jersey.

Eisenhardt, K. (1989), "Building Theories from Case Study Research", *The Academy of Management Review*, Vol.14, No.4, pp. 532-550.

Ferriera, L.D. and Merchant, K.A. (1992), "Field Research in Management Accounting and Control: A Review and Evaluation", *Accounting, Auditing and Accountability Journal*, Vol.5, No.4, pp. 3-34.

Filstead, W.J. (1970), *Qualitative Methodology*, Chicago: Rand McNally.

Gronhaug, K. and Olson, O. (1999), "Action research and knowledge creation: merits and challenges", *Qualitative Market Research*, Vol. 2, No. 1, pp. 6-14.

Gummesson, E. (2000), *Qualitative Methods in Management Research*, Sage, Thousand Oaks, CA.

Halfpenny P. (1979), "The Analysis of Qualitative Data", *Sociological Review*, Vol.27, No.4, pp. 799-825.

Harris, M. and. Harris, J. (2001), "Achieving organizational collaboration in the nonprofit sector: an action research approach", *Organization Development Journal*, Vol. 20, No. 1, pp. 28-35.

Hopper, T. M. and Powell, A. (1985), "Making Sense of Research into Organizational and Social Aspects of Management Accounting: A Review of its Underlying Assumptions", *Journal of Management Studies*, Vol.22, No.5, pp. 429-436.

Hopper, T. M., Cooper, D.J., Lowe, T., Capps, T. and Mouritsen, J. (1986), "Management Control and Worker Resistance in the NCB: Financial Control in the Labour Process", in Knights, D. and Willmot, H. (eds), *Managing the Labour Process*, Aldershot: Gower.

Hopper, T. M., Storey, J. and Willmot, H. (1987), "Accounting for Accounting: Towards the Development of a Dialectical View", *Accounting, Organizations and Society*, Vol.12, No.5, pp. 437-456.

Kaplan, R.S. (1983), "Measuring Manufacturing Performance: A New Challenge for Managerial Accounting Research", *The Accounting Review*, October, pp. 686-705.

Kaplan, R.S. (1984), "The Evolution of Management Accounting", *The Accounting Review*, July, pp. 390-418.

Kaplan, R.S. (1986), "The Role for Empirical Research in Management Accounting", *Accounting, Organizations and Society*, Vol.11, No.4/5, pp. 429-452.

Karmin, K. (2001), "Assessing the strengths and weaknesses of action research", *Nursing Standard*, Vol. 15, No. 26, pp. 33-35.

McKay, J. and Marshall, P. (2001), "The dual imperatives of action research", *Information Technology and People*, Vol. 14, No. 1, pp. 46-59.

McNicholas, P. and Barrett, M. (2005), "Answering the emancipatory call: an emerging research approach 'on the margins' of accounting", *Critical Perspectives on Accounting*, Vol. 16, No. 4, pp. 391-414.

McNicholas, P. and Humphries, M. (2005), "Decolonization through critical career research and action", *Australian Journal of Career Development*, Vol. 14, No. 1, Autumn.

Miles, M.B. and Huberman, A. (1984), *Qualitative Data Analysis: A Source Book of New Methods*, Beverly Hills, CA: Sage Publications.

Morgan, G. (1980), "Paradigms, Metaphors and Puzzle Solving in Organisation Theory", *Administrative Science Quarterly*, Vol.25, pp. 605-622.

Morgan, G. (ed.) (1983), *Beyond Method: Strategies for Social Research*, Beverly Hills, CA: Sage.

Morgan, G. and Smircich, L. (1980), "The Case for Qualitative Research", *The Academy of Management Review*, Vol.5, No.4, pp.491-500.

Meyer, J. (2000), "Using qualitative methods in health related action research", *British Medical Journal*, Vol. 320, No. 7228, pp. 178-181.

Mumford, E. (2001), "Advice for an action researcher", *Information Technology and People*, Vol. 14, No. 1, pp. 12-27.

Naslund, D. (2002), "Logistics needs qualitative research-especially action research", *International Journal of Physical Distribution and Logistics Management*, Vol. 32, No. 5, pp. 321-338.

Olesen, K. and Myers, M. D. (1999), "Trying to improve communication and collaboration with information technology: an action research project which failed", *Information Technology and People*, Vol. 12, No. 4, pp. 317-332.

Patton, M.Q. (1987), *How to Use Qualitative Methods in Evaluation*, Beverly Hills, CA: Sage.

Reason, P. (1999), "Integrating action and reflection through co-operative inquiry", *Management Learning*, Vol. 30, No. 2, pp. 207-226.

Reason, P. and Bradbury, H. (2001), *Handbook of Action Research: Participative Inquiry and Practice*, Sage Publications, UK.

Robson, C. (1993), *Real World Research: A Resource for Social Scientists and Practitioner-Researchers*, Blackwell, Oxford.

Rock, T. C. and Levin, B. (2002), "Collaborative action research projects: enhancing preservice teacher development in professional development schools", *Teacher Education Quarterly*, Vol. 29, No. 1, pp. 7-21.

Sax, C. and Fisher, D. (2001), "Using qualitative action research to effect change: implications for professional education", *Teacher Education Quarterly*, Vol. 28, No. 2, pp. 71-80.

Scapens, R.W. (1990), "Researching Management Accounting Practice: The Role of Case Study Methods", *The British Accounting Review*, Vol.22, pp. 259-281.

Silverman, D. (1985), *Qualitative Methodology and Sociology*, Gower.

Schein, E. H. (1999), *Process Consultation Revisited, Building the Helping Relationship*, Addison-Wesley, Reading, MA.

Smith, L. T. (1999), *Decolonizing Methodologies*, University of Otago Press, Dunedin.

Tinker, A.M. (1980), "A Political Economy of Accounting", *Accounting, Organizations and Society*, Vol.5, No.1, pp.147-160.

Tomkins, C. and Grove, R. (1983), "The Everyday Accountant and Researching His Reality", *Accounting, Organizations and Society*, Vol.8, No.4, pp. 361-374.

Van Maanen J., Dabbs, J.M. and Faulkner, R.R. (1982), *Varieties of Qualitative Research,* Beverly Hills, CA: Sage.

Whyte, W.F. (1988), *Learning from the Field: A Guide from Experience,* London: Sage.

Willmott, H.C. (1983), "Paradigms for Accounting Research: Critical Reflections on Tomkins and Groves' "Everyday Accountant and Researching His Reality", *Accounting, Organizations and Society,* Vol.8, No.4. pp. 389-405.

Yin, R.K. (1981), "The Case Study Research: Some Answers", *Administrative Science Quarterly,* Vol.1, No.26, pp. 58-65.

Yin, R.K. (1984), *Case Study Research: Design and Methods,* Beverly Hills, CA: Sage.

Yin, R. K (2003), *Case Study Research: Design and Methods,* Sage Publications; Thousand Oaks.

Ziegler, M. (2001), "Improving practice through action research", *Adult Learning,* Vol. 12, No. 1, pp. 3-4.

18

THE QUALITATIVE RESEARCH TRADITION

Jodie Moll
University of Manchester, UK

Maria Major
ISCTE – Business School, Portugal

Zahirul Hoque
Deakin University, Australia

Abstract: In recent years, businesses have witnessed dramatic changes in the business environment. The complexity of this environment and the more prominent role attributed to accounting has resulted in an increase in the use of qualitative methodology based on its ability to provide fresh and interesting insights to the way that accounting interacts with its environment. This chapter has been written to provide a general overview of the current qualitative landscape and some practical guidance to any student embarking on research for the first time. It draws on our personal experiences and relevant literature to help students to develop the research skills that are necessary to successfully conduct research in this tradition.

Keywords: Research methods, research design, qualitative research, field study, case study.

1. Introduction

Those who strongly advocate the qualitative methodology or case study methods in accounting research (e.g. Hopwood, 1983; Otley, 1984; Hopper and Powell, 1985; Covaleski and Dirsmith, 1983, 1990; Kaplan, 1984, 1986; Scapens, 1990; Roberts and Scapens, 1985) claim this strategy can make substantial contributions to the study of how accounting and control systems interact with their environment. This chapter is concerned with such research methodology. It provides a practical guide to qualitative research. In particular, in this chapter the methodological issues underpinning qualitative research approaches are discussed along with the steps outlining the various qualitative research methods and processes. The chapter draws on the experience of the authors and literature on qualitative research. It is designed to be read in conjunction with Chapter 17 'Case Studies and Action Research' and Chapter 22 'Reliability and Validity in Field Study Research'. To avoid confusion, methodology is used in this chapter to refer to the theory of how research should be undertaken, whereas method relates to the tools or techniques used to collect and analyse data.

The remainder of the chapter is divided into six main sections. In section one we provide a general discussion of the qualitative landscape, with the intention of providing some clarity on what it is and how it differs from quantitative research. In the second section we provide a historical review of the emergence of accounting research in the qualitative tradition to demonstrate how it has become an important accepted basis for helping us to understand the roles that accounting plays in organisational life. Choosing your research methodology is a critical stage of any piece of research. To help you to identify where your own personal philosophical assumptions lie so that you can make more informed choices about what methods and theories are appropriate for your research, we focus on this issue in section three. In the fourth section we provide a general overview of the research methods that provide qualitative evidence. Section five of the chapter is designed to provide you with some detailed and practical guidance on the common protocols of qualitative research. Specifically, the way to choose and access a case, some of the methods that can be used to collect and analyse data and tips on how to write up and publish are the focus of this section. Section six concludes the chapter.

2.   The Qualitative Landscape

... qualitative research is difficult to define clearly. It has no theory or paradigm that is distinctly its own ... nor does qualitative research have a distinct set of methods or practices that are entirely its own (Denzin and Lincoln, 2000, p. 6).

To Patton (1987, p. 301) qualitative methods provide:

... detailed descriptions of events, situations and interactions between people and things providing depth and detail.

Others (e.g. Hopper and Powell, 1985; Covaleski and Dirsmith, 1990) see qualitative methods as a strategy that can be employed to analyse the social realities of a phenomenon. While definitions of qualitative research vary a common feature of the strategy is that it aims to provide a richer understanding of processes and social realities.

Qualitative approaches are derived most directly from the ethnographic and field study traditions of anthropology and sociology (Pelto and Pelto, 1978). In this sense, the philosophical and theoretical frames underpinning qualitative methods include: phenomenology (Bussis *et al.*, 1973; Carini, 1975); symbolic interactionism and naturalistic behaviourism (Denzin, 1978); ethnomethodology (Garfinkel, 1967); and, ecological psychology (Barker, 1968). Patton (1987) argues an integrative theme of these perspectives is that the study of human beings is different from other scientific inquiries. As Strike (1972, p. 28; quoted in Patton, 1987) pointed out:

Human beings can be understood in a way that other objects of study cannot. Men have purposes and emotions, they make plans, construct cultures, and hold certain values, and their behaviour is influenced by such values, plans, and purposes. In short, a human being lives in a world which has 'meaning' to him, and, because his behaviour has meaning, human actions are intelligible in ways that behaviour of nonhuman objects is not. The opponents of this view, on the other hand, will maintain that human behaviour is to be explained that way as is the behaviour of other objects of nature. There are laws governing human behaviour. An action is explained when it can be subsumed under some such law, and, of course, such laws are confirmed by empirical evidence.

The philosophical roots of qualitative methods emphasise the importance of understanding the meanings of human behaviour and the organisational context of social interaction. This includes developing empathetic understanding based on subjective experience, and understanding the connections between personal perceptions and behaviour.

One useful way to conceptualise qualitative research is to distinguish it from qualitative methodology. It is common for students to be confused by the differences between qualitative and quantitative methodology since they are often contrasted in the literature as belonging to different methodological paradigms. However, the two are not mutually exclusive. Qualitative research is a term used to describe the type of evidence collected, not the type of research design (i.e. qualitative research is usually based on words, sentences, and narratives). Consequently, some quantitative research methods are common to both quantitative and qualitative research methodology. Typically, qualitative approaches are employed to explore and identify relevant influencing variables for testing using quantitative approaches. Alternatively, they can also be used as a complement to quantitative studies by providing more in depth explanations of statistical relationships. Maxwell (2005) provides a clear distinction of the two approaches:

Quantitative and qualitative researchers tend to ask different kinds of causal questions. Quantitative researchers tend to be interested in whether and to what extent variance in x causes variance in y. Qualitative researchers, on the other hand, to ask how x plays a role in causing y, and what the process is that connects x and y.

Qualitative studies are useful when researchers seek to understand how accounting phenomena are produced, experienced, and interpreted by social actors within complex social world (Mason, 2002). The multifaceted nature of many accounting practices can only be analysed when qualitative methods are adopted. The roles that accounting plays in the dissolution, reconstruction and operation of new organisational forms, such as networks and interfirm alliances, for instance, can only be described and understood using a qualitative approach.

In comparison, quantitative studies rule out the possibility of studying in-depth issues which are usually related to 'why' and 'how' accounting practices come to exist. Instead, detail is often replaced by scope within quantitative research tradition. These studies are aimed at explaining phenomenon variance by making systematic comparisons, and thus measurement and analysis of causal relationships between variables are central (Silverman, 2005; Denzin and Lincoln, 2000).

Depending on the research problems needing to be addressed, either of the methodological strategies may be valid. For instance, if a researcher is interested in studying the phenomenon of ABC diffusion in UK firms either quantitative or qualitative research may be appropriate depending on the research questions raised. Quantitative research should be employed if the main aim of the investigation is to identify variance and to make inferences to wider populations based on samples. In this case a limited number of variables are identified and statistically analysed. Conversely, qualitative research should be adopted if the study is mostly concerned with obtaining rich descriptions and explanations from organisational actors on their perceptions about why ABC was adopted and how it is used in particular firms.

3.   Closing the Gap between Practice and the Textbooks

Accounting research traditionally involved the application of financial economics to accounting problems supported by research methods used in economics (Ryan et al., 2002). Such studies test theory in the form of mathematical models using data sets. The ease with which quantitative data can be replicated earned it a reputation for providing 'objective' research.

The nature of quantitative inquiry is, however, suggestive of a narrow view of reality: organisations are depicted as coherent units that are oriented to achieving specific goals, employees are described as behaving in a consistent and purposeful manner towards rational ends, and accounting is considered as an information system that provides aid to decision-making (Hopper and Powell, 1985). In recognition of this, in the late 1970s academics began debating the methodology of accounting research, with the intention of exploring alternative methodological approaches to overcome the simplified and highly structured explanations of accounting offered by such positivistic methods and in turn with the intention of addressing the gap between textbooks and practice (Baker and Bettner, 1997). This led researchers to recommend the adoption of alternative research approaches such as behavioural and organisational, interpretive and critical, to study the nature and practices of accounting (Dent et al., 1984; Hopwood, 1983; Scapens, 1990; Tomkins and Groves, 1983; Willmott, 1983). Such theories enable investigators to explain accounting practices by emphasising their social, cultural and political construction (Lukka and Granlund, 2002; Humphrey and Scapens, 1996; Scapens and Roberts, 1993). In recognition of these new alternative research approaches, a call was made for the research methodology (i.e. the process of doing research) to be dictated by the nature of the phenomena to be researched (Tomkins and Groves, 1983). Since then the number of accounting studies adopting a qualitative tradition, especially management accounting, has been on the rise (Lukka and Kasanen, 1995).

4. Making the Link between your Philosophical Assumptions and Determining the Appropriate Research Method(s)

The ability to carry out research successfully lies partly in a familiarity with the philosophical traditions described in this chapter, and by thinking through your own philosophical assumptions about the way in which you view the world. This is important not least because while qualitative and quantitative methodologies may both be designed to understand behaviour, each holds different assumptions about phenomena. Many students believe that qualitative research is easier to conduct than statistically based research and thus choose to undertake research of this nature. Those academics who have undertaken qualitative research would be quick to disband such beliefs, emphasising that understanding your philosophical assumptions is required in order to identify the appropriate theoretical backing and research methods for a study (Bryman, 1984; Hopper and Powell, 1985; Hussey and Hussey, 1997). Failure to consider your personal assumptions implies that the research methods determine the form of research (Morgan and Smircich, 1980). Furthermore, understanding what your personal philosophical assumptions are and which set of assumptions best represents a piece of research is important if you want to be able to defend your chosen methodology (i.e. qualitative or quantitative) or to identify new or different areas of investigation which may improve your research strategy (Hopper and Powell, 1985; Tomkins and Groves, 1983). Understanding the various sets of diverse assumptions is also critical for appreciating others research (Morgan, 1983; Baker and Bettner, 1997).

Your philosophical assumptions can be classified as belonging to two main categories; those about social science and about society (Burrell and Morgan, 1979). According to Chua (1986, p. 603) social science assumptions refer to those 'about the ontology of the social world (realism vs nominalism), epistemology (positivism vs anti-positivism), human nature (determinism vs voluntarism), and methodology (nomothetic vs ideographic)'. Past research has found it useful to conceptualise society as either being logical and ordered or disorderly and open to dispute.[74] Your philosophical assumptions can be located within one of the following four paradigms – functionalist, interpretive, radical humanist and radical structuralist (see Figure 1).

---

[74] As noted by Hopper and Powell (1985) such dichotomous classifications are useful but may not necessarily represent the full breadth of assumptions available.

Figure 1
The Sociological Paradigms

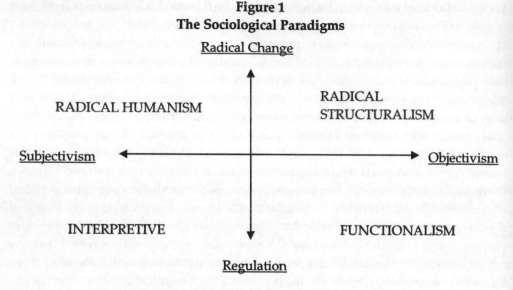

Radical Change

RADICAL HUMANISM

RADICAL
STRUCTURALISM

Subjectivism ←——————————————→ Objectivism

INTERPRETIVE

FUNCTIONALISM

Regulation

Source: Adapted from Burrell and Morgan, 1979, pp. 29-30.

Briefly, the functionalist perspective is associated with pluralism, social systems theory and objectivism. Each of these theories assumes that controls are an objective conception of reality and that human behaviour is to varying degrees constrained by the wider social environment. Objectivism assumes that organisations operate with a set of unitary goals and staff members operate in a rational fashion towards the achievement of those goals. Social systems theory, a more complex theory, concentrates on providing explanations for how extra-organisational factors influence organisational control and offers a wider range of responses for how organisational members respond to the organisational environment. Pluralism can be differentiated from the other functionalist perspectives since it assumes that a set of unitary organisational goals is inappropriate. This perspective attempts to understand organisations by looking more closely at the sectional groups that comprise the organisation. Control according to the pluralist perspective assumes that groups will comply with the organisations network of rules and regulations (Hopper and Powell, 1985).

The interpretive perspective assumes that the social world is socially constructed. As discussed in Chapter 8 of this book, in order to understand the social world, the interpretive perspective suggests that the focus of study must be on the meanings and perceptions of those who inhabit it. It is aimed at understanding the shared realities of individuals (Hopper and Powell, 1985). Implicit in this view is the assumption that the researcher is never entirely sure that they have acquired the views of the subjects of study.

Radical theorists, both structural and humanist, aim to explain the social and economic world by focusing on wider social relationships underpinning societies such as the power and class relationships. The difference between the two theories is dependent on the epistemological Marxist position adopted. The structural approach suggests that the social world exists independently of any of its inhabitants. According to Hopper and Powell (1985) it concentrates on fundamental conflict between industrial structures and economic relationships, whereas the humanist perspective concentrates on individual perceptions and how they are subject to ideological influence. To make these paradigms more meaningful to accounting research, Ryan *et al.* (2002) link these to three categories of accounting research: mainstream, interpretive, and critical.

Mainstream research which is quantitative in nature is most closely linked to the functionalist perspective because of its concern for an 'objective' view of the world. It aims to generalise and predict cause and effect relationships. To the positivist, only phenomena which are observable and measurable are considered to be knowledge.

Interpretive accounting research, on the other hand, assumes that any action is given meaning by the actors around it and thus must be studied within its wider social framework (Ansari and Bell, 1991; Hopper and Powell, 1985). Thus, it rejects the objective stance on the role of human nature. Instead, this paradigm assumes that any one interpretation of the phenomenon of study is limited or bound by an individual's ability to understand fully the complexities surrounding it and thus it cannot be represented to be an objective representation of reality. Since no one individual is thought to provide an accurate representation of reality, the interpretive approach relies on the commonalities of experience amongst the case subjects and multiple methods to build up a trustworthy picture of the phenomenon being studied (Smith, 2003; Stoner and Holland, 2004). As discussed in Chapter 8, the interpretive paradigm focuses on how actors use accounting numbers, not as an objective representation of reality, but as an 'interpretive' or 'subjective' art. It explores how accounting interacts with its environment and is designed to provide a better understanding of how it can be used to make sense of situations and everyday practice. This includes how it interacts with other organisational processes (Hopper and Powell, 1985) and how it can be used to rationalise the adoption of a particular course of action (Morgan, 1988, 1997). Put another way, the perspective assumes that accounting practices are not natural phenomena and as such they can be changed or modified by those carrying them out (Ryan *et al.*, 2002). By improving our understanding of accounting in practice, Chua (1986, p. 615) argues that it increases 'the possibility of mutual communication and influence'. Morgan's (1988) comments suggest a similar view:

> *Skilled managers develop the knack of reading complex situations with various scenarios in mind, and of forging actions appropriate to the understandings obtained.*

Critical research, the term used to describe 'radical structuralist' and 'radical humanist' accounting research, offers a basis for social critique and/or promotes forms of radical change (Ryan *et al.*, 2002). Similar to interpretive research approaches its focus is less concerned with the 'technicalities' of accounting practice. It builds on interpretive approaches by locating accounting within its social context, but involves significant self-reflection on the grounds of observation to offer plausible explanations (Smith, 2003). Social theories such as those by Marx, Latour, Foucault and Habermas are commonly used by Critical theorists (Chapter 13) to explain the roles of accounting in society in relation to issues of conflict, domination and power (Covaleski et al., 1996). For instance, both Marxist labour process theories (Chapter 14) and Foucault theories provide explanations of how accounting, as a social practice, can control how individuals act. In this regard, science and knowledge are never seen to be value-neutral (Smith, 2003). The most common criticism of critical theorists is that any conclusions drawn from their research are known in advance of the study (Jonsson and Macintosh, 1997).

5. Research Methods Providing Qualitative Evidence

Qualitative evidence can be collected using a variety of diverse approaches. The common theme among these approaches is that they involve collecting evidence and analysing a natural setting such as an organisation or at an event (Burgess, 1994). Some scholars therefore use the term 'field research' as an umbrella term for any of the methods which can be used to collect qualitative evidence.[75] Chapter 22 discusses the basic features of a field research (see also, Ferreira and Merchant, 1992, p. 4).

Ahrens and Dent (1998) point out the motivations and methods of field research conducted in accounting are diverse; some scholars have focused on describing accounting in practice, others have focused on the linkages between accounting practices and organisational process and some have chosen to focus on single cases while others have focused on multiple cases. Atkinson and Shaffir (1998) categorise the published accounting field research as being aimed at providing a description of practice, testing a theory developed elsewhere, or developing a theory. Three types of field research are common to the study of accounting practice: case study, field studies, and field experiments.[76] A brief description of these is now provided.

5.1. Case Studies

The case study is said to be the preferred research strategy when 'how' and 'why' questions are the focus of research, when the researcher has little control over the events or circumstances of the phenomenon being investigated and when the research has some real life context (Yin, 2003). For further details on the case study strategy, refer to Chapters 17 and 22.

---

[75] Ferreira and Merchant (1992) argue that the interchangeable use of the terms 'field research' and 'qualitative research' is problematic since many field research studies supplement their qualitative evidence with quantitative evidence.

[76] There are other research strategies available, such as life or oral histories, and ethnography; however, these are not commonly employed by accounting academicians.

The unit of analysis of a case study is an individual, a group, a department or an organisation. The case study is normally limited to a specific stage of an organisational life, or an incident. Its purpose is to identify and explain relevant information about each case of interest and is most useful when a topic remains unexplored or for providing preliminary evidence for surveys (Patton, 1990). The case research approach involves a combination of data collection methods such as archives (i.e. annual reports, minutes to meetings, memos), interviews, questionnaires and observations (Eisenhardt, 1989; Yin 1981). Through case analysis this raw data is reduced and sorted either chronologically or topically into what is referred to as a case study narrative – a report or publication on the case. The main criticism of this research method is its lack of generalisability (Ferreira and Merchant, 1992).

Kajuter and Kulmala (2005) in their paper on open-book accounting in networks, for example, conducted a case study of a German car manufacturer to describe open-book accounting practice in detail. The studies of Seal *et al.* (1999) and Ahrens and Chapman (2002) also utilise the single case based approach. Seal *et al.* employed this approach to understand the role of management accounting in the construction of a strategic partnership of two UK manufacturing companies, while Ahrens and Chapman used a single case study (a restaurant chain) to help explain how organisations can balance mechanistic and organic controls in the pursuit of efficiency and flexibility.

5.2. Field Studies

Field studies, whilst similar in nature to the case study, involve limited depth studies of two or more organisations (Smith, 2003; Lillis and Mundy, 2005). A distinguishing feature of the field study method is that it usually involves less intensive data collection than the single case study. One version of this approach is the comparative case method. The purpose of this field work is to observe and compare a particular phenomenon in its social context to improve the generalisability of findings. According to Lillis and Mundy (2005, p. 120) this method is most useful for theory refinement, 'where there is significant extant theory but doubt or disagreement about either the nature of the constructs on which the theory is built, the relations among these constructs, or their empirical interpretation'. An example of this strategy is Norris (2002) who compared the use of activity based techniques and information in two British banks to understand the different outcomes of implementation that may arise. Another example is that of Carr and Tomkins (1998) who analysed 51 case studies in the UK, US and Germany to understand the application of strategic cost management in practice.

5.3. Field Experiments

Field experiments are easily distinguished from other research methods because they involve the researcher observing a strict predefined range of behaviour under controlled conditions (Birnberg *et al.*, 1990; Jankowicz, 2005). In other words, they concentrate on providing evidence of causal relations between variables. As such this method can offer a high degree of generalisability (Birnberg *et al.*, 1990). However, it is often criticised because of the inability of the researcher to have sufficient control over the conditions of the experiment to draw any meaningful conclusions about the data set. Furthermore, it is common that when students are used as the data set, the results have poor generalisability for the population of interest (Brownell, 1995). Unlike other disciplines such as audit (as examples, see O'Donnell, 2002; Tsui, 1996) and financial accounting (as an example, see Sharma and Iselin, 2003), this method remains largely under-utilised in management accounting (Brownell, 1995; Schulz, 1999).[77] An example of this strategy in management accounting is Roodhooft and Warlop (1999) who conducted a field experiment with manager of health care organisations to determine their commitment to internal procurement versus outsourcing through specific investigation of sunk costs and asset specificity. Waller and Bishop (1990) provide a second example of this research method use in the management accounting discipline. They conducted two experiments to examine the effects of alternative incentive pay schemes for controlling unit manager behaviour in intrafirm resource allocation situations.

6. The Field Research Process

Becker (1998, p. 2) suggests that the qualitative researcher can be likened to a 'brocoleur', a quilt maker, who 'uses the aesthetic and material tools of his or her craft, deploying whatever strategies, methods, or empirics are at hand'. This metaphor implies that the researcher is vital to the success of any qualitative study, regardless of methods utilised since they are the 'measurement device'. For instance, they need to be capable of building sufficient trust with key informants in the case to enable them to enter the field when necessary, to ask any difficult questions which may be pertinent to the subject of study, and to be able to assess when sufficient data has been collected (Miles and Huberman, 1994).

Unlike quantitative research, qualitative research has a multi-method focus and the choice of research methods is not necessarily determined in advance allowing relevant data collection and analysis methods to be drawn upon. Research methods that are too rigid and standardised are unable to capture social phenomena in their full complexity and as a result the qualitative methods of data generation tend to be flexible and sensitive to context (Burgess, 1994). For instance, accounting historians because of the retrospective nature of their research are more likely to rely on documents as the primary data collection technique due to the unreliability of interviewee recall, whereas a study of a change in accounting process is likely to rely more heavily on interview evidence to understand process and the meanings attributed to the new and the discarded systems.

In this section we consider the protocols associated with the field research process, since this is the qualitative method with which we have been formally

---

[77] For a list of experimental research published prior to 1983 see Swieringa and Weick (1982).

trained and have personal experience. While there is no one best way to undertake qualitative research, we distinguish four separate steps in this section that are common to all field research: (1) choosing and accessing the case; (2) collecting the data; (3) analysing the data; and (4) writing and publishing field research. As we will discover, there are a number of issues and protocols to be considered in each step. These steps are designed to provide a general framework for conducting a field study but are not intended to provide an exhaustive guide to all of the qualitative research strategies. Furthermore, in a routine situation the steps will not necessarily occur in the sequences provided, but are complex interactive processes that may be repeated or overlapped with other processes (see also Ryan *et al.*, 2002). The protocols described in this section are intended to be broad and they are inherently based on our own experiences with field research; more extensive commentary on the protocols required for specific types of field research, such as case study is described elsewhere in this text.

6.1. Choosing and Accessing the Data

Unlike much research conducted in a quantitative tradition, collecting data in the qualitative tradition is not as simple as purchasing the latest data set, it requires you to spend prolonged periods in the field (Bédard and Gendron, 2004). In choosing a case, multiple cases in field study research, or whom to include in your research sample it is important to consider the ability of each of the cases and in turn the individuals to either extend our knowledge of a phenomenon such as management accounting or replicate an existing study for generalisability (Eisenhardt, 1989; Ryan *et al.*, 2002). In other words, there needs to be some justification for the choice of case organisations, such as their economic importance, their ability to offer new techniques, or their size. Ferreira and Merchant (1992) suggest that in securing sufficient access to organisations for case based researchers it is common to have a 50% success rate. Others, however, have reported this to be as low as 17% (see Bédard and Gendron, 2004). There can be many reasons for a lack of support of research including previous bad experiences with academic research, time constraints, or unsuitably identified cases. If possible, it can be useful to use existing contacts to help you to gain entry into a case (Jankowicz, 2005). If this is not possible you can expect the identification and negotiation of appropriate cases to be very time consuming. Furthermore, when access is a problem, your research may be subject to the criticism of representativeness. Bédard and Gendron (2004) suggest that one way to deal with this criticism is to highlight it as a limitation of study.

In many cases, as pointed out by Ahrens and Dent (1998), access to the case will follow from an initial discussion by the researcher with a member(s) of an organisation to identify issues/processes which they believe to be of some relevance to the organisation. In other words, a qualitative researcher does not start with a fixed set of ideas. (S)he examines the responses to develop ideas that seem fruitful (see also Glaser and Strauss, 1967; Van Maanen, 1979; Jick, 1979). It is important to enter a case already having analysed that data that is available in the public sphere on the organisation to demonstrate your commitment to understanding the organisation (Silverman, 2005). Initial ideas about organisational issues can stem from a range of sources such as newspaper clippings, professional agency publications, research on comparable organisations, and the internet or through commentary with employees in less formal settings. It is important as a researcher to enter the case with some understanding of potential issues, but also have an open mind and to realise that your initial conception about what could make an interesting contribution might not be the same as the organisations. You may find that the data collection process will identify more pressing organisational issues which will make a more substantive contribution to both the literature and to the organisation (Ferreira and Merchant, 1992). The negotiation process thus, will involve not only access to the organisation, but also the settings, events, processes and individuals who can contribute knowledge and offer representative views about the research topic (Miles and Huberman, 1994). This means that unlike quantitative research the research questions are not likely to be identified at the outset and may emerge from interaction with the field and once your theoretical and methodological options become clearer.

In the field, your role of the researcher may vary from a complete participant, participant-as-observer, observer-as-participant, or complete observer (Atkinson and Shaffir, 1998; Burgess, 1994). The negotiation of access should involve what your role in this regard will be. Will participants know that you are collecting data, or are you to be employed by the organisation and collect data as an employee? Will you be given access to all of the employees and locations of the company? Defining your role in the organisation is necessary to distinguish what research methods are appropriate and the level of information that participants will be provided about the study. In our experience a complete observer or observer-as-participant tends to be the roles which organisations are most comfortable with.

Once access to the organisation has been negotiated and the topic of study has been established, a review of existing research literature is required to define the study's research question, including defining the unit(s) of analysis and the criteria for interpreting the findings. The literature review will also help you to determine how to proceed with the data collection process. It is also necessary for identifying the type of evidence that is required to successfully complete the study.

6.2. Collecting the Data

Qualitative research relies on multiple methods such as artefacts, documents, interviews, and observation to provide answers to research questions.[78] The choice of methods will be determined by the research question and purposes of study. They should be used to validate existing evidence or help build a richer description of the phenomena. Individually, methods can be unreliable or unable to offer a holistic picture. For instance, while interviews may give an indication of how people

---

[78] Questionnaires and surveys may also be used as part of the qualitative research approach.

'see things' they tend to attach limited importance to 'how people do things', which requires alternative forms of data collection such as observation. Using multiple data collection techniques can be messy and produce an overwhelming amount of data so it is in your interest to keep a project diary to record your ideas and reflections about the direction of your research and how the various pieces of information collected helps to answer your research question.

6.2.1. Interviews. One of the most commonly used field research methods is the interview (Burgess, 1994). Interviews can take numerous forms including face-to-face individual or group interchange, mailed or administered questionnaires and telephone surveys. Irrespective of form, the interview research method is fundamental to field research based on its ability to provide an understanding of complex situations. In accounting research, in our experience and from the research published the most common form of interview used is individual face-to-face interviews.

Ahrens and Dent (1998) consider 'spreading the net' and talking to a wide range of organisational participants in various positions and locations to be necessary to understand the organisational complexities so that a rich understanding of the phenomenon of study can be built up. Again, it is important not to underestimate the time that this phase of the process may take as gaining interviews with individuals, for whom the research project is unlikely to be a priority can mean that they are unwilling to talk to you immediately because of their other commitments.

Interviewing skills are the key to successfully collecting evidence on the phenomenon of interest (Burgess, 1994). Prior to conducting the interview, you need to consider the interview approach you intend to use. Fully structured techniques involve asking respondents or participants a set of predetermined questions and responses. This approach will provide a limited set of data. For an inexperienced researcher this interview strategy can be useful to ensure that the interview discussion runs smoothly and that the amount of data is kept to a manageable level (Miles and Huberman, 1994). The comparability of cases may rely on a more structured approach. For case study research, semi-structured, open-ended techniques may be more relevant if the intended purpose of the research is to understand the meanings that interviewees link to issues and situations. General interview themes will have been identified in advance of the interview, but these will be used only as a guide allowing the interviewer to probe the interviewee and provide stories about how and why particular meanings attached to phenomenon. This interview approach, while offering no generalisability provides sufficient flexibility for you to build up a richer understanding of the complexities of the research setting because respondents are encouraged to answer in their own words. In choosing the interview approach, you also need to consider the knowledge of your subjects and their involvement with the phenomena of study. Understanding such participant characteristics will help to determine the type of questions that are relevant and how they should be worded.

A good way to begin the interview is to open with more general questions. For instance, ask the participant about their job and what it entails. This helps to put the respondent at ease so that they will more willingly participate in the discussions which will follow. In the interview, you also need to be mindful of how your own comments and stories may influence the participant responses and be sensitive to any of the non-verbal signals exhibited. Paying close attention to non-verbal signals is especially important for understanding the boundaries of the topics that participants are willing to be questioned about (Jankowicz, 2005).

You need to devise an interview schedule to conduct interviews during your fieldwork. An interview schedule serves several purposes: it introduces the purpose and methods of the research to your interviewees; it emphasises the importance placed on the views of each of the respondents; it stresses the confidentiality of the information provided; perceptions and attitudes of interviewees towards control systems; and it provides a basic checklist during the interview to make sure that all relevant topics are covered (for further details, see Miles and Huberman, 1994).

It is suggested (Patton, 1987) that before going into the field a researcher should consider: what questions to ask; how to sequence questions; how much detail to solicit; how long to make the interview; and, how to word the actual questions. These are all measurement questions affecting the quality of interview responses. Some questions could be similar for every interviewee; some might seek clarification about the interviewee's own responsibility, interactions with other people in the organisation and the types of controls to which the interviewee has subjected and used to control his/her subordinates.

Where possible, interviewees should be asked clear, precise, singular open ended questions, which avoid putting any unnecessary or unfair burden of interpretation on the interviewees. For instance, if you were investigating the change in a management control system, your questions might follow a sequence similar to the following:

Can you describe the management control system in your organisation?
[Interviewee responds].
How and why has the management control system changed in the past five years?
[Interviewee responds].

Depending on the level of description given, you might ask the following probing questions, to build up a richer account of the system:

Now I'd like to ask you to reflect on the control system's strengths and weaknesses, then to suggest possible improvements and changes. First, then, what do you consider the system's strengths?
[Interviewee responds].
OK, what about weaknesses?
[Interviewee responds].

What changes would you recommend improving the system?
[Interviewee responds].

As implied above, the interview schedule should be used flexibly. If an interviewee shows special interest in an issue and wishes to develop it he/she should be allowed and encouraged to do so. If, on the other hand, he/she appears uninterested or uneasy about a line of questioning it should be dropped. This should provide interviewees with sufficient encouragement to make them more open in discussion. This technique also serves, *'inter alia'*, to build confidence and give the interviewer an assurance that all of the relevant topics are discussed.

Field notes should be kept of each interview. These will be the key to developing your understanding of whether there is consensus in the views of the participants. Field notes commonly include details such as the date of the interview, the name of the interviewee and any other individuals present, where the interview was conducted, what social interactions occur, any observations (i.e. non-verbal signals such as body language or appearance), follow up ideas or new or interesting questions that should be posed to other participants, and pre/post interview banter (Patton, 1987). Such small details can be very helpful for trying to recollect the interview at a later date (Ahrens and Dent, 1998). Miles and Huberman (1984, see p. 57) provide an interview summary form, which may provide further guidance on this. These summary forms are useful not only for recording what went on in the interview but also for planning the issues that need to be discussed in future interviews (Miles and Huberman, 1984).

In addition, the interviews, where possible, should be tape recorded to allow for specific quotes to be used in the write up to improve the credibility of inferences drawn. Tape recording interviews has both advantages and disadvantages. The primary advantage is that it allows all that is said to be recorded permitting the interviewer to be more attentive to the interviewee. Thus, the interviewer is free to concentrate on the responses and the more subtle interactional aspects of the interview. This encourages the meaning attached to responses to be discovered more easily. On occasions it can even increase rapport between interviewer and interviewee.

These tapes should be transcribed verbatim at the nearest opportunity while the interview is still fresh in the researcher's mind so they can add in their own notes on observations or possible theoretical links. Bear in mind, transcribing a single one hour interview can be time consuming and as a result in our experience this is probably the most painful part of the qualitative process!

Note that there may also be certain drawbacks in using the tape recorder during interview. In particular, it can affect the interviewee's reception to the research, with in extreme cases a refusal to be interviewed. The behaviour and responses of an interviewee may also be affected by the presence of a recorder, and in some cases, respondents may decline to comment on confidential or sensitive issues.

6.2.2.   Documents and records. Documents and records are also important sources of information for providing insight into social events and phenomena. These can usually be obtained relatively easily and at a low cost to the researcher, however, they do not provide the opportunity for interaction.

6.2.3.   Observation. Observation is important for its ability to offer a richer understanding of how people do things and the way systems work in practice. It is possible, for instance, that observation of the layout of a factory floor may provide a much better understanding of how costs are accumulated in an organisation than a description offered in an interview or by looking at a document such as a general ledger. In negotiating access you need to be clear about the particular research issue which you intend to observe. A number of issues need to be considered if observation is to be used as a research method, such as how to build up trust with the participants being observed, the level of participation in the field setting and how and when you will withdraw from the field. The value of this research method, similar to interviews relies on the researcher skills to accurately document their observations. Because we are limited in our capacity to observe all of the ingredients of a process, supplementing observations with interview evidence is useful for providing a better understanding.

6.3.   Methods of Analysis

How best to analyse and order the overwhelming amount of qualitative data collected so that it is both convincing but also representative of the phenomena under study is a question that confronts even the most experienced researcher.

The various types of qualitative data implies that there is no uniform approach to carrying out this process. Initially, your analysis will begin by reading interview transcripts, observations, notes, or documents. Each piece of evidence or data should be assessed to in terms of its reliability and validity. Chapter 22 comments on the criteria that are commonly used to assess the reliability and validity further. Following this, three interactive processes are commonly used to bring the data to publication: data reduction, data display and conclusion drawing and verification (Silverman, 2005). These processes begin when data collection commences and continues through to the write up of the case study.

As a researcher, you always run the risk that you will choose an overly simplistic or inaccurate framework to help make sense of the data. For this reason it is important to review case information routinely to assess its validity and reliability and any inferences you might have drawn.

The analysis of qualitative data can be done in either an inductive or deductive fashion. Using an inductive approach, also called grounded theory, means that you will attempt to build up a theory using your case materials through careful analysis of text to identify processes, actions, assumptions and consequences. While this strategy can produce fresh useful insights on a phenomenon, it can be problematic for an inexperienced researcher who may be overcome with the vast quantities of data and as a result may find it difficult to draw any inferences about the themes that are emerging from the case materials. The inductive nature of the grounded theory approach also means that it is likely to be a more time consuming process.

Using a deductive approach involves drawing on existing or pre-ordained theories to provide a frame of reference for analysing your case material. Apart from providing a basis for starting the analysis process, the deductive approach means that your research will already be linked with an existing body of knowledge in the subject area. In the first phase of deductive analysis, it is common to develop categories for sorting the data. These categories develop from your theoretical framework or will emerge from a content analysis of the data collected. Content analysis of documents and interview transcripts involves searching the text for recurring themes and patterns to help to reduce the amount of data and to identify consistencies and meanings. Once categories have been identified, you should go back and re-read the data and code sections or bits of it according to the categories. These sections or bits may be complete sentences, paragraphs or diagrams (Saunders *et al.*, 2003). This can be done by placing a category code in the margins of the paper, followed by each category being cut and re-arranged according to the category. (It is advisable to use photocopies for this purpose, not the originals). Arranging data in this manner is a form of analysis that can be useful for integrating related data from multiple sources of evidence and for helping to assess the level of detail of your information. This is important because qualitative research strategies, such as field studies, are designed to provide richer insights to accounting in organisational life (Ahrens and Dent, 1998). This approach will also help you to identify any alternative explanations which do not conform to the patterns of data being tested.

There are also various Computer-Assisted Qualitative Data Analysis Software (CAQDAS) software packages available to help manage and sort qualitative data including Nudist, NVivo and Atlas. Case analysis of accounting studies has, however, up until this point tended to rely on the manual processes described in this section.[79] There are many plausible reasons for this including the lack of research training in using these programs and the fact that they provide a basis for managing data but do not ensure that the important themes or patterns are identified.

Once the data is arranged in categories you need to try and identify patterns in the data. This phase is used to understand how the different perspectives in any one category are related to each other and to help cumulatively to understand the phenomena being studied. Ryan *et al.* (2002) recommend the use of diagrams or charts at this stage to link the themes and categories. These diagrams and charts can also be useful for comparing the emerging case explanations with available theories.

---

[79] See Seale (in Silverman, 2005) and Weitzman (in Denzin and Lincoln, 2000) for further discussion on the use of computers to analyse qualitative data.

An important process of the analysis step is to look for negative patterns and to identify any rival explanations which may explain the phenomenon (Miles and Huberman, 1994).

6.4. *Writing and Publishing Qualitative Research*

Writing up research is never a neutral process (for details, see Chapter 25). The purpose of the writing process is to provide accurate and reliable answers to the research question. The format, language and the choice of which narratives provide representative examples of what went on and how people see things is, however, left to the researcher's discretion. And, the nature of qualitative research means there is no generally recognised structure for writing up qualitative papers making the process messy, challenging and time consuming process. Ryan *et al.* (2002), for instance, estimate that it takes equal time to set up the study, carry out the field work and write up the study.

When writing up, a useful starting point is to clarify who you expect your target audience to be. Is it going to be academics? Is it going to be practitioners? Is it going to be a mixture of academics and practitioners? Is it going to be students or policy makers? Consideration of the target audience is required for determining the type of language, the depth of detail that is required, and the length of the report. Once you have determined who the target audience is, you need to consider your publication outlet. Is the research going to be published in an accounting journal, magazine, monograph or other? The nature of academy requires some publication in academic journals.

Despite the criticisms raised towards the limitations of neoclassical economics to inform 'good' research in management accounting and the successive calls for more qualitative studies informed by interpretative and critical perspectives (Kaplan, 1984) positivism and quantitative studies still dominate published literature. This is particularly true in the US. The American academy is considered by some to be rather conservative; any new theoretical and methodological perspectives other than those based on positivism and quantitative models of research are seen as inferior (Lee, 2004). Qualitative case study research is often considered as 'unscientific' and therefore regarded as lacking quality. For American researchers, the use of statistical techniques to test data relationships is considered to be indispensable to investigate management accounting issues. Research training programs continue to focus on providing scholars with a toolkit of various calculative techniques for testing accounting relationships. Research questions are expected to be posed and answered by quantitative means following a positivist and empirical model, otherwise research is not considered to be trustworthy. As a result accounting studies based on qualitative research are a rarity in the US. Major American journals, such as *The Accounting Review, Journal of Accounting Research* and *Journal of Accounting and Economics*, and the editors of these journals spur the publication of empirical investigation based on quantitative research (Lee, 2004).

Regardless of the dominance of quantitative studies, the last two decades have signalled important progress in the development of qualitative studies. A range of European and Asia Pacific journals including *Accounting, Organisations and Society* (AOS), *Management Accounting Research* (MAR), *Accounting, Auditing and Accountability Journal* (AAAJ), the *Journal of Accounting and Organisational Change* (JAOC) and *Qualitative Research in Accounting and Management* (QRAM) have been known to publish significant numbers of qualitative papers. Many of these journals also publish special issues which may be more sympathetic to qualitative research.[80] Each of these has a set of criteria for the layout of the manuscript which should be adhered to in the write up of the case.

Apart from familiarising yourself with the journal submission requirements, you will find it helpful to review other case studies published on the subject in a similar outlet. These can give hints as to the composition of the report, the writing style, and the appropriate length (Yin, 2003). If the case is to be written as a dissertation, for instance, the format is vastly different than a publication for an academic journal such as AOS.

It is also important to be mindful of any agreements that you have negotiated to gain access to the case in the writing up phase. For instance, if the name of the company and any participants are to remain anonymous, then consideration needs to be given in the writing up stage as to how you intend to disguise their identity.[81]

In accounting, the case based write ups have in the past been criticised for
(1) misused or weak attempts to link the literature to the contribution the case;
(2) excessive focus on conclusions; and
(3) poor communication of ideas because of over use of complex theoretical terms (Ferreira and Merchant, 1992).

To overcome these criticisms it is useful to first test your ideas on how you think your field evidence explains the phenomena of study by sending drafts of the manuscript to key participants for verification. From a theoretical standpoint, it is also useful to give any case write ups to your supervisor or other academics who are familiar with the theoretical standpoint to test the applicability of the theoretical framework for explaining the case. Getting the right balance between the theory and field materials is difficult and can require much reflection and a return to the case evidence to test theoretical patterns and themes. In addition, it is important to make use of quotations from interviews and organisational documentation in the write-up. Ahrens and Dent (1998) suggest that identifying key quotes or events in the analysis phase can provide a useful way to compose a manuscript. Such dialogue also helps the reader of the manuscript to understand the participant's frame of reference. The conclusion section of the write-up should focus on answering the research question, it should tease out the implications of the research and it should

---

[80] See Guthrie *et al.* (2004) for other possible publishing outlets.
[81] For a more complete treatment of confidentiality issues see Irvine (2003).

present any limitations of the research. Depending on the nature of the study, the descriptions can be equally if not more important than the conclusion because this is where the 'rich' description about the phenomena is provided. This is particularly important when the purposes of the qualitative research are to illustrate new or innovative accounting techniques.

Generally, three criteria can be used to assess whether you have been successful in your case write-up; authenticity, plausibility, and criticality (Ryan *et al.*, 2002). Authenticity refers to the extent to which you have demonstrated that the study findings are grounded in the case evidence. In order to do this rich descriptions must be provided of the evidence to support any assertions made. Plausibility is determined by linking the case interpretations with existing theories and literature. Criticality is assessed via an assessment of the new research ideas and/or questions raised in the paper. Does the paper, for instance, make a contribution to the existing knowledge of a subject? Alternatively, the research may be assessed based on theory generation where theories are assessed based on their ability to hold some explanatory power for other cases.

7.   Summary

In academe, qualitative research has emerged as an alternative and popular way of doing research, providing fresh insights to the way that management accounting interacts within its environment. In the new and increasingly complex business environment, this research tradition has much to offer to improve our understanding of the role of accounting has played in the construction of this environment. This chapter was written for the novice researcher, providing an overview of the qualitative landscape including a review of its history in the discipline, its philosophical assumptions and the protocols that are commonly used to carry out one type of qualitative study, the field study.

References

Ahrens, T. and Chapman, C. (2002), "The structuration of legitimate performance measures and management: day-to-day contests of accountability in a UK restaurant chain", *Management Accounting Research*, Vol. 13, No. 2, pp. 151-171.

Ahrens, T. and Dent, J. F. (1998), "Accounting and organizations: realizing the richness of field research", *Journal of Management Accounting Research*, Vol. 10, pp. 1-39.

Ansari, S. and Bell. J. (1991), "Symbolism, collectivism and rationality in organisational control", *Accounting, Auditing and Accountability Journal*, Vol. 4, No. 2, pp. 4-27.

Atkinson, A. A. and Shaffir, W. (1998), "Standards for field research in management accounting", *Journal of Management Accounting Research*, Vol. 10, pp. 41-67.

Baker, C. R. and Bettner, M. S. (1997), "Interpretive and critical research in accounting: a commentary on its absence from mainstream accounting research", *Critical Perspectives on Accounting*, Vol. 8, No. 4, pp. 293-310.

Barker, R. G. (1968), *Ecological Psychology*, Stanford University, Stanford.

Becker, H. S. (1998), *Tricks of the Trade: How to Think About Your Research While You Are Doing It*, University of Chicago Press, Chicago.

Bédard, J. and Gendron, Y. (2004), "Qualitative research on accounting: some thoughts on what occurs behind the scene", in Humphrey, C. and Lee, B. (Eds.), *The Real-Life Guide to Accounting Research*, Elsevier, Oxford, pp. 191-206.

Birnberg, J., Shields, M. D. and Young, S. M. (1990), "The case for multiple methods in empirical management accounting research (with an illustration from budget setting)", *Journal of Management Accounting Research*, Vol. 2, Fall, pp. 33-66.

Brownell, P. (1995), *Research Methods in Management Accounting*, Coopers & Lybrand, Australia.

Bryman, A. (1984), "The debate about quantitative and qualitative research: a question of method or epistemology?", *The British Journal of Sociology*, Vol. XXXV, pp. 75-92.

Burgess, R.G. (1994), *In the Field: An Introduction to Field Research*, Routledge, London.

Burrell, G. and Morgan, G. (1979), *Sociological Paradigms and Organizational Analysis: Elements of the Sociology of Corporate Life*, Heinemann Educational Books Ltd, London.

Bussis, A., Chittenden, E. A. and Amarel, M. (1973), *Methodology in Educational Evaluation Research*, Educational Testing Service (Mimo), Princeton, NJ.

Carini, P. F. (1975), *Observation and Description: An Alternative Methodology for the Investigation of Human Phenomena*, North Dakota Study Group on Evaluation Monograph Series, University of North Dakota, Grand Forks.

Carr, C. and Tomkins, C. (1998), "Context, culture and the role of the finance function in strategic decisions. A comparative analysis of Britain, Germany, the U.S.A. and Japan", *Management Accounting Research*, Vol. 9, No. 2, pp. 213-239.

Chua, W. F. (1986), "Theoretical constructions of and by the real", *Accounting, Organizations and Society*, Vol. 11, No. 6, pp. 583-598.

Covaleski, M. A. and Dirsmith, M. W. (1983), "Budgeting as a means for control and loose coupling", *Accounting, Organizations and Society*, Vol. 8, No. 4, pp. 323-340.

Covaleski, M. A. and Dirsmith, M. W. (1990), "Dialectic tension, double reflexivity and the everyday accounting researcher: on using qualitative methods", *Accounting, Organizations and Society*, Vol. 15, No. 6, pp. 543-573.

Covaleski, M. A., Dirsmith, M. W. and Samuel, S. (1996), "Managerial accounting research: the contributions of organizational and sociological theories", *Journal of Management Accounting Research*, Vol. 8, pp. 1-35.

Dent, J. F., Ezzamel, M. and Bourn, M. (1984), "Reflections on research in management accounting and its relationship to practice: an academic view", in Hopwood, A. and Schreuder, H. (Eds.), *European Contributions to Accounting Research: The Achievements of the Last Decade*, Free University Press, Amsterdam, pp. 233-253.

Denzin, N. K. (1978), *Sociological Methods: A Sourcebook*, McGraw-Hill, US, in Denzin, N. and Lincoln, Y. (2000) (Eds.), *Handbook of Qualitative Research*, 2nd edition, Sage Publications, Thousand Oaks, CA.

Eisenhardt, K. (1989), "Building theories from case study research", *The Academy of Management Review*, Vol. 14, No. 4, pp. 532-550.

Ferreira, L. D. and Merchant, K. A. (1992), "Field research in management accounting and control: a review and evaluation", *Accounting, Auditing and Accountability Journal*, Vol. 5, No. 4, pp. 3-34.

Garfinkel, H. (1967), *Studies in Ethnomethodology*, Prentice-Hall, Englewood Cliffs, NJ.

Glaser, B. G. and Strauss, A. L. (1967), *The Discovery of Grounded Theory: Strategies for Qualitative Research*, Aldine Press, Chicago.

Guthrie, J., Parker, L. D. and Gray, R. (2004), "Requirements and understandings for publishing academic research: an insider view", in Humphrey, C. and Lee, B. (Eds.), *The Real-Life Guide to Accounting* Research, Elsevier, Oxford, pp. 411-432.

Hopper, T. and Powell, A. (1985), "Making sense of research into organizational and social aspects of management accounting: a review of its underlying assumptions", *Journal of Management Studies*, Vol. 22, No. 5, pp. 429-465.

Hopwood, A. (1983), "On trying to study accounting in the contexts in which it operates", *Accounting, Organizations and Society*, Vol. 8, pp. 287-305.

Humphrey, C. and Scapens, R. (1996), "Methodological themes: theories and case studies of organisational accounting practices: limitation or liberation?", *Accounting, Auditing and Accountability Journal*, Vol. 9, No. 4, pp. 86-106.

Hussey, J. and Hussey, R. (1997), *Business Research: a Practical Guide for Undergraduate and Postgraduate Students*, Macmillan Business, London.

Irvine, H. (2003), "Trust me! A personal account of confidentiality issues in an organisational research project", *Accounting Forum*, Vol. 27, pp. 111-131.

Jankowicz, A. D. (2005), *Business Research Projects*, Thomson, London.

Jick, T. D. (1979), "Mixing qualitative and quantitative methods: triangulation in action", *Administrative Science Quarterly*, Vol. 24, No. 4, pp. 602-611.

Jonsson, S. and Macintosh, N. B. (1997), "Cats, rats and ears: making the case for ethnographic accounting research", *Accounting, Organizations and Society*, Vol. 22, No. 3/4, pp. 367-386.

Kajuter, P. and Kulmala, H. I. (2005), "Open-book accounting in networks: potential achievements and reasons for failures", *Management Accounting Research*, Vol. 16, No. 2, pp. 179-204.

Kaplan, R. S. (1984), "The evolution of management accounting", *The Accounting Review*, July, pp. 390-418.

Kaplan, R. S. (1986), "The role for empirical research in management accounting", *Accounting, Organizations and Society*, Vol. 11, No. 4/5, pp. 429-452.

Lee, T. A. (2004), "Accounting and auditing research in the United States", in Humphrey, C. and Lee, B. (Eds.), *The Real-Life Guide to Accounting* Research, Elsevier, Oxford, pp. 57-72.

Lillis, A. M. and Mundy, J. (2005), "Cross-sectional field studies in management accounting research – closing the gaps between surveys and case studies", *Journal of Management Accounting Research*, Vol. 17, pp. 119-141.

Lukka, K. and Kasanen, A. (1995), "The problem of generalizability: anecdotes and evidence in accounting research", *Accounting, Auditing and Accountability Journal*, Vol. 8, No. 5, pp. 71-90.

Lukka, K. and Granlund, M. (2002), "The fragmented communication structure within the accounting academia: the case of activity-based costing research genres", *Accounting, Organizations and Society*, Vol. 27, No. 1/2, pp. 165-190.

Mason, J. (2002), *Qualitative Researching*, 2nd edition, Sage Publications, London.

Maxwell, J. A. (2005), *Qualitative Research Design: An Interactive Approach*, Sage Publications, Thousand Oaks, CA.

Miles, M. B. and Huberman, A. M. (1984), *Qualitative Data Analysis: A Sourcebook of New Methods*, Sage Publications Inc., Beverley Hills, CA.

Miles, M. B. and Huberman, A. M. (1994), *Qualitative Data Analysis: A Sourcebook of New Methods*, Sage Publications Inc., Beverley Hills, CA.

Morgan, G. (1983), "Social science and accounting research: a commentary on Tomkins and Groves", *Accounting, Organizations and Society*, Vol. 8, No. 4, pp. 385-388.

Morgan, G. (1988), "Accounting as reality construction: towards a new epistemology for accounting practice", *Accounting, Organizations and Society*, Vol. 13, No. 5, pp. 477-485.

Morgan, G. (1997), *Images of Organization*, Sage Publications, Thousand Oaks, CA.

Morgan, G. and Smircich, L. (1980), "The case for qualitative research", *Academy of Management Review*, Vol. 5, No. 4, pp. 491-500.

Norris, G. (2002), "Chalk and cheese: grounded theory case studies of the introduction and usage of activity based information in two British banks", *The British Accounting Review*, Vol. 34, No. 3, pp. 223-255.

O'Donnell, E. (2002), "Evidence of an association between error-specific experience and auditor performance during analytic procedures", *Behavioral Research in Accounting*, Vol. 14, pp. 179-195.

Otley, D. T. (1984), "Management accounting and organization theory: a review of their inter-relationship", in Scapens, R., Otley, D. T. and Lister, R. (Eds.), *Management Accounting, Organizational Theory and Capital Budgeting: Three Surveys*, Macmillan, London, pp. 96-164.

Patton, M. Q. (1987), *How to Use Qualitative Methods in Evaluation*, Sage, Beverly Hills, CA.

Patton, M. Q. (1990), *Qualitative Evaluation and Research Methods*, Sage Publications, Beverly Hills, CA.

Pelto, P. J. and Pelto, G. H. (1978), *Anthropological Research: The Structure of Inquiry*, Cambridge University Press, Cambridge.

Roberts, J. and Scapens, R. (1985), "Accounting systems and systems of accountability – understanding accounting practices in their organisational contexts", *Accounting, Organizations and Society*, Vol. 10, No. 4, pp. 443-456.

Roodhooft, F. and Warlop, L. (1999), "On the role of sunk costs and asset specificity in outsourcing decisions: a research note", *Accounting, Organizations and Society*, Vol. 24, No. 4, pp. 363-369.

Ryan, B., Scapens, R. W. and Theobold, M. (2002), *Research Method and Methodology in Finance and Accounting*, 2nd edition, Thomson, London.

Saunders, M., Lewis, P. and Thornhill, A. (2003), *Research Methods for Business Students*, Pearson Education Limited, Essex, England.

Scapens, R. W. (1990), "Researching managing accounting practice: the role of case study methods", *British Accounting Review*, Vol. 22, No. 3, pp. 259-281.

Scapens, R. W. and Roberts, J. (1993), "Accounting and control: a case study of resistance to accounting change", *Management Accounting Research*, Vol. 4, pp. 1-32.

Schulz, A. (1999), "Experimental research method in a management accounting context", *Accounting and Finance*, Vol. 39, pp. 29-51.

Seal, W., Cullen, J., Dunlop, A., Berry, T. and Ahmed, M. (1999), "Enacting a European supply chain: a case study on the role of management accounting", *Management Accounting Research*, Vol. 10, No. 3, pp. 303-322.

Sharma, D. S. and Iselin, E. R. (2003), "The decision usefulness of reported cash flow and accrual information in a behavioural field experiment", *Accounting and Business Research*, Vol. 33, No. 2, pp. 123-135.

Silverman, D. (2005), *Doing Qualitative Research: A Practical Handbook*, Sage, London.

Smith, M. (2003), *Research Methods in Accounting*, Sage Publications, London.

Stoner, G. and Holland, J. (2004), "Using case studies in finance research", in Humphrey, C. and Lee, B. (Eds.), *The Real-Life Guide to Accounting Research*, Elsevier, Oxford, pp. 37-56.

Strike, K. (1972), Explaining and Understanding: The Impact of Science on our Concept of Man. *Philosophical Redirection of Educational Research: The Seventy-first Yearbook of the National Society for the Study of Education*. L. G. Thomas. Chicago, University of Chicago Press.

Swieringa, R. J. and Weick, K. R. (1982), "An assessment of laboratory experiments in accounting", *Journal of Accounting Research*, Vol. 20, pp. 56-101.

Tomkins, C. and Groves, R. (1983), "The everyday accountant and researching his reality", *Accounting, Organizations and Society*, Vol. 8, No. 4, pp. 361-374.

Tsui, J. S. L. (1996), "Auditors' ethical reasoning: some audit conflict and cross cultural evidence", *The International Journal of Accounting*, Vol. 31, No. 1, pp. 121-133.

Van Maanen, J. (1979), "Reclaiming qualitative methods for organizational research: a preface", *Administrative Science Quarterly*, Vol. 24, No. 4, pp. 520-526.

Waller, W. and Bishop, R. (1990), "An experimental study of incentive pay schemes, communication and intrafirm resource allocation", *The Accounting Review*, Vol. 65, No. 4, pp. 812-836.

Willmott, H. C. (1983), "Paradigms for accounting research: critical reflections on Tomkins and Groves' everyday accountant and researching his reality", *Accounting, Organizations and Society*, Vol. 8, No. 4, pp. 389-405.

Yin, R. K. (1981), "The case study crisis: some answers", *Administrative Science Quarterly*, Vol. 26, No. 1, pp. 58-65.

Yin, R. K. (2003), *Case Study Research: Design and Methods*, Sage Publications, Inc., Thousand Oaks, CA.

19

PROTOCOL ANALYSIS

David Campbell
University of Newcastle upon Tyne, UK

Abstract: This chapter discusses protocol analysis and its prior and potential employment in accounting research. It places the method within its epistemological context and reviews the principal ways in which it has been employed by accounting researchers who have sought to dissect and understand the behavioural and cognitive aspects of accounting expertise. Finally, the chapter discusses method issues and then examines limitations, developments and future research opportunities.

Keywords: Protocol analysis; Content analysis; Expertise; Deconstruct

1. Introduction

Engagement with practitioners, policy makers, capital market participants and others has been in the ascendant in accounting research in recent years. The purposes behind such encounters vary but where engagement is for the purposes of examining professional practice, 'expertise' or work study, protocol analysis offers a potentially useful framework for analysis.

It offers the possibility of making explicit, and helping to externalise, the often highly internalised tacit knowledge constructs resident within an 'expert' in a given area. By probing the construction of an expertise, the understanding of that expertise can be enhanced. This, in turn has the potential benefits of informing work study analyses, identifying and transferring best practice, and facilitating greater understanding of that expertise. In accounting research, it has been used to dissect and deconstruct the behavioural and cognitive components of activities such as audit, financial analysis and loan decision-making.

In the most frequently employed version, protocol analysis is a research method that involves a practitioner speaking aloud as he or she undertakes a task. The task is usually of some complexity and typically involves a decision to make or a problem to solve. When recorded, transcribed and content analysed, the processes by which the practitioner has undertaken the task can be dissected by various means so as to understand its execution in a way that would not have been possible by alternative methods such as, for example, mere observation. The complex construction of expertise and the highly internalised nature of tacit knowledge, often cultivated over many years and decades of practice, presents a challenge to those seeking to deconstruct and understand it. Protocol analysis offers such an opportunity. It differs from other engagement methods (such as interview) in that it is formal or semi-formal and that it requires the active participation of the subject (person being studied). The subject must agree not only to give up time for the encounter but also to engage actively with the research. In situations where access to subjects *at all* is an issue, this additional requirement may be significant.

Simple, if reductionist, examples of protocol analysis may serve to clarify its meaning. In their influential book on protocol analysis, Ericsson & Simon (1993) give the example of a person conducting a simple piece of mental arithmetic. The person could be asked, for example, to mentally calculate 24 multiplied by 36. A researcher might observe the subject arriving at the answer by non-verbal observation - perhaps by watching the subject as he or she thinks and then finally announces the answer. Alternatively, by asking the subject to verbalise the mental processes by which they arrive at the answer, the observer can gain an appreciation of the protocols employed that would not have been otherwise possible: "24 times 36? Well 6 times 4 is 24, so put in the 4 and carry the 2. 3 times 4 is 12, add the 2 makes 14. So the first line is 144. Now put in the 0 on the right hand side, 2 times 6 is 12, carry the 1, etc." until finally the subject announces, "so the answer is 864." By asking the subject to verbalise as he or she carries out the mental arithmetic, the observer learns the procedures employed in the calculation process in a way that would not have been otherwise possible.

Imagine also a scene where a motorist speaks to an experienced mechanic about a disturbing knocking noise in his car engine. The motorist might ask the mechanic in advance what he intends to do to diagnose the fault and repair it but such an approach would be unlikely to elicit a helpful response. This would be partly due to the reluctance of the subject (the mechanic) to explain in detail what might be a complex job to a non-specialist and partly because, in all likelihood, the mechanic does not approach such jobs in a manner amenable to detailed advanced prescription. If, instead, the mechanic agrees to describe the entirety of the job as he conducts it in 'real time', then some insight into the expertise of the mechanic can be gained. A full description of each stage, or protocol, could be used not only to establish time allocations per protocol but also the intellectual processes undergone to diagnose the knocking noise and ascertain how to expedite the repair. An experienced mechanic would be likely to go about this task in a different manner from a novice and an analysis of the protocols employed would be a way of understanding the nature of the expertise of the experienced mechanic.

Protocol analysis is superficially, therefore, a simple research method to understand. In practice however, the emphases placed, nuances examined and methods of deconstruction explored differ according to the research question being asked, the levels of resolution sought and the type of expertise being dissected. This chapter is intended to introduce the method, to review its epistemic and methodological underpinnings and then to briefly consider how it has been employed by accounting researchers.

2. Epistemological Context

The links between ontological assumption, epistemic and method have been discussed for some time in the broader accounting literature and in many other areas of academic enquiry. Early attempts to rationalise the paradigms employed in accounting research found an over-emphasis on methodologies stressing the supposed knowability of truth using broad scientific approaches. Employing the continuum of methodological assumptions described in Morgan & Smircich (1980), Tomkins & Groves (1983) highlighted the numbers of studies using the continuum points, 'reality as concrete structure' and 'reality as concrete process' and showed that these studies had dominated accounting research up to that point. Such positions tended to privilege method employing scientific assumptions with regard to the use of dependent and independent variables where each variable is assumed capable of, usually parametrically, accurately describing a reality:

1. reality as a concrete structure
2. reality as a concrete process
3. reality as a contextual field of information
4. reality as symbolic discourse
5. reality as social construction
6. reality as projection of human imagination

Source: Morgan and Smircich (1980, p. 492).

It was the points towards the other end of the continuum that Tomkins & Groves argued were potentially more useful ontological perspectives for the exploration of a complex social science like accounting. Inasmuch as accounting activities, broadly defined, are human activities, involving human decision making and problem solving, assumptions of reality other than accounting as 'concrete' construct are more valid in some research spaces. Such assumptions suggest that methodologies relying on psychological rather than economic constructions of reality may be more appropriate probing instruments when seeking to understand behavioural or cognitive issues.

Where human understanding, or, at a deeper level, *'verstehen'* is a prominent motive in a research task, Tomkins & Groves (1983) argued that 'interpretive humanistic' methods were demonstrably more appropriate than any based on reality as anything more 'concrete' (Morgan & Smircich, 1980) than social constructionism. "In so far as accounting research is concerned with the effects of accounting practices upon social action...there is a strong case for examining 'naturalistic' research approaches." (Tomkins & Groves, 1983: 367)

The recognition of these early thinkers of the need for different epistemologies to address different research questions was not an original observation, of course. Some of the more penetrating critiques of positivist methodology had been made before. Blumer (1956), for example, noted that, "for certain types of research problems concerning social behaviour, the 'scientific' model is not just difficult to manage, but is manifestly inappropriate," especially when the research need was for "feeling one's way inside the experience of the actor" in order to gain an understanding (*verstehen*) of the research subject's subjective perspectives in specific decision contexts (Tomkins & Groves, 1983).

Perhaps unsurprisingly, the major theoretical descriptions of protocol analysis have been made by psychologists (Newell & Simon, 1972; Payne, 1976; Payne et al. 1978; Einhorn et al, 1979; Ericsson & Simon, 1980; Ericsson & Simon, 1993) and it is they who have most penetratingly sought to theoretically underpin protocol analysis whilst also examining its empirical possibilities. In method (rather than methodological) terms, protocol analysis can be seen to have been derived from, and be linked to, a number of areas of prior studies including work study, ethnomethodology, knowledge theory and learning behaviour and as such is an eclectic method and one potentially subject to critique from a range of perspectives.

The origin of protocol analysis as a recognised research method appears to be rooted in the 1970s with Nisbett & Wilson (1977), Newell & Simon (1972) and Ericsson & Simon (1980) being influential in its development. Newell & Simon (1972) derived a protocol-based method substantially from data processing theory and process tracing, which "proclaims man to be an information processing system, at least when he is solving problems... [It] posits a set of processes or mechanisms that produce the behaviour of thinking humans" (p. 9) which, explicitly, are accessible to comprehension using protocol analysis. It is, thus, an unambiguously idiographic way to probe aspects of human behaviour and cognition. It can be understood at the level of the individual, and processes observed in one individual patently need not be evident in another. Newell & Simon drew substantially in what was (at the time) a relatively new understanding of information processing that arose from the need to programme computers to perform tasks. It is likely that post-Aristotelian assumptions of thought as a temporal quasi-linear sequence of mental events underpin the theory – a point made explicit by Ericsson & Simon (1993). Human behaviour can, Newell & Simon argued, be conceptualised in an equivalent manner: problem spaces are identified which an individual seeks to develop internal (sometimes linear-rational) programmes to solve. The development of such internal programming may have contributed to the development of what later became understood as tacit or implicit knowledge – development of increasing cognitive abilities to facilitate the solving of increasingly complex problems.

The initial epistemological contribution of Ericsson & Simon (1980) was operationalised as protocol analysis in the first edition of their book of the same name in 1984 (second edition is cited here as Ericsson & Simon, 1993). The version of protocol analysis as described here is substantially rooted in ethnomethodology carrying with it the assumptions implicit in the premise of reality as social construction. The ethnomethodologist as a researcher (Garfinkel, 1967) is concerned with self-image, underlying personal assumptions and, crudely but accurately, "he is not... very interested in moving beyond the viewpoint of the person studied." (Tomkins & Groves: 370). This approach represents a challenging but potentially highly rewarding (in data terms) approach to research: challenging inasmuch as traditional method 'values' such as sample size, variable definition and measurement are subjugated in favour of understanding, evaluation and probing; rewarding in terms of the extent to which human expertise can be explored and, perhaps, celebrated. These aspects were well described by Bouwman et al (1987: 2): "traditional research methodologies are typically limited to the analysis of well-defined, well-structured tasks, whereas protocol analysis can be applied to [an] ill-structured, ambiguous environment... as [subjects] dig through stacks of available information" to solve problems and undertake other complex tasks.

3. Protocol Analysis in Accounting Research: Issues Explored

Accounting as a profession has long traded on its claims of expertise, knowledge and skill in respect to a number of aspects of finance, governance, control, analysis, reporting and audit. The profession would argue that expertise in each of these areas is capable of being learned, developed, taught and, ultimately, mastered by the most able practitioners of the craft. In exploring elements of that expertise, protocol analysis offers the opportunity to not only comprehend and dissect the composition of expertise but also to discriminate between those of varying competence.

Accounting researchers have employed a number of approaches to protocol analysis in seeking to understand elements of the expertise of one or more components of professional practice. In reviewing this literature it is evident that there is an agreement in general approach but a divergence on matters of detail. This may be in substantial part due to differences in the objectives pursued in each study and the adjustment of method to best match those objectives. The work reviewed in this section is merely illustrative of this corpus of work and should not be read as an exhaustive treatment.

A number of studies have explored various aspects of auditing expertise by interrogating the components of auditing process. The early work of Ashton (1974a; 1974b) and Ashton & Kramer (1980) involving the provision of information cues to audit students and practitioners was influential in later studies. Subjects were examined, using a protocol analysis method, for intra-sample agreement and consistency over time. Klersey & Mock (1989) helpfully reviewed seven prior studies in protocol-based process tracing techniques that examined expertise in auditing. Bedard (1989), which also provided a useful literature review at the time, distinguished between behavioural and cognitive differences between experienced and novice auditors. He noted that behaviourally, novices and experts followed the same or similar protocols and thus concluded that differences between experts and novices are best explained in terms of cognition. Lauer & Peacock (1993) conducted a protocol analysis experiment on 14 audit managers and found a difference between 'scanning' activity and the more intellectually demanding 'diagnostic' activity. The use of diagnostic activity by auditors was, unlike scanning activity, found to vary with the financial health of the firm being audited.

The appeal of financial analysis as an area for the receipt of attention from protocol analysts is due in substantial part to its prominence in the skill set of the accounting profession as well its import to those who rely upon this aspect of accounting expertise. In general terms, everybody in the information supply chain from the immediate buy side to the individual pension or trust holder has a potential interest in how experts to varying degree manifest or develop this particular expertise. Perhaps not surprisingly, then, it is this application of protocol analysis that has most appealed to researchers and journal editors.

Table 1
Selected Previous Uses of Protocol Analyses in Accounting Research

Reference	Sample	Comments
Bouwman, Frishkoff and Frishkoff (1987)	12 buy side analysts (in US).	Examines the decision making processes of professional financial analysts who are screening prospective investments.
Larcker and Lessig (1983)	31 faculty members and MBA students (split not given)	An investment decision task using a range of information sources.
Biggs (1984)	11 analysts	Assessing the 'earning power' of five companies.
Bouwman (1984)	Novice and expert financial analysts (students and qualified accountants)	To identify the protocols used by novices and experts in evaluating the financial condition of a company based on a given case and supporting financial data.
Lauer and Peacock (1993)	14 'manager level' auditors	Studying auditors' acquisition of information.
McAulay et al. (1997)	21 UK financial directors	Analysing FDs' approaches to a number of financial accounting tasks.
Bedard (1989)	Review paper	Examining behavioural and cognitive differences between expert and novice auditors.
Day (1986)	15 analysts (different sectors)	Analysing use of annual reports and forecasting techniques.
Birt et al. (1997)	6 analysts and 6 accountants	An interdisciplinary approach to a number of complex scenarios.
Anderson and Potter	4 'experienced' analysts	Analysts asked to perform an

(1998)		'unstructured' valuation task.
Anderson (1988)	4 'professional' analysts and 3 'non-professional' analysts (but who had 'extensive business and investment experience').	Subjects invited to talk through the way in which they evaluated a real but anonymised IPO prospectus and associated information.

A number of researchers have examined the decision making behaviour of financial analysts as a group of professionals upon whose forecasts significant capital flows can depend. Biggs (1984), Bouwman (1984), Day (1986), Bouwman, Frishkoff & Frishkoff (1987), Anderson (1988), Birt et al (1997) and Anderson & Potter (1998) are among those that used protocol analysis to examine the tasks undertaken by financial analysts. The specific purposes of these, and similar analyst studies, have varied. Some have sought to understand the development of analytical skills from novice to expert, some the sources of information that analysts use in making investment decisions, some the processes by which forecasts are generated from reporting data and others still, analysts' valuation techniques.

Other applications of protocol analysis (other than for examining audit and analysis) have included an analysis of the protocols involved in evaluating loan decisions (Campbell, 1984), the expertise of financial directors (McAulay, Russell & Simms, 1997) and, outwith the accounting literature, it has been used in some product buying decision analysis (Hannu, Spence, & Kanto, 1998). It has been used in a range of analyses in other areas of human behaviour and cognitive inquiry but these are beyond the scope of this chapter.

4. Protocol Analysis in Accounting Research: Method Issues and Limitations

Accounting researchers have interpreted the basic principles of protocol analysis in a number of ways but all have predictably involved elements of verbalisation and semi-structured interview. Those that have used elements of it have interpreted the general approach broadly. Helpfully, some papers have provided elements of self-critique at the conclusions to the studies.

One area of concern, and one that also applies to all methods involving elements of content analysis and narrative semantic interrogation, is the resolution of coding. How small a behavioural or cognitive process should be defined as a protocol? The answer is likely to different in each research case and is likely to be suggested by the research question being asked. Birts et al (1997) examined the processes involved in accounting decisions by two sets of financial experts – accountants analysing university accounts and analysts examining financial and press information for a soft drinks manufacturer. The method involved coding at the level of the "individual idea or statement" (p. 76) although they later described this as being too limited as it was too over-resolved in coding detail. Bouwman (1984: 325) explained how he "start[ed] with splitting up protocols into phrases, and classifying [coding] those phrases with respect to the decision making *activity* that they display," - a resolution of detail at the level of the phrase. He then proceeded to give examples of such activities: "computing a trend, comparing two items, making an inference and summarising findings." (ibid)

Bouwman *et al* (1987), a study that examined the protocols used by financial analysts, divided transcribed text up into 'topic lines' which were defined as (pages 7-8): "manageable pieces of text that deal with a single action, a single item of information, or single comment. For example: 78. Now I'm quickly going to calculate the profit margin; 79. and uh the return on assets, by division; 80. OK, container profit margin of 6% (Analyst S13, topic lines 78-80)." As in other areas of content analysis, it is important, when selecting coding resolutions, to work at the level of hermeneutic significance. Is it necessary, for example (referring to the topic lines used by Bouwman *et al* (1987) to know the precise calculation being made (as it may well be) or is it sufficient to record that the analyst is conducting a number of ratio recalculations from the annual report? It is a matter of academic judgment as to which resolution provides sufficient meaning and which provides no more return for the increased investment made in data capture.

The processes employed by researchers in interview and analysis also differs from study to study. Again, the challenge for the individual researcher is to arrive at a model that facilitates the answering of the research question being posed – finding a method that fits the enquiry. It is not necessary and is conceivably undesirable to emulate previous studies in detail. An illustration of selected approaches will serve to demonstrate the different models employed.

In examining the ways in which financial analysts used annual report data in making forecasts, Day (1986) divided up face-to-face encounters between a formal protocol analysis (what she called the *evaluation stage*) and a follow-up *questioning stage*, where issues raised by the evaluation stage could be explored. Campbell (1984) was typical of others in her breakdown of protocols for further analysis: "(a) Analysis by components - answers the question 'what information items were used?'; (b) Analysis by processes - answers the question 'how were the information items used?'" (p. 332). Bouwman (1984) divided verbal protocols into those describing *activities*, those identifying *goals* and those describing *processes*.

An early point of discussion in the literature concerned issues of the timing of verbalisations (concurrent or retrospective). A concern with any research involving engagement, especially where it is semi or highly invasive of the subject (person) being studied, is that the process of data capture may interfere with the process being analysed. This, in turn would challenge the validity of the findings. This has been an issue for ethnomethodologists for many years, of course. Whilst the study of, say, birds in the wild is unlikely to interfere with birds' behaviour (because the birds are unaware they are being watched), anthropologists engaging with primates in their natural habitats may change primate behaviour by their very presence. As soon as a researcher makes a demand of a subject such as, "please describe what you are doing," (as they might do in concurrent protocol analysis) the assumption is being made that such a commentary can be made without influencing the process being analysed. It is conceivable, for example, that some professionals need all of their concentration simply to perform the task (such as a surgeon conducting a complex operation). In such a situation, verbalisation would materially change the progress of the task being studied. This, in turn, would conceivably invalidate the experiment.

This potential limitation gave rise to a discussion of whether retrospective verbalisation would be a more reliable method of protocol analysis (Ericsson & Simon, 1993). Notwithstanding this, almost all empirical studies have opted for the concurrent verbalisation approach. One notable exception was Larcker & Lessig (1983) who employed post-experimental verbal reports to dissect the processes involved in a decision task. Whilst agreeing that both concurrent and post-experimental approaches are valid, they conceded in their conclusions that retrospection "may not allow [full] access to the subject's mental process (p. 60)" and makes assumptions on the capacity of subjects' short term memories and articulacy of recall. It is likely that retrospection may be more appropriate where protocol coding takes place at a low resolution and perhaps the subject therefore need only recall a small number of protocols. Where a more highly resolved coding instrument is required and a decision making or problem solving task may require many separate protocols, issues of recall and reporting accuracy would militate against retrospection. It is for this reason that most previous researchers have employed a concurrent protocol analysis method.

5. Further Research

Protocol analysis, or a variant thereof, can be employed wherever understanding is sought of an expertise, a problem-solving scenario or a complex decision task. As a general purpose analytical tool, its application is under-developed and there is ample scope for developing the method itself or applying it to hitherto under-researched situations

In terms of developing the method, the way that protocol analysis and content analysis marry to provide a cohesive hermeneutic instrument is rarely discussed in the literature. Content analysis, the method of inferring meaning from narrative by representing information content in numerical or codified form, is the 'next stage' in processing verbal protocols and interpreting their meaning. Issues of coding and content measurement are not well developed in protocol analysis and this would be an opportunity for research albeit at a cognitive and conceptual level.

There is also scope for applying protocol based interrogative to hitherto less-explored areas of accounting and business research. Although researchers have so far concentrated on audit and financial analysis, it could conceivably by applied to such areas as accounting education, learning, internal audit, control, risk management, corporate governance and ethical issues.

References

Anderson, M. J. (1988), "A comparative analysis of information search and evaluation behavior of professional and non-professional financial analysts", *Accounting, Organizations and Society*, Vol. 13. No. 5. pp. 431-446.

Anderson, M. J. & Potter, G. S. (1998). On the use of regression and verbal protocol analysis in modeling analysts' behavior in an unstructured task environment: a methodological note. *Accounting, Organizations and Society*, Vol. 23, No. 5/6, pp. 435-450.

Ashton, R. H. (1974a), "An experimental study of internal control judgments", *Journal of Accounting Research*, Vol. 12. No. 1. pp. 143-157.

Ashton, R. H. (1974b), "Cue utilization and expert judgments: a comparison of independent auditors with other judges", *Journal of Applied Psychology*, Vol. 59. No. 4. pp. 437-444.

Ashton, R. H. and Kramer, S. S. (1980), "Students as surrogates in behavioral accounting research: some evidence", *Journal of Accounting Research*, Vol. 18. No. 1. pp. 1-15.

Bedard, J. (1989), "Expertise in auditing: myth or reality?", *Accounting, Organizations and Society*, Vol. 14, Nos. 1/2, pp. 113-131.

Biggs, S. F. (1984), "'Financial analysts' information search in the assessment of corporate earning power", *Accounting, Organizations and Society*, Vol. 9. No. 3/4, pp. 313-323.

Birts, A., McAulay, L., Pitt, M., Saren, M. and Sims, D. (1997), "The expertise of finance and accountancy: an interdisciplinary study", *British Journal of Management*, Vol. 8. pp. 75-83.

Blumer, H. (1956), "Sociological analysis and the 'variable'", *American Sociological Review*, December.

Bouwman, M. J. (1984), "Expert vs novice decision making in accounting: a summary", *Accounting Organizations and Society*, Vol. 9, No. 3/4, pp. 325-327.

Bouwmann, M. J., Frishkoff, P. A. and Frischkoff, P. (1987), "How do financial analysts make decisions? A process model of the investment screening decision", *Accounting, Organizations and Society*, Vol 12, No. 1, pp. 1-29.

Campbell, J. E. (1984), "An application of protocol analysis to the 'little GAAP' controversy", *Accounting, Organizations and Society*, Vol. 9, Nos. 3/4, pp. 329-342.

Einhorn, H., Klemmuntz, D. and Klemmuntz, B. (1979), "Linear regression and process-tracing models of judgment", *Psychological Review*, pp. 465-485.

Ericsson, K. and Simon, H. (1980), "Verbal reports as data", *Psychological Review*, pp. 215-251.

Ericsson, K. A. and Simon, H. A. (1993), *Protocol Analysis. Verbal Reports as Data*, MIT Press, Cambridge, MA.

Day, J.F.S. (1986). 'The use of annual reports by UK investment analysts'. Accounting and business research. Autumn. pp. 295-307.

Garfinkel, H. (1967), *Studies in Ethnomethodology*, Prentice Hall, Englewood Cliffs, NJ.

Hannu, K., Spence, M. T. and Kanto, A. J. (1998), "Expertise effects on prechoice decision processes and final outcomes. A protocol analysis", *European Journal of Marketing*, Vol. 32., No. 5/6, pp. 559-576.

Klersey, G. F. and Mock, T. J. (1989), "Verbal protocol research in auditing", *Accounting, Organizations and Society*, Vol. 14, Nos. 1/2, pp. 133-151.

Larcker. D. F. and Lessig, V. P. (1983), "An examination of the linear and retrospective process tracing approaches to judgment modeling", *The Accounting Review*, Vol. 58, No. 1, pp. 58-77.

Lauer, T. W. and Peacock, E. (1993), "Experienced auditors' information acquisition: a research note utilizing questioning methodology", *British Accounting Review*, Vol. 25, No. 3, pp. 243-256.

McAulay, L., Russell, G. & Sims, J.M. (1997). *Inside financial management*. London: Chartered Institute of Management Accountants.

Morgan, G. and Smircich, L. (1980), "The case for qualitative research", *Academy of Management Review*, Vol. 5, No. 4, pp. 491-500.

Newell, A. and Simon, H. A. (1972), *Human problem solving*, Prentice Hall, Englewood Cliffs, NJ.

Nisbett, R. and Wilson, T. (1977), "Telling more than we can know. Verbal reports on mental processes", *Psychological Review*, May, pp. 231-259.

Payne, J. (1976), "Task complexity and contingent processing in decision making. An information search and protocol analysis", *Organizational Behavior and Human Performance*, pp. 366-387.

Payne, J., Braunstein, L. and Carroll, J. (1978), "Exploring predecisional behavior. An alternative approach to decision research", *Organizational Behavior and Human Performance*, pp. 17-44.

Tomkins, C. and Groves, R. (1983), "The everyday accountant and researching his reality", *Accounting, Organizations and Society*, Vol. 8, No. 4, pp. 361-374.

20

FINANCIAL RATIOS IN QUANTITATIVE DATA ANALYSIS: A PRACTICAL GUIDE

Susanne Trimbath
STP Advisory Services, LLC, USA

Abstract: The proliferation of easily accessible, searchable databases of financial statements in the last 20 years has made it simpler than ever to test theories of the firm and the market for corporate securities. In this chapter we offer practical advice for using income and balance sheet data, along with an example using STATA commands for analysis. This chapter also offers some cautionary tales. Despite the theoretical underpinnings for the use of equity and earnings in empirical analysis, certain financial ratios are not suited for large-sample models. In particular, when reported shareholder's equity and/or earnings are less than zero, an inverse relationship can exist between financial ratios and actual firm performance. Although certain earnings ratios can be corrected, adjustments to ratios involving negative book values for equity will result in severe sample bias, erroneous results, and consequently misleading conclusions.

Keywords: Quantitative methodology; methodology for collecting, estimating, and organising financial accounting data; corporate finance.

1.   Introduction

Many theoretical questions in corporate finance can be examined through the use of accounting data and financial ratios. The ordinary balance sheet and income statement are fairly common reporting for businesses around the globe. As the world's financial centres have grown increasingly interconnected, corporations and borrowers have looked beyond their home country's borders for capital. The general adoption by the world's largest economies of the standards put forth by the International Accounting Standards Committee (IASC) provides for information that is comparable, transparent and reliable no matter where a company is headquartered, incorporated or does business.

When gathering data to test a theory, whether that question is in accounting, economics or finance, researchers often turn to financial ratios as measures of corporate performance. Many ratios, like return on assets, are commonly used to evaluate the company in a variety of settings. Public corporations include financial ratios in their annual reports to shareholders. Investment analysts provide them for investors who are considering the purchase of a firm's securities. Newspapers report them everyday. Many researchers routinely incorporate these measurements into models of the performance of companies, industries and market economies, especially in order to make their results accessible to practitioners.

While many of the most common financial ratios are well suited to statistical modelling, others can lead to disastrous mathematical results. Unfortunately, some researchers have found it necessary to use certain ratios in order to make their empirical results comparable to earlier studies that used the same financial ratios. The erroneous use of results based on meaningless financial ratios is perpetuated by the need to make comparisons to previous studies on the same subject in order to compare the underlying theoretical issues being tested. This blind following of precedent has led to a situation where important theories of firm performance may be accepted or rejected based on misleading financial ratios. In addition to discussing the proper use of financial ratios in quantitative analysis in this chapter, we will discuss the implications for quantitative modeling and inference that result from the misuse of equity and earnings as measures of firm performance.

2. Accessing Financial Statement Data

One of the most commonly used databases for company financial information is COMPUSTAT, either North America (from Standard and Poor's Investment Services, a division of McGraw-Hill, Inc.) or Global (from Wharton Research Data Services). COMPUSTAT North America is a primary source of financial information for academic researchers examining US corporations. It is also becoming commonly used by the institutional investment community around the world. COMPUSTAT is a standardised database delivering fundamental and market data on over 54,000 securities listed on the US and Canadian stock exchanges (now or in the past) plus market information on more than 24,000 active and inactive publicly held companies, including foreign companies that either list direct or through American Depositary Receipts. COMPUSTAT provides more than 300 annual and 100 quarterly Income Statement and Balance Sheet data items, in both annual and quarterly formats with historical and restated data. For most companies, data is readily available for a maximum of 20 years although academic systems can usually access longer datasets.

COMPUSTAT Global provides financial and market data covering publicly traded companies in more than 80 countries, representing over 90% of the world's market capitalisation, more than 96% of European market capitalisation and 88% of Asian market capitalisation. Hundreds of data items, ratios and concepts and up to 12 years of annual history is included. International data sets such as this have been designed to reflect the varieties of actual reporting practices used across the globe, while allowing for minimal normalisation and establishing consistency on an item by item basis. For example, financial items in COMPUSTAT Global are stored using a scaling factor due to variation in company size and reporting currency. Therefore, the scale value that corresponds to each data record must be used to place all reported financial data items into the same scale. (Note that the scale of millions is used consistently in the North America COMPUSTAT set, whereas in the Global set some companies report in thousands.) If you are careful to include the scale factor in your dataset, the techniques discussed in this chapter can be applied to both North American and Global corporate financial data.

Although examples in this chapter will be based on COMPUSTAT, there are many other sources which provide data on a set of corporations that include both domestic (continental) and global. Securities Data Corporation provides financial data for companies around the globe, plus specific datasets on mergers, acquisitions and initial public offerings. The Wharton Research Data Services provide a wide variety of databases, including sets devoted to companies in emerging market economies and the European Union. In Australia, Aspect Huntley maintains comprehensive equity research and information operations. Their databases include DatAnalysis, FinAnalysis and annual reports for Australian companies.

3. Selecting Firms

Even if your research interest is in only one or a few firms, it will usually be necessary to select some benchmark group for comparison. COMPUSTAT provides some ready-made groupings by including a data item for the Fortune 500 rank, exchange listing, geographic location, and standard industry classification of each company. COMPUSTAT carries both the Standard Industry Classification code (data item DNUM) and the North American Industry Classification System (data item NAICS). When selecting companies based on the industry codes, be sure to check the historical codes (data item DATA324), as some companies change their primary industry after reorganisations or major corporate control events that alter their product mix. Standard and Poor's, in collaboration with Morgan Stanley Capital International (MSCI), developed a Global Industry Classification Standard (GICS) to further align the international classification of companies, industries and sectors. According to the developers, 'GICS was developed in response to the financial community's need for one complete, consistent set of global sector and industry definitions. The GICS standard can be applied to companies globally, in both developed and developing markets, and currently comprises a universe of over 25,000 companies worldwide'. GICS simplifies the selection of a performance benchmark for sample companies because each company belongs to only one group at any level of GICS.

In studies where samples include a control group, selection bias can occur if the performance being studied is correlated with unmeasured, stable characteristics of the sample members. This contamination bias is common in non-experimental data sets. To avoid that bias in quantitative analysis, apply a fixed-effects model to a sample that has some common element, like membership in a group that is non-self-selecting. The S&P 500 and industry groups are good examples, whereas exchange listing is a self-selecting process that could induce bias into the study. One advantage of using firms with commonality is that the coefficients resulting from estimation of the model are directly attributable to the effect being studied and not the difference between firms belonging to different groups (e.g. industry or size). Selection bias can still occur in the fixed-effects model if the performance being studied is associated with some transitory variation in the other performance variables. However, by carefully defining the population from which the sample is drawn, a major source of bias can be avoided. (On this point, see Palepu (1986) for corrections relevant to binary state prediction models, i.e. probit and logit regressions, in the context of criticism of models for predicting takeover targets.)

4.   Time-Series Versus Static Analysis

The next choice to make in setting up the analysis is whether to examine the data across firms, across time or both. The proliferation of desktop computers and graphic interfaces for data search and analysis programs has greatly enriched the tools available to today's analyst. For example, in the 1970s, most research into corporate financial data used either multiple discriminant analysis or univariate analysis. Although higher order techniques were well described in the literature on mathematics, empirical investigation of more complex event analysis required computing power not generally available. Even by the 1980s, probability analysis was limited to linear techniques like probit and logit regression analysis. At the same time, there was greater recognition of the heterogeneity of firms and temporal changes in performance, putting even greater demands on quantitative analysis.

Up to that point, most studies were limited to examining performance measures either for one year, or perhaps comparing two time periods to each other. However, with today's computing power at our fingertips, the bar has been raised quite high. Hazard analysis and full multivariate regression models are moving to the forefront as the preferred analytical technique in finance and economics. Hazard analysis is used in studies examining the characteristics of a group of firms all experiencing some event (e.g. mergers) while multivariate analysis allows an examination of the relationships among many performance measures.

Accessing COMPUSTAT data through Standard and Poor's Research Insight interface, the researcher now can easily select to examine one company over time, many companies for one time period, or a full panel of data covering multiple companies across time for several variables. Research Insight has extensive functionality and a broad selection of data items to customise data modelling. It has a library of 'canned' spreadsheets to analyse the relationship among multiple variables but is especially flexible regarding the output of the data files. The output is fully customisable and completely accessible through Microsoft® Excel, in addition to the delimited text output required by more sophisticated analytical tools like SPSS, STATA and SAS.

5. Selecting Profitability Measures

There are several options available for calculating profitability based on the income statement, including return on gross assets (ROA), return on equity (ROE), return on invested capital (ROI), etc. The numerator in these ratios can range from net sales at the top of the income statement to net income at the bottom and practically every step between the two. Earnings Before Interest, Taxes, Depreciation and Amortisation was popularised in the 1990s by its acronym 'EBITDA'. However, more classical analysis often will consider only the top or bottom of the income statement, that is, either revenue generated (net sales) or bottom line profits (net income). The choice of denominator, however, requires careful consideration within the context of the study. A good reference for measuring cash flow, for example, is Lang et al. (1991), who presents ten different ratios in the context of one study, with details on how each measure can be calculated. Similar to sample selection problems, however, bias can be introduced into quantitative analysis through an ill-selected scaling factor (see next section, Pitfalls in Financial Ratios for specific advice).

The choice of which performance measure to use in quantitative analysis developed in parallel to the changes in technology available. Until the early 1980s, with corporate financial statements generally only available in print, analysts were limited to calculating a few accounting rates of return. With the proliferation of access to the security price data maintained by the Center for Research in Security Prices (CRSP), and the CRSP/COMPUSTAT merged database, researchers beyond academia were able to easily match financial data to security price data for large sample analysis. During this time, several researchers put efforts into testing the accuracy of these databases, reporting problems and getting corrections made (for example, see Bennin, 1980). These databases are now widely believed to have a high degree of accuracy. Toward the end of the 1980s, shareholder return studies virtually replaced accounting return studies.

Beginning in the 1990s, researchers took the final step toward matching accounting data with shareholder return data in order to begin testing theories of free cash flow, wealth transfers, etc. Two very good references resulted from an examination of the empirics involved in these tests. Lewellen and Badrinath (1997) examine three different ways to calculate Tobin's Q, a classic measure of firm value. Magenheim and Mueller (1988) offer a clear presentation of the myriad methodological problems associated with measuring firm value as gains to shareholders in stock price studies. Finally, Gregory (1997) offers an interesting perspective by lining up six different stock return methodologies on the same sample.

6. Pitfalls in Financial Ratios

Many quantitative studies of firm performance rely on one of two popular performance measures. One is Return on Assets (ROA), defined as the ratio of earnings to assets. The other is Return on Equity (ROE), defined as the ratio of earnings to equity. Equity itself is defined as the difference between assets and liabilities. Equity represents the owners' claims against or interests in the assets of the firm. In the case of public corporations, this is equivalent to stockholders' equity on the balance sheet. ROE is a theoretically popular measure, primarily because it takes into account a firm's liabilities and pays homage to the dispersed ownership represented by shareholders. In addition, studies using ROE have been more successful in finding statistically significant results. We can demonstrate, however, that negative values for the book value of equity and reported earnings will provide contrary evidence when used for absolute rankings, despite being theoretically interesting for ranking relative firm performance.

The reasons can be made obvious in a few sentences. Firms that report very low book values for equity are likely to be over-leveraged, though they can have a high ROE ratio which may not be excluded by any systematic search for outliers in a large sample study. The book value of equity can also be negative when liabilities exceed assets, resulting in a ratio that has no meaning in financial analysis. Eliminating firms with negative equity means eliminating (potentially) the worst performing firms (those whose liabilities exceed their assets), a serious source of sample bias in studies examining firm performance. Finally, when both earnings and equity are negative, these firms will display a 'falsely-positive' ROE, resulting in the most egregious of the errors generated by the inappropriate use of a financial ratio in quantitative analysis. In the following sections, we give real life examples of these pitfalls, along with explanations of the performance scenarios that generate the statistical bias.

7.   Rising ROE with Falling Income

Shareholder's equity is one item on the balance sheet that is calculated rather than measured. Quite simply, when liabilities exceed assets, the book value of equity is negative and the firm with negative equity is technically bankrupt: they owe more than they own, at least from an accounting perspective. An econometric model using equity as the scaling factor for profitability would necessarily input a negative number for ROE.

Negative return on equity is meaningless as a measure of firm performance. Financial statements and analysts' reports usually note the ratio resulting from negative equity as 'not meaningful' and do not report a figure. Unfortunately, available databases (including Research Insight, which has built in ratio calculations) will output a negative number for return on equity when the ratio is requested. In a quantitative model, although the figure is not truly meaningful, at least it would rank the technically bankrupt firm as having worse performance than any firm with positive equity. Therefore, one might consider that it could at least be used as a measure of relative firm performance. Unfortunately, this is not actually the case.

An example will clarify the point. Note that equity generally falls toward zero before going negative. As equity falls, ROE rises. Looking at the data in Table 1, it appears that the Coca-Cola Bottling Companies took on some additional liabilities during 1992. ROE, however, increased from 1.4% to a healthy-looking 8.1%. But ROE is deceiving in this case. Net income actually decreased by about 30%. Because assets remained about the same, there was a decrease in return on assets (ROA). This problem is exacerbated through the point where reported equity equals zero. Note that although it is unlikely that a firm would report literal zero for equity, the figure may be small enough that data services like COMPUSTAT would register US$0 millions before the number is small enough that it triggers the 'I' (insignificant) footnote. (Although I found no examples of zero equity in the sample discussed later, I did recover one observation with literal zero from COMPUSTAT for Net Income and for Earnings per Share.)

Table 1
Coca-Cola Bottling Companies: Return on equity rises as income falls

Date	Income	Assets	Liabilities	Equity	ROE	ROA
1990	0.229	467.972	299.877	168.095	1.36%	0.05%
1991	2.936	785.196	572.49	212.706	1.38%	0.37%
1992	2.083	785.871	760.065	25.806	8.07%	0.26%

ROE and ROA may not calculate exactly due to rounding This example is far more serious than concerns about earnings management or financial disclosure requirements. This is a serious issue for the quantitative analyst which calls into question the use of ROE to measure firm performance in empirical studies. Indeed, as we take the next logical step in the examination of ROE, you will see that the worst kind of error occurs when the firm with negative equity also has negative net income.

8. Disasters with Negative Equity and Negative Earnings

The following example will make this clear. Comcast Corporation reported negative net income every year from 1990 through 1995 (see Table 2). In addition, the book value of equity was positive in only one of those six years: 1991. Now, in this example, most simple methods for eliminating outliers would have dropped Comcast in the years 1990–1992 when ROE was +/- 100%. However, despite their dreadful performance in 1993–1995, any econometric model would have identified Comcast as having a healthy, positive return on equity when in reality Comcast (1) was technically bankrupt, and (2) had costs that exceeded revenue. The same is true of Continental Airlines in 1991–1992, Eli Lilly in 1992, Dynacore Holdings in 1998–1999, Freeport McMoran in 1993, Interlake Corporation in 1990–1994, etc., etc. In fact, using data from 1990 through 1999 on a sample of firms that were ranked by Fortune magazine among the top 500 for sales, 14.4% of the non-missing observations were for negative net income and 3.8% were for negative equity. The results for return on equity are disastrous: 2.6% of the non-missing positive ROE observations were calculated over *negative income and negative equity*.

Table 2
Comcast Corporation, Return on Equity is Positive When Income is Negative

Date	Income	Equity	ROE	ROA
1990	-178.41	-21.69	822.6%	-7.3%
1991	-155.57	19.48	-798.6%	-5.6%
1992	-217.94	-181.64	120.0%	-5.1%
1993	-98.87	-870.53	11.3%	-2.0%
1994	-75.32	-726.79	10.4%	-1.1%
1995	-37.85	-775.53	4.6%	-0.4%

ROE and ROA may not calculate exactly due to rounding.

9. Deceptions in Significance

In another example of how ROE is a deceptive measure of firm performance, consider that Coca-Cola Bottling Companies had ROA of around 2% in the years from 1993 to 1997 (Table 3). Compared to other firms who had similar ROA performance in those years, Coca-Cola Bottling had an exceptionally high ROE: 74% versus 13% on average for firms with similar ROA performance. Specifically, compare Coca-Cola Bottling's performance to that of Cabot Corporation (Table 4) who maintained increasing equity and kept ROA above 2%. The ratio ROE rises as the firm takes on more debt, that is, as equity approaches zero in the denominator of the ratio. ROE has the potential to produce rates of return that are just large enough to avoid elimination as outliers during a period of time when the firm's performance is deteriorating. This could, in fact, be the reason that ROE produces statistically significant results when ROA does not.

Table 3
Coca-Cola Bottling Companies, Falling Income From Rising Assets

Date	Income	Assets	Liabilities	Equity	ROE	ROA	Change in income	Change in assets
1993	14.83	648.45	618.82	29.63	50.1%	2.3%	612%	-17%
1994	14.15	664.16	630.18	33.98	41.6%	2.1%	-5%	2%
1995	15.54	676.57	637.60	38.97	39.9%	2.3%	10%	2%
1996	16.16	702.40	680.13	22.27	72.6%	2.3%	4%	4%
1997	15.27	778.03	768.76	9.27	164.6%	2.0%	-6%	11%
1998	14.88	825.23	809.44	15.79	94.2%	1.8%	-2%	6%
1999	3.24	1,110.92	1,078.48	32.44	10.0%	0.3%	-78%	35%

Results may not calculate exactly due to rounding.

Table 4
Cabot Corporation Under-Performs Coca-Cola Bottling While Increasing Equity and Income

Date	Income	Assets	Liabilities	Equity	ROE	ROA	Change in income	Change in assets
1993	37.41	1,489.47	1,047.20	442.27	9.0%	3.0%	-40%	-4%
1994	78.69	1,616.76	1,054.27	562.49	14.0%	5.0%	110%	9%
1995	171.93	1,654.33	969.33	685.00	25.0%	10.0%	118%	2%
1996	194.06	1,857.58	1,112.65	744.93	26.0%	10.0%	13%	12%
1997	92.75	1,823.59	1,095.80	727.79	13.0%	5.0%	-52%	-2%
1998	121.60	1,805.20	1,099.70	705.50	18.0%	7.0%	31%	-1%
1999	97.00	1,842.00	1,136.00	706.00	14.0%	5.0%	-20%	2%

Results may not calculate exactly due to rounding.

10.   Sample Bias

If eliminating outliers is insufficient to prevent this misuse of return on equity as a measure of firm performance, what adjustments are possible? In other contexts, researchers have dropped firms (or observations) with negative equity values. However, if we eliminate all the firms that report negative equity, we are eliminating the worst performers from our sample. This is sample bias at its worst: using a measure of firm performance to eliminate observations from a study of firm performance. As an alternative, eliminating all firms/observations with negative income is just as bad.

The next logical question is: does it matter? As Table 4 and Table 6 show, the answer is a resounding 'yes'. The calculated mean ROE figures are statistically significantly different ($p < 0.001$) in all cases except where only the false positives are excluded. Yet even in that case, the p-value for the t-test is 0.11.

Table 5
Descriptive Statistics for Return on Equity

	Unadjusted	No Negative Equity	No FALSE Positives	Both Corrections
Min	-7608.85	0.002	-7608.85	0.002
Median	13.024	14.678	12.867	14.5145
Mean	10.294	22.855	6.431	18.647
Max	3,334.42	3,334.42	936.842	936.842
N	4,335	3,703	4,240	3,608

Unadjusted ROE uses all observations. No Negative Equity removes all observations where negative equity is reported. No False Positives removes all observations where both income and equity are negative. Both Corrections removes all observations where negative equity is reported and where both income and equity are negative.

Table 6
t-Tests for Equality of Means with Unadjusted Value of ROE

	Unadjusted	No Negative Equity	No FALSE Positives	Both Corrections
Mean	10.29	22.86	6.43	18.65
Obs	4,335	3,703	4,240	3,608
d.f.		8,036	8,573	7,941
t		-4.56	-1.22	-3.24
P(T<=t)		0.000002	0.11	0.0006

Unadjusted ROE uses all observations. No Negative Equity removes all observations where negative equity is reported. No False Positives removes all observations where both income and equity are negative. Both Corrections removes all observations where negative equity is reported and where both income and equity are negative.

11.   Other Problems with Negative Equity

Similar problems occur with other equity ratios, though none are as damaging as those involving income. For example, the ratio of debt-to-equity will be affected by values of negative equity. Here, again, the question is whether or not the resulting ratio is a reasonable measure of firm performance. Putting aside the question of absolute value, a poor performing firm, i.e. one with negative stockholders' equity, would rank lower than any with positive equity. However, here the relative performance ranks are inverse. In most situations, we consider whether a firm is over- or under-leveraged. Let's say that two firms have the same quantity of long-term debt, US$10 million. Further, the two firms are of comparable size, US$100 million in assets. These firms should rank similarly for leverage. But suppose there is some discrepancy in short-term debt or other liabilities. If one has positive equity of US$10 and the other has negative equity of US$10, the 'better' firm (i.e. the one with positive equity) would have a leverage ratio of one while the 'worse' firm (i.e. the one with negative equity, which is surely over-leveraged) would have a relatively lower leverage ratio of negative one. Again, some of the leverage ratios resulting from negative equity would be eliminated as outliers, for example, where liabilities exceed assets by some small amount (resulting in an absurdly high absolute value for leverage). A similar inversion of rankings occurs when using the price-earnings ratio over negative income. The danger, as before, is when the difference results in an 'econometrically reasonable' figure that is 'absolutely unreasonable'.

12. Academic Usage of Equity

We have demonstrated that there is no mathematical, statistical or econometric adjustment that makes return on equity a useable measure of firm performance. It simply should not be used in large sample econometric models. Unfortunately, because of pressure to conform to editorial demands, many fine researchers include balance sheet equity in their studies in order to gain access to the top academic journals.

For example, nine articles printed in the *Journal of Finance* in 2000 used the book value of equity in measures of firm performance (Chaplinsky and Ramchand; D'Mello and Shroff; Data, Iskandar-Datta and Patel; Davis, Fama and French; Detragiache, Garella and Guiso; Haushalter; Kang, Shivdasani and Yamada; La Porta, Lopez-de-Silanes, Shleifer and Vishny; and Schwert; all 2000). In this section, we cite several of these papers as examples of research that potentially suffered from the use of 'tried and true' financial ratios like return on equity. This does not in any way imply that only research published in the *Journal of Finance* suffered from this problem. It is more likely that the editorial subject matter more often requires the use of measures for firm performance than articles published in other journals. For example, there were only a few articles published in 2000 in any of the *American Economic Review*, the *Journal of Financial Economics*, the *Journal of Economic Literature* or the *Quarterly Journal of Economics* that measured firm performance. Those that did used profit/revenue or similar measure; return on equity was not used.

The majority of the *Journal of Finance* papers attempted to make some adjustment to account for the unusual values generated by the use of equity ratios. Schwert (2000) eliminates 'extreme outliers' with ROE ratios greater than 100. D'Mello and Shroff (2000) 'excluded … 10 firms with negative book values [for equity] …'. Davis, Fama and French (2000) 'do not use negative BE [book value of equity] firms when calculating the breakpoints for BE/ME [ratio of BE to market value of equity] or when forming the size- BE/ME portfolios'.

However, as demonstrated in this chapter, such adjustments are insufficient to correct for the problems that occur with using equity for performance measures in empirical studies. Another example can be found in Haushalter (2000) where firm value is calculated as:

> *market value of assets = (Number of common shares outstanding * End of year price per share) + (Book value of total assets − Book value of equity).*

In this case, negative book values for equity would actually have *increased* the value of the firms in this study of oil and gas producers. Finally, Davis, Fama and French (2000) report that firms with higher book values for equity have higher average share price returns. Because the capital asset pricing model does not explain this pattern, they say 'it is typically called an anomaly'. What needs to be revisited is whether or not this 'anomaly' is the result of the unusual ranking of firm performance that results when equity is used in financial ratios.

13.   Conclusion

In this chapter we used net profit return on equity to demonstrate how certain financial ratios can give statistical results that run contrary to logic. In general, we make the point that the book value of equity and reported earnings should be used cautiously if at all in large sample statistical studies because negative values, while potentially meaningful to rank *relative* firm performance, can provide contrary evidence when used for *absolute* rankings. Further, some uses of equity cannot even be used to make relative rankings of firm performance.

Adaptations have been made for some financial ratios. For example, scaling factors other than equity can be used to measure leverage with reported values of debt. In the *Journal of Finance* during 2000, Detraigiache, Garella and Guiso used the ratio of debt to sales; Data, Iskandar-Datta and Patel used debt to assets, as did Haushalter. These papers point the way toward more fruitful and less misleading studies of firm performance. The cautions presented here are intended not only to instruct the analyst preparing to examine a sample of firms, but also to guide the researcher who is reviewing the literature of existing quantitative studies. Bad empirics can be used to reinforce bad theories; but if the researcher and the analyst are careful then the results will be worth the extra effort needed to select the firms and performance measures for examination in quantitative analysis.

13.1.   Example: Panel-data models in STATA

(This section presents an advanced description of data modeling, which may be skipped without loss of content). This example is drawn from Trimbath (2002) in which the performance of pairs of merged companies are examined for changes from before the merger to after the merger. The original research generated a database from the companies in the annual ranking of the 500 largest companies done by Fortune magazine. The database is comprised of 10,784 annual observations on 896 firms who engaged in 276 takeovers from 1981 through 1997. From this set, we selected 162 merged pairs with 1,194 observations for detailed event analysis.

13.1.1. Data structure: Each pair of firms (one buyer and one target) has up to 10 annual observations from five years before the takeover through five years after (excluding the year of the takeover). Some pairs are missing observations (unbalanced panels). We choose to treat each takeover as a separate pair (non-repeating events). Some pairs have overlapping *ex post* observations. The dates of the observations coincide with different *ex post* years for each overlapping pair because no buyer in the sample has multiple takeovers in the same year.

13.1.2. Fixed-effects model: In the context of our data setting, we wish to estimate the effect of the takeover as changes from pre-takeover performance to post-takeover performance. In economic studies, fixed-effects models are usually applied to samples that include a group that has not experienced the event (control group) (Hsiao, 1986; Heckman and Hotz, 1989). We draw on the application of these models in sociology where event effects are estimated by the same method and no control group is included (Allison, 1994).

We calculate the 'takeover effect' from the regression equation

$$Y_{it} = \alpha_0 + \alpha_i + X_{it}\beta + W_{itsd}\delta_{sd} + \varepsilon_{it},$$

where $i = 1, 2, \ldots, n$ is the number of pairs, $t = 1, 2, \ldots, T$ is time relative to the takeover, $s = 1, 2, \ldots, S$ is the target's economic sector and $d = 1980, 1981, \ldots, D$ is the calendar date of the observation. The model assumes that no one firm experiences an event before $t = 1$. Y_{it} is the column vector of annual observations on pair performance. The α_is are 'nuisance' parameters representing differences across pairs that are constant over time and can be thought of as summarising the effects on Y of all unmeasured, stable characteristics of the pairs. One pair dummy variable is omitted to avoid perfect collinearity.

X_{it} is the treatment variable, equal to zero for $t \leq 5$ and equal to one for $t \geq 6$. That is, the treatment variable is equal to one for all *ex post* observations. β is the parameter of interest and it measures the effect of the takeover on Y_{it} that is common to all pairs (cross-sectional units). We are primarily interested in the effect of a takeover at time t_0 on the quantitative variable Y_t, where t can vary continuously. Our specification assumes that the effect of the takeover is an immediate, additive and permanent change in the level of Y. Formally, we say that $Y_t = \mu$ for $t < t_0$ and $Y_t = \mu + \beta$ for $t > t_0$. Thus β can be regarded as the effect of the takeover on the performance characteristics of the firm.

W_{itsd} represents the S^*D dummy variables for the target's economic sector and the date of the observation. One sector-year dummy variable is omitted to avoid perfect collinearity. The sector-year specific effects δ_{sd} are estimated. The combination of the sector with the date allows us to include the sectoral effect in our specification, since time constant variables cannot be estimated in the fixed-effects model. ε_{it} is the 'usual' residual, the serially uncorrelated, transitory component of performance. The ε variables represent time-specific random disturbances that are assumed to be independent of the measured explanatory variables, of α_i, and of each other.

Efficient estimation can be accomplished by a single application of OLS to the 'change-score' transformation (Allison, 1994). For each variable at each point in time, we subtract the pair-specific mean for that variable over time. Thus, we calculate

$$(Y_{it} - \bar{Y}_i + \bar{\bar{Y}}) = \alpha + (Z_{it} - \bar{Z}_i + \bar{\bar{Z}})\phi + (\varepsilon_{it} - \bar{\varepsilon}_i + \bar{v}) + \bar{\bar{\varepsilon}}$$

where

$$\bar{Y}_i = \frac{1}{T}\sum_{t=1}^{T} Y_{it} \text{ and}$$

$$\bar{\bar{Y}} = \frac{1}{nT}\sum_i\sum_t Y_{it}.$$

Z, representing the K explanatory variables, and v_i, the pair specific error terms, are similarly transformed. Then OLS regression is applied to the deviation scores for pooled individual time periods. Therefore, $\hat{\beta}$ in $\hat{\phi}$ measures the average change in performance for pairs post-takeover, that is, the 'within' pair-level deviation from its mean across time. The dummy variable coefficients can be recovered as

$$\alpha_i = (\bar{Y}_i - \bar{\bar{Y}}) - \hat{\phi}'(\bar{Z}_i - \bar{\bar{Z}})$$

(Greene, 1993) and estimates of individual error terms are obtained as:

$$\hat{v}_i = \bar{Y}_i - \hat{\alpha} - \bar{Z}_i\hat{\phi} .$$

This method yields exactly the same coefficient estimates as the dummy variable method. Only the standard errors and degrees of freedom need to be adjusted for the fact that one is implicitly estimating a constant for each pair. Each standard error must be multiplied by $[(nT - K)/(nT - n - K)]^{1/2}$ where K is the number of coefficients in the model *including* the intercept. When using the t distribution, the number of degrees of freedom is $nT - n - K$. The resulting estimators are unbiased and fully efficient under the fixed-effects assumption (Allison, 1994). As usual, if the ε disturbance terms have a multivariate normal distribution, the OLS estimator is also the unconditional maximum likelihood estimator.

STATA will estimate the fixed effects model described here with the following command where terms in brackets [] are replaced by performance measures and firm identifiers:

> *xtreg [performance variable of interest] [event marker in time series] [dummy combining year and industry] , fe i([unique identifier for each firm]).*

STATA does not report estimates for the individual α_is, though it provides a test statistic that can be used to test the null hypothesis that all the α_is are zero.

Acknowledgements

The author received support and encouragement for this research from Professors D. Glen Whitman and Hilton Root. The description of databases and industry classifications benefited, especially, from the comments and suggestions of an anonymous reviewer.

References

Allison, Paul D. (1994), "Using panel data to estimate the effects of events", *Sociological Methods and Research*, Vol. 23, No. 2, November, pp. 174-199.

Bennin, R. (1980), "Error rates in CRSP and COMPUSTAT: a second look", *Journal of Finance*, Vol. 35, No. 5, pp. 1267-1271.

Chaplinsky, S. and Ramchand, L. (2000), "The impact of global equity offerings", *Journal of Finance*, Vol. 55, No. 6, pp. 2767-2789.

D'Mello, R. and Shroff, P. K. (2000), "Equity under-valuation and decisions related to repurchase tender offers: an empirical investigation", *Journal of Finance*, Vol. 55, No. 5, pp. 2399-2424.

Data, S., Iskandar-Datta, M. and Patel, A. (2000), "Some evidence on the uniqueness of initial public debt offerings", *Journal of Finance*, Vol. 55, No. 2, pp. 715-743.

Davis, J. L., Fama, E. F. and French, K. R. (2000), "Characteristics, covariances, and average returns: 1929 to 1997", *Journal of Finance*, Vol. 55, No. 1, pp. 389- 406.

Detragiache, E., Garella, P. and Guiso, L. (2000), "Multiple versus single banking relationships", *Journal of Finance*, Vol. 55, No. 3, pp. 1133-1161.

Gregory, A. (1997), "An examination of the long run performance of UK acquiring firms", *Journal of Business Finance and Accounting*, Vol. 24, No. 7/8, pp. 971-1007.

Greene, W. H. (1993), *Econometric Analysis*, Macmillan Publishing Company, New York.

Haushalter, G. D. (2000), "Financing policy, basis risk, and corporate hedging: evidence from oil and gas producers", *Journal of Finance*, Vol. 55. No. 1, pp. 107-152.

Heckman, J. J. and Hotz, J. V. (1989), "Choosing among alternative nonexperimental methods for estimating the impact of social programs: the case of manpower training", *Journal of the American Statistical Association, Applications and Case Studies*, Vol. 84, No. 408, pp. 862-880.

Hsiao, C. (1986), *Analysis of Panel Data*, Cambridge University Press, New York.

Kang, J., Shivdasani, A. and Yamada, T. (2000), "The effect of bank relations on investment decisions: an investigation of Japanese takeover bids", *Journal of Finance*, Vol. 55, No. 5, pp. 2197-2218.

La Porta, R., Lopez-de-Silanes, F., Shleifer, A. and Vishny, R. W. (2000), "Agency problems and dividend policies around the world", *Journal of Finance*, Vol. 55, No. 1, pp. 1-33.

Lang, L. H. P., Stulz, R. M. and Walkling, R. A. (1991), "A test of the free cash flow hypothesis", *Journal of Financial Economics*, Vol. 29, pp. 315-335.

Lewellen, W. G. and Badrinath, S. G. (1997), "On the measurement of Tobin's Q", *Journal of Financial Economics*, Vol. 44, pp. 77-122.

Magenheim, E. B. and Mueller, D. C. (1988), "Are acquiring-firm shareholders better off after an acquisition", in Coffee, J. C. Jr., Lowenstein, L. and Rose-Ackerman, S. (Eds.) (1988), *Knights, Raiders and Targets: The Impact of Hostile Takeovers*, Oxford University Press, New York, pp. 171-193.

Palepu, K. G. (1986), "Predicting takeover targets: a methodological and empirical analysis", *Journal of Accounting and Economics*, Vol. 8, pp. 3-35.

Schwert, G. W. (2000), "Hostility in takeovers: in the eyes of the beholder?", *Journal of Finance*, Vol. 55, No. 6, pp. 2599-2640.

Trimbath, S. (2002), *Mergers and Efficiency: Changes Across Time*, Kluwer Academic Publishers, Boston.

21

CONDUCTING SURVEY RESEARCH IN MANAGEMENT ACCOUNTING

Jamal Nazari
University of Calgary, Canada

Theresa Kline
University of Calgary, Canada

Irene Herremans
University of Calgary, Canada

Abstract: In this chapter, the psychometric issues regarding the design, implementation and analysis of mail surveys are discussed. When researchers follow the methodological procedures suggested in the first section of this chapter, the results provide a valid and interpretable source of data for analysis. Then, using these same procedures, we critically evaluate how survey instruments have been used in selected published studies in the management accounting field. To improve the quality of survey research in this field, we make several recommendations based on the methodological deficiencies observed in the survey research we reviewed. Researchers are encouraged to apply sound methodological procedures such as random sampling and more widespread application of reliability and validity assessment to improve the quality of survey research in accounting.

Keywords: Mail survey; survey design; survey implementation; management accounting.

1. Introduction

This chapter is divided into two major sections. After a brief discussion of boundary conditions for designing survey questions in the accounting literature, the first section is devoted to describing how to create and assess survey instruments as a meaningful way to collect data, and the second section is an examination of how surveys have been used in accounting research for the past 11 years. To the extent possible, both sections discuss the same major steps regarding surveys: designing, implementing, and analysing data (with special emphasis on reliability and validity). Elaborating on the work done by Van der Stede *et al.* (2005) and using 61 articles published in major accounting journals within an 11-year period, we empirically examine to what extent researchers actually practise sound methodological procedures when using surveys for research. Finally, we end with a summary of where the discipline is with regard to survey research and where it should move to in the future.

Although the survey method has had an important impact on accounting, it has been the subject of heavy criticism, especially by some management accounting researchers. Reliability of the survey method has been the fundamental concern (Van der Stede *et al.*, 2005; Young, 1996). Van der Stede *et al.* (2005) conducted an analysis similar to ours, which is an excellent source of survey information. However, our study builds on Van der Stede *et al.* (2005) and offers several additional contributions to the discipline as listed below.

First, we develop the survey design framework to inform researchers inclined to use survey methods of sound methodological procedures. Second, we empirically review the survey literature to provide useful information about the trends of survey studies and the appropriateness of the survey method. Third, in our review we separately assess the type of samples used in each study. Fourth, we scrutinise the reliability and validity issues in accounting survey to an extent that it has not been done before. And finally, our study provides an update (covering years 1994-2004) to Van der Stede *et al.*'s study (covering years 1981 through either 2000 or 2001).

2. Boundary Conditions for Designing Questions for Mail Surveys

The survey method has been one of the most commonly used methods in social sciences to study the characteristics and interrelationships of sociological and psychological variables. Researchers use surveys to collect data on a variety of topics such as accountants' perceptions, evaluations of new performance measurement systems, gauging attitudes towards a new costing program, and measurement of effective responses to organisational change, to name just a few. The design of survey instruments could easily be the topic of an entire volume. However, because this book devotes only a single chapter to its description, we have restricted the discussion to a particular type of survey. This type is characterised as self-reported assessments of attitudes, values, beliefs, opinions, and/or intentions. The survey items are answered with closed-ended, numerical responses through mail surveys. We have also limited the discussion to information obtained from surveys used to assess differences between individuals rather than within the same individual. We do not discuss surveys used in experimental studies, interviews, or case studies, and we focus solely on mail surveys as the data collection technique. An additional reason to confine the focus of this chapter to mail surveys is that they are the survey method most frequently used in managerial accounting research (Van der Stede *et al.* 2005).

3. Section 1: Methodological Procedures

3.1. *Epistemological Assumptions in Survey Research*

There are several underlying assumptions in survey research using self-reports of attitudes, values, beliefs, opinions and/or intentions. One is that respondents are the most reliable source for certain types of information. When the beliefs, attitudes, values, opinions and intentions of individuals are the topics of interest, then the most appropriate sources for that information are the survey respondents themselves. A second assumption is that these subjective perceptions actually matter. This is a valid assumption in that while perceptions may not be real, perceptions of reality are more powerful than reality itself because people act on their perceptions.

This leads to the third assumption, which is that these perceptions can be demonstrated to be linked to outcomes of interest to organisations. That is, attitudes influence behaviours and those behaviours have real consequences for organisations. Research strongly suggests that this assumption is quite tenable. Fishbein and Ajzen (1975) asserted that 'the best single predictor of an individual's behaviour will be a measure of his intention to perform that behaviour' (p. 369). They further supported this contention (Ajzen and Fishbein, 1977) calling the phenomenon the Theory of Reasoned Action. The theory was updated and broadened by Ajzen (1991, 1996) and called the Theory of Planned Behaviour to address complex behaviours that require planning, arranging resources, and obtaining cooperation of others.

If researchers agree that the assumptions above are tenable, then they can conclude that surveys offer a promising avenue for obtaining valuable information. However, a critical hurdle must be overcome in that the questions on a survey must be designed to adequately assess the phenomenon of interest. That is, instruments must assess perceptions with a high degree of fidelity. To do so requires careful consideration and considerable effort; this process is discussed next.

3.2. *Designing a Survey*

The aim of survey research in management accounting is to measure certain attitudes and/or behaviours of a population or a sample. The surveys can be used either for exploratory or confirmatory purposes. Exploratory surveys are used to find basic facts and become familiar with the subject of study. Exploratory surveys usually focus on finding out what constructs to measure and how to best measure them (Pinsonneault and Kramer, 1993). The purpose of confirmatory survey research is to test theory and assess relationships between constructs that have been defined in previous research studies.

3.2.1. Construct development. The first step in designing any type of survey is to define the construct. Constructs are ideas that are self-defined synthesised impressions. Generating a list of what is going to be included and excluded from the construct is often helpful.

For example, if a survey of employee satisfaction with a new cost accounting system is to be developed, it might include every point of contact employees have with the system beginning with determining the internal customers' needs for making the system useful for decision making to following up with any problems the internal customer has six months after implementing the new system. The survey may not include external auditors' assessment of the security of the system or vendor selection for installing the system. By defining the inclusion criteria for a construct, it will be clear to those who use the survey, or the information from the survey, which construct it was designed to measure.

A construct should be valid or free of deficiency and contamination. Measurement of a construct is deficient if the entire domain of interest is not covered. If an employee satisfaction survey has no items that ask about the user friendliness of the system and efficiency of the system, then the survey might be considered deficient. Contamination occurs when the survey contains information that should not be part of the construct. If the employee satisfaction survey contained items referring to satisfaction with the size of an employee's office, then it might be considered contaminated. Construct deficiency must be demonstrated rationally, whereas contamination can be detected using statistical procedures.

An important consideration in survey development is whether or not the survey is designed to assess a single or multiple constructs. For example, is the employee satisfaction survey to be developed assuming that the construct is a single, general attitude or are there multiple constructs (such as satisfaction with the ease of interpreting information from the system versus satisfaction with interactions with staff that provide training on the system) embedded within the notion of employee satisfaction? There is no right answer to whether assessing single or multiple constructs is a better approach. Instead, a survey is developed that is consistent with the needs of those who will be using the information. Multiple constructs are more difficult to assess because in addition to measuring each of the constructs individually, subsequent issues about how the constructs work together and relate to one another must be understood. This adds a layer of complexity to the construction and design of items as well as to the analyses of data collected.

3.2.2. Item development. The first place researchers would look to determine what items should be included in a survey to assess a construct is the extant literature. Continuing with the example of a survey to assess satisfaction with a new costing system, the relevant literature (in both printed and electronic forms of reports and journal articles) should contain the salient aspects of the construct that are consistently discussed as important. These aspects are likely to be developed into items to include in the survey. In addition, there may be employee satisfaction surveys on costing systems that have been previously developed. The researcher will examine these already existing instruments and determine what constructs the authors were attempting to measure with these items.

A fruitful source of information about the construct is found in subject matter experts (SMEs). SMEs can represent many stakeholder groups. Sales staff, managers, accountants, and others who interact with the costing system or use information from the system would all provide various perspectives about satisfaction with the system. Interviews or focus groups conducted with these SMEs about the construct help to define its salient aspects. In addition, when searching the existing literature, it is likely that some researchers' names will keep cropping up. Contacting these SMEs about the construct is often a very useful exercise as they are often willing to assist in survey construction. One question comes up when conducting interviews with SMEs: how many should be interviewed? The researchers should interview as many as necessary until no new perspectives or information is obtained. Usually this occurs after about 10-12 in-depth interviews.

Once the constructs are clear, then a number of items are created that should query the respondent about the construct. When writing items for a survey, the researcher needs to be as clear as possible. If items are unclear, respondents could provide inaccurate answers, leading to validity and reliability concerns. Some guiding principles in item writing cited in Ghiselli, Campbell, and Zedek (1981) and Nunnally and Bernstein (1994) include:

1. Deal with only *one* central thought in each item.
2. Be precise and brief.
3. Avoid awkward wording and irrelevant information.
4. Present items in positive language and avoid double negatives.
5. Avoid terms like 'all' and 'none'.
6. Avoid indeterminate terms like 'frequently' or 'sometimes'.

One consideration in designing surveys is to determine whether the items should be questions or declarative statements. Regardless of what type of item approach is taken, the researcher should stay with the same pattern for the entire instrument. There should be as many items on the survey as is necessary to properly assess the construct. It is likely that at least 5–10 items will be needed to perform even the most rudimentary analyses on the data, with some requiring no fewer than 20 items. In addition, some items will prove to be more useful than others, and so usually more items are created than will eventually be retained on a final version of a survey. However, the researcher should consider the time it will take the respondents to complete the survey; if it is too long, few people will participate in the survey, resulting in a low response rate and possibly compromising the representative nature of the survey. Thus, the final decision about how many items to include is based on rational, statistical, and administrative concerns. It is extremely useful to test out the set of items to be used in a 'pilot test' (discussed shortly). The results of the pilot test will also provide input into the decision of the number of items it is reasonable for respondents to complete in a given time frame.

3.2.3. Response development. In a survey, individuals will respond to items. The responses are usually coded with a number that then provides information allowing inferences to be made about the construct. For example, in the employee satisfaction survey, a series of questions will be designed to operationalise the construct of satisfaction with the costing system. Responses to each of the items will have a number attached to it. The numbers can then be used to generate a total score on the construct 'employee satisfaction'.

Social scientists have been interested in assessing attitudes for almost a hundred years. Various methods to attach numerical values to attitudes have been developed. But in 1932 Rensis Likert revolutionised the way that attitudes are measured and his work permeates most current survey designs. He published a method for scaling response categories that were distinct and separate from the questions (stimuli). Likert evaluated many attitude statements using five response categories: 1 = strongly approve; 2 = approve; 3 = undecided; 4 = disapprove, and 5 = strongly disapprove. He demonstrated that his approach could be used to assess respondents – not items (Likert, 1932). By taking the simple sum across each of the responses using this 5-point scale, the strength of the respondent's attitude could be determined.

Scales that use a 5-point format like the one described are called Likert scales. Variations on the original Likert scale are called summated rating scales or Likert-type scales. While Likert used 'strongly approve' to 'strongly disapprove' to anchor the ends of his 1 – 5 scale, many scales use variations on this such as 'strongly agree' to 'strongly disagree' or 'extremely difficult' to 'extremely easy'. Research has shown that these variations are not problematic (Bass, Cascio and O'Commor, 1974; Spector, 1976). The number of categories has also been a subject of controversy, but somewhere between 3 and 9 is sufficient for assessing attitude strength (Anderson, 1991; Champney and Marshall, 1939; Symonds, 1924). It is important to ensure that there are clear descriptors for each of the category options, and that the categories allow for an even distribution of negative versus positive response options.

Whether to have a midpoint on a summated rating scale (e.g. the 3 in a 1 – 5 scale) has also received some attention. There are no compelling statistical reasons to include or exclude the midpoint on a response scale. However, if there is no midpoint, respondents are forced to choose to agree or disagree with a statement. This may not be appropriate and may frustrate the respondents. Sometimes in a survey it is important to include a 'don't know' descriptor, because if respondents truly do not know, then they will leave the item blank, or worse provide responses that don't characterise their perceptions accurately. When respondents indicate 'don't know' the most frequent way to deal with the response is to insert the mean for the value. For example, if an employee is asked a series of questions about their attitude towards a new costing system, and the response categories are rated from 1 – 5, then a substitution of '3' would be made for a 'don't know' response. This has the virtue of being the most conservative way to deal with missing data.

Survey designers must determine whether to create items with a negative valence (a negative tone to them, such as 'I am dissatisfied with the costing system').

If the construct to be assessed is satisfaction, then the responses to this item have to be 'reverse coded'. For example, in a 5-point scale, a '1' would be changed to a '5', and a '2' would be changed to a '4', while the '3' would remain the same. Sometimes survey designers are cautioned to add such items to make sure that respondents are paying attention to the items, but respondents often find these types of items confusing (e.g. DeVellis, 2003; Netemeyer, Bearden and Sharma, 2003). If respondents are under a lot of time pressure or not used to answering surveys, then it is not advisable to use negative valence items. If such items are added, be sure to add many of them, not just one or two. Doing this will help to ensure more accurate answers to the survey items.

Another general issue that arises in creating Likert-type scales is whether to ask the respondent for intensity information (e.g. agreement) or frequency information (e.g. how often ...). If the response options ask for frequency information (i.e. never, sometimes, frequently, and almost always) a problem surfaces in that what the test developer meant by 'sometimes' or 'almost always' may very well not be what the respondent means by 'sometimes' or 'almost always.' In fact, each and every respondent may have a different interpretation of these terms. Some surveys require frequency information; for example, indicating how frequently managers complain about the system not providing information needed to make good decisions. However, survey researchers must be very explicit about what the response categories mean so that all respondents are working from the same frame of reference, increasing the reliability of the survey responses. Survey researchers need to know what the typical frequency is for a given question so that the categories can be formed appropriately. This typical frequency should be identified through interviews or focus group discussions prior to the pilot study (e.g. 'sometimes' may mean every few months, 'frequently' means monthly, 'almost always' means weekly, and 'always' is daily).

3.3. Implementing the Survey

3.3.1. Pilot testing. Pilot testing surveys is a crucial step in the surveying process. Small groups of individuals should be asked to complete the draft survey, pointing out where the survey may be confusing, which items may be problematic, and noting how long it takes to complete the survey. It is important to pilot test the survey using individuals who are representative of the population that will complete it in the future. These individuals should be recruited for their willingness to provide constructive feedback. This feedback will help the designer modify the final survey so that it is easy to complete by the sample participants of the target population. It may be that the survey will undergo more than one iteration in its development and will need to be pilot tested several times.

3.3.2. Sampling. Decisions regarding sampling are of two types: representativeness and size. Making inferences about the population based on the sample data collected can only be done with confidence if the sample adequately represents the population. There are two general types of sampling strategies: probability and non-probability. In probability sampling, each person has an equal probability of being sampled and that probability is known in advance. In probability samples, the error due to sampling can be estimated based on probability theory. This is not the case in non-probability samples.

The most common forms of probability samples include: simple random, stratified random, disproportionate stratified random sampling, and proportionate stratified random sampling. Systematic and multi-stage (cluster) sampling approaches are also used in large survey efforts. Non-probability samples characterise much of the more modest sample survey research. One example of such a sample is a quota sample. Snowball and convenience (also known as accidental, fortuitous, and opportunity) sampling are also all non-probability. Samples based on responses that come from mail out surveys (or email and Internet delivered surveys) are also non-probability samples. Theoretical or purposive sampling is a deliberate non-probability sampling procedure used in theory development by qualitative researchers. With non-probability samples one cannot simply assume that the results generalise to the population. Consumers of the results of the survey will need to be convinced that the findings are generalisable.

The other sampling decision is one of size. Often the data collected via a survey are to be used to assess relationships with other variables of interest. Tests to determine the statistical significance of such relationships are strongly affected by the sample size. In addition, assessments of the fidelity of the survey instrument itself often require sample sizes of at least 100. Turning to the issue of statistical significance first, there is a relationship between the alpha level, effect size, and power of any statistical test. The alpha is the amount of Type I error (i.e. incorrectly rejecting the null hypothesis) the researcher is willing to allow and is usually set at 0.05. The effect size is the amount of variance in the dependent variable that should be accounted for by the independent variable. Effect sizes vary dramatically depending on the research area and are often estimated based on past research findings. Power is the probability of rejecting the null hypothesis (or alternatively, the probability of being able to find support for the alternative hypothesis) and is usually expected to be about 0.80 (Cohen, 1988). The statistical results of the power of the test take into account both effect size and sample size in most statistical software programs. As the sample size increases and/or the alpha level is made more liberal, the power of a statistical test increases. Because the alpha levels are usually set by convention, researchers are restricted to changing the sample size to increase power. Power tables, such as those provided in Cohen (1988) assist in determining the sample size required for a given effect size and desired power.

3.3.3. Responses rates, follow-up procedures and non-responses. Generally, the researcher receives fewer completed surveys than were mailed-out, emailed, or Internet delivered. This has given rise to the need to report response rates from such surveys. Typical response rates to unsolicited surveys are about 30%, while response rates to national surveys are usually much higher (70%-95%) (Madow *et al.* 1983).

These numbers indicate that many more surveys should be sent out than need to be returned to secure the desired sample size. To encourage respondents to reply, Madow *et al.* (1983) suggest making the survey as short and effortless as possible, sending out reminders, providing incentives, and guaranteeing information privacy. Noting that ethics clearance has been obtained from a reputable Research Ethics Board is often an added incentive for individuals to complete the survey, as the process for securing ethics clearance for human subjects is often quite stringent. Finally, researchers should collect demographic information so that the final sample can be compared to the population to which the researcher wants to generalise.

Once surveys are returned, it is common for some of the items to be left unanswered. Missing data can be handled in a variety of acceptable ways. Tabachnick and Fidell (2001) claim that the pattern of the missing data indicates the relative seriousness of the problem. For example, if 5% of the data points are missing and are scattered randomly throughout the data set, this does not pose a serious problem. A draconian approach to missing data is to delete all cases that have any missing data. Another option is to leave cases with the missing data in the data set and run the various analyses only on those cases with all of the data for those analyses. Another commonly used option is to replace the missing values with the mean or median value of the variable across cases. If a case is missing only one or two responses in a survey of 20 items, then one could alternatively substitute that respondent's mean or median score within the survey. It is worthwhile running analyses where the researcher both removes the cases with the missing data and also inserts substitutions. If the results are similar using both approaches, then the substitution procedure is acceptable. After screening the data set for such issues as non-responses, the researcher then turns to assessing the reliability and validity of the scale scores.

3.4. Data Analyses (Reliability and Validity)

3.4.1. Item reliability. Descriptive statistics for each item on the survey should be examined as a first step in the data analyses process. Item responses should be normally distributed, and deviations from normality will result in attenuated relationships. Items that have very little variance (e.g. respondents all select '3' on a 1 – 5 Likert-type scale) are useless items and should be removed from further analyses.

Next, the internal consistency of the items must be established. That is, the items purporting to assess a single underlying construct should be related to one another. To assess this feature, corrected item-to-total correlations should result in values of at least 0.30 for each item. In addition, an overall index such as the Cronbach's alpha needs to be conducted on a set of items that assess a similar construct. Values of 0.70 are acceptable for surveys to be used for research purposes (Nunnally and Bernstein, 1994). If we continue with our example of employee satisfaction with a costing system survey, we would expect that items would correlate with one another (i.e. respondents rating one item highly are likely to rate other items highly), indicating high internal consistency.

Finally, to demonstrate that the internal relationships among the items are operating as expected, a principal components analysis is likely to be employed. Specifically, if one construct is anticipated, then the principal components analyses should statistically 'find' a single underlying component that is predicted reliably and thus significantly by all of the items. If the survey is expecting to assess more than one construct, then the internal consistency evaluations should be conducted within each of the sets of items making up each construct separately. Additionally, a common factor analysis is likely to be employed to determine which items are associated with each underlying construct or 'factor.'

In the aforementioned analyses, an exploratory approach can be taken using conventional principal components or common factor analysis programs. Alternatively, a more confirmatory approach can be taken using more sophisticated structural equation modeling programs. Regardless of the approach taken, items are expected to load substantially on the respective underlying construct. In exploratory approaches usually this means that items have loadings above 0.30. In confirmatory approaches, this means that the item loadings are statistically significant and the purpose of the analysis is to confirm the 'goodness of fit' of the items under the theorised constructs (e.g. Bollen, 1989).

If more than one construct is assumed, then correlations between the total scores on the constructs should be examined for evidence of multicollinearity. For example, if in the employee satisfaction survey, items are developed about information derived from the system and items are developed about servicing of the system, it might be inferred that the items are assessing unique constructs. However, if the correlation between the scores on the constructs is high (i.e. 0.90 or more) then it is more reasonable to assert that the items are all assessing a single construct.

3.4.2. Validity of scores. Often researchers will use the total scores on a survey to relate to other variables of interest (e.g. employee position). In addition, survey scores are often *not* expected to be related to other variables (e.g. gender or age). The next step in assessing the integrity of the survey is to conduct a series of analyses that will demonstrate the expected relationships.

Correlation or regression analyses are frequently used to determine whether the survey scores are useful. For example, scores on service surveys might be correlated with number of times an employee uses the system, the employee's level of education or experience in accounting. Tests of mean differences on surveys with respect to demographic variables also shed light on when the survey is most useful and when it is likely not useful. For example, perhaps young employees rate the system more positively than do older employees. Alternatively, women employees may rate the system more positively than do men. If this is the case, then the information itself is useful. However, care must be taken then to subject the data to analyses after first separating it into its demographic groups. As an illustration, assume that women and men rate the costing system differently on user-friendliness. Then correlating the employee satisfaction survey scores with both the men and women data points combined may mask true relationships.

The assessment of a set of survey items is a long and laborious process. It often takes several attempts with several samples to reduce the items to a set that accurately and succinctly measures the construct of interest.

4. Section 2: Empirical Evaluation of Accounting Survey Research

4.1. Source of Data

In this section of the chapter, we review how surveys have been developed, used, and their scores interpreted over the past 11 years within the mainstream accounting literature.

Of the five accounting journals that are frequently top ranked, only *Accounting, Organizations and Society* (AOS) tends to accept survey research. *Contemporary Accounting Research, The Accounting Review,* and *Journal of Accounting Research* did not publish any survey research articles and *Journal of Accounting and Economics* published only one (Keating, 1997) in our study period. Therefore, we used 61 articles published in three accounting journals: 37 from *Accounting, Organizations and Society* (AOS), 11 from *Behavioral Research in Accounting* (BRIA), and 13 from *Journal of Management Accounting Research* (JMAR). Although there are many journals that publish management accounting studies, we believe the data from the three selected well-known journals should be a good indicator of the survey research trends in the management accounting discipline.

Table 1
Survey Research in AOS, BRIA and JMAR (1994-2004)

Journal	Study	Subject	Respondents population	Respondents	Type of sampling	Resp. rate	Follow up	Non resp analysis	Reliability	Validity	Type of dependent variable
BRIA	Wentzel (2002)	Budgeting	A large urban hospital	88 cost centers managers	Selective (all)	84%	No	Yes	Cronbach alpha of .8 to .93	Factor analysis, SEM and based on previous studies	Self rating of performance using Mahoney (1963)
AOS	Baines and Langfield-Smith (2003)	Strategic management accounting	Australian manufacturing companies	700 business managers	Random	20%	Yes	No	Cronbach alpha of .74 to .85 and item correlations analysis	Based on previous studies and SEM	Self rating of organisational variables as antecedents to management accounting change
AOS	Arunachalam (2004)	Management accounting systems	Organisations registered as Electronic Data Interchange users	1400 organisations	Selective (All)	32%	No	No	Not reported	Not reported	Self rating on EDI usage
AOS	Cavalluzzo and Ittner (2004)	Performance measurement	US General Accounting Office	1300 middle and upper level managers	Random	40%	Yes	Yes	Cronbach alpha of .65 to .93	Factor analysis	Self rating of the performance measurement system
AOS	Widener (2004)	KM and management control system	Different industries in US	800 CFOs	Random	15%	Yes	Yes	Cronbach alpha of .64 to .88 and inter item reliability	Factor analysis and SEM	Self rating on the components of management control systems
AOS	Chalos and O'Connor (2004)	Management control system	US-Chinese Joint Ventures	742 managers	Random	35%	Yes	No	Cronbach alpha of .65 to .94	Factor analysis	Self ratings on management controls
BRIA	Chenhall (2004)	Activity based management	18 organisations that recently introduced ABM in Australia	64 SBU managers	Selective	88%	Yes	Yes	Cronbach alpha of .74 to .90	Factor analysis, SEM and based on previous studies	Self rating on the usefulness of ABM in 5 areas (Based on literature)

Journal	Study	Subject	Respondents population	Respondents	Type of sampling	Resp. rate	Follow up	Non resp anal-ysis	Reliability	Validity	Type of dependent variable
AOS	Gul and Chia (1994)	Managerial Performance	Different industries in Singapore	100 Sub-Unit Managers	Random	48%	No	No	Cronbach Alpha of .66 to .88	Factor analysis	Subjective measure of managerial performance developed by Mahoney et al. (1963)
AOS	Ross (1994)	Trust and performance measurement	Different Australian Organisations	308 Managers in Australian Organisations	Selective	70%	No	No	Cronbach Alpha of .81 to .86	Not reported	Self rating of performance developed by Hopwood (1972)
JMAR	Foster and Gupta (1994)	Cost management	Marketing executives attending annual seminar	220 managers from Australia, Canada, UK and US	Selective (all)	23%	No	No	Not reported	Not reported	Exploratory
JMAR	Shields and Young (1994)	Cost management	Four large chemical firms in US	285 R & D professional	Not reported	56%	No	No	Cronbach alpha of .47 to .58	Not reported	Self rating of cost consciousness
AOS	Abernethy and Stoelwinder (1995)	Management control systems	A large Australian hospital	100 Physicians and subunit managers	Selective	91%	No	No	Cronbach Alpha of .77 to .84	Based on previous studies	Self rating of role conflict using Rizzo et al. (1970), Self rating of performance using single global rating, self rating of job satisfaction using Dewar Werbel (1979)
AOS	Lau et al. (1995)	Performance measurement	Different manufacturing firms in Singapore	240 functional heads from 80 companies	Random	47%	Yes	Yes	Cronbach Alpha of .48 to .87	Based on Previous studies	Self rating of performance developed by Mahoney (1965)
AOS	O'Conner (1995)	Budgeting	62 Manufacturing firms in Singapore	282 Singaporean Managers	Not reported	44%	Yes	No	Cronbach Alpha of .81 to .90	Based on previous studies and criterion related validity of .52	Self rating of behavioral variables using Hofstede (1980)

Journal	Study	Subject	Respondents population	Respondents	Type of sampling	Resp. rate	Follow up	Non resp analysis	Reliability	Validity	Type of dependent variable
AOS	Magner et al. (1995)	Budgeting	International managers attending at a 10 week executive seminar in Europe	56 international managers	Selective	95%	No	No	Cronbach Alpha of 70 to .86	Based on previous studies	Self rating of attitudes towards supervisor using Read (1962)
JMAR	Shields (1995)	Activity based costing	143 different firms	143 financial managers	Selective	Not reported	No	No	Not reported	Factor analysis	Self rating of overall ABC success and financial benefits of ABC
AOS	Firth (1996)	Management accounting systems	Chinese firms that participate in a joint venture company with a foreign partner	1254 CFOs in Chinese firms	Not reported	29%	No	Yes	Not reported	Not reported	Self rating of management accounting systems variables partly based on previous studies
AOS	Chow et al. (1996)	Management control systems	A large manufacturing firm (Toshiba) in Japan	37 Toshiba's division managers	Selective	76%	No	No	Cronbach Alpha of .77 to .89	Based on previous studies and factor analysis	Self rating of control tightness and dysfunctional behaviour using Merchant's (1985) questionnaire
BRIA	Collins et al. (1995)	Budgeting	A large charitable organisation in US	344 non-supervisory employees	Selective	50%	No	Yes	Cronbach alpha of .70 to .84	Factor analysis SEM	Self rating of organisational commitment developed by Mowday et al. (1979)
AOS	Fisher (1996)	Management information systems	Nine different industry groups in the area of Hobart, Australia	143 managers	Random	69%	No	No	Cronbach Alpha of .65 to .71	Based on previous studies and factor analysis	Self rating of the information characteristics developed by Chenhall and Morris (1986)

Journal	Study	Subject	Respondents population	Respondents	Type of sampling	Resp. rate	Follow up	Non resp anal-ysis	Reliability	Validity	Type of dependent variable
AOS	Chong (1996)	Management accounting systems and performance measurement	Manufacturing companies in Western Australia with more than 100 employees	78 senior managers	Random	54%	No	Yes	Cronbach Alpha of .92	Not reported	Self rating of performance developed by Mahoney (1965)
BRIA	Nouri and Parker (1996)	Budgeting	A large multinational chemical firm in US	203 managers	Selective	67%	No	No	Cronbach alpha of .75 to .86	Based on previous studies	Self rating of propensity to create budgetary slack developed by Onsi's (1973)
JMAR	Foster and Sjoblom (1996)	Cost management	Electronic companies in US	2000 members of American Society for Quality Control	Not reported	14%	No	No	Not reported	Not reported	Self rating of production related variables as the cause of quality problem
JMAR	Libby and Waterhouse (1996)	Management accounting systems	70 organisations in Canada	70 controller	Random	34%	No	Yes	Cronbach alpha of .63 to .75	Factor analysis	Self scoring of the number of changes in management accounting system
JMAR	Sangster (1996)	Management accounting systems	Professionally designated management accountants in U.K	4238 members of CIMA	Not reported	25%	No	No	Not reported	Not reported	Exploratory to find the extent of expert system diffusion
AOS	Gosselin (1997)	Activity based costing	Canadian Manufacturing firms	415 strategic business units	Selective	39%	Yes	Yes	Cronbach Alpha of above .60	Factor analysis and criterion related validity using correlation	Self rating of adoption of ABM and ABC (Yes or No)
AOS	Abernethy and Brownell (1997)	Management control systems	A large Australian company and a major US scientific organisation	150 senior research officers in R&D division	Selective	85%	No	No	Cronbach Alpha of .82 to .91 and a maximum inter-item correlation of .20	Based on previous studies and factor analysis	Self rating of performance developed by Mahoney (1965)

Journal	Study	Subject	Respondents population	Respondents	Type of sampling	Resp. rate	Follow up	Non resp analysis	Reliability	Validity	Type of dependent variable
AOS	Perera et al. (1997)	Performance measurement	Manufacturing firms in Australia	200 managers	Random	53%	No	No	Cronbach Alpha of .56 to .82	Not reported	Self rating of performance used by Chenhall (1993)
BRIA	Choo and Tan (1997)	Budgeting	10 US firms in light industry	156 managers	Selective	70%	No	No	Cronbach alpha of .85 to .90 and comparison with previous studies	Factor analysis and based on previous studies	Self rating of performance using Mahoney (1963)
JMAR	Foster and Swenson (1997)	Activity based costing	Company sites that were using ABC	750 respondents (Not obvious who they are)	Not reported	22%	No	No	Cronbach alpha of .78 to .93	Factor analysis	Self rating of ABC success determinants
AOS	Chenhall and Langfield-Smith (1998)	Management accounting systems	Manufacturing firms in Australia	140 Financial Controller, Senior managers or chief executives	Selective	56%	Yes	Yes	Not reported	Based on previous studies and factor analysis	Self rating of organisational performance developed by Govindarajan (1988)
AOS	Nouri and Parker (1998)	Budgeting	A large multinational corporation	203 managers and supervisors	Selective	67.00 %	Yes	Yes	Cronbach Alpha of .84 to 89	Based on previous studies and factor analysis	Self rating of performance developed by Govindarajan and Gupta (1985)
JMAR	Krumwiede (1998)	Activity based costing	Members of Cost Management Group of IMA	778 members	Not reported	31%	Yes	Yes	Cronbach alpha of .68 to .91	Content validity using experts and factor analysis	Self rating of the stage of ABC implementation
JMAR	Sim and Killough (1998)	Management accounting systems	Electronic industry in U.S	1500 directors of manufacturing	Random	6%	Yes	No	Cronbach alpha of .63 to 83	Based on previous studies	Self rating of customer and quality performance developed by Lynch and Cross (1991)
AOS	Kalagnanam and Lindsay (1999)	Management control system	Canadian manufacturing plants	1580 plant managers	Random (All)	13%	Yes	Yes	Correlation analysis to test the internal reliability	Content validity analysis and factor analysis	Self rating on the implementation type of JIT

Journal	Study	Subject	Respondents population	Respondents	Type of sampling	Resp. rate	Follow up	Non resp analysis	Reliability	Validity	Type of dependent variable
AOS	Vandenbosch (1999)	Accounting information systems	3 US and 15 Canadian organisations who adopted executive support system	612 (Not obvious)	Selective	56%	No	Yes	Measure of internal consistency of more than .8 Using Fornell and Larcker convergent validity	Convergant and discriminant validity	Self rating on the type of executive use of management information
AOS	Scott and Tiessen (1999)	Performance measurement	12 for-profit and 15 not-for-profit organisations in different industries	583 managers	Selective based on ease of access	43%	No	No	Cronbach Alpha of .8 to 87	Based on previous studies and factor analysis	Self rating of team performance
AOS	Chow et al. (a) (1999)	Culture and Management control systems	6 Japanese-Taiwanese, and US-Owned firms	391 top level managers	Selective	41%	No	No	Cronbach Alpha of .63-.93	Based on previous studies	Self ratings on the kind of control based on a number of previous studies
AOS	Chow et al. (b) (1999)	Culture and management information systems	13 Taiwanese and 14 Australian companies in different industries	102 middle level managers	Selective	Not mentioned	Yes	No	Based on previous studies	Based on previous studies	Self rating of cultural elements using Hofstede (1980)
AOS	Guilding (1999)	Competitor-focused accounting	New Zealand's largest companies	217 chief accountants	Random	52%	Yes	Yes	Based on previous studies	Based on previous studies	Self rating of CFA adoption and helpfulness using the constructs developed in previous studies
AOS	Malmi (1999)	Activity based costing	Different industries in Finland	1240 employees	Random	40%	No	Yes	Not reported	Not reported	Exploratory
BRIA	Comerford and Abernethy (1999)	Budgeting	A large Australian teaching hospital	100 physicians and nurse managers	Selective	88/%	No	No	Cronbach alpha of .72 to .90	Factor analysis and based on previous studies	Self rating of role conflict using the instrument developed by Rizzo (190)

Journal	Study	Subject	Respondents population	Respondents	Type of sampling	Resp. rate	Follow up	Non resp analysis	Reliability	Validity	Type of dependent variable
JMAR	Widener and Selto (1999)	Management control systems	Companies with more than 500 employees in Compustat	600 employees	stratified random	14%	Yes	Yes	Inter-rater reliability and Cronbach alpha of 45 to .98	Content validity using experts and factor analysis	Self scoring of internal auditing out-sources hours
AOS	Otley and Pollanen (2000)	Budgeting and performance measurement	Administration of universities and colleges in Ontario, Canada	176 administrators	Selective	72%	Yes	Yes	Based on previous studies and Cronbach Alpha of .64 to .85	Based on previous studies and Factor analysis. Also comparative study	Self rating of performance developed by Mahoney, Jerdee and Carroll (1963)
AOS	Vagneur and Peiperl (2000)	Performance measurement	British-based business units of 20 international companies	82 managers	Random	82%	No	No	Based on previous studies	Based on previous studies, factor analysis and criterion related validity	Both objective measure and self rating of performance developed by steers
AOS	Van der Stede (2000)	Budgeting	A large firm in Belgium	341 business unit managers	Selective	45%	Yes	Yes	Cronbach Alpha of .67 to .83	Based on previous studies, factor analysis and criterion related validity	Both objective measure and self rating of performance
AOS	Stone et al. (2000)	Management accounting knowledge	Three different industries in US	5932 management accountants in different levels	Random	50%	No	Yes	Cronbach Alpha of .43 to .97 and based on previous studies	Factor analysis	Exploratory to find the level of management accounting knowledge
AOS	Hunton et al. (2000)	Management accounting knowledge	Three different industries in US	5933 management accountants in different levels	Random	50%	No	Yes	Based on previous study	Based on previous study and SEM	Exploratory to find the level of management accounting knowledge

Journal	Study	Subject	Respondents population	Respondents	Type of sampling	Resp. rate	Follow up	Non resp analysis	Reliability	Validity	Type of dependent variable
BRIA	Chalos and Poon (2000)	Budgeting	A large multinational US firm	190 project managers	Selective	93%	No	No	Cronbach alpha of .68 to .93 and interrater reliability of .66 to .83	Factor analysis and SEM	Self rating of performance using Mahoney (1963)
BRIA	Chalos and Poon (2000)	Budgeting	A large multinational US firm	190 project managers	Selective	93%	No	No	Cronbach alpha of .68 to .93 and interrater reliability of .66 to .83	Factor analysis and SEM	Self rating of performance using Mahoney (1963)
JMAR	Hoque and James (2000)	Performance measurement	Australian manufacturing firms	188 CFOs and financial controllers	Random	35%	Yes	Yes	Cronbach alpha of .62 to .81	Factor analysis and based on previous studies	Self appraising of fine dimensions of organisational performance using Merchant (1984)
AOS	Moores and Yuen (2001)	Management accounting systems	Clothing and footwear industry in Australia	337 CEOs	Random	14%	No	Yes	Based on previous studies	Based on previous studies and factor analysis	Self rating of organisational characteristics
AOS	Williams and Seaman (2001)	Management accounting systems	Different industries in Singapore	206 personnel directors and CFOs	Random	45%	Yes	Yes	Cronbach alpha of .68 to .80 and based on previous studies	Based on previous studies and factor analysis	Self rating changes in management accounting and control systems using scale developed by Libby and Waterhouse (1996)
BRIA	Clintion and Huntono (2001)	Budgeting	Accounting professionals attending annual conference from different US industries	1710 accounting personnels (89% managers)	Selective (all)	23%	No	No	Cronbach alpha of .84 to .87	Based on previous studies and factor analysis	Self scoring of organisational performance using Shields & Young (1993)
JMAR	Abernethy and Lilis	Management control	A large Australian hospital	149 CEOs and medical directors	Selective	58%	No	Yes	Cronbach alpha of .68 to .84	Factor analysis	Self rating of organisational outcomes

Journal	Study	Subject	Respondents population	Respondents	Type of sampling	Resp. rate	Follow up	Non resp analysis	Reliability	Validity	Type of dependent variable
JMAR	Kennedy and Affeck-Grave (2001)	Activity based costing and performance systems	Top UK firms	853 finance directors	Selective	27%	Yes	Yes	Not reported	Criterion related validity	Objective measure of performance: increase in shareholders' wealth measured by stock returns
AOS	Fullertone and McWatters (2002)	Performance measurement	US manufacturing firms	447 manufacturing executives	Random	57%	Yes	Yes	Cronbach alpha of .70 to .90	Factor analysis split sample cross validation	Self rating on the degree of JIT implementation
AOS	Guiding and McManus (2002)	Strategic management accounting	Top 300 Australian listed companies	300 chief accountants and marketing managers in 251 companies	Selective (All)	49%	Yes	Yes	Cronbach alpha of .86 to .91	Factor analysis	Self rating on CA practices and managerial merit of CA
BRIA	Almer and Kaplan (2002)	Organisational behaviour	Public accountants employed in 5 public accounting firms	646 employees working in the firms (60%) Managers	Selective	48%	Yes	No	Cronbach alpha of .67 to .93	Factor analysis and based on previous studies	Self rating of job outcomes using Hppock's scale
BRIA	Chong and Chong (2002)	Budgeting	80 Australian manufacturing companies in different industries	150 middle level managers	Random	53%	Yes	Yes	Cronbach alpha of .70 to .94 and Item reliability measures	Convergent and discriminant validity using factor analysis and SEM based on previous studies	Self rating of performance using Mahoney (1963)
BRIA	Hooks and Higgs (2002)	Organizational behaviour	Client service professionals in one of Big 5	9765 partners, middle-managers and experienced consultants	Selective (all)	11%	No	No	Not mentioned	Not mentioned	Self rating of workplace environment (Instrument based on interviews)

Complementing the discussion in the first section of sound methodological procedures, in the empirical evaluation we follow the same three major steps of designing the survey, implementing the survey, and analysing the data. We also discuss the same topics falling under each of these steps to the extent that these topics were available for evaluation in the published accounting studies.

4.2. Designing a Survey

Of the topics falling under designing a survey, the topic of construct development receives the most emphasis in our empirical evaluation, as item and response development are rarely discussed extensively in published survey research.

4.2.1. Construct development. As discussed in the first section of this chapter, the purpose of the survey can be either exploratory or confirmatory. In analysing our 61 studies, if the research studied the interrelationship of variables based on existing theories, the research was classified as confirmatory. If no pre-existing theory or specific hypotheses were noted, then the research was classified as exploratory. Atkinson and Shaffir (1998) argued that studies aimed at either developing or testing theory attract the most attention in management accounting literature. Consistent with their suggestion, the results of our analysis indicated that 90% (n=55) of the selected studies were confirmatory. We rarely found an article that attempted to build theory using the survey method. Anderson and Widener, (in press) also maintain that the use of numeric data and quantitative analysis benefits all forms of field research, whether exploratory, theory building or confirmatory.

Researchers use survey research to study a wide variety of topics (see Table 2). Our analysis indicated that budgeting, activity based costing/management (ABC/M), performance measurement, and management control systems were the most popular topics using survey research. Other, less popular topics were accounting information system and strategic management accounting. In general, BRIA tended to publish survey research on budgeting, AOS tended to publish research on performance measurement, management control systems, ABC/M, and some budgeting, and JMAR tended to publish research on ABC/M, with a few studies on management control systems, and performance measurement systems. All journals had research that fell in the 'other' category.

Table 2
Subject of Studies

Subject	AOS (n=37)	BRIA (n=11)	JMAR (n=13)	Total (n = 61)
Performance measurement	10 (27%)	-	1 (8%)	11 (18%)
Management control system	8 (22%)	-	2 (15%)	10 (16%)
Budgeting	4 (11%)	8 (73%)	-	12 (20%)

Activity Based Costing/Management	7 (19%)	1 (9%)	4 (31%)	12 (20%)
Other	8 (21%)	2 (18%)	6 (46%)	16 (26%)

4.2.2. Item and response development. An important consideration in survey research, when developing items for a survey, is to determine the unit(s) of analysis upon which the data rest (Pinsonneault and Kraemer, 1993). Common units of analysis include individual, department, and organisation. Which unit is used in a particular research study is generally determined by the research objectives and hypotheses.

Table 3
Unit of Analysis

Unit of Analysis	AOS (n = 37)	BRIA (n = 11)	JMAR (n=13)	Total (n=61)
Individuals	14	9	3	26 (42%)
Department	6	-	-	6 (10%)
Organisation	17	2	10	29 (48%)

Table 3 shows that most surveys used the individual (42%) or organisation (48%) as the unit of analysis. Researchers should be cautious in interpreting their findings if a survey is completed by an individual, but the unit of analysis is the organisation. The individuals who are representing the organisational perspective may be biased in their responses. For example, a favoured employee within the organisation may not be the most suitable employee to complete a survey (Young, 1996). Collecting objective data as well as survey data when the unit of analysis is at the organisational level might help to validate the results.

In most of the studies (n=52) upper and middle level managers in the organisations were targeted as respondents. Even though organisational managers may be the best source of knowledge on a given topic, potential respondents with other functional responsibilities would provide further organisational insight into a particular research question.

4.3. Implementing the Survey

In our empirical evaluation, we discuss the same topics of sampling, response rates, follow-up procedures, and non-responses as in the methodological procedures section of this chapter, as these topics are subject to the greatest criticism in published survey research. We do not discuss pilot testing as this topic is not discussed as extensively in published survey research. In addition, it is rarely noted in studies whether and to what degree pilot testing has been conducted.

4.3.1. Sampling. Selecting an appropriate sample frame (those individuals or organisations from which one selects the actual sample for the survey) is not often discussed even though it is usually more important than the selection of the sample itself. Sampling in the majority of the articles in our analysis was based on convenience (selective) rather than theoretical justification. Most convenient samples were drawn from organisations from which the researchers had easy access to respondents, helping to increase the final response rate. Many studies did not justify their sampling frame or the theoretical reason for drawing their desired sample. Table 4 presents the type of sampling used in the articles analysed.

Table 4
Type of Sampling

Sampling Type	AOS (n = 37)	BRIA (n = 11)	JMAR (n = 13)	Total (n = 61)
Selective	17	10	4	31 (51%)
Random	18	1	4	23 (38%)
Not reported	2	-	5	7 (11%)

The majority of selected papers did not use probability (random) sampling to collect the data. Inappropriate sampling methods can cause problems in generalising the research findings. In some of the studies using selective sampling, researchers used the entire population under investigation as the sample. Proper random sampling and statistical sampling techniques could have reduced the resources needed to conduct these studies.

A weakness that we found in the studies was the failure to report the sample size necessary to have the appropriate power in conducting statistical analyses.

4.3.2. Response Rates. The average number of respondents in the studies was 859 with a standard deviation of 1654. The high standard deviation indicates there were wide differences in the range of sample sizes. For example, Hooks and Higgs (2002) used 9,756 respondents for their analysis while Chow et al. (1996) used 37 respondents. As mentioned in the methodological procedures, assessment of the fidelity of the survey instrument often requires sample sizes of at least 100. However, we found that 13% (n=8) of the studies had sample sizes less than this level.

There are many ways to determine a response rate (Asch et al., 1997). However, we used a ratio of the number of usable surveys returned to the number of surveys distributed as our measure. The mean survey response rate for the studies we reviewed was 48%. Surprisingly, two of the selected studies did not report the response rate, and 22% (n=14) of the studies had response rates of less than 30%. High response rates have many advantages (Fox et al., 1988): increased sample size for data analysis, generalisability of results, reduced costs associated with follow-up procedures, and reduced concerns over non-response bias.

4.3.3. Follow-up procedures. A low response rate is the major reason why mail survey research findings have a poor image (Dillman, 1991). To ensure the highest response rate possible, Dillman (1978) has suggested the following survey components and characteristics: easy survey layout, short length, appropriate use of color, enclosing return postage, and an invitational cover letter. One of the most powerful tools for increasing response rate is to use incentives, follow-ups or reminders. Examples of these tools include: monetary incentives, non-monetary incentives, well-timed personalised follow-up correspondence, follow-up reminders, timing of the follow-up, personalisation of correspondence, and ensuring the anonymity of respondents (Dillman 1978). Harvey (1987) suggested, however, that the incentive and follow-up methods used should be appropriate for each research situation. Table 5 shows the use of follow-up procedures used in the studies we reviewed. Only six out of the fourteen studies that had low response rates (below 30 %) used follow-up procedures.

Table 5

Response Rate and Follow-up Procedures

Response Rate	Papers using Follow-up Procedures			
	AOS (n=37)	BRIA (n=11)	JMAR (n=13)	Total (n=61)
Below 30% (n= 14)	3 (60%)	None	3 (42%)	6/14= 42%
30% to 50% (n = 20)	8 (53%)	1 (50%)	2 (67%)	11/20= 55%
Above 50% (n = 25)	5 (31%)	2 (28%)	None	7/25=28%
Not Reported (n = 2)	1 (100%)	None	1 (100%)	2/2= 100%

Non-responses. Non-response error or bias happens when some of the potential respondents with different attitudes from the respondents do not respond to the survey (Dillman, 1991). Researchers are usually not aware of the possible differences between respondents and non-respondents and therefore should analyse the data for non-respondent bias that might potentially affect the implications of the findings.

In the studies we reviewed, just under half (49%; n=30) analysed non-responses. Armstrong and Overtone (1977) describe three different methods to estimate non-response bias: comparisons with known values for the population, subjective estimates, and statistical extrapolation. Because values for the population are not usually known beforehand, subjective estimates have been overused and heavily criticised (Armstrong and Overtone, 1977). Statistical extrapolation is a rigorous method to assess non-response bias. Detailed discussion of the different methods is beyond the scope of this chapter. However, some suggestions are provided in the first part of the chapter.

4.4. Data Analyses (Reliability and Validity)

4.4.1. Item reliability and validity of scores. To have confidence in the statistical results and to make valid inferences about the research question, it is important that measures of the variables are both reliable and valid. Reliability is a necessary but not sufficient precondition for validity. It refers to the consistency or reproducibility of a measure. Validity of scores is not an all or nothing phenomenon, rather, it is the degree to which we can have confidence in the knowledge claims we make about our data. One way to increase the utility of survey findings is to use well-established measures that have demonstrated good reliability and validity. However, using existing measures of constructs does not absolve researchers from conducting their own psychometric assessments on the data that they collect. In several of the studies reviewed we noticed that researchers relied solely on previous studies to demonstrate the reliability and validity of their survey. Detailed discussion of reliability and validity measurement is beyond the scope of this chapter, but can be found elsewhere (e.g. Kline, 2005). In the studies we examined, Cronbach's alpha (in some cases, factor analysis) was primarily the method used to assess survey instrument reliability and validity. Some of the studies did not report any psychometric assessment of their survey instrument (see Table 1 for details). To increase the precision and generalisability of survey studies, psychometric properties of instruments should be reported.

4.4.2. Subjective dependent variables. As noted in Table 1, self-ratings were the most widely used type of dependent variable in the studies we assessed. For example, 16 studies (26%) used a self-reported measure of performance as the dependent variable. However, self-ratings of performance have been criticised by some accounting researchers. Mia (1989) contends that self-ratings are overly lenient. Young (1996) argues that self-ratings of performance might be substantially different from actual performance. Young (1996) also argues that different organisations apply different measures of performance and have different norms for performance. This issue might affect the equivalence of self-reported performance survey results that have been collected in different organisations using the same survey instrument.

Van der Stede *et al.* (2005) have suggested using both objective and subjective measures of performance. The use of objective measures of performance as a dependent variable can increase the reliability of the self-rating measures. As explained earlier, correlating the objective measures with subjective measures would increase the reliability of the instrument. In the studies we reviewed, only three studies (Vagneur and Peiperi, 2000; Vand der Stede, 2000 and Kennedy and Affeck-Grave, 2001) used both objective and subjective measures in their variable measurements, and all were conducted in 2000 or later. While the trend towards both objective and subjective measures may be increasing, the method is still not extensively used.

5. Conclusions, Problems and Recommendations

In the first section of this chapter, we provided a framework (including design, implementation, and analysis of data) for sound methodological procedures for researchers using the survey method when conducting accounting research. We then used that framework as a standard to evaluate the published survey research in some of the top ranking management accounting journals.

We have observed that certain top-rated journals in the field of accounting have rarely (if at all) published survey research over the past 11 years. For those journals that do publish survey research, certain research subjects tend to migrate to certain journals: AOS tended to publish the broadest range of subject areas (as well as the largest absolute number) including (in rank order of absolute numbers) performance measurement, management control systems, ABC/M and budgeting. However, BRIA published the greatest absolute number of research studies on budgeting. In JMAR, the subject area of ABC/M ranked highest for the journal, but the absolute number of ABC/M articles was less than those published by AOS on this subject.

We also observed that the organisation tended to be the preferred unit of analysis (48%), but we were not able to determine what precautions were taken to ensure that the individual respondent was capable of answering accurately for the entire organisation. Researchers are thus cautioned to consider the unit of analysis when determining constructs and developing items for the survey instrument to ensure that responses by an individual respondent will be an accurate reflection of the entire organisation.

Regarding survey implementation, selective or convenience sampling (rather than random) tended to be the preferred sampling method; however, 11% of the studies did not report the type of sampling used. Type of sampling used should always be disclosed. Also statistical sampling should be used when appropriate to ensure generalisability of the findings. Researchers should also report the power as well as effect sizes to assist readers in the interpretation of findings. Of the studies reviewed, 24% had response rates below 30%. One might attribute low response rate to lack of follow-up procedures. Indeed, the number of studies with follow-up procedures in the below 30% response rate category (n=6) was lower than the number of studies with follow-up procedures in the 30%-50% category (n=11). However, it is interesting that for studies where the response rate was 50% or lower few researchers used follow up procedures (only 28%) or if they did, they did not indicate that they used them, which tends to go against suggested best practices for increasing response rates. We suggest that researchers should actively engage in follow-up practices when conducting survey research to minimise low response rates by building it into the study design. Furthermore, any follow-up procedures used should be discussed in the final published article. In the studies we reviewed, fewer than a majority (49%) analysed non-responses. To increase the validity of the results, researchers are encouraged to apply more extensive use of non-response analyses. Statistical extrapolation is a rigorous method to assess non-response bias, and we encourage its use.

Regarding reliability and validity of data, only three studies (published in 2000 or later) used both objective and subjective measures in their variable measurements of the dependent variable in their analysis. The use of objective measures of performance as a dependent variable can increase the reliability of the self-rating measures. To increase the precision and generalisability of survey studies, psychometric properties of survey instruments should be reported.

In the future, if researchers follow the methodological framework suggested in this chapter and apply careful attention to designing and implementing survey instruments and analysing survey responses, it may help to minimise the criticisms regarding this research method.

References

Abernethy, M. A. and Stoelwinder, J. U. (1995), "The role of professional control in the management of complex organizations", *Accounting, Organizations and Society*, Vol. 20, No.1, pp. 1-17.

Abernethy, M. A. and Brownell, P. (1997), "Management control systems in research and development organizations: the role of accounting, behavior and personnel controls", *Accounting, Organizations and Society*, Vol. 22, No. 3-4, pp. 233-248.

Abernethy, M. A. and Lillis, A. M. (2001), "Interdependencies in organization design: a test in hospitals", *Journal of Management Accounting Research*, Vol. 13, pp. 107-129.

Ajzen, I. (1991), "The theory of planned behaviour", *Organizational Behavior and Human Decision Processes*, Vol. 50, pp. 179-211.

Ajzen, I. (1996), "The directive influence of attitudes on behaviour", in Gollwitzer, P. M. and Bargh, J. A. (Eds.), *The Psychology of Action: Linking Cognition and Motivation to Behavior*, Guildford, New York, pp. 385-403.

Ajzen, I. and Fishbein, M. (1977), "Attitude-behavior relations: A theoretical analysis and review of empirical research", *Psychological Bulletin*, Vol. 84, pp. 888-918.

Almer, E. D. and Kaplan, S. E. (2002), "The effects of flexible work arrangements on stressors, burnout, and behavioral job outcomes in public accounting", *Behavioral Research in Accounting*, Vol. 14, pp. 1-34.

Anderson, N. H. (1991), *Contributions to Information Integration Theory*, Erlbaum, Hillsdale, NJ.

Anderson, S. W. and Widener, S. K. (2005), *Doing Quantitative Field Research in Management Accounting*, Forthcoming in the Handbook of Management Accounting Research, Vol. 1 Chapman, C., Hopwood, A. and Shields, M. (Eds.).

Armstrong, J. S. and Overton, T. S. (1977), "Estimating nonresponse bias in mail surveys", *Journal of Marketing Research*, Vol. 14, pp. 396-402.

Arunachalam, V. (2004), "Electronic data interchange: an evaluation of alternative organizational forms", *Accounting, Organizations and Society*, Vol. 29, No. 3-4, pp. 227-241.

Asch, D. A., Jedrziewski, M. N., Christakis, N. A. (1997), "Response rates to mail surveys in medical journals", *J Clin Epidemiol*, Vol. 50, pp. 1125-1136.

Atkinson, A. A. and Shaffir, W. (1998), "Standards for field research in management accounting", *Journal of Management Accounting Research*, Vol. 10, pp. 41-68.

Baines, A. and Langfield-Smith, K. (2003), "Antecedents to management accounting change: a structural equation approach" *Accounting, Organizations and Society*, Vol. 28, No. 7-8, pp. 675-698.

Bass, B. M., Cascio, W. F. and O'Connor, E. J. (1974), "Magnitude estimations of expressions of frequency and amount", *Journal of Applied Psychology*, Vol. 59, pp. 313-320.

Bollen, K. A. (1989), *Structural Equations with Latent Variables*, John Wiley and Sons, New York.

Cavalluzzo, K. S. and Ittner, C. D. (2004), Implementing performance measurement innovations: evidence from government", *Accounting, Organizations and Society*, Vol. 29, No. 3-4, pp. 243-267.

Chalos, P. and Poon, M. C. C. (2000), "Participation and performance in capital budgeting teams", *Behavioral Research in Accounting*, Vol. 12, pp. 199-229.

Chalos, P. and O'Connor, N. G. (2004), "Determinants of the use of various control mechanisms in US-Chinese joint ventures", *Accounting, Organizations and Society*, Vol. 29, No. 7, pp. 591-608.

Champney, H. and Marshall, H. (1939), "Optimal refinement of the rating scale", *Journal of Applied Psychology*, Vol. 23, pp. 323-331.

Chenhall, R. H. and Langfield-Smith, K. (1998), The relationship between strategic priorities, management techniques and management accounting: an empirical investigation using a systems approach", *Accounting, Organizations and Society*, Vol. 23, No. 3, pp. 243-264.

Chenhall, R. H. and Morris, D. (1986), "The impact of structure, environment, and interdependence on the perceived usefulness of management accounting systems", *The Accounting Review January*, Vol. 61, No. 1, pp. 16-35.

Chenhall, R. H. (1993), *Reliance on Manufacturing Performance Measures, Strategies of Manufacturing Flexibility, Advanced Manufacturing Practices, and Organizational Performance: An Empirical Investigation*. Paper presented at the Strategic Management Accounting Seminar, Macquarie University, Sydney.

Chenhall, R. H. (2004), "The role of cognitive and affective conflict in early implementation of activity-based cost management", *Behavioral Research in Accounting*, Vol. 16, pp. 19-44.

Chong, V. K. (1996), "Management accounting systems, task uncertainty and managerial performance: a research note", *Accounting, Organizations and Society*, Vol. 21, No. 5, pp. 415-421.

Chong, V. K. and Chong, K. M. (2002), "Budget goal commitment and informational effects of budget participation on performance: a structural equation modeling approach", *Behavioral Research in Accounting*, Vol. 14, pp. 65-86.

Choo, F. and Tan, K. B. (1997), "A study of the relations among disagreement in budgetary performance evaluation style, job-related tension, job satisfaction and performance", *Behavioral Research in Accounting*, Vol. 9, pp. 199-218.

Chow, C., Kato, Y. and Merchant, K. (1996), "The use of organizational controls and their effects on data manipulation and management myopia: A Japan vs U.S. comparison", *Accounting, Organizations and Society*, Vol. 21, No. 2-3, pp. 175-192.

Chow, C., Shields, M. and Wu, A. (1999), "The importance of national culture in the design of and preference for management controls for multi-national operations", *Accounting, Organizations and Society*, Vol. 24, No. 5-6, pp. 441-461.

Chow, C. W., Harrison, G. L., McKinnon, J. L. and Wu, A. (1999), "Cultural influences on informal information sharing in Chinese and Anglo-American organizations: an exploratory study", *Accounting, Organizations and Society*, Vol. 24, No. 7, pp. 561-582.

Clinton, B. D. and Hunton, J. E. (2001), "Linking participative budgeting congruence to organization performance", *Behavioral Research in Accounting*, Vol. 13, pp. 127-141.

Cohen, J. (1988), *Statistical Power Analysis for the Behavioral Sciences*, Lawrence Erlbaum, Hillsdale, NJ.

Collins, F. and Lowensohn, S. H. (1995), "The relationship between budgetary management style and organizational commitment in a not-for-profit organization", *Behavioral Research in Accounting*, Vol. 7, pp. 65-79.

Comerford, S. E. and Abernethy, M. A. (1999), "Budgeting and the management of role conflict in hospitals", *Behavioral Research in Accounting*, Vol. 11, pp. 93-110.

Davila, T. (2000), An empirical study on the drivers of management control systems' design in new product development", *Accounting, Organizations and Society*, Vol. 25, No. 4-5, pp. 383-409.

DeVellis, R. F. (2003), *Scale development: Theory and applications*, 2nd edition, Sage, Thousand Oaks, CA.

Dillman, D. A. (1978), *Mail and Telephone Surveys: The Total Design Method*, Wiley, New York.

Dillman, D. A. (1991), "The design and administration of mail surveys", *Annual Review of Sociology*, Vol. 17, No. 1, pp. 225-249.

Firth, M. (1996), "The diffusion of managerial accounting procedures in the People's Republic of China and the influence of foreign partnered joint ventures", *Accounting, Organizations and Society*, Vol. 21, No. 7-8, pp. 629-654.

Fishbein, M. and Ajzen, I. (1975), *Belief, Attitude, Intention, and Behaviour: An Introduction to Theory and Research*, Addison-Wesley, Reading, MA.

Fisher, C. (1996), "The impact of perceived environmental uncertainty and individual differences on management information requirements: A research note", *Accounting, Organizations and Society*, Vol. 21, No. 4, pp. 361-369.

Foster, G. and Gupta, M. (1994), "Marketing, cost management and management accounting", *Journal of Management Accounting Research*, Vol. 6, pp. 43-77.

Foster, G. and Sjoblom, L. (1996), "Quality improvement drivers in the electronics industry", *Journal of Management Accounting Research*, Vol. 8, pp. 55-86.

Foster, G. and Swenson, D. W. (1997), "Measuring the success of activity-based cost management and its determinants", *Journal of Management Accounting Research*, Vol. 9, pp. 109-141.

Fox, R. J., Crask, M. R. and Kim, J. (1988), "Mail survey response rate: A meta-analysis of selected techniques for inducing response", *Public Opinion Quarterly*, Vol. 52, pp. 467-491.

Fullerton, R. R. and McWatters, C. S. (2002), "The role of performance measures and incentive systems in relation to the degree of JIT implementation", *Accounting, Organizations and Society*, Vol. 27, No. 8, pp. 711-735.

Ghiselli, E. E., Campbell, J. P. and Zedek, S. (1981), *Measurement Theory for the Behavioral Sciences*, W. H. Freeman, New York.

Gosselin, M. (1997), "The effect of strategy and organizational structure on the adoption and implementation of activity-based costing", *Accounting, Organizations and Society*, Vol. 22, No. 2, pp. 105-122.

Govindarajan, V. (1988), "A contingency approach to strategy implementation at the business-unit level: integrating administrative mechanics with strategy", *Academy of Management*, Vol. 31, pp. 828-853.

Govindarajan, V. and Gupta, A. K. (1985), "Linking control systems to business unit strategy: impact on performance", *Accounting, Organizations and Society*, pp. 51-66.

Guilding, C. (1999), "Competitor-focused accounting: an exploratory note", *Accounting, Organizations and Society*, Vol. 24, No. 7, pp. 583-595.

Guilding, C. and McManus, L. (2002), "The incidence, perceived merit and antecedents of customer accounting: an exploratory note", *Accounting, Organizations and Society*, Vol. 27, No. 1-2, pp. 45-59.

Gul, F. A. and Chia, Y. M. (1994), "The effects of management accounting systems, perceived environmental uncertainty and decentralization on managerial performance: A test of three-way interaction", *Accounting, Organizations and Society*, Vol. 19, No. 4-5, pp. 413-426.

Harvey, L. (1987), "Factors affecting response rates to mailed questionnaires: A comprehensive literature review", *J. Market Res. Society*, Vol. 29, pp. 342-353.

Hofstede, G. H. (1980), *Culture's Consequences: International Differences in Work-Related Values*, Sage, Beverly Hills, CA.

Hooks, K. L. and Higgs, J. L. (2002), "Workplace environment in a professional services firm", *Behavioral Research in Accounting*, Vol. 14, pp. 105-127.

Hopwood, A. G. (1972), "An empirical study of the role of accounting 8 data in performance evaluation", *Journal of Accounting Research, Supplement*, pp. 156-182.

Hoque, Z. and James, W. (2000), "Linking balanced scorecard measures to size and market factors: impact on organizational performance (Cover story)", *Journal of Management Accounting Research*, Vol. 12, pp. 1-17.

Hunton, J. E., Wier, B. and Stone, D. N. (2000), "Succeeding in managerial accounting. Part 2: a structural equations analysis", *Accounting, Organizations and Society*, Vol. 25, No. 8, pp. 751-762.

Kalagnanam, S. S. and Lindsay, R. M. (1999), "The use of organic models of control in JIT firms: generalizing Woodward's findings to modern manufacturing practices", *Accounting, Organizations and Society*, Vol. 24, No.1, 1-30.

Keating, A.S. (1997), "Determinants of divisional performance evaluation practices", *Journal of Accounting and Economics*, Vol. 24. No. 3, pp. 243-273.

Kennedy, T. and Affleck-Graves, J. (2001), "The impact of activity-based costing techniques on firm performance", *Journal of Management Accounting Research*, Vol. 13, pp. 19-45.

Kline, T. J. B. (2005), *Psychological Testing. A Practical Approach to Design and Evaluation*, Sage: Thousand Oaks.

Krumwiede, K. R. (1998), "The implementation stages of activity-based costing and the impact of contextual and organizational factors", *Journal of Management Accounting Research*, Vol. 10, p. 239.

Lau, C., Low, L. and Eggleton, I. (1995), "The impact of reliance on accounting performance measures on job-related tension and managerial performance: additional evidence", *Accounting, Organizations and Society*, Vol. 20, No. 5, pp. 359-381.

Libby, T. and Waterhouse, J. H. (1996), "Predicting change in management accounting systems", *Journal of Management Accounting Research*, Vol. 8, pp. 137-150.

Likert, R. (1932), "A technique for the measurement of attitudes", *Archives of Psychology*, No. 40.

Lynch, R. and Cross, K. (1991), *Measure Up! Yardsticks for Continuous Improvement*, Blackwell Business, Cambridge, MA.

Madow, W. G., Nisselson, H. and Olkin, I. (1983), *Incomplete Data in Sample Surveys Volume 1 Report and Case Studies*, 1st edition, Academic Press, New York.

Magner, N., Welker, R. and Campbell, T. (1995), "The interactive effect of budgetary participation and budget favorability on attitudes toward budgetary decision makers: A research note", *Accounting, Organizations and Society*, Vol. 20, No. 7-8, pp. 611-618.

Mahoney, T. A., Jerdee, T. H. and Carroll, S. J. (1965), "The job(s) of management", *Industrial Relations*, Vol. 4, No. 2, pp. 97-110.

Mahoney, T.A., Jerdee, T. H. and Carroll, S. J. (1963), *Development of Managerial Performance: A Research Approach*, South-Western Publishing, Cincinnati, OH.

Malmi, T. (1999), "Activity-based costing diffusion across organizations: an exploratory empirical analysis of Finnish firms", *Accounting, Organizations and Society*, Vol. 24, No. 8, pp. 649-672.

Merchant, K. (1985), Organizational controls and discretionary program decision making: a field study", *Accounting, Organizations and Society*, Vol. 10, pp. 67-85.

Merchant, K. (1984), "Influences on departmental budgeting: an empirical examination of a contingency model", *Accounting, Organizations and Society*, Vol. 9, No. 3/4, pp. 291-307.

Mia, L. (1989), "The impact of participation in budgeting and job difficulty on managerial performance and work motivation: A research note", *Accounting, Organizations and Society*, Vol. 14, No. 4, pp. 347-357.

Moores, K. and Yuen, S. (2001), "Management accounting systems and organizational configuration: a life-cycle perspective", *Accounting, Organizations and Society*, Vol. 26, No. 4-5, p. 351-389.

Mowday, R. T., Porter, L. W. and Steers, R. M. (1982), *Employee-Organization Linkages*, Academic Press, New York, NY.

Netemeyer, R.G., Bearden, W.O. and Sharma, S. (2003), *Scaling procedures: Issues and applications*, Sage, Thousand Oaks, CA.

Nouri, H. and Parker, R. J. (1996), "The effect of organizational commitment on the relation between budgetary participation and budgetary slack", *Behavioral Research in Accounting*, Vol. 8, pp. 74-86.

Nouri, H. and Parker, R. J. (1998), "The relationship between budget participation and job performance: the roles of budget adequacy and organizational commitment", *Accounting, Organizations and Society*, Vol. 23, No. 5-6, pp. 467-483.

Nunnally, J. C. and Bernstein, I. H. (1994), *Psychometric Theory*, 3rd edition, McGraw-Hill, New York.

O'Connor, N. G. (1995), "The influence of organizational culture on the usefulness of budget participation by Singaporean-Chinese managers", *Accounting, Organizations and Society*, Vol. 20, No. 5, pp. 383-403.

Onsi, M. (1973), "Factor analysis of behavioural variables affecting budgetary slack", *The Accounting Review*, Vol. 48, No. 3, pp. 535-548.

Otley, D. and Pollanen, R. M. (2000), "Budgetary criteria in performance evaluation: a critical appraisal using new evidence", *Accounting, Organizations and Society*, Vol. 25, No. 4-5, pp. 483-496.

Perera, S., Harrison, G. and Poole, M. (1997), "Customer-focused manufacturing strategy and the use of operations-based non-financial performance measures: A research note", *Accounting, Organizations and Society*, Vol. 22, No. 6, pp. 557-572.

Pinsonneault, A. and Kraemer, K.L. (1993), "Survey research methodology in management information systems: an assessment", *Journal of Management Information Systems*, Vol. 10, No. 2, pp. 75-106.

Rizzo, J. R. (1970), "Role conflict and ambiguity in complex organizations", *Administrative Science Quarterly*, pp. 150-163.

Ross, A. (1994), "Trust as a moderator of the effect of performance evaluation style on job-related tension: A research note", *Accounting, Organizations and Society*, Vol. 19, No. 7, pp. 629-635.

Sangster, A. (1996), "Expert system diffusion among management accountants: a U.K. Perspective", *Journal of Management Accounting Research*, Vol. 8, pp. 171-182.

Scott, T. W. and Tiessen, P. (1999), "Performance measurement and managerial teams", *Accounting, Organizations and Society*, Vol. 24, No. 3, pp. 263-285.

Shenhar, A. J. and Dvir, D. (1996), "Toward a typological theory of project management", *Research Policy*, Vol. 25, pp. 607-632.

Shields, M. D. and Young, S. M. (1993), "Antecedents and consequences of participative budgeting: evidence on the effects of asymmetrical information", *The Journal of Management Accounting Research*, Vol. 5, pp. 265-280.

Shields, M. D. and.Young, S. M. (1994), "Managing innovation costs: a study of cost conscious behavior by r&d professionals", *Journal of Management Accounting Research*, Vol. 6, pp. 175-196.

Shields, M. D. (1995), "An empirical analysis of firms' implementation experiences with activity-based costing", *Journal of Management Accounting Research*, Vol. 7, pp. 148-166.

Sim, K. L. and Killough, L. N. (1998), "The performance effects of complementarities between manufacturing practices and management accounting systems", *Journal of Management Accounting Research*, Vol. 10, p. 325.

Spector, P. E. (1976), "Choosing response categories for summated rating scales", *Journal of Applied Psychology*, Vol. 61, pp. 374-375.

Stone, D. N., Hunton, J. E. and Wier, B. (2000), "Succeeding in managerial accounting. Part 1: knowledge, ability, and rank", *Accounting, Organizations and Society*, Vol. 25, No. 7, pp. 697-715.

Steers, R. M. (1975), "Problems in the measurement of organizational effectiveness", *Administrative Science Quarterly*, Vol. 20, pp. 546-558.

Symonds, P. M. (1924), "On the loss of reliability in ratings due to coarseness of the scale", *Journal of Experimental Psychology*, Vol. 7, pp. 456-461.

Tabachnick, B. G. and Fidell, L. S. (2001), *Using Multivariate Statistics*, Allyn and Bacon, Boston, MA.

Vagneur, K. and Peiperl, M. (2000), "Reconsidering performance evaluative style", *Accounting, Organizations and Society*, Vol. 25, No. 4-5, pp. 511-525.

Van der Stede, W. A. (2000), "The relationship between two consequences of budgetary controls: budgetary slack creation and managerial short-term orientation", *Accounting, Organizations and Society*, Vol. 25, No. 6, pp. 609-622.

Van der Stede, W. A., Young, S. M. and Chen, C. X. (2005), "Assessing the quality of evidence in empirical management accounting research: The case of survey studies", *Accounting, Organizations and Society*, Vol. 30, No. 7-8, pp. 655-684.

Vandenbosch, B. (1999), "An empirical analysis of the association between the use of executive support systems and perceived organizational competitiveness", *Accounting, Organizations and Society*, Vol. 24, No. 1. pp. 77-92.

Wentzel, K. (2002), "The influence of fairness perceptions and goal commitment on managers' performance in a budget setting", *Behavioral Research in Accounting*, Vol. 14, pp. 247-271.

Widener, S. K. and Selto, F. H. (1999), "Management control systems and boundaries of the firm: why do firms outsource internal auditing activities?", *Journal of Management Accounting Research*, Vol. 11, pp. 45-73.

Widener, S. K. (2004), "An empirical investigation of the relation between the use of strategic human capital and the design of the management control system", *Accounting, Organizations and Society*, Vol. 29, No. 3-4, pp. 377-399.

Williams, J. J. and Seaman, A. E. (2001), "Predicting change in management accounting systems: national culture and industry effects", *Accounting, Organizations and Society*, Vol. 26, 4-5, pp. 443-460.

Young, S. M. (1996), "Survey research in management accounting: a critical assessment", in Richardson, A. J. (Ed.), *Research methods in accounting: Issues and debates*, CGA Canada Research Foundation.

22

RELIABILITY AND VALIDITY IN FIELD STUDY RESEARCH

Anne M. Lillis
The University of Melbourne, Australia

Abstract: This chapter addresses issues of valid and reliable measurement and inference in field research. The recommendations in this chapter try to strike a balance between realising the richness of field research through open-mindedness and flexibility of approach, with the researchers' obligations to be rigorous and unbiased in the execution of their research. The chapter addresses:

- construct validity – how theoretical constructs are operationalised in messy real-world data;
- internal validity – the extent to which theoretical linkages in the data are rigorously tested and rival hypotheses admitted;
- external validity – generalisability to theory and practice, and
- reliability – minimisation of error and bias.

Keywords: Field studies; validity; reliability.

1.   Introduction

The design and conduct of field studies in accounting has elements of both art and science (Ahrens and Dent, 1998). There is an art to constructing interesting and probing stories about real organisational functioning and linking these stories to the theoretical basis of accounting. An important motivation for field research is to depart from the rigors of scientific method to capture with greater realism the phenomena we study. When we address complex behavioural issues in organisations such as the drivers of managerial choice, the influence of particular kinds of information, the role of accounting in facilitating or hindering organisational adaptation and learning, and the management control of transactions that cross organisational boundaries, the science of strict construct definition, clearly defined measurement scales and robust hypothesis tests becomes problematic. The application of pure science may significantly compromise our capacity to represent with any sense of realism the phenomena under study. However, it is dangerous to assume that field studies are all art and no science. Field study researchers have the same obligations that any other researchers have to be rigorous and unbiased in the execution of their research (Ahrens and Dent, 1998). Thus it is important to consider the nature of rigorous field research. This chapter contributes to resolving two questions relating to rigorous field research. First, how do field researchers establish that their findings are not only interesting, but also rigorously distilled from extensive real-world observation in a reliable, unbiased way? Second, how do researchers ensure that their observations are rigorously and neutrally assessed against theory? (Marshall, 1985; Ahrens and Dent, 1998).

This chapter addresses the key issues of establishing reliability and validity in field study research. Field study researchers face significant threats to reliability and validity at both the data collection and data analysis phases. As field research covers a range of different research forms, we commence by defining the types of studies addressed by this chapter. The chapter then addresses construct, internal and external validity and reliability in data collection and analysis.

2. Defining Case Study/Field Research

Yin's (2003) definition of a case study remains one of the most descriptive and commonly used definitions. Yin describes a case study as:

> ... an empirical inquiry that investigates a contemporary phenomenon within its real-life context, especially when the boundaries between the phenomenon and context are not clearly evident (Yin, 2003, p. 13).

Ferreira and Merchant (1992) draw on Yin's definition and elaborate on the distinguishing features of field studies:

> In field research studies:
> 1. The researcher has direct, in-depth contact with organizational participants, particularly in interviews and direct observations of activities, and these contacts provide a primary source of research data.
> 2. The study focuses on real tasks or processes, not situations artificially created by the researcher.
> 3. The research design is not totally structured. It evolves along with the field observations.
> 4. The presentation of data includes relatively rich (detailed) descriptions of company context and practices.
> 5. The resulting publications are written to the academic community.
>
> (Ferreira and Merchant, 1992, p. 4).

Ferreira and Merchant's (1992) extensions are designed to exclude pilot studies, ex-post clarifications of statistically-analysed data, archival studies, and case studies not aimed at the research community. A notable attribute of these definitions is that they blur the distinction between case studies and field studies and focus on the substantive aims of the method. If there is a natural distinction between case studies and field studies, it is in the definition of a unit of analysis. The term 'case study' implies a single unit of analysis that focuses on the organisation or organisational sub-unit (Spicer, 1992). The term field study is broader and almost certainly embraces case studies within it (Lillis and Mundy, 2005). More importantly, the distinction is unimportant in consideration of method attributes such as validity and reliability, as the data are qualitatively similar. In this chapter, the term field study is used as a generic term which captures the type of studies described by Yin (2003) and Ferreira and Merchant (1992).

It is also important to specify the epistemological domain of a chapter relating to field studies. There are significant debates in the literature that challenge the role of theory, the objective observability of accounting practice in organisational settings and the broad role of field study research (Chua, 1996; Scapens, 1990, 1992; Llewellyn, 1992). By challenging the underlying principles of scientific method, the role of the researcher and the notion of data as something other than a social construction, researchers within a social constructionist paradigm would challenge the assumptions that underpin many of the discussions here regarding validity and reliability. This chapter takes a perspective that is predominantly aligned with positivism. It is assumed that accounting practices are realities that can be observed and studied by researchers, albeit within a social context that is an integral part of that reality. Theory is treated as both informing and being informed by observation (Humphrey and Scapens, 1996), and the researcher is assumed to be capable of relatively objective observation and analysis of accounting and organisational phenomena. The discussion of validity and reliability in this chapter apply within a positivist paradigm as it is assumed that 'a key to successful discovery is the careful application of data analysis routines which minimise prejudice and idiosyncratic bias' (Chua, 1996, p. 212). It would also apply to some interpretive or critical research, as the social and political context of accounting may be legitimate subjects of study within this framework. It is, however, less applicable to strong forms of social constructionist research.

Finally, the approach taken here favours field research in management accounting. While field study research in financial accounting and auditing is not deliberately excluded, the chapter focuses on data derived from in-depth contact with organisational participants. There is less imperative for field studies utilising deep insights from organisational participants in financial accounting and auditing, and less history of such studies as a source of theory development.

3. Validity in Field Research

Having defined field studies such that research data will emerge from direct and in-depth contact between the researcher and organisational participants and that the collection of the data will be at least somewhat unstructured and rich in detail, many attributes generally associated with research science become less relevant. There is little standardisation in each research encounter. There is no control group against which research observations can be evaluated for theoretical authenticity. Furthermore, even the fundamental building blocks of research – clearly defined constructs – are likely to be subject to redefinition in the field. Nonetheless, the essential evaluation criteria of scientific research – validity and reliability – do apply to field research. This section addresses the attributes of construct, internal and external validity as they apply in a field research setting.

3.1. Construct Validity

Construct validity is defined as 'the extent to which the constructs of theoretical interest are successfully operationalised in the research' (Abernethy et al., 1999, p. 8). From a practical perspective, construct validity in field research is about how the researcher observes constructs in the data. In quantitative research, the demand for demonstration of construct validity is satisfied by clear construct definitions, and clear statements about the way these constructs are operationalised. Faithfulness to the underlying construct is tracked through definition, operationalisation and measurement. An important issue confronting quantitative researchers is the inevitable slippage from a construct which is inherently complex in its organisational manifestation through quantitative operationalisation which sheds some of the realistic complexity of the construct, through to measurement, which again compromises on realistic complexity. For example, a complex construct such as competitive strategy is operationalised based on a specific definition (e.g. prospector/defender) and measured on a five-point scale with the archetypes forming the scale end-points.

Much of the motivation for field research rests on the desire to reduce the compromise involved in capturing real-world complexity in the constructs we use (Lillis and Mundy, 2005). In fact, it could be argued that construct validity is potentially the greatest strength of field research. Field researchers can argue that by capturing more of the subtle complexities associated with a construct they end up with a description and analysis that captures the construct more effectively than any quantitative operationalisation can hope to do (Atkinson and Shaffir, 1998). While this is potentially the case for field research, high construct validity cannot simply be taken as a given. It is still incumbent on the researcher to demonstrate that the constructs are indeed observable in the data collected. A researcher may have collected a wealth of rich data on management control practices and yet not be able to argue convincingly that the data adequately distinguishes, for example, diagnostic and interactive levers of control, or the relative impact of accounting and other controls on decision making and organisational learning, or the role of controls in fostering or impeding organisational adaptation. The motivation for a field study will relate to theoretical constructs and their inter-relationships. The researcher needs to address the question of how these constructs are observable in the messy real-world data collected.

Constructs are measured in qualitative data by identifying an occurrence of the construct in the data. From an expansive field conversation or extensive observational notes, how does a researcher studying the control of inter-organisational relationships reliably identify an occurrence of, for example, 'reliance on results control'? Ideally, a field study researcher will use multiple sources of evidence (Brownell, 1995; McKinnon, 1988). In the above example, relevant data sources might include contracts, documents exchanged between parties and performance monitoring reports, as well as interview evidence. While triangulation of multiple data sources is highly desirable, not all research questions in management accounting lend themselves to examination through document analysis, and documents do not necessarily convey important attributes of constructs such as 'reliance' rather than 'existence of'. Regardless of the data source, or how many sources there are, the question of construct identification and measurement still arises. How is the construct actually observed in the data?

The themes observed in the data and the names given to these themes are generally conditioned by theory (Abernethy et al., 1999; Brownell, 1995; Yin, 2003). The key to establishing construct validity is clear construct definition and a set of decision rules that clarify how and when the theoretical construct is observable in the data. For example, in a detailed narrative description of control practices, what decision rules does the researcher use to identify whether the control mechanisms are diagnostic or interactive, whether it is a case of use of accounting data in performance measurement, whether controls are tight or loose? Clear decision rules for making classifications of this kind enhance both construct validity and reliability. They provide the link between real-world data and theoretical constructs (construct validity) as well as enhancing reliability (reproducibility) in the process of matching data with constructs.

Once definitions are clear and decision rules established to discriminate between different constructs in the research then the identification of an occurrence of a construct in data is generally achieved through coding[82]. A coding structure is established containing theoretical categories or constructs on which the researcher has set out to collect data. The application of coding techniques to enhance construct validity overlaps issues of reliability. The section in this chapter relating to reliability contains further discussion of reliable construct measurement and coding.

It is also critically important that the researcher utilises the field research opportunity to *enhance* construct validity. The field researcher has the opportunity to expand the domain of observables relating to particular constructs and to be on the look-out for attributes missing in the literature. An important strength of field research is the ability to identify complex empirical attributes that define constructs. For example, Simons (1990) defined the basic elements of interactive and programmed levers of control based on field study data relating to control systems in different strategic settings, and researchers have subsequently used field data to refine the attributes of these levers (e.g. Davila, 2000). This ability to delve into constructs and avoid simplistic definition is a key advantage of field research and an important way for field researchers to contribute to the literature (Lillis and Mundy, 2005).

---

[82] At this stage, coding simply refers to identifying themes in the data. It is not necessarily a computerised process, although this is now common.

Thus, there are two elements to construct validity. One is taking advantage of the opportunity presented in the field to build our understanding of the attributes of key constructs we use in our research. The other aspect is forming a rigorous attachment of data to constructs such that the decision rules used to identify occurrences of constructs in the data are evident to readers.

3.2. *Internal Validity*

Internal validity is defined as 'the extent to which the research permits us to reach causal conclusions about the effect of the independent variable on the dependent variable' (Abernethy *et al.*, 1999, p. 8). While causal inferences are always problematic in cross-sectional studies, researchers generally infer causality from theory in the presence of evidence of predicted co-variation between dependent and independent variables. Quantitative researchers defend the internal validity of their research by focusing on the robustness of the analysis that links variables together. Well-established multivariate techniques, control variables and robustness tests are used to satisfy the reader that the researcher's theoretical perspective on the findings is rigorously tested in the data.

There are contrasting perspectives on issues of internal validity in field research. On the one hand, field researchers face considerable challenges in establishing the internal validity of their research. They lack the accepted and well-understood statistical methods and terminology to establish that the conclusions reached are supported by independent, rigorous analysis of the data, and that rival explanations have been tested and eliminated. On the other hand researchers observing and questioning participants in the field are potentially confronted by many challenges to their theory simply because of their presence in the field. These are challenges that are unobserved by researchers that collect or experiment with data detached from its field origins (Chua, 1996; Becker, 1970; Atkinson and Shaffir, 1998; Eisenhardt, 1989). This perspective suggests that field research may have an inherent advantage in identifying rival explanations for findings. Nonetheless, *demonstrating* internal validity is an area of significant difficulty for field study researchers. While many establish coding reliability, it is really lack of bias in forming conclusions about how variables relate to one another that is potentially most subject to question, and most rarely verified.

Generally, field studies make their links to theory and report findings based on patterns within and across cases (Eisenhardt, 1989; Lillis and Mundy, 2005; Ahrens and Dent, 1998; Scapens, 1990). However, most field study researchers disclose little of how these patterns emerge and the processes that were used to test and eliminate rival hypotheses (Lillis and Mundy, 2005; McKinnon, 1988):

> ... *no researchers admit to wearing blinkers and almost none of the studies provide enough data for the reader to draw alternate conclusions* (Ferreira and Merchant, 1992, p. 20).

Does the analysis allow for challenges to emerge from the data in the form of rival hypotheses? How are such challenges treated? A disciplined analytical process has several attributes. It is important to ensure that all data are analysed, and that all data are treated equally in the analysis (Miles and Huberman, 1994; Lillis, 1999). It is too easy in qualitative analysis to be swayed by the attraction of the data that fit the theory perfectly, or those wonderful quotes that capture exactly what the researcher wants to capture in the field!

There are a variety of models of data analysis. The matrix approach used by Miles and Huberman (1994) is excellent for ensuring completeness in data analysis, and exposing contrary cases within the existing theoretical frame of reference (Lillis, 1999; Lillis and Mundy, 2005). For example, a matrix that links themes of belief and boundary controls within and across cases will readily expose the regularity in the cases studied in which these phenomena occur as substitutes or complements. An alternative approach based on the notion of method triangulation is proposed by Abernethy *et al.* (2005) who use multiple causal maps derived in various ways from the data and tested for consistency. They use a mechanical method based on computerised searching for codes in proximity (proximity being suggestive of relationships), an ethnographic approach based on researcher intuition, and a third approach using the insights of field participants to directly link the variables together. A common approach is to triangulate multiple sources of evidence (Brownell, 1995) provided these sources of evidence are clearly related to the issue of how the themes under study at the research site relate to each other. Another alternative is to use multiple researchers to independently assess the underlying patterns in the data. However, this is difficult. Multiple researchers working on a project jointly are rarely sufficiently independent in assessing causal linkages in the data if they have jointly established their theoretical positioning on the topic. Competent independent researchers who will actually process entire research database for the purposes of establishing reliability and veracity in the assignment of linkages among constructs are rare and expensive. In light of these difficulties, it is important to note that the use of multiple *coders* (see following section on coding reliability) is not equivalent to enhancing internal validity and few qualitative researchers provide any independent evidence of the veracity of the theoretical linkages they establish.

The approaches above all seek to find common patterns in a disciplined way. Fundamentally, a researcher analysing field data should be alert to challenges to existing theory that reside in the observations that do not fit the theory. In reality, it is much more interesting to analyse the case that challenges existing theory or the researcher's own emerging theory. There are good examples in the accounting literature of studies built on challenges to existing theory, not necessarily envisaged at the outset (e.g. Merchant and Manzoni, 1989).

3.3. *External Validity*

External validity is defined as 'the generalisability of results from the research to the wider population, settings or times' (Abernethy *et al.*, 1999, p. 8). In general terms field study researchers do not undertake field research in order to produce generalisable findings. Such studies naturally compromise on the breadth of data collection and random selection of participants within a clearly defined sampling frame which are the essential building blocks of statistical generalisability. Field researchers generalise to theory. This is commonly stated, but what does it mean? Field researchers review their findings and restate the contribution of their study in abstract theoretical terms. For example, patterns in real-life descriptions of management decisions and the influences on them are converted into 'levers of control' and propositions are raised about the relative strength of those levers when they are found together in practice (Simons, 1990). Alternatively, real-life descriptions of the way firms implement flexibility are translated into schemas for classifying firms strategically and structurally – for the use of other researchers (Abernethy and Lillis, 1995). These explicit links to theory are what sets field research apart from stories. However, the links are often not explicit and it has been a source of frustration in the literature that these links are not adequately made (Ferreira and Merchant, 1992; Keating, 1995).

The use of matrices for analysis, as described earlier, assists in making links between observations and theory because the structure of thematic matrices is naturally theory driven. They form the means by which real-world descriptions of control practices are organised around themes such as 'levers of control' or 'accounting and non-accounting controls'. In completing the matrices the researcher is collecting the data around abstract theoretical themes, and the step to writing up findings in theoretical, abstract terms should be straightforward. However, generalising to theory requires additional effort beyond the use of theoretical, abstract terms to describe findings. It requires the researcher to identify the contribution of the study to the literature. Does it elaborate on the empirical attributes of existing theoretical constructs? Does it illustrate the application of theory in an interesting practical setting? Does it identify potential new linkages between constructs that are not yet evident in extant theory?

While contributions to theory will be of interest to the literature, readers also need a sense of potential generalisability beyond the specific field research site. Without potential generalisability, theoretical contributions have little sustainable interest (Eisenhardt, 1989). There are clearly notable contributions in the form of unique, rich stories both within and outside the management literature (Ahrens and Dent, 1998). However, most field studies in accounting tend to draw on Eisenhardt's (1989, 1991) comparative logic rather than story telling through single cases (e.g. Simons, 1990; Merchant and Manzoni, 1989; Davila, 2000). Even using comparative logic, the field researcher is not able to make statements about generalisability. However, readers will be more comfortable if there is a *sense* of generalisability about the phenomena studied and reported. Multiple case designs have a natural advantage in conveying generalisability, simply because the phenomenon is observed multiple times, or subject to multiple tests of its observability (Eisenhardt, 1991; Scapens, 1990).

Replications may be theoretical or literal (Yin, 2003). Literal replications try to reproduce the setting of a prior field study as faithfully as possible. The recurrent observation of new construct attributes or new relations among constructs in similar settings goes some way to reassuring readers that the phenomenon observed is not simply a site-specific anomaly. Alternatively, theoretical replications seek to vary the essential characteristics of the site in order to test the phenomenon where it should not be present, or where it should be present in a different form. Such tests also provide the reader with a sense of the link between the observation within a specific case and the more generalisable contextual co-variates of the phenomenon.

Thus, external validity also has two aspects. The first is that the contribution to theory must be evident, and the second is that the *contribution* extracted from the field study should be *potentially* generalisable. It is not necessary for the researcher to demonstrate generalisability. The notion of generalisability should, however, have some credibility with readers.

4. Reliability in Field Research

Reliability is defined as 'measurement of a variable on one dimension with minimal error' (Brownell, 1995, p. 47). In quantitative research, reliability is interpreted as consistency. A construct is captured reliably if multiple measures of the same construct produce similar results. For example, a student essay is reliably graded if two or more independent assessors produce the same grade. A construct like reliance on accounting performance measures is reliably measured if multiple items consistently suggest a similar level of reliance. These notions of reliability provide the reader with assurance that the findings of a study are not simply an artefact of a study design or the particular survey questions used. They are, in fact, reproducible. This raises an interesting question for field researchers – will an independent researcher who follows exactly the same procedures to perform a field study arrive at the same conclusions? The answer to this question is in all honesty – probably not! As Otley (2001) suggests, 'our facts are social facts generated by the perceptions and attitudes of the participants themselves, and coloured by the social and cultural context within which they are set. Further, these conditions change quite rapidly over time'. (Otley, 2001, p. 248). Field researchers are faced with a problem. The more realistic the problems we study, and the greater our reliance on perceptions of field participants, the less stable our observations are likely to be over time and across different settings. Factual data about organisational events, processes and outcomes may be stable and reproducible, but perceptions of individuals within organisations are inherently unstable. Re-examine a range of field study findings represented in the literature, and ask whether the perceptual data reported would be likely to be represented in the same way on repeated occasions. It is certainly possible that individuals have stable perceptions but there is no guarantee of this, and few ways of assessing the reliability of perceptual data.

It is also important to see the reliability issue in context. This is not peculiarly a problem with field study research. In quantitative research, there are established mechanisms to measure reliability and to determine whether variables are measured with sufficient consistency to be deemed reliable (e.g. Cronbach's Alpha). Note, however, that this is a very narrow measure of reliability – do various ways of measuring a variable such as 'reliance on accounting performance measures' produce consistent scores? The challenge posed in the prior paragraph regarding reliability in field study research raises a much broader question. If we posed the challenge to *quantitative* researchers to guarantee that other researchers conducting the same study would reach similar conclusions, we would expose the fact that quantitative researchers make all sorts of judgements about the variables used to measure constructs, the attributes of the constructs that are measured, and the degree of genuine challenge to reliability in the way the alternative measures of the variable are framed. In other words, quantitative researchers may measure unique aspects of constructs very reliably. However, multiple researchers will not necessarily agree on the choice of construct attributes or measures. These are issues of construct validity, which were addressed in the prior section. They are raised here only to juxtapose the inevitable reliability issues associated with field study research within a framework of reliability and validity trade-offs that plague empirical accounting research in general. Nonetheless, threats to reliability are endemic in field research, both in data collection and analysis.

There are practical ways to avoid major threats. Practical advice is generally contained within guidebooks related to interviewing, observing, analysing document content and so forth. From the higher level design perspective, it is critical to maintain a detailed field study protocol and database in which data collection and analysis procedures are documented (Yin, 1994; Brownell, 1995). The records within the field study protocol and data base provide the important foundation for reproducibility (even though actual replications are rare). In this database, the researcher can keep not only a record of procedures undertaken but also an audit trail of decisions made as multiple sources of evidence are evaluated and compared, definitions are revised, decision rules created and modified, coding schemes tested and altered and productive and unproductive thematic analyses undertaken. Such a database provides a rich record of the research process which also potentially enhances the final write-up by allowing the researcher to convey at least the important research ideas that did not work, as well as those that did (Ferreira and Merchant, 1992). The following sub-sections address specific issues relating to reliability (lack of error and bias) in data collection and analysis.

4.1. Reliability in Data Collection
In field research there is little distance between the researcher and the execution of the research, and the influence of the researcher is powerful and difficult to control (McKinnon, 1988). Even in relatively short interviews, relationships develop between researchers and participants. Participants want to be helpful and appear

knowledgeable, so they may 'tell more than they really know' (Atkinson and Shaffir, 1998; McKinnon, 1988). Researchers want to be helpful to participants – you are after all, grateful for their time! Casual repartee in the course of an interview can convey a great deal about the researcher's agenda. Alternatively, if participants perceive the research to be delving into sensitive areas of organisational life, they may provide the unknowing researcher with a sanitised view of reality (Young and Selto, 1993; McKinnon, 1988). All of these are major threats to data quality and reliability. Findings threatened in this way are simply not reproducible except in the most constrained circumstances because they are an invented product of the interaction between researcher and participant, and not genuine reflections of the underlying reality.

How can these threats be minimised? The first step is to acknowledge the theoretical foundations of the study – the lens and perspective the researcher brings to the problem. There is no such thing as 'immaculate perception' (Mahoney, 1993, p. 182) and it is these preconceived theories and beliefs that introduce significant potential for bias in observation and data collection (Atkinson and Shaffir, 1998). The second step is to acknowledge the need for objectivity and distance from these preconceptions in order to observe and accept challenges to them. Ahrens and Dent (1998) caution against researchers becoming so caught up in their compelling story from the field and its connection with theory, that they:

... *obscure the inescapable truth that the reality conveyed, however carefully researched, is only one of a possible number of interpretations* (Ahrens and Dent, 1998, p. 10).

The third step is to ensure that researchers embarking on this type of research are aware of the nature of the threats to reliability, and that they study interviewing and observations methods. Field studies are not in any sense an easy option for the untrained researcher (Brownell, 1995). Good references on field study practice abound. These references address key issues such as the collection of data from multiple sources (Brownell, 1995; McKinnon, 1988); preparation of an interview protocol, with pre-planned questions and prompts to avoid leading explanations (Brenner, 1985; McCracken, 1988); guaranteeing confidentiality, and modelling this in the way data are collected (Scapens, 1990); and logically separating the processes of data collection and theorising (McKinnon, 1988; Ahrens and Dent, 1998).[83]

---

83 It is not suggested here that all field research should have two completely disconnected stages – data collection and theorising. It is frequently good research practice to evaluate early findings against extant theory, consider emerging theory and then return to the field with a modified theoretical lens. The important point is not to drive that theory into the data collection process. Even in multiple field iterations based on evolving theory, the time at the field site is devoted to clean data collection, not theorising.

4.2.   Reliability in Data Analysis

Data analysis in field study projects involves an exhaustive process of data classification, reduction, interpretation and development of links with theory. There are two key stages – attaching data to constructs, and drawing linkages between constructs. There are threats to reliability at both stages.

The section on construct validity discussed the importance of decision rules for attaching data to constructs in order to replicate the definition/ operationalisation/measurement protocols that drive construct validity assessments in quantitative research. The use of clear decision rules for attaching data to constructs also enhances reliability. Using the same set of decision rules, other researchers ought to expect to see the same occurrences of themes in the data. Many field researchers use multiple coders in order to demonstrate reliability in the coding phase. The discipline imposed by using multiple coders also has consequences for construct validity. Difficulties and disagreements among coders will expose unclear or inappropriate definitions and meanings assumed by the researcher that are not shared by others viewing the same data. These discussions among competent coders add greatly to ensuring lack of bias in observing constructs in the data, and doing so reliably within and across cases.

It is important to distinguish different kinds and stages of coding (Siedel and Kelle, 1995). Thematic codes are used to index data for easy retrieval around important research themes (or constructs). Segments of text are indexed to themes by identifying sentences about, for example, 'use of diagnostic control', 'reliance on accounting performance measures' or 'an internal business process within a BSC model'. In more interpretive coding, researchers are observing motives, causes or effects of an event in the data, or they are evaluating the event qualitatively. In interpretive coding researchers ask whether this sentence indicates that 'managers are weighting information from source x more highly than information from source y', or that 'accounting performance measures are used because they are entrenched'. All field research studies progress beyond indexing large tracts of text or observational data to making inferences about the relations among constructs embodied in the text. However, this progression can occur in a variety of ways. Coding can simply be used as an indexing method. The data are then retrieved around the themes of interest and analysed qualitatively, perhaps by constructing matrices to examine the co-variation of themes (Lillis, 1999). Indexed data can also be analysed using the network building tools within qualitative analysis software (e.g. Malina and Selto, 2001; Abernethy et al., 2005). Alternatively, the coding process itself can become progressively more interpretive as it is used as an heuristic device for discovery (Siedel and Kelle, 1995).

The distinction between types and purposes of coding is integral to the question of reliability in data analysis. Reliability in data analysis in field research is often established by a measure of inter-coder reliability. However, such measures are generally quite limited really in what they say about the reliability of the underlying research. The calculation of inter-coder reliability is illustrated in Malina and Selto (2001) and Abernethy *et al.* (2005). However, the reality of determining inter-coder reliability is more problematic than suggested in these examples. First, the type of coding used determines to some extent the degree of reliability that should be expected. Thematic (index-style) coding should produce significantly higher reliability than interpretive coding. Second, it is difficult to determine what constitutes a match as coders code differently. If one coder picked up three sentences in a single narrative passage as relevant to the code and another picked up only one of these – is that an agreement? If similarly coded passages overlap but do not match exactly, is that an agreement? Is agreement measured at the major code or minor sub-code level? For example, both coders may recognise an instance of 'internal business process measures', but may not agree on which attributes of internal business processes are being measured (e.g. productivity/ efficiency/throughput) because of increasingly subtle distinctions at the minor sub-code level. Generally inter-coder reliability measures deteriorate between major and minor sub-code levels of analysis. There is little guidance available as to how to resolve these issues, but they do affect the inherent stability and reliability of the inter-coder reliability metric.

Most importantly, a high level of reliability in thematic coding says nothing about the reliability of inferences made regarding the inherent relationships in the data. The importance of this step and the lack of attention given to it in extant field research was discussed under the section relating to internal validity.

5. Conclusion

Despite the increased popularity of field research in the management accounting literature, field study researchers still lack a common language of reporting and conveying their attention to validity and reliability in study design. Yet for many field studies executed within a positivist paradigm, the methodological science is no different for field studies. The data and level of contextualisation differ considerably from surveys and laboratory studies. However, the concerns of valid and reliable measurement and inference remain critical to publishability and credibility. This chapter has attempted to address the specific application of the criteria of science to field study research. Ultimately, assessments of rigour in the execution of field research require attention to all aspects of validity and reliability. Quantification of inter-coder agreement addresses only one aspect of reliability and will not be sufficient without also being able to demonstrate strong construct validity and lack of bias in drawing inferences. Similarly, quantifying the number of field sites studied or the number of participants at each site will not be sufficient without also establishing the veracity of hypothesis building and testing, and the efforts made to discover and eliminate rival hypotheses. There are established techniques in the broad literature relating to all of these issues in the design and conduct of field studies and the analysis of qualitative data. Slowly but surely the applications of these methods are permeating the management accounting literature.

References

Abernethy, M. A., Chua, W. F., Luckett, P. F. and Selto, F. H. (1999), "Research in managerial accounting: learning from others' experiences", *Accounting & Finance*, Vol. 39, No. 1, pp. 1-27.

Abernethy, M. A., Horne, M., Lillis, A. M., Malina, M. A. and Selto, F. H. (2005), "A multi-method approach to building causal performance maps from expert knowledge", *Management Accounting Research*, Vol. 16, pp. 135-155.

Abernethy, M. A. and Lillis, A. M. (1995), "The impact of manufacturing flexibility on management control system design", *Accounting, Organizations and Society*, Vol. 20, No. 4, pp. 241-258.

Ahrens, T. and Dent, J. F. (1998), "Accounting and organizations: realizing the richness of field research", *Journal of Management Accounting Research*, Vol. 10, pp. 1-39.

Atkinson, A. A. and Shaffir, W. (1998), "Standards for field research in management accounting", *Journal of Management Accounting Research*, Vol. 10, p. 41-68.

Becker, H. S. (1970), *Sociological Work: Method and Substance*, Aldine, Chicago, IL.

Brenner, M. (1985), "Intensive interviewing", in Brenner, M., Brown, J. and Canter, D. (Eds.), *The Research Interview: Uses and Approaches*, Academic Press, London.

Brownell, P. (1995), *Research Methods in Management Accounting*, Coopers & Lybrand, Melbourne.

Chua, W. F. (1996), "Issues in substantive areas of research: field research in accounting", in Richardson, A. J. (Ed.), *Research Methods in Accounting: Issues and Debates*, CGA-Canada Research Foundation, Vancouver.

Davila, T. (2000), "An empirical study on the drivers of management control systems' design in new product development", *Accounting, Organizations and Society*, Vol. 25, No. 4-5, pp. 383-409.

Eisenhardt, K. M. (1989), "Building theories from case study research", *Academy of Management Review*, Vol. 14, No. 4, pp. 532-550.

Eisenhardt, K. M. (1991), "Better stories and better constructs: the case for rigor and comparative logic", *Academy of Management Review*, Vol. 16, No. 3, pp. 620-627.

Ferreira, L. D. and Merchant, K. A. (1992), "Field research in management accounting and control: a review and evaluation", *Accounting, Auditing & Accountability Journal*, Vol. 5, No. 4, pp. 3-34.

Humphrey, C. and Scapens, R. W. (1996), "Methodological themes – theories and case studies of organizational accounting practices: limitation or liberation?", *Accounting, Auditing & Accountability Journal*, Vol. 9, No. 4, pp. 86-106.

Keating, P. J. (1995), "A framework for classifying and evaluating the theoretical contributions of case research in management accounting", *Journal of Management Accounting Research*, Vol. 7, pp. 67-86.

Lillis, A. M. (1999), "A framework for the analysis of interview data from multiple field research sites", *Accounting & Finance*, Vol. 39, No. 1, pp. 79-105.

Lillis, A. M. and Mundy, J. (2005), Cross-sectional field studies in management accounting research – closing the gaps between surveys and case studies", *Journal of Management Accounting Research,* Vol. 17, pp. 119-141.

Llewellyn, S. (1992), "The role of case study methods in management accounting research: a comment", *British Accounting Review,* Vol. 24, pp. 17-31.

Mahoney, J. T. (1993), "Strategic management and determinism: sustaining the conversation", *Journal of Management Studies,* Vol. 30, No. 1, pp. 173-191.

Malina, M. A. and Selto, F. H. (2001), "Communicating and controlling strategy: an empirical study of the effectiveness of the balanced scorecard", *Journal of Management Accounting Research,* Vol. 13, pp. 47-90.

McCracken, G. (1988), *The Long Interview,* Sage Publications, Newbury Park.

McKinnon, J. (1988), "Reliability and validity in field research: some strategies and tactics", *Accounting, Auditing & Accountability Journal,* Vol. 1, No. 1, pp. 34-54.

Marshall, C. (1985), "Appropriate criteria of the trustworthiness and goodness for qualitative research on educational organizations", *Quality and Quantity,* Vol. 19, pp. 353-373.

Merchant, K. A. and Manzoni, J.-F. (1989), "The achievability of budget targets in profit centers: a field study", *The Accounting Review,* Vol. 64, No. 3, Vol. 539-558.

Miles, M. B. and Huberman, A. M. (1994), *Qualitative Data Analysis: An Expanded Sourcebook,* 2nd edition, Sage Publications, Thousand Oaks, London and New Delhi.

Otley, D. (2001), "Extending the boundaries of management accounting research: developing systems for performance management", *British Accounting Review,* Vol. 33, pp. 243-261.

Scapens, R. W. (1990), "Researching management accounting practice: the role of case study methods", *British Accounting Review,* Vol. 22, pp. 259-281.

Scapens R. W. (1992), "The role of case study methods in management accounting research: a personal reflection and reply", *British Accounting Review,* Vol. 24, pp. 369-383.

Seidel, J. and Kelle, U. (1995), "Different functions of coding in the analysis of textual data", in Kelle, U. (Ed.), *Computer-aided Qualitative Data Analysis: Theory, Methods and Practice,* Sage Publications, London, Thousand Oaks and New Delhi.

Simons, R. (1990), "The role of management control systems in creating competitive advantage: new perspectives", *Accounting, Organizations and Society,* Vol. 15, No. 1/2, pp. 127-143.

Spicer, B. H. (1992), "The resurgence of cost and management accounting: a review of some recent developments in practice, theories and case research methods", *Management Accounting Research,* Vol. 3, No.1, pp. 1-37.

Yin, R. K. (2003), *Case Study Research: Design and Methods,* 3rd edition, Sage Publications, Thousand Oaks, London and New Delhi.

Young, S. M. and Selto, F. H. (1993), "Explaining cross-sectional workgroup performances differences in a JIT facility: a critical appraisal of a field-based study", *Journal of Management Accounting Research,* Vol. 5, pp. 300-326.

23

TRIANGULATION APPROACHES TO ACCOUNTING RESEARCH

Trevor Hopper

Manchester Business School, UK; Stockholm School of Economics, Sweden; and Victoria University of Wellington, New Zealand

Zahirul Hoque

Deakin University, Australia

Abstract: Multiple theoretical perspectives or research methods permit a wider and richer understanding of accounting practice than methodologically a singular approach. This claim, by some accounting researchers, advocates the use of a variety of theories and research methods, namely 'triangulation', as a way of taking advantage of their complementariness and building a more holistic analysis. This chapter illustrates the various forms of triangulation that can be applied in accounting research. The message of this chapter is that whilst conventional 'paradigms' can usefully explain qualitative, case study research, they need to be located in analyses embracing subjective and institutional factors for an adequate understanding of their import. As well as being a plea for greater theoretical plurality, the chapter also suggests a variety of research methods which can be developed jointly within a single study.

Keywords: Theory-triangulation;   data-triangulation;   investigator-triangulation; multiple perspectives.

1.   Introduction

Some accounting researchers in recent years have become interested in using a variety of theoretical perspectives or research methods developed jointly to understand an organisational phenomenon such as management accounting practice (Ansari and Euske, 1987; Berry *et al.*, 1991; Ansari and Bell, 1991; Hoque and Hopper, 1994; Covaleski, et al., 1985; Carpenter and Feroz, 2001). This approach was prompted by the perceived inadequacies of a single theory or research method for tapping the wider aspects of management accounting practice. Multiple approaches to research can lead to a more holistic understanding of how a management accounting system operates within its context. This chapter introduces the various forms of triangulation that can be applied to study accounting practice. As argued in the chapter, triangulation approaches have the potential to provide us with better understandings of management accounting practice.

The remainder of this chapter is organised as follows. The next section introduces the meaning of triangulation. Section three discusses the various forms of triangulation. Section four outlines the limitations of triangulation approaches. The last section provides conclusions.

2. Meaning of Triangulation

The Collins English Dictionary and Thesaurus (1993, p. 1237) defines triangulation as 'a method of surveying in which an area is divided into triangles, one side (the base line) and all angles of which are measured and the lengths of the other lines are calculated trigonometrically'. It has long been used by navigators and military strategists as a strategy that uses multiple reference points to locate an object's exact position (Smith, 1981). In social science research, the term 'triangulation' refers to the use of multiple strategies in the study of the same phenomenon (Campbell and Fiske, 1959; Denzin, 1978, 1983; Jick, 1979). A triangulation approach draws from multiple theoretical perspectives and research methods and can help a researcher capture a comprehensive, holistic and contextual portrayal of events or the social phenomena under study (Vidich and Shapiro, 1955; Webb *et al.*, 1966; McCall and Simmons, 1969; Sieber, 1973). As Bouchard (1976, p. 268) argued, such an approach enhances our belief that the results (empirical) are valid and not a methodological artefact.

3. Forms of Triangulation

Various types of triangulation can be employed for studying management accounting practice namely theory triangulation, data triangulation and investigator triangulation. These are discussed in turn.

3.1. *Theory Triangulation*

Theoretical triangulation involves using various factors from a variety of theoretical perspectives simultaneously to examine the same dimension of a research problem. Considerable accounting research advocates this form of research approach (see, for example, Covaleski *et al.*, 1985, 1996; Ansari and Euske, 1987; Berry *et al.*, 1991; Ansari and Bell, 1991; Carpenter and Feroz, 1992, 2001; Hoque and Hopper, 1994; Hoque *et al.*, 2004; Abernethy and Chua, 1996; Geiger and Ittner, 1996; Klumpes, 2001). These researchers believe that a single theoretical paradigm is inadequate for tapping into a comprehensive understanding of accounting practice.

There can be two types of theoretical triangulation. One type of theoretical triangulation can be 'within-same tradition' that uses multiple theories with no differences in their epistemological, ontological and philosophical assumptions. Examples of this would be the use of technical-rational choice models (Chapter 1), human-relations theory (Chapter 2), contingency approach (Chapter 3), and agency theory (Chapter 4) to research management accounting practice in an organisation.

A more ambitious and difficult form of theoretical triangulation is the use of theories, which have fundamentally different assumptions. It is not the intention to debate this issue here – it is simply too vast. Instead the chapter wishes to state its position in this regard and its consequences for such a triangulation approach. First, the chapter does not accept the existing view that theories with fundamentally different ontologies and epistemologies cannot be merged into one integrated approach without the researcher's abandoning core methodological beliefs (Burrell and Morgan, 1979). Second, given the general conclusions of the philosophy of science it is impossible to 'prove' the superiority of one theoretical approach over another (Lakatos, 1976; Feyerabend, 1978, 1990). No theory has the prerogative of truth. Third, dichotomies between objective and subjective reality, hard and soft theories, are essentially language games for privileging theories (Latour, 1999). Their basis is dubious and not helpful – all knowledge is socially created but this does not mean that conventional scientific inquiry has no validity or is not useful. Fourth, what is true is a social creation relying on the conviction of potential users – this will offer perceptions of whether a study effectively pursued methods consistent with its philosophical underpinnings or it can also be a product of relations within social milieu (Lakotos, 1976). Fifth, purposeful individuals base choice of theories on moral, pragmatic and social grounds. Pragmatically the choice of methods and use of results is a consequence of perceived usefulness to problems under scrutiny (Chua, 1986; Humphrey and Scapens, 1996; Rorety, 1999). Individuals can and do construct useful knowledge that does not normally dichotomise between its theoretical source. The essential message is that theoretical hypocrisy is normal, useful in everyday-life (though not without a moral dimension) and realisation of this is liberating for researchers and practitioners intent on informing practical problems.

Perhaps the most prevalent attempt in theoretical triangulation approach is in researcher's efforts to integrate different perspectives into the study of the same phenomena, which helps enrich our understanding of everyday accounting practice. Further, the most challenging effort in the use of theoretical triangulation is to assess whether or not results analysis from multiple perspectives has converged. It should be, however, noted that due to the differing nature of different perspectives the determination of the effectiveness of theoretical triangulation would be subjective.

A theory-triangulation approach offers alternative interpretations of the same phenomena. Because each theory can reflect distinctive insights on various dimensions of accounting and control practices in organisations, and a single theory would have been captured a little on these multidimensional issues in organisations. Theory- triangulation can help one to take advantage of the complementariness of different theories and gain alternative interpretations of the same phenomena.

A major dilemma confronting a researcher new to this area is how to choose a theoretical perspective to begin with or which theoretical perspective is most apt? One way of resolving this dilemma is to review a number of theoretical perspectives in advance, choose one, and then test its efficacy in the field with a view to confirming, modifying or rejecting it. Another is to carry a variety of possible perspectives into a pilot study to establish which is most meaningful in content for later use in the main study. This emergent strategy carries the danger of theoretical eclecticism and a lack of focus, but it has the advantage of creating theory from the extant situation and, as was found to be the case in prior research, to permit the insights of a various theoretical approaches to inform the actual problem simultaneously.

There has been interesting management research on theoretical triangulation (see Academy of Management Review, October 1989 and October 1999), which accounting research has neglected (see Modell, 2005, for exceptions). This invites questions of how one can combine theories with different ontological and epistemological assumptions. Can intuitive observation that competing theories each contain some validity be pursued without losing theoretical coherence? Works by Gioia and Pitre (1990) and Lewis and Grimes (1999) on theoretical triangulation are useful here. They recognise the impossibility of integrating theories with irreconcilable assumptions. Instead they advocate a dialectic that compares results and explanations from divergent theories to establish paradoxes, conflicts, and contradictions. The insights from alternative theories help extend or revise one's own theoretical stance and understanding of the topic under scrutiny. Lewis and Grimes'(1999) strategy for multi-paradigm research proceeds by ascertaining the different assumptions of each paradigm: then analyses data using codes from the constructs and protocols of each; and rebuilds one's focal theory by comparing and contrasting each set of results to establish differences and contradictions.

To the best of our knowledge no accounting research has consciously followed a theoretical triangulation strategy from the outset but examples of work in this genre exist. Ansari and Euske's (1987) research on the use of accounting information in a US military organisation employed three theoretical perspectives: the technical-rational theory, socio-political perspective and institutional theory. They pointed out that the alternative theoretical perspectives coexist insofar as different individuals use the accounting data differently in an organisation. Likewise, Berry et al. (1991), in their study of control in a financial services company, used a variety of different theoretical perspectives namely, management control model, cybernetic approach, behavioural approach and contingency theory. According to Berry et al., multiple theoretical perspectives, with their different epistemological assumptions, can be seen as complementary in that they offer alternative explanations of the same empirical data. Carpenter and Feroz's (1992 and 2001) work on the decision-making process in the state of New York employed four theoretical perspectives: economic consequences theory, traditional-rational theory, power-political theory and institutional theory. They demonstrated that various theoretical perspectives can complement each other and add richness to the analysis. Hoque and Hopper's (1994, 1997) work, concerning management control in a

Bangladeshi jute mill, is a good example of research in this category. By using technical-rational model, human-relations approach, interpretive theory and political economy approach, Hoque and Hopper provide evidence to support earlier research claiming that multiple theoretical perspectives facilitate accounting research in identifying and explaining the many factors causing failure of formal accounting and control systems in an organisation. Berry *et al.* (1991, p. 137) suggest that each approach offers something different and appears to offer something practical and organisationally helpful − if not always individually helpful. They claim that multiple approaches (whatever their limitations) can provide windows into organisational activity and allow one to achieve a wider and richer understanding of accounting and control procedures.

In summary, a theory-triangulation strategy can provide accounting researchers with a number of opportunities. First, it allows a researcher to build a wider explanation of the phenomena. Second, it helps uncover the deviant or off-quadrant dimension of a phenomenon. Third, the strategy builds in means of testing a whole range of plausible theoretical interpretations (Smith, 1981). Finally, this strategy permits individual learning in the field and has the advantage of creating theory from an extant situation (Hoque and Hopper, 1994). However, this requires new researchers to be aware and skilled in more than one theoretical approach. Also, whilst it is not claimed here that any researcher enters a site value free and is not influenced by previous theoretical exposure and predilections, it requires a discipline of scepticism and open-mindedness to build theory bottom up from the field.

A theory-triangulation from conflicting perspectives is useful since one perspective may be complementary to the other without being theoretically integrated. Overall, by employing a theoretical triangulation approach to future accounting research, more meaningful results can be provided, enabling the discipline to advance at a faster rate and a more soundly manner than the single theoretical approach. There is no correct way to gain knowledge or to understand a phenomenon because the achievements of such knowledge or understanding are based upon diverse approaches. Philosophers see theories as tools for predictions (Popper, 1963; Lakatos, 1976) and, surely a theoretical triangulation approach drawing insights from multiple perspectives not only lay down prescriptions by which accounting can proceed, they also provide a basis for a descriptive rational reconstruction of how accounting disciplines often evolve. As for philosophers, there is virtue in every idea (see Lakatos, 1976; Feyerabend, 1978; for a review of this literature, see Ardill, 2000). In fact, the issue here is methodological differences and theoretical triangulation with approaches with mutually exclusive philosophical assumptions. This then raises the big question of relativism and choice of a research theory in a particular setting. The nature of the inquiry and the user's perceived usefulness of the problem-based approach are important in judging where a theoretical triangulation approach might be useful. Clearly, there is much to be explored in the empirical field around these substantive issues.

3.2. Data triangulation

Data triangulation involves using a variety of data sources within a single study (Denzin, 1978). The strategy mixes both qualitative and quantitative methods including interviews, detailed observations and shadowing, documentary evidence and questionnaires to help the researcher to generate a rich source of field data with internal checks on its validity (Webb et al., 1966; Gross et al., 1971; Denzin, 1978; Yin, 1981).

As discussed in Chapter 18, qualitative methods (such as observations and interviews) derive from the ethnographic and field study traditions of anthropology and sociology (Pelto and Pelto, 1978; Silverman, 1985). In this sense, the philosophical and theoretical frames underpinning qualitative methods include: phenomenology (Bussis et al., 1973), symbolic interactionism and naturalistic behaviourism (Denzin, 1978), ethnomethodology (Garfinkel, 1967), and ecological psychology (Barker, 1968). The central notion behind these perspectives is that the study of human beings is different from other scientific inquiries.

Data-triangulation can assist a researcher to take advantage of the strong points of each type of data, cross-check data collected by each method, and collect information that is available only through particular techniques. Moreover, a research strategy embracing quantitative and qualitative methods can, as Lukka and Kasanen (1989) argue, alleviate the problems of generalisation from case study research in accounting (for a detailed review on this issue, see Modell, 2005).

3.3. Investigator triangulation

Investigator triangulation involves using multiple researchers in collect data (Denzin, 1970, p. 303). Smith (1981) suggests that investigator triangulation centres on the validity rather than reliability checks. Investigators with differing perspective or paradigmatic biases may be used to check out the extent of divergence in the data each collects. Under such conditions, if data divergence is minimal, then one may feel more confident in the data's validity. On the other hand, if their data are significantly different, then one has an idea as to possible sources of biased measurement that should be further investigated.

Investigator triangulation can be employed in a variety of ways, for example, interviews in a case study research can be conducted by employing more than one interviewer. Berry et al.'s (1985) work within an area of the UK coal industry well illustrates this category. Techniques, for instance, may include: one can be responsible for asking questions, one to make notes (besides a tape recorder) and a third to observe and pick up potentially interesting themes. Berry et al. suggest that something like built-in validity and reliability checks can thus be obtained because several interviewers/field workers are exposed directly to similar or identical data. This strategy, however, cannot be applied in a doctoral research where a doctoral candidate works on his/her own.

4. Limitations of Triangulation Approaches

Triangulation approaches, especially theory-triangulation and data-triangulation have limitations. A fundamental concern about the use of these two approaches is that they carry the danger of using theories and methods with different philosophies that can lead to theoretical and methodological opportunism and incoherence. Furthermore, the application of a triangulation approach is likely to be time consuming and costly. Nevertheless, these are practical difficulties that need to be overcome, rather than fundamental objections to this emergent 'triangulation' approach *per se*.

5. Conclusions

This chapter sought to demonstrate that triangulation approaches have a potentially important role to play in accounting research. The basic point in this paper is that no singular theory can fully explain the complexity of accounting practices. This expectation is consistent with the thesis put forwarded by Lakatos (1976) and Feyerabend (1978, 1990) where it has been suggested that no theories can have a monopoly on explanation because there is some virtue in each individual theory, and collectively, they add to an understanding that accounting is indeed a paradoxical phenomenon (see also Morgan, 1988; for details, see Ardill, 2000).[84] The chapter argues that the use of theoretical triangulation means that the weaknesses in each single theory will be compensated by the counter-balancing strengths of another. Multiple theories within a theoretical triangulation approach, however, are not to be taken as mutually exclusive; they complement each other (Klumpes, 2001). Data triangulation can provide the researchers powerful solutions to offset the problems of relying too much on any single data source or method by increasing the validity and credibility of the research findings of their study(s). This suggests, for example, that accounting researchers can use quantitative data in research that is essentially qualitative and interpretive in design. The use of multiple field researchers behoves the researcher to take full advantage of the opportunity to seek confirmation of 'factual' data in the situation under study providing the researchers have different background, training, etc.

References

Abernethy, M. A. and Chua, W. F. (1996), "A field study of control system change: the impact of institutional inducement on managerial choice", *Contemporary Accounting Research*, Vol. 13, No. 2, pp. 569-595.

Ansari, S. L. and Euske, K. J. (1987), "Rational, rationalizing and reifying uses of accounting data in organizations", *Accounting, Organizations and Society*, Vol. 12, No. 6, pp. 549-570.

---

[84] It is to be pointed out that it is not the aim of the chapter to convince colleagues that they need to re-evaluate their methodologies. Rather, the aim is to demonstrate how a better understanding might be possible with such an approach in order to further our theoretical knowledge in the area.

Ansari, S. L. and Bell, J. (1991a), "Symbolic, behavioral and economic roles of control in organizations and society", in Bell, J. (Ed.), *Accounting Control Systems: A Technical, Social and Behavioral Interaction*, Markus Wiener Publishing Inc., New York, pp. 9-24.

Ansari, S. L. and Bell, J. (1991b), "Symbolism, collectivism and rationality in organizational control", *Accounting, Auditing and Accountability Journal*, Vol. 4, No. 2, pp. 4-27.

Ardill, A. (2000), "The ideology and rhetoric of positive accounting theory", *Accounting, Accountability and Performance*, Vol. 6, No. 2, pp. 1-26.

Barker, R.G. (1968), *Ecological Psychology*, Stanford: Stanford University Press.

Berry, A. J., Capps, T., Cooper, D. J., Ferguson, P., Hopper, T. M. and Lowe, E. A. (1985), "Management control in an area of the NCB: rationales of accounting practices in a public enterprise", *Accounting, Organizations and Society*, Vol. 10, No. 1, pp. 3-28.

Berry, A. J., Laughton, E. and Otley, D. T. (1991), "Control in a financial services company (RIF): a case study", *Management Accounting Research*, Vol. 2, No. 2, pp. 109-139.

Bouchard, T.J. Jr. (1976), "Unobtrusive measures: an inventory of uses", *Sociological Methods and Research*, Vol. 4, pp. 267-300.

Burrell, G. and Morgan, G. (1979), *Sociological Paradigms and Organizational Analysis*, Heinemann, London.

Bussis, A., Chittenden, E.A. and Amarel, M. (1973), *Methodology in Educational Evaluation and Research*, Princeton, N.J.: Educational Testing Service.

Campbell, D. T. and Fiske, D. W. (1959), "Convergent and discriminant validation by the multitrait multimethod matrix", *Psychological Bulletin*, Vol. 56, pp. 81-105.

Carpenter, V. L. and Feroz, E. H. (1992), "GAAP as a symbol of legitimacy: New York's decision to adopt generally accepted accounting principles", *Accounting, Organizations and Society*, Vol. 17, No. 7, pp. 613-644.

Carpenter, V. L. and Feroz, E. H. (2001), "Institutional theory and accounting rule choice: an analysis of four US state governments' decisions to adopt generally accepted accounting principles", *Accounting, Organizations and Society*, Vol. 26, pp. 565-596.

Chua, W.-F. (1986), "Radical developments in accounting thought", *The Accounting Review*, October, pp. 601-632.

Covaleski, M. A., Dirsmith, M. W. and Jablonsky, S. F. (1985), "Traditional and emergent theories of budgeting: an empirical analysis", *Journal of Accounting and Public Policy*, Vol. 4, pp. 277-300.

Covaleski, M.A., Dirsmith, M.W. and Samuel, S. (1996), "Managerial accounting research: the contributions of organizational and sociological theories", *Journal of Management Accounting Research*, Vol. 8, pp. 1-35.

Denzin, N. K. (1978), "The logic of naturalistic inquiry", in Denzin, N. K. (Ed.), *Sociological Methods: A Sourcebook*, McGraw-Hill, New York.

Denzin, N. K. (1983), *Beyond Method Strategies for Social Research*, London, Sage Publications.

Feyerabend, P. (1978), *Against Method*, Verso, London.

Feyerabend, P. (1990), *Farewell to Reason*, Verso, London.

Garfinkel, H. (1967), *Studies in Ethnomethodology*, Englewood Cliffs, NJ: Prentice-Hall.

Geiger, D. R. and Ittner, C. D. (1996), "The influence of funding source and legislative requirements on government cost accounting practices", *Accounting, Organizations and Society*, Vol. 21, No. 6, pp. 549-567.

Gioia, D. A. and Pitre, E. (1990), "Multiparadigm perspectives on theory building", *Academy of Management Review*, Vol. 15, No. 4, pp. 584-625.

Gross, N., Giacquinta, J.B. and Bernatein, M. (1971), *Implementing Organizational Innovation*, New York: Basic Book.

Hoque, Z. and Hopper, T. (1994), "Rationality, accounting and politics: a case study of management control in a Bangladesh jute mill", *Management Accounting Research*, Vol. 5, pp. 5-30.

Hoque, Z. and Hopper, T. (1997), "Political and industrial relations turbulence, competition and budgeting in the nationalised jute mills of Bangladesh", *Accounting and Business Research*, Vol. 2, Spring, pp. 125-144.

Hoque, Z., Sharee, A. and Alexander, R. (2004), "Policing the police service: An exploratory case study of the rise of "new public management' within an Australian police service", *Accounting, Auditing and Accountability Journal*, Vol. 17, No. 1, pp. 59-84.

Humphrey, C. and Scapens, R. W. (1996), "Theories and case studies of organizational accounting practices: limitations or liberation"?, *Accounting, Auditing and Accountability Journal*, Vol. 9, No. 4, pp. 86-106.

Jick, T. D. (1979), "Mixing qualitative and quantitative methods: triangulation in action", *Administrative Science Quarterly*, Vol. 24, pp. 602-611.

Klumpes, P. J. M. (2001), "Implications of four theoretical perspectives for pension accounting research", *Journal of Accounting Literature*, Vol. 20, pp. 30-61.

Lakatos, I. (1976), "Methodology of scientific research programmes", in Lakatos, I. and Musgrave, A. (Eds.), *Criticisms and the Growth of Knowledge*, Cambridge University Press, London.

Latour, B. (1999), *Pandora's Hope: Essays on the Reality of Social Science Studies*, Harvard University Press, Mass., Cambridge.

Lewis, M. W. and Grimes, A. J. (1999), "Metatriangulation: building theory from multiple paradigms", *Academy of Management Review*, Vol. 24, No. 4, pp. 672-690.

Lukka, K. and Kasanen, E. (1995), The problem of generalizability: anecdotes and evidence in accounting research, *Accounting, Auditing and Accountability Journal*, Vol. 8, No. 5, pp. 71-90.

McCall, G. and Simmons, J. (1969), *Issues in Participant Observation* Reading, MA: Addison-Wesley.

Modell, S. (2005), "Triangulation between Case Study and Survey Methods in Management Accounting Research: An Assessment of Validity Implications", *Management Accounting Research*, Vol. 16, pp. 231-254.

Morgan, G. and Smircich, L. (1980), "The case for qualitative research", *The Academy of Management Review*, Vol. 5, No. 4, pp. 491-500.

Morgan, G. (1988), "Accounting as reality construction: towards a new epistemology for accounting practice", *Accounting, Organizations and Society*, Vol. 13, pp. 477-486.

Pelto, P.J. and Pelto, G.H. (1978), *Anthropological Research: The Structure of Inquiry*, 2nd Edition, Cambridge: Cambridge University Press.

Popper, K. R. (1963), *Conjectures and Refutation: the growth of knowledge*, London: Cambridge University Press.

Rorety, R. (1999), *Philosophy and Social Hope*, Penguin, London.

Sieber, S. D. (1973), "The integration of fieldwork and survey methods", *American Journal of Sociology*, Vol. 78, pp. 1335-1359.

Silverman, D. (1985), *Qualitative Methodology & Sociology*, London, Gower.

Smith, H.W. (1981), *Strategies of Social Research* Englewood Cliffs, NJ: Prentice-Hall.

Vidich, A. J. and Shapiro, G. (1955), "A comparison of participant observation and surveys data, *American Sociological Review*, Vol. 20, pp. 28-33.

Webb, E. J., Campbell, D. T., Schwartz, R. D. and Sechresr, L. (1966), *Unobtrusive Measures: Non-reactive Research in the Social Science*, Rand McNally, Chicago.

Yin, R. K. (1981), "The case study research: some answers", *Administrative Science Quarterly*, Vol. 1, No. 26, pp. 58-65.

24

DEALING WITH HUMAN ETHICAL ISSUES IN RESEARCH: SOME ADVICE

Zahirul Hoque
Deakin University, Australia

Abstract: Any research involving human and animal subjects requires ethical clearance from the relevant institution. All educational and research institutions have research and ethics policies and requirements. The ethics policy requires that the researcher take the utmost care or safety of the research participants involved to avoid any detriment – or risk of detriment – to any person or entity directly involved. This chapter provides some advice on how to deal with human subjects in research. It also outlines some key issues.

Keywords: Human ethics; ethics policy; ethical issues in research.

1. Introduction

Ethics and ethical principles extend to all spheres of human activity. They apply to our dealings with each other, with animals and the environment. They should govern our interactions not only in conducting research but also in commerce, employment and politics.[85] In value-free social science, codes of ethics for professional and academic associations are the conventional format for moral principles (Christians, 2000, p. 138). Ethical clearance for academic research projects and other research proposals such as student assignments and higher degrees by research (HDR) which involve human subjects, including animal species, now becomes a requirement. However, ethical clearance is not required for any archival research based on information in the public domain, unless such research involves materials likely to affect human or statistical data from which the identity of an individual may be inferred.

If you are an academic researcher or a HDR student, your research involving human and animal subjects will require the approval of the relevant University ethics committee, in accordance with the University policies. All research and

---

[85] Australian Government – National Statement on Ethical Conduct in Research Involving Humans: http://www7.health.gov.au/nhmrc/publications/synopses/e35syn.htm

educational institutions in Australia have research and ethics policies and requirements. In addition to these, there might be other ethical requirements for research. For example, in the Northern Territory of Australia, legislation requires permits to enter Aboriginal land to carry out excavations or to remove artefacts or samples in several jurisdictions, Commonwealth, Northern Territory and State. If your research involves such an attempt, you must acquaint yourself with this legislation and comply with its requirements where relevant. The purpose of this chapter is to discuss the following issues in research involving human subjects:

- Basic ethical principles
- Ethical requirements in human subjects research
- Informed consent for research
- Anonymity and confidentiality
- How to write an application for human ethics approval?

Australian Government Health and Human Research Ethics committee states: 'It is expected that all research involving, or impacting on humans is performed in an ethical manner'.[86] Accounting research has now been bombarded with fieldwork, qualitative research where innumerable ethical issues would be involved. Qualitative research includes developing empathic understanding based on subjective experience of actors (such as accountants and managers) in an organisational setting, and understanding the connections between their personal perceptions and behaviour. In a qualitative case study, pseudonyms and disguised locations are often recognised by readers. It now becomes an ethical issue as to how a qualitative researcher can overcome such a problem. This chapter is an attempt to address such an important but neglected area of qualitative research in accounting.[87]

2. Basic Ethical Principles[88]

In one of the early reflective documents on research ethics, the authors of the Belmont Report[89] identify three basic ethical principles: those general judgments that serve as a basic justification for particular ethical prescriptions and evaluations of human action. The first of these is *respect for persons*. This suggests that individuals should be treated as autonomous agents and that persons with diminished autonomy are entitled to protection. If respect for persons is equivalent to treating others as autonomous agents then we cannot show respect for those

---

[86] Australian Government Heath and Human Research Ethics:
http://www7.health.gov.au/nhmrc/ethics/human/index.htm

[87] The author is grateful to one of the reviewers of this chapter for bring this issue to his attention.

[88] Source: http://www7.health.gov.au/nhmrc/publications/humans/preamble.htm#Import
For details, see "The Belmont Report: Ethical Principles and Guidelines for the Protection of Human Subjects of Research", April 18, 1979 by The National Commission for the Protection of Human Subjects of Biomedical and Behavioral Research (http://www.nihtraining.com/ohsrsite/guidelines/belmont.html)

whose autonomy we recognise to be diminished. But we clearly can show such respect.

The second is *beneficence* that suggests the obligations to maximise possible benefits and minimise possible harms. Harm, in this context, extends beyond physical harm to a wide range of psychological or emotional distress, discomfort and economic or social disadvantage. Researchers exercise beneficence in assessing the risks of harm and potential benefits to participants, in being sensitive to the rights and interests of people involved in their research and in reflecting on the social and cultural implications of their work. 'Professional etiquette uniformly concurs that no one deserves harm or embarrassment as a result of intensive research practices' (Christians, 2000, p. 139).

The third principle is *justice*, addressing the resolution of the question of who ought to receive the benefits of research and bear its burdens. In the early twentieth century, it was recognised as unjust that, while the burdens of serving as medical research subjects fell largely on public patients, the benefits of improved medical care flowed largely to private patients. In contemporary times, researchers should recognise the potential for injustice where some groups are regularly selected as research subjects because of convenience and without regard to the frequency of research with those populations or to whom the benefits of the research flow. One example of such practice would be using indigenous peoples who are a particularly exploited groups in regards to research (for details, see Smith, 1999). Questions of justice can also arise in relation to the use of public funds for research.

3. Ethical Requirements in Human Subjects Research

There are several ethical issues that you need to consider when designing research that involves participants who are human beings.

- The ethics policy requires that you take the utmost care or safety of the research participants involved to avoid any detriment – or risk of detriment – to any person or entity directly involved. You can do so by carefully considering the risk/benefit ratio, using all available information to make an appropriate assessment and continually monitoring the research as it proceeds.
- If you represent an institution, your institution also expects you to adhere to a code of behaviour that reflects credit on you, as well as on your institution.
- You must obtain informed consent from each research participant in writing after your participants have had the opportunity to carefully consider the risks and benefits and to ask any pertinent questions.
- You must enumerate how privacy and confidentiality concerns will be addressed. You must be sensitive to not only how information is protected from unauthorised observation, but also if and how participants are to be notified of any unforeseen findings from the research that they may or may not want to know.

- You must consider how adverse events will be handled; who will provide care for a participant injured in a study and who will pay for that care are important considerations.

3.1.   Informed Consent for Research

Researchers (e.g. Christians, 2000; Soble, 1978; Veatch, 1996) suggest that human subjects in research must agree voluntarily to participate and they must be told the duration, methods, possible risks, and the purpose of their study. You must submit evidence to the research ethics committee that your research proposal has received the informed consent of the subject organisation. This consent should be in writing and demonstrate that the following steps have been completed:

- An introduction to the researchers involved with their institutional affiliation.
- A summary explanation of the research, its purpose, the data collection procedures, the expected benefits to the participant organisation.
- An estimate of the total amount of time required on the part of the subject(s).
- A description of any reasonably foreseeable risks or discomforts to the subject(s).
- A statement that participation is entirely voluntary, that the subject(s) may choose not to participate at all, or may discontinue participation at any time.
- Instructions on whom to contact with questions regarding the research, generally the Executive Officer of the University's Research Ethics Committee.
- Information about, and clarification of, the proposed use of research information about, and clarification of, ownership of the results, consistent with the relevant institution's policy on intellectual property rights.
- Your informed consent document must be written in simple language, avoiding any technical jargon.

In most cases, the above information can be communicated to the research human subjects using a PLAIN LANGUAGE STATEMENT. Appendix 1 provides an example. Appendix 2 provides an example of a consent form.

3.2.   Anonymity and Confidentiality

Your research proposal must contain your steps in maintaining anonymity and confidentiality. You must spell out clearly what you mean by anonymity and confidentiality. Refer to the example below:

All information collected will remain:

ANONYMOUS: Participants' names and addresses must be known to the researcher, so he can find them, but it will never be mentioned in the report of the research. Here the researcher assures the participants that he/she will conceal the identity of the participants in all written documents.

CONFIDENTIAL: All personal details will be locked away, quite separate from the other material. Here the researcher ensures that the information collected will be stored securely.

In a case study research when conducting 'face-to-face' interviews with people, you must assure the participants the confidentiality of the information. Bulmer (1982, p. 217) suggests that 'neither ethically justified or nor practically necessary, nor in the best interest of sociology as an academic pursuit' (see also Punch, 1994; cited in Christians, 2000, p. 139). To maintain such confidentiality your results must be analysed in aggregate form only and no individual participant should be identified in the report or paper. Also, you must be careful when you study government agencies or educational institutions or health organisations in presenting your field data because there could be some confidential, sensitive information. Christians (2000, p. 134) comments: 'when government agencies or educational institutions or health organisations are studied, what private parts ought not to be exposed? And who is blameworthy if aggressive media carry the search further.'

4. Application for Human Ethics Approval – Some Tips

It is now widely accepted that all kinds of research involving or impacting upon humans should conform to the highest standards of academic integrity and ethical practice. The Australian Research Council (ARC), which is the major Australian funding body for research outside the fields of clinical medicine and dentistry, has recently been concerned to develop a code of ethics that will be applicable to all forms of research which either involve humans directly or impact upon them directly or indirectly (Australian Government: National Health and Medical Research Council:

www7.health.gov.au/nhmrc/publications/humans/preamble.htm#Import).

To comply with this requirement, a researcher must submit an application for ethics approval before he/she commences his/her project. In general, the human ethics committee assesses this application. Remember, your application must be written in simple language for panel members as some of them may not be experts in your field.

There is a specific standard form for research ethics application. You must ensure that you strictly follow the set procedures. In most cases, there is a cover sheet, which contains all contact details of the researchers. A typical university application process requires the following:[90]

4.1. Project title: In general the title should reflect the theme of the research and it must be free from contractions or acronyms.

4.2. Objectives and intended outcomes of the research: The research objectives and intended outcomes should be spelled out clearly with plain language. Some researchers use dot points to outline their research objectives.

---

[90] Adapted from Deakin University human research ethics website, Guidelines for completing the DU-HREC Application Form
(http://www.deakin.edu.au/research/admin/ethics/human/index.php)

4.3. Introduction and background to the research: This part should contain the context for your research. That is, why it is important to study the proposed topic further in the context of existing research on the subject.

4.4. Methodology/procedures: You should clearly outline your research methodology, which should indicate any theoretical basis and how the data will be collected. If your research involves any interviews with human subjects, you should indicate the following:

- The place of the interview
- The length of the interview
- How the interview will be recorded
- Interview schedule (list of questions or themes)
- Feedback to the interviewee (whether the interviewee will be offered the opportunity to check his/her interview data)
- Data storage policy (whether the recorded data will be destroyed after the certain period or whether the permission will be sought to archive the data).

  If you use questionnaire surveys, you need to outline how you will distribute and collect them. If your survey is to be an anonymous, you need to explain how you will protect the anonymity of the participants. This can be done by not identifying any codes to link the participants to their identity.

4.5. Data collection and storage: Your ethics application should include:

- How the data will be collected and stored
- Who will have access to the data, and what safeguards will be used to prevent unauthorised access
- Confidentiality or anonymity – how either will be arranged and preserved
- The form in which results be available to participants
- The form in which results will be published.

4.6. Ethical Issues: In general, you need to address the following in your application:

Risks: If there are any risks, emotional or physical, involved in your project, you must inform the participants right 'up front' and outline how you are going to minimise them.

Coercion: You should not force people to participate in your study because of pre-existing relationships (such as between friends, workmates or students and teachers).

Stress or burden: In general, your project should not cause any stress to the participants.

Privacy/confidentiality/anonymity: As discussed earlier, you must clearly outline how you will maintain privacy, confidentiality or anonymity.

4.7. Duration of your project: Your application should provide a timetable for the research.

4.8. Proposed budget/funding sources: You should indicate your proposed budget, its sources and how it will be used.

4.9. **Profile of the researchers:** Details of each researcher including: name, title and contact details (including phone number and email address); academic qualifications and summary of experience; institutions and employment details.

5. Some Examples

Below are some examples of good ethical practice from ethical guidelines prepared by the British Sociological Association (BSA), the British Psychological Society (BPS), and the Association of Social Anthropologists (ASA) of the UK.[91]

5.1. **BSA 'Statement of Ethical Practice' on Anonymity, Privacy and Confidentiality**

'Research participants should understand how far they will be afforded anonymity and confidentiality and should be able to reject the use of data-gathering devices such as tape-recorders and video cameras'. 'Sociologists should be careful, on the one hand, not to give unrealistic guarantees of confidentiality and, on the other, not to permit communication of research films or records to audiences other than those to which the research participants have agreed'.

5.2. **BPS 'Ethical Principles for Conducting Research with Human Participants' Regarding Confidentiality (paragraph 7):**

'Subject to the requirements of legislation, including the Data Protection Act, information obtained about a participant during an investigation is confidential unless otherwise agreed in advance. Investigators who are put under pressure to disclose confidential information should draw this point to the attention of those exerting such pressure. Participants in psychological research have the right to expect that information they provide will be treated confidentially and, if published, will not be identifiable as theirs. In the event that confidentiality and/or anonymity cannot be guaranteed, the participant must be warned of this in advance of agreeing to participate'.

5.3. **ASA 'Ethical Guidelines for Good Research Practice' Regarding Confidentiality and Anonymity (paragraph 5):**

- 'Be sensitive to cultural variations;
- Take care not to infringe on private space (locally defined) of the individual or group;
- Anticipate threats to confidentiality and anonymity;
- Consider not even recording certain information, and store it carefully if you do;
- Use appropriate technical solution to problems of privacy;

---

[91] Adapted from Lancaster University Faculty of Social Sciences Committee on Ethics website.

- Make clear that guarantees may be unintentionally compromised. Some attributes can be difficult to disguise;
- Guarantees must be honoured unless there are overriding reasons not to do so. Make sure subjects are aware that it is rarely legally possible to ensure total confidentiality.'

6. Conclusion

This chapter suggests that ethics and ethical principles are important in any human activity. When submitting an application for ethical clearance, ensure that your application is written in simple language for panel members as some of them may not be experts in your field. It is your obligation as a researcher to respect each participant as a person capable of making an informed decision regarding participation in the research study. You must fully disclose the nature of your study, the risks and benefits associated with it. These must be outlined in the informed consent document.

It has been suggested in this chapter that there involves "less ethical issues in survey research" and "more complex ethical issues in 'ethnographic,' field research where the researcher is a complete participant." In such a complex environment, the complete morality of the researcher, mutual trusts, and a set of mutual agreements between the researcher and the participants must be developed, maintained and articulated. Future work may be undertaken to address such complexities in qualitative research, especially in accounting.

Appendix 1

PLAIN LANGUAGE STATEMENT
Re: (Insert project title here)

I/we, ... of
(insert institute's names) am conducting a research project on ....
The purpose of this study is to

_____

The primary source of data for this study will be

_____

I/we invite you to participate in this study. The information collected will only be presented in aggregate form and no information from any sources will be attributed to a particular individual in research publications. I/we would be happy to provide you with a summary of my/our aggregated results. There will be no potential personal/social/professional risks, stresses, discomfort, etc. to you as a participant in this study.

Please note that participation in this study is COMPLETELY VOLUNTARY. You are free to withdraw your consent at any time during the study, in which event your participation in the research study will immediately cease and any information obtained from you will not be used.

If, during the course of the project, you have any concerns about the conduct of this research project, please contact the Executive Officer, Ethics Committee, (insert contact details including telephone, fax and email address).

If you decide to participate please fill in the attached consent form and sign it.

Thank you in advance for taking the time to consider this proposal.

....
....
....
(Insert Researchers' details here)

Appendix 2

CONSENT FORM – For Organisations

I, (insert CEO or nominee's name) .... of (organisation's name)

Hereby give permission for _____

to be involved in a research study being undertaken by

Insert the researchers' names with institutions _____

and I understand that the purpose of the research is

Insert a summary of the research issues and data collection process.

All information collected will remain:

1. ANONYMOUS: Participants' names and addresses must be known to the researcher, so he can find them, but it will never be mentioned in the report of the research.
2. CONFIDENTIAL: All personal details will be locked away, quite separate from the other material.

    The same care will be taken with the names or characteristics of anyone participants mention in the interview.

    There will be no potential personal/social/professional risks, stresses, discomfort, etc. to participants

and that involvement for the institution means the following:

I acknowledge

1. That the aims, methods, and anticipated benefits, and possible risks/hazards of the research study, have been explained to me.
2. That I voluntarily and freely give my consent for the institution/organisation to participate in the above research study.
5. That I am free to withdraw my consent at any time during the study, in which event participation in the research study will immediately cease and any information obtained through this institution/organisation will not be used if I so request.
3. I understand that aggregated results will be used for research purposes and may be reported in scientific and academic journals.

I agree that

4. The institution/organisation MAY / MAY NOT be named in research publications or other publicity without prior agreement.
5. I / We DO / DO NOT require an opportunity to check the factual accuracy of the research findings related to the institution/organisation.
6. I / We EXPECT / DO NOT EXPECT to receive a copy of the research findings or publications.

    Signature: .... Date: _ _/_ _/_ _ _ _

References

Bulmer, M. (1982), "The merits and demerits of covert participant observation", in Bulmer, M. (Ed.), *Social Research Ethics*, Macmillan, London, pp. 217-251.

Christians, C. (2000), "Ethics and politics in qualitative research", in Denzin, N. K. and Lincoln, Y. S (Eds.), *Handbook of Qualitative Research*, Second Edition, Sage Publications, Thousand Oaks.

Punch, M. (1994), "Politics and ethics in qualitative research", in Denzin, N. K. and Lincoln, Y. S. (Eds.), *Handbook of Qualitative Research*, Sage Publications, Thousand Oaks.

Smith, L. T. (1999), *Decolonizing Methodologies*, Dunedin, University of Otago Press.

Soble, A. (1978), "Deception in social science research: is informed consent possible?", *Hastings Centre Report*, pp. 40-46.

Veatch, R. M. (1996), "From Nuremberg through the 1990s: the priority of autonomy", in Vanderpool, H. Y. (Ed.), *The Ethics of Research in Human Subjects: Facing the 21st Century*, University Publishing Group, Fredrick, MD.

Further Suggested Reading

Banyard, P. and Flanagan, C. (2005), *Ethical Issues and Guidelines in Psychology*, Routledge, New York, NY.

Thomas, D., Werhane, P. H. and Cording, M. (Eds.), (2002), *Ethical Issues in Business: A Philosophical Approach*, 7th edition, Prentice Hall, Upper Saddle River, N.J.

Cheney, D. (Ed.) (1993), *Ethical Issues in Research*, University Publishing Group, Frederick, MD.

Edward, E., Gendin, S. and Kleiman, L. (1994), *Ethical Issues in Scientific Research: An Anthology*, Garland, New York.

Sales, B. D. and Folkman, S. (2000), *Ethics in Research with Human Participants*, American Psychological Association, Washington, DC.

Sieber, J. E. (1992), *Planning Ethically Responsible Research*, Sage Publications, Newbury Park.

25

METHODOLOGICAL ISSUES REGARDING RESEARCH ON ACCOUNTING ETHICS

C. Richard Baker

Adelphi University, New York, USA

Abstract: In this chapter I shall examine some of the more significant methodological issues pertaining to research on accounting ethics. To that end, the term 'ethics' shall be confined to mean the ethics of the 'public accounting profession'. This is obviously a restricted meaning for both accounting and for ethics, but it is necessary to establish a boundary for the topic so that it will be manageable within one chapter. Likewise, 'methodological issues' is defined to mean both the principal theories and objectives underlying the discipline or field in which the research takes place and the primary types of evidence and methods of analysis chosen to undertake the research. The focus of the chapter will be on those disciplines in which there has been some prior research on accounting ethics and, in particular, on the psychological theory of cognitive moral development, where there has been a great deal of prior research.

Keywords: Research methodologies; research on accounting ethics; professional ethics; cognitive moral development.

1. Introduction

This chapter deals with methodological issues pertaining to research on accounting ethics. To begin with, it is necessary to define what is meant by 'research on accounting ethics', and secondly to explain what is meant by 'methodological issues' within this context. In the interest of placing some limits on the topic, research on accounting ethics is confined to mean the ethics of the 'public accounting profession'. This is, of course, a rather restricted meaning for both 'accounting' and for 'ethics'. However, the limitation in scope will prove useful, as it averts confusion regarding the variety of meanings given to both terms (i.e. accounting and ethics) in academia and in practice. Likewise, our meaning of 'methodological issues' refers to (1) the primary theories, arguments and objectives underlying the research; (2) the nature of the evidence and data utilised, and (3) the types of analysis and methods chosen to undertake the research. The focus of the chapter is also on the range of disciplines and sub-disciplines in which there has been some prior research on accounting ethics. In particular, special attention is given to the psychological theory of cognitive moral development where there has been a great deal of prior research.

The public accounting profession differs from other professions in that while public accountants receive fees for services rendered to persons and organisations whom they refer to as their clients, public accountants also assume responsibilities to third parties and to the public generally. This unusual arrangement poses an ethical dilemma for public accountants. Most research on accounting ethics focuses on explaining in one way or another how public accountants deal with this dilemma. The remainder of the chapter is organised as follows. In the first section, there will be a brief discussion of traditional accounting history research in which the establishment of codes of ethics for the public accounting profession has played a prominent role. Following that, 'new' accounting history is discussed, wherein a critical stance is taken regarding codes of ethics within the professionalism project of the public accounting profession. After that, various social science approaches to research on accounting ethics will be discussed, including: economics, in which there has little ethics research; psychology, in which there has been a great deal of ethics research; sociology, which is sub-divided into various sub-disciplines like sociology of the professions, organisation theory, critical theory, and postmodern theory. The section after that, will address a major research paradigm within psychology, namely the cognitive moral development paradigm. A great deal of research on accounting ethics has been done within this paradigm, particularly in North America. Table 1, provides a summary of the different approaches to research on accounting ethics, identifying: the primary theory underlying the research; the primary objective of the research; the primary evidence gathered, and the primary method used to analyse the evidence gathered.

Table 1
Methodological Approaches to Research on Accounting Ethics

Discipline	Primary Theory	Primary Objective	Primary Evidence	Primary Method
Traditional History	Teleological	Objective Interpretation	Documentary Archives	Discursive Interpretation
New History	Critical or Marxist	Persuasion	Selected Archives	Persuasive Interpretation
Economics	Economic Theory	Discovery of Relationships and Testing of Theory	Numerical data	Mathematical Modeling
Psychology	A specific psychological theory	Discovery of relationships and testing of hypotheses	Numerical data	Statistical tests

Sociology of the Professions	A specific theory of the professions	To articulate theory	Archives, secondary sources, surveys	Discursive Interpretation
Organisation Theory	A specific organisation theory	To articulate theory	Archives, case studies, participant observation	Discursive Interpretation
Critical Theory	Critical Theory	To combine theory and practice	Archives, field and case studies	Persuasive Interpretation
Postmodern Theory	Postmodern Theory	To reveal the faults of modernity	Secondary sources	Persuasive Interpretation

2.   Traditional History and the Public Accounting Profession

The emergence of the public accounting profession has been accompanied by the creation of codes of ethics (Littleton, 1933; Carey, 1966; Loeb, 1978). The main purpose of these codes has been to regulate the conduct of professional accountants and to set forth the kinds of behaviour expected of practicing professionals (Lee, 1991; Preston *et al.*, 1995). The theory underlying this area of research has, in the main, been teleological in that it has focused on enhancing and preserving the professional status of the public accounting profession. At the same time, the primary objective of traditional accounting history research has been on the interpretation of documentary archives in a neutral and objective manner. Nevertheless, because the underlying teleological orientation has been directed more towards the creation of professional status for public accounting practices, histories of codes of ethics have often presented an idealised picture of the evolution of the accounting profession. This idealised picture has tended to equate the ethics of the public accounting profession with concepts like integrity, honesty, objectivity, fairness, and competence (Carey, 1966; Montagna, 1973, 1974; Parker, 1986; Lee, 1991). This confinement of traditional accounting history research to a celebration of the rise of the public accounting profession has led to numerous criticisms (Preston *et al.*, 1995; Mitchell *et al.*, 1993; Parker, 1986; Walker, 1995). As a result of such criticisms, this type of research is now regarded as being somewhat antiquated.

3.   New History and Critique of the Public Accounting Profession

In recent years, a number of researchers have questioned whether it is possible to interpret accounting history in a neutral and objective manner (Parker, 1994; Preston *et al.*, 1995). There has also been criticism of the purpose of professional codes of ethics, suggesting that such codes may involve self-interested values. It is argued that self-interested values create social closure around the public accounting profession which excludes unwanted members and thwarts unwanted competition (Kedslie, 1990; Walker, 1995). Evidence is cited regarding the fact that codes of ethics have often included restrictions on accounting practice which prohibit members from engaging in any activity apart from public accountancy, as well as prohibitions against advertising and solicitation of new business, hiring staff away from other firms, competitive bidding for new clients, and so forth (Preston *et al.*, 1995). New accounting researchers have challenged the accounting profession's code of ethics on grounds ranging from its ineffectiveness to its hidden ideological purpose in acting as a smokescreen for private interests and capitalist hegemony (Briloff, 1978; Tinker *et al.*, 1982; Mitchell *et al.*, 1993; Parker, 1994). Among the new accounting historians, any pretense regarding objective interpretation of historical facts has been replaced by a more or less explicit interpretive framework such as *Marxism* (Tinker *et al.*, 1982), *Critical Theory* (Michell *et al.*, 1993; Walker, 1995), *Structuration Theory* (Macintosh, 1995; Dillard and Yuthas, 2001, 2002) or *Post-modern Theory* (Preston *et al.*, 1995). Successful publication in this area of research requires not only an ability to interpret primary archives and secondary sources, but a willingness to apply a particular theoretical framework to a critical interpretation of the historical evidence (Carmona *et al.*, 2004).

4. Social Science Approaches to Research on Accounting Ethics

4.1. Economics-based Methodologies

While economics-based research methodologies underpin most accounting research (eg. capital markets research), there have only been a few research studies focusing on accounting ethics which have used economics-based approaches (see, for example, Noreen, 1988; Elias, 2004; Carcello and Nagy, 2004). This lack of research using economics-based methodologies may present an opportunity for accounting researchers who would like to use economics theories to investigate issues pertaining to accounting ethics. Economics is relatively unified around the neo-classical theory which assumes that markets move towards an equilibrium of supply and demand. The overall goal of economics-based approaches is to investigate relationships between economic variables, such as market prices of shares and accounting variables, and to test economic theory. The evidence gathered in economics-based approaches to research is almost exclusively numerical, and the analysis is based on mathematical models of economic theory. For example, Elias (2004) surveyed practicing public accountants regarding earnings management. Their results indicated that public accountants employed in firms with high (low) ethical standards viewed earnings management activities as more unethical (ethical). In another type of research on accounting ethics utilising an economics-based approach, Carcello and Nagy (2004) found that fraudulent financial reporting is more likely to occur during the first three years of the auditor-client relationship. They did not find evidence that fraudulent financial reporting is more likely given long auditor tenure. Their results are consistent with the argument that mandatory audit firm rotation might have adverse effects on audit quality. Experimental markets methods constitute a third example of research using economics-based approaches. Schatzberg *et al.* (1996) performed an experimental market study of auditor independence. The subjects were students, and the setting was highly abstracted from reality. The results indicated that certain economic conditions, such as an auditor's ability to profit from lack of independence, were necessary for an ethical lapse to take place.

4.2. *Psychological Approaches*

In recent years, particularly within the American context, research on accounting ethics has often been conducted through methodologies derived from psychology. In a relative sense, psychological theory is not unified; there are many theories about the nature of mental processes and the influence of mental process and factors like genetics, personality, and social setting, on human behaviour. Any given piece of research is highly dependent on the theoretical paradigm underlying the research and the specific features of the psychological instrument used to conduct the research. In research on accounting ethics, it is frequently assumed that ethical behaviour is determined by attitudes, beliefs, values, personality factors, or levels of cognitive moral development that are inherent to a particular individual. For example, the theory of cognitive moral development involves an individual's choice of reasons why a particular type of ethical behaviour should be followed or not followed. These reasons are then classified into a hierarchy of levels of moral development.

Kohlberg (1969) was the primary figure in the development of the psychological theory of cognitive moral development. His theory was derived from a psychological model derived from Piaget. According to Piaget (1932), a child develops cognitively through a series of stages over time. Kohlberg (1984) elaborated on these stages of development to explain the variables that cause an individual to behave in a certain way. Kohlberg described his theory of cognitive moral development as consisting of a series of steps. According to this theory, a person's moral development moves through a series of stages over time which are influenced by factors inherent to the individual, as well as education and other factors.

Based on Kohlberg's theory, James Rest (1986b) developed the Defining Issues Test (DIT), a self-administered multiple choice questionnaire that provides a specific measure of an individual's level of cognitive moral development (Louwers *et al.*, 1997). A great deal of research on accounting ethics has been done using the DIT. Some of this research will be discussed in a later section of this chapter. In addition, certain specific methodological issues pertaining to the DIT will be discussed. In general, it can be seen that psychological approaches to research on accounting ethics focus on testing hypotheses through statistical distinctions between numerical data like those produced by psychological instruments such as the DIT (see studies like Ryan, 2001; Radtke, 2000).

4.3. *Sociological Approaches*

Research on accounting ethics has also been based on methodologies derived from sociology. An ongoing theoretical debate in the sociological literature deals with the reality concept, that is whether sociological variables such as organisations, institutions, class, power, position or influence constitute 'real' variables (i.e. the realist position) or whether they are socially constructed (i.e. the constructivist position). Among the different sociological approaches, different researchers have taken quite varied approaches to research on accounting ethics, ranging from the realist, structural-functionalist theories put forth in the sociology of professions and organisation theory literatures to the constructivist theories that inform critical theory and post-modern approaches.

4.4. Sociology of Professions

The sociology of professions literature focuses on identifying characteristics that define a profession and explaining how these characteristics serve the functions of both advancing the profession and serving the public interest. The sociology of professions literature defines a profession as having (among other attributes): a defined body of knowledge, specific recognition by society, a code of ethical conduct and a defined cultural tradition. Historically, persons have become members of professions by joining guilds or institutes that imposed codes of ethical conduct on the members. These codes of conduct address both technical and ethical issues, and violations of the codes might constitute grounds for taking disciplinary actions against the offending member. The disciplinary actions could range from warnings and reprimands to harsher penalties, including expulsion from the guild or institute. Threats of expulsion from the professional guild or institute and the corresponding loss of status and income generally suffice to cause the member of the profession to abide by the written and unwritten codes of ethical conduct.

As mentioned previously, the public accounting profession differs from other professions in that while public accountants receive fees for services rendered to persons and organisations whom they refer to as their clients, public accountants also assume responsibilities to third parties and to the public generally. The underlying assumption of the sociology of professions literature is that the ethical dilemmas faced by accountants can be resolved by creating appropriate social structures such as codes of ethics that will influence professional behaviour (Carey, 1966; Loeb, 1978; Baker, 1993; Ketz and Miller, 1998). While there has been a great deal of research done in the sociology of professions literature, this avenue of research is now seen as being somewhat limited. More recent research has moved in the direction of critiques of the ideology of professionalism (Mitchell *et al.*, 1993).

4.5. Organisation Theory Approaches to Research on Accounting Ethics

Another approach to research on accounting ethics with methodological roots in sociology is organisation theory. These types of studies focus on ethical dilemmas faced by accountants and discuss how organisational structure variables act to resolve or exacerbate these dilemmas. The studies also maintain that organisational and cultural variables have an impact on ethical behaviour, regardless of the individual characteristics of the participants. The general conclusion of this line of research is that the organisational and cultural settings in which accountants find themselves are determinative of their behaviours regardless of individual ethical beliefs or attitudes. Because of this assumption, the organisation theory approach can be seen as articulating a particular theory (i.e. ontological position) regarding the significance and importance of social settings. The evidence gathered in this area of research is diverse, ranging from archives and documents to surveys, case studies and participant observation data (see, for example, Montagna, 1973, 1974; Baker, 1993, 1999; Louderback, 1994; Shapeero et al., 2003), and the methods of analysis generally involve discursive interpretation of empirical data.

4.6. Critical Theory Approaches

Critical theory approaches to ethics are based on the idea that contradictions within capitalism cause ethical dilemmas to persist and that only the evolution of society away from the capitalist form of economic organisation will allow a resolution of these ethical dilemmas. Critical theory is founded on the principle that it is possible to change the nature of society to achieve greater justice for all. The central thesis is that human discourse creates views of the world about social relationships and about the status of individuals within the world (i.e. the life-world). Human discourses also create organisations and social structures that reflect the life-world (i.e. systems). Finally, human discourses create mechanisms to help the systems reflect the needs of the life-world (i.e. steering media). As long as the systems of society and the steering media are determined by the freely conducted discourses of human beings operating in the life-world, then society can move forward toward a freer and more just status. However, if the steering media take over, they can dominate the systems and control the life-world to the detriment of human freedom. Recent studies reveal the complex interplay between accounting systems and the steering media of society. If accounting systems are not designed in an open and discursive manner (i.e. an ideal speech situation), then they are likely to be used by the steering media in a manner that reduces human freedom. Since the principal emphasis of critical theory is social change, the primary objective of this approach is to combine theory and practice (see, for example, Dillard and Yuthas, 2001, 2002; Huss and Patterson, 1993; Lehman, 1992; Lehman and Tinker, 1987; Tinker, Merino and Neimark, 1982). Because of its combination of theory and practice, this approach often relies on field and case studies interpreted persuasively through a particular theoretical lens.

4.7. Postmodern Approaches

In a general sense, a postmodern approach is defined as a set of beliefs regarding the outmoded nature of modernity (Covaleski et al., 1998; Macintosh, 1993). The primary theoretical claim of this approach is that the meta-narratives that constitute modernity have lost their effectiveness and no longer represent reality. The postmodern stance is one of incredulity with respect to meta-narratives. Second, postmodernism argues that modernity has not always been socially progressive. Instead, the modern world has produced a mechanised society which may have reduced freedom. Third, the modern era, spanning the 19th and most of the 20th century, has been a period marked by deadly warfare. Fourth, the postmodern perspective sees a new political order emerging which may produce more space for those who have been previously left out of the mainstream (e.g. women, minorities, etc.) Finally, postmodernism argues that the development of new information technologies may open up opportunities to increase the level of democracy in political and social life, but that simultaneously, these new technologies pose threats to personal privacy and freedom. Postmodernism essentially rejects the notion that there is such a thing as moral or ethical truth and it views arguments in favour of moral truth as essentially a means of controlling the less powerful in society.

While Michel Foucault (1986) did not accept classification of his work within the postmodern genre, he did address the question of ethics in an intriguing way which sheds some light on the postmodern perspective. Foucault viewed morality as a type of meta-concept which incorporates various sub-concepts. These sub-concepts include: moral codes, moral behaviour, and ethics. The moral code refers to the set of laws, values and rules of action that are specified for individuals by entities such as religious authorities, families, schools and so forth. The moral code stipulates the rules that must be followed on pain of sanction. However, these rules exist within a 'complex interplay of elements that counterbalance and correct one another, and cancel each other out on certain points, thus providing for compromises and loopholes' (Foucault, 1986). Because Foucault did not subscribe to the belief that the moral code is immutable, nor is it necessarily the same moral code in all places at all times, there is a significant difference between Foucault's definition of the moral code and a typical deontological view of ethics.

Moral behaviour, according to Foucault, consists of the actual behaviour of individuals in relationship to their moral code. The questions to be addressed here are whether individuals comply more or less fully with a rule, the manner in which they obey or resist an interdiction or a prescription, and the manner in which they respect or disregard a set of values. From Foucault's perspective, ethics is concerned with the kind of relationship a person ought to have with himself or herself and the manner in which the individual constitutes himself or herself as a moral subject. Thus, ethics can be distinguished from moral behaviour and the moral code. Ethics concerns the manner in which a person conducts himself or herself in order to become the 'right kind' of person. Ethics is concerned with disciplinary practices of the self and self-formation as an ethical subject (Foucault, 1986).

From a public accounting perspective, the self-forming aspect of ethics is not as evident with respect to the code of ethics as it is with regard to the various self-disciplining practices that commence early in the career of a prospective professional accountant, ranging from difficult examinations, to the social rituals associated with accounting institutes and associations, and to the recruitment rituals of the public accounting firms. These ritualised activities constitute self-forming and disciplinary practices that shape the prospective public accountant into an idealised ethical being; not an ethical being who conforms to the code of ethics, but rather an ethical being who is disciplined and self-formed into the idealised member of the public accounting firm. The disciplinary and self-forming practices of the public accounting profession are closely associated with the kind of person to which an individual aspires when he or she behaves in a moral manner. In accounting, this would be the partner in the large public accounting firm who is an ethical being, not in the sense of conforming closely to the code of ethics, but one who is able to satisfy clients, bring in new business, be technically astute, all the while providing an image of action in the highest ethical manner (Covaleski *et al.*, 1998; Baker, 1993, 1999). A postmodern view of ethics then reveals the fault-lines underlying modernity. Its evidence consists primarily of secondary sources, while its method of analysis is persuasive interpretation.

5. The Theory of Moral Development and Research on Accounting Ethics

Because of the large amount of prior research that has used the psychological theory of cognitive moral development, this section focuses on that theory and its application to accounting research. Kohlberg's (1969) theory of cognitive moral development comprises three levels with each level sub-divided into two stages for a total of six stages. The six stages are organised into a hierarchy, with each successive stage being higher than previous stage. At the Pre-Conventional level of moral development, there are two stages. Individuals assessed as being at Stage 1 utilise moral reasoning which focuses on obeying rules in order to avoid punishment, whereas at Stage 2, an individual obeys rules primarily to gain personal rewards from others. After Stage 2, individuals enter into the Conventional level of moral development, which is divided into Stages 3 and 4. At Stage 3, an individual obeys rules based on loyalty to a particular group, whereas at Stage 4, an individual abides by established laws out of a sense of participating in a valid social order. The highest level of moral development is the Post-Conventional level, divided into Stages 5 and 6. At Stage 5, an individual abides by a code of ethical conduct based on an underlying ethical theory such as religious or natural law or utilitarianism. Finally, Stage 6 involves unwritten principles of justice and human rights (Kohlberg, 1969, 1984).

Most of the research on accounting ethics that has used the theory of cognitive moral development has also used the Defining Issues Test (DIT). The DIT includes six narratives describing moral dilemmas. These narratives are first read by subjects who are then asked to respond to twelve questions for each narrative regarding potential reasons for resolving the moral dilemma in a particular way. The subjects select the relative importance of each reason using a four-point scale (much importance, some, little or none). Because the DIT is a proprietary instrument, researchers must pay a fee to have it scored by the Centre for the Study of Ethical Development at the University of Minnesota. After scoring, the Centre provides several diagnostic reports to the researcher, among which is the P-score.

ETHICAL ISSUES

The P-score ranges from 0 to 99. It is intended to measure the relative importance a subject assigns to reasons corresponding to Stages 5 and 6 of Kohlberg's theory of cognitive moral development (i.e. the Post-Conventional level of moral reasoning). The DIT has demonstrated high test-retest reliability rates (in the high 80s) and high internal reliability (Rest, 1994).

Ponemon (1990, 1992a, 1992b, 1993; Ponemon and Glazer, 1990; Ponemon and Gabhart, 1990) has been highly influential in the introduction of Kohlberg's theory and the use of the DIT in accounting research. Ponemon's studies have touched on a number of different issues. For example, Ponemon and Glazer (1990) found that P-scores of senior level accounting students and alumni of accounting programs were higher than lower level accounting students at the same institution, and that students and alumni from a university offering primarily a liberal arts curriculum had higher P-scores than students at a university with primarily an accounting curriculum. In another study, Ponemon (1993) found that ethics education did not cause an increase in accounting students' P-scores. In the same study, he found that economic free-riding (i.e. unethical behaviour) was associated with both very low and very high P-scores, while less free-riding behaviour was associated with middle level P-scores. In a third study, Ponemon (1992a) found that practising auditors' P-scores increased from the staff to the supervisory levels, but decreased in the manager and partner ranks.

Ponemon's work has raised questions about the appropriateness of the theory of cognitive moral development and the use of the DIT in accounting and auditing. Based on Kohlberg's theory, the P-score provides a measure of moral reasoning at Post-Conventional Stages 5 and 6 in Kohlberg's theory. While Post-Conventional moral reasoning may be appropriate for certain professionals, it may be more appropriate for public accountants and auditors to comply with generally accepted rules of accounting and auditing. This type of expectation for professional accountants may be more congruent with Kohlberg's Stages 3 or 4. Lampe and Finn (1992) have argued that public accountants and auditors should be expected to demonstrate less willingness to deviate from rules in order to follow abstract ethical principles. As an area for further research on accounting ethics, it might be useful to investigate whether there are differences in the level of moral development between different levels of staff in public accounting firms and whether this makes a difference to accounting practice.

Gender effects have also been a controversial issue in the theory of cognitive moral development and the use of the DIT. This is because Kohlberg's theory is viewed by some researchers as biased in favour of masculine values (e.g. justice). Gilligan (1982) has proposed an alternative theory of moral development, which is oriented more towards caring values than the justice orientation that underlies Kohlberg's theory. There is some support for Gilligan's theory in empirical research. For example, Lyons (1983) argues that females are more concerned about caring for others compared with males who are more rights-oriented. However, a number of studies of moral reasoning have also indicated that the P-scores of females are at least equal to, and in some studies significantly higher than, those of males. For example, Thoma (1986) indicates that while females outscored males on the P-score the difference has not been statistically significant. Similar results have been reported for accounting students and practicing auditors, where some studies have shown gender effects and others have not. For example, female students in Abdolmohammadi and Reeves (2000) had higher P-scores than male students. Bernardi and Arnold (1997) also reported that female auditors had higher P-scores than the male auditors, but, Abdolmohammadi et al. (2003) did not find significant differences between males and females. Thus, it is unclear whether there may be gender effects when using the DIT. In addition, the gender effects that may have been present in the prior studies may have been dissipated by subsequent developments in recruitment and training of public accounting professionals. This may present an opportunity for further research on accounting ethics (see also Radtke, 2000).

Another issue that might be investigated with respect to the use of the DIT in research on accounting ethics is the political question. Some researchers have argued that Kohlberg's model is based on a distinction of political ideology rather than cognitive moral development. In other words, individuals with a liberal political orientation may have higher P-scores than those with a conservative political orientation. Of course, the question then becomes, does a political orientation cause the P-score, or does the level of cognitive moral development cause the political orientation (i.e. do conservatives have a lower level of cognitive moral development). This is a controversial issue, which has not been resolved in the literature. With respect to research on accounting ethics, Hill et al. (1998), Eynon et al. (1997) and Sweeny (1995) have all found that auditors who have relatively lower P-scores also have more conservative political orientations.

Another issue concerning the theory of cognitive moral development and the use of the DIT is whether the P-score is connected with ethical behaviour. The relationship between moral reasoning and ethical behaviour was reviewed by Thoma (1994). He indicates that moral reasoning is significantly related to ethical behaviour but that the extent of variation in ethical behaviour that is caused by moral reasoning is not great (i.e. about 15 percent) (Thoma, 1994). Some research on accounting ethics has provided support for this conclusion. For example, using Chinese auditors as subjects and a survey questionnaire, Gul et al. (2003) found that there was a negative relationship between the P-score and unethical behaviour. As mentioned previously, Ponemon (1993) also found that the relationship between the P-score and unethical behaviour was quadratic instead of strictly linear, meaning that subjects with both low and high P-scores were more likely to engage in unethical behaviour than those in the middle. Bay and Greenberg (2001) replicated Ponemon's study. Their experiment involved undergraduate business students in a simulated trade of playing cards of varying quality with the opportunity to increase their payment by lying to buyers and making them pay higher prices for low quality cards. Their results were consistent with those of Ponemon (1993), however, Bay and Greenberg's (2001) results appeared to have been driven by the behaviour of male subjects. Female subjects demonstrated an unexpected negative relationship between moral reasoning and ethical behaviour. Specifically, they had a decreasing level of ethical behaviour as the P-score increased. Thus, there seems to be conflicting results in these studies, thereby providing an opportunity for further research investigating the relationship between levels of moral reasoning and ethical behaviour and the possible confounding effects of gender (see also Ryan, 2001).

6. Conclusion

This chapter has reviewed methodological issues pertaining to research on accounting ethics. The focus has been on those disciplines in which there has been prior research on accounting ethics. In particular, there has been a focus on the theory of cognitive moral development and the use of the DIT in accounting research. The public accounting profession has long relied on its reputation for integrity and veracity as justification for its professional status and monopoly privilege. This reliance has been predicated on claims of acting in the public interest. If such status and privilege are to be justified and sustained, serious consideration of what constitutes ethical conduct and behaviour is imperative for the profession. Traditionally, research on accounting ethics has tended to be quite narrow, failing to recognise the social and psychological context of behaviour. Such research has also failed to identify and recognise the public interest aspect of the accounting profession and has not articulated processes through which the public interest could be identified. Generally, the research literature on accounting ethics has taken superficial view of accounting ethics, focusing mainly on artifacts like the code of ethics. The chapter has tried to take a broader view. Overall, the approaches and theories mentioned above allow for an enhanced ability to appreciate the pertinence and importance of ethics and ethical behaviours within the public accounting profession.

References

Abdolmohammadi, M. J. and Reeves, M. (2000), "Effects of education and intervention on business students' ethical cognition: a cross sectional and longitudinal study", *Teaching Business Ethics*, Vol. 4, August, pp. 269-284.

Abdolmohammadi, M. J., Read, W. and Scarbrough, D. (2003), "Does selection-socialization help to explain accountants' weak ethical reasoning?", *Journal of Business Ethics*, Vol. 42, January, pp. 71-81.

Baker, C. R. (1993), "Self-regulation in the public accounting profession: the response of the large, international public accounting firms to a changing environment", *Accounting, Auditing & Accountability Journal*, Vol. 6, No. 2, pp. 68-80.

Baker, C. R. (1999), "Theoretical approaches to research on accounting ethics", *Research on Accounting Ethics*, Vol. 5, pp. 115-134.

Bay, D. D. and Greenberg, R. R. (2001), "The relationship of the DIT and behavior: A replication", *Issues in Accounting Education*, Vol. 16, No. 3, pp. 367-380.

Bernardi, R. A. and Arnold, D. F. (1997), "An examination of moral development within public accounting by gender, staff level, and firm", *Contemporary Accounting Research*, Vol. 14, Winter, pp. 653-668.

Briloff, A. (1978), Codes of conduct: their sound and their fury", in De George, R. and Picher, J. (Eds.), *Ethics, Free Enterprise and Public Policy: Original Essays on Moral Issues in Business*, Oxford University Press, London.

Carcello, J. V. and Nagy, A. L. (2004), "Audit firm tenure and fraudulent financial reporting", *Auditing: A Journal of Practice & Theory*, Vol. 23, No. 2, September, pp. 55-71.

Carey, J. (1966), *The Ethical Standards of the Accounting Profession*, AICPA, New York.

Carmona, S., Ezzamel, M. and Guttierez, F. (2004), "Accounting history research: traditional and new accounting history perspectives", *Spanish Journal of Accounting History*, Vol. 1, December, pp. 24-53.

Covaleski, M. A., Dirsmith, M. W., Heian, J. B. and Samuel, S. (1998), "The calculated and the avowed: techniques of discipline and struggles over identity in Big Six public accounting firms", *Administrative Science Quarterly*, Vol. 43, No. 2, June, pp. 293-328.

Dillard, J. F. and Yuthas, K. (2001), "A responsibility ethic for audit expert systems", *Journal of Business Ethics*, April, p. 337.

Dillard, J. F. and Yuthas, K. (2002), "Ethical audit decisions: a structuration perspective", *Journal of Business Ethics*, March, pp. 49-65.

Elias, R. Z. (2004), "The impact of corporate ethical values on perceptions of earnings management", *Managerial Auditing Journal*, Vol. 19, No. 1, January, pp. 84-98.

Eynon, G., Hill, N. and Stevens, K. (1997), "Factors that influence the moral reasoning ability of accountants: implications for universities and the profession", *Journal of Business Ethics*, Vol. 16, pp. 1297-1309.

Foucault, M. (1986), *The History of Sexuality, Volume 2*, Vintage Books, New York.

Gilligan, C. (1982), *In a Different Voice*, The Harvard University Press, Cambridge, MA.

Gul, F. A., Ng, A. Y., Yew, M. and Tong, J. (2003), "Chinese auditors' ethical behavior in an audit conflict situation", *Journal of Business Ethics*, Vol. 42, February, pp. 379-392.

Hill, N., Stevens, K. and Clarke, P. (1998), "Factors that affect ethical reasoning ability of U.S. and Irish small-firm accountancy practitioners", *Research on Accounting Ethics*, Vol. 4, pp. 145-166.

Huss, H. F. and Patterson, D. M. (1993), "Ethics in accounting; values education without indoctrination", *Journal of Business Ethics*, Vol. 12, No. 3, March, pp. 235-244.

Kedslie, M. J. M. (1990), "Mutual self-interest – a unifying force; the dominance of societal closure over social background in the early professional accounting bodies", *The Accounting Historians Journal*, Vol. 17, pp. 1-9.

Ketz, J. E. and Miller, P. B. W. (1998), "Character is destiny: the value of ethics in accounting", *Accounting Today*, Vol. 12, No. 11, June, pp. 14-16.

Kohlberg, L. (1969), "Stages and sequences: the cognitive developmental approach to socialization", in Goslin, D. (Ed.), *Handbook of Socialization Theory and Research*, Rand McNally, Chicago, IL.

Kohlberg, L. (1984), *Essays on Moral Development*, Harper & Row, San Francisco.

Lampe, J. C. and Finn, D. W. (1992), "A model of auditors' ethical decision process", *Auditing: A Journal of Practice and Theory*, Vol. 11 (Supplement), pp. 33-66.

Lee, T. A. (1991), "A review essay: professional foundations and theories of professional behavior.", *The Accounting Historians Journal*, Vol. 18, pp. 193-203.

Lehman, C. (1992), *Accounting's Changing Roles in Social Conflict*, Markus Wiener Publishing, Inc., New York.

Lehman, C. and Tinker, T. (1987), "The real cultural significance of accounts", *Accounting, Organizations and Society*, Vol. 12, pp. 503-522.

Littleton, A. C. (1933), *Accounting Evolution to 1900*, Russell & Russell, New York.

Loeb, S. (1978), *Ethics in the Accounting Profession*, John Wiley & Sons, New York.

Louwers, T., Ponemon, L. and Radtke, R. (1997), "Examining accountants' ethical behavior: a review and implications for future research", in Arnold, V. and Sutton, S., *Behavioral Accounting Research: Foundations and Frontiers*, American Accounting Association, Sarasota, FL.

Louderback, W. T. (1994), "Concrete process analysis (CPA) and living systems process analysis (LSPA)", *Behavioral Science*, Vol. 39, No. 2, April, pp. 137-169.

Lyons, N. P. (1983), "Two perspectives: oneself, relationships, and morality", *Harvard Educational Review*, Vol. 53, May, pp. 125-145.

Macintosh, N. B. (1993), *A Research Proposal to Investigate the Possibility of Poststructuralist Accounting Thought*, Queen's University, Kingston, ON.

Macintosh, N. B. (1995), "The ethics of profit manipulation: a dialectic of control analysis", *Critical Perspectives on Accounting*, Vol. 6, pp. 289-315.

Mitchell, A., Puxty, T., Sikka, P. and Willmott, H. (1993), "Ethical statements as smokescreens for sectional interests: the case of the U.K. accountancy profession", *Journal of Business Ethics*, Vol. 13, No. 1, pp. 39-51.

Montagna, P. (1973), "The public accounting profession: organization, ideology and social power", in Freidson, E. (Ed.), *The Professions and Their Prospects*, Sage, Beverly Hills, CA.

Montagna, P. (1974), *Certified Public Accounting: A Sociological View of a Profession in Change*, Scholars Books Co., Houston.

Noreen, E. (1988), "The economics of ethics: a new perspective on agency theory", *Accounting, Organizations and Society*, Vol. 13, No. 4, pp. 359–370.

Parker, R. H. (1986), *The Development of the Accountancy Profession in Britain to the Early Twentieth Century*, Academy of Accounting Historians, University, AL.

Parker, L. (1994), "Professional accounting body ethics: in search of the private interest", *Accounting, Organizations and Society*, Vol. 19, pp. 507-525.

Piaget, J. (1932), *The Moral Development of the Child*, Free Press, New York, NY.

Ponemon, L. A. (1990), "Ethical judgments in accounting: a cognitive-developmental perspective", *Critical Perspectives in Accounting*, Vol. 1, No. 2, pp. 191-215.

Ponemon, L. A. (1992a), "Ethical reasoning and selection-socialization in accounting", *Accounting, Organizations and Society*, Vo. 17, No. 3/4, pp. 239-258.

Ponemon, L. A. (1992b), "Auditor underreporting of time and moral reasoning: an experimental lab study", *Contemporary Accounting Research*, pp. 171-189.

Ponemon, L. A. (1993), "Can ethics be taught in accounting?", *Journal of Accounting Education*, Vol. 11, pp. 185-209.

Ponemon, L. A. and Glazer, A. (1990), "Accounting education and ethical development: the influence of liberal learning on students and alumni in accounting practice", *Issues in Accounting Education*, pp. 21-34.

Ponemon, L. A. and Gabhart, D. R. L. (1990), "Auditor independence judgments: a cognitive developmental model and experimental evidence", *Contemporary Accounting Research*, pp. 227-251.

Preston, A., Cooper, D., Scarbrough, P. and Chilton, R. (1995), "Changes in the code of ethics of the U.S. accounting profession, 1917 and 1988: the continual quest for legitimation", *Accounting, Organizations and Society*, Vol. 20, No. 6, pp. 507-546.

Radtke, R. P. (2000), "The effects of gender and setting on accountants' ethically sensitive decisions", *Journal of Business Ethics*, Vol. 24, No. 4, April, pp. 299-313.

Rest, J. (1986b), *Moral Development: Advances in Research and Theory*, Praeger Publishers, Inc., New York.

Rest, J. (1994), "Background: theory and research", in Rest, J. R. and Narvaez, D. (Eds.), *Moral Development in the Professions*, Erlbaum, Hillsdale, NJ, pp.1-26.

Ryan, J. J. (2001), "Moral reasoning as a determinant of organizational citizenship behaviors: a study in the public accounting profession", *Journal of Business Ethics*, Vol. 33, No. 3, October, pp. 233-254.

Schatzberg, J., Sevcik, G. and Shapiro, B. (1996), "Exploratory experimental evidence on independence impoariment conitions: aggregate and individual results", *Behavior Research in Accounting*, Vol. 8 (supplement), pp. 173-195.

Shapeero, M., Koh, H. C. and Killogy, L. N. (2003), "Underreporting an premature sign-off in public accounting", *Managerial Auditing Journal*, Vol. 18, No. 6/7, pp. 478-490.

Sweeny, J. (1995), "The ethical expertise of accountants: an exploratory analysis", *Research in Accounting Ethics*, Vol. 1, pp. 213-234.

Thoma, S. J. (1986), "Estimating gender differences in the comprehension and preference of moral issues", *Developmental Review*, Vol. 6, pp. 165-180.

Thoma, S. (1994), "Moral judgments and moral action", in Rest, J. R. and Narvaez, D. (Eds.), *Moral Development in the Professions*, Erlbaum, Hillsdale, NJ, pp. 199-211.

Tinker, T., Merino, B. and Neimark, M. (1982), "The normative origins of positive theories: ideology and accounting thought", *Accounting, Organizations and Society*, Vol. 7, No. 2, pp. 167-200.

Walker, S. P. (1995), The genesis of professional formation in Scotland. A contextual analysis", *Accounting, Organizations and Society*, Vol. 20, No. 4, pp. 285-310.

ETHICAL ISSUES

26

PUBLISHING IN ACADEMIC ACCOUNTING: PRACTICAL ADVICE AND HEALTHY ICONOCLASM

Timothy Fogarty
Case Western Reserve University, USA

Abstract: What separates successful and not successful accounting academics? Most would say that it is the ability to publish at and beyond standards set by universities. Although this may be somewhat reductionistic, this type of activity is at least a necessary condition of success. This essay offers practical advice in all aspects of the research and publication process. This ranges from generic aspects of approaching research to more focused treatments of the norms and conventions surrounding the endeavour.

Keywords: Publishing, research, peer review.

1.   Introduction

Last August marked twenty years wherein I have given over at least some time of nearly everyday thinking about publishing in the accounting literature. During that time, I have to believe that I have learned something worth sharing in print. My purpose is to provide a practical guide that mixes elements of the conventional wisdom with my personal perspective. Since I have built a career mostly on the outskirts of the mainstream, I would like to suggest that the 'party line' will be appropriately qualified. For the benefit of those not familiar with this literature, I could recommend Kinney (1986), Ashton (1998) and Zimmerman (1989), as well as presentations made before any consortia of doctoral students.

Why should you listen to me? Allow me one paragraph to outline the basis of my 'credentials' to impart advice. There are about 175 pieces with my name on them that have been published somewhere. This includes the highly prestigious academic journals within and outside accounting, and highly applied practitioner outlets. This corpus has tended to defy functional classification. Currently, I am somewhere 'in process' with another 30 projects. Perhaps more importantly, I review more than 75 papers every year for an equally diverse set of publications around the world. I have worked in an editorial capacity for special issues of journals and for academic meetings. Although the conduct of this work has transitioned me from a young scholar to an old one, I remain completely (and perhaps insanely) committed to this work.

The construction of a practical guide strongly suggests a set of subtopics that are chronologically organised. These are provided in the middle eight sections. The journey here starts with the development of an idea and ends with the periodic inevitability of dealing with rejection. The main body of the paper is sandwiched by a preface that develops the personal and institutional context, and ending material that addresses the ongoing management of a portfolio of research projects.

2. Contexts of Scholarship

This chapter is not the first 'advice' piece in the literature. One of my unpublished 30 projects is a 'deconstruction' of the advice that has preceded this. In a nutshell, where this departs from the wisdom of previous elders is in my unwillingness to make the assumption that the market for accounting studies is efficient. In other words, I do not subscribe much to the notion that 'good' research gets published and 'bad' research does not. An imperfect process cannot be described as cream rising to the top. The world is too complex to reduce to a bromide such as that. Such a worldview would tend to give insufficient attention to self-fulfilling prophecies and to the humans who have their hands on the wheels that create results.

While the world is not a fair place, it never tires of trying to convince people that it is just. Research of a calibre consistent with the published literature fails for a variety of reasons that depart widely from the merits. On the other hand, very few pieces are so superlative that they demand publication. There is, in the parlance of the business, no shortage of Type I and Type II error. The existence of such a state of nature does not gainsay the tireless efforts at the management of its occurrence.

The 'gatekeeping' bias in favour of the graduates and faculty at elite schools in the USA as it pertains to publishing in journals as the *Journal of Accounting Research*, the *Journal of Accounting and Economics* and *The Accounting Review*, is strong and pervasive (see Williams and Rodgers, 1995; Lee, 1996). This seems to fall disproportionately to the detriment of scholars outside the USA (Beattie and Goodacre, 2004). The absence of a level playing field does not appear to be so extreme in other academic disciplines. Put bluntly, there does not seem to be any advantage to pretending that some players are not *ex ante* advantaged and disadvantaged.

There are other numbers that are encouraging. The fact that most accounting faculty do not attempt to publish increases the odds of any particular paper being accepted. In a world that has made publishing a journal much more affordable, there will continue to be significant demand. Assuming that one is not tilting at windmills, you have to believe that your work is wanted. The question is whether you can answer the call, or will that chance go to somebody else.

3.   Personal Assumptions

Although every author confronts a finite and somewhat inflexible structure of opportunity, that pales in importance with the personal factors. These include motivation, skills and rewards.

Many will claim to be motivated to work on research, but the empirical truth is that most have a half-hearted inclination. A person who is truly motivated does not pursue publications as time permits or just when there is a lull in other endeavours. Publishing is what sociologists call 'a greedy institution' in reference to its ability to consume all available time and yet be unsated. If one does not have a fire in one's belly for this, then success will be left very much to happenstance.

Research utilises a diverse set of skills that are not too commonly represented in the population. This runs the gamut from a knack for seeing what is interesting, to knowing what to do about it. Although the temptation is to slough this ability set off on doctoral training, I believe that it has to be well-developed before then. For example, writing is a skill that defies complete codification and is therefore a meta-skill. Whereas statistical skill would seem more mechanical, a touch for the appropriate use of this language cannot be dismissed as mere technique. Although skills of these sorts are not uniformly distributed, neither are they dispositive of success.

Perhaps the ultimate skill is one that can only develop over time and through trial and error processes. Emotional maturity to persevere through the adversity imposed by the work and by those that discourage it, is difficult to overestimate in value. This attribute needs to be in abundant supply to prevent hubris and to allow one to know when the time comes to change course.

The assumption that potential authors have access to those physical resources that have become necessary to conduct research has to be made. In addition to data sets and processing equipment, it is difficult to imagine research where legitimate out-of-pocket expenses are not reimbursed. Nonetheless, in the new austerity of higher education, faculty cannot expect to head teams of talented staff. Support should include, however, meaningful recognition for distinguished research success. We all need the occasional pat on the back.

4.   Project Conceptualisation

Although the question of where ideas come from may be classic banter for the philosophically inclined, the inquiry also embeds very mundane issues. Those that falter here never really have the opportunity to experience the rest of the process. Although that truism certainly holds, a worse mistake is to vest this step with more grandeur than it deserves.

A good idea represents the confluence of the author's *ex ante* interests, the cumulative position of the literature and wherewithal to make progress on the idea. Lacking a sufficient 'score' on any of these dimensions causes an idea to fail.

I critique doctoral education for straight-jacketing students unnecessarily into their choice of topics. Many talented people have been convinced that the price they must pay for admission to the academic accounting community is to strictly winsorize the problems upon which they believe they should work. For many, this limitation creates tension because they never become the idea machine that they need to be. As a result, the passion for the idea often just is not present. A good idea is one that the author truly believes demands resolution.

The literature could be conceived as an unfinished brick wall. The workable idea, as the next brick, has to find fit within this structure. Although the writer has the ability to describe the wall of previous work in various ways, it represents certain constraints to the acceptability of additions. Thus, the good idea is one that is neither redundant nor unmoored to previous published work. This criterion validates the personal interest that the author has in the idea.

In the abstract, many ideas would be both interesting and valuable contributions to the literature. However, lacking the ability to push them forward, they do not represent feasible ideas. Often times, the absence of data is what takes an otherwise good notion off the table. Since an idea is only as good as the search that it sets in motion, many have to be stillborn until data becomes available.

Without a doubt, extensive critical reading enables ideas to be sorted and weighed. This investment must continue throughout one's career in order that a worthy set of ideas can be harvested. This facilitates each part of the trinity proposed above. Without reading, one's interests become stagnant and therefore antiquated. Without reading, one does not know what might be a logical extension for that which exists in print. Without reading, one cannot discover the creative answers others are finding to the data problem. Although this can be somewhat strategic and purposeful, the value of a good portion of reading can never be elevated above the serendipitous. This suggests that often one just has to await good fortune to strike. With enough waiting (and reading), it does.

Ideas can be large or small. The former demands more accommodation by readers, but is likely to generate considerable enthusiasm. The small idea, often referred to as a new 'wrinkle' or a 'tweak' would appear to be a more conservative strategy. Whereas the small idea should pose little identification problems, it runs the significant risk of being insufficiently eye-catching. Work in this tradition may be difficult to execute because little tolerance for methodological shortfalls is likely to be extended. On the other hand, large ideas often enjoy considerable leeway since they tend to be first impressions into untilled soil. A place exists for both the large and the small idea, if authors are sufficiently self-conscious to realise what they offer.

The complaint that all the good ideas have been taken is often heard in one version or another. Whereas this indicates a serious creativity deficiency on the part of its proponents, it also suggests high functional fixity. Some of the best ideas come from the relaxing of an assumption that most believed essential. Taking the usual structure for research and rotating it often creates something that is at the same time familiar and novel, and therefore is a double victory.

Whereas ideas are usually considered the sole product of author ingenuity, they sometimes reflect the contribution of editors and reviewers. Although officially in place to judge and evaluate quality, one of these readers might find an idea that is better than the one the author put forth. Obviously, the author is free to adjust accordingly or to ignore such a vision. Although many of these suggestions are not offered in complete seriousness or with the full awareness of the inherent difficulties, they are potential gifts that should not be completely ignored.

The best ideas have a sharp critical edge. They challenge the existing order in a way that causes readers to prick up their ears. The discipline does not need ongoing revolution, but it does need research that rattles the cage albeit in small ways. While this can be done in all of accounting's subfields, it has stronger credence in those areas that have more tightly coalesced around paradigmatic touchstones.

Good ideas have to be the core of the paper from the beginning. This premise is not defeated by the admittedly interactive relationship between ideas and findings. There are many instances of counter-intuitive results that demand a re-conceptualisation that is richer and better nuanced than original thoughts. Occasionally a reviewer even provides an insight that leads to a material re-conceptualisation. However fortuitous, these possibilities cannot be expected.

5. Data

There is no excuse for the failure to publish if data is good. Quality data creates an obligation to publish. Whereas the poor soul that lacks the proof of the pudding can be pitied, the person that has it and either fails to know it or to exploit it, is extended no such embrace.

With regard to archival data on the securities markets and the regulatory-required corporate information that exists in its wake, this is certainly the golden age of acquired data the likes of which could only have been imagined just a few years ago. This availability has levelled the publishing field considerably, to the great advantage of those who were not inside the circles where early versions of such had been previously distributed. At the same time, the rapid and wide availability of public company data de-emphasises the importance of the data itself. For people working in the financial accounting area, the possession of big databases is similar to having the use of a computer. While essential, it is not going to make you special.

The problem with the data that everyone has is that everyone has it. The most obvious question that can be answered with it will be done rapidly and then effectively debased. Although all understands the value of replication to the integrity of the discipline, this work will never command sufficient respect such that they will create an independent use for data. Therefore, those that feed at this increasingly crowed trough have to be nimble. This might include the more ambitious arguments that the common place should not be taken at its face value but instead be accepted as a proxy for a less tangible concept. Authors should also investigate more approaches that create combinations of multiple pieces of data such that a new meaning is created.

The finite nature of the purchased or free data that is often used in the accounting discipline should make it difficult for those that limit themselves to this data to sleep well at night. Seeing 'your' idea appear in print under somebody else's name happens with frightening regularity when there is such a strong consensus on what is interesting in the field. One way out of this box is to hand-collect at least one central variable from a different source. The more labour-intensive this is, the more it creates an entry barrier for others. Data collected 'the old fashioned way' represents an investment by the author that elevates the ante for others. This work also may take projects to a point where the author dare not fail.

For those that do not work in the mainstream of accounting, data must be created. Those that see everything of importance in the world to be the product of humans, consider survey and experimental means to get at underlying cognitive processing and consequential attitudes. This data is only as good as the care that goes into its collection. Researchers are well-advised to never forget the old adage, 'once run, done' that suggests that collection design errors cannot be revisited or compensated. 'Fatal flaws' are not academic versions of urban legends, but appear with considerable frequency. The one that I see the most has many faces. 'Demand effects' reserves for the author an unfair advantage to find what is desired. By giving respondents no reasonable choice but to use the hypothesised relevant information, experiments are particularly susceptible to bring about a product of the artificial situation rather than produce a reflection of the world. Surprisingly, many researchers also act indifferently to strong social desirability bias. Unless the objective is to determine if people want to be perceived in a favourable light, the alternative reading will undermine more substantive propositions.

Behavioural researchers are routinely on the horns of an agonising dilemma. In order to entice more subjects to co-operate, that which is requested from them often is reduced. I believe this is an overreaction to the sample size dimension. Whereas more subjects dominate fewer subjects, it does not when it comes at the cost of squeezing the substance out of the instrument. I have regrettably researched the conclusion 'what a waste of postage!' after quickly getting to the end of a questionnaire. Often, there are so few questions that I am sure nothing useful can be made out of it. With ample dollops of subtlety and complexity, unexpected good things are quite possible.

Educational research presents special data dimensions. The captive audience that students will continue to present for studies of pedagogical effectiveness is without parallel. Although human subject protection constraints now exist, faculty members can still convert components of their teaching work into data generating machines. It is unusual for data to be less of a constraint than the ability to use it. There are no shortages of validity and reliability issues to cope with, however, they are surmountable.

For those that work in especially marginalised areas, of which education may be one, the word is awash with data. The practice community, as well as academe is constantly creating information that describes phenomenon of interest. In the right hands, this can be grafted upon our nascent understanding of relationships. Data of this sort may be so compelling that it alone may bring a previously uncontemplated paper into existence.

6. Theory

More than any other dimension of the research undertaking, theory and its appreciation separates academics and practitioners in accounting. That academic accountants should align themselves with theory, and work to further it, may contribute to the schism with professional practice yet also lie at the heart of our distinctiveness. Theory is also that which separates the practitioner and academic literatures.

One of the reasons that outsiders find doctoral training in accounting to be quixotic is that the field has not developed its own theory. The systematic borrowing that has taken place has been the subject of study for several (Reiter and William, 2002; Williams, 2005). For the most part, economics has been the mothership. A large cadre of professors can imagine no theory that is not neoclassical utility maximisation in its origin. Still for many of these people, economics itself is a vague murmur that does little other than establish the range and set the assumptions.

Good papers should have highly explicit theory that does not rely upon readers' power of inference. The absence of theory abdicates the author's responsibility to link the observation with a particular worldview that is somewhat honest about what it is likely to see and what it cannot reach. Theory makes sense of the choices in a broad historical vein. To do otherwise is tantamount to an assertion that the data speaks for itself. It never does, apart from choices made by authors.

Properly deployed, theory organises the major thrusts of a paper. This is done primarily through the articulation of the hypotheses. These specific expectations should be drawn from theory. Although this is often easier said than done, the author should aspire to the level of plausibility in this. Without such linkages, the theory appears to be free-standing, as if it had been inserted in a pre-packaged obligatory module. Perhaps worse, the hypotheses that have not been sufficiently tethered appear as whimsical ideas driven more by the convenience of the author than any preordained plan. The reader is then left to wonder why these relationships, as opposed to many others. Theory therefore facilitates flow and induces closure.

Theory imposes higher demands on the author's descriptive abilities. Theory, typically more abstract in the original, has to be partially translated to make it useful to applications. The difficulty of this is exacerbated by the need to cross disciplinary lines to import theory into accounting. Since it is the theory that transcends the specifics of the article, this section of the exposition represents the part of the paper that has the most potential to inform the uninitiated reader. Therefore, well done, it proselytises for the theory at the expense of other theories. This only works if the author can invoke the best elements of the theory in a parsimonious and effective manner.

Whereas many authors have learned to draw upon theories to launch their work, the effort is not complete unless they also suggest the ways that they have informed the theory. The theory is neither complete nor stable. Therefore, it exists primarily as a set of successful applications. Through their differences, these build a mosaic that is more or less convincing and aesthetically pleasing. To contribute here, the author should ask what is so special about the context or the data so that we can say that the theory is more or less robust.

Authors that are not wedded to standard economics may find themselves at the early stages of a theory's migration into accounting. Although this suggests that more resistance to the theory's acceptability will be encountered, it also promises the advantages of novelty. In such a virgin field, there are fewer 'dead bodies' to work around. More will depend upon the rhetorical powers of the author to deliver the incremental insights that new theory makes possible. No matter what stage of development an author finds theory, a distinct advantage is possessed by those able to keep abreast of theoretical developments outside of accounting.

Both psychology and sociology have immense untapped potential as a source of new theory. Their realisation in accounting work is partially constrained by the inadequacies of doctoral training in the United States. This situation makes importations much less likely and much more expensive for US scholars, but opens an opportunity for others.

I have been impressed at how portable a single theory can be. Even when I am not engaged in writing a paper, theory explains the world to me and enables me to coherently have a perspective that I can share with others. After all, professors are expected to 'profess' and to do so without much cognitive struggle. One size does not fit all, but it does merit the occasional fitting.

7. Analysis

The possession of strong theory and quality data tees up the need for appropriate analysis. Although certain theories are regularly tested in particular ways, the more typical association links the data with the ideal type of analysis. Although the idea that the data works within one type of analysis and fails within another should be a Statistics 101 lesson, it is easily forgotten or ignored.

What the data is presupposes the method that was used to acquire or develop it. For the most part, this section assumes that the data is either archival (and has been collected in an unobtrusive manner) or has been made archival-like through the experimental or quasi-experimental reduction of subject responses to categories and measures. Case studies open the definition of data to the reactive, the qualitative and the judgemental. This produces a world unto itself and is mostly beyond the scope of this essay.

Analysis starts with the care shown for the data. Nothing erodes the confidence of the reviewers more than anything short of absolute perfection in this regard. Since all data comes with inherent limitations that can be forgiven, the author must expend every effort to preclude additional threats that could be avoided. The best adage I have heard on this point is 'Never let anyone else touch your data'. Having only oneself to blame is the best place to be, if blame is necessary.

Modern statistical analysis packages have transferred much of the wizardry of analysis to the machine. Becoming proficient with these tools has become a foundational skill for the academic. Although these processing capabilities may enable researchers to focus more on 'higher end' skills, it may make analysis less valid. Increased automation allows researchers to be less conscious of the circumstances surrounding their use. As a result, less concern is given to the assumptions of the technique. *Ceteris parabus*, more misuse is likely to occur when analysis is relatively painless. In addition to violated assumptions, this problem may also occur when researchers uncritically accept a program's default processing parameters.

Statistical conclusions are much more precarious than we would like to admit. Often not much separates the $p<.045$ relationship and the $p<.055$ one, even though we imbue the former with the glorifying label 'significant' that we withhold from the latter. The thinness of the edge of this razor demands that the author offer robustness tests as additional analysis. This might involve the use of an alternative measurement, or the revisitation of how the dataset was delimited. To withhold such obvious variations invites suspicion.

Whereas ANOVA and multiple regressions provide very serviceable methods of analysis, they will not create a competitive advantage for the person that uses them. At best, these methods are passable. Most researchers choose not to invest in the knowledge of other methods that have stronger upside potential. For example, the various programs that employ a structural equations approach would seemingly enable the user to argue that better analysis had to be conducted. Structural equations methods such as LISREL, AMOS and EQS offer two major advantages: the ability to test a group of hypotheses together as a single model of effects, and the extraction of the common variance of multiple measures to form the construct that is used in the analysis. Although these methods are appearing with more frequency than a decade ago, the movement in this direction has not been very rapid. Improvements in the software have reduced the entry cost of using these analysis methods from the legendary to the acceptable.

One of the major reasons that researchers cannot hit every nail with the same methodological hammer is sample size. A modest number of observations is more of a problem for some methods than others. For example, structural equations methods should only be used with relatively large datasets. More generally, the relationship between the number of measured observations and the number of model parameters to be estimated needs to be problematised. Even with a relatively simple technique such as multiple regressions, researchers often push the limits of this balance when a long laundry list of independent variables is used in the name of completeness.

Multicollinearity serves as another reason why researchers are advised against developing overly large groups of variables. Although there may be a plausible connection between two variables, it may have been effectively undermined by another hypothesised relationship. In other words, relationships demand a separate space or their co-existence in an analysis will cause interpretation problems.

Most of the issues pertaining to quantitative data have been well understood for some time. Whereas this makes their continuing violation difficult to comprehend, it also suggests that the future action is elsewhere. I believe that the analysis of qualitative data, such as that provided by words, represents the new frontier of analysis. Software such as N6 (nee NUDIST) brings rigour to content analysis by unearthing patterns in texts that would not otherwise be visible. Programs like DICTION make the tonality of words become something about which we might want to be conscious. In a field like accounting, we need to pay more attention to the language than we have in the past.

8. Writing

Stripped to its essence, every paper is a collection of paragraphs. Unless the paragraphs are acceptable, the paper does not get published. Bad writing can undo good substance. Therefore, the calibre of the exposition is a very important aspect of any research project.

Unlike data analysis, writing is not the product of considerable consensus or explicit training. There are many, many rules for writing. Clarity of exposition, soundness of argumentation and the flow that results from a tight and visible structure should not be diminished in importance. However, following them all does not necessarily yield a well-written document. This shows that writing is an art, rather than a science. Writing improves with practice and cannot be changed through mere appreciation. The inability to reduce writing to mechanics also explains that there may be active disagreement over the quality of writing.

The first step toward good writing is the habit of writing. If writing is the subject of apprehension, it will not get done. We can all think of a hundred things that just have to be accomplished before we sit down to write. If it does get done under such psychological circumstances, it will be sub-standard. The habit of writing engenders a certain comfort level with words and sentences. Even though this implies that it ought not be painful, writing will always remain a craft that requires discipline and diligence. Understanding that it is not an art that demands inspiration, demystifies it and enables it to be produced in less than ideal circumstances. Above all else, waiting for the mood or for a large block of uncompromised time is a recipe for not writing anything.

Getting writing into your soul means that it should not be relegated to infrequent episodes. The only way to write is to write every day. The only way to write every day is to manage a large number of simultaneous research projects at different stages of development and to look for non-research academic projects that require written output. This would include contributions to newsletters and journal article reviews. I often think of myself as a writer who happens to be a professor rather than a professor who happens to write.

Writing the academic article does not present the challenge of writing the novel or the short story. Our task is more like the technical writer than the storyteller. We have a well-understood model that we can use to guide our efforts. The idea of what the article should look like provides structure that makes the blank page feel considerably less blank. Young academics are well-advised to master the form that applies with fullest force to empirical studies. This will allow any deviations that are necessary to be purposeful decisions rather than ignorant choices.

A few worthy aspects of this template merit mention. A swift but striking motivation of the topic precludes our tendencies to waffle about what is important and to even temporarily evade the 'so what?' challenge. A review of the literature should be the general conveyance for the transition from theory to applied studies to specific hypotheses. The hypotheses must be highly crystallised expressions of the empirical work, and must precisely resolve the tension that the author has constructed between that which has been done and that which needs to be done. Patience should be exercised so that a separation is forged between the results ('just the facts, ma'am') and the discussion (which can include both reasoned interpretations and modest speculation). Needless to say, any worthwhile study paves a road toward needed future research. For the most part, the liberties that one should take should be *inside* the form rather than *of* the form.

Non-empirical academic pieces present more of an open-ended invitation. Lacking specific hypotheses to support, measurements to defend, a study design to elaborate and results to describe, there is no strict organisational logic. Without so much substance, simple declarative sentences will often not be good enough. One's ability to communicate a more esoteric set of ideas calls for a stronger vocabulary and a self-designed analytic division of a field. The writer needs to be self-absorbed in the techniques of rhetoric, even down to much smaller matters such as word selection. Unless one at least fancies themselves a good writer, this should be eschewed. At the micro level this often translates with willingness to attempt to write cognitively demanding sentences and envelop-pushing paragraphs that do not collapse under their own weight.

Writing for a practitioner audience is a different mastery. In many ways this objective is irreconcilable with other areas. A great premium is placed on brevity. Furthermore, one must write with the assumption that readers want to consume less than the entirety of even a brief article. This demands 'Executive Summaries' and boxed set-asides that are capable of some alternative stand-alone value. Practitioner articles enforce the demand for simplicity and for practicality, two attributes that usually are liabilities in academic writing.

9.   Pulling the Trigger: Journal Submission

Nothing has ever been published that has not first been submitted for publication. Many have failed, not because of inherent quality problems with their work or because of an inability to produce work, but due to the unwillingness to offer the work to the critical scrutiny of others.

The objective of the initial submission is to avoid outright rejection. Given the fact that exceptionally few manuscripts are accepted outright in their initial form, any goal more grandiose should not be entertained. Once the paper is good enough to not be found irredeemably hopeless, the result obtained, whether one submits now or much later, is likely to be the same.

Premature submission imposes a risk of rejection that can be partially managed. Younger authors ought to fear this fate more since their placement of manuscripts in the hierarchy of journals has greater consequence. They also lack the feel for likely utility functions of reviewers. The question they must face is the degree of improvement on material dimensions that they can reasonably make in a reasonable allotment of time.

My advocacy of earlier submission accomplishes a couple of worthwhile objectives. First, it prevents authors from their own worst tendencies. Many of us are perfectionists in that we believe that everything is under our control, waiting to be made better. Unless checked, this is a regrettable and potentially fatal affliction. The perfect paper will never be done. Second, prompt submission squeezes down the prospects of being 'scooped' by other writers. Generally, property rights adhere to an idea only after its publication. Third, submission frees the author to start new projects. Many authors find it difficult to think about other research while there is anything at all to do on an earlier one. I have never sent a paper unaccompanied by a feeling of liberation, even if short-lived.

The conventional wisdom includes the belief that one should solicit feedback for manuscripts prior to their submission. In a perfect world, there would be plentiful colleagues ready, willing and able to perform this service. In the imperfect world, readers with the time are unlikely to have substantive feedback, and those with good ideas will not have the time to give for a good informal read. Therefore, delaying submission in the hope of improvements made possible in this way is a poor strategy. I might attenuate this conclusion for very novice authors who might not know the template and the norms surrounding the production of research, and for those that have some sort of relationship (i.e. friend, dissertation committee member) that increases the odds of a prompt and worthwhile response. Young authors should realise that most senior authors want to help them, but often lack the time to do so. They should also accept that receiving help commits them to giving help in like measure. The hopes that the pass around of manuscripts can be effective to co-opt potential reviewers has always seemed far-fetched to me.

The absence of external readers has to be compensated for by a commitment by the author to do more preparatory work with the manuscript before its release. Although papers can retain errors through multiple readings, the number of these mistakes can be reduced to an acceptable threshold with enough iteration. Both too few and too many run throughs can be problematic. In the process, it helps to adopt the perspective of a vaguely informed reader. This demands a reasonably high level of clarity in the manuscript and works to the disadvantage of jargon and cryptic abbreviations in the text. Even if the paper is to be electronically submitted, a paper version should be inspected. This allows appearance problems to be isolated and addressed.

As the author moves toward submission, he or she will encounter such work that is inherently tedious. This might include tasks such as running down references, reformatting tables and figures, and conforming the paper to a journal's style guide. If a person hates something enough, it may not get done, or at best, slow down the progress. I recommend that the author outsource this work if it would present an obstacle. This might include even more work and not be limited to the terminal stages of the project (e.g. word processing, editing). The key point is to understand one's self in relationship to the work. If some part of it is likely to be time consuming and unrewarding, reasonable options should be sought.

A submission is only as good as the destination. In other words, considerable thought should be given to the characteristics of a journal as they relate to the reception that a manuscript is likely to receive. Only when a good match exists does the author put the project in its best position to be ultimately accepted. Out-of-match papers look worse than they actually are from any particular journal's unique perspective. *Ceteris paribus*, poorly matched papers stand a higher chance of rejection that increases the opportunity cost for the author.

Journal selection has become increasingly important in the competition among schools for institutional prestige. As influenced by the dangling of extrinsic rewards, faculty members are well advised to tailor their project *ab initio* to the tastes of the journals of their choice. This can only be done by a careful contemplation of the contents over several years-worth of editions. For these purposes, one should observe the types of papers that do not appear as closely as what does. Protestations of open-mindedness toward all types of research are often an empty promise.

I have never worried too much about other people's conceptions of journal quality. If a project is interesting, feasible and marketable, I want to do it. I will try to make it as good as I can fully realising that it might not have 'A' journal potential. I believe that it is a pity that many good projects have never been published because, lacking an 'A' journal profile, their authors have no incentive to pursue their completion. Contributions to the general knowledge can be made at many places less ratified. However, this sort of strict rationality may be ameliorated by tenure, after which professors can pursue their personal interests more feverishly.

Authors are well-advised to appreciate the personal interests of journal editors. These individuals are key gatekeepers and cannot be expected to be absolutely neutral on issues of content and method. Although there are limits to the value that can be extracted from this knowledge, author indifference risks unnecessary conflict. Although hardly any journal editors demand homage, some respect is entirely appropriate. Just as one would not pursue employment without doing some research, one should not blindly submit manuscripts.

Another specific condition worthy of note is the special edition of a journal. Often supervised by a guest editor, these opportunities provide better odds for those that have content consistent with the desired theme. The trick is to convince the reviewer that this consistency is strong and not fanciful. This appears worthwhile if it can be done as a re-packaging of a pre-existing research intention rather than being tantamount to a substantive deviation in focus. Working toward a special edition invitation also requires the surrender of the timing of the project. Specific and often tight deadlines must be adhered to as a condition of the initial submission. Revisions also are likely to be demanded on a more exacting basis. I have always welcomed the artificiality of such deadlines as a means to ensure that work that one has intended to do is actually done.

Authors also face submission decisions for academic meetings. Similar to special editions, the attendant deadlines can be valuable to focus effort in a way that pushes the work along. However, placing a paper at a meeting typically does not further its prospects for publication. Meetings are not structured to accomplish much due to the lead times that are needed for the organisation. That most of the audience has not read the paper prior to its presentation also precludes a knowledgeable dialogue with conference attendees. Therefore, submission to meetings may come at a cost if it delays the ultimate objective of submission for publication. Nonetheless, these submissions and presentations are valuable in building a reputation as a scholar and an authority on a particular set of topics in the field.

10.   Revise and Resubmit

Since the best that can result from a submission is the avoidance of total failure, the author routinely must confront a revision process. The revisions that are suggested by editors and reviewers can vary from minor to the equivalent of working on a different paper. In the case of the latter, the revision process can be more difficult than constructing the initial draft.

The first task for the author is to ensure that the editorial response is, in fact, a 'revise and resubmit' result. For these purposes, the label given the outcome by the editor is not necessarily conclusive. In an effort to be courteous, editors sometimes suggest that a closed door actually is ajar. Sometimes one must read between the lines to ascertain that one has been given a chance to attempt the impossible. Sometimes this can be inferred from the tone of the editor's letter in which some hint about priorities might be extended.

One of the great impairments of human capital in the professoriate occurs following the receipt of the reviews of one's 'dissertation paper.' Harshly negative responses to the work that the new faculty person has invested heart and soul over a number of years, presents to all too many an invitation to suspend efforts as a researcher. No episode illustrates better the emotionally charged circumstances of the review process. Since this psychological battle is re-engaged for every paper, the need to achieve some degree of equanimity about it is of paramount importance.

Authors need to remember that reviewers will never understand the research under review as well as the author. Therefore, reviewers' opinions about it are likely to be less informed and less valid. Therefore, the review process is not an epistemological one. Once the author realises that the discourse about truth is only a way that the debate is dressed, the ego-intensive dynamics can be mostly diffused. Authors are invited to explore alternative metaphors and philosophies to supplant the official line. Fogarty and Ravenscroft (2000) offer a few for consideration.

Many have advised that authors put review comments aside to achieve a 'cooling off period'. I would join them for several reasons. Temporal distance will allow one to get beyond the knee-jerk emotional response to comments that are not likely to be conducive to a successful revision. More practically, time allows the author to fit the work into a schedule that does not interrupt the ongoing completion of other projects. Third, it may take some time to decide what to do. Often, that which at first blush appears unrealistic becomes only difficult with the passage of time. I believe that even the relatively easy revisions should be put aside for some time. Authors should give their minds, even on an unconscious level, some respite to consider the possibilities. Besides, a proper amount of revision time provides reviewers with respect, least they come to the realisation that they did not set the bar sufficiently high.

The obvious objective of the revision is to do everything requested by the reviewers. If possible, more should be attempted. The former is itself a best case scenario that can only be achieved if the reviewers do not provide incompatible content. Young authors are often stunned by the dissensus among reviewers, and even more aghast to learn that it is not uncommon. When Reviewer A says 'Cut X' and Reviewer B says 'X is the best part, expand it' the conflict cannot be ignored. Surprisingly, editors do not often intervene and therefore authors cannot achieve the ideal of full compliance.

Making more changes than specifically requested has to be looked at with favour by editors and reviewers. As a good faith demonstration of commitment to the improvement process, this realisation transcends the desire to be published. If one senses a direction that the reviewers favour, the author should push for a point beyond the literal. If the revision has to be substantive as a matter of necessity, not much more work is often needed to reach this point of impressive changes beyond the call of obligation.

Whether specifically requested or not, the author should create a schedule of responses to the reviewer. This is an excellent opportunity to shape the minds of the reviewers towards a more sympathetic disposition. This is especially important if you cannot do as they suggest. Make the most of this conversation using whatever 'emotional intelligence' you may possess.

When presented with a difficult but not impossible revision, my bias is to recommend its attempt. I dislike admitting defeat without a struggle. By not going quietly into that good night, a pleasant surprise occasionally comes your way. This *never* happens to those that walk away from the challenge presented by a revision.

11. Moving on

Rejection is a fact of life. Not everything that you do will be well received. You can only hope that some of one's work will be liked well enough. Rejection provides opportunities for learning that are not sought but might be valuable nonetheless. This state can be reached only if rejection can be looked at as a timeout, rather than an end.

Why do manuscripts get rejected? It would be easy to say that they lacked quality. However, it would be more accurate to say that they did not possess the type of quality favoured by the journal. If quality is assumed to be a multidimensional matrix rather than a binary attribute, one has to conclude that managing the fit of the manuscript and the journal is the most important process. In other words, manuscripts get rejected because they are wrong for the journal considering them. Beyond that, rejection results from an imperfect enactment of the norms and rules that govern the publication pursuit (many of which are addressed above). Although these categories carve out most of the episodes, we should never deny that some rejection is random. There is ill will in the minds of some decision makers, and there is bad timing and there is some degree of honest mistake that mars the process.

Sooner or later, you will have to accept the unfavourable outcome. It probably is not to the author's advantage to think of a rejection as the opinion of a lower court that can be reversed upon appeal. First, remember that rejection is the editor's decision, and therefore supposedly already reflects a weighing of the testimony provided by the reviewers. To convince an editor to reverse a decision requires more than an argument that the reviewer erred. If there is a monitoring structure in place over the editor's work (e.g. the Publications Committee of the AAA), even more convincing will be needed. The editor was selected to exercise judgement and others are unlikely to constrain this prerogative except in the most blatant cases of procedural inadequacy. One factor that should console us that we are playing for long-run success. Therefore, we need to suffer occasional injustices to construct a reputation of reasonableness within the small community of academic accountants.

Rejections could be looked at as 'revise and do not resubmit' outcomes. The reasons provided for the unfavourable outcome often contain useful ideas that could lead to manuscript improvement if taken to heart. Thus, there are 'good' rejections and 'bad' rejections based on the calibre of useful and feasible ideas that are contained therein. However, implementing these suggestions often proves emotionally difficult given the fact that there will be no return to that journal. The first inclination is always to ignore the comments. This not only saves time, but appears psychologically pleasing, as it achieves some sort of primitive vindication over the ideas that led to the unfavourable outcome. Experienced authors gradually come to recognise how childish this behaviour is at its core. Perhaps this has to be learned the hard way when the same problems are encountered at the next journal. Even worse is the non-trivial possibility, given our small world, that the second journal will send the manuscript to the same person that reviewed it for the first journal.

What one does with a rejected manuscript should reflect the balance of extrinsic and intrinsic reward faced by the author. If the resort to a second journal seriously erodes the former, it may not be rational to continue the struggle. Often, journals of equivalent prestige can be found and no loss (other than time) occurs. If this is not the case, one's time might be better spent beginning a new project. When intrinsic rewards predominate, such a harsh logic may not be so appealing. Here, a rejection allows the author to decide whether or not the ideas within the paper are sufficiently enjoyable to continue to think about. A new submission of a rejected paper entails the deepening of a certain cognitive investment that could otherwise be redeployed.

The resubmission of a rejected manuscript can be thought of as an application of the lessons of cost accounting. The rejected manuscript represents a sunk cost that should be irrelevant to subsequent decisions. The advisability of another submission should be a function of the incremental revision effort going forward. This would include changes suggested by the rejection communication, alterations made necessary by the focus or audience of the new journal and format changes to conform the draft to the style guide of the new journal. One also should take into account the possible new environment created by the times. A manuscript that once addressed a 'hot' topic may have gone stale in the time consumed by the initial rejection. While it is doubtful that the academy has gained closure on the issue, the effort that may be necessary to get readers to care about the past may be monumental. At a minimum, authors should freshen the literature cited by the manuscript to avoid the tell-tale sign that the paper has been 'around the block.'

The cost/benefit calculus of submitting a paper to a new journal should include an honest evaluation of its failure at the previous target. If a paper has a serious validity or reliability problem, a resubmission is tantamount to a prayer that future reviewers will be less competent or less diligent. Since there is not much support for an efficient market in reviewing, that position has to be seen as a long shot. At the other extreme, a rejection caused by a misunderstood paper or by an editor that has been influenced by collateral considerations, suggests more promise in a new submission. Authors are advised not to be excessively self-lenient in these assessments. If the objective is to maximise success through the efficient allocation of effort, creating a hollow ego boost through a fanciful re-submission may be a step in the wrong direction.

If one has made the decision to try one's luck at another journal, one should attempt to do so on an expeditious basis. Although it may take a little time to be able to dispassionately review the details of the rejection decision, and even more time to respond meaningfully to them, the turnaround time has to be proactively managed. As noted above, topics do not always wait patiently to be worked upon. Even if they did, time elapsed always translates into opportunity costs. If a new submission is viable, the perceived extra work that is needed to make it ready will increase as time passes. When this happens, the temptation to forego this work, and send it out unaltered, grows. If succumbed to, this approach increases the prospects of failure at the second journal.

12. A Note on Co-authors

The progress of a piece of accounting research often depends upon the ability of a group of people to work together. This essay has suppressed this reality in order to highlight the inherent features of the topics and the other elements of the process. Nonetheless, one cannot ignore the fact that fewer and fewer articles are the product of a single person.

Co-authors are rarely equal, and that is a good thing. I believe that expecting equality is a bad place to start. Some individual has to be the driver or the destination will never be reached. Co-authors with roughly equivalent skill sets also do not make good choices. As a general rule, complimentary aptitudes and competitive advantages add better and produce 'zones of influence' that yield more and better output. In the real world, however, you 'go to war' with the co-authors that you can find. As a result, you live and learn, often trusting the wrong people.

The possession of co-authors creates interpersonal obligations that heighten our sense of diligence. The flesh is weak enough that we will often welsh on the promises that we have made to ourselves. This is more difficult to do to another human being, especially if you know that they have 'skin in the game' regarding the outcome of the efforts.

Co-authorship provides the author with an excellent opportunity for self discovery. Despite ample evidence to the contrary, I remain sanguine about my fellow academics believing that they will do their part and push the project along on a reasonable timetable. Fearing no evil, I rarely approach any explicit understanding about ownership or possible termination consequences. In a way, I admire those that rely less on the norms of proper behaviour and more on contractual reasoning. Then again, I do have a distinct preference for co-authors that make their contribution first.

Young authors should be vigilant about those that would exploit them. We are a business whose primary stock in trade is ideas and their manifestation in intangible products such as data. As such, young authors should realise the need to be wary, especially about those that they would be inclined to trust. Although national practices vary, dissertation supervisors do not have an automatic co-authorship privilege. This should be a unilateral decision by the freshly minted PhD based upon an understanding that a correspondingly significant amount of future work will be done by the supervisor on the project(s) that originate in dissertations.

13. Managing the Portfolio

One idea, especially if it has been reduced to a publication, breeds other ideas. Multiplied thus, authors should therefore soon possess a portfolio of research projects that have advanced to any of the various stages of completion. Perhaps there are too many to manage well, but it is an embarrassment of riches. To me, it is a joy to not fully anticipate what work will be done in any day.

I believe that the obligation of academics is to write for audiences beyond other academics. This suggests an occasional 'translation' for practitioners. I also believe in the importance of the scholarship of teaching. I also recommend escape from the characteristic ways that our countries look at things by publishing globally. Together these forces have pushed me out of the boundaries that others find comfort within. However, even the less promiscuous should have a well-stocked portfolio.

If you enjoy working with other people, doing projects that they are more keen on than you are initially, is a wonderful learning experience. If you are not personally addicted to learning, you should seriously wonder why you are in education. After tenure is achieved, one no longer has to subscribe to other people's ideas of intellectual coherence.

14. Conclusion

Research is a life style. The pursuit of the new and its communication provides structure to one's existence. The extrinsic rewards that are bestowed upon those that do it are mostly beside the point, and much less than one could make in consulting. However, I do not think I would trade it for anything else. Research keeps me young at heart and in the same breath, it makes the time pass quickly.

This essay is an impressionistic collection of 'do's' and 'don'ts' that I hope either have strong intuitive appeal or are food for thought in controversial places. Throughout, no attempt has been made to analytically separate basic logic, theoretical positions and my own personal experience. This is a limitation, but may be a necessary one.

In this essay, I have tried to describe the behaviours that are needed to live in the world that I see. More than anything, academic research requires personal passion. With that, anything is possible. Knowledge of the norms and the preferences that have been institutionalised into the subculture pale in comparison. Happy trails!

References

Ashton, R. (1998), "Writing accounting research for publication and impact", *Journal of Accounting Education*, Vol. 16, pp. 247-260.

Beattie, V. and Goodacre, A. (2004), "Publishing patterns within the UK accounting and finance academic community", *British Accounting Review*, Vol. 36, pp. 7-44.

Fogarty, T. and Ravenscroft, S. (2000), "Peering at power: a critical analysis of journal reviewing practices in accounting", *Critical Perspectives on Accounting*, Vol. 11, pp. 409-432.

Kinney, W. (1986), "Empirical accounting research design for Ph.D. students", *The Accounting Review*, Vol. 61, No. 2, pp. 338-350.

Lee, T. (1996), "Anatomy of a professional elite: the Executive Committee of the American Accounting Association 1916-1996", *Critical Perspectives on Accounting*, Vol. 6, pp. 241-261.

Reiter, S. and Williams, P. (2002), "The structure and progressivity of accounting research: the crisis in the academy revisited", *Accounting, Organizations and Society*, Vol. 27, No. 4, pp. 575-607.

Williams, P. (2005), "Academic reputations, behavioral accounting research and the next generation of elites", unpublished working paper, North Carolina State University.

Williams, P. and Rodgers, J. (1995), "The accounting review and the production of knowledge", *Critical Perspectives on Accounting*, Vol. 6, June, pp. 263-287.

Zimmerman, J. (1989), "Improving a manuscript's readability and likelihood of publication", *Issues in Accounting Education*, Vol. 4, pp. 458-466.

INDEX

accountability, xvii, xviii, xxiii, 3, 98, 149, 156, 178, 180, 196, 213-221, 225, 232, 240, 244, 281, 291, 294, 298, 301, 306, 309, 316, 318-321, 324, 327-329, 337, 348-349, 352-353, 355, 357-358, 369, 394, 397

accounting research, xv, xxi, xxii, 1, 3-5, 12-13, 19, 29-31, 53, 55-57, 64, 77, 84, 89-91, 99, 130-131, 133, 148, 155, 157, 170, 175, 183-184, 186, 189, 195, 198, 201, 207, 208, 218, 219, 223-228, 239-241, 247-248, 253-254, 256-258, 260-263, 266, 268, 278, 279, 339, 340, 352, 361, 362, 365, 375, 376, 378, 381, 387, 394-399, 401, 408, 427, 428, 452, 459, 470, 475, 477, 478, 480, 481, 483-485, 502, 507, 508, 510, 532, 534

action research, xiii, 4, 361, 365, 366, 367, 368, 369, 370, 371, 372, 373

agency costs, 55, 61-63, 67, 75, 78-79, 89-90

agency theory, 11, 12, 55, 89, 90-91, 195, 220, 478, 512

bounded rationality, 2, 7, 9, 15, 31, 32, 65, 66, 84-86, 89, 108, 186, 196

budgets, 19, 30, 32, 34, 74, 75, 116, 193, 194, 244, 348, 352, 354

case study, xvi, 4, 10, 16, 100, 148, 158, 193, 201, 202, 243, 350-351, 353, 355, 358-359, 361-369, 375, 382-383, 385, 387, 390, 392, 395, 397, 398, 462, 474, 475, 477, 482, 484, 485, 486, 488, 491

classical management theory, 20, 21

collaboration, 105, 109, 117-119, 204, 260, 366, 368-369, 371, 372, 413

community expectations, 161-164, 178

complementarity theory, 105, 117-119

contingency theory, 2, 35, 42, 52, 53, 125, 253, 264, 480

control, xv, xviii, xix, xx, xxi, xxiii, 1-4, 8, 12, 13, 15-16, 20, 22, 27, 29, 31-32, 35, 40, 41, 43-46, 51-54, 56, 58, 60, 63, 75, 78-80, 83-84, 86, 88-92, 95-103, 105-126, 132, 144, 148-151, 156, 158, 168, 189-193, 195, 196, 199, 202, 203, 214, 233, 241, 242, 244, 250, 251, 253, 267, 271-274, 276-278,

280-289, 291-292, 294, 298, 300, 304, 306, 308-309, 314-316, 318, 323-324, 326, 329, 339, 340, 342-344, 346, 348, 349, 351, 352-354, 357-359, 362-365, 368-369, 375, 380, 382, 384, 388, 394, 395, 398, 403, 407, 408, 413, 422, 447, 452-456, 459, 461, 463-468, 470, 472, 474-475, 479-480, 483-485, 505, 512, 526

corporate disclosure, 157, 161, 162, 165, 171, 177, 178

critical accounting project, xxii, 247, 248, 253, 254, 261, 262, 282

data-triangulation, 477, 483

decision making, xvii, 7-16, 26, 31, 55, 57, 62-63, 76-77, 101, 130, 131, 135, 196, 210, 323, 325, 349, 358, 401, 404-409, 430, 457, 464

dialectic, 291, 298, 299, 304, 307, 312, 317, 329, 349, 480, 512

divergence of grounded theory method, 130

emancipatory intent, 247, 259

employee compensation, 55

enabling accounting, 247, 260-263, 266, 271, 282

Feyerabend, Paul, 479, 481, 483, 484

field study, xx, 5, 52, 121, 192, 199-200, 242, 356, 375-376, 383, 385, 394, 457, 462-475, 482, 483

Foucault, Michel, 223-224, 227, 230-231, 240, 242, 254-255, 276, 349, 350, 382, 506, 511

fragmentation, 147, 291, 299, 308, 310, 312, 315-316, 318, 327, 329-331

Gailbraith, John K., 33

Gandhi, Mahatma xxii, 3, 291-293, 296-298, 300-303, 305-320, 328-329, 332-337

governance, xvi, xx, xxiii, 2, 12, 61, 64-66, 75, 78, 80, 81, 83, 84, 86, 88-91, 95-97, 99-100, 102-103, 114, 118, 186, 207-208, 217-218, 231, 288, 317, 403, 407

Gramsci, Antonio, 249, 250, 253, 264, 268

Also from Spiramus

Handbook of
Cost and Management Accounting

General Editor: Zahirul Hoque, Deakin University

Published 2005   Price £75.00   ISBN: 1-904905-01-3

In order to survive in the changing business environment, organisations should rethink their strategic philosophy and the role of management accounting. While some businesses continue to use conventional methods of costing, performance measurement and cost analysis, increasing numbers are adopting activity-based cost allocation system, strategic-oriented investment decisions models, and multiple performance measures such as the Balanced Scorecard. This handbook helps with both conventional and contemporary issues in cost and management accounting.

The book is a useful reference source for practicing accountants, senior executives and managers working in human resources, operations, and accounting divisions. As the principal focus of this book is on conceptual foundations, it would also be ideal for courses in graduate programs such as master's degree, MBA or Executive MBA.

"Read this book! Whether you take a conventional performance measurement and cost analysis approach to management accounting or prefer a more contemporary approach, this book has it covered" PayAdvice Magazine, December 2005.

About the author

Zahirul Hoque is Professor and Chair of Accounting at Deakin University, Australia. He earned his PhD from University of Manchester in 1993, and also has B.Com and M.Com from the University of Dhaka. He edits and contributes to a number of international accounting journals.